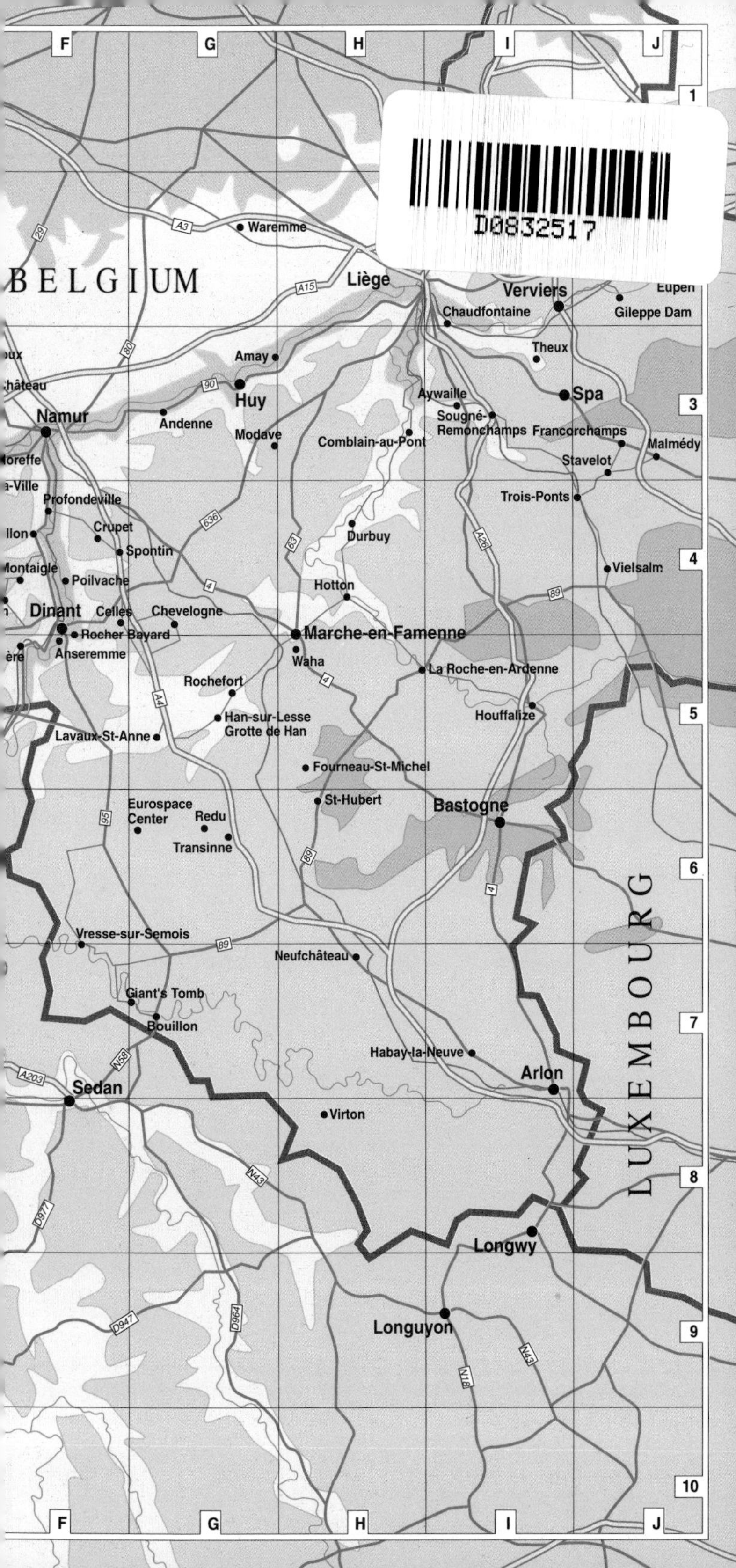

F
G
H
I
J
1
D0832517
A3
Waremme
29
BELGIUM
A15
Liège
Verviers
Eupen
Chaudfontaine
Gileppe Dam
Theux
80
Amay
90
Huy
Spa
3
Namur
Andenne
Aywaille
Sougné-
Remonchamps
Francorchamps
Modave
Comblain-au-Pont
Malmédy
Stavelot
Profondeville
Trois-Ponts
636
Crupet
Durbuy
Spontin
63
A26
4
Vielsalm
Poilvache
Hotton
89
Dinant
Celles
Chevelogne
Rocher Bayard
Marche-en-Famenne
Anseremme
Waha
La Roche-en-Ardenne
Rochefort
A4
Han-sur-Lesse
Grotte de Han
Houffalize
5
Lavaux-St-Anne
Fourneau-St-Michel
Eurospace
Center
Redu
St-Hubert
Bastogne
95
Transinne
6
LUXEMBOURG
Vresse-sur-Semois
Neufchâteau
Giant's Tomb
Bouillon
7
Habay-la-Neuve
N58
A203
Sedan
Arlon
Virton
N43
8
D977
Longwy
D947
D964
Longuyon
9
N18
10

It was in Belgium, in 1836, that the first railway line in continental Europe was built. Public transport (here, the omnibus serving Brussels and Wavre) has long played a vital role in the economic prosperity of Brussels and southern Belgium.

RE - BRUXELLES

At the turn of the century two worlds, poles apart from each other, coexisted: the south and the east of the country lived according to the secular rhythms of the peasant communities of the Ardennes; the regions of the Sambre, Meuse and Brussels, on the other hand, played the card of industrialization and progress.

Top: *Le Vieux Trottoir*, Charleroi.
Left: Brussels in 1930.
Main picture:
the Ardennes in winter.

“The elm-lined track, twisting to the left and right as it descends still further, is lost from view in the crook of a valley, then reappears in the distance, where the dwarfed elms climb in symmetrical rows to meet the sky.”
Hubert Krains

For over one hundred years the area around Mons, La Louvière and Charleroi has constituted a large industrial basin, based on two main activities: the iron and steel industries, and coal. Seen here are the haulers of Charleroi.

Everyman Guides
Published by David Campbell Publishers Ltd, London

Brussels and southern Belgium – ISBN 1-85715-867-9

Numerous specialists and academics have contributed to this guide. This guide has been made possible by the help of: les Relations Extérieures; L'Assemblée de la Commission Communautaire Française de la Région de Bruxelles-Capitale; Le Commissariat Général aux Relations Internationales de la Communauté Française de Belgique; L'Office de Promotion du Tourisme; La Communauté Française, Ministère de la Culture et des Affaires Sociales; La Société de Développement Régional de Bruxelles; Les Services de la Programmation de la Politique Scientifique du Gouvernement Fédéral Belge.

Editors: Anne Cauquetoux and Julie Wood
Assisted by Pierre-Gilles Bellin, Odile George, Clarisse Deniau (architecture), Odile Simon (nature)
Nature coordination: Philippe J. Dubois and Frédéric Bony
Architecture coordination: Bruno Lenormand
Maps: Vincent Bruno
Photography coordintation: Eric Guillemot and Patrick Léger
Layout: Béatrice Desrousseaux, Carole Gaborit, Michèle Bisgambiglia (nature)
Picture research: Véronique Legrand
Coordinators in Belgium: Sabine Cartuyvels, Gaby Castel (Gedif SA), Louis-Pierre Nevelsteen

Institutions: Xavier Mabille
Nature: Philippe Goffart (encyclopedia and itineraries), Ann-Kirstin de Caritat
History: Xavier Mabille
Language: Jean Lechanteur
Art and traditions: Ann Chevalier, Le Centre Belge de la Bande Dessinée, Elsje Janssen, Andrée Longcheval, Michel Revelard, Jacques Stiennon, Mme Ter Assatouroff, Jean-Pierre Van Roy, Jean-Louis Verdebout
Architecture: Philippe Bragard, Thomas Coomans, Alain Forti, Philippe Goffart, Gérard Michel, Guido Vanderhulst, Anne Van Loo
Belgium as seen by painters: Jacques Stiennon
Great masters and schools of painting: Jacques Stiennon
Belgium as seen by writers: Lucinda Gane

Itineraries:
In and around Brussels: L'ASBL Arcadia, Claire Billen, Pierre-Paul Dupont, Xavier Duquesnne, Laure Eggerickx, Eric Hennaut, Anne Van Loo, Fabrice de Kerhove, Bernard Vandendriessche, Manoëlle Wasseige
In and around Namur: Philippe Bragard, Ingrid Nachtergael, Jacques Toussaint
In and around Liège: Nicole Darding, Mme Deblanc-Magnée, André Henrard, Yves Hurard, Jacques Stiennon, Christine Swings
In and around Saint-Hubert: Louis Lefebvre, Ingrid Nachtergael, André Neuberg
In and around Charleroi: Jean-Louis Delaet, Ingrid Nachtergael
In and around Mons: Marcel Capouillez, Jean-Louis Delaet, Christiane Piérard, Robert d'Ursel, Jean-Louis Vanden Eynde
In and around Tournai: Jacques Pycke

Illustrations
Nature: Jean Chevallier, François Desbordes, Bernard Duhem, Claire Felloni, Jean Guiol, Catherine Lachaud, Alban Larousse, Dominique Mansion, Pascal Robin, John Wilkinson
Architecture: Jean-Marie Guillou, Jean-Claude Sené, Claude Quiec, Jérôme Deborde, J.-M. Ballay, Michel Sirier, Maurice Pommier, Valérie Gevers, Françoise Lenormand, Pierre de Hugo, Jean-Sylvain Roveri
Itineraries: P.-E. Dequest, Alban Larousse, Claire Feloni, Dominique Mansion
Practical information: Maurice Pommier
Maps: Stéphane Girel, Éric Gillion,
Colorists: Christine Adam, Carole Picard, Catherine Totems, Olivier Verdy
Computer graphics: Paul Coulbois, Florence Picquot, Patrick Alexandre, Xavier Garnerin (Latitude), Emmanuel Calamy , Patrick Mérienne (nature)

Photographers: Christine Bastin, Michel Bockiau, Jacques Évrard, Benoît Roland, Jean-Jacques Rousseau

We would also like to thank:
Vincent Cartuyvels, L'Échevinat duTourisme (Charleroi), M. Philippekin, François Cochin, l'association Le Fuseau, René Pechère, Mme Thys-Clément.

Translated by Laura Ward and Susan Mackervoy.
Edited and typeset by Book Creation Services, London.
Printed in Italy by Editoriale Libraria.

Everyman Guides
79 Berwick Street
London W1V 3PF

BRUSSELS
AND SOUTHERN BELGIUM

EVERYMAN GUIDES

CONTENTS

▲ Brussels and southern Belgium

9. Dinant
10. Huy
11. Waremme
12. Liège
13. Marche-en-Famenne
14. St-Hubert
15. Neufchâteau
16. Virton
17. La Roche-en-Ardenne
18. Verviers
19. Eupen
20. Bastogne
21. Arlon

Below: interior of the Théâtre de la Monnaie in Brussels. Bottom: the courtyard of the Bishop's Palace, Liège.

SOUTHERN BELGIUM

As a result of the institutional reform that has dominated the recent history of Belgium, Wallonia (southern Belgium) has become one of the constituent parts of the new federal state. The region extends across southern Belgian to the south of the language frontier separating the "Latin" from the "Germanic" sections of the community. It is comprised of the provinces of Hainaut, Liège, Luxemburg and Namur, and includes the newly formed Walloon Brabant, created on January 1, 1995. The names of these modern provinces evoke those given to the principalities of the Ancien Régime, although there are marked differences between them in territorial terms, and not one institution dating from the time of the principalities has survived. The roots of the modern-day provinces can be traced to the French *départements* created in 1795 ● *35*.

The Théâtre de la Monnaie.

SOME FACTS ABOUT SOUTHERN BELGIUM
Southern Belgium has a population of 3,255,711 (census of March 1, 1991) and covers an area of 10, 468 square miles – in other words, it comprises nearly one-third of the total population of Belgium and 56 percent of the total territory. The region includes the German-speaking cantons (67,818 inhabitants, on 530 square miles), situated in the western area of the Liège province: this "germanophone community", an integrated part of southern Belgium, forms one of the constituents of the federal state ▲ *242*.

BRUSSELS

Brussels is a city whose history dates back some thousand years: it is thought to have been founded between 977 and 979. It has been the capital of the Kingdom of Belgium since 1830. Previously Brussels was capital of the Duchy of Brabant during the Middle Ages; the center of the communal institutions of the hereditary principalities for the whole of the Low Countries during the 15th and 16th centuries, then solely of the southern Low Countries during the 17th and 18th centuries; head of the *département* of the Dyle during French rule; and the capital (alternating with the Hague) of the Kingdom of the Netherlands between 1814 and 1830. The population of the Brussels agglomeration has grown dramatically since the late 19th and early 20th centuries. This conurbation now constitutes the region of Bruxelles-Capitale, one of the constituent parts of the new federal state that has emerged from Belgium's most recent institutional reforms.

SOME FACTS ABOUT BRUSSELS
On March 1, 1991 the population was 954,045, spread over 100 square miles. Brussels is the seat of a number of European institutions (for example, the European Commission) and one of the seats of the European Parliament.

Below, the Brussels parliament.

The structure of the federal state

The levels	The institutions		
Federal level	Federal institutions: The Chamber of Representatives, the Senate, the King and the Federal Government		
Community level	The German-speaking community	The French-speaking community	The Flemish community
		The Commission of the French community	The Commission of the Flemish community
Regional level	Southern Belgium (Wallonia)	The Bruxelles-Capitale region	The Flemish region
Provincial level	The five Walloon provinces	The bilingual territory of Brussels-Capital	The five Flemish Provinces
Communal level	The Walloon communes	The nineteen Brussels communes	The Flemish communes

The political institutions

The Belgian state is a federal state composed of communities and regions (1st Article of the Constitution). The federal institutions are: the king and the government (who exercise executive power) and the Chamber of Representatives and Senate (who, together with the king, exercise legislative power). During the course of the latest institutional reforms, however, a profound change in the bicameral regime (instituted in 1831) occurred, and a new division of parliamentary duties between the Chamber of Representatives and the Senate was drawn up. In southern Belgium (Wallonia) and the region of Bruxelles-Capitale, the regional institutions are: the regional government (which exercises executive power) and the regional council (which, jointly with the regional government, exercises legislative power). The members of Wallonia's regional council combined with the French-speaking members of the council of the Bruxelles-Capitale region, together make up the Council of the French Community, which in turn has its own government. There is also a political body composed solely of the French-speaking citizens of Brussels, known as the Commission of the French Community, which has an assembly of French-speaking members from the regional council and a college composed of the French-speaking members of the regional government.

HOW TO USE THIS GUIDE

(Sample page shown from the guide to Venice)

The symbols at the top of each page refer to the different parts of the guide.

■ NATURAL ENVIRONMENT

● KEYS TO UNDERSTANDING

▲ ITINERARIES

◆ PRACTICAL INFORMATION

The itinerary map shows the main points of interest along the way and is intended to help you find your bearings.

The mini-map locates the particu[lar] itinerary within the wider area covered by the guide.

●▲■◆ The symbols alongside a title or within the text itself provide cross-references to a theme or place dealt with elsewhere in the guide.

★ The star symbol signifies that a particular site has been singled out by the publishers for its special beauty, atmosphere or cultural interest.

At the beginning of each itinerary, the suggested means of transport to be used and the time it will take to cover the area are indicated:

- By car
- By boat
- On foot
- By bicycle
- Duration

THE GATEWAY TO VENICE ★

PONTE DELLA LIBERTA. Built by the Austrians 50 years after the Treaty of Campo Formio in 1797 ● *34,* to link Venice with Milan. The bridge ended the thousand-year separation from the mainland and shook the city's economy to its roots as Venice, already in the throes of the industrial revolution, saw

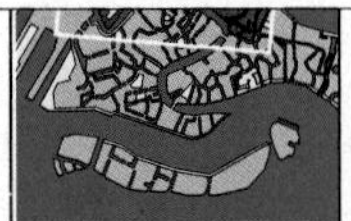

Half a day

BRIDGES TO VENICE

Nature

Birch

Alder

Peat bogs occur in cold and humid areas and on impermeable soils such as clay. In these conditions dead organic matter formed by the slow decomposition of sphagnum mosses and marsh rushes accumulates as peat. In the Upper Ardennes some of these plant formations, known as raised peat bogs, are as much as 23 feet thick; their origins date back between 8,000 and 9,000 years. The flora and fauna associated with this habitat include species of northern origin.

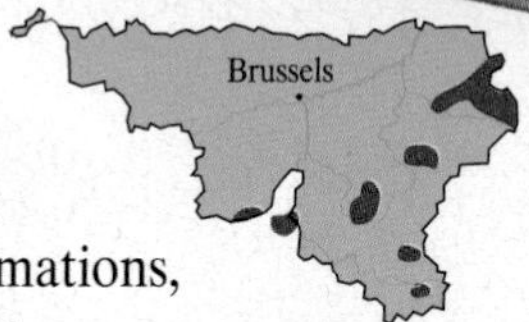

Brussels

In southern Belgium peat bogs occur mainly on the upper plateaux of the Ardennes ▲ *244* and in the Lorraine ▲ *266*.

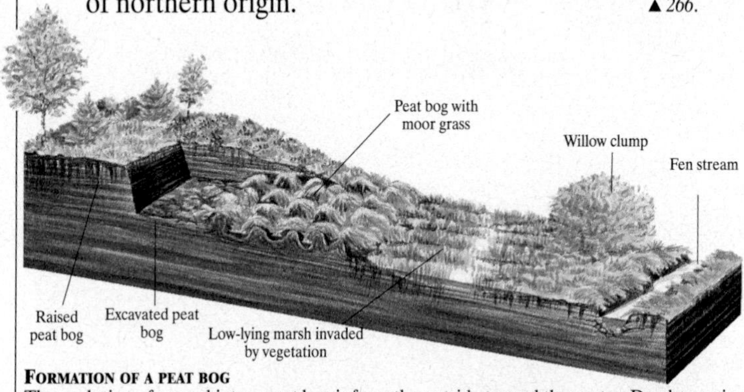

Peat bog with moor grass

Willow clump

Fen stream

Raised peat bog

Excavated peat bog

Low-lying marsh invaded by vegetation

FORMATION OF A PEAT BOG

The evolution of a pond into a peat bog is from the outside toward the center. Dead organic matter slowly decomposes at the bottom and forms peat. If the climate is mild enough and evaporation is less than the amount of rainfall, a mound of sphagnum moss develops. Human exploitation of peat has led to a significant reduction in the number of plant species, due to the drying out of the substrate: moor grass encroaches onto the excavated areas, while heather appears on the edges of the higher parts of the peat bog.

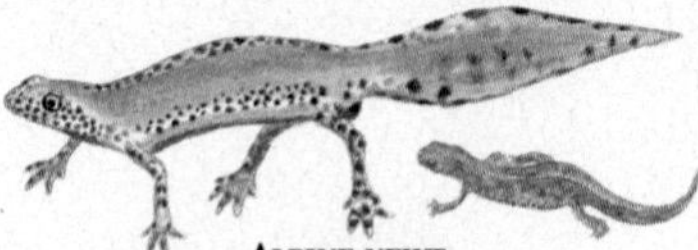

ALPINE NEWT
Highly adaptable, it can live happily in the poor, acidic waters of the peat bogs of the Upper Ardennes, but prefers the waters richer in nutrients found at lower altitudes.

LARGE COPPER
Its caterpillars feed on a plant found in peat bogs.

COMMON AESHNA
This dragonfly reproduces in the stagnant, acid waters of the peat bogs.

Carpets of sphagnum moss and various other plants colonize and eventually choke the ponds in low-lying bogs.

Moor grass forms characteristic humps, which encroach on dried-out peat bogs.

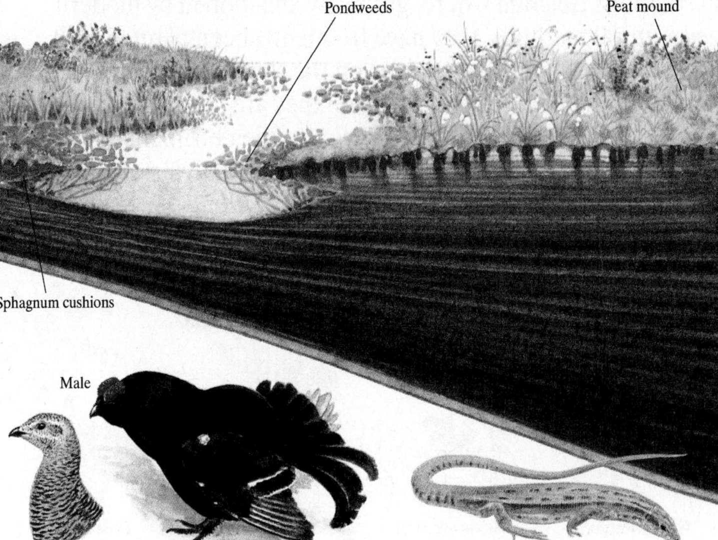

Black grouse
A typical bird of the moors and peat bogs of southern Belgium. The males perform spectacular communal nuptial displays.

Viviparous lizard
This small reptile is commonly found in peat bogs, where it seeks out the driest humps on which to sun itself.

Meadow pipit
Extremely common in fen lands; its characteristic flight is a "parachute fall".

Redpoll
This passerine is known primarily by its twittering when in flight.

Grasshopper warbler
Its long, continuous song resembles that of a grasshopper.

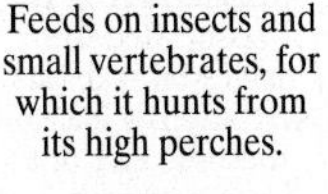

Great gray shrike
Feeds on insects and small vertebrates, for which it hunts from its high perches.

Cranberry
The berries of this deciduous shrub are sought after by the black grouse.

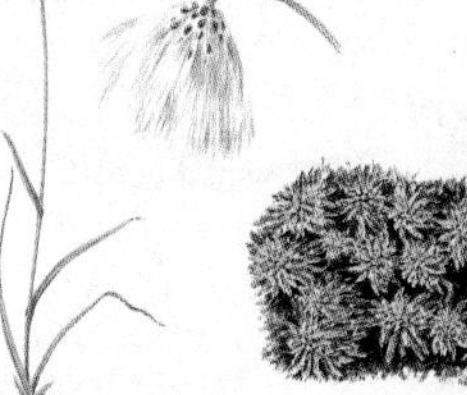

Cotton grass
Grows near ponds and in the dampest areas of the peat bogs.

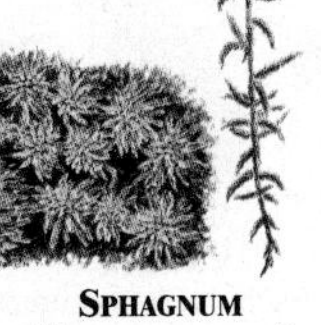

Sphagnum
These mosses, of northern origin, can absorb up to 30 times their weight in water.

Cross-leaved heath
Unlike heather, this grows in the damper parts of the peat bog.

Water meadows appear where alluvial forests have been cleared. In the past these would have been mown between June and July, and then grazed on the second crop, between August and September. They are to be found in numerous valleys in southern Belgium where, gradually abandoned by modern agricultural methods, they have frequently been planted with poplars, in low areas, or spruces on the slopes of the Ardennes massif. In the absence of cultivation they are often taken over by willows, alders and silver birches – to the detriment of the rich indigenous flora and fauna. The finest surviving meadows are now managed and protected using traditional husbandry techniques (mowing and extensive grazing).

RAGGED ROBIN
Very common. It is said that its flowers mark the arrival of the cuckoo.

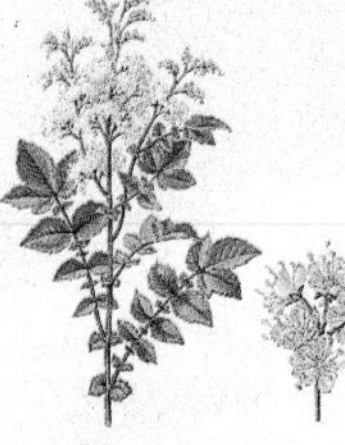

MEADOWSWEET
Widespread on abandoned valley floors; the cream flowers emit a strong almond scent.

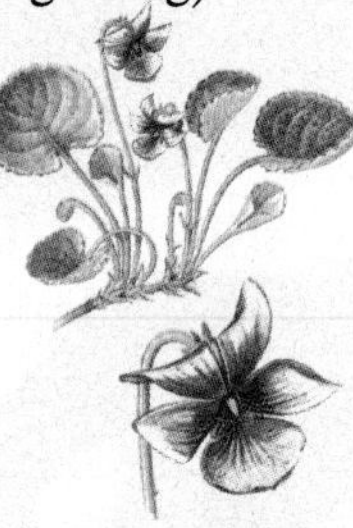

BOG VIOLET
The solitary flowers open in May; it grows on water meadows and swampy ground low in nutrients.

COMARUM
This member of the rose family is found in water meadows and acid swamps.

MARSH FRITILLARY
Associated with devil's-bit scabious, this butterfly has now become rare due to progressive loss of its habitat.

BISTORT COPPER
A rare European butterfly, this is still found in the Ardennes and the Lorraine.

SMALL PEARLY-BORDERED FRITILLARY
In fine weather, the males can be seen flitting swiftly, low over the ground, in search of females.

FIERY COPPER
Its caterpillar feeds on small reeds.

FIELD VOLE
This rodent is mainly found on damp ground, but it tends to avoid overly exposed areas.

SHREW
Each day it consumes the equivalent of half its own weight – if not more – in insects and worms.

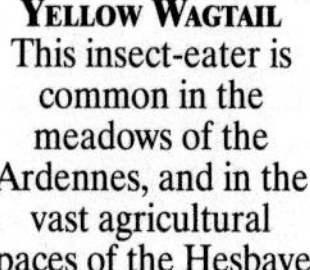

YELLOW WAGTAIL
This insect-eater is common in the meadows of the Ardennes, and in the vast agricultural spaces of the Hesbaye.

WHINCHAT
Changes in the pasture lands of the Ardennes and the Lorraine have led to the decline of this pretty bird.

Stoat

This small carnivore, averaging 8 inches in length, is the only mammal in the region whose pelt radically changes color according to the season. In summer, the black tip of its tail distinguishes it from the weasel.

Grass snake

This harmless snake feeds mainly on frogs and fish. It is becoming increasingly rare in the valleys of southern Belgium.

Dry grasslands

Scrubby vegetation began to grow over the slopes once they were no longer being grazed by sheep.

The microclimate of these grasslands, which is particularly warm and dry, is determined by their rocky limestone substrate and the south-facing aspect of their slopes, on which a flora – some of it originating from more southerly climes – has established itself. The grasslands appeared once the ancient forests were cleared, and were kept cropped by grazing sheep. Many of these grasslands, now gradually abandoned as pasture lands, have once again been taken over by shrubby vegetation.

Brussels

These grasslands are to be found on the hills of the Calestienne region ▲ *211*, in the Meuse valley ▲ *204*, and in the southernmost parts of Belgian Lorraine ▲ *266*.

A Mediterranean flora
In May and June the dry, rocky slopes of the limestone hills are particularly colorful, thanks to the simultaneous flowering of a multitude of plants from southern climes. The resulting impression calls to mind parts of Provence.

Scarce swallowtail
Its caterpillars feed on the blackthorns that grow on the gentle exposed slopes, where they benefit from a warm microclimate.

Common whitethroat
Still widespread, this warbler thrives in the bushy vegetation of the grasslands.

Red-backed shrike
This predatory passerine has now forsaken the dry grasslands for the hedges and trees.

Woodlark
Reafforestation of the grasslands has caused the departure of this pasture-loving bird.

Stonechat
Grasslands and shrubs once provided an ideal habitat for this increasingly scarce bird.

Smooth snake
This lizard-loving predator is particularly fond of the sunny, rocky slopes of the limestone hills known locally as *tiennes*.

Rabbit
Once extremely common, rabbits kept the vegetation cropped low – but their population was decimated by myxomatosis.

Bloody cranesbill
In June and July this wild geranium produces carpets of scarlet flowers on the rocky limestone.

Box
This shrub forms copses on some of the slopes in the Meuse, Viroin and Sambre valleys.

Rockrose
A plant belonging to a Mediterranean family, in Belgium it only flourishes in the wild in the Meuse valley.

Great burnet
This widespread member of the rose family is pollinated principally by wasps and bumblebees.

BANDED AGRION DAMSELFLY
The males defend their territory along the banks of fast-flowing rivers, and perform a display in front of the females.

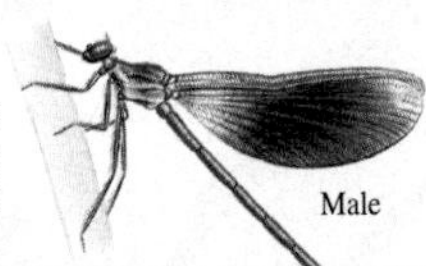

In a rainy region such as southern Belgium fresh water constitutes one of the most precious resources. Yet natural environments such as rivers and streams are most vulnerable to human activity and various pollutants. Left undisturbed, the course of a river is constantly being modified by erosion and alluvial deposits, thus providing diverse habitats for the numerous creatures in it. These may live up or down stream, depending on the speed of the current and the water conditions (such as chemical composition and temperature).

The fauna of the clear waters of the tiny rivers of the Ardennes is still richly varied, with numerous different fish, dragonflies and insect larvae.

YELLOW WATER LILY
It thrives in deep, slow-flowing or still waters.

COMMON ALDER
The roots of this tree are home to a number of fish species, and also help to shore up the river banks.

Gudgeons

Dipper (which runs along the river bottom to catch its prey)

Gray wagtail

KINGFISHER
Common along clear running rivers and streams, in which it dives for small fish and larvae. Its nest is built in a hole dug into the river bank.

GRAY WAGTAIL
Widespread, it hunts for insects along the river banks.

DIPPER
Associated with swift-flowing streams, in which it hunts for insects and molluscs.

SALMON
It spawns in cold, swift-flowing waters, primarily in the streams of the Ardennes.

CHAR
A sedentary, gregarious member of the salmon family, commonly found in fast-flowing rivers.

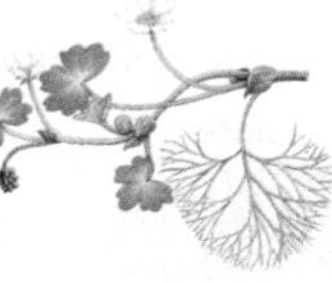

SALICARIA
Fairly common, it grows at the foot of sunny river banks.

CLUB RUSH
It flowers from June to August along undisturbed and well-exposed riverbanks.

COMMON WATER CROWFOOT
Thrives in rich, even slightly polluted, waters.

YELLOW IRIS
In summer beautiful clumps of this plant brighten the sunny river banks along shallow streams.

EUROPEAN OTTER
Hunted for its fur and affected by the pollution of its watery habitat, this fish-eating mammal has become as rare in southern Belgium as in other parts of western Europe.

WATER SHREW
This tiny insect-eating mammal, active by day and by night, has webs of fur between its paws which help it to swim.

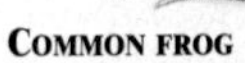

COMMON FROG
Living on land outside its reproductive period, it comes to lay its eggs in still reaches of the river.

Salmon

Forests

The man-managed broadleaved forests provide a habitat for flora and fauna closest to that of the original forests.

Up until Roman times southern Belgium was almost completely covered with broadleaved forests. Tree-clearing and intense exploitation of wood resources (for heating, building and fuel) meant that by the 18th century these had been considerably depleted. Thanks to a program of planting coniferous trees (mainly spruce and pine) embarked upon during the 19th century, forested areas are now increasing in size. Today, spread over a total area of more than 1 million acres, half of which is planted with non-indigenous conifers, they cover more than 30 percent of southern Belgium. Plantations of broadleaved trees are home to a much richer plant and animal life than the coniferous plantations.

Beech
In the absence of human intervention beech is the predominant species in the forests of southern Belgium, where it is found among the oldest stands. It can grow to over 100 feet.

Oak
Oaks offer an attractive environment for animal life: from birds to insects, approximately 400 animal species can be associated with this noble tree.

Silver birch
This tree is referred to as a "pioneer" species, since it is one of the first trees to take root in clearings with poor soils, such as sand or schist.

Aspen
The rustling of the rounded leaves of this tree justifies its scientific name, *Populus tremula*. Its foliage is home to the caterpillars of some superb forest butterflies.

Hornbeam
This tree, which can tolerate shade and pollarding, often forms copses underneath oak trees, providing the soil is sufficiently rich.

HAZELHEN
This species of grouse is a shy, retiring bird. It is now increasingly rare because of the disappearance of the copses that provided it with sustenance and shelter.

Forests are home to a diverse, although somewhat timid, animal life. The numerous birds in the copses and foliage signal their presence primarily by their song. The forest mammals are usually nocturnal animals. Insects, which play an important part in the forest ecosystem (notably in the decomposition of organic matter) are hidden in the leaves or trunks, or in the leaf litter.

Male

WHITE ADMIRAL
The wings of this butterfly change color according to the light.

CAMBERWELL BEAUTY
Associated with the birches and willows of the great broadleaved forests, and now increasingly rare.

BANK VOLE
Common in forests with a rich leaf litter, it hunts for its food on the ground but also up trees, the trunks of which it sometimes climbs.

Woodcock

Bank vole

Badger

Hind (female)

Stag (male)

BADGER
This omnivorous mammal digs vast sets, or occupies ones already lived in by previous generations. It has been badly affected by campaigns to gas earths, directed against rabies-carrying foxes.

RED DEER
Its populations are now confined to the great forest-covered massifs of the Ardennes ▲ *256*, Famenne and Condroz regions, which are more or less cut off from one another by motorway networks.

Red squirrel
The pelt of this rodent sometimes changes color, going from a red shade to almost black.

Black woodpecker
It frequents the tops of tall beeches and pines. During the last century it colonized most of the forests of southern Belgium.

Chaffinch
One of the most common birds found in forests, whether broadleaved or coniferous.

Robin
One of the few insect-eaters that remains in southern Belgium throughout the winter.

Red squirrel
This diurnal mammal can often be seen in the treetops, where it busies itself building its nest of twigs.

Fire salamander
This amphibian breeds in spring waters and in small forest streams (mainly in beech groves). After giving birth it leads a terrestrial existence. Following rain storms it can occasionally be seen in large numbers.

Blackcap
This migrant warbler is notable for its melodious song.

Roe deer
Needing less space than the red deer, it lives in forests with dense undergrowth, where it leads a relatively sedentary life either alone or in family groups. Only the male, or stag, has antlers, which it loses each year.

Wild boar
This omnivorous mammal is still fairly common in the broadleaved forests to the south of the Meuse and Sambre. A system of rearing followed by release into the wild, for hunting purposes, explains its frequency.

KESTREL
As in other European towns, this bird of prey has proved remarkably adaptable and even nests in crevices in public buildings.

There are numerous semi-natural habitats in Brussels, either vestiges of older landscapes or areas abandoned by man and reclaimed by nature. But Brussels' greatest asset is without doubt the Forest of Soignes, a magnificent beech grove situated along the southeastern edge of the city. The soil and relief of what was once a huge forest still bear witness to a landscape formed by the last Ice Age.

House martin's nest

ROSE-RINGED PARAKEET
Approximately forty of these birds were released in 1974. Their subsequent proliferation has presented a problem for some of the indigenous wildlife.

HOUSE MARTIN
A prime example of an urban species associated with buildings, it is nonetheless on the verge of extinction in Brussels.

EUROPEAN SPARROWHAWK
More than fifty pairs nest in and around Brussels; this population is one of the largest in Europe.

RED FOX
This predator reappeared in the Forest of Soignes ▲ *188* around 1950, and is increasingly common in the districts bordering the forest.

History and language

-5000	-1000	-500	-100	0	500	700

Bronze Age

-57 Caesar invades northern Gaul

458–480 Tournai the capital of Childeric I

6TH CENTURY Separation of Neustria from Austrasia

The Megaliths of Wéris

-50 Gaul is finally conquered

4TH AND 5TH CENTURIES Settlement of the Franks

481–511 Clovis I completes the reunification of Gaul

THE BEGINNINGS

Very early settlements can still be traced from certain sites in southern Belgium – for example, at Sprimont, south of Liège, and at Spiennes, south of Mons. Recorded history, however, begins with the Roman conquest in 57 BC, when Caesar used the term *Belgae* to describe the inhabitants of the northern part of Gaul, established between the Seine and the Rhine. In the early Roman Empire this area was the province of *Gallia Belgica*, but was subsequently subdivided under Flavian rule into *Belgica Prima* (capital: Trier) and *Belgica Secunda* (capital: Reims). This frontier region remained Romanized until Frankish peoples settled here during the 4th and 5th centuries. In fact there are those who maintain that the language frontier separating the Germanic languages of the north from the Romance languages of the south dates from the great Frankish invasion of 406.

MEROVINGIANS AND CAROLINGIANS

Childeric I (458–80) was the first of the Merovingian kings to choose Tournai as his capital. It was from this town that Clovis I, who ruled between 481 and 511, undertook the reunification of Gaul. During his reign the diocese of Tournai was founded. In the 6th century the Frankish kingdom split into Neustria in the west and Austrasia in the east. In 751 the last of the Merovingians, Childeric III, was deposed. Pepin III (also known as Pepin the Short) became King of the Franks and founded the Carolingian dynasty; the Carolingians themselves originated from the Meuse region. The family of Charlemagne (below) owned an estate at Herstal, close to Liège.

After Gaul had been conquered it was divided into three provinces: Gallia Aquitania, Gallia Lugdunensis, and Gallia Belgica. The territory which was to become modern-day Belgium was divided into *civitates*, or cities, that corresponded more or less to ancient ethnic divisions. The process of Romanization included the establishment of a network of roads during the reign of Augustus. Three cross-provincial parallel roads passed through Bavay to link the Rhine with the Channel. Today's freeway follows roughly the same route as the Roman road from Bavay to Cologne.

725 Episcopal see of Liège situated at Maastricht

751 Pepin the Short founds the Carolingian dynasty

843 Treaty of Verdun

925 Absorption of Lotharingia into the Empire

972 Notger becomes Bishop of Liège

1066 Town charter of Huy

1316 Peace of Fexhe: absorption of the "commonality" by the principality of Liège

1338 First meeting of the Estates of Hainaut

800 | 900 | 1000 | 1200 | 1400

THE EARLY EMPIRE

Under the Treaty of Verdun in 843 the Carolingian Empire was divided up. Much of present-day southern Belgium was actually part of Lotharingia, which was itself finally absorbed into the Empire in 925. Notger, who was Bishop of Liège, was appointed temporal Prince of the city by the Emperor in 972. The real development of the city, and of the Prince-Bishopric of which it formed the center, dates from this period. The years between 976 and 979 witnessed the birth of Brussels, which was situated at the junction of the north–south and east–west trade

routes. Urban development forced the feudal regime to make certain concessions; and town charters, with their liberties and franchises, began to multiply. The oldest of these to have survived is that of the town of Huy (1066). Between the 10th and 12th centuries principalities under the dynasties of local princes began to appear. At around this time – or shortly afterward – the first representative institutions began to emerge: the Peace of Fexhe (1316) brought the "commonality" under the rule of the principality of Liège, while in around 1338 the first meeting of the Estates of Hainaut was held.

The hereditary principalities had common institutions. The sovereign, if resident abroad, was represented by a Governor-General of the Low Countries.

THE HOUSES OF BURGUNDY AND HABSBURG

Between 1419 and 1448 the Duke of Burgundy, Philip the Good (right), who was already Count of Flanders and Artois, succeeded to his other hereditary principalities: the duchies of Brabant, Limbourg and Luxembourg, together with the counties of Hainaut and Namur. These were to remain under a common sovereign until the end of the Ancien Régime. Initially this was the Duke of Burgundy – then, from the time of Charles V (left), the King of Spain and, eventually, the Emperor. All of them ruled by virtue of their local titles (as Duke of Brabant in Brabant, Count of Hainaut in Hainaut, and so on). In 1526 the Treaty of Madrid dissolved the feudal ties that still linked Flanders and Artois with France. Following the Compromise of Augsburg in 1548 (sometimes called the Interim of Augsburg) the principalities of the Low Countries formed a distinct "circle" within the Empire – the "Burgundian Circle". After the Pragmatic Sanction of 1549, they also formed a single, indissoluble inheritance. The only areas that remained outside this territorial grouping were two ecclesiastical principalities: the Prince-Bishopric of Liège and the Prince-Abbotship of Stavelot-Malmedy, which were joined with another province of the Empire, that of Westphalia. Finally a new hereditary principality, the Duchy of Bouillon, attained its independence during the 18th century.

1500 | 1515 | 1530 | 1545 | 1560 | 1575

1526 Treaty of Madrid: dissolution of the feudal ties joining Flanders and Artois with France

1548 Compromise of Augsburg: establishes the "Burgundian Circle"

1549 Pragmatic Sanction: the principalities constitute an indivisible territorial unit

1559 Creation of new dioceses, including Namur

1576 Pacification of Ghent

1579 Peace of Arras: submission of Artois, Hainaut, Namur and Luxemburg to the King of Spain

THE REFORMATION AND ITS CONSEQUENCES

The 16th century was marked by the Reformation and the Counter-Reformation. The campaigns of the Duke of Alba (right), governor of the Low Countries, were directed both against the reformers and the moderate Catholics suspected of sympathizing with them. In 1579 the Peace of Arras recognized the confederation of Artois with Hainaut, the recovery of Namur and of Luxembourg and, lastly, the submission of these principalities to the King of Spain. In 1588 the break with the United Provinces occurred. Between 1598 and 1621 the Archduke Albert and Archduchess Isabella reigned as sovereigns of the Low Countries. There are those who see in this event the seeds of a future independent Belgian state being sown. In 1612 the Society of Jesus, known as the Jesuits, arrived in the Low Countries and established two "provinces", including Gallia Belgica to the south of the linguistic border, whose territory corresponded to that of today's southern Belgium and northern France. In 1648 the Treaty of Westphalia recognized the break with the United Provinces.

THE EUROPEAN SCENE

Toward the end of the 17th century France annexed the southern part of Flanders (including Lille and Douai), Artois, the south of Hainaut (with Valenciennes) and the regions of Given, Montmedy and Thionville. In 1695 the troops of Marshal de Villeroy bombarded Brussels ▲ *148*, destroying the Grand-Place, which was later rebuilt in its original style. From 1700 onward the War of the Spanish Succession paved the way for the rule of the House of Anjou, first under the Duke of Anjou, Philip V, and then under the reign of Maximilian-Emmanuel of

Bavaria, as nominal sovereign of the Low Countries. In 1713 the Treaty of Utrecht recognized the conquests of Louis XIV, while transferring the sovereignty of the Low Countries to the Emperor Charles VI. Between 1746 and 1748 the War of the Austrian Succession led to military occupation by the French. In 1789 two "revolutions" occurred: in Brabant, arising from opposition to reforms attempted by the Emperor Joseph II (below, right, with his brother Leopold, the future Emperor); and in Liège, sparked by the French Revolution. In 1790 a treaty of union was signed between the united Belgian states, which excluded both Liège and Luxembourg. Nevertheless, Austrian rule was re-established in December 1790. In 1792, after the victory of Jemappes, the Revolutionary armies invaded as liberators; but the following year the Austrian armies, fresh from their victory at Neerwinder, reconquered the country and re-established the Ancien Régime. In 1798 the Revolutionary armies, after a further victory at Fleurus, arrived in Brussels as conquering heroes. After a period of military occupation the country was formally annexed to France, a situation that endured until 1814–5. Under French rule the country was divided

1598–1621 Albert and Isabella joint sovereigns of the Low Countries

1612 The Jesuits establish the province of Gallia Belgica south of the linguistic border

1600 | **1700** | **1750** | **1790** | **1830**

1745–8 French military occupation

1787–9 Revolt in Brabant

1789 Revolt in Liège

1790 Creation of the united Belgian states

1815 Following Battle of Waterloo, Kingdom of Netherlands created (including present-day Belgium).

1830 Revolution and independence

into *départements,* including those of Dyle (Brussels), Jemappes (Mons), Sambre-et-Meuse (Namur), Ourthe (Liège) and les Forêts (Luxembourg). In 1814 the coalition of European powers against France established the Kingdom of the Netherlands. The troubled times spanning the late 18th and early 19th centuries coincided with the beginnings of the Industrial Revolution.

Industrialization arrived early in southern Belgium – particularly in Liège and Verviers – as it did in Hainaut: the textile industries in the east and the coal and iron industries in the Sambre and Meuse areas were the driving forces behind the economy.

The Revolution of 1830

A transitional period of more than one-third of a century elapsed following the end of the Ancien Régime, with almost twenty years of French rule and some fifteen years of Dutch rule. This period of transition was one of decisive change in the economic sphere, since it corresponded with the years of the Industrial Revolution, which particularly affected certain areas of the southern Belgium (Hainaut, Liège, Verviers). It was also a time of political upheaval, as it coincided with two successive attempts at centralization without national independence. Under Dutch rule (1815–30), much of Belgian public opinion was opposed to the use of the Dutch language, as well as the religious and educational policies of the government. The unity of the Kingdom of the Netherlands, as it had been conceived by the European powers (chief of which was Great Britain) at the end of the revolutionary wars, was broken from the moment two hitherto opposed groups – first-generation Catholics and first-generation liberals – came together in coalition. The Catholics, who could no longer hope for the return of the Ancien Régime, had come to distrust the government of two successive regimes, and perceived an advantage in assuming – and exercising – their liberties (particularly those of education and of free association). The liberals, for their part, no longer had reason to fear a return of the Ancien Régime, and felt that the state should cease to pursue the degree of constraint and intervention that had been deemed necessary while such a threat existed. It was this generation which, in 1830, following the September days, flexed its muscles by bringing to a close the period of transition that had prevailed since the end of the Ancien Régime, and establishing a truly modern constitutional government ● *38.*

1830

FEBRUARY 8, 1831 Promulgation of the Constitution

JULY 21, 1831 Leopold of Saxe-Coburg-Gotha takes the oath as the first King of the Belgians

1840

1843 Commission of enquiry into "the condition of the working classes and child labor"

1846 Constitution of the Liberal Party

1847–1914 Catholics and liberals alternate in power

1850

1860

1864 Brussels branch of the International Workers' Party founded

1870

1873 First language law

From the time of its declaration of independence (1830) up until formal recognition of it (1839), Belgium was run by coalition governments founded on an alliance between liberals and Catholics prior to their formation into separate and distinct parties.

THE SOCIAL QUESTION

The creation in 1885 of the Belgian Labour Party, the political voice of the socialist movement, sprang from the condition of the working classes. The socialist movement also took shape in the form of unions, friendly societies and co-operatives. However, a number of working class organizations were also Christian in origin. Grave social unrest developed during the course of 1886 in the industrial centers of southern Belgium, the area around Liège and in the Hainaut district, and the government called out the army to suppress the disturbances. Not only were there widespread arrests, but some twenty dead and a number of wounded. In the aftermath of these events the government was pushed to introduce the first social reforms. The workers' movement was to maintain its pressure and to agitate, in particular, for the extension of the franchise.

THE BIRTH AND DEVELOPMENT OF THE WALLOON MOVEMENT

The word "Wallonia", used for the first time in 1844 by Charles Grandgagnage, was picked up in 1886 by the poet Albert Mockel, and used in the title of a magazine founded by him at around this time. It was he who, in an article in the *Mercure de France* of April 1897, launched the slogan: "Wallonia for the Walloons, Flanders for the Flemings, and Brussels for the Belgians." The first Walloon Congress was held in 1890, and from this time the Walloon movement grew in popularity, without as yet being representative of the main body of public opinion of the region – any more than the Flemish movement to which it was opposed. A forceful declaration of Walloon feeling was made by the socialist Jules Destrée ▲ *275* in his "Letter to the King" of 1912: "You reign over two peoples. In Belgium, there are Walloons and there are Flemings; there are no Belgians." The author called for a "Belgium built on the union between two free and independent peoples, united precisely because of their mutual independence."

1885 Creation of the Belgian Labour Party

1890 First Walloon Congress

1898 Language legislation (the "law of equality")

1908 The Congo a Belgian colony

1914–18 The Catholic government brings in liberals and socialists

1880 | 1890 | 1895 | 1900 | 1910

1880 Breaking of diplomatic relations with the Holy See (the "war of the schools")

1886 Serious unrest in the areas around Liège and in Hainaut

1893 Strikes for universal suffrage; abolition of property qualifications for the vote

1912 Jules Destrée's "Letter to the King"; first meeting of the Walloon Assembly

Clericals and Anticlericals

The opposition between Catholics and liberals on all questions concerning the relationship between the Catholic church and the state has long dominated political life in Belgium. The crisis reached its head under the liberal government in power between 1878 and 1884. The second law to introduce primary education in 1879 was dubbed the "Loi de Malheur" (the "invidious law") by the Catholics. On January 31, 1879, a mandamus of the bishops closed with the prayer: "from schools without God and from teachers without faith, Lord deliver us." In 1880 the Catholic church's hierarchy refused to take official part in the celebrations marking the fiftieth anniversary of Independence. In the same year, diplomatic relations between Belgium and the Holy See were broken off. During subsequent elections, however, held in 1884, the Catholic party was returned to power for a further thirty years.

World War One

Although Belgian neutrality had been guaranteed by the European powers since 1831, German troops nevertheless marched into Belgium on August 4, 1914. This act of aggression resulted in Great Britain's entry into the war on the side of France. Belgian territory was occupied, in its virtual entirety, by the German troops. With the return of peace, a number of important reforms were introduced: universal suffrage and social reforms to meet the demands of the Labour movement, together with language reforms in response to the demands of the Flemish movement. Below: soldiers from the Belgian army.

1815: Waterloo reshapes the political map of Europe

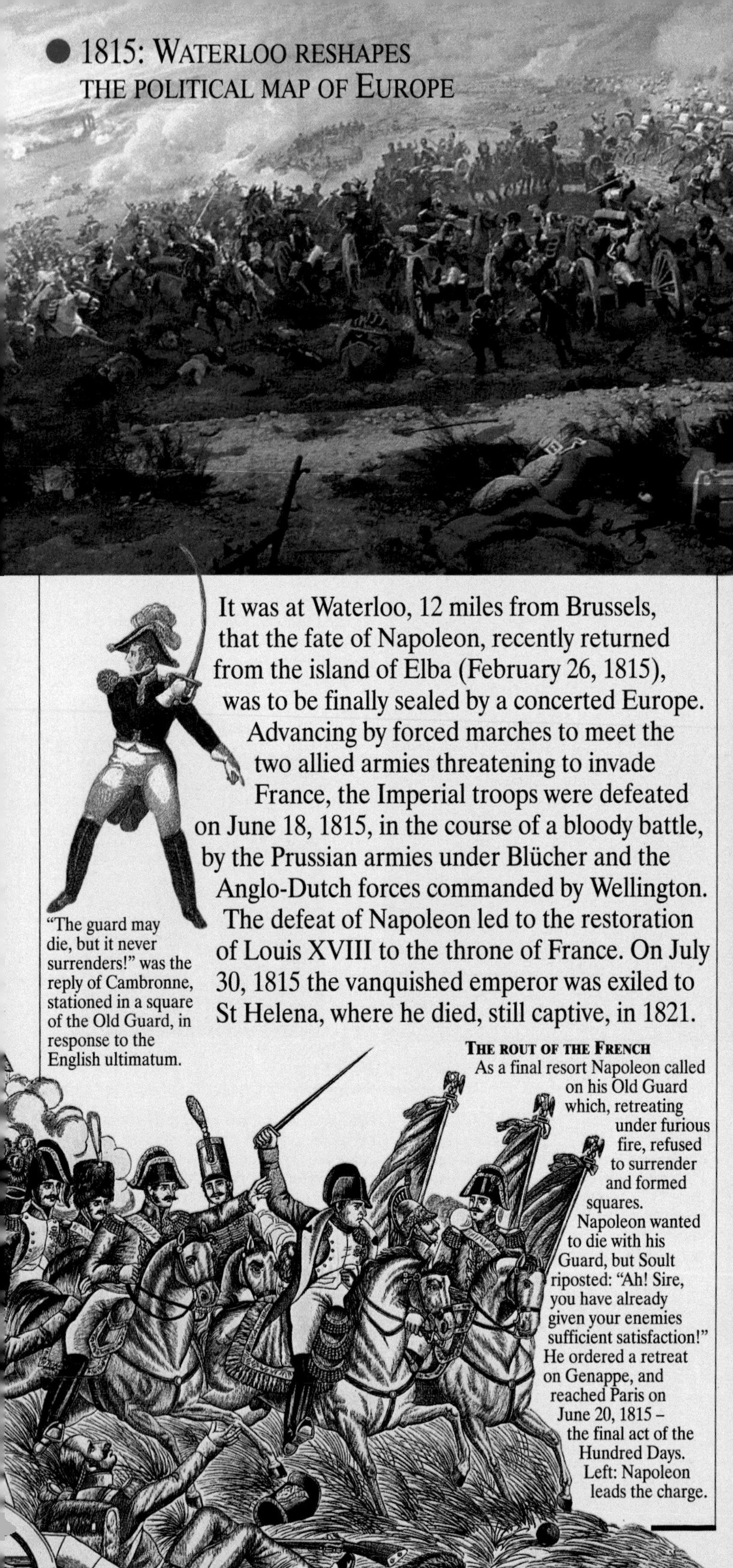

It was at Waterloo, 12 miles from Brussels, that the fate of Napoleon, recently returned from the island of Elba (February 26, 1815), was to be finally sealed by a concerted Europe. Advancing by forced marches to meet the two allied armies threatening to invade France, the Imperial troops were defeated on June 18, 1815, in the course of a bloody battle, by the Prussian armies under Blücher and the Anglo-Dutch forces commanded by Wellington. The defeat of Napoleon led to the restoration of Louis XVIII to the throne of France. On July 30, 1815 the vanquished emperor was exiled to St Helena, where he died, still captive, in 1821.

"The guard may die, but it never surrenders!" was the reply of Cambronne, stationed in a square of the Old Guard, in response to the English ultimatum.

The rout of the French
As a final resort Napoleon called on his Old Guard which, retreating under furious fire, refused to surrender and formed squares. Napoleon wanted to die with his Guard, but Soult riposted: "Ah! Sire, you have already given your enemies sufficient satisfaction!" He ordered a retreat on Genappe, and reached Paris on June 20, 1815 – the final act of the Hundred Days. Left: Napoleon leads the charge.

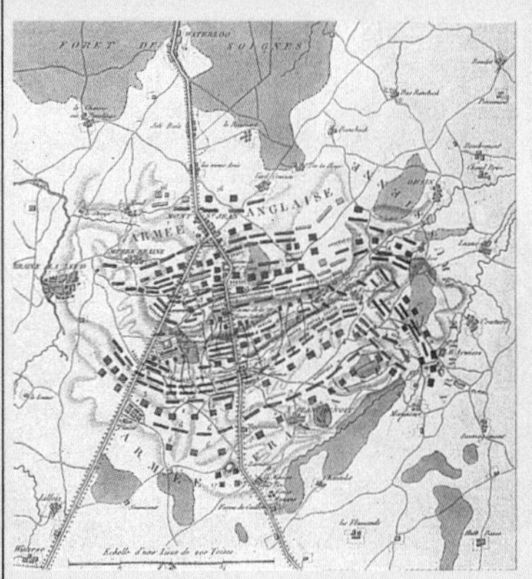

The battle

Napoleon, encamped at the farm of Caillou, only decided to attack on June 18, owing to the heavy rain. He finally launched his offensive toward noon, and took the farm of Hougoumont; then the enemy line was broken with the capture of the farms of La Haie-Sainte and La Papelotte. But cannons sounded from the left, in the direction of Wavre: the Prussians, who had routed Grouchy, were coming to the rescue of the English. Napoleon found himself hemmed in on the Sunken Road. An appalling melee ensued, resulting in the defeat of the Imperial army. The victors, Blücher and Wellington, exchanged congratulations at La Belle Alliance farm. Above and below: the battle in progress.

Plan and positions

Mont St-Jean, where Wellington's army was established, is on an elevated plateau. The left wing, at La Haie-Sainte, had open lines of communication with Blücher's Prussians in the direction of Wavre, but the rear was blocked by the Forest of Soignes. Napoleon intended to force the enemy back against the latter: Grouchy would attack at Wavre, while he himself would advance from the front. Above: a plan of the battle positions.

Wellington, the Iron Duke

Napoleon had underestimated the resolve of Wellington, who gained his nickname the "Iron Duke" at Waterloo. Endowed with great physical endurance and an unbreakable will, he withstood the attack of the horse guards and the cavalry corps of Kellerman and Ney, brought in by Napoleon.

"Mournful plain . . .

"Bodies, weapons, all were confused, heaped up upon each other, pressing and crushing each other." (Gourgaud) Right: a Highlander engaging a French cuirassier.

THE REVOLUTION OF 1830

Making the first Belgian flag.

In 1830 a revolutionary wave, presaged by events in Ireland and Greece, swept through Europe, changing the political map that had existed since the Congress of Vienna. It was the July Revolution in France which, because of its proximity and blare, had the most decisive impact on the evolution of political ideas and attitudes in Belgium. Disturbances on August 25, 1830 snowballed in a matter of days. One month later the Dutch withdrew, and Belgium gained its independence.

THE SPARK
On August 25 there were disturbances in Brussels after a performance of *La Muette de Portici*, an opera describing the insurrection in Naples of 1647 ▲ *167*. The patriotic aria *Amour Sacré* ("Sacred Love") had the effect of a signal, unleashing street demonstrations.

DEPARTURE OF THE VOLUNTEERS OF LIÈGE
On September 23 Brussels was attacked by Dutch troops. Workers from all over Belgium – but particularly from Liège under the leadership of Charles Rogier (right) – came to support the citizens of Brussels.

THE TROOPS WITHDRAW
On September 24 a provisional administrative commission was established. After four days of fighting, the Dutch troops left Brussels during the night of September 26.

REVOLUTION SWEEPS THE COUNTRY
At the end of August the middle-class citizens of Brussels formed a militia to re-establish order; nevertheless, revolt soon swept the country. Above: a combatant of 1830 (artist unknown).

The provisional government
This was partly composed of leaders of the opposition. On October 4 an edict was issued proclaiming that "the provinces of Belgium, wrested by force from Holland, constitute an independent state." Independence, however, was not to be formally established until 1839.

Street fighting
At the beginning of 1830, although the opposition had included both Catholics and liberals, no desire for independence had been voiced. As the riots continued, however, demands began to crystallize.

The new institutions
The Conference of London, consisting of representatives of the European powers, debated the fate of Belgium for a period of several months. A constituent assembly – the National Congress – elected on November 3, 1830, drafted a constitution that was adopted on February 7, 1831. This constitution, drawn up in French, established the long-term institutions: a constitutional monarchy, bicameralism, and communes and provinces subject to the authority of the central government.

Which king?
The National Congress was also called upon to choose the first head of state. It first opted for the Duke of Nemours, son of Louis-Philippe. This choice, however, came to nothing, and on June 4, 1831 the National Congress, after a regency lasting several months, finally elected Prince Leopold of Saxe-Coburg-Gotha ● *42*.

"Peg-leg" Charlier, a hero of the events of 1830 in Liège.

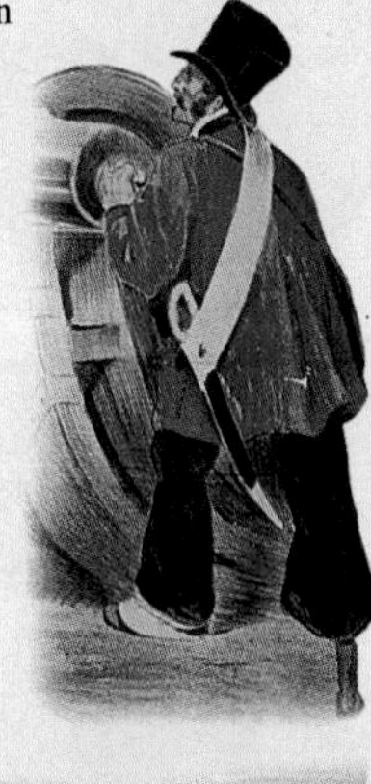

On November 22, 1830 the National Congress charged with drawing up the constitution of the new state decided by 174 votes to 13 that Belgium would be a hereditary constitutional monarchy. The King of the Belgians thus fills both a political and a representative role; the principal of ministerial responsibility, however, leaves no room for the exercise of personal power. The Queen is joined with him in this representative role. Between 1831 and 1991 women were excluded from the succession to the throne.

LEOPOLD II (1835–1909) Son of Leopold I. He was married to the Archduchess of Austria, Marie-Henriette.

LEOPOLD I (1790–1865) Duke of Saxony and Prince of Saxe-Coburg, Belgium's first king took the oath of office on July 21, 1831. Widower of Charlotte, Princess of Wales, he took as his second wife Louise-Marie, Princess of Orléans, daughter of the French king Louis-Philippe.

ALBERT I (1875–1934) He succeeded his uncle Leopold II on December 23, 1909. His wife Elizabeth (1876–1965) was Duchess of Bavaria. He died tragically in a climbing accident at Marche-les-Dames ▲ *214*.

Albert II. Brother of Baudouin I, Albert II was born in 1934 and succeeded to the throne on August 9, 1993. In 1959 he married Paola Ruffo di Calabria, born in 1937.

Baudouin I (1930–93)
He exercised royal power under the title of Prince Royal from August 10, 1950 to July 16, 1951 and was only crowned on July 17, 1951. He married Fabiola de Mora y de Aragón in 1960.

Leopold III (1901–83)
Son of Albert I, he was crowned on February 23, 1934. His first wife was Princess Astrid of Sweden (1905–35); his second wife, Mary Lilian Baels, never had the title of Queen and their children do not appear in the line of succession. He was forced to abdicate on July 16, 1951 ● *44*. His brother Charles (1903–83) was Regent between September 2, 1944 and July 20, 1950.

Queen Astrid, the future King Baudouin, and Princess Josephine-Charlotte.

1920

1920–1 Second revision of the Constitution

1930

1932 New language legislation

SEPTEMBER 1944 Liberation

1940

1945 Walloon Congress at Liège

1950

1919 First elections to the Chamber of Representatives under universal male suffrage

MAY 10, 1940 Troops of the Third Reich invade Belgium

1945–50 The "Royal Question"

1949 Women given the vote

1950–8 The "Schools Question"

WORLD WAR TWO

On May 10, 1940 the armies of the Third Reich marched into Belgium; the country's entire territory remained occupied until September 1944. Subsequently the political rift between King Leopold III, who remained in the country after the army's capitulation, and his ministers, who left first for France and then for London, was at the root of the "Royal Question". Following the war, there were again important reforms, including currency reform and the creation of a social security system.

THE "ROYAL QUESTION"

King Leopold III was deported to Germany in June 1944, and had still not returned – despite having the opportunity to do so – by the time of his country's liberation. When his return seemed imminent, in May 1945, liberals, socialists and Communists opposed it, denouncing the King for his conduct during the war and, in particular, for his meeting with Hitler in November 1940. A referendum was held in March 1950, in which 57.68 percent of the populace declared themselves in favor of the return of Leopold III; in Brussels and southern Belgium, however, a majority of the voters were against it. After the King's return on July 22, an opposition movement formed, which manifested itself in strikes and violent clashes – particularly in the industrial centers of southern Belgium – and the threat of a march on Brussels loomed. After the incidents of Grâce-Berleur, which left three dead, and in response to mediation by leaders of the National Confederation of Political Prisoners, the King decided to withdraw from the public eye, announcing that he would abdicate after one year should a compromise be found in the person of his son, Baudouin.

LE ROI LEOP

1960 Independence of the Congo

1958–93 Dismantlement of Belgium as a unified state; series of institutional reforms introduced

1993 Formal establishment of a federal state

1960 | 1970 | 1980 | 1990

1962 Language frontier established by law

WINTER OF DISCONTENT 1960–1

After the Congo finally gained its independence on June 30, 1960, the Belgian government set about instituting a number of major social, economic and financial reforms. Its "unified law program" provoked strong opposition among socialist and union circles. Between the middle of December 1960 and the middle of January 1961 a wave of strikes unfurled. These strikes mainly took place in Wallonia, and they prompted a fresh resurgence of the Walloon movement. This had begun to develop toward the end of the 19th century, in reaction to the Flemish movement which had been steadily growing stronger since Belgian independence. From 1961 onward the combined pressure of the Flemish and Walloon movements paved the way for institutional reforms.

THE TRANSITION FROM UNITARY TO FEDERAL STATE

This occurred in four stages: 1970, 1980, 1988–9 and 1992–4, with the Belgian state eventually adopting a federal structure. Within this framework the autonomy of the Walloon, Flemish and German-speaking regions was recognized, as were the Flemish, French and German communities. These regions and communities would henceforth be components of a federal state, and would possess their own representative and administrative institutions. The emergence of a federal state was achieved partly by constitutional amendments and partly through the enactment of institutional reforms.

LD CAPITULE

● The Walloon language

Below, the linguistic divisions of Wallonia (southern Belgium).

Walloon: "the Latin of the North"

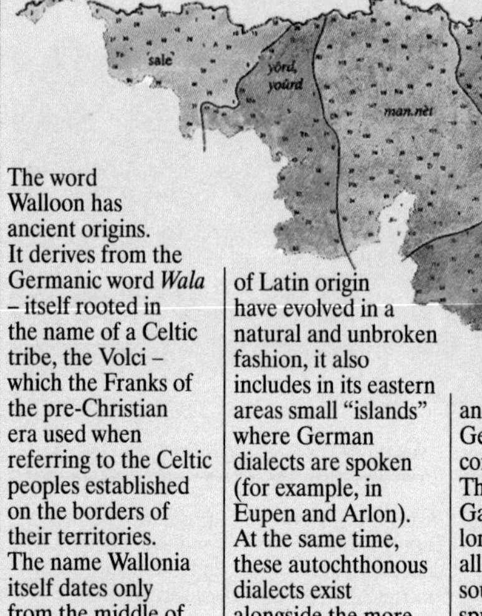

The word Walloon has ancient origins. It derives from the Germanic word *Wala* – itself rooted in the name of a Celtic tribe, the Volci – which the Franks of the pre-Christian era used when referring to the Celtic peoples established on the borders of their territories. The name Wallonia itself dates only from the middle of the 19th century. Although Wallonia, or the Walloon region, essentially corresponds to the area in Belgium within which dialects of Latin origin have evolved in a natural and unbroken fashion, it also includes in its eastern areas small "islands" where German dialects are spoken (for example, in Eupen and Arlon). At the same time, these autochthonous dialects exist alongside the more widespread official languages of Belgium: French (in Brussels and the greater part of the Walloon region), Dutch (in Flanders) and German (in the German-speaking community ▲ *242*). The Romanization of Gaul – which was long-established and all-pervading in the south – steadily spread northward, and particularly northeastward via the Rhone and Saône valleys and through the Vosges and Lorraine as far as the Meuse, the Moselle and the Rhine (Aix-la-Chapelle and Cologne). Consequently the final boundary of the Latin language eventually came to be fixed on an axis running through the center of Belgium, and the commune of Eben-Emael (to the north of Liège) became the northernmost point of the Latin world.

The dialects of Wallonia

These are divided into a number of sub-groups. Those of the Hainaut region are related to the dialect of Picardy and, for example, retain the Latin "c" sound before the letter "a": *canter* (to sing), *car* (cart). Those of the Virton district ▲ *267* are, under the designation "gaumais", a variant of the dialect of the Lorraine. Several communes of the Bohan district ▲ *266*, however, are related to the dialect of Champagne. The Walloon dialect is spoken in the remaining areas, and encroaches slightly into France via Givet and Fumay; in the 19th century it was also spoken in part of America (Wisconsin), where it survives to this day. Wallonia itself is divided into two main, relatively homogeneous dialects, centered around Liège and Namur: the "west Walloon" of Liège and the "central Walloon" of Namur. In addition to this there are two hybrid dialects, marking in the west and the south the transition into the dialects of Picardy and Lorraine.

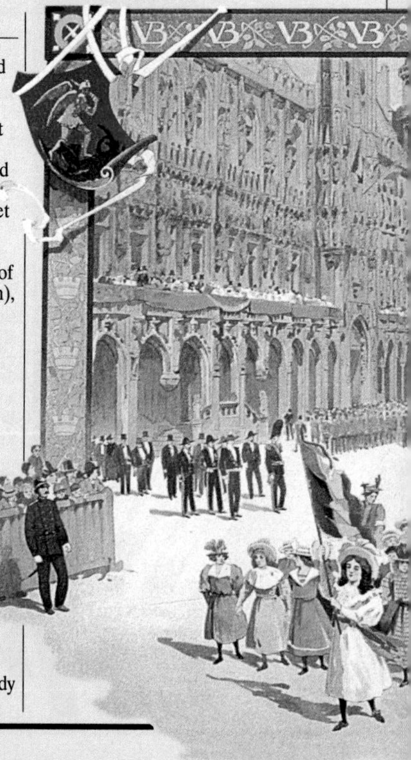

Walloon characteristics

The Walloon dialect, while having Latin as its principal source, has also been strongly influenced by the Germanic languages. It has borrowed from the Franks a larger number of words than from the dialects of the more southern and western regions, and retained them for longer: in the Liège district, for example, words such as *foûre* (hay), *banse* (manna) or *hêtî* (good health). In addition, it has continued to import from the north and east a large number of Flemish and German words: again in Liège, Flemish and German importations into the local dialect include *snoufe* (snuff), *toûbak* (tobacco), *crompîre* (potato) and *pot'kése* (potted cheese).

Nevertheless, the language has also preserved Latin words: in the Liège dialect, *faw* (beech tree) from the Latin *fagus* and *sa* (willow) from the Latin *salix*. Wallonia has long been and continues to be much influenced by French, which for centuries was the language of culture; but in return it has donated a number of words to the French language, especially in the area of mining: *houille* (coal), *terril* (slag heap), *bure* (homespun), *faille* (seam), and so on. Today the widespread use of the French language – which has increased since World War Two – presents a serious threat to the survival of Walloon. Monolingual speakers of Walloon have disappeared, and the number of young people who do not speak the dialect at all has now increased to the point where measures are being considered to save it from extinction.

Written and spoken language

No one dominant Walloon tongue has emerged from the numerous dialects, with the result that these have remained local phenomena. However, this has not precluded the emergence of a considerable body of Walloon literature. Works began to appear in the late 1500's, but it was only in the 19th century, under the influence of the Romantic movement, that they really took on any importance. The Liège Society of Walloon Literature, founded in 1856, in this respect played a role similar to that of the Félibres in Provence; and in 1885 the success of the play *Tatî l'Pèriquî* (*Gauthier the Wig Maker*) by Edgar Remouchamps sparked the "awakening of the Walloon spirit" (Jean Haust, compiler of the *Atlas linguistique de la Wallonie*, far left). While theater and song were more popular in the 19th century, it was the poets who produced the most enduring contributions (Louis Remacle, Albert Marquet, Gabrielle Bernard, Willy Bal and others).

French as spoken in Belgium

Le Jeune Albert, a bilingual comic strip in French and "Bruxellois".

The French language in Brussels

Although officially bilingual, today Brussels is mainly French-speaking, and is the third-largest French-speaking city in the world. French influence arrived later in Brussels than in Wallonia, and under very different circumstances, since French in Brussels was superimposed onto a Germanic rather than a Latin dialect. What the French regard as a typical Belgian accent is in fact the accent of Brussels. This is characterized by its intonation and certain Germanic sounds. At the same time, some Flemish words have been introduced into the French of Brussels, and their influence is also apparent in certain grammatical conjunctions: *ça je sais pas* (I don't know), from the Flemish *dat week ik niet*, instead of the French *je ne sais pas*; *je ne peux pas de ma mère* (in French, *ma mère me l'a interdit* – my mother forbade me); *est-ce que tu veux une fois écouter* (here *une fois* – once – is the Flemish *eens*, which in French would be *enfin*, or finally); *il est deux ans marié* (in French, *il est marié depuis deux ans* – he has been married for two years), and so on.

A mini-dictionary

Brussels dialect
baes: boss
half en half: 50/50
ketje: kid
smeerlap: scoundrel
zievereer: gossip-mongerer
zwanze: joke
prober: to try

Walloon dialect
drache: rain
maquée: fromage blanc
sacoche: handbag
posture: statue
vidange: empty glass
chicon: chicory
endive: endive
pralines: chocolates

Those who are keen to learn more about this subject are advised to visit one of the Toone puppet shows ▲ *161* or, if possible, to see the well-known play by Fonson and Wicheler – or indeed, to read, carefully observing the pronunciation, some of the novels of Leopold Courouble (*La Famille Kaekebroek*, 1902) or the stories of Marcke Ten Driessche (*Les Fables de Pitje Schramouille*, 1923). See also French/Flemish glossary ◆ *346*.

The French language in southern Belgium

French gained a foothold in southern Belgium at an early date. While local dialects were used for everyday speech, the first public and private records, dating from the 13th century, were written in French. From this time on, French gradually became the language of everyday speech alongside the local patois. Its growth – especially rapid during the 19th century – was accelerated by education and the growth of the media. While the French language of southern Belgium has now lost

many of its local characteristics, it still retains many idioms. Some of these – both official terms, such as *bourgmestre* (mayor) and *athénée* (high school), and more general ones such as *septante* (seventy) and *nonante* (ninety) – apply to the whole of southern Belgium; whereas others are purely local – such as *soirer* (to spend the evening, from the French word *soirée*, meaning evening) used in Liège.
The pronunciation of French in southern Belgium tends to be lazier than in France. The Walloons usually ignore any difference between words such as *enfuir* and *enfouir*, pronouncing them both as *enfouir*; but, unlike the French, they distinguish between "w" and "v" and also maintain the distinction between the sounds *un* and *in*. The people of Hainaut nasalize the vowel "è" before a nasal consonant (the word *laine* thus becomes *linne*), while the people of Liège aspirate the "h" in words of Germanic origin (*hache* and *hêtre*). Home to grammarians such as Grevisse and Hanse, and writers such as Simenon and Marchaux, who have enriched the French language as a whole, Wallonia has also produced literary masterpieces more firmly rooted in its native soil, such as *Les Ceux de chez nous* by Marcel Rémy and the novels of Aimé Quernol.

ART AND TRADITIONS

“From Carolingian times until the mid 12th century, Mosan art was hardly matched in brilliance by any other cradle of art in western Europe.” (Lucien Febvre)

Miniature painting from the Floreffe Bible (1150–70).

Mosan art flourished in the southern districts of the old diocese of Liège, where cultural and economic life followed the course of the Meuse river. The main centers of artistic activity were the towns of Liège, Huy, Namur and Dinant. Between the 11th and 13th centuries the influence of Mosan art spread as far afield as Flanders, France, Rhineland and even Poland. Its incontestable achievements were in working gold and other metals, and its greatest artists Renier de Huy (first quarter of the 12th century), Godfrey de Huy (middle of the 12th century), Nicolas de Verdun (active between 1181 and 1205), Jourdain de Liège (c. 1200) and Hugo d’Oignies (c. 1230).

NOTGER IVORY
(Musée Curtuis, Liège, ▲ *226*)
This ivory (c. 980), considered to be the first Mosan work of art, displays the profound influence of Byzantine traditions.

CHALICE OF GILLES DE WALCOURT
(Oignies Treasury, Namur ▲ *198*)
This carved chalice provides the fullest expression of Hugo d’Oignies’ goldworking skills.

BAPTISMAL FONT
(St-Barthélemy, Liège ▲ *225*)
This is without doubt the most accomplished masterpiece (1107–18) of Mosan art, as much for the harmony of its proportions (classical Antiquity bends here, for the first time, to serve a Christian spirituality) as for the richness of its iconography, which centers entirely on the sacrament of Baptism. The whole is executed in bronze by the lost-wax process. The great themes central to Mosan art – water (the Meuse and Sambre) and fire (for melting metal) – are handled to perfection. For was it not predicted in the Gospels that John would baptize with water, whereas Jesus would baptize with fire?

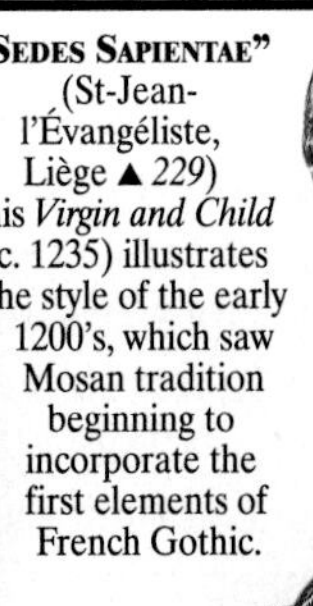

“Sedes Sapientae”
(St-Jean-l’Évangéliste, Liège ▲ *229*)
This *Virgin and Child* (c. 1235) illustrates the style of the early 1200’s, which saw Mosan tradition beginning to incorporate the first elements of French Gothic.

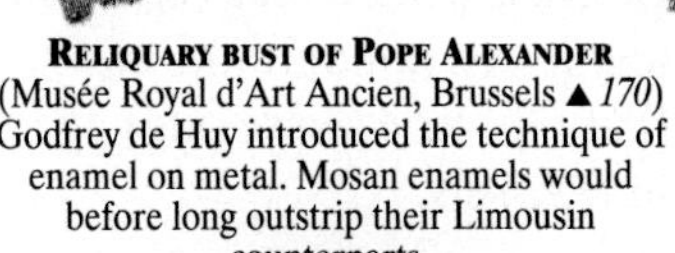

Reliquary bust of Pope Alexander
(Musée Royal d’Art Ancien, Brussels ▲ *170*)
Godfrey de Huy introduced the technique of enamel on metal. Mosan enamels would before long outstrip their Limousin counterparts.

Virgin and Child attributed to Dom Rupert
(Musée Curtuis, Liège ▲ *226*)
This relief carved in graywacke sandstone (above), dating from c. 1150, places Mary within a doorway whose threshold, forbidden to men, was to be crossed only by God – to save mankind. Mosan iconography called on the erudite notions of the great theologians of the Liège schools. It often combined, with great ingenuity, the teachings of the Old and New Testaments.

For nearly four centuries tapestry making was undeniably the leading luxury trade in the southern Low Countries. The art of tapestry found its fullest expression during the 16th century when artists as renowned as Raphael and Bernard Van Orley produced their cartoons, an activity that was taken up in the 17th century by masters such as Rubens and Jordaens. Tapestry production was concentrated in two weaving centers: Tournai in the 15th century, and Brussels during the centuries that followed. During the 18th century, however, the influence and competitiveness of France forced the last Brussels workshop to close its doors (in 1794), and it was not until the early 20th century that tapestries were once again being woven in Brussels.

Brussels tapestry is characterized by a large border decorated with swags of flowers and fruit, which become increasingly exuberant over the centuries.

TOURNAI TAPESTRY
During the 15th century the city of Tournai was a center of prime economic and cultural importance ▲ *310*. Tapestries, mostly of historical scenes, were woven on vertical looms (a method known as *haute lisse*). In each scene figures were piled up one upon the other in rich profusion within a wide band, with just a narrow strip of horizon at the top. The tapestries were without borders, and the composition ignored perspective. Above: the *Battle of Roncevaux*.

Brussels tapestry
Brussels tapestries of the pre-Renaissance combined Gothic elements (three-paneled composition, richly dressed figures) and Renaissance innovations: candle-lit interiors, a concern with realism and the inclusion of landscape detail (right, *Mourning at the Foot of the Cross*, from the first quarter of the 16th century). Subsequently, influenced by the Italian Renaissance and following the example of Raphael in his series of *Acts of the Apostles*, figures became increasingly expressive and moved more freely within a monumental setting (above, *The Story of Jacob*, c. 1530).

Anti-fraud device. In the early part of the 16th century the more difficult parts of a tapestry were sometimes dyed. In order to put a stop to this, and guarantee the high quality of Brussels tapestries, the mark of the town weavers (B-B) was made obligatory from 1528 (top left).

Evolution of a style
In the 17th century historical or allegorical subjects and scenes of daily life were all equally popular. The style of the Baroque tapestries, for which Rubens often made preparatory sketches, explored sweeping movements, powerful gestures and theatrical poses. During the following century public preference turned instead to pastoral scenes and mythological subjects. The rendering of perspective was fully mastered, and the chromatic values were so richly varied that tapestries almost perfectly imitated paintings.

Characterized by pieces assembled on a foundation of braids, mesh and tulle, lacemaking in Brussels reached its height during the 17th and 18th centuries. The superlative quality of the design and finish of Brussels lace accounted for its success. This luxury commodity was highly sought after in foreign markets, making it the most important industry both in terms of workforce numbers and export figures. The European courts were the main clients of the Brussels workshops.

THE LACEMAKER
The design, once transposed onto a pattern (known as the *patron*), is given to the lacemakers who make the lace by hand. A new technique using appliqué perfected during the 17th century enabled large-scale works to be produced in a short space of time.

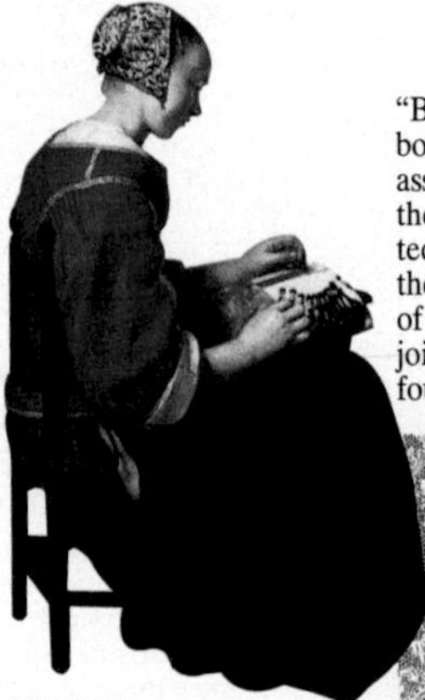

BRUSSELS LACE
(17th–18th century)
"Brussels lace" was a bobbin-produced lace assembled by using the appliqué technique (see left): the various elements of the design are joined together on a foundation of net or braids with picots. Toward the end of the 18th century lace design became much lighter, at which point lacemaking technique in Brussels was compelled to adapt to the new fashion.

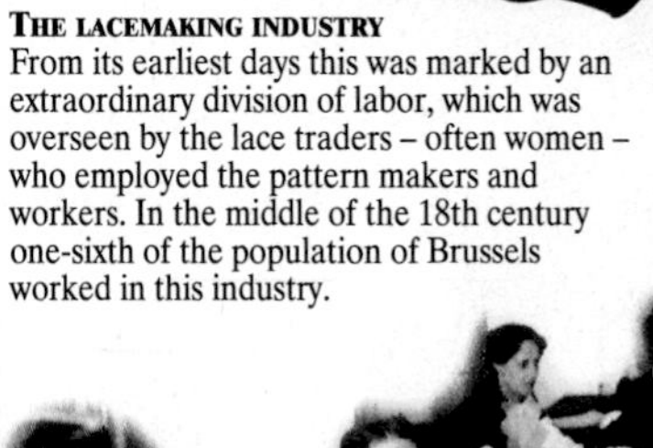

THE LACEMAKING INDUSTRY
From its earliest days this was marked by an extraordinary division of labor, which was overseen by the lace traders – often women – who employed the pattern makers and workers. In the middle of the 18th century one-sixth of the population of Brussels worked in this industry.

English point (19th–20th century)
This term was applied, around 1850, to a new type of mixed lace. The typical gauze foundation and circular decorative elements were produced by needlepoint, while the floral motifs picked out with ribs were bobbin-made.

Brussels appliqué (19th–20th century)
The motifs (made with a bobbin or needlepoint) were stuck or stitched onto a foundation that was made separately. Originally this was a foundation of braids with picots, but toward the end of the 18th century it became a foundation of narrow bobbin-made strips (known as *drochel*) which were joined invisibly by a "tack". Very light with muted contrasts, the *drochel* was unique to Brussels lace. From the second half of the 19th century, machine-made tulle took over, at greatly reduced cost.

Duchesse lace (19th–20th century)
This bobbin-made lace derives its name from the Duchess of Brabant's title before her marriage to Leopold II. Inspired by Brussels lace, Duchesse lace is composed of a tight pattern of flowers and leaves with raised ribs, sometimes picked out by a thread border.

Gauze point, or rose point (19th–20th century)
This Brussels needlepoint lace was created in the mid 19th century; it has sometimes been called "rose point" after its floral pattern (often with superimposed rose petals). The extremely delicate gauze foundation is made from a network of nets produced with a single continuous thread.

Celtic glassmaking knowledge – in existence long before the Roman conquest – and the superb production of Venetian-style glassware in the 16th and 17th centuries paved the way for southern Belgium's perfect mastery of a technique that was to culminate in the manufacture of crystal from the end of the 18th century. The early experiments of Sébastien Zoude in Namur in 1761 laid the foundations for the extraordinary success of Aymé-Gabriel d'Artigues who in 1802, at Vonêche, created the first crystal factory in continental Europe. In 1826 its engineers, François Kemlin and Auguste Lelièvre, opened the prestigous factory of Val-St-Lambert at Seraing, near Liège, which was to become famous for its fine cutting and for its research into colored double and triple crystal.

THE GLASS INDUSTRY
Glassmaking flourished at Charleroi during the 19th century, thanks to the abundant supply of coal (the new source of fuel) available locally.

VONÊCHE CRYSTAL
Between 1802 and 1830 d'Artigues produced crystal of exceptionally high quality at Vonêche. The crystal – the first to rival British counterparts – was cut by Cappelemans in Brussels, or in Paris (below).

THE GLASSBLOWER
In the sweltering atmosphere of the hall the glassblower (right), with the help of a blowpipe (a long hollow tube), takes a blob of molten glass called the *paraison* from the oven and, aided by an assistant called a *gamin* ("boy") or an older youth, shapes the glass by blowing air into it. The master glassblower, aware of the great skill he employs, jealously guards his privileges: he is always the one who adds the glass stem and the foot, which is the last part of the hot work. The decoration (engraving, cutting or pantography) is done once the glass has cooled.

Gothic glass
The decoration consists of embossing or ribbing; here skillful coloring has been used to produce a beautiful shade of green.

"Dusk"
In this piece of multi-layered crystal (left) from Val-St-Lambert, the craftsman Philippe Wolfers created the pattern of two bats (1902) using a dentist's drill. The glassworkers of Val-St-Lambert mastered the art of producing layers of crystal in different colors (here applied with consummate skill), which allowed artists to produce pieces using shapes, engraving or acid-etching.

Liège glass
Despite the edicts of the Venetian Republic, the glass workshops of Murano exported Venetian-style glass throughout Europe. In 1568 the first northern workshop to produce Venetian-style glass opened in Liège. The real impetus, however, was to come from Guy Libon and his associate Jean Bonhomme in the 17th century.

HAN!

The Belgian comic strip can claim to follow in the footsteps of the classic serial, with its weekly dose of cliff-hanging suspense. Started by Hergé, creator of Tintin, it exploded in popularity after World War Two: many authors and creators started out under the Occupation, when American comics were banned. Two fertile grounds for talent, the weeklies *Tintin* and *Spirou*, played a decisive role. The former favored suspense and adventure (Blake and Mortimer, Alix), while the latter opted for humor (the Smurfs, Gaston Lagaffe). Today the monthly *À Suivre* ("to be continued") keeps the "ninth art" alive.

TINTIN
The most famous hero of the comic strip, or "BD" (*bande dessinée*), as it is called in French, was "born" in 1929, the brainchild of Hergé, who created a hallmark style for his protagonist: simple caricaturized portrayals and bold, bright blocks of color. Tintin's success was equally due to the exciting plots, which combined numerous adventures with a plethora of secondary, entertaining oddball characters, such as Captain Haddock, Professor Sunflower and Bianca Castafiore. Defender of widows and orphans, this tireless reporter fights against the imperialism of arms and the power of money. He travels the world in search of good causes to embrace. Tintin is translated into 51 languages and dialects worldwide. His success has never waned, even after the death of his creator in 1983. A testimony to Tintin's enormous popularity are the 200 million or more Tintin books that have been sold.

LUCKY LUKE
From the Gold Rush via the coming of the railroad, the adventures of the Pony Express, the discovery of oil, the newspaper era and the exodus of farmers to the West – every "episode" of the history of the United States has been brought to life in this lively parody of the Wild West legend. The charm of the strip, invented by Morris, lies in the crazy humor of Jolly Jumper, the hero's trusty steed, and the hilarious mixture of real-life characters (among them Calamity Jane, Billy the Kid, Jesse James, the Dalton brothers and Sarah Bernhardt) who are unlucky enough to cross Lucky Luke's path over the course of his adventures.

M'ENFIN!?

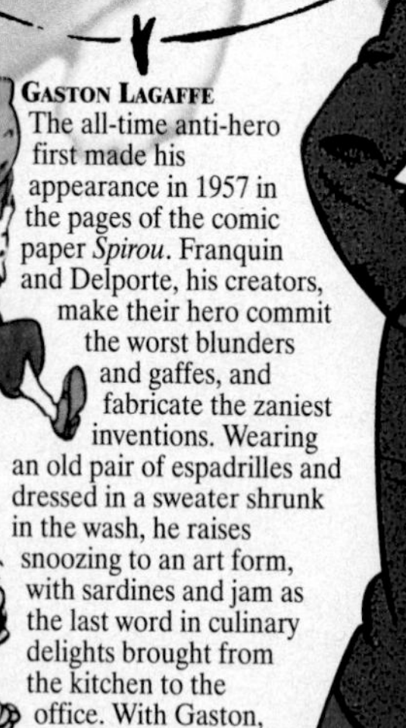

GASTON LAGAFFE
The all-time anti-hero first made his appearance in 1957 in the pages of the comic paper *Spirou*. Franquin and Delporte, his creators, make their hero commit the worst blunders and gaffes, and fabricate the zaniest inventions. Wearing an old pair of espadrilles and dressed in a sweater shrunk in the wash, he raises snoozing to an art form, with sardines and jam as the last word in culinary delights brought from the kitchen to the office. With Gaston, Franquin creates a doodle that is lively and energetic and free of all constraint.

"Les Schtroumpfs" (the Smurfs)
Created in 1958 as secondary characters in a separate strip entitled *Johan et Pirlouit*, the Smurfs – small blue dwarfs inspired by the *nutons* (some of the "little people" said to live in the Ardennes Forest ▲ *257*) – are symbols of an ideal society in which each person has their task to fulfill in nature's plan. The Smurfs are all equal and identical (apart from the Chief Smurf, dressed in red) and speak "Smurfish". This microcosm allowed Peyo, their creator, to slice through the layers of society. Artistically the strip succeeded in combining a simple form with a clear-cut yet subtle portrayal.

Comès. Breaking away from the serial, Comès writes contemporary novels that mark a return to the highly effective black-and-white techniques of the early days. In 1979 he made his mark with *Silence*, a mordant tale on the subject of communication. Since then he has produced a series of powerful works based on light and shadow.

Alix
Since 1948, under the highly researched and scholarly pen of Jacques Martin, Alix has lived out his adventures as the young, Romanized Gaulish slave, meeting Caesar, Cleopatra and Vercingetorix on his travels through the ancient world.

Spirou and Fantasio
Started in 1938, this strip was relaunched by Franquin in 1947. The Comte de Champignac, the Marsupilami, the lively Seccotine, and also the "atomic" graphic style (linked with the Atomium ▲ *173* and a certain notion of progress), the futuristic architecture and objects such as "turbotraction": all these inventions add up to a delightful serial, constituting one of the finest examples of Belgian comic strips.

Blake and Mortimer
For this mythical "ninth art" strip Edgar-Pierre Jacobs dreamed up, in 1946, an attractive and very appealing mixture of sharply realistic drawing, English humor, extensive research and Hitchcockian suspense.

Musical folklore is characterized by oral transmission from generation to generation and by its appropriateness to everyday situations, days of the calendar and festivities. A land passed through by countless armies, southern Belgium adopted, then adapted to its musical tradition, tunes borrowed from France, Germany and Britain. The instruments, often basic (reed pipe, rattle), but occasionally more sophisticated (spinet, hurdy-gurdy, bagpipes), accompanied holidays and village dances, and are today being rediscovered. As for the traditional songs known by all, these still punctuate many of the larger public gatherings.

THE "CRAMIGNON"
The name has its origins in the word *cramillon* (from *crémaillère*, meaning a house-warming party in Old French) and refers both to a serpentine dance and the singing that accompanies it. Still common in the streets of Liège on saints' days, this leaping human chain of men and women winds in and out of cafés and homes. The words of the song describe in playful terms lovers' trysts or scenes of daily life.

A LIFE IN SONG
In days gone by, winter evenings were filled with music; evening songs were often lovers' laments whose tunes were adapted from courtly Medieval ballads. Between 1794 and 1830 the history of Namur's streets was thus put to music each New Year's day with the singing of the lamplighters (below).

THE MIRLITON. This is a tube closed with a vibrating membrane and pierced with a hole, through which the player blows to obtain a nasal sound. Once made from reeds, but today more commonly plastic, it holds pride of place in many a whimsical orchestra, such as that of the Quarante Molons at Namur ▲ *194*.

THE SACRED AND PROFANE. Certain songs accompanied special moments in village life. At Mons during the Lumeçon battle ▲ *291*, each person sang the tune of the *Doudou* (above).

THE FIFE, VIOLA AND SPINET
The viola was widely used to accompany dances during the 15th century, particularly in and around Liège and the Hainaut region, where it became the prized instrument of traveling musicians, many of whom were blind. The spinet, a sort of primitive cithara, was played during the 19th century and early 20th century in watermen's families of the Borinage and of the Mouscron region. As for the fife, this was widespread throughout the Sambre-Meuse *marches* ▲ *280*.

THE BAGPIPES
Known from the 13th century onward in France, this was called a *muchosa* or *muchafou* in the Hainaut region, where it was most commonly used. From the 15th century, bagpipes enlivened the village *kermesses* (right). Used solely by shepherds in the previous century, the bagpipes disappeared around 1900.

For a long time puppet shows were put on by itinerant troupes. These once traveled to the four corners of Europe, depending on economic, political or even religious circumstances (during the 17th century in southern Belgium a puppeteer was burnt as a witch). With the arrival of the Industrial Revolution, in the 19th century puppetry settled down, and numerous theaters sprang up in the larger towns. This was the poor man's theater, where shows were enacted using the dialect of their working-class audiences. Two traditions have survived to this day: in Liège that of Tchantchès, the eternal true Liègois, a hearty bon viveur; and in Brussels that of the Toone Theater, led by the outrageous Woltje, the street urchin from the Marolles district.

THE TRADITIONAL BRUSSELS PUPPET
The body of the Brussels puppet is made from tightly stuffed fabric, with the rod firmly attached to the chest. The legs move at the hips. A long wire attached to the wrists creates the rapid arm movements essential for sword fights.

THE REPERTOIRE
In 19th-century Brussels plays were usually put on in episodes, matching the serials in the popular newspapers: for example, the *Three Musketeers* was put on over three weeks, while the *Dame de Monsoreau* was played over thirty-two episodes. Today television fulfills this function. While respecting the traditional methods, puppeteers have therefore been keenly aware of the need to adapt to a contemporary audience: nowadays, for example, puppet plays are generally put on over a single evening. Under the aegis of Brussels' Toone VII, cloak-and-dagger stories have broadened out to encompass the works of Shakespeare as well as new plays. In Liège ▲ 224, the repertoire consists mainly of medieval plays inspired by epics from the time of Charlemagne, historical novels such as the *Six Cents Franchimontois* and religious plays like *Li Naissance.*

TOONE. The Toone dynasty was established by the puppeteer Antoine (Toone) Genty around 1830: Toone VII is the worthy descendant. The Toone Theater is the last traditional puppet theater in Brussels.

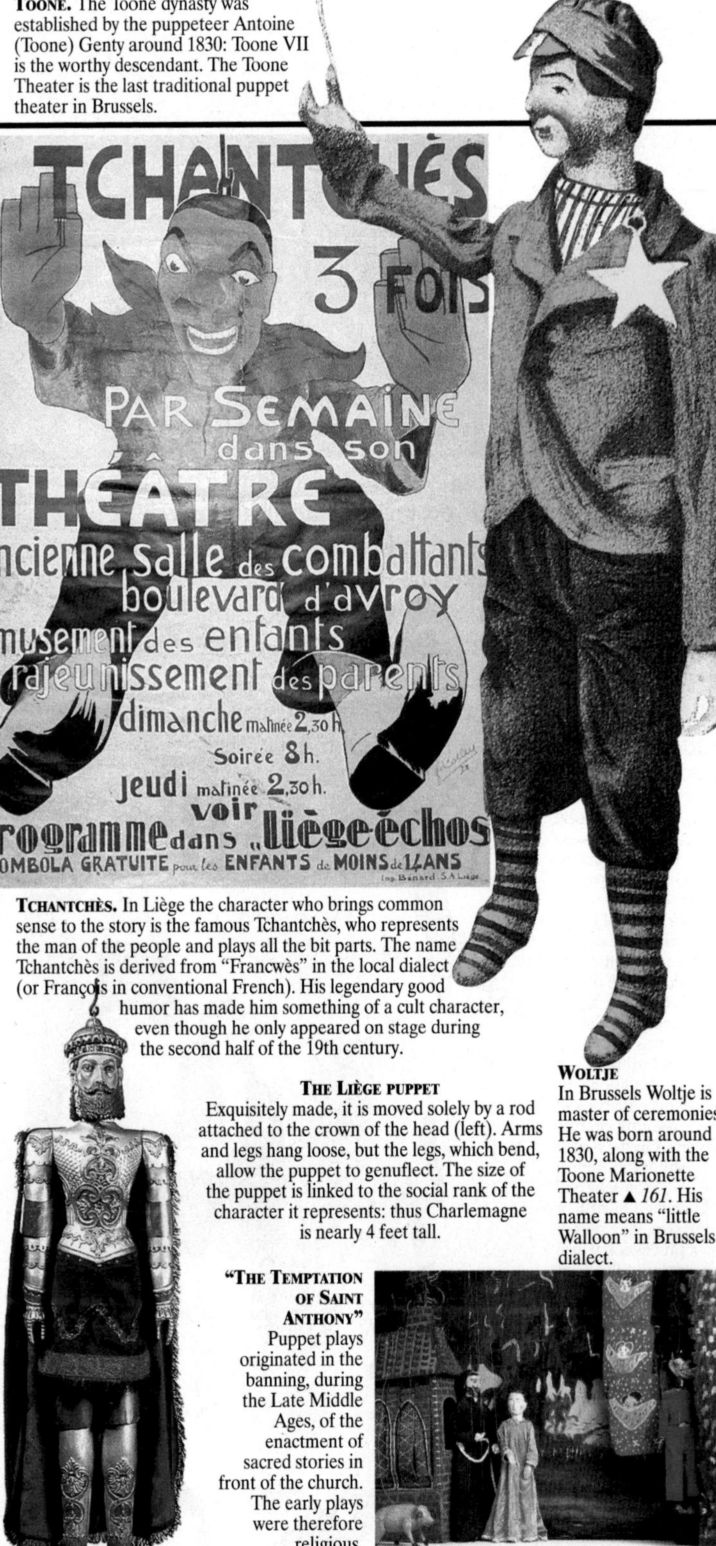

TCHANTCHÈS. In Liège the character who brings common sense to the story is the famous Tchantchès, who represents the man of the people and plays all the bit parts. The name Tchantchès is derived from "Francwès" in the local dialect (or François in conventional French). His legendary good humor has made him something of a cult character, even though he only appeared on stage during the second half of the 19th century.

WOLTJE
In Brussels Woltje is master of ceremonies. He was born around 1830, along with the Toone Marionette Theater ▲ *161*. His name means "little Walloon" in Brussels dialect.

THE LIÈGE PUPPET
Exquisitely made, it is moved solely by a rod attached to the crown of the head (left). Arms and legs hang loose, but the legs, which bend, allow the puppet to genuflect. The size of the puppet is linked to the social rank of the character it represents: thus Charlemagne is nearly 4 feet tall.

"THE TEMPTATION OF SAINT ANTHONY"
Puppet plays originated in the banning, during the Late Middle Ages, of the enactment of sacred stories in front of the church. The early plays were therefore religious.

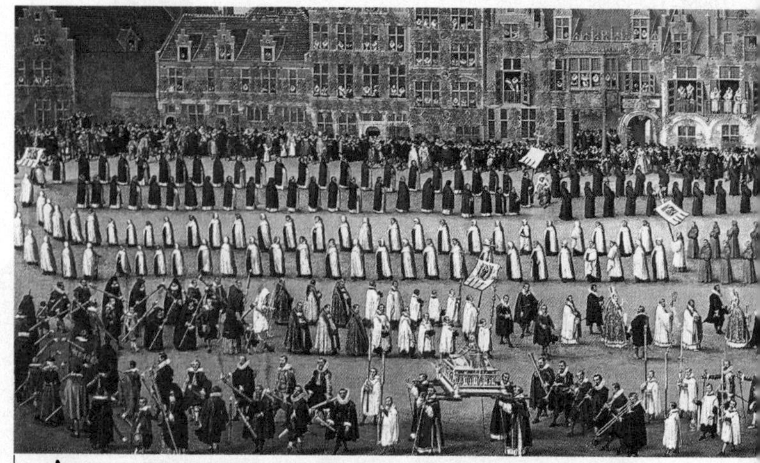

The towns and villages of Belgium have always revered their protecting saints with conspicuous fervor; often these were the patron saints to whom the parish churches were dedicated. The saint's feast day, or *ducasse* as it is called in southern Belgium, combines the sacred with the profane. This faith and popular rejoicing is a feature of French-speaking Belgium, where the festive calender is marked by pilgrimages, marches and processions, often with games and parades.

THE GIANTS
Many local communities possess their own giants, which they parade through the streets. For many of them, this is a relatively recent tradition. In the region of Ath ▲ *302*, however, this is not the case, since it was one of the original birthplaces of the tradition – its giants date back to the 15th century (right). On the fourth Sunday in August Monsieur and Madame Goliath, or Gouyasse, take part in a procession which includes the giant Samson, Ambiorix the Terrible, Mam'zelle Victoire, and Bayard the horse ▲ *268*. The evening culminates in the marriage of "Monsieur et Madame Gouyasse", and the young shepherd David confonts Monsieur Gouyasse in a symbolic battle.

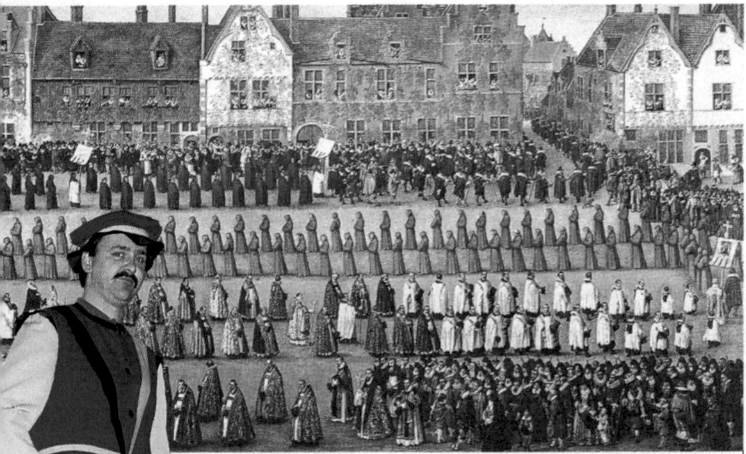

THE "OMMEGANG"
In Brussels at the beginning of July the Ommegang ▲ *158* procession takes place in commemoration of the parade held in honor of Charles V in 1549.

THE "DOUDOU" AT MONS
On Trinity Sunday in Mons the Car d'Or ▲ *288* procession is accompanied by the only processional game still enacted in southern Belgium – the battle of the Lumeçon (below). Saint George fights the Dragon, affectionately called "Doudou"; after the battle "lucky" hairs are plucked from his tail ▲ *291*.

THE "MARCHES" OF SAMBRE-ET-MEUSE
South of Charleroi almost every village has its "company" – a group of soldiers, often dressed in Empire costume, who circle the relics of the patron saint as these are exhibited. These folkloric soldiers, organized in squads of Zouaves (fools), or platoons of firemen carrying arms, march to the orders of the "officer corps", an honor that is bought. The most famous parades are those of Thuin, Gerpinnes, Walcourt ▲ *281* and Fosses ▲ *282*, and Jumet's Marche de la Madeleine ● *69*.

TOWERS AND DEVOTIONALS
The saint's dedication is commemorated each year by a procession of the statue or relics of the patron saint. The sequence of events is always the same, whether propitiatory (the fertility of the fields) or commemorative (here, at Andenne ▲ *216*).

Walloon popular traditions, still very much alive today, surface on numerous occasions throughout the year, though primarily at the end of winter and beginning of spring. Candlemas, called *chandeleur* (February 2), marks the start of masquerades when the populace, wearing masks, crowds onto the streets. This general rejoicing is particularly lively in the Geer valley, at Malmédy and Stavelot, at Fosses, in the Viroin valley, around Binche and in many villages in the heart of the Hainaut, where carnivals go on for three months.

FOOD HUNTS
Carnival time has always been marked by an excessive overindulgence in food before the period of fasting during Lent. Eating and drinking well are thus inseparable from carnival rituals. The "food hunts" which occur in the valley of the Geer or in the Sambre-Meuse region are enduring forms of an ancient rural carnival tradition. Thus the "Houres" of the Geer valley and the inhabitants of Vierves collect eggs and distribute a giant omelette as the carnival procession parades through the streets.

THE TRANSVESTITES
In the past the festivities were somewhat restrained, with participants restricting themselves to simple or naive disguises. Men dressing up as women was a common occurrence. This tradition can still be found today, especially at Binche where the custom of dressing up as the "Mam'zelle binchoise" has become a standard ritual (left).

CARNIVAL TIME
The carnival season, dating back to the old tradition of winter masquerades, is organized around several variable key dates linked with Ash Wednesday, Lent and Easter. Thus the days around Mardi Gras (Shrove Tuesday) mark the peak of the more traditional carnivals, such as that at Binche (above).

THE "GRAND FEU"
The bonfire tradition is still very much alive in southern Belgium, notably in the provinces of Liège, Luxembourg and Namur. At Bouge, near Namur, the members of the "Grand feu" confraternity, wearing scarlet hoods, build a spectacular bonfire on the rocks of the Grands Malades, overlooking the Meuse river. A lively procession accompanies the figure of a Snowman, representing Carnival, which is carried on a cart to the bonfire.

CARNIVAL SNOWMAN
Stuffed with straw, the Carnival Snowman is a fall guy. At Treignes he is the object of a mock trial, after which he is condemned to drowning and then hauled onto a bonfire, or "Grand Feu", around which dances a masked saraband. Left: the Snowman at Bouge. Right: the carnival at Binche ▲ *294*.

THE "CWARMÉ" AT MALMÉDY ▲ *246*
This is preceded by the *cràs djudis* – the *quatre jeudis* (four Thursdays) prior to Quinquagesima Sunday – during which masked children and adults indulge in intrigues. The Saturday signals the start of the carnival. The Trouv'lè, equipped with his ladle or scoop (*trouv'lè* in the Walloon dialect) to preside over the festivities, then makes his entrance accompanied by two Djoupsènnes and a rural policeman. The Trouv'lè is followed by masked fools, including Big Heads, Long Noses and Long Arms (above, right) who delight in teasing the spectators . But the most important figure of all makes his appearance on the following day. This is the Haguète (right and top left), wearing a cowl and hat with multi-colored plumes, who terrorizes his victims with his man-snatcher. On the Monday, satirical plays are performed.

THE "BLANCS MOUSSIS" CARNIVAL
Mid Lent at Stavelot ▲ *247* sees the appearance of Blancs Moussis (below), meaning "dressed in white" in the local dialect. In 1947 a group of students gave new life to the masquerade ritual, a feature of the Ancien Régime that was moved during the 19th century to the days between Shrove Tuesday (Mardi Gras) and mid Lent. A confetti-firing cannon is a recent addition to the Blanc Moussi's battery of pranks, among which are posting satirical tracts on walls, jeering giants, and terrorizing passers-by with inflated pigs' bladders or fishing rods with kippers attached.

THE BLANC MOUSSI'S COSTUME
Traditionally the Blanc Moussi sported an improvized costume made from a pillow case and a bed sheet. In 1947 the costume was standardized: white trousers and shirt or sweater, under the bed sheet (worn as a cape), plus a white hood and a long-nosed mask.

THE BINCHE CARNIVAL ▲ *294*
This is the best known carnival of all, dominated by its characteristic Gilles, whose origins date back to a distant past. Organized by twelve societies, it follows strict rules established by successive generations.

THE FOSSES CARNIVAL
The small town of Fosses ▲ *282*, in the province of Namur, celebrates carnival in mid Lent. "Doudous" and "Chinels" are its traditional symbols. The Doudous (below) wear a costume of white cloth decorated with red buttons, stuffed with straw and equipped with bells. These are, in fact, a reincarnation of the ancient Chinel, the rural version of Polichinelle, popularized by the traveling theater.

THE "CHINEL"
Around 1869 a more sophisticated Chinel (left and below) made its appearance decked in satin and lace, graced with tinkling bells and polished slippers. The costume of the old Chinel was then called "Doudou" as a term of derision.

Traditional games have not always had a purely sporting function, and many of them can be traced back to ancient ritualistic origins. Like carnivals and processions, they provide an occasion for the entire community to let itself go. In days gone by there was no such thing as a passive onlooker, simply participants with a single collective voice of excitement; nowadays, however, these games are increasingly eclipsed by sports where there is a clear division between players and supporters. In order to survive, the oldest games (ball games, shooting and skittles) have had to adopt this model, while others (pigeon fancying and cock crowing) now accept bets.

THE STILT MEN OF NAMUR
A drum roll sounds and opposing teams confront each other. The object of the game, recorded as far back as the Middle Ages, is to topple your opponents.

PIGEON FANCYING
This sport, which originated in the Liège-Verviers-Herve triangle at the end of the 18th century, was widespread throughout Belgium by about 1820. Homing pigeons are released hundreds of miles from their lofts; the winner is the fastest bird, taking into account the distance traveled. Only pigeon owners can place bets. The headquarters of the World Federation of Pigeon Fanciers is in Brussels.

GOOSE DECAPITATION. This ritualistic game has its roots in medieval custom. Mainly practiced in the Hainaut region, the lower Meuse valley and the eastern regions of Belgium, it consists of decapitating a goose suspended by the neck (sometimes by the feet, or occasionally buried in the ground) with a stick or sickle. At one time the goose was hung up alive, but nowadays it is presented dead to the competitors.

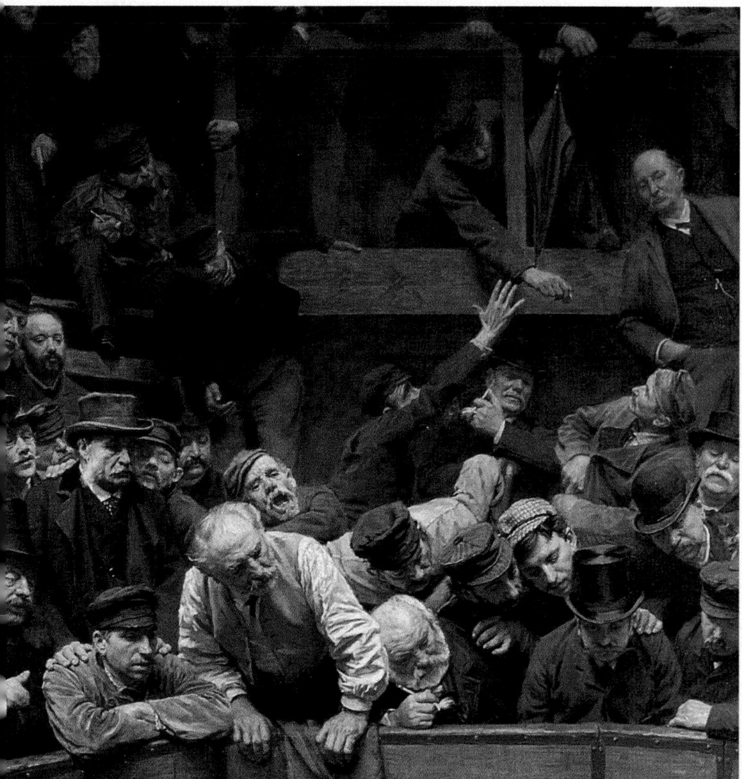

THE GAME OF PELOTA
This ball-and-glove game is much practiced in the Hainaut, Brabant and Namur provinces. A modern-day version of medieval real tennis, pelota is primarily a street sport and is mainly played during local festivities, although the ground marks are often permanent. The scoring system is similar to that used for tennis.

COCK FIGHTING
Once widespread in the Hesbaye and around Liège, cock fights are now illegal, but are nonetheless profitable because of the entry fees charged and amount of bets placed. A less savage game, that of cock crowing, consists of betting on the exact number of times a cock will crow at a specified hour.

The social situation of the worker at the end of the 19th century enticed him into drinking establishments, the false eldorado of the working man. Living in discomfort and poverty, he sought refuge in "his" estaminet (bistro or café) in order to find congenial company and also to seek warmth. The estaminet was not solely a low-life establishment: it was in the back rooms of these cafés, around tables laden with frothing beer, that the first trade unions were formed and also, during the same period, that friendly societies and cooperative savings societies were born.

WHY "ESTAMINET"?
The name is said to have its root in *étamine* (muslin cloth), and the establishment where one smoked and drank was indeed indicated by a small cloth flag. It may also be derived from the German *Stammtisch* (meaning the "host's table" or "table of regulars").

FROM "ESTAMINET" TO "CABARET"
Up until the 18th century the estaminet was a quality establishment where only beer was drunk. But overcrowding in certain towns and the industrial manufacture of alcohol led to a cheapening of the traditional estaminet, which became a "cabaret" – or, as it was known in Brussels, a *caber-douche* (a drinking establishment of ill repute).

The drinks
Beer was only consumed in significant quantities after 1919, when the Vandervelde Law was passed. This placed a total ban on the consumption of spirits in cafés.

A political arena
Following the events of 1830 ● *40*, the first political meetings took place in estaminets since assemblies on public thoroughfares were forbidden. Nowadays, especially in small villages, cafés are often the seat of a political party, in which case they are frequented solely by those affiliated to the party in question.

Games
Games were a feature of estaminet life: card games (whist, rummy and *couyon*) and dice ("421", known as *pitchesbak* in Brussels) were played; and *vogelpik*, an early version of darts in which the projectile was a tiny wooden bird with an iron beak. On Sunday mornings, the back yards would be taken over by archers with bows and arrows.

The "zwanze" ("joke" in Brussels dialect)
In Brussels all estaminets have one thing in common. The *zwanze* – the spirit of Brussels, where wit and subterfuge are the order of the day – reigns unchallenged.

An instrument of change
The estaminet was also the driving force behind a social revolution: it was here that the workers' societies for collective savings gathered from 1820 onward, as did the first friendly societies around 1860. In the early days the estaminet owner was the society secretary, responsible for subscriptions and paying out money. It was only in 1885, with the creation of the Belgian Labour Party, that the savings and mutual societies became properly regulated. Nowadays, toward the end of the 20th century, several bistros still maintain the traditional role of a savings' society.

Where else would one consume beer if not in Belgium? Pale, frothy, dark, slightly fizzy, light or strong, bitter or sweet, Belgium offers the beer lover a wealth of beers from which to choose. Despite the rapid expansion of the big breweries, the number of labels has multiplied – bewilderingly and not always with favorable results. As with wine, a sound knowledge is therefore essential prior to tasting.

LAMBIC (PRODUCED BY SPONTANEOUS FERMENTATION ▲ *76*)
Lambic is in effect a grain-based wine, or "still beer". Nowadays its consumption is extremely rare.

THE SEASONS
Seasonally produced beers have always been a specialty of the Hainaut region. In days gone by, these were brewed in farms during the winter when work was at a standstill. They were then drunk during the summer months, after their period of fermentation. Nowadays, these highly fermented beers are brewed all year round. Spices are added to them during the course of production.

LOW FERMENTATION
This is achieved at around 46°F, and takes between seven and ten days. All the yeast is deposited on the floor of the fermentation vat. A typical beer of this type is pils.

HIGH FERMENTATION
More rapid than low fermentation, this takes place between 64°F and 72°F. Most of the yeast rises to the surface of the wort. These beers are more aromatic and heavier than the low-fermentation beers.

The Brewing Pavilion at the Universal Exhibition in 1897.

Kriek
In order to expand their range of beers, brewers hit on the idea of macerating fruit in their lambic – particularly Morello cherries (called *kriek* in Flemish) and raspberries. In the Brussels estaminets drinkers would have at their disposal two lumps of sugar and a stirrer to sweeten the lambic to their taste. Nowadays the kriek beers are sweetened and pasteurized, and aromatized too.

Gueuze. A fizzy sparkling beer, gueuze is produced by a true "champenoise" method; that is to say, from a mixture of lambics from several vintages (from one to three years of age). The lambics that are between one and two years old are refermented in bottles, which produces gueuze after five or six months in the cellar. However, to produce a really good gueuze, a period of at least one year in the bottle should elapse. At that point the sugar content has dropped to zero, and the gueuze is nearly 100 percent proof.

"Bières spéciales"
The designation *bières spéciales* is used to indicate beers of high fermentation. They may be dark or clear, and their density also varies. These beers are considered to be local specialties.

Trappist beers
These are beers of a high density and high fermentation. The description "Trappist" is given to beer that has been brewed by a Cistercian Trappist abbey. True Trappist beers produced in southern Belgium are those of the abbeys at Orval, Rochefort and Chimay. The last two produce two types of beer, whereas Orval produces just the one.

Abbey beers
During the Middle Ages monasteries alone had the right to brew beer, whereas today the monastic designation tends to be purely a marketing ploy. Abbey beers are beers of high fermentation, and are frequently strong. They are mostly produced in ordinary breweries.

● BREWING LAMBIC

Beer making has changed dramatically since the end of the 19th century, when the work of eminent microbiologists such as Pasteur and Hanssen meant that brewers were able to innoculate the wort with colonies of selected yeasts, and thus industrialize production. The traditional brewing methods – in other words, by spontaneous fermentation – are nonetheless still practiced in the Cantillon family brewery in Brussels.

MAKING LAMBIC THE TRADITIONAL WAY

The ingredients are wheat, barley and mature hops (**1**). The wheat is a raw grain; the barley comes from the maltings, where it has been malted (its starch has been transformed into a simple broken-down sugar).

After painstaking crushing of the grains, a grain that is fine enough for brewing is obtained (**2**). The grain is tossed into hot water and mixed. The starch is liquefied by enzyme action, which transforms it into

The latter is sterilized by cooking, and its volume reduced through evaporation (**6**). Thus the final concentration of sugar will determine the future alcoholic content of the lambic. Here, finally, is the key to the

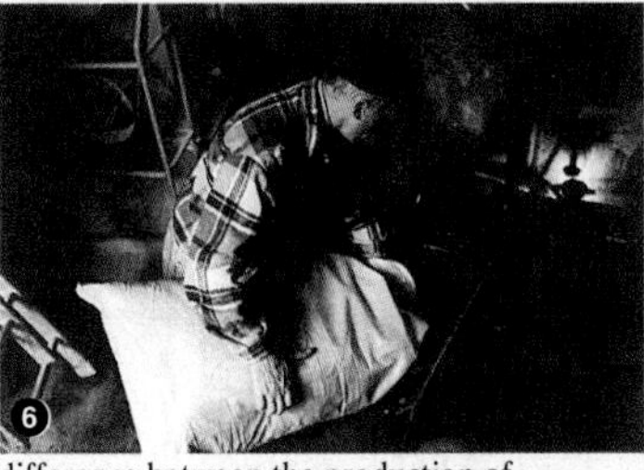

difference between the production of traditional gueuze-lambic and that of other beers (**7**): the air so dreaded by brewers of low and high fermentations now becomes the great ally of the gueuze brewer.

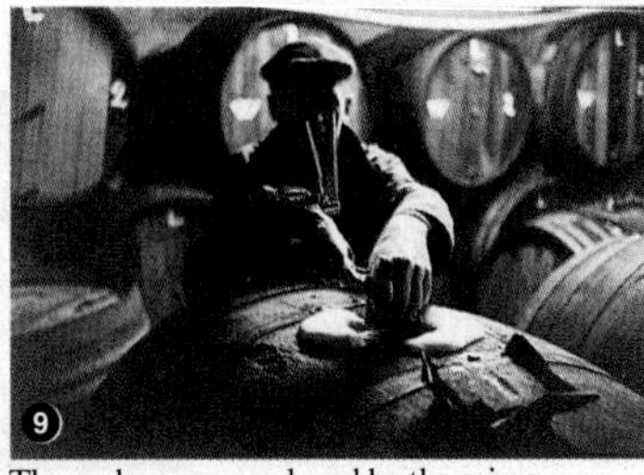

The carbon gas produced by the micro-organisms provokes a veritable eruption of the wort (**9**). This first fermentation is followed by a slow transformation of the sugar (three years). Evaporation is critical: the volume is reduced from 172 to 132 gallons.

GUEUZE & KRIEK
DE LA MAISON
CANTILLON
RUE GHEUDE, 56-58 BRUXLLES

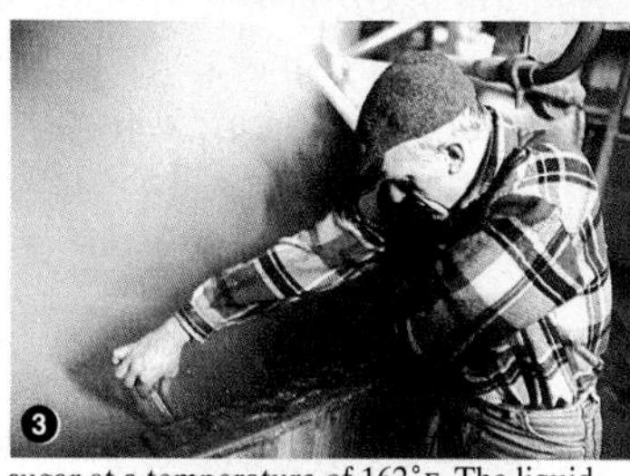

sugar at a temperature of 162°F. The liquid and solid portions of the brew (the mix) separate (**3**). The sugary wort is filtered and sent to the cooking vats (**4**). The solid remains (the "dredges") are recycled as cattle feed (**5**).

The next stage is where the hops are added. Hops, which play a vital role in the preservation of lambic, must be extremely dry and at least three years old in order to minimize the bitterness they bring to the wort.

The wort cools for one whole night in an enormous shallow tank, in order to reach a temperature of 64°F by the morning. Such an operation can only be carried out between the end of October and early April.

The cold season also favors a good sowing of the wort by numerous airborne fermentators. The beer is then stored in barrels (**8**).

Industrial beer making at the turn of the century.

Beer tasting at Orval.

Salade Liègeoise

There is not just one Brussels and Walloon gastronomic tradition, but as many specialties as there are provinces. The traditional cuisine of Liège and the surrounding area, for example, is based on plain family cooking and uses readily available, straightforward ingredients. The jewel of this rustic gastronomy is Salade Liègoise.

Ingredients: 4 slices streaky bacon
4 slices smoked bacon
1 cup spirit vinegar
1 cup wine vinegar
3 cups crème fraîche
2 pounds of green beans
12 new potatoes
2 onions (chopped)
Tarragon and parsley (chopped)
Ground pepper

1. Clean the beans and cook them in salted water. Drain. Peel the potatoes and cook in salted water. Drain.

2. Cut the slices of bacon into small cubes of approximately 1 inch.

3. Fry the bacon cubes in a non-stick frying pan. Remove the excess grease.

4. Deglaze the chopped onions and the vinegars.

5. Cook until the quantity of liquid has been reduced by about one-third.

6. Add the crème fraîche, and stir until the required consistency is obtained.

7. Once all the ingredients have been well mixed together, season with pepper (no salt).

Mix the beans and the warm potatoes in a salad bowl, together with the reduced onion, cream and vinegar mixture. Add the cooked bacon and serve warm, having garnished with chopped parsley and tarragon.

"COUQUES" These are hard, flattened sweet biscuits made from honey. A specialty of the area around Dinant ▲ *208*, they are baked in carved wooden molds to give them a decorative shape (above, that of a wild boar).

THE "PÉKÈT" OF LIÈGE This juniper-based form of alcohol is the favorite tipple of Tchantchès ▲ *231*. It is the prized beverage at festivals in and around Liège.

AUX SANS PAREILS
BERNARDINS FLEURUSIENS
SPÉCIALITÉ UNIQUE DE
Piraux Etienne
MARQUE DEPOSÉE RECONNUE DEPUIS PLUS DE 100 ANS
MÉDAILLE D'OR
BRUXELLES 1880
ANVERS 1885

"BAISERS" ("kisses") The romantic name refers to the small macaroons filled with fondant that are a specialty of southern Belgium ▲ *255*.

HERVE CHEESE A specialty of the pastural lands in the region of Herve ▲ *236*, it comes in the form of a small orange cube and has a distinctive odor.

BEERS. These are too numerous to mention ● *74*. The best-known are those made in the trappist monasteries. Above: beer from Chimay ▲ *282* and Maredsous ▲ *207*.

BELGIAN CHOCOLATES These cream-filled chocolates, known as *pralines*, have an international reputation ◆ *333*.

LIÈGE SYRUP This extremely sugary "paste" made from quinces is eaten, spread on *tartines* (slices of bread), for breakfast.

"SPECULOOS" These small spiced biscuits, eaten at coffee time, come in handy-sized pieces. They are especially popular in Brussels.

SPA WATERS The renowned spring waters from Spa ▲ *250* may be either still or sparkling. Spring water from Chaudfontaine ▲ *238* is also sold in bottles.

SPA
SPA

ARCHITECTURE

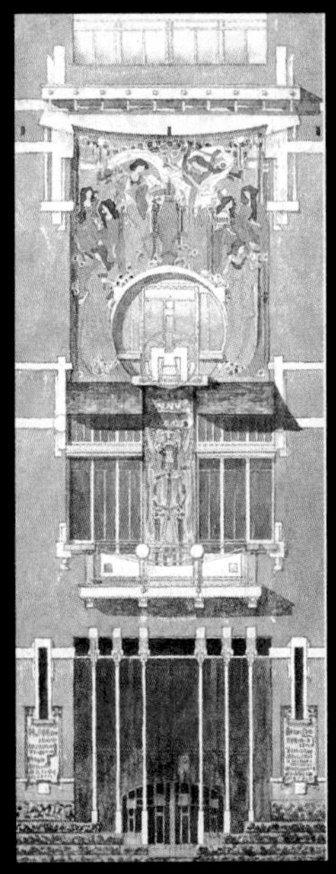

In the 11th and 12th centuries two styles of architecture emerged in the region that is modern Belgium. To the south, the Meuse valley, with the episcopal town of Liège at its heart, formed part of the Germanic Empire; Mosan style was therefore influenced by the Ottonian and Romanesque traditions of Rhenish architecture. To the north, where the Escaut (or Scheldt) valley and the episcopal town of Tournai was under French control, the Scaldian school instead took its cue from an Anglo-Norman architectural vocabulary.

THE CRYPT. This underground vaulted chamber is situated beneath the choir, and houses the relics of a saint. Access to it is via two lateral flights of steps. The crypt of Notre-Dame at Huy (1066) ▲ *217* is a veritable underground church, with three naves and apses.

THE MOSAN WEST FRONT ("WESTBAU") A feature of larger churches, this is a tall imposing structure crowned by towers at the western end of the church. It contains an additional choir for special religious ceremonies, a grand tribune and, occasionally, a crypt. Below: west front of St-Barthélemy in Liège (late 12th century) ▲ *225*.

Ste-Gertrude at Nivelles.

STRUCTURE OF THE CHURCH
1. West front
2. Apse
3. Crypt
4. Access to the crypt
5. Nave and roof vault
6. Transept

BICEPHALOUS PLAN The Cathedral of St-Lambert in Liège ▲ *223* (1015) exerted a major influence on a number of Mosan buildings. Today nothing but the foundation survives, which is based on a rational modular plan consisting of two transepts and two choirs with crypts at either end of the naves.

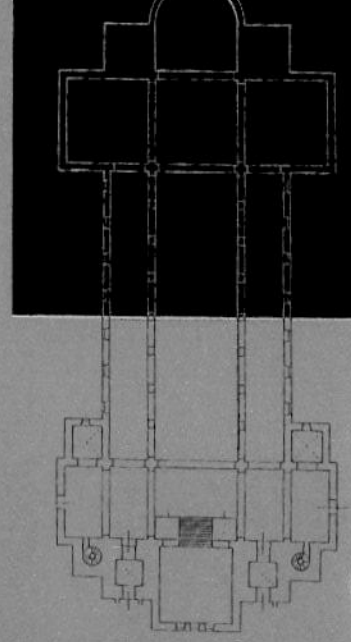

St-Hadelin at Celles-en-Condroz ▲ *211* typifies, on a reduced scale, the Mosan style of the 11th century.

The Mosan church
The only large surviving Mosan church, Ste-Gertrude at Nivelles ▲ *203* (dedicated in 1046) marks one of the high points of 11th-century architecture. While its ground plan is similar to that of Liège Cathedral, its elevation affords a true appreciation of the use of space, which here is resonant, unadorned and luminous.

Tournai Cathedral.

The Scheldt church
While the nave and gallery at Tournai Cathedral ▲ *313* is the crowning achievement of 12th-century Scaldian Romanesque, the extraordinary apsidal transept with five towers already hints at an articulated Gothic structure with ribbed vaulting.

Capitals
A. In Mosan architecture, which is sculptural and austere, the capitals are spheroidal cubes with plain bells.
B. Tournai capitals, in local limestone, are more decorative. The curved-bell capital shown here has a stylized foliate motif.

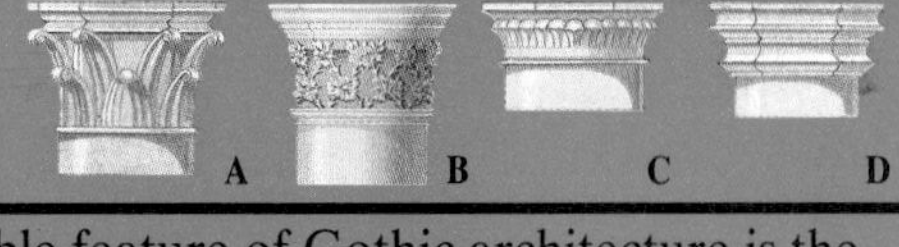

A notable feature of Gothic architecture is the ribbed vaulting, which allowed higher, better-lit churches to be built. The Tournai region rapidly cultivated its own style in the 13th century, but it was only in the 14th century that a truly native school took root in Brabant. This produced a number of major buildings, and Flamboyant (Late Gothic) features were only tentatively adopted toward the end of the 15th century. In the 16th century the influence of Brabantine Gothic spread still further, while local variations emerged in the Meuse and Hainaut regions.

A GOTHIC BUILDING
At Villers-la-Ville ▲ *202* the Cistercians erected a new church between 1210 and 1267 (above, the abbey choir). The light openings here are still restricted, in spite of the perfect grasp of Gothic masonry techniques and load-bearing principles.

CAPITALS
A. Tournai region (Tournai, St-Jacques).
B. Brabant region (Brussels, St-Michel).
C. Meuse region (Liège, St-Paul).
D. Hainaut region (Marcq-lez-Enghien, St-Martin).

TOURNAI TRIPLE LANCET
Tournai ▲ *313* developed its own style of Gothic architecture, which spread through the Escaut valley in the 13th century. One characteristic was the triple lancet window, with tracery made from local limestone.

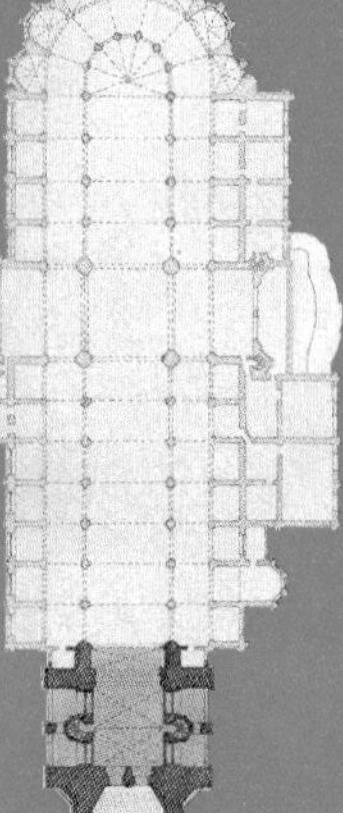

BRABANTINE PLAN
The plan of the Collegiate Church of Ste-Waudru at Mons ▲ *288* conforms to a true cathedral plan and illustrates the vitality of the regional style.

GOTHIC BAYS
A. Three distinct levels (Tournai Cathedral, choir).
B. Three levels linked by a screen extending the bays into the triforium (Brussels Cathedral).

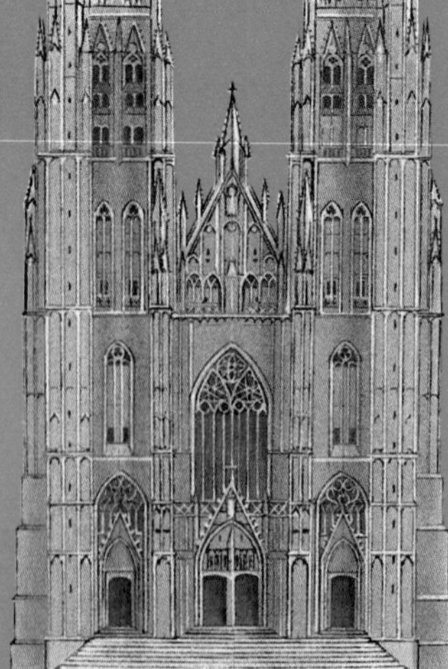

FAÇADE
The façade of the Cathedral of St-Michel in Brussels (often called Ste-Gudule) ▲ *161* was completed in the 15th century. With its twin towers, the cathedral conforms to traditional Gothic rather than pure Brabantine style, which tends to have only one tower. However, the elevation of the nave corresponds to the typical Brabantine formula.

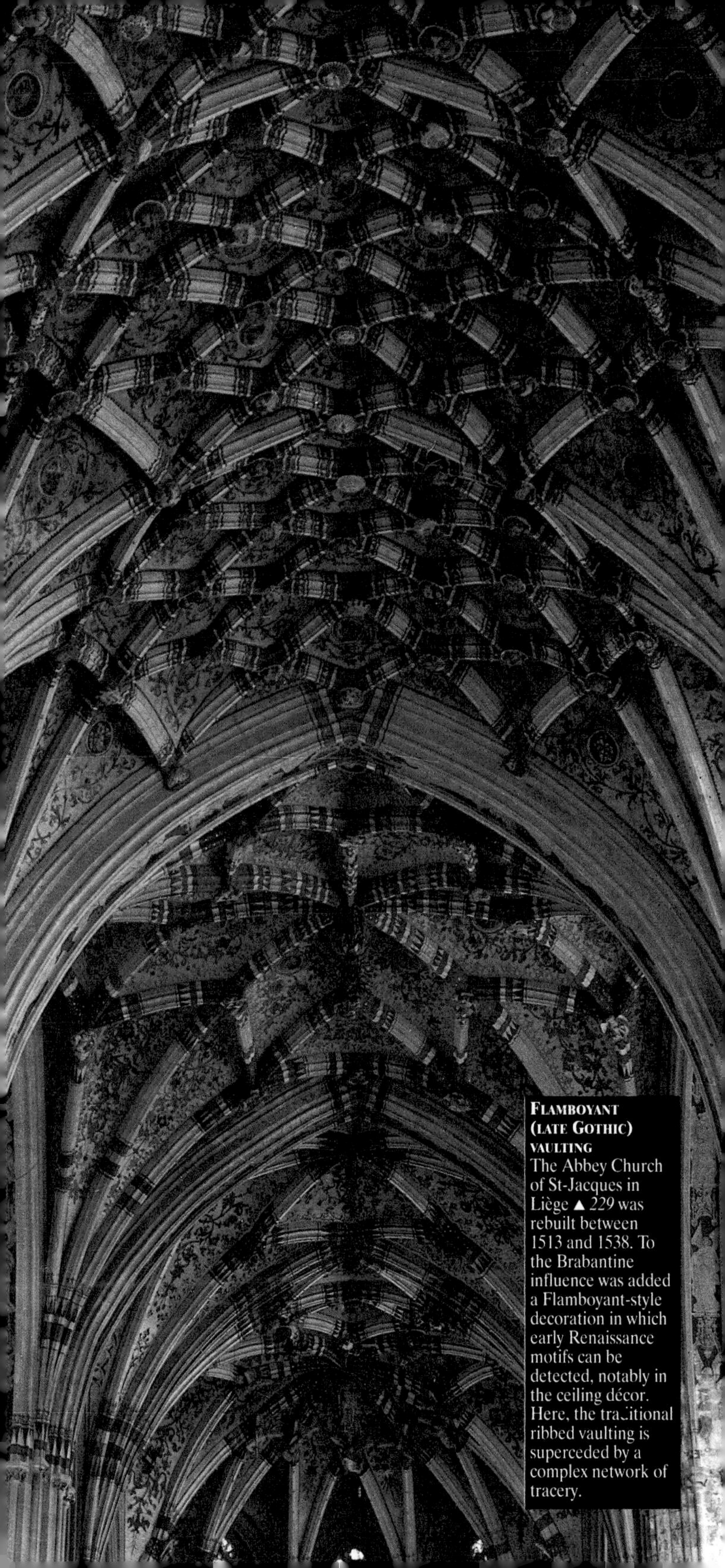

Flamboyant (late Gothic) vaulting
The Abbey Church of St-Jacques in Liège ▲ *229* was rebuilt between 1513 and 1538. To the Brabantine influence was added a Flamboyant-style decoration in which early Renaissance motifs can be detected, notably in the ceiling décor. Here, the traditional ribbed vaulting is superceded by a complex network of tracery.

Early 13th-century capital, from the Abbey at Villers.

The widespread growth of the monastic orders was a phenomenon that affected the whole of Christian Europe. The abbey, the heart of a self-sufficient community dedicated to prayer and labor, consisted of monastic and domestic buildings (such as workshops, mills and barns) as well as the church. Very few pre-13th-century monastic complexes have survived. It was only with the 18th century and a second monastic golden age that major building projects were once again embarked upon. The secularization of society in 1796, following the French Revolution, brought in its wake sales and demolitions.

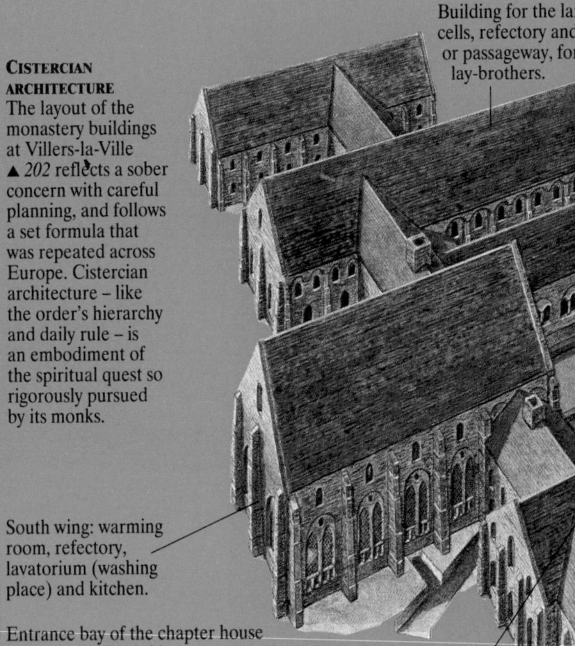

CISTERCIAN ARCHITECTURE
The layout of the monastery buildings at Villers-la-Ville ▲ 202 reflects a sober concern with careful planning, and follows a set formula that was repeated across Europe. Cistercian architecture – like the order's hierarchy and daily rule – is an embodiment of the spiritual quest so rigorously pursued by its monks.

Entrance bay of the chapter house at Villers, cloister side.

CHOICE OF SITE
The monks always selected the sites on which to found their abbeys judiciously. A nearby water supply was essential for sanitation and hygiene, as well as for drinking and cooking; it was also needed to power the forges and mills.

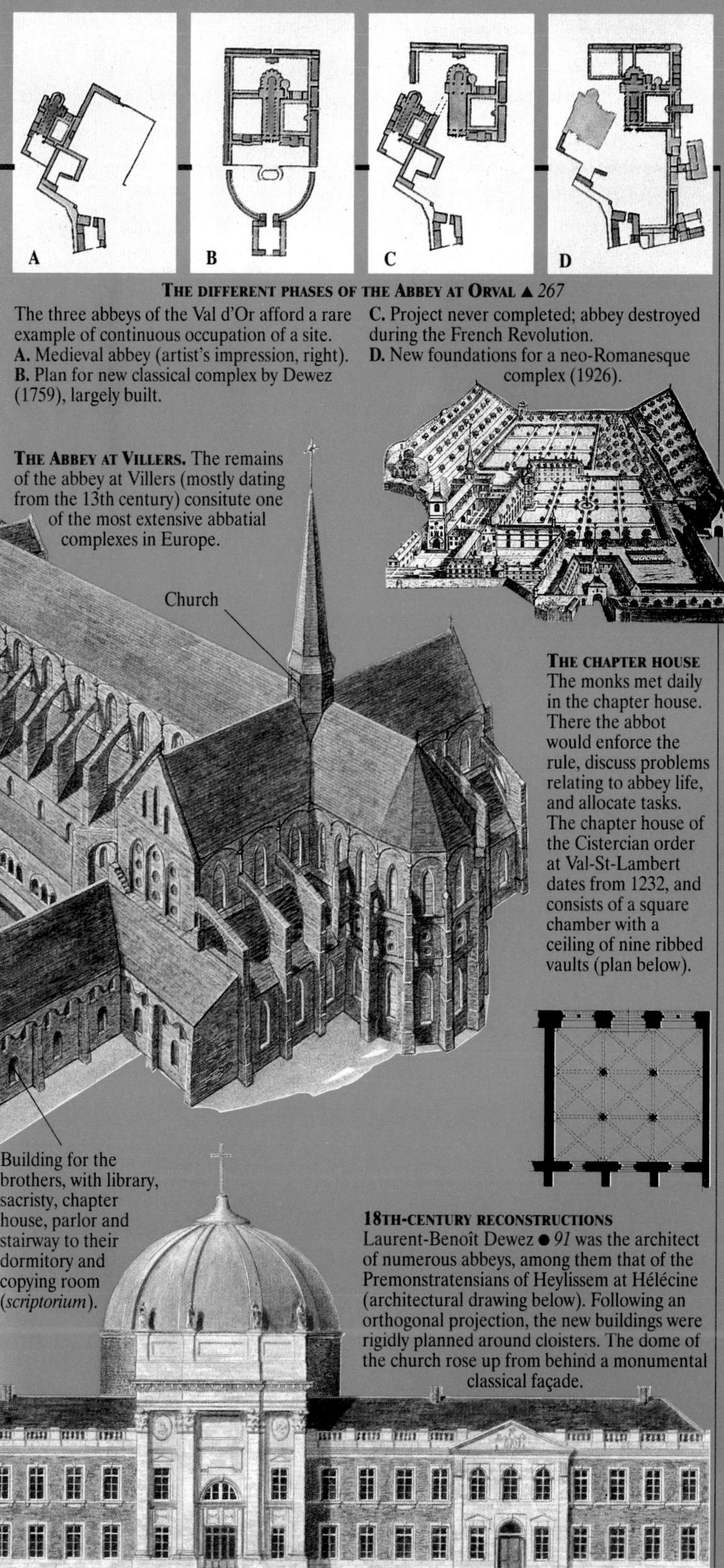

The different phases of the Abbey at Orval ▲ *267*

The three abbeys of the Val d'Or afford a rare example of continuous occupation of a site.
A. Medieval abbey (artist's impression, right).
B. Plan for new classical complex by Dewez (1759), largely built.
C. Project never completed; abbey destroyed during the French Revolution.
D. New foundations for a neo-Romanesque complex (1926).

The Abbey at Villers. The remains of the abbey at Villers (mostly dating from the 13th century) consitute one of the most extensive abbatial complexes in Europe.

Building for the brothers, with library, sacristy, chapter house, parlor and stairway to their dormitory and copying room (*scriptorium*).

The chapter house
The monks met daily in the chapter house. There the abbot would enforce the rule, discuss problems relating to abbey life, and allocate tasks. The chapter house of the Cistercian order at Val-St-Lambert dates from 1232, and consists of a square chamber with a ceiling of nine ribbed vaults (plan below).

18th-century reconstructions
Laurent-Benoît Dewez ● *91* was the architect of numerous abbeys, among them that of the Premonstratensians of Heylissem at Hélécine (architectural drawing below). Following an orthogonal projection, the new buildings were rigidly planned around cloisters. The dome of the church rose up from behind a monumental classical façade.

During the Middle Ages southern Belgium consisted of a mixture of towns and feudal domains that were alluring targets for the great European ruling houses, as well as sources of mutual envy. Fortifications and castles sprang up at this time. Three types of feudal construction predominated. Between the 12th and 15th centuries keeps and towers were erected; hilltop fortresses were built between the 10th and 15th centuries, and castles on lower ground between the 13th and 15th centuries. While a castle could be built within a few years, the construction of urban fortifications could stretch over a century or more. Well into the 12th century these were still being built from wood and earth; stone was not widely used until the 13th century.

A

B

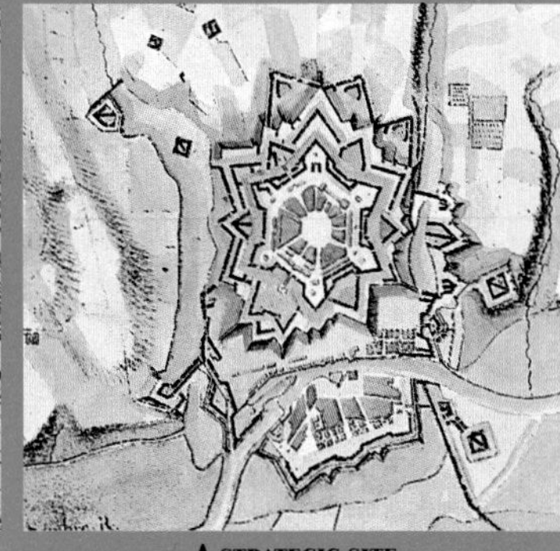

FORTIFIED TOWNS
In the 16th century the Italians introduced fortified bastions. These were pentagonal structures, with bastions projecting from curtain walls made of earth faced with stone or brick. The fortified towns of Mariembourg ▲ *284* (**A**) and Philippeville ▲ *284* were both built following this principle. The streets were planned so that they radiated out from the center. Charleroi (**B**) ▲ *274*, built in 1666, was to adopt the same arrangement.

A STRATEGIC SITE
Because of its strategic position, the area around Bouillon ▲ *266* was fortified from the time of the Franks. In the 11th century Godfrey of Bouillon erected a fortress on the rocky promontory overlooking the bed of the Semois river. It was destroyed during the 16th century, but was rebuilt soon after. Under Louis XIV the town itself was fortified by Vauban. Below: a 19th-century view of Bouillon, from across the river.

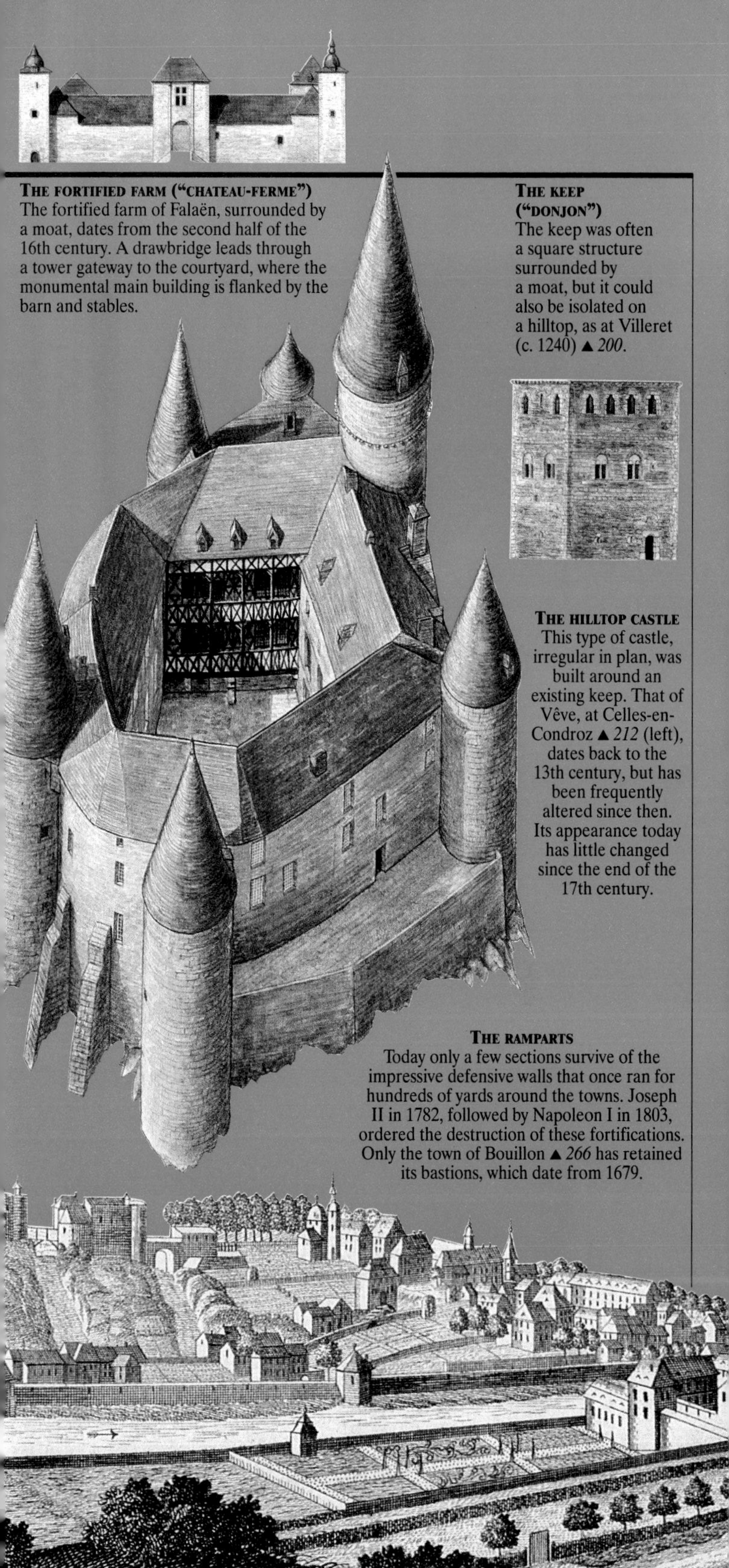

The fortified farm ("chateau-ferme")
The fortified farm of Falaën, surrounded by a moat, dates from the second half of the 16th century. A drawbridge leads through a tower gateway to the courtyard, where the monumental main building is flanked by the barn and stables.

The keep ("donjon")
The keep was often a square structure surrounded by a moat, but it could also be isolated on a hilltop, as at Villeret (c. 1240) ▲ *200*.

The hilltop castle
This type of castle, irregular in plan, was built around an existing keep. That of Vêve, at Celles-en-Condroz ▲ *212* (left), dates back to the 13th century, but has been frequently altered since then. Its appearance today has little changed since the end of the 17th century.

The ramparts
Today only a few sections survive of the impressive defensive walls that once ran for hundreds of yards around the towns. Joseph II in 1782, followed by Napoleon I in 1803, ordered the destruction of these fortifications. Only the town of Bouillon ▲ *266* has retained its bastions, which date from 1679.

The turbulent years of the Middle Ages were succeeded by the more peaceful Renaissance era, which brought with it new refinements in social manners and a desire for comfort. Up to the end of the 17th century the fortified castles were progressively transformed into more habitable residences: large windows were installed, roofs were enhanced with gables and onion-shaped domes, and flights of steps were added. These castles nevertheless retained their defensive aspect since the region, in spite of itself, was still an arena of European battle. With the 18th century a period of calm set in, and many of the castles were rebuilt or converted to a more classical style. Finally, with the 19th century, a period of major restoration commenced.

SUCCESSIVE ALTERATIONS
Like many other castles, that of Spontin (13th–16th century) ▲ *204* underwent numerous alterations over the course of the centuries, becoming gradually more comfortable with each century's flurry of renovation. A section of the medieval wall was destroyed, and an imposing *corps de logis* and a farm were added.

CONVERSIONS
During the 16th century a corner tower and an overhanging upper story, in brick and half-timbering, was added to the medieval keep of Crupet (13th century) ▲ *205* (above, top).

REFURNISHING
The furniture of many great castles ransacked during the French Revolution has gradually been replaced since.

RESTORATION
In the 19th century numerous châteaux (Spontin, Jehay) were restored, occasionally with dramatic results, after the fashion of Viollet-le-Duc.

16TH-CENTURY FAÇADE
In the early part of the 16th century the main building of the Château de Jehay ▲ *218* was erected over the remains of an earlier fortified manor. It was provided with an extraordinary two-tone façade, Gothic windows, and slate spires crowned with bulbous domes.

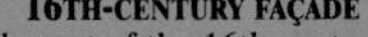

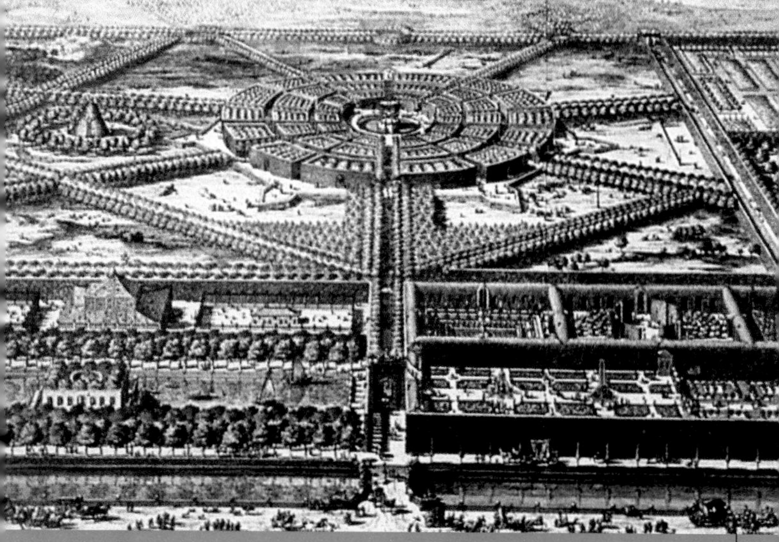

Parks and gardens
In the early 17th century Charles d'Arenberg, Prince of Enghien, relaid his park ▲ *307* in the spirit of an Italian Renaissance garden. What had probably been a hunting ground was transformed into a green "town", with pathways, ponds and fountains, and a sizable population of statues. (Above, an engraving dating from the end of the 17th century.)

French-style architecture
In the 17th century the Château of Modave ▲ *217*, wrecked by troops from the Lorraine, was rebuilt by French architect Jean Goujon. Under his supervision Modave adopted the classical style, well ahead of the 18th-century vogue that was to sweep across Belgium.

Italian-style architecture
This series of rounded arches (above) supported by Tuscan columns, at the Château of Fernelmont (Noville-Les-Bois), reveals the discreet application of Italian Renaissance motifs in the aristocratic architecture of the 17th century.

The second half of the 18th century
The Château of Seneffe ▲ *296*, built between 1763 and 1768, was designed by the architect Laurent-Benoît Dewez soon after returning from Italy. It displays the neoclassical features of Enlightenment architecture, but also owes much to the influence of English Palladianism. (Below, the courtyard façade.)

The Gothic Hôtel de Ville in Brussels ▲ *155*.

Secular architecture in Brussels and southern Belgium is largely the by-product of the various artistic currents that have left their trace on the area that is modern Belgium. In the 16th-century Gothic towns began to draw on Renaissance influences imported from France and, to a lesser extent, Italy. The 17th century saw the arrival of the Baroque style from the Flemish regions; then in the 18th century secular architecture finally turned for its inspiration to the French classical style, which it blended with German Rococo.

THE RENAISSANCE COURT
At the palace of the Prince-Bishops in Liège ▲ *223* the two arcaded courts evoke the Italian palaces of the *quattrocento*.

THE RENAISSANCE PALACE
In 1526 the Prince-Bishop of Liège, Érard de La Marck, determined to rebuild his war-torn palace. Although constructed along the finest Gothic lines, this hybrid building (above) was nevertheless endowed with the first seeds of Renaissance style.

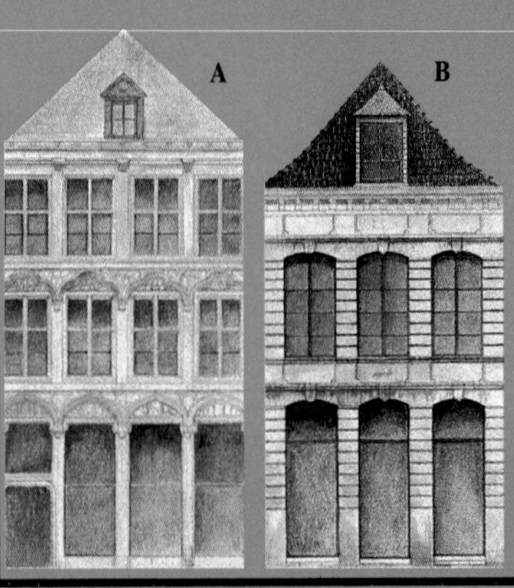

HOUSES IN MONS
▲ *290*
The "Blanc Levrié" house (1530) **(A)**, although Gothic in moldings and style, is one of the rare houses in Mons from this period to have been built in stone. The "Au Renard" house (1724) **(B)**, with its curved lintels, each struck with a keystone, is a classic Mons-style house.

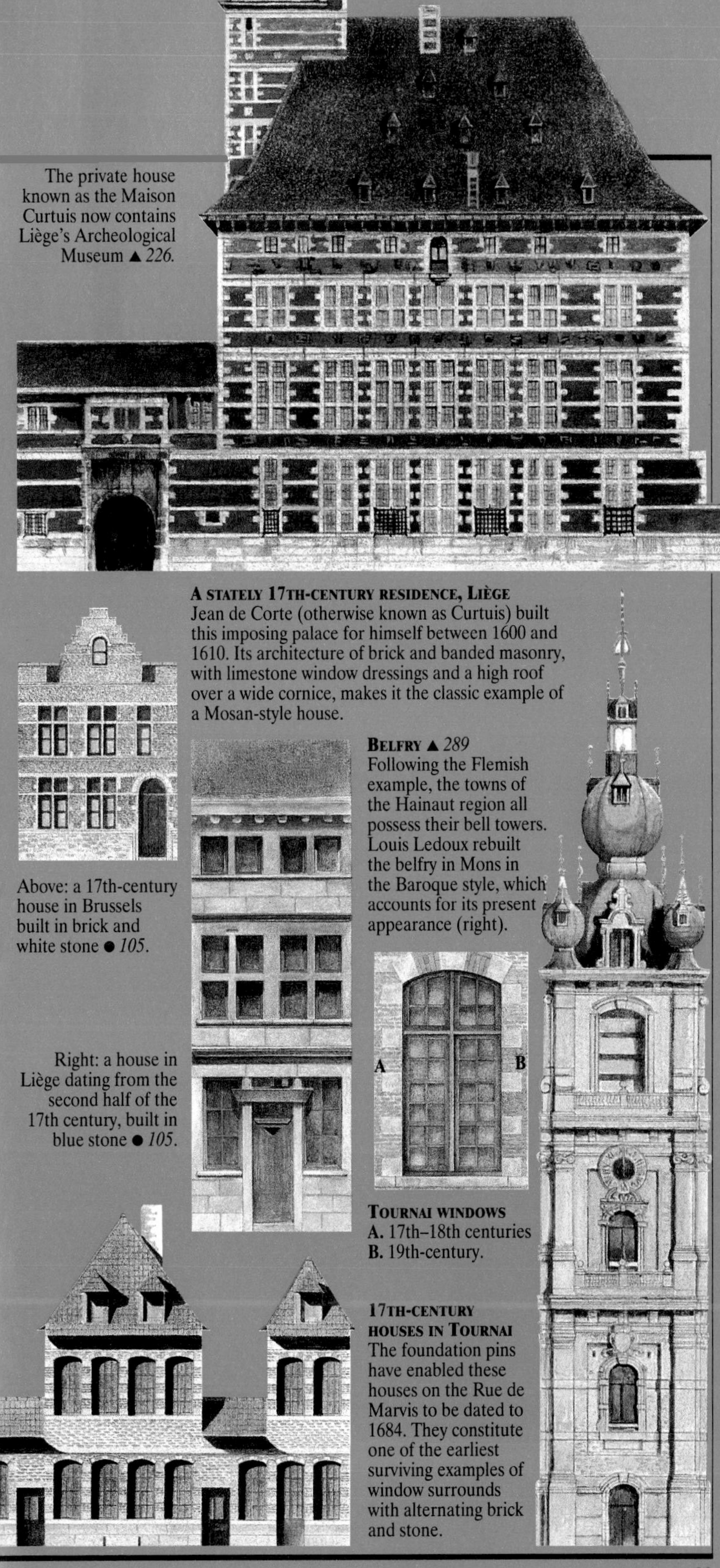

The private house known as the Maison Curtuis now contains Liège's Archeological Museum ▲ *226.*

A stately 17th-century residence, Liège
Jean de Corte (otherwise known as Curtuis) built this imposing palace for himself between 1600 and 1610. Its architecture of brick and banded masonry, with limestone window dressings and a high roof over a wide cornice, makes it the classic example of a Mosan-style house.

Above: a 17th-century house in Brussels built in brick and white stone ● *105.*

Belfry ▲ *289*
Following the Flemish example, the towns of the Hainaut region all possess their bell towers. Louis Ledoux rebuilt the belfry in Mons in the Baroque style, which accounts for its present appearance (right).

Right: a house in Liège dating from the second half of the 17th century, built in blue stone ● *105.*

Tournai windows
A. 17th–18th centuries
B. 19th-century.

17th-century houses in Tournai
The foundation pins have enabled these houses on the Rue de Marvis to be dated to 1684. They constitute one of the earliest surviving examples of window surrounds with alternating brick and stone.

In the first half of the 19th century southern Belgium was transformed by a new landscape of factories. These sprang up in response to the inherent needs of the industrial revolution, and were frequently built from the materials that industry was to mass-produce, such as iron, cast iron, bricks and – in the 20th century – reinforced concrete. Many of these buildings – factories, annexes and laborers' cottages – display a sober rationalism. Others reveal more formal concerns, and either look to the past for inspiration or attempt a new architectural style.

THE MODEL TOWN
The idea of a model town for laborers stemmed from the need to attract a permanent workforce by offering a level of comfort that was, by contemporary standards, quite exceptional. Right: a view of the Grand-Hornu ▲ *298*, built between 1822 and 1835.

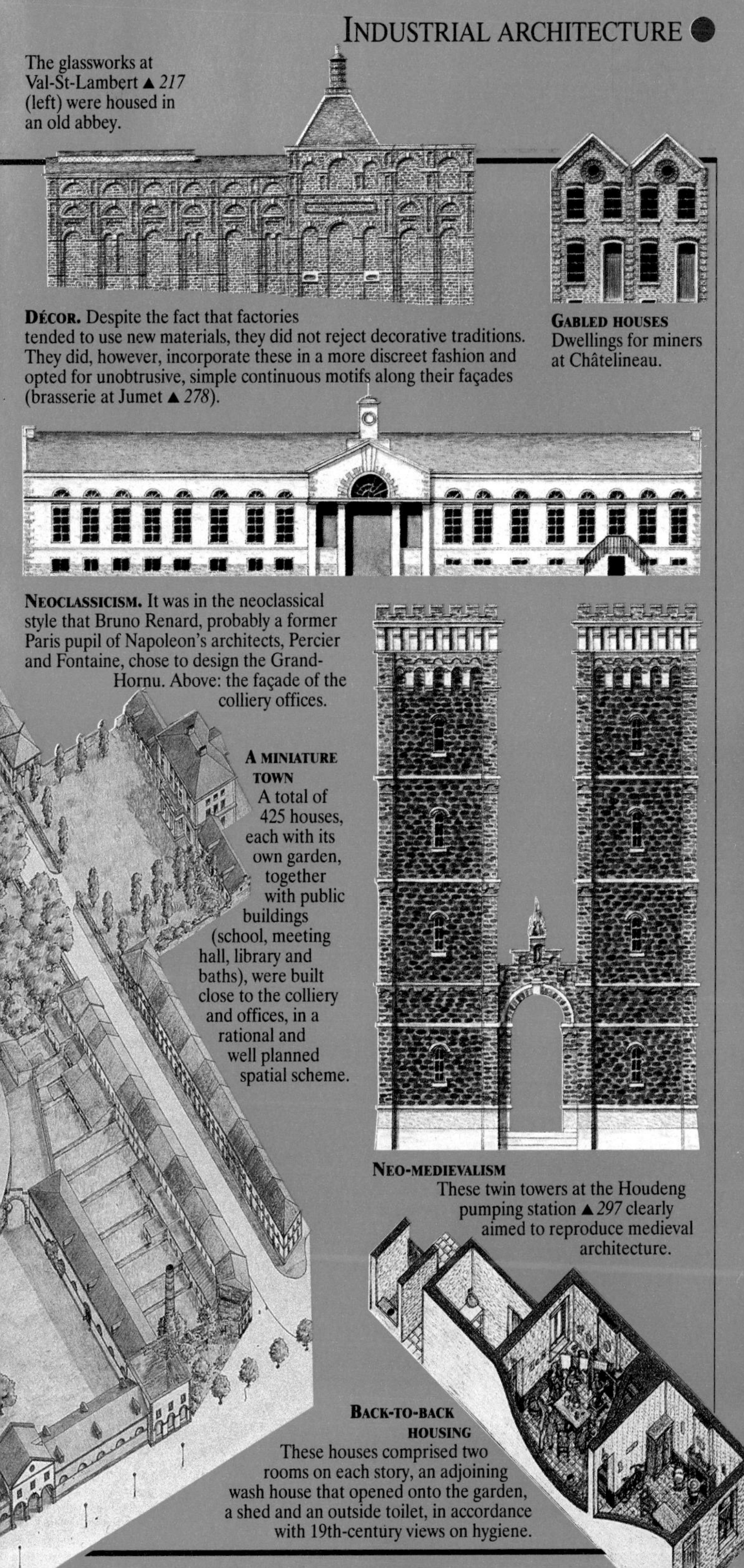

The glassworks at Val-St-Lambert ▲ *217* (left) were housed in an old abbey.

DÉCOR. Despite the fact that factories tended to use new materials, they did not reject decorative traditions. They did, however, incorporate these in a more discreet fashion and opted for unobtrusive, simple continuous motifs along their façades (brasserie at Jumet ▲ *278*).

GABLED HOUSES Dwellings for miners at Châtelineau.

NEOCLASSICISM. It was in the neoclassical style that Bruno Renard, probably a former Paris pupil of Napoleon's architects, Percier and Fontaine, chose to design the Grand-Hornu. Above: the façade of the colliery offices.

A MINIATURE TOWN A total of 425 houses, each with its own garden, together with public buildings (school, meeting hall, library and baths), were built close to the colliery and offices, in a rational and well planned spatial scheme.

NEO-MEDIEVALISM These twin towers at the Houdeng pumping station ▲ *297* clearly aimed to reproduce medieval architecture.

BACK-TO-BACK HOUSING These houses comprised two rooms on each story, an adjoining wash house that opened onto the garden, a shed and an outside toilet, in accordance with 19th-century views on hygiene.

In southern Belgium, coal mining was for a long time a seasonal activity, alternatin with working in the fields. Mining was limited to small pits, known as *bures* or *cayats*. The invention of the steam-powered pump (the Newcomen Engine) in 1705 solved the problem of water extraction and meant that deeper, previously inaccessible, seams could be exploited. During the 19th century the enormous energy demands of a burgeoning heavy industry, coupled with technical advances and the intervention of financiers, made coal mining the core industrial activity along the Haine-Sambre-Meuse axis.

The mining levels
Photomontage dating from 1892. (In reality the tunnels are dozens or, in some cases, even hundreds of yards apart.)

Silicosis
Mechanization was gradually introduced ▲ 300 – but, although this technical advance made the work less strenuous, it was also responsible, by creating extra dust, for silicosis, the disease commonly known as the "miner's malady".

Transport
In the early days the coal trucks were hauled either by ponies or by women or children.

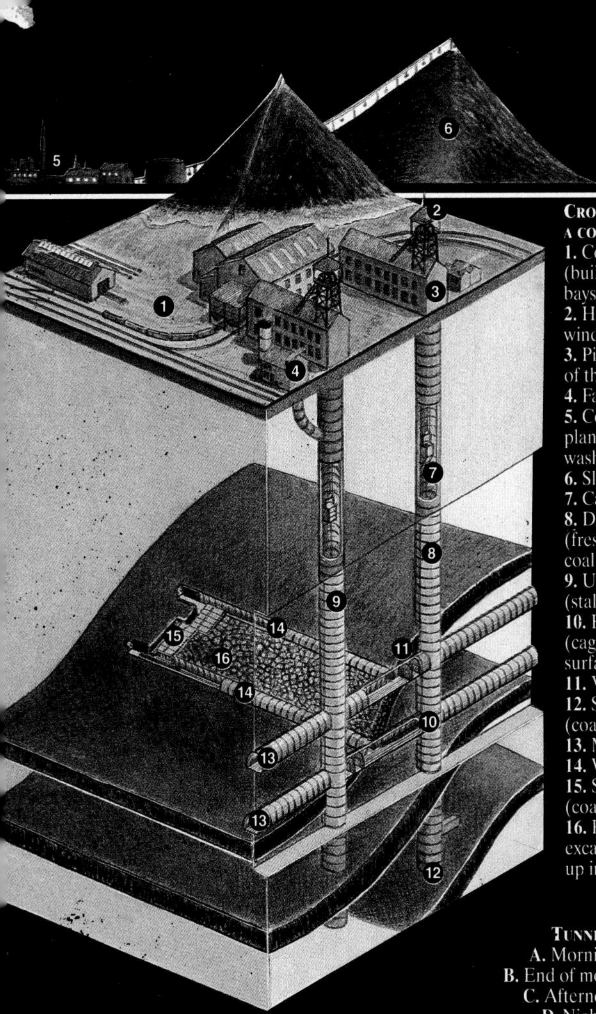

Cross section of a colliery

1. Coal yard (buildings, loading bays).
2. Head frame, or winding house.
3. Pithead (arrival of the cages).
4. Fan house.
5. Coal preparation plant (sorting and washing).
6. Slagheaps.
7. Cage.
8. Downcast shaft (fresh air flows in; coal is carried out).
9. Upcast shaft (stale air removed).
10. Hitching point (cages return to the surface).
11. Ventilation doors.
12. Shaft bottom (coal face).
13. Main roadways.
14. Work tunnels.
15. Site of excavation (coal face).
16. Previously excavated area, built up into "pack" walls.

Tunneling

A. Morning shift.
B. End of morning shift.
C. Afternoon shift.
D. Night shift.

At the coal face

The coal is dislodged using a pneumatic pick, then undercut along the bottom of the seam. After the coal has been extracted, ceiling props are put in place.

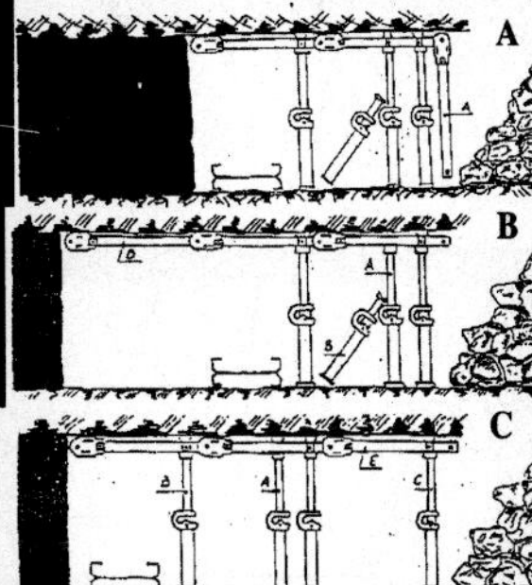

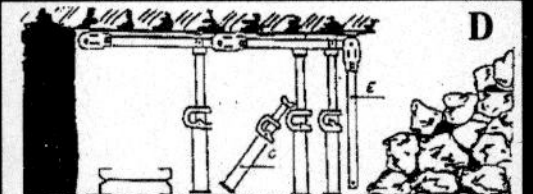

At the foot of the tunnel the "won" coal falls onto a conveyor belt, which carries it to the trucks for transportation to the surface.

Publicity poster for Hankar (1894).

Brussels was a pioneer of Art Nouveau, and it was here that this ornamental style, inspired by floral and geometric patterns, first appeared in Belgium (1893). It was born out of new political, economic and social conditions (industrial prosperity, massive exploitation of colonial resources and the growth of a liberal middle class keen to emphasize its identity), but also out of a reaction against the eclecticism of historical styles. Art Nouveau reached its extraordinary peak at the turn of the century, then began to decline in the early years of the 20th century when technical developments gave way to a decorative explosion and an amalgam of styles. Ironically, this was the very kind of eclecticism that the leaders of the movement – Victor Horta, Paul Hankar and Henry van de Velde – had so criticized.

EARLY DAYS
The elegant house (left) that Victor Horta built for Professor Tassel ▲ *179* in Brussels in 1893 is considered to be the "manifesto" of Art Nouveau architecture in Belgium. The symmetrical façade is enlivened by a wrought-iron bow window – but the house's originality lies inside, above all in the distribution of the rooms and the theatricality of the décor.

DEPARTMENT STORES
These acted as highly visible advertisements for Horta's designs. Below: Waucquez, which now houses the Comic-Strip Museum.

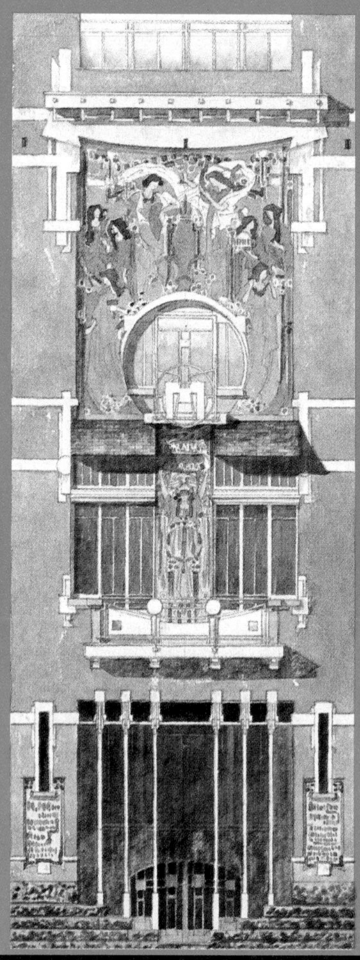

A SYMBOLIST DÉCOR. Right: the Brussels home (1905) of the painter Paul Cauchie, decorated with pre-Raphelite inspired sgraffito.

Sgraffito
Below: detail of the sgraffito, representing the five Muses, on the exterior of Paul Cauchie's house. This technique of wall decoration consisted of producing a design by using scrapers to scratch through superimposed layers of different colored paints.

Paul Hankar and the ornamental façade
While Victor Horta's work is characterized by interior design, Paul Hankar's concentrates on polychrome schemes, as demonstrated by this "poster" façade covered in a monumental sgraffito design painted (1897) by the artist Albert Ciamberlani for his own house in Brussels ▲ *179*.

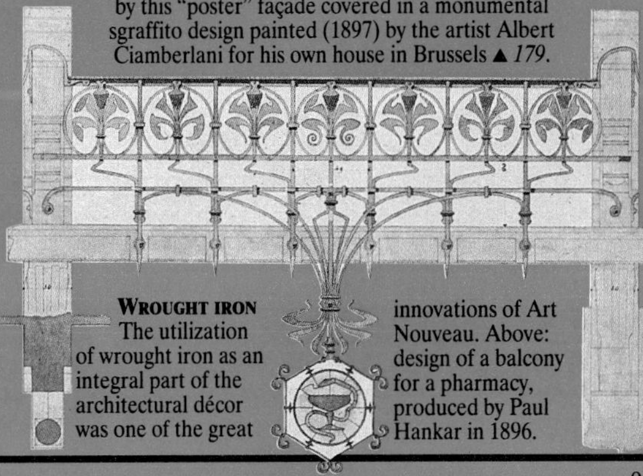

Wrought iron
The utilization of wrought iron as an integral part of the architectural décor was one of the great innovations of Art Nouveau. Above: design of a balcony for a pharmacy, produced by Paul Hankar in 1896.

For the younger generation keen to follow in the footsteps of the Art Nouveau pioneers, the sobriety of Austrian architecture extolled by the Viennese Secession (1897–1907) offered an attractive compromise. However, the desire to emphasize a social and collective dimension found only limited expression in the formal subtleties of the Secessionists, and that desire began to fade with the advent of the Modern Movement (1910). This broke with all notions of style or décor and found, in the aftermath of World War One, a fitting application in the construction of social housing.

A RATIONALIST FAÇADE
The Brussels clinic (above) of Dr Van Neck, designed in 1910, ushered in the Modernist movement in Belgium. The rationalist façade of the building is reinforced by the vertical lines of the ventilation shafts. Its designer, the architect Antoine Pompe, a formidable personality, later renounced the functionalist esthetic.

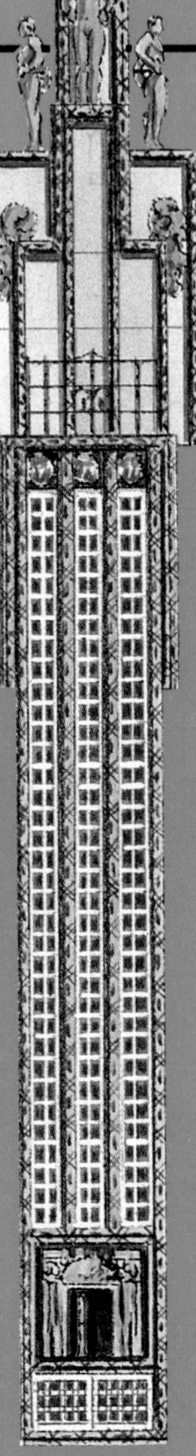

THE PALAIS STOCLET
The four sculpted heroes, by Franz Metzner, and demisphere that crown the Palais Stoclet (right and below) bear witness to the importance of the decorative arts in the genesis of this building – long nicknamed the "Crematorium" by the citizens of Brussels because of its stark façades.

SECESSIONIST DÉCOR
At the Palais Stoclet ▲ *183*, a Secessionist structure built by the Viennese architect Josef Hoffmann between 1906 and 1911, the walls clad in white Norwegian marble and framed by gilded metal moldings serve to emphasize the strict volumetric design of the building.

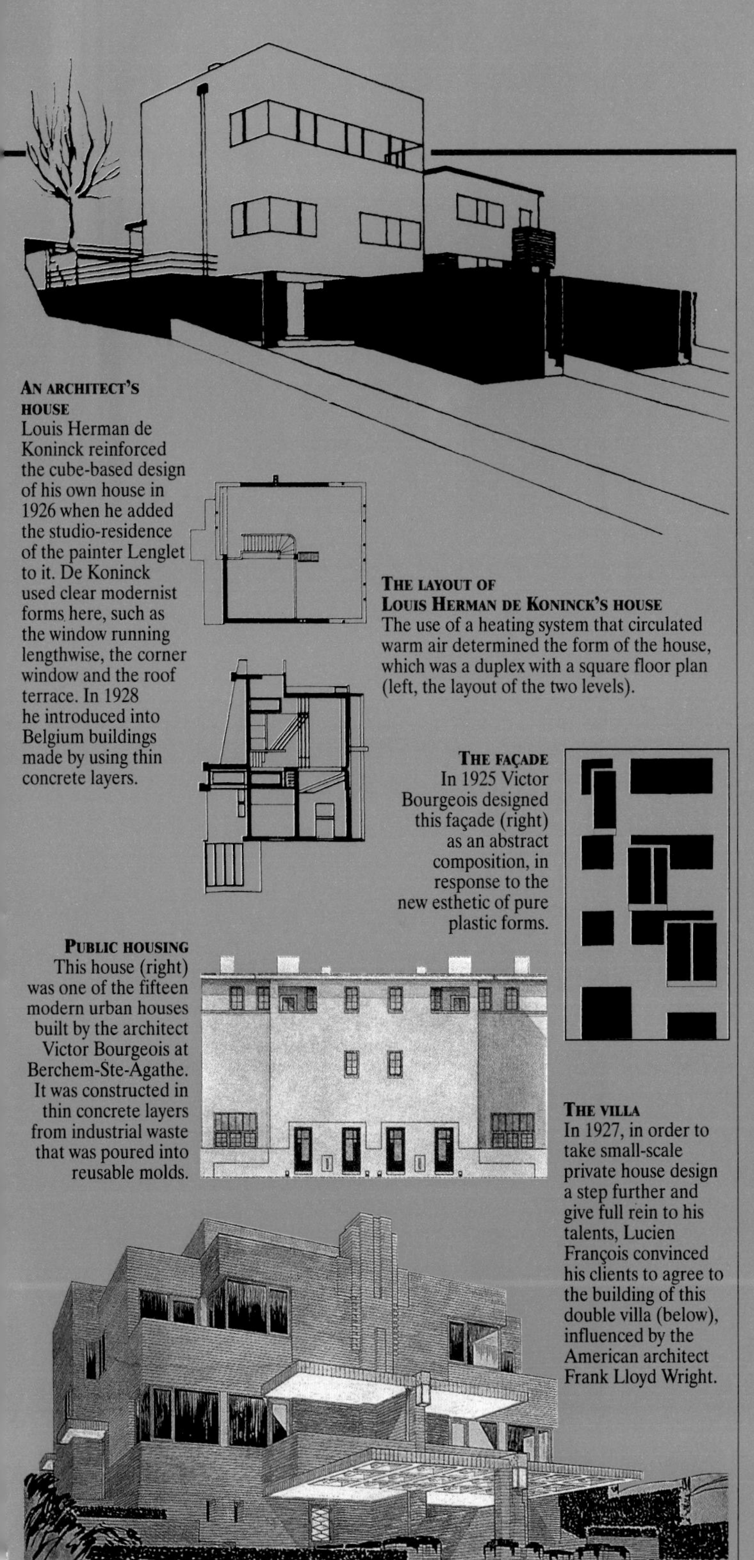

An architect's house
Louis Herman de Koninck reinforced the cube-based design of his own house in 1926 when he added the studio-residence of the painter Lenglet to it. De Koninck used clear modernist forms here, such as the window running lengthwise, the corner window and the roof terrace. In 1928 he introduced into Belgium buildings made by using thin concrete layers.

The layout of Louis Herman de Koninck's house
The use of a heating system that circulated warm air determined the form of the house, which was a duplex with a square floor plan (left, the layout of the two levels).

The façade
In 1925 Victor Bourgeois designed this façade (right) as an abstract composition, in response to the new esthetic of pure plastic forms.

Public housing
This house (right) was one of the fifteen modern urban houses built by the architect Victor Bourgeois at Berchem-Ste-Agathe. It was constructed in thin concrete layers from industrial waste that was poured into reusable molds.

The villa
In 1927, in order to take small-scale private house design a step further and give full rein to his talents, Lucien François convinced his clients to agree to the building of this double villa (below), influenced by the American architect Frank Lloyd Wright.

Belgium was badly hit by the 1914–18 war, and in its aftermath the young generation of modernists concentrated on urban regeneration. Influenced by what had been done in England and Holland, they developed plans for garden cities to solve the housing problem. From 1920 to 1926 – when the program began to lose momentum – this urban model offered a broad scope for technical and formal experimentation.

THE "CITÉS"
The planning of the garden cities was overseen by cooperative societies which tried to promote a new community-based way of life. At Cité Floréal, the urban planner Louis Van der Swaelmen conceived an interplay between public and private space within an extraordinary urban landscape.

Artist's impression of a section of Cité Floréal (1922–35), in Watermael-Boitsfort commune.

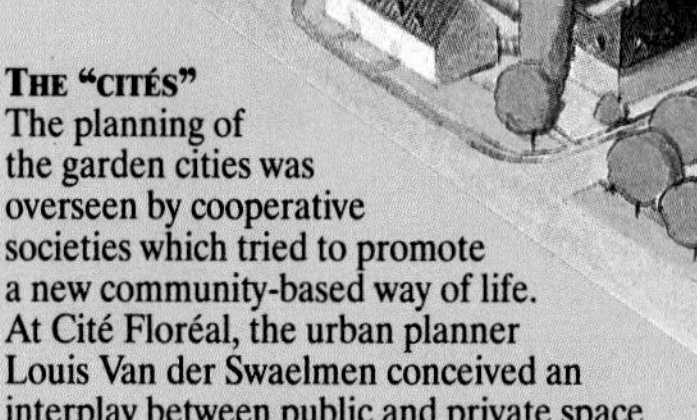

THE SHOPPING CENTER
The "Fer à cheval" (Horseshoe), a 1927 shopping center overlooked by a water tower, is one of the landmarks of Cité Floréal and Cité du Logis ▲ *187*.

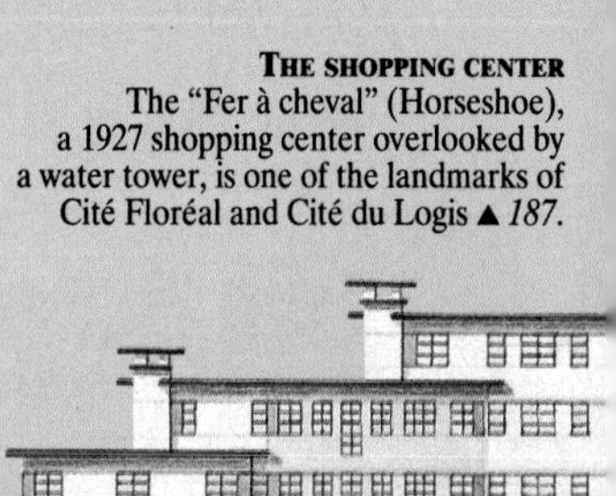

THE HOUSES
At Cité Floréal strict guidelines on the upkeep of houses and gardens were drawn up by the cooperative society, which stipulated the color of façades, doors and frames. Above, semi-detached "cottage" style house.

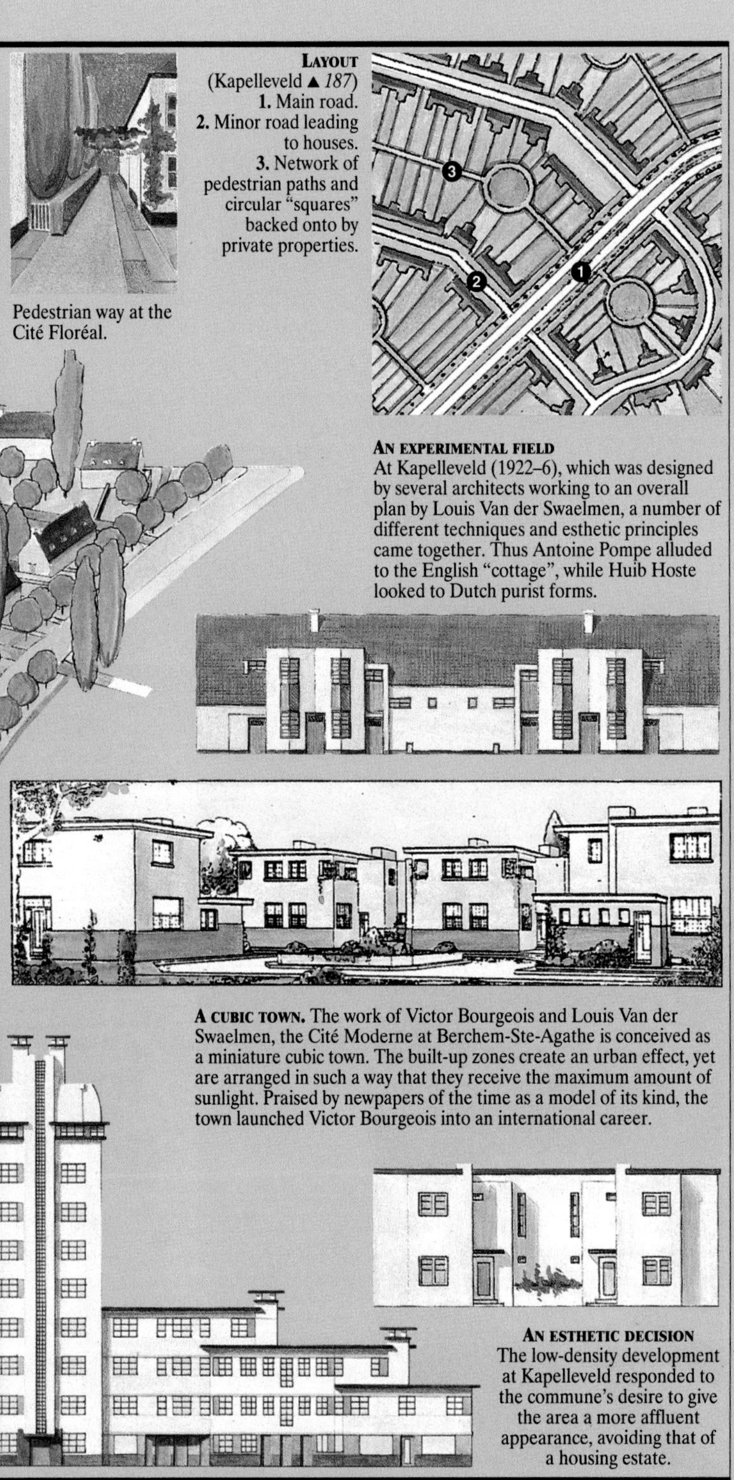

Layout
(Kapelleveld ▲ *187*)
1. Main road.
2. Minor road leading to houses.
3. Network of pedestrian paths and circular "squares" backed onto by private properties.

Pedestrian way at the Cité Floréal.

An experimental field
At Kapelleveld (1922–6), which was designed by several architects working to an overall plan by Louis Van der Swaelmen, a number of different techniques and esthetic principles came together. Thus Antoine Pompe alluded to the English "cottage", while Huib Hoste looked to Dutch purist forms.

A cubic town. The work of Victor Bourgeois and Louis Van der Swaelmen, the Cité Moderne at Berchem-Ste-Agathe is conceived as a miniature cubic town. The built-up zones create an urban effect, yet are arranged in such a way that they receive the maximum amount of sunlight. Praised by newpapers of the time as a model of its kind, the town launched Victor Bourgeois into an international career.

An esthetic decision
The low-density development at Kapelleveld responded to the commune's desire to give the area a more affluent appearance, avoiding that of a housing estate.

The exceptional diversity of southern Belgium in terms of climate and geology provides the area with a huge range of materials that can be used for construction. Local stone holds pride of place in the region's architectural heritage, and variations in color can often be traced to nearby rock deposits. In the silt-laden plateaus of Brabant and Hainaut brick is widespread because of the clay soil, and occasional outcrops of white or blue stone also occur. In the fluvial valleys of the Meuse and Sambre and in the Condroz the rock includes sandstone, blue stone (limestone) and marble; in the massif of the Ardennes phyllite (metamorphosed schists), sandstone and occasionally arkose can be found.

SANDSTONE
1 and **2.** Types of psammite sandstone from the Condroz.
3 and **4.** Types of sandstone schists. These are widely used in rubble walls and paving.

MARBLE
Left: samples of Belgian marble quarried c. 1766 (Palace of Charles de Lorraine, Brussels, ▲ *170*).
1. Red and gray marble.
2. Gray marble.
3. Gray-pink Byzantine marble.
4. Royal-red marble.

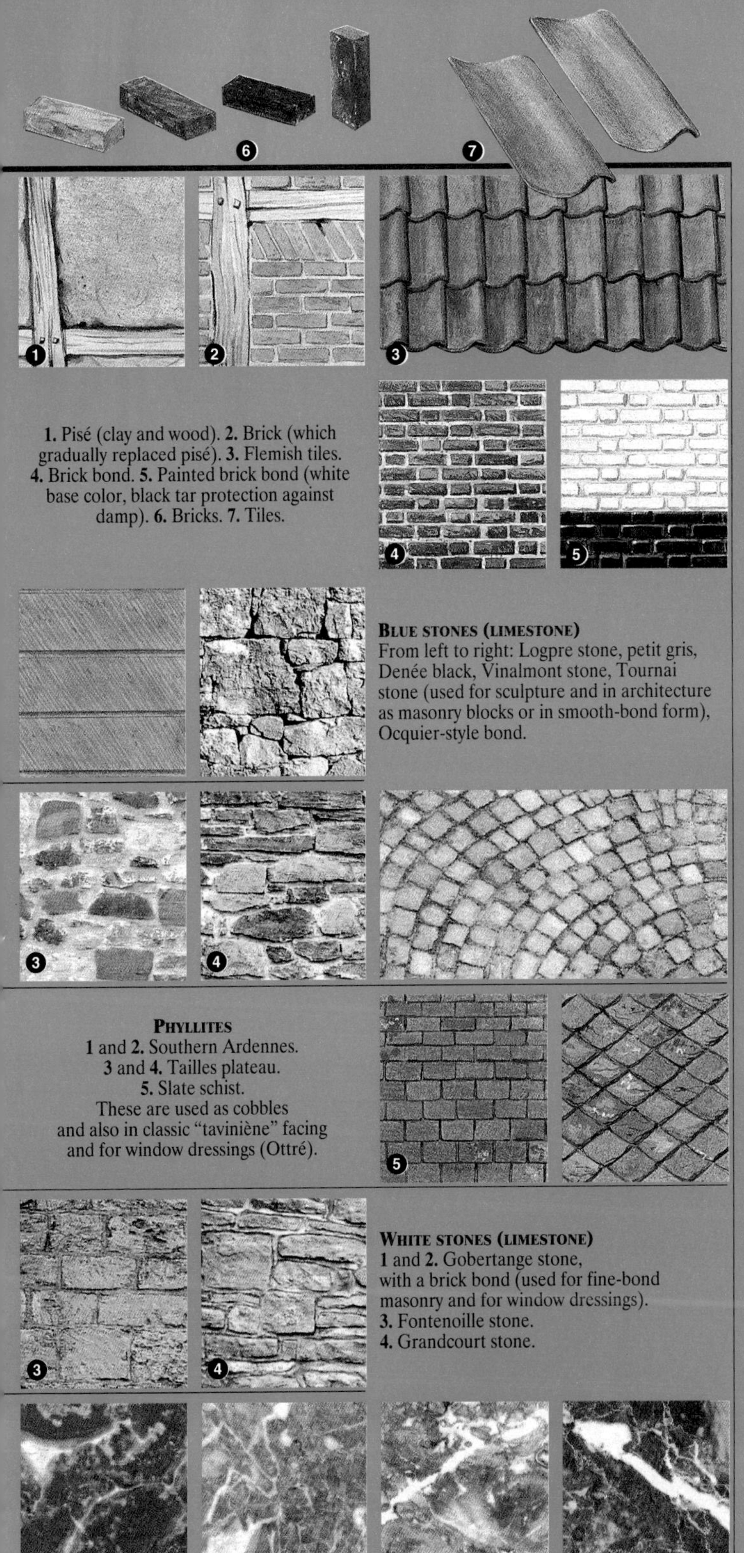

1. Pisé (clay and wood). 2. Brick (which gradually replaced pisé). 3. Flemish tiles. 4. Brick bond. 5. Painted brick bond (white base color, black tar protection against damp). 6. Bricks. 7. Tiles.

Blue stones (limestone)
From left to right: Logpre stone, petit gris, Denée black, Vinalmont stone, Tournai stone (used for sculpture and in architecture as masonry blocks or in smooth-bond form), Ocquier-style bond.

Phyllites
1 and 2. Southern Ardennes.
3 and 4. Tailles plateau.
5. Slate schist.
These are used as cobbles and also in classic "tavinière" facing and for window dressings (Ottré).

White stones (limestone)
1 and 2. Gobertange stone, with a brick bond (used for fine-bond masonry and for window dressings).
3. Fontenoille stone.
4. Grandcourt stone.

Southern Belgium is made up of a variety of landscapes. The forbidding Ardennes massif is in stark contrast to the fertile Condroz plateau or the clay terrain north of the Meuse. Determined by soil and climate, and also by local custom, each district of southern Belgium has produced its own individual architectural style. In the south the relatively plain farmhouse block is widespread, whereas in the north the more elaborate courtyard farm is common. But throughout southern Belgium – with only rare exceptions and irrespective of the type of farm or village – because of the crop-rotation system the houses are clustered together.

The village of Ottré specializes in carving the fine local slate. Above: Ottré tombstone.

FARMHOUSE BLOCK
This Ardennes farmhouse is above all a functional building. Under one roof are grouped together, in different "cells", all the various constituents of rural life, from human lodging and shelter for the animals to storage for harvested produce and farming equipment. The living area faces south, while the barn forms a thick protective barrier against cold north winds.

ROOF
The roof is covered with schist tiles that are laid diagonally, using clay on a flat plank.

GROUND PLAN
The farmhouse's proportions are almost perfectly square.

WINDOWS
Framed in wood or slate, the windows mostly open into the gabled living area.

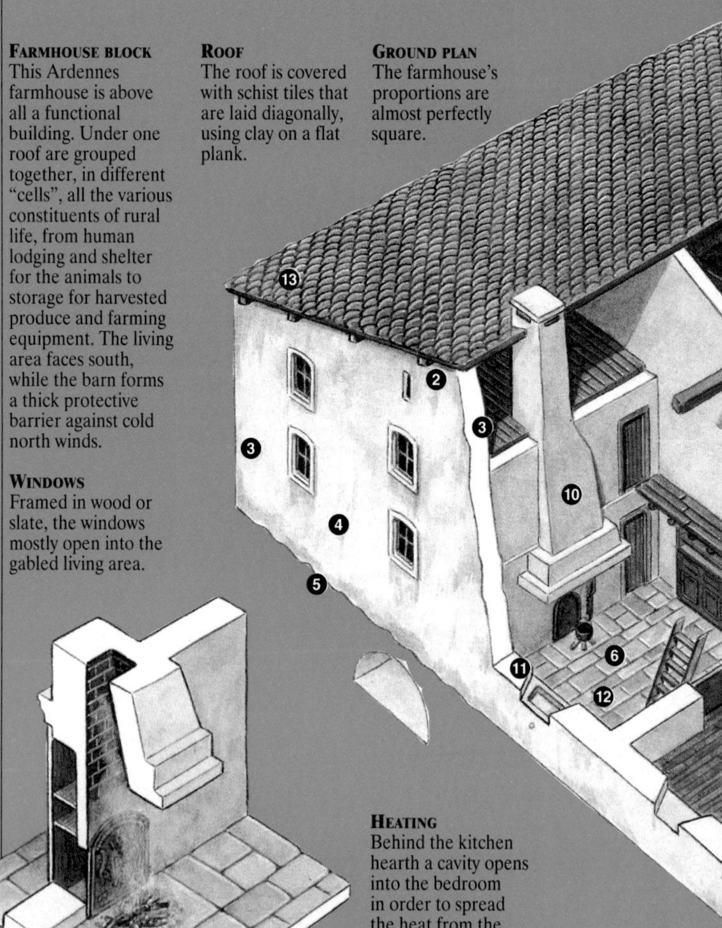

HEATING
Behind the kitchen hearth a cavity opens into the bedroom in order to spread the heat from the huge funnel-shaped chimney.

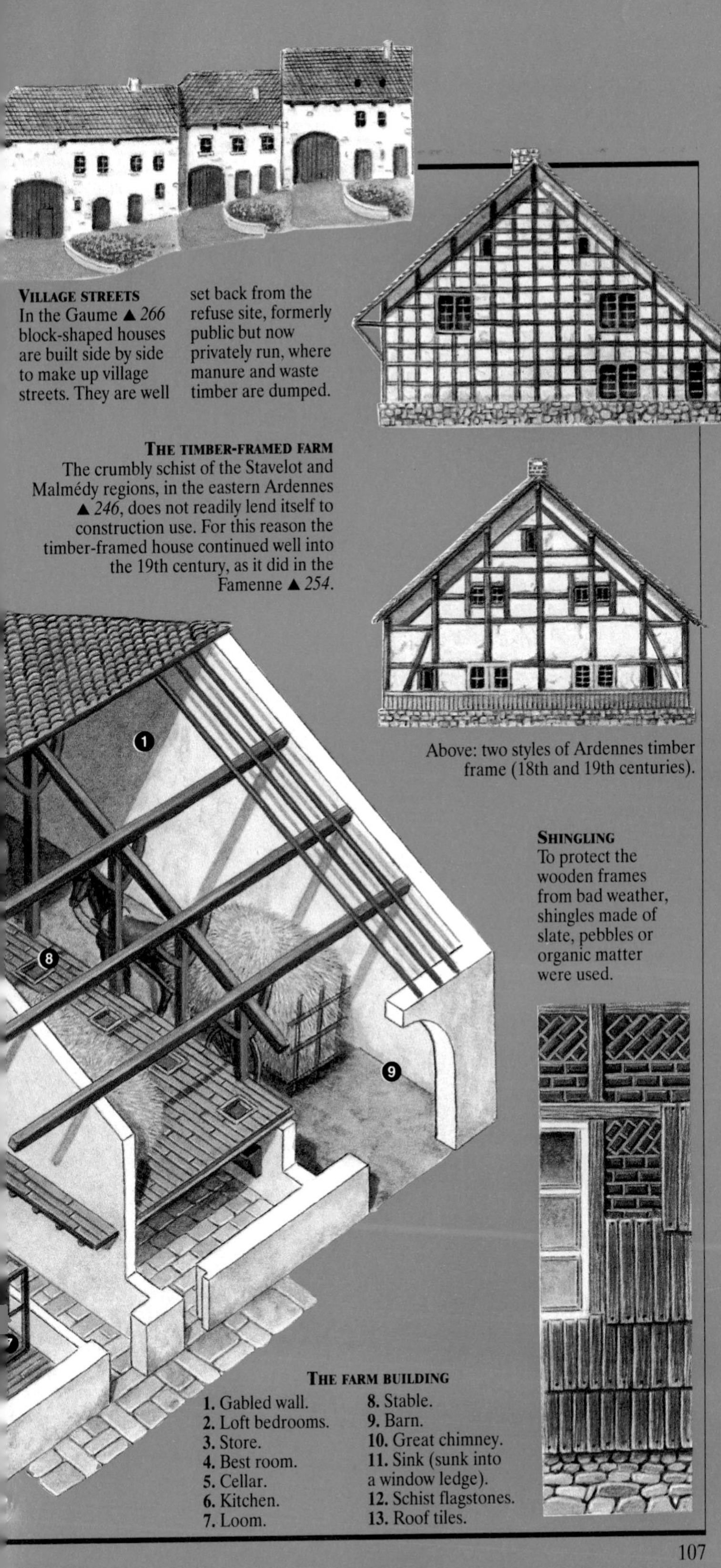

Village streets
In the Gaume ▲ *266* block-shaped houses are built side by side to make up village streets. They are well set back from the refuse site, formerly public but now privately run, where manure and waste timber are dumped.

The timber-framed farm
The crumbly schist of the Stavelot and Malmédy regions, in the eastern Ardennes ▲ *246*, does not readily lend itself to construction use. For this reason the timber-framed house continued well into the 19th century, as it did in the Famenne ▲ *254*.

Above: two styles of Ardennes timber frame (18th and 19th centuries).

Shingling
To protect the wooden frames from bad weather, shingles made of slate, pebbles or organic matter were used.

The farm building

1. Gabled wall.
2. Loft bedrooms.
3. Store.
4. Best room.
5. Cellar.
6. Kitchen.
7. Loom.
8. Stable.
9. Barn.
10. Great chimney.
11. Sink (sunk into a window ledge).
12. Schist flagstones.
13. Roof tiles.

THE COURTYARD FARM
Country estates in southern Belgium, a prime source of income for the nobility and church under the Ancien Régime, were conceived along the same lines as the courtyard farm (above). This type of farm centered on a square courtyard, around which were arranged the farmhouse and a variety of agricultural buildings; an enormous barn occupied the length of one side.

THE FARM LAYOUT
1. Dovecote and entrance gateway.
2. Cowshed and stables beneath a hayloft.
3. Farmhouse.
4. Hayloft, outhouse and pigsty.
5. Barn.
6. Sheep pen.
7. Manure heap.

Below: a farm of considerable size at Loupoigne (Brabant).

Belgium as seen by painters

As early as the 15th century ROBERT CAMPIN (c. 1375–1444), known as the Master of Flémalle, captured in the background of *The Nativity* (**1**) the gentle charms of the Mosan valley at the small town of Huy, which was the secondary residence of the Prince-Bishops of Liège. The castle, collegiate church, ramparts, vines and welcoming inns, as well as a silvery stretch of the Meuse river, are all depicted. In the following century a painter from Louvain, LUCAS VAN VALCKENBORCH (c. 1530–97), in *Huy Seen from Ahin* (**3**), chose to paint the same river, but from further upsteam. He turned his eye to the massive rocks, pastoral activities and the coming and going of traffic on the life-giving Meuse. At around the same time a Mosan artist who had settled in Antwerp, HENRI BLÈS (c. 1480–after 1550), exaggerated the rocky banks of the Meuse in his *Mosan Landscape* (**2**) in order to create a hallucinatory universe, given over to the plundering of nature. As an antidote to this view of nature as somehow violated, *First Frost* (**4**) by ALBERT RATY (1889–1970) focuses on the massive dark shapes of the virgin Ardennes Forest where the Semois river carves its way through the tall hills near Bouillon like an icy flow of liquefied emerald.

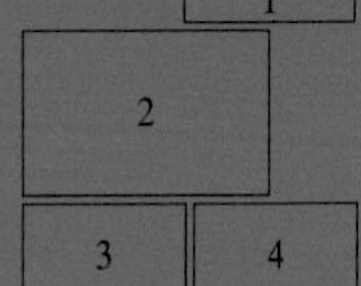

COROT

FÉLICIEN ROPS ▲ 196 (1833–98), whose caricatures of women could be caustic, rediscovered in his tiny paintings of the Mosan landscape around Namur and Anseremme (right, *The Coléby Valley at Freyr*) the simplicity of a rustic environment where the flora communes with the Mosan limestone massifs. Before him, GILLES CLOSSON (1796–1852) had consciously chosen a more homely rural scene (left).

The landscapes of southern Belgium are extremely varied, and in no way do they match the *plat pays* ("flat country") rendered famous by Jacques Brel in his songs about Flanders. CAMILLE COROT (1796–1875) managed nonetheless to erase the rugged aspects of the Ardennes, deliberately retaining only an impression of peaceful solitude and rolling wooded hills. Below: *Souvenir of the Ardennes*.

Nowhere other than in southern Belgium, where coal and iron so radically transformed the landscapes around Liège and Charleroi, have art and industry come together to forge such creative talent: the "one [having] illustrated the other; the second

[having] on occasion nourished the first" (Claude Gaier). Swept along by the prevailing positivist ideas, certain artists of the last century pinned high hopes on mechanization – whereas others were more inclined to point an accusing finger at social injustices or the blackened landscapes now hostile to man. Thus, if you pass through the Sambre valley in winter, the Black Country may be covered with dirty snow – as in *The Tow Horse* (**3**), a powerful composition by Pierre Paulus (1881–1959). In this painting the artist has deliberately focused on the strain of the animal pulling the barge and the crushing bleakness of the factories beneath the sooty sky.

MAXIMILIEN LUCE (1858–1941) in *Slagheaps* (**2**) selects one of the most striking features of the industrial landscape of the Sambre-Meuse valley: the *terrils* (slagheaps, or coal tips) ▲ *278*; these pyramids of slag, which punctuate the landscape with their pointed triangular shapes, are sometimes dusty, sometimes wooded.

C Meunier

Although all this acitivity belongs to a bygone era, even today anyone entering the gigantic workshops at Cockerill-Sambre can easily recapture the overwhelming impression experienced by CONSTANTIN MEUNIER (1831–1905) (**4**) when he painted *Casting at Ougrée* (**1**) and the straining nobility of toiling metal workers.

4 1 2 3

The Grand-Place in Brussels has, more than any other landmark, been the preferred theme of artists seeking to evoke the capital of the Brabant region. The choice is understandable, given the symbolic force of this masterpiece of urban architecture.

Nevertheless, some artists have approached their chosen subject with unaccustomed restraint.

JAMES ENSOR (**3**) (1860–1949), for example, although one of the most daring painters of his generation, tackled his subject – in *Hôtel de Ville in Brussels* (**1**) – from the rooftops of an adjoining street in order to best capture its main feature: the soaring spire of the town hall, symbol of regional and metropolitan pride. Other, more intimate angles, however, have also caught the artistic eye. Brussels-born Jean-Jacques Gaillard (1890–1976) provides proof of this in his painting *Rue des Trois-Têtes in Brussels* (**2**), which portrays Brussels as a working-class provincial town that keeps the hidden poetry of its narrow streets to itself.

2 1 3

"THE HÔTEL DE VILLE IN BRUSSELS IS A JEWEL TO RANK WITH THE SPIRE OF CHARTRES."

VICTOR HUGO

The Surrealist imagination of RENÉ MAGRITTE (1898–1967) ● *122* visualized the Forest of the Ardennes as thrusting its branches and foliage into the recesses of man's memory – while, at the same time, turning into a petrified object that is also functional.

Great masters and schools of painting

By a noteworthy coincidence it was at the very time of the first recorded use of the name Walloon, in Mons in 1447, that Walloon art – and more particularly Walloon painting – was born. The latter is represented by two figures of international renown: Robert Campin and Rogier de la Pasture (or Van der Weyden), whose works, venturing beyond religious symbolism, draw closer to realism and begin to include landscape details and everyday representations of people. The current of realism running through the 15th century was to merge with the resurgence of humanism in the Renaissance art of the following century, embodied by artists such as Joachim Patenier, Henri Blès, Nicolas de Neufchâtel, Jean Provost and Lambert Lombard.

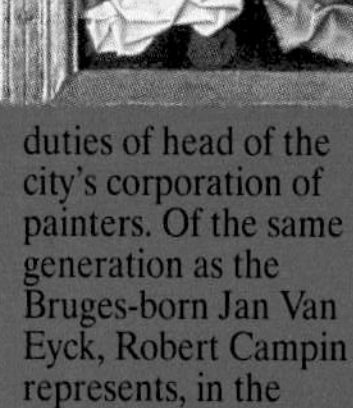

ROBERT CAMPIN was born at Valenciennes in the Hainaut between 1375 and 1378, but settled while young in Tournai, where in 1423 he assumed the duties of head of the city's corporation of painters. Of the same generation as the Bruges-born Jan Van Eyck, Robert Campin represents, in the sculptural plasticity of his figures, a contrast to the refinements of the latter's style. He was influenced by the contemporary sculpture of Tournai, and his style retains notable echoes of its monumentality; yet it is nonetheless imbued with an internalized, meditative quality, particularly notable in this *Annunciation* (**1**). In comparison, the esthetic ideals of his pupil Rogier de la Pasture (Tournai 1399/1400–Brussels 1464), whose name was transcribed into its Flemish version, ROGIER VAN DER WEYDEN, by Brussels clerks of the period, are very different. From the peaceful world of Campin, the viewer is transported into a universe filled with dramatic tension and human tragedy. What is most notable about Rogier van der Weyden's paintings is the recurrent motif of

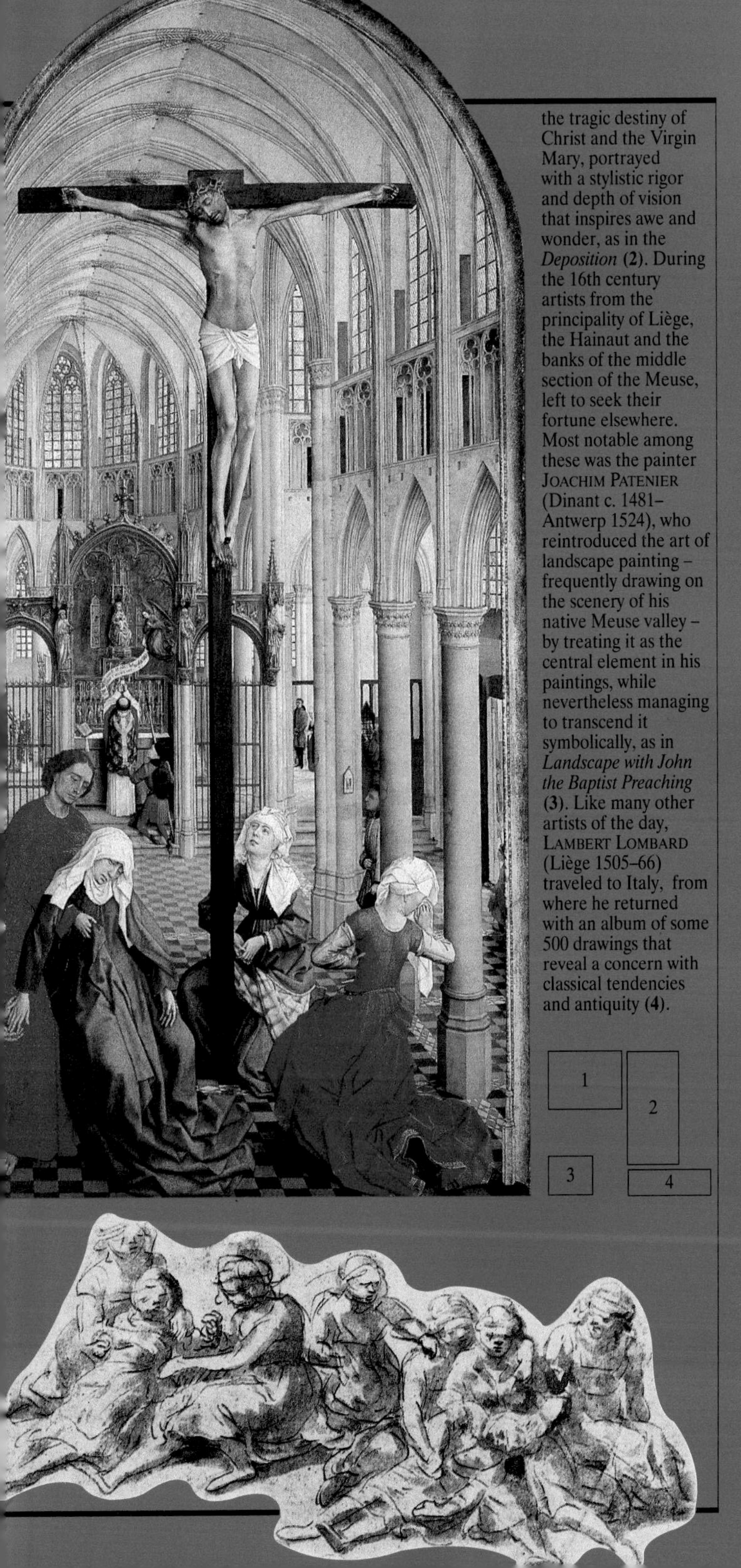

the tragic destiny of Christ and the Virgin Mary, portrayed with a stylistic rigor and depth of vision that inspires awe and wonder, as in the *Deposition* (**2**). During the 16th century artists from the principality of Liège, the Hainaut and the banks of the middle section of the Meuse, left to seek their fortune elsewhere. Most notable among these was the painter JOACHIM PATENIER (Dinant c. 1481–Antwerp 1524), who reintroduced the art of landscape painting – frequently drawing on the scenery of his native Meuse valley – by treating it as the central element in his paintings, while nevertheless managing to transcend it symbolically, as in *Landscape with John the Baptist Preaching* (**3**). Like many other artists of the day, LAMBERT LOMBARD (Liège 1505–66) traveled to Italy, from where he returned with an album of some 500 drawings that reveal a concern with classical tendencies and antiquity (**4**).

1	2
3	4

Belgian 20th-century art offers a fertile pictorial tradition. The Surrealist movement – essentially a French creation – gained recognition through Magritte from 1926, and was invigorated by the dream-like art of Delvaux. After World War Two the artists of "Young Belgian Painting" – a self-proclaimed collective and national enterprise – paved the way for a new, international movement: Cobra (COpenhagen–BRussels–Amsterdam).

René Magritte (Lessines 1898–1967) was a leading figure within the extraordinary movement of Walloon Surrealism. His work is exemplified by disturbing juxta-positions between titles and paintings, and the logic of *Ceci n'est pas une pipe*; the illusoriness of a frame, a window and nature; fetish objects such as an apple or a bow tie; emblems of portent, mystery, and occasionally anxiety. Right: *The Empire of Light*. Paul Delvaux (Antheit 1897–St-Idesbald 1994), on the other hand, opted for a dream-like universe in which three themes return: nudes, skeletons and stations. The recurrent motif of the last train, as in *Evening Trains* (below), evokes the irreversibility of time.

The movement known as "Young Belgian Painting" originated in Brussels in the aftermath of the Liberation after World War Two, and consisted of a dozen or so young artists who wanted, above all, to champion contemporary art and free use of color. The group had no precise objectives, but was bound together by a common taste for freedom and the breaking down of barriers, and travel. Some of them, such as Serge Creuz, whose work resonates with post-Cubist influences, opted for figurative art. Others chose to explore the possibilities of abstraction: perceived as lyrical by Louis van Lint; purified by Anne Bonnet who, increasingly over her career, emphasized the importance of line; powerful and colorful by Antoine Mortier, whose vigorous discourse draws him closer to Expressionism. The movement was disbanded in 1948, following the death of the group's president, René Lust.

SERGE CREUZ
Woman with a Basket, 1946

ANNE BONNET
The Golden Town, 1955–6

ANTOINE MORTIER
Man, 1947–8

A masked ball organized by the "Young Belgian Painting" group, in Brussels, in 1947. Jean Milo is dressed as a clown; Willy Anthoons is sitting astride the barrel; and Louis van Lint is wearing the large hat.

Cobra

Cobra, the international movement created in 1948 by the Belgian, Christian Dotrémont – and dissolved in 1951 – reacted against all forms of dogmatism, and favored spontaneity, richness of imagination and children's drawings. As the Dane Asger Jorn explained: "Our experiments seek to release spontaneous thoughts from all rational constraints."

The movement had an extraordinary impact on the intellectual milieu of the time, and writers and poets also participated in the adventure.
Its main exponents were from Brussels and southern Belgium, notably PIERRE ALECHINSKY (above, *The Sad Dragon*), but also included Pol Bury, Corneille, Georges Collignon, Marcel Havrenne and Roaul Ubâc.

Members of the Cobra group reunited for the Second International Exhibition of Experimental Art, at Liège, in 1951.

Belgium
as seen by writers

SEPARATE CULTURES

THE THREE PARTS OF FLANDERS

Florentine traveler Lodovico Giucchardini (1523–89) provides a descriptive account of the towns and peoples of Flanders in the 16th century.

❝This countrey is devided into 3. partes though of quantitie unequall, namely, *Flanders Flamade* or *Flamingante*, so named because in it the Flemish language is used, and this is the principall part of the countrey and the most respected. The second is *Flanders Gallicane*, so called, because the wallon language which is a bastard French is their mother toong. And the thirde is *Flanders* Imperial, so named because many yeares it was under the obedience of the Empire. . . . *Flanders Gallicant* is very small but the soile therof verie good, fatt, and frutefull of all things especially of wheate, it produceth also mather and excellent good oade, though no great quantitie, but of goodly pastures for Cattell great plentie are in it. . . . In this parte of *Flanders* are contayned the fayre Townes of *Le Isle, Douay*, and *Orchies*. The mightie Seniorie of *Tournay*, with divers other places worthy of memorie. . . . *Tournay* standeth upon *Shelde* which runneth through it. It is a faire, great, rich, mightie, and strong towne with a strong fort. The houses are fine and comely built, the monasteryes, churches and Convents, very statelye and magnificent. It is a great towne of traffique and replenished with an infinite number of Artisans, makers of Sarges and other Mercerie stuffe, so that in all there are 72. companies. . . .

Liege standeth in a pleasant Valley upon the *Meuse*, being environed with hilles on all sides, the *Meuse* entereth into it with two branches, and maketh many pleasant Iles within the town all the which are inhabited. . . .

The cittie is replenished with people, but those very idle, yet fierce and naturallie inclined to armes. This towne hath also produced many learned men. The *Liegeoys* language is Frenche, but verie corrupt. . . .

Namur is bounded with *Brabant*, *Haynault*, *Luxembourg* & *Liege*. The countrey is verye small yet abounding with all graces & riches, it is replenished with people, and those very industrious, true, and faithfull to their prince. The Nobility is valiant, flourisheth in all militarie discipline, and is given to all exercises fit for their degree. The aire is very holsome, & the countrey is watered with many Rivers and brookes especially the *Meuse* and the *Sambre*, which besides the commoditie of portage, furnish the countrey with great plenty of excellent good fish.❞

LODOVICO GUICCHARDINI, *THE DESCRIPTION OF THE LOW COUNTREYS*,
PUB. THEATRUM ORBIS TERRARUM LTD, AMSTERDAM, 1976

BELGAE

The complex origins of the people of Belgium are explained by Edith Mary Wightman (d. 1983).

❝The *Belgae* and *Belgium* of Caesar – the words are Celtic, and Belgae are 'the proud' or 'the boasters' – present different, not unrelated, problems. Of the people included by Caesar among the Belgae, some, such as Morini and Menapii, are clearly located in the transition zone. So too are the Eburones and perhaps others whom he classifies not as Belgae but rather as left-bank Germani. Other Belgae, the Ambiani, Caletes, Bellovaci, Suessiones and Remi certainly lie to the south of it, while there is doubt over Atrebates, Viromandui and Nervii. Some passages of Caesar, however, give a narrower meaning to Belgium, excluding Menapii, Morini, Nervii and Remi, so that Suessiones, Viromandui and Ambiani are left forming a heartland, with one or two immediate neighbours on either side. Two conclusions follow. The first is that the heartland of Belgium is quite distinct from the 'zone of transition' with which it has sometimes been connected. The second is that Caesar's broader (and more usual) definition of the Belgae was probably grounded on the political conditions which he met in 57 BC, while the narrower Belgium he learned about later. Yet this does not explain why Caesar's Belgae should be different from the other Gauls, nor do place-names or broad archaeological differences at present promise a solution. It will however be seen that northeastern Gaul was less developed socially and economically than the centre of the country, and this, along with the differences of dialect and custom likely in so large a country, might be reason enough for his statement.”

EDITH MARY WIGHTMAN, *GALLIA BELGICA*, PUB. B.T. BATSFORD LTD, LONDON, 1985

THE TWO CULTURAL IDENTITIES

Jacques DeDecker (b. 1945) explains how the two populations of Belgium have affected the culture of the country.

“Belgium comprises two populations, two cultures which, since the Roman occupation at the start of the Christian era, have had different cultural destinies. It is remarkable to note, in effect, that the line of demarcation which separates the two languages that are spoken on its territory (French and Dutch, with the plethora of local dialects of either coming in under the heading of Walloon and Flemish respectively) continue to correspond, practically two thousand years later, to the route the Latin colonizers had traced between Bavai, in the North of present-day France, and Cologne. . . . All the richness and all the problematicness of Belgium are there, naturally: both Germans and Latins people it. And both were handed, over a map in the course of a single international conference, by the major powers, one common national identity. If this measure was accepted on paper without too much difficulty, it was because, in 1830, the Flemish had no say in the matter. . . . The first century of Belgium's history is from that moment forth marked by a struggle of the Flemish population to obtain recognition of its identity. This combat, which did not run out of steam any too fast, was led primarily by intellectuals, who brought all their efforts to bear on the recognition of a tradition which, since the Middle Ages, had distinguished itself with great accomplishments in the arts and letters. The Spanish occupation, the persecution of the Protestants which followed, and above all, the massive exile of thinkers and creative individuals to the newly consitituted Netherlands, had in disturbing proportions impoverished the cultural life of Flanders. The role of those instrumental in the *Vlaamse Beweging* (Flemish Movement) was to get back in touch with those centuries of artistic prosperity which had seen the appearance of such dominant personalities as the theologian Ruusbroeck, the encyclopedist Maerlant, the poetess Hadewijch, and the brilliant painters of the Primitive School and Renaissance.”

JACQUES DEDECKER, *BELGIUM, A COUNTRY WITH TWO FACES*, from *AN ANTHOLOGY OF CONTEMPORARY BELGIAN PLAYS, 1970–1982*, ED. DAVID WILLINGER, PUB. THE WHITSTONE PUBLISHING COMPANY, TROY, NEW YORK, 1984

An unhappy exile

In 1857 Charles Baudelaire (1821–67) published his "Les Fleurs du mal", a collection of 101 poems which is widely accepted as his greatest work. However, he was fined and six of the poems were banned as being offensive to public morals. Hence, perhaps, some explanation of his annoyance with the Belgian "rabble" who crowded around him because of it. The following extract is from a letter to his friend Ancelle on October 13, 1864.

❝From my trip to Belgium I shall have gained only the acquaintance of the most stupid people on earth (this at least is presumable), a very strange little book which will perhaps serve as bait for a publisher and induce him to buy others; and lastly the habit of a complete and prolonged chastity (laugh, if you will, at this vulgar detail), which *moreover is far from being a merit*, since the sight of the Belgian female repels any idea of pleasure. . . . Imagine, my dear friend, what I'm enduring. Winter has come suddenly. Here one doesn't see any fire, since the fire is in a stove. I work yawning – when I work. Think what I am enduring, I who find Le Havre a black and American port, I who came to know the sea and the sky in Bordeaux, in Bourbon, in Mauritius, in Calcutta; think what I endure in a country where the trees are black and *where the flowers haven't any perfume*. As for the cooking, you will see I have devoted a few pages of my little book to it! As for conversation, the great, the sole pleasure of an intelligent person, you could travel through Belgium in every direction without finding a soul who *talks*. Many *gaping*, curious people have crowded around the author of *Les Fleurs du Mal.* The author of the *Fleurs* could only be a monstrous eccentric. All that rabble took me for a monster and when they saw I was cold, restrained and polite – and that I had a horror of free-thinkers, of progress, and of all modern foolishness – they decided (this is supposition on my part) that I was not *the author of my book* . . . . What a comic confusion between the author and the subject! That accursed book (*of which I am very proud)* must be very obscure, very unintelligible! I shall suffer a long time for having dared to paint evil with some talent.

Moreover, I must confess that for two or three months I have relaxed my hold on my temper, I have taken a special enjoyment in giving offence, in showing myself *impertinent*, a talent in which I excel when I wish. But here that doesn't suffice. One must be *coarse, to be understood.*

What a pack of scoundrels! – and I, who thought that France was an absolutely barbarous country, here I am forced to admit that there is a country more barbarous than France!❞

Charles Baudelaire,
Baudelaire: A Self-Portrait – Selected Letters,
trans. and ed. Lois Boe Hyslop and Francis E. Hyslop,
pub. Oxford University Press, London, 1957

Advice to all protestants

Despite her poor opinion of the Belgians, Charlotte Brontë (1816–55) stayed in Belgium with her sister Emily for longer than the six months they had originally planned. She describes her feelings in this letter of 1842.

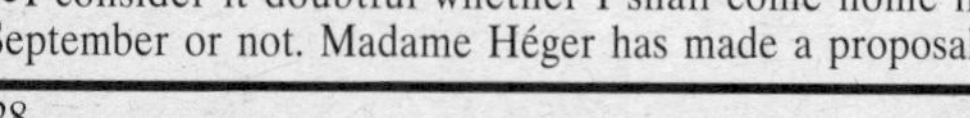

❝I consider it doubtful whether I shall come home in September or not. Madame Héger has made a proposal for both me and Emily to stay another half year, offering to dismiss her English master, and take me as English teacher; also to employ Emily some part of each day in teaching music to a certain number of the pupils. For these services we are to be allowed to continue our studies in French and German, and to have board, etc., without paying for it; no salaries, however, are offered. The proposal is kind, and in a great selfish city like Brussels, and a great selfish school, containing nearly ninety pupils (boarders and day-pupils included), implies a degree of interest which demands gratitude in return. I am inclined to accept it. What think you? I don't deny I sometimes wish to be in England, or that I have brief attacks of home-sickness; but, on the whole, I have borne a very valiant heart so far; and I have been happy in Brussels, because I have always been fully occupied with the employments that I like. Emily is making rapid progress in French, German, music, and drawing. Monsieur and Madame Héger begin to recognise the valuable parts of her character, under her singularities. If the national character of the Belgians is to be measured by the character of most of the girls in this school, it is a character singularly cold, selfish, animal, and inferior. They are very mutinous and difficult for the teachers to manage; and their principles are rotten to the core. We avoid them, which it is not difficult to do, as we have the brand of Protestantism and Anglicism upon us. People talk of the danger which Protestants expose themselves to, in going to reside in Catholic countries, and thereby running the chance of changing their faith. My advice to all Protestants who are tempted to do anything so besotted as turn Catholics is, to walk over the sea on to the Continent; to attend mass sedulously for a time; to note well the mummeries thereof; also the idiotic, mercenary aspect of all the priests; and *then*, if they are still disposed to consider Papistry in any other light than a most feeble, childish piece of humbug, let them turn Papists at once – that's all. I consider Methodism, Quakerism, and the extremes of High and Low Churchism foolish, but Roman Catholicsm beats them all. At the same time allow me to tell you, that there are some Catholics who are as good as any Christians can be to whom the Bible is a sealed book, and much better than many Protestants.❞

E.C. GASKELL, *THE LIFE OF CHARLOTTE BRONTË*, PUB. J.M. DENT, LONDON, 1908

POOR FLEMINGS

Thomas Jefferson Hogg (1792–1862) seems to agree with Baudelaire's poor opinion of Flemish women and Charlotte Brontë's disdain for the Catholic faith.

❝We reached Brussels at half-past seven. I was handed out of the carriage by an officer of police, and I repaid his politeness by showing him my passport. The market before the Hotel de Ville was quite amazonian – a hundred women to one man. The museum, or picture gallery, has nothing but saints and saintesses: these, shown in Flemish pictures, are cruelly uninteresting. I entered several large and handsome churches: in France, women only are to be found in the churches; here, although there is a majority of the fair sex, yet there are some men, and even a few well-dressed men, or at least

men who may be considered so here. It is remarkable that whilst even the indifferent Protestant, in walking about their churches to look at the painting, treads as lightly as he can, the men and women who are employed in bringing and taking away the chairs make as much noise as they can; they being, nevertheless, good Catholics. On one church, in a side chapel dedicated to St Anthony, a priest was saying mass. That I might see the thing perfectly, and thus be able to judge for myself, I stood as near to him as I could; the good man seemed to be annoyed by this, but as I had as much right, under the present state of things, to stand as he had to kneel, I did not care that, for one kind look he gave his holy tackle, he gave me five cross looks, and I kept my place. A fine little girl, seven or eight years of age, who was kneeling at the rails, kept looking at me with great curiosity; her eyes seemed to say, 'How his bones will crack in the fire for this.'

The poor Flemings are very unlucky; they try to resemble the French, who laugh at them, and with reason. They are joined to the Dutch; they pay a part of their debt, and are subjected to the inconvenience of the Dutch currency and government, and the Dutch hate them for their pains. I conversed at dinner with a Dutchman, who was sunk deep in the sulks; he said that Amsterdam is a much finer city than this; that the houses there are built not of gloomy stone but of nice, cheerful brick, the streets paved with smooth clinkers, and so on. I could not agree with him; but he seemed so much annoyed at my dissent that I was obliged to back out, and to say that I only differed from him for the sake of conversation. To please him, I assented also to his notion that we make no good cheese in England, but import Dutch cheese because our Cheshire and Stilton are uneatable.

They show many reliques in the churches here, but none that are of great curiosity or interest. I was told that at Cologne they have the first animal that drew blood, and thus broke the general peace, viz. the flea that bit Eve the night after her fall, and to her great dismay; for it is said to be nearly as large as a well-grown prawn. I cannot say that I believe this entirely; yet I have seen so many wonderful things, I cannot say that I disbelieve it. The unusual size of the creature is in favour of the truth of the story, and of the antediluvian origin of the insect, for there were giants in those days, and men reached a prodigious age; but since the deluge, both ourselves and our fleas are a stunted, short-lived, aguish race.

We dined at two. A German cut his finger, and bled like a pig. A beautiful Flemish lady was at table, tall, with a fine figure and clear complexion, black eyes and hair; but she looked stiff and stupid. Women in these countries do not seem as if they could make love. I suppose they increase and multiply, and look sulky all the time.”

THOMAS JEFFERSON HOGG, *TWO HUNDRED AND NINE DAYS*,
QUOTED IN *ABROAD – A BOOK OF TRAVELS*, ED. JON EVANS,
PUB. VICTOR GOLLANCZ LTD, LONDON, 1968

FLEMISH MANNERS

After the success of her caustic book entitled "Domestic Manners of the Americans", Frances Trollope (1780–1863), mother of the English novelist Anthony Trollope, was commissioned to write about the Belgians. On the whole, her impressions were favorable.

“Before leaving Belgium, I must say a few farewell words

respecting it. Not many among us are, I believe, fully aware how peculiarly rich this country is in objects of every kind that can most interest and delight a traveller; provided, indeed, that he be not journeying post to the Rhine, but have time and inclination to pause and look about him. People who love pictures know that Flanders possesses many *chef-d'œuvres* of the art; and people who love churches are aware that the Low Countries are famed for Gothic architecture; nevertheless, but few of our yearly tourists pause long enough to enjoy fully the exceeding richness of Belgium in all that can gratify the eye of taste, or 'awaken the enthusiasm of the antiquary.' Where can be found such a constellation of fine old cities as Bruges, Ghent, Antwerp, Louvain, Brussels, Namur, and Liege? each assisting to illustrate the history of the others, and all within so small a space, that they may be visited in succession, and revisited again half-a-dozen times in the course of as many weeks; and that, perhaps, at a less expense, than if the same time were spent at a fashionable watering-place in England.

Of genuine Flemish manners it is not easy to form any accurate judgment by merely passing a few weeks in the country, and going only into the society that good travelling introductions lead to: for therein will be found the same uniform tone of European good breeding which distinguishes the well-educated from those who are not so, in every country; but which has too little characteristic variety to be considered as purely national in any. I took some pains, and not quite without success, to look a little more behind the scenes, and whenever I did so, the conformity in habits and character of the present race, with the portraits made familiar to us in the history of ages past, was most striking.

It should seem that even the soil and air had an influence on the tailors, stocking-weavers, and shoemakers; for there are still the self-same outlines, nay, the self-same colours, and, as it should seem, the identical materials, with which they wrought. Nor are the healthy, comely, lusty weaves more changed. No people, I think, bear a stronger national impress on their features than the peasants of Flanders: and their admirable painters have made us all sufficiently familiar with them.

Of their manners I saw enough to show me that they were industrious, clean, cheerful, and kindhearted; and if beer and tobacco-smoke constitute a larger portion of their happiness than might be wished, it should be remembered that it is better to smoke than chew the loathsome herb; and that barley may be taken in a more pernicious form than that of Flemish ale.❞

FRANCES TROLLOPE, *BELGIUM AND WESTERN GERMANY IN 1833*,
PUB. JOHN MURRAY, LONDON, 1835

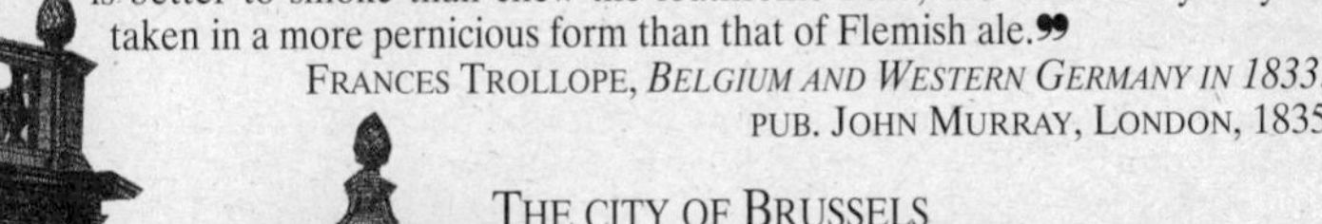

THE CITY OF BRUSSELS

A WALK AROUND THE TOWN

John Evelyn (1620–1706) traveled in Belgium in 1641.

❝We arriv'd at Bruxelles at 9 in the morning. The State house, neere the market-place, is for the carving in freestone a most laborious and finished piece, well worthy observation. The flesh-shambles are also built of stone. I was pleased with certain small engines by which a girl or boy was able to draw up, or let downe, greate bridges, w[eh] in divers parts of this Citty crossed y[e] channell, for the benefit of passengers. The walls of this Town are very intyre, and full of towers at competent distances. The Cathedrall is built upon a very high and exceeding steepe ascent, to which we mounted by faire stepps of stone. Hence I walked to a Convent of English Nunns, with whom I sate discoursing most part of the afternoone. . . .

I went to see the Prince's Court, an ancient, confus'd building, not much unlike the Hofft at the Hague; there is here likewise a very large Hall, where they vend all sorts of wares. Through this we passed by the Chapell, which is indeed rarely arch'd, and in the middle of it was the hearse or catafalco of the late Arch-Dutchesse, the wise and pious Clara Eugenia. Out of this we were conducted to the lodgings, tapistry'd with incomparable arras, and adorn'd with many excellent pieces of Rubens, old and young Breughel, Titian, and Stenwick, with stories of most of the late actions in the Netherlands.

By an accident we could not see the Library. There is a faire terrace which looks to the Vineyard, in which, on pedestalls, are fix'd the statues of all the Spanish Kings of the House of Austria. The opposite walls are paynted by Rubens, being an history of the late tumults in Belgia; in the last piece the Arch-Dutchesse shutts a greate payre of gates upon Mars, who is coming out of hell, arm'd, and in a menacing posture: which with that other of the Infanta taking leave of Don Philip the Fourth, is a most incomparable table.

From hence we walk'd into the Parke, which for being intirely within the walls of the Citty is particularly remarkable; nor is it less pleasant than if in the most solitary recesses, so naturally is it furnish'd with whatever may render it agreeable, melancholy, and country-like. Here is a stately heronry, divers springs of water, artificial cascades, rocks, grotts; one whereof is composed of the extravagant rootes of trees cunningly built and hung together with wires. In this Parke are both fallow and red deere.

From hence we were led into the Manege, and out of that into a most sweete and delicious garden, where was another grott, of more neate and costly materials, full of noble statues, and entertaining us with artificial musiq; but the hedge of water, in forme of lattice-worke, which the fontanier caused to ascend out of the earth by degrees, exceedingly pleased and surpris'd me, for thus with a pervious wall, or rather a palisad hedge, of water, was the whole parterre environ'd.

There is likewise a faire Aviary, and in the court next it are kept divers sort of animals, rare and exotic fowle, as eagles, cranes, storkes, bustards, pheasants of several kinds, and a duck having 4 wings. In another division of the same close, are rabbits of an almost perfect yellow colour.❞

JOHN EVELYN, *MEMOIRS, VOL 1*, PUB. HENRY COLBURN, LONDON, 1827

GREAT TREASURES

Albrecht Durer (1471–1528) stayed in Brussels from August 26 to September 3, 1520. The previous year Hernan Cortez had begun his assault on the Aztec empire in Mexico and treasures from that part of the world had begun to arrive in Europe.

❝In the golden chamber in the Townhall at Brussels I saw the four paintings which the great Master Roger van der Weyden made. And I saw out behind the King's house at Brussels the fountains, labyrinth, and Beast-garden; anything more beautiful and pleasing to me and more like a Paradise I have never seen. Erasmus is the name of the little man who wrote out my supplication at Herr Jacob de Bannisis' house. At Brussels is a very splendid Townhall, large, and covered with

beautiful carved stonework, and it has a noble, open tower. I took a portrait at night by candlelight of Master Konrad of Brussels, who was my host; I drew at the same time Doctor Lamparter's son in charcoal, also the hostess.

I saw the things which have been brought to the King from the new land of gold (Mexico), a sun all of gold a whole fathom broad, and a moon all of silver of the same size, also two rooms full of the armour of the people there, and all manner of wondrous weapons of theirs, harness and darts, very strange clothing, beds, and all kinds of wonderful objects of human use, much better worth seeing than prodigies. These things were all so precious that they are valued at 100,000 florins. All the days of my life I have seen nothing that rejoiced my heart so much as these things, for I saw amongst them wonderful works of art, and I marvelled at the subtle *Ingenia* of men in foreign lands. Indeed I cannot express all that I thought there.

At Brussels I saw many other beautiful things besides, and especially I saw a fish bone there, as vast as if it had been built up of squared stones. It was a fathom long and very thick, it weights up to 15 cwt., and its form resembles that drawn here. It stood up behind on the fish's head. I was also in the Count of Nassau's house which is very splendidly built and as beautifully adorned. . . .

In the chapel there, I saw the good picture that Master Hugo van der Goes painted, and I saw the two fine large halls and the treasures everywhere in the house, also the great bed wherein 50 men can lie. And I saw the great stone which the storm cast down in the field near the Lord of Nassau. The house stands high, and from it there is a most beautiful view, at which one cannot but wonder; and I do not believe that in all the German lands the like of it exists.❞

LITERARY REMAINS OF ALBRECHT DURER, ED. WILLIAM MARTIN CONWAY, TRANS. LINA ECKENSTEIN, PUB. CAMBRIDGE UNIVERSITY PRESS, CAMBRIDGE, 1889

UPPER AND LOWER PARTS

Washington Irving (1783–1859) visited Brussels in September 1805 and described his impressions in a journal. At this stage, he was not yet known as a writer, and had in fact trained as a lawyer.

❝The upper part of Bruxelles, which is built on a hill is extremely beautiful. It is the residence of the Beau monde and the buidings are large & elegant built of a whitish stone that retains its color well and is peculiarly fine for building. The Hotel where we put up is situated on the *place royal*, which is one of the handsomest squares that I have seen in Europe. The centre of the principal side is dignified by the noble façade of a church, in the composite order. The houses that form the rest of the Square are spacious and uniform of simple and excellent architecture; several of them are hotels, the rest are the houses of individuals, but they all have the appearance of palaces. From one side of this Square you pass by a short but noble street, into the Park. Here we took a stroll this morning. It is laid out with admirable taste and tho much smaller yet I think it superior by far even to the boasted Tuilleries of Paris. The walks are spacious well gravelled and ornamented with statues busts &c. But what I chiefly admired was, that from what ever centeral spot you turned your eyes either a magnificent edifice or an extensive and beautiful view presented itself. In one part of the Park a little portion of ground is laid out as a place of recreation – Here there is a fine saloon for refreshments – several billiard rooms – Different kinds of amusements as swings – flying horses &c &c At the latter some ladies and Gentlemen were diverting themselves, we were very liberal in our praises of the beauty of a fine girl in the company when to our astonishment we heard them speak english, and our valet de place told us that they were some Irish emigrants who resided at Bruxelles[.] fortunately we had said nothing with which the ladies could possibly be displeased. It was delightful once more to hear my native language spoken by a pretty girl.

After amusing ourselves suffciently in the Park we went to the *Ecole Centrale* in the antient palace of the court. Here is to be seen a cabinet of Physic & natural history – a Botanic Garden – a Liberary and a gallery of paintings. We only visited the latter which contains several paintings by Vandyck – Rubens & his scholars &c

and a painting by Raphael in his second manner, which possesses much merit particularly the figure of two children in the bottom of the picture.

We afterwards walked to the Square [*blank*] no less worth of attention than the *place Royal* tho in a completely different style. The architecture that surrounds it is chiefly gothic – One side is occuped by the *Hotel de Ville* an immense Gothic pile with a lofty steeple: this edifice is a fine specimen of that species of architecture. Opposite to it is another large public building in the same style and probably built about the same time.

The lower part of Bruxelles is far inferior to that which I have already discribed – The streets where business is stirring – are muddy and as there are no side walks the foot passenger is as badly off as in paris. The houses are built very much in the dutch style and are remarkably clean – the windows well washed – the floor sanded and in the shops – the scales measures &c highly polished. The lower class speak the Flemish language, but among the better educated & polite the French is universal. The Houses in the lower parts are of Brick generally but painted or whitewashed so as to have a cleanly appearance. A small river which runs thro Brussels furnishes water for a canal by which they have communication with Antwerp and different parts of Holland. There is a very fine view from a bridge that crosses this canal at the [*blank*] end of the town. On one side you have the little port of Bruxelles crowded with canal vessels some of which are of a very respectable size, tho all of the clumsy dutch form – beyond you over look part of the city and catch a glimpse of its principal buildings – on the other side you have before you a long stretch of the canal and its verdant banks enrichd with walks of stately trees – and you have a partial view of the rich environs of Bruxelles. After having made a tour of the finest parts of the city we returned along the ramparts to our hotel. The walls are old and of no further service excepting as they form a delightful promanade that formerly extended round the city. The french however, when they took Bruxelles, demolished part of the Ramparts and cut down many of the trees. The inhabitants alarmed for the b[e]loved walkes made such representations as put a stop to their violactions [violations]. Our old *valet de place* expatiated upon these outrages with particular earnestness. I soon found that the french were no favorites with him. He told me that they had experienced wretched times but that matters were now assuming a happier appearance. We passed one place where they were about erecting an arch in honor of the Emperor.❞

WASHINGTON IRVING,
JOURNALS AND NOTEBOOKS, VOL. 1, 1803–1806,
ED. NATHALIA WRIGHT, PUB. UNIVERSITY OF
WISCONSIN PRESS, MADISON/MILWAUKEE/LONDON, 1969

APPEARANCES

Henry Smithers was a British resident of Brussels in the early 19th century.

❝The shops in the principal streets of Brussels make a very respectable appearance; the shopkeepers generally, are wealthy and independent, and seldom submit to make much abatement from the prices they demand, except in articles of luxury: many of them endeavour to take advantage of English purchasers, but with some few exceptions, the latter are treated with courtesy. Very few new houses are to be seen; the precarious state of the country, which has so often been the seat of war, accounts for this. Should peace continue, security will be re-established; and the once magnificent cities of the Netherlands may be expected to increase in population, and resume in some degree their ancient splendor. It strikes an English traveller with surprize that houses of a superior class, having in front, on each floor, from ten to fourteen plate glass windows, are frequently found in secondary streets, and even in lanes; and in the best streets, large buildings adjoin others of a very mean appearance, such as cabarets or public-houses and inferior shops. The streets are well lighted in the evenings. Some few of the houses are built of brick, covered with plaister, which requires to be annually re-coloured. This is done with some taste with an argillaceous earth, or a light tea-green hue, found near Namur, which, when properly prepared, produces a pleasing effect. . . .

The long alliance that has subsisted between France and Belgium, has had considerable influence on the habits and manners of the latter. The Belgians are fond of appearances, and magnify every object connected with their own country. In their degrees of comparison they make great use of the superlative. . . .

Brussels lace obtains the highest prices, the patterns are the most elegant, and it is consequently most in demand; but considerable quantities are made at Mechlin, Ghent, Bruges, and other cities. An ounce of the finest thread for making the Brussels lace is worth two hundred francs or ten Napoleons, about eight pounds sterling, more valuable than gold of the same weight. The best flax grows near Courtrai, and at Soigny, and Braine la-leud. Children begin at six and seven years of age to work at lace making; good workwomen can earn ten francs each day in making the fine laces.

Amongst the manufacturing concerns of the city of Brussels, the lace fabrics of M. Antoine Troyaux deserve notice, for elegance of design, strength and durability: he has received the sanction and patronage of their Royal Highnesses the Dukes of Kent and Cambridge, and the Princess Elizabeth of Hesse Hombourg: the magnificent lace of the dresses in which they appeared at Court after their respective marriages were manufactured by him. He employs a great number of hands, many of which may be seen employed in making the lace at the manufactory, Rue de Parchemin, Brussels, near the Park.”

HENRY SMITHERS, *OBSERVATIONS MADE DURING A RESIDENCE IN BRUSSELS*, PUB. THE BRITISH PRESS, BRUSSELS, 1820

FASHIONABLE SOCIETY

Elizabeth Fry's niece, Elizabeth Gurney, kept a diary of their journeys around Europe. They arrived in Brussels by train on February 30 (sic), 1840 and stayed there until March 6.

❝We have been much pleased with Belgium whilst flying across it. The cultivation is so beautiful, far exceeding what you ever see abroad. It is by some travellers called 'the Garden of Europe' from the great care that is taken with every inch of the ground. I saw many people weeding large wheatfields *on their knees*. No country was ever better made for a Chemin de Fer. It is one universal flat but very prettily wooded in some parts. The people look poor and not well clothed as is almost always the case in Catholic Countries....

Papa and I walked in the *Parc.* A large square, well wooded. The Palaces of the King & Prince of Orange, the Chamber of Deputies and other fine Buldings round it. This is the Promenade of the town and we had a good view of the

fashionables of Brussels much to our amusement and reminding us both of the Jardins at Paris. The nurses in costume and gaily dressed children took our fancy very much playing about amongst the trees while the sedater papas et mamans with their spyglasses and tiny parasols sauntered up and down the walks with a truly Parisian air. We dined at the table d'hôte which was an unwise plan not only for the length of time it takes but our party is rather too conspicuous a one to eat in public. Mons. and Madame Panchard a delightful Minister and his wife whom both my Aunt and Papa previously knew in France were much with us. About 50 English came to our Reading in the evening. Our room was so small that we opened the large doors into our Aunt's bedroom to give more room. Papa read as usual and afterwards William Allen, Josiah Forster and our Aunt addressed them. I was with Lucy Bradshaw in the bedroom and we were astonished how quietly and attentively all the people stood. Many very gaily dressed people expressed to us their extreme interest in having heard our Aunt and anxiously enquired whether she would 'preach again' before leaving Brussels....

Not much worth seeing in the Cathedral. The Pulpit and painted windows fine. The shops good. The carnival going on here so that we could not venture down the principal streets. Spent the evening at the Baron Bois de Ferrierès. A 'sweet man' and a pleasant party mostly English to meet us: his rooms hung round with the richest paintings of the Dutch School which were a treat to see. There are many private individuals who possess some of the first Dutch pictures which any stranger is allowed to see....

We drove to the Palace in a handsome carriage that Papa had hired for us during our stay here and entering the Square palace yard our dear party were ushered in amidst a crowd of scarlet livery servants. Luch Bradshaw and I remained in the carriage and watched them ascend the broad flight of steps and then we were left to our own meditations. We waited half an hour when Papa came down for us and mentioned the king's permission that we should go up. At the top of the stairs stood a few Aides de Camps and servants one of which threw open the door and Papa presented us each to His Majesty. He came forward to us, asked me if I had ever been in Brussels before and whether I admired the town. He is a particularly pleasing looking man. Rather older that I expected and a figure that was much shown off by his Military dress, a profusion of 'golden Orders' on his breast. The whole of the party were standing but this was the only show of Court Etiquette as they conversed very easily together. . . . Papa and I spent a pleasant hour in walking about the town. We skaited in slippers about the Palace of the Prince of Orange. Heard a debate in the Chambre des Députés; watched the proceedings of the Carnival, bought a large box of Bonbons to send home to you &c.❞

ELIZABETH GURNEY, *ELIZABETH FRY'S JOURNEYS ON THE CONTINENT 1840–41*, PUB. JOHN LANE/THE BODLEY HEAD, LONDON, 1831

BELGIAN COUNTRYSIDE

BY CANAL

Robert Louis Stevenson (1850–94) traveled through Belgium on the Willebroek Canal.

❝It was a fine, green, fat landscape; or rather a mere green water-lane, going on from village to village. Things had a settled look, as in places long lived in. Crop-headed children spat upon us from the bridges as we went below, with a true conservative feeling. But even more conservative were the fishermen, intent upon their floats, who let us go by without one glance. They perched upon sterlings and buttresses and along the slope of the embankment, gently occupied. They were indifferent like pieces of dead nature. They did not move any more than if they had been fishing in an old Dutch print. The leaves fluttered, the water lapped, but they continued in one stay like so many churches established by law. You might have trepanned every one of their innocent heads, and found no more than so much coiled fishing line below their skulls. I do not care for your stalwart fellows in india-rubber stockings breasting up mountain torrents with a salmon rod; but I do dearly love the class of man who plies his unfruitful art, for ever and a day, by still and depopulated waters.

At the last lock just beyond *Villevorde*, there was a lock mistress who spoke French comprehensibly, and told us we were still a couple of leagues from *Brussels*. At the same place, the rain began again. It fell in straight, parallel lines; and the surface of the canal was thrown up into an infinity of little crystal fountains. There were no beds to be had in the neighboourhood. Nothing for it but to lay the sails aside and address ourselves to steady paddling in the rain.

Beautiful country houses, with clocks and long lines of shuttered windows, and fine old trees standing in groves and avenues, gave a rich and sombre aspect in the rain and the deepening dusk to the shores of the canal. I seem to have seen something of the same effect in engravings: opulent landscapes, deserted and overhung with the passage of storm.

And throughout we had the escort of a hooded cart, which trotted shabbily along the tow-path, and kept at an almost uniform distance in our wake.❞

ROBERT LOUIS STEVENSON, *AN INLAND VOYAGE*, PUB. CHATTO & WINDUS, LONDON, 1907

COLORS OF BELGIUM

❝I have undergone some misery in the Belgian 'black country', and my health has not been very good lately . . .❞

VINCENT VAN GOGH, LETTER TO THEO, BRUSSELS, OCTOBER 15, 1880

❝I love Belgium for I love green & mauve.❞

KATHERINE MANSFIELD, LETTER TO GARNET TROWELL, APRIL 28–30, 1909

THE FOREST OF SOIGNY

Robert Southey (1774–1843) traveled through Soigny on October 21, 1815.

❝The forest of Soigny is very striking. It has none of the beauty of a natural forest; but because it is an artificial one, it has a character of its own, not always becoming, impressive where it is upon a large scale. The trees are so straight that they look as if they had grown under the superintendence of a Drill Sergeant. An oak which stands on the verge of the forest, where it has room to spread its arms in natural growth, really appeared like a deformed and monstrous being, from its utter unlikeness to all the other trees. They stand in many parts so close that the interstices look only like straight lines of green light. The road is in many parts raised considerably above the level of the forest. Labouring men and boys were seated by the wayside at breakfast, and spreading their dark brown bread with a white substance, which whether it be lard, or a sort of inferior butter, or curd, we have not yet learnt, tho' we have frequently seen it thus used. Saw one horse with a comb attached to the trappings of his neck; another with red tassels pendant over his face, which must be useful against the flies.❞

ROBERT SOUTHEY, *JOURNAL OF A TOUR IN THE NETHERLANDS*, PUB. WILLIAM HEINEMANN, LONDON 1903

WATERLOO

BEFORE THE BATTLE

"Vanity Fair" by William Thackeray (1611–63) is set at the time of the Napoleonic wars and gives a satirical picture of society. The two main characters, Becky Sharp and Amelia Sedley, travel to Belgium with their husbands, who are in the army, and Amelia's brother Jos.

"This flat, flourishing, easy country never could have looked more rich and prosperous than in that opening summer of 1815, when its green fields and quiet cities were enlivened by multiplied red-coats: when its wide *chaussées* swarmed with brilliant English equipages: when its great canal-boats, gliding by rich pastures and pleasant quaint old villages, by old châteaux lying amongst old trees, were all crowded with well-to-do English travellers: when the soldier who drank at the village inn, not only drank, but paid his score; and Donald, the Highlander, billeted in the Flemish farmhouse, rocked the baby's cradle, while Jean and Jeannette were out getting in the hay. As our painters are bent on military subjects just now, I throw out this as a good subject for the pencil, to illustrate the principle of an honest English war. All looked as brilliant and harmless as a Hyde Park review. Meanwhile Napoleon, screened behind his curtain of frontier-fortresses, was preparing for the outbreak which was to drive all these orderly people into fury and blood; and lay so many of them low.

Everybody had such a perfect feeling of confidence in the leader (for the resolute faith which the Duke of Wellington had inspired in the whole English nation was as intense, as that more frantic enthusiasm with which at one time the French regarded Napoleon), the country seemed in so perfect a state of orderly defence, and the help at hand in case of need so near and overwhelming, that alarm was unknown, and our travellers, among whom two were naturally of a very timid sort, were, like all the other multiplied English tourists, entirely at ease. The famous regiment, with so many of whose officers we have made acquaintance, was drafted in canal-boats to Bruges and Ghent, thence to march to Brussels. . . . So prodigiously good was the eating and drinking on board these sluggish but most comfortable vessels, that there are legends extant of an English traveller, who, coming to Belgium for a week, and travelling in one of these boats, was so delighted with the fare there that he went backwards and forwards from Ghent to Bruges perpetually until the railroads were invented, when he drowned himself on the last trip of the passage-boat. . . .

We of peaceful London City have never beheld – and please God never shall witness – such a scene of hurry and alarm as that which Brussels presented. Crowds rushed to the Namur gate, from which direction the noise proceeded, and many rode along the level *chaussée*, to be in advance of any intelligence from the army. Each man asked his neighbour for news; and even great English lords and ladies condescended to speak to persons whom they did not know. The friends of the French went abroad, wild with excitement, and prophesying the triumph of their Emperor. The merchants closed their shops, and came out to swell the general chorus of alarm and clamour. Women rushed to the churches, and crowded the chapels, and knelt and prayed on the flags and steps. The dull sound of the cannon went on rolling, rolling. Presently carriages with travellers began to leave the town, galloping away by the Ghent barrier. The prophecies of the French partisans began to pass for facts. 'He has cut the armies in two,' it was said. 'He is marching straight on Brussels. He will overpower the English, and be here to-night.' 'He will overpower the English,' shrieked Isidor to his master, 'and will be here to-night.' The man bounded in and out from the lodgings to the street, always returning with some fresh particulars of disaster. Jos's face grew paler and paler. Alarm began to take entire possession of the stout civilian. All the champagne he drank brought no courage to him."

William Makepeace Thackeray, *Vanity Fair*,
ed. Eleanor Melville Metcalf,
pub. Smith, Elder & Co., London, 1904

The aftermath

An Englishwoman, Charlotte Eaton, visited the battlefield in 1817.

"On the morning of Saturday the fifteenth of July, we set off to visit the field of the ever-memorable and glorious battle of Waterloo . . .

The road, the whole way through the forest of Soignies, was marked with vestiges of the dreadful scenes which had recently taken place upon it. Bones of unburied horses, and pieces of broken carts and harness were scattered about. At every step we met with the remains of some tattered clothes, which had once been a soldier's. Shoes, belts, and scabbards, infantry caps battered to pieces, broken feathers and Highland bonnets covered with mud were strewn along the road-side, or thrown among the trees . . .

Before we left the forest, the Church of Waterloo appeared in view, at the end of the avenue of trees. It is a singular building, much in the form of a Chinese temple, and built of red brick. On leaving the wood, we passed the trampled and deep-marked bivouac, where the heavy baggage-waggons, tilted carts, and tumbrils had been stationed during the battle, and from which they had taken flight with such precipitation.

Even here, cannon-balls had lodged in the trees, but had passed over the roofs of the cottages. We entered the village which had given its name to the most glorious battle ever recorded in the annals of history . . .

After leaving Waterloo, the ground rises: the wood, which had opened, again surrounded us, though in a more straggling and irregular manner – and it was not till we arrived at the little village of Mont St Jean, more than a mile beyond Waterloo, that we finally quitted the shade of the forest, and entered upon the open field . . .

Nothing struck me with more surprise than the confined space in which this tremendous battle had been fought: and this, perhaps in some measure contributed to its sanguinary result. The space which divided the two armies from the farm-house of La Haye Sainte, which was occupied by our troops, to La Belle Alliance, which was occupied by theirs, I scarcely think would measure three furlongs. Not more than half a mile could have intervened between the main body of the French and English armies: and from the extremity of the right to that of the left wing of our army, I should suppose to be little more than a mile . . .

In many places the excacavations made by the shells had thrown the earth all around them; the marks of horses' hoofs, that had plunged ancle deep in clay, were hardened in the sun; and the feet of men, deeply stamped into the ground, left traces where many a deadly struggle had been. The ground was ploughed up in several places with the charge of the cavalry, and the whole field was literally covered with soldiers' caps, shoes, gloves, belts, and scabbards, broken feathers battered into the mud, remnants of tattered scarlet cloth, bits of fur and leather, black stocks and havresacs, belonging to the French soldiers, buckles, packs of cards, books, and innumerable papers of every description . . . The quantities of letters and of blank sheets of dirty writing paper were so great that they literally whitened the surface of the earth . . .

We crossed the field from this place to Château Hougoumont, descending to the bottom of the hill, and again ascending the opposite side. Part of our way lay through clover; but I observed, that the corn on the French position was not nearly so much beaten down as on the English, which might naturally be expected, as they attacked us incessantly, and we acted on the defensive, until that last, general, and decisive charge of our whole army was made before which theirs fled in confusion."

Charlotte Eaton, *Narrative of a Residence in Belgium*, quoted in *Unsuitable for Ladies – An Anthology of Women Travellers,* selected by Jane Robinson, pub. Oxford University Press, Oxford, 1994

Itineraries around Brussels and southern Belgium

Buildings beside the Sambre in Namur ▲

Fountains in the gardens of the Château de Freyr ▲

The bulbous bell tower of the collegiate church at Dinant ▲

The gardens of Brussels' Musée Van Buuren ▼ Fall at Belœil ▲

The Giant's Tomb in the Semois valley ▲ Contrasting foliage in the Ardennes ▼

The Condroz under snow ▼

Winter ▲ and fall, in the Ardennes ▼

Hills and valleys in the Ardennes ▼

The glasshouses at Laeken ▲ A baroque façade on Brussels' Grand-Place ▼

A café scene in Brussels ▼

In and around Brussels

The covering of the Senne
The medallion below commemorates the covering of the Senne. The river was canalized and covered over in the 19th century in order to improve living conditions in the lower part of the city. Another river, the Maelbeek, also vanished after 1875.

Reconstruction in the 18th century
Brussels was bombarded by French artillery in 1695, during the War of the Grand Alliance (1690–7). The scale of the destruction was enormous (below). After the siege the city was, for the first time, rebuilt according to an overall plan: a decree laid down the standards to be met by houses on the Grand-Place, and neighboring streets were widened and straightened. The Place des Martyrs and the Coudenberg were rebuilt, in French neoclassical style, between 1770 and 1780.

Few of Europe's medieval cities have undergone so much alteration as Brussels. The city is the capital of both Belgium and Europe, as well as being an autonomous region among the federal Belgian states. It is the meeting place of two languages, two cultures and a multitude of conflicting interests.

The city's landscape

Brussels' natural landscape began to be transformed almost from the outset and is now barely recognizable. The city's name derives from *bruocsella*, a Frankish word signifying a settlement on marshland. The town grew up on an alluvial plain in which erosion had produced a series of hills and valleys with steep west-facing slopes. As the town spread over the slopes of the hills, two distinct areas emerged: the upper and the lower town. The hills were mostly leveled out in the 18th and 19th centuries, leaving only a huge horizontal shelf running from the Palais de Justice to the Jardin Botanique. Today the difference between the upper and the lower towns is scarcely perceptible, except in three places: on the esplanade of the Palais de Justice ▲ *174*, at the Sablon ▲ *175* and on Place Royale ▲ *169*. The depressions separating the three main hills (the Galgenberg, Coudenberg and Treurenberg) were filled in during the 18th and 19th centuries.

The medieval city

The earliest references to Brussels date from the end of the 10th century. At the end of the Middle Ages the city was organized around three main centers: the marketplace (the commercial center and home of the Hôtel de Ville, the symbol of civic rights), the castle on the Coudenberg (the medieval center of political power, still a center of power today) and the church dedicated to St Michael and St Gudula (the religious center). Two city walls were built during the 12th and 14th centuries to meet the defensive needs of the fast-growing town. Today the ring of boulevards known as the Pentagon follows the outline of the second rampart.

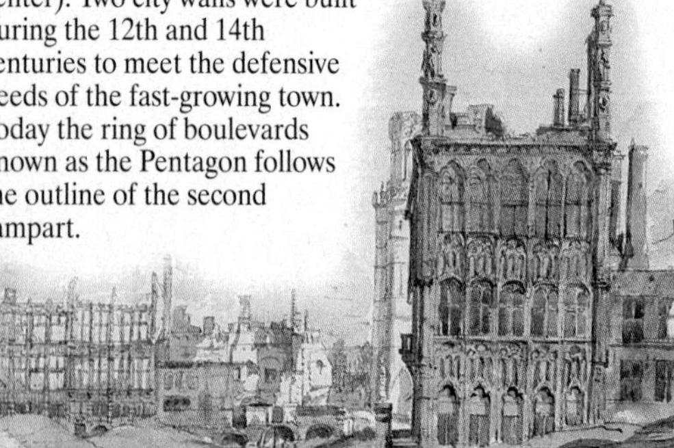

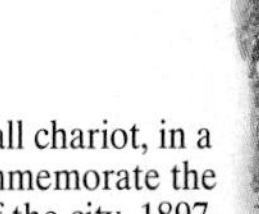

Town-hall chariot, in a procession to commemorate the rebuilding of the city, 1897.

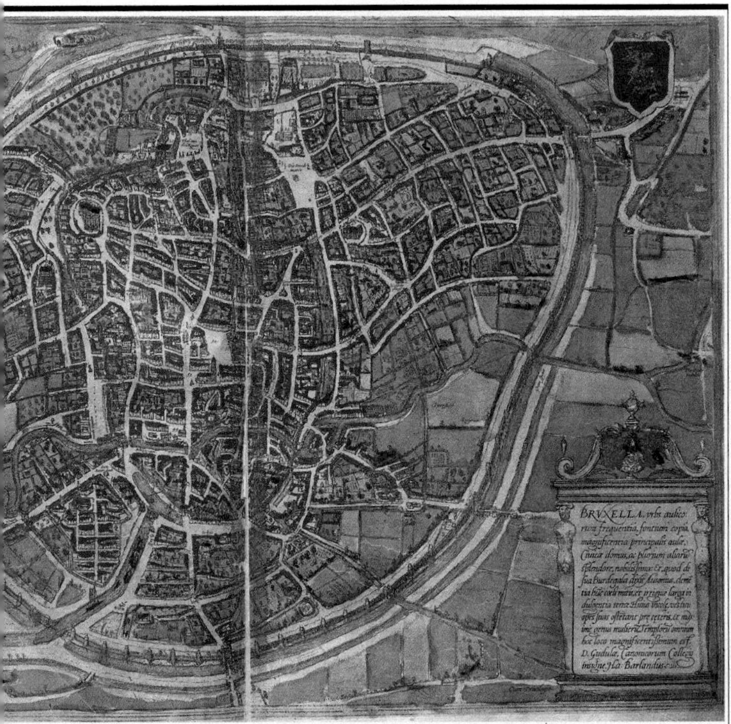

Brussels in 1576.

A PORT AT BRUSSELS

In 1561 the Willebroek Canal was opened to shipping, connecting Brussels to the sea via the Escaut river. An inland port was built to the northwest of the town: this continued to be the commercial heart of the city up to the 19th century. When a new section of canal was built between Brussels and Charleroi (1832) and the city's industrial activities began to move out to the suburbs, the port fell into decline. All the docks were filled in between 1850 and 1911.

MODERN EXPANSION

In 1830 Brussels became the capital of an independent Belgium: this led to an influx of civil servants and the rapid expansion of the city's industrial suburbs. Large-scale building projects were undertaken to affirm Brussels' status as capital city, including the Palais de Justice and the covering of the Senne. In the 20th century the historical fabric of the city has been damaged and partly destroyed by major construction works, such as the linking up of the Gare du Nord and Gare du Midi and the building of urban freeways. As many of its inhabitants left the city for greener areas on the outskirts, Brussels fell prey to property speculators: office blocks sprang up everywhere. When the northern quarter was demolished in 1967 and, more recently, when residential districts were destroyed to make way for European Community offices, angry protests were heard from residents' committees and heritage conservation groups.

THE CITY TODAY
At a time when the preservation and restoration of the national heritage is a highly topical issue, the ancient fabric of the city is still being torn apart by vast building sites.

1. Grand-Place
2. Church of St-Nicolas
3. Galeries St-Hubert
4. Cathedral of St-Michel
5. Church of Notre-Dame-du-Bon-Secours
6. Chapel of La Madeleine
7. Galerie Bortier
8. Manneken Pis
9. Place St-Géry
10. Church of Notre-Dame-aux-Riches-Claires
11. Bourse du Commerce
12. Place Ste-Catherine
13. Tour Noire
14. Church of St-Jean-Baptiste
15. Place de Brouckère
16. Théâtre de la Monnaie
17. Church of Notre-Dame-de-Finistère
18. Place des Martyrs
19. Palais de Justice
20. Square du Petit-Sablon
21. Palais d'Egmont
22. Place du Grand Sablon
23. Church of Notre-Dame-du-Sablon
24. Church of Notre-Dame-de-la-Chapelle
25. Cité Reine-Astrid
26. Place du Jeu-de-Balle
27. Porte de Hal
28. Place Royale
29. Church of St-Jacques-sur-Coudenberg
30. Parc Royal
31. Musée Royal d'Art Ancien
32. Musée Royal d'Art Moderne
33. Mont des Arts
34. Palais des Beaux-Arts
35. Palais Royal
36. Palais des Académies
37. Colonne du Congrès
38. Jardin Botanique
39. Avenue Louise
40. Centre de la Bande dessinée (Comic-strip Center)
41. Musée du Costume et de la Dentelle (Museum of Costume and Lace)

Map of the historical center of Brussels, known as the Pentagon ▲ *148*.

West side:
7. "Le Renard" (The Fox)
House of the Haberdashers (rebuilt in 1699). Four reliefs show cupids performing the guild's various trades.

6. "Le Cornet" (The Horn)
House of the Boatmen. Hence the pediment shaped like a ship's poop, incorporating sea gods, two sailors, and a medallion of the King of Spain surrounded by the four winds.

5. "La Louve" (The She-Wolf)
House of the Archers, one of the five military companies of the town. Built in stone in 1644, but not completed until 1692, it survived the bombardment of 1695 almost intact. At the top is a phoenix rising from the ashes, a reference to the building's many reconstructions.

4. "Le Sac" (The Sack)
House of the Carpenters and Cabinetmakers.

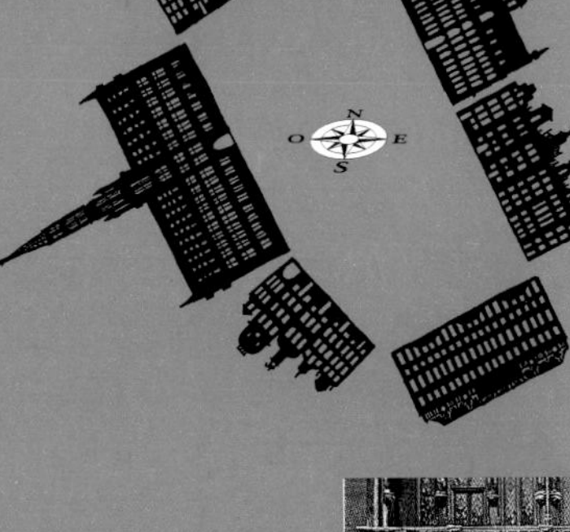

"Maison du Roi"
Built during the last flourishing of Late Gothic style (around 1504–36), the house was completely rebuilt from 1873 onward. The two stories of galleries and the central tower which were added to the original façade, appear to have been planned in medieval times.

Hôtel de Ville
The town hall was built in two main phases: the left wing was built in 1401, the right wing in 1444.

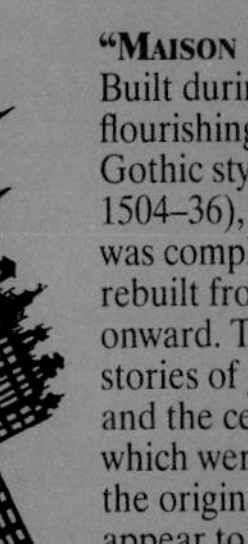

East side:
13. "Maison des Ducs de Brabant"
The name refers to the nineteen busts of Dukes of Brabant standing at the base of the pilasters. In fact this huge building is made up of six separate houses joined by a monumental façade (1696–7).

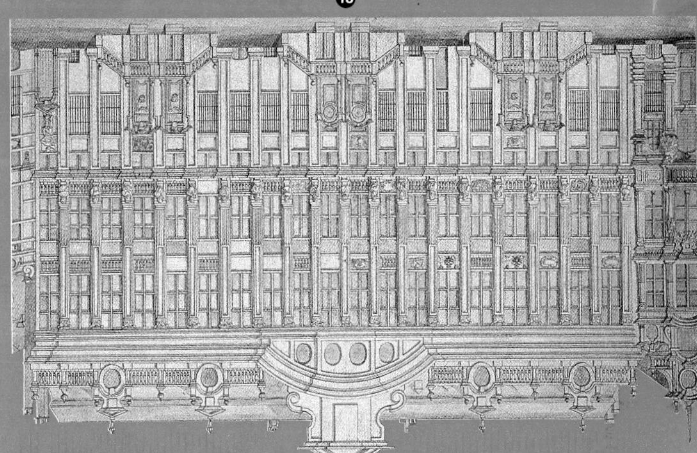

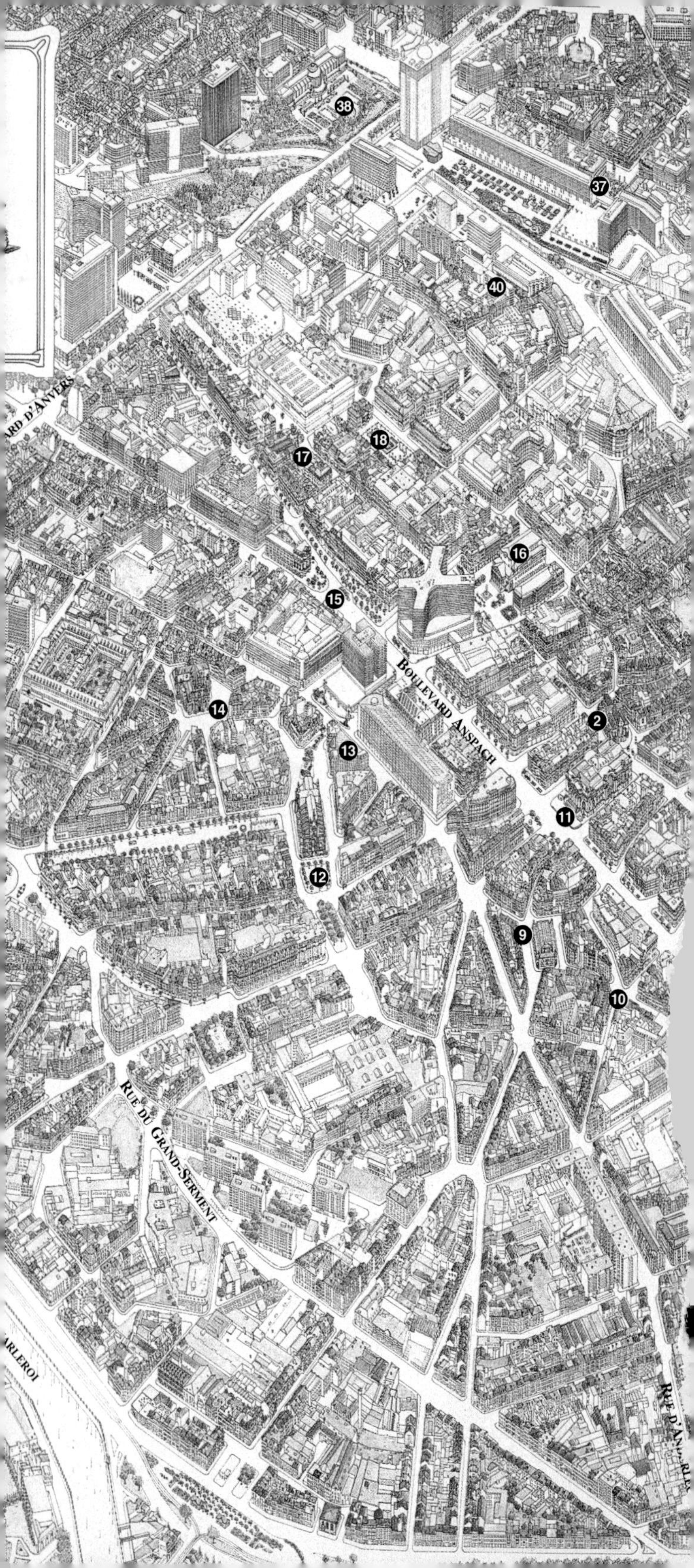

38
37
40
ARD D'ANVERS
18
17
16
15
BOULEVARD ANSPACH
14
2
13
11
12
9
10
RUE DU GRAND-SERMENT
ARLEROI

Rue de la Loi
Place des Palais
Boulevard de l'Empereur
36
37
30
35
4
28
29
34
32
31
33
3
6
7
23
20
22
1
41
24
8
5

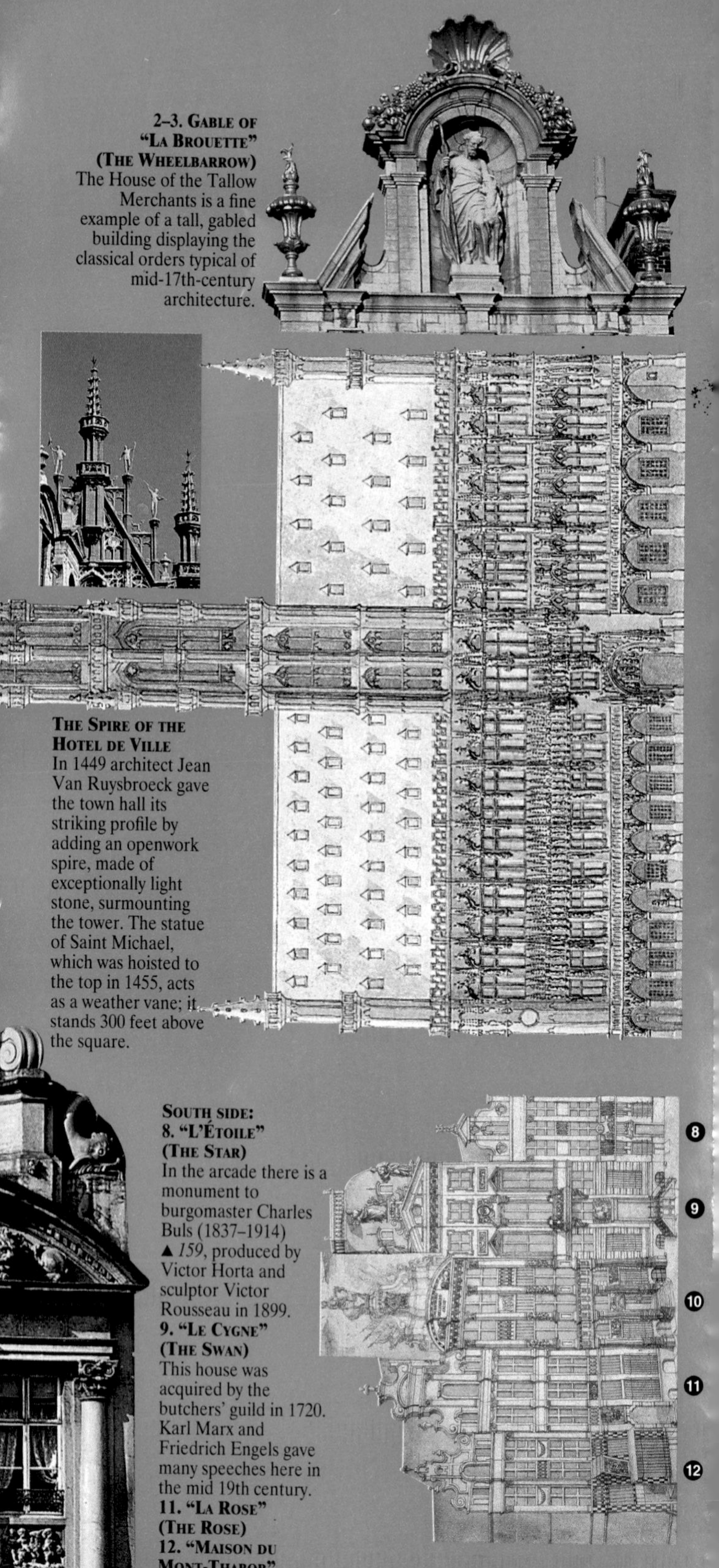

2–3. GABLE OF "LA BROUETTE" (THE WHEELBARROW)
The House of the Tallow Merchants is a fine example of a tall, gabled building displaying the classical orders typical of mid-17th-century architecture.

THE SPIRE OF THE HOTEL DE VILLE
In 1449 architect Jean Van Ruysbroeck gave the town hall its striking profile by adding an openwork spire, made of exceptionally light stone, surmounting the tower. The statue of Saint Michael, which was hoisted to the top in 1455, acts as a weather vane; it stands 300 feet above the square.

SOUTH SIDE:
8. "L'ÉTOILE" (THE STAR)
In the arcade there is a monument to burgomaster Charles Buls (1837–1914) ▲ *159*, produced by Victor Horta and sculptor Victor Rousseau in 1899.
9. "LE CYGNE" (THE SWAN)
This house was acquired by the butchers' guild in 1720. Karl Marx and Friedrich Engels gave many speeches here in the mid 19th century.
11. "LA ROSE" (THE ROSE)
12. "MAISON DU MONT-THABOR"

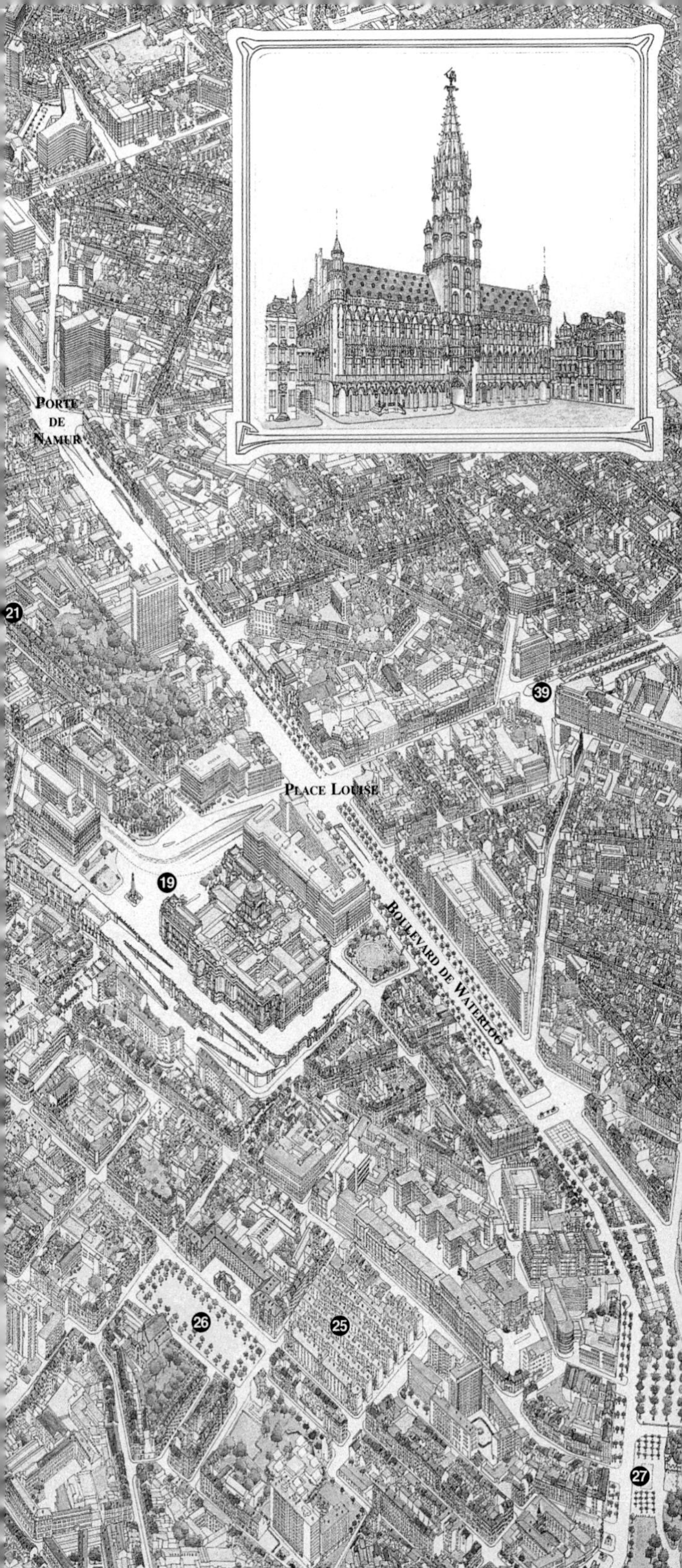

Porte de Namur
21
39
Place Louise
19
Boulevard de Waterloo
26
25
27

The Grand-Place, which Jean Cocteau called "the most beautiful theater in the world", is lined on all four sides by magnificent Baroque façades, surrounding two masterpieces of Gothic architecture on opposite sides of the square: the Hôtel de Ville (Town Hall) and the Maison du Roi (King's House). The square was destroyed by French bombardment in 1695; within a few years it had been rebuilt in its present form.

The Grand-Place on Fire during the Bombardment of 1695 (anonymous painter).

10. FAÇADE OF THE "MAISON DES BRASSEURS" (THE BREWERS' HOUSE)
The lower sections of the columns are decorated with hop leaves and spikes of corn; three reliefs depict the harvest, transportation of beer, and hop picking. It was here on July 10, 1873 that an argument flared up between the poets Rimbaud and Verlaine, who shot Rimbaud twice. On the roof is a statue of the governor Charles de Lorraine.

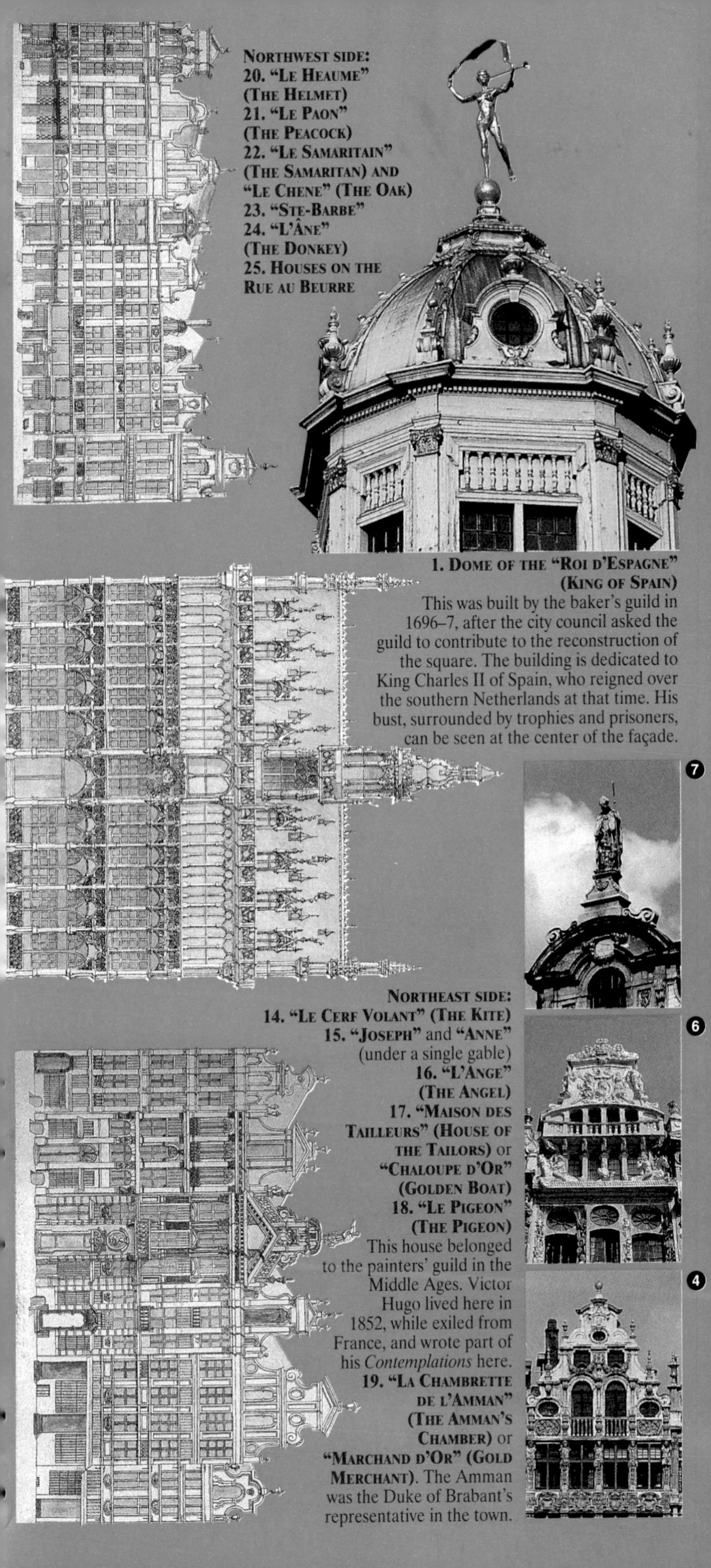

NORTHWEST SIDE:
20. "LE HEAUME" (THE HELMET)
21. "LE PAON" (THE PEACOCK)
22. "LE SAMARITAIN" (THE SAMARITAN) AND "LE CHENE" (THE OAK)
23. "STE-BARBE"
24. "L'ÂNE" (THE DONKEY)
25. HOUSES ON THE RUE AU BEURRE

1. DOME OF THE "ROI D'ESPAGNE" (KING OF SPAIN)
This was built by the baker's guild in 1696–7, after the city council asked the guild to contribute to the reconstruction of the square. The building is dedicated to King Charles II of Spain, who reigned over the southern Netherlands at that time. His bust, surrounded by trophies and prisoners, can be seen at the center of the façade.

7

NORTHEAST SIDE:
14. "LE CERF VOLANT" (THE KITE)
15. "JOSEPH" and "ANNE" (under a single gable)
16. "L'ANGE" (THE ANGEL)
17. "MAISON DES TAILLEURS" (HOUSE OF THE TAILORS) or **"CHALOUPE D'OR" (GOLDEN BOAT)**
18. "LE PIGEON" (THE PIGEON) This house belonged to the painters' guild in the Middle Ages. Victor Hugo lived here in 1852, while exiled from France, and wrote part of his *Contemplations* here.
19. "LA CHAMBRETTE DE L'AMMAN" (THE AMMAN'S CHAMBER) or **"MARCHAND D'OR" (GOLD MERCHANT)**. The Amman was the Duke of Brabant's representative in the town.

6

4

THE "OMMEGANG"
This historical festival goes back to the 14th century, when a young woman, under the influence of divine inspiration, stole a miraculous statue of the Virgin Mary from Antwerp and took it to the Sablon ▲ *176*. Each year a parade is held in her honor, bringing all the guilds and public officials together in a single procession. In 1549 Emperor Charles V was present at an especially brilliant version of the Ommegang: this event is now reproduced every year in a huge historical pageant.

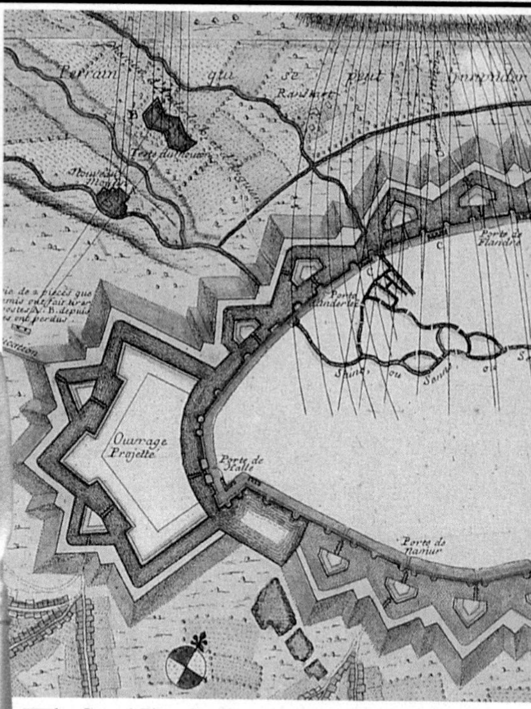

The Grand-Place has been the geographical, economic and political heart of the city since the Middle Ages. Its history is virtually the history of Brussels itself. Through the centuries the square has witnessed all the principal events in the city's history: the citizens' oath of allegiance to the new Dukes of Brabant, celebrations and tournaments, political riots and public executions. From the balcony of the Hôtel de Ville, kings and other dignitaries watched festivities held in their honor, magistrates pronounced laws and decrees, and officials announced peace treaties or pardons. It is on the Grand-Place that the Ommegang is held every summer ● *65*.

ECONOMIC AND POLITICAL CENTER

Historical records indicate that the first commercial center, consisting of three markets (for bread, cloth and meat), was established early in the 13th century in the area between what are now the Maison du Roi and Rue du Marché-aux-Herbes ▲ *160*. The markets flourished, and soon the commercial activities spilled over into the surrounding streets, which still bear names reminiscent of the old markets for cheese, coal, poultry, butter, pepper, herrings, leather, clothes and herbs. At the beginning of the 15th century work was started on the Hôtel de Ville: a masterpiece of secular Gothic architecture

“NEVER WAS THERE A MORE AWFUL SPECTACLE, NEVER ANYTHING SO SIMILAR TO WHAT IS RECOUNTED OF THE BURNING OF TROY.”

THE DUKE OF BERWICK

marking the peak of civic power. The sculptural ornamentation on the façades of the building dates mainly from the 19th century; originally there were just eight figures of prophets on the arches of the porch, plus figures in the vaulting of the galleries. Some of the original sculptures are preserved in the Musée de la Ville. The classical wing at the back was built by the Brabant States between 1706 and 1719; its second story houses a remarkable suite of state rooms decorated with Brussels tapestries from the early 18th century, depicting key events of the duchy of Brabant (in the Salle du Conseil) and the story of Clovis, based on drawings by Charles le Brun (Salle Maximilienne). After the guilds seized a major role in the city's administration in 1421 they soon began to build their houses around the new town hall.
A century later, when the Dukes of Burgundy imposed a centralized power structure they too made a symbolic demonstration of their power over the marketplace by building the ostentatious edifice later known as the Maison du Roi.

CHANGING FORTUNES

THE BOMBARDMENT OF 1695. The town was bombarded by the French army under Maréchal de Villeroi in August 1695, entirely destroying the square. Only the walls and the tower of the Hôtel de Ville survived, along with the shell of the Maison du Roi and the lower part of some façades on the east side which had been built in stone in the 17th century. When the city was rebuilt, reconstruction of the Grand-Place was given priority. Guilds and private citizens exerted themselves to the utmost, incurring huge debts in order to create within just a few years a sumptuous Baroque décor that would efface memories of the disaster.
RESTORATION. Badly damaged by the French Sans-Culottes in 1793–4, the square later deteriorated further through the negligence of proprietors. It was eventually saved from ruin toward the end of the 19th century, when art-loving burgomaster Charles Buls ordered the systematic restoration and conservation of all the façades.

MUSÉE DE LA VILLE
The Maison du Roi has housed the city's historical museum since 1887.
A magnificent collection of altarpieces, tapestries, faïence

and porcelain attests the splendor of the decorative arts in Brussels. Models, maps and engravings illustrate the evolution of the town. Above: detail from an engraving depicting the funeral procession of Charles V in Brussels in 1559.

FLOWER MARKET
A flower market is held every day on the Grand-Place; in addition, a bird market is held there on Sundays.

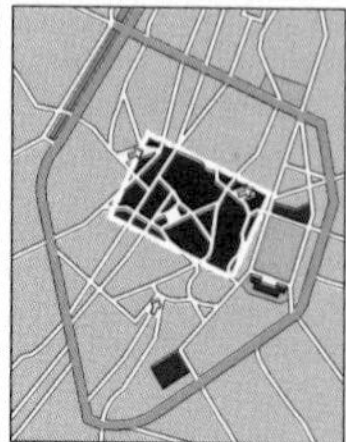

Half a day

A large area around the Grand-Place, stretching between the foot of the Mont des Arts and the boulevards of the city center, was entirely rebuilt after the bombardment by Louis XIV's armies in 1695. Despite economic constraints at this time, nearly four thousand houses were rapidly rebuilt within a few years. At the same time the medieval street pattern was regularized, and building standards were greatly improved. Most of the streets that have narrow gabled houses built of stone and brick were constructed during this period. Many bear a date in the middle of the façade, attesting the speed with which the reconstruction work was carried out.

THE HEART OF THE CITY

Rue au Beurre and the Church of St-Nicolas after the French siege ● *34*.

THE CHURCH OF ST-NICOLAS. This church is dedicated to the patron saint of merchants, and its history is closely intertwined with the growth of the civic center around the Grand-Place. The Gothic building bears the mark of numerous restorations. A fortified tower once stood in front of the church, acting as a bell tower for many years. Inside, the decorations date mainly from the 18th century. They include interesting Baroque altarpieces and woodcarvings; a *Descent from the Cross* attributed to the school of the Carracci (around 1600); paintings by the Belgian school (S.-J. Van Helmont, V. Janssens, B. Van Orley, G. Herreyns); and a remarkable wrought-iron grille in front of the choir.

RUE DU MARCHÉ-AUX-HERBES. This street formed the backbone of the old town, winding through Brussels on an east-west axis, connecting the ducal Coudenberg Palace (now Place Royale) to the Senne and the docks, and finally meeting the road to Ghent and Flanders. Halfway along the road stood the Grande Boucherie (below), today replaced by a building with a portico. One of the earliest commercial establishments on the Grand-Place (13th century), it faced the butchers' quarter of the town, which is now one of the city's gastronomic centers.

GALERIES ST-HUBERT ★. These galleries were built by architect Jean-Pierre Cluysenaer in 1847 following a plan which dated from 1836. At the time of their completion they formed the largest covered walkway in Europe. This modern addition in the heart of the old town was an immediate success: with their luxury stores, restaurants and theaters, the galleries became a focal point for the city's social life.

17TH-CENTURY HOUSES
The Rue du Marché-aux-Herbes still has many houses built soon after the bombardment. They include no. 36 (1697); no. 42, "L'Agneau Blanc" (The White Lamb) (1696); nos. 82–4; and nos. 89–111, a remarkable group dominated by the large "Au Char d'Or" (The Golden Chariot) (1697), shown below.

"THE CARVED-WOOD PULPIT BY HENRY VERBRUGGEN . . . IS CREATION ITSELF, IS ALL PHILOSOPHY, ALL POETRY. . . ."

VICTOR HUGO

THE TOONE MARIONETTE THEATER
Impasse Scuddeveld (next to 23, Petite-Rue-des-Bouchers) leads to a house built in 1696: this is the home of Brussels' celebrated Toone Marionette Theater ● *62*.

GALERIES ST-HUBERT
These galleries, with façades in Italian Renaissance style, form a magnificent indoor street more than 200 yards long.

CATHEDRAL OF ST-MICHEL ★

Today's cathedral was built on the site of a Romanesque church founded by Count Lambert Baldéric in 1047. Baldéric established a chapter of canons, and had the relics of Saint Gudula ▲ *163* transferred here. The church was then dedicated to Saint Michael and Saint Gudula, the patron saints of the town.

THREE CENTURIES OF BUILDING WORK. Reconstruction in the Gothic style began under Henri I, Duke of Brabant. The work started with the ambulatory and apse around 1220, but was not completed until the reign of Charles V. The duration of the project explains the coexistence of different phases of Brabant Gothic style: Romano-Gothic (ambulatory), Early Gothic (choir), High Gothic and Flamboyant (nave, west façade and windows). The towers and portals were restored by T.-F. Suys in 1839, statues of saints and Brabant nobles being placed in the niches at this time. The first known telegraph system – a semaphore signalling system – was installed in one of the towers after the 1830 Revolution. The most striking features of the building are its massive columns, huge triforium and wide windows. Over the nave there is ribbed vaulting. The stunning BAROQUE PULPIT OF TRUTH, carved by Hendrik Verbruggen in 1699, depicts the fall of Adam and Eve and the Redemption. The statues of apostles on the piers of the nave were created

The cathedral, now separated from the old city by modern boulevards.

Above: the Church of Notre-Dame-du-Bon-Secours. Below: the Galerie Bortier, home of second-hand booksellers, built by Jean-Pierre Cluysenaer in 1847. (The entrance to the gallery is through 55, rue de la Madeleine.)

THE "MANNEKEN PIS" One of the popular symbols of Brussels, this bronze statuette (less than 24 inches high) was made in 1619 by Jérôme du Quesnoy senior.

In 1747 Louis XV gave the statue an embroidered suit and awarded him the Cross of Louis XIV to make amends for his soldiers' disrespectful behavior. Since then the Manneken has amassed an extensive wardrobe (Musée de la Ville ▲ *159*).

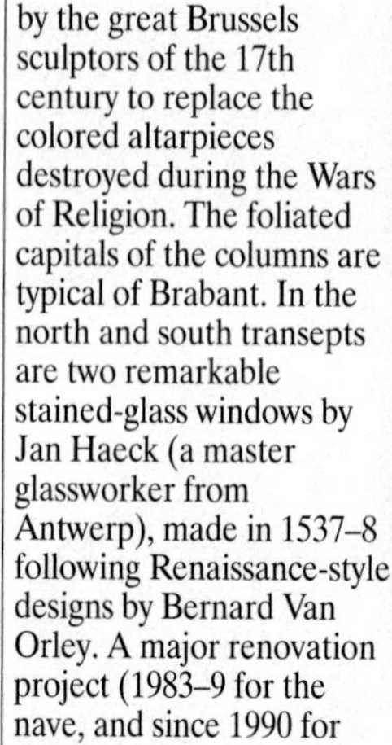

by the great Brussels sculptors of the 17th century to replace the colored altarpieces destroyed during the Wars of Religion. The foliated capitals of the columns are typical of Brabant. In the north and south transepts are two remarkable stained-glass windows by Jan Haeck (a master glassworker from Antwerp), made in 1537–8 following Renaissance-style designs by Bernard Van Orley. A major renovation project (1983–9 for the nave, and since 1990 for the choir) has restored the building to its former splendor. While this work was in progress the remains of the first Romanesque building were uncovered (the *westbau*, or western façade, pillars and walls of the nave). A Romanesque crypt was also discovered, under the present-day chancel.

AROUND THE CHAPEL OF LA MADELEINE

THE CHAPEL OF LA MADELEINE. The elegant steeple of this 15th-century chapel was rebuilt after 1695. To the left-hand side is the façade of the former Chapel of Ste-Anne – built in the mid 17th century at one end of Rue de la Montagne, then re-erected when the railway junction was built in 1956.

NOTRE-DAME-DU-BON-SECOURS. This church was once attached to a small hospice dedicated to Saint John, whose symbols (shell, beggar's bag and pilgrim's hat) decorate the pier of the door and the façade. The luminous interior, which has a centralized floor plan, is one of the most original and elegant examples of Belgian Baroque architecture.

Underneath the hexagonal dome are three semi-circular apses separated by pointed pillars that highlight the dynamism of the overall structure.

QUARTIER ST-GÉRY ★

PLACE ST-GÉRY. This square stands on the site of the island where Brussels is thought to have been founded. Charles, Duke of Lower Lotharingia, is supposed to have had a *castrum* built here in 977, as well as a chapel dedicated to Saint Géry, into which he transferred the relics of Saint Gudula (these had previously been kept in the abbey at Moorsel). The first houses were built around a port on the Senne (Rue de la Vierge-Noire) and a market (Place de la Bourse). The town's political and ecclesiastical leaders left St-Géry in 1047, when the chapter of St-Michel was established and a castle erected on the Coudenberg hill. LES HALLES (the central market) was built in 1881, on the site of a church destroyed during the Revolution ● *40*. The exterior, decorated with neo-Renaissance Flemish motifs, is in contrast with the interior (opposite page), which features a metal structure combining modern technical and decorative innovation.

NOTRE-DAME-AUX-RICHES-CLAIRES. This church (1665) is all that remains of a convent set up in the quarter after the Wars of Religion. Its Baroque style illustrates the importance of the Counter-Reformation in Brussels. The building is striking for its lack of a screen façade. The choir and transept end in semicircles crowned by gables with volutes, similar to those which can be seen on houses of the period. The church was damaged by fire and is currently being restored.

THE FALSTAFF AND THE CIRIO
On either side of the Bourse de Commerce are two famous Brussels cafés. The Falstaff is the fashionable place to meet: intellectuals and artists gather in its Art Nouveau interior. The Cirio is a typical 19th-century café which is decorated in the eclectic style, and the original décor has survived more or less intact.

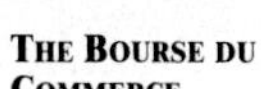

THE BOURSE DU COMMERCE
Built by Leon Suys in 1871, on the site of a Recollect convent, the Stock Exchange, with its magnificently eclectic ornamentation, stands in a prominent position on the boulevards. Its decorative motifs celebrate Belgium's prosperity in the second half of the 19th century, with allegories of Commerce and Industry, cupids, and garlands of fruit and flowers. Some of the figures were carved by Rodin, working under Carrier-Belleuse.

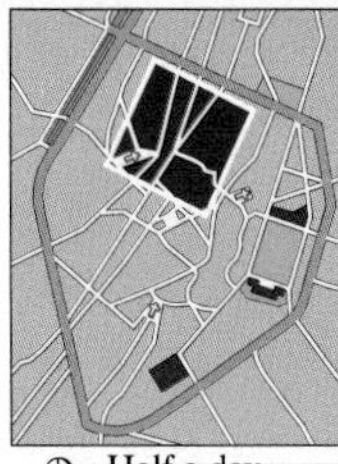

◷ Half a day

The Tour Noire
The Tour Noire (Black Tower) stands on Place du Samedi, behind the Church of Ste-Catherine. It is one of the few remains of the first city wall.

The fish market
The old Bassin des Marchands (Merchants' Dock) became the fish market in the 19th century. In 1979 one of the city's first major restoration projects was undertaken here, during work on the metro network.

The old ports ★

The Ste-Catherine quarter grew up outside the city wall, along the old trading route joining Flanders to the Rhine. In the 16th century the docks here (1584) were the focus of the city's maritime and river traffic; the new port connected Brussels with the Willebroek Canal, excavated in 1550. Subsequently, in the 19th century, the canal, which was no longer wide enough, was diverted to the north. The church and the Place Ste-Catherine form one of the focal points of this area; others are the Beguine convent and Pachéco Hospice, still charming havens of peace at the heart of a busy city.

Place Ste-Catherine. When the docks were filled in, in 1853, the architects J. Poelaert and W. Jannsens built a new Church of Ste-Catherine here. Poelaert drew inspiration from the Church of St-Eustache in Paris for his design. The eclectic style matches the hybrid character of the building, with its flying buttresses and Gothic rose window alongside a classical portal and Baroque aedicules. The old Church of Ste-Catherine was demolished in 1893: the only remains are the Baroque tower and a section of wall from the choir which backed onto the city wall. On Rue Ste-Catherine Haussmann-style apartment blocks have replaced the façade of the church. Place Ste-Catherine and the Marché aux Grains (Grain Market) present an exceptional architectural group: the harmonious proportions of the 18th- and 19th-century houses, the terraces planted with trees, the lively fish market and the bistros around it all combine to create an area of great charm.

Rue Ste-Catherine. This street, which was the backbone of the medieval town, is the oldest trading street in Brussels. The contrasting façades are striking. On the even-numbered side, 17th-century houses illustrate the evolution of the gable, from the traditional model with tiers to the Baroque gable with volutes;

whereas the 19th-century eclecticism of the odd-numbered side is reminiscent of the city-center boulevards. The street continues into RUE DE FLANDRE, in a quarter which still has the narrow winding streets of the medieval town. In the courtyard of no. 46, rue de Flandre is MAISON LA BELLONE (below), now the home of the Maison du Spectacle (an exhibition and information center). The style of the façade (1697) combines the austerity of French classicism with Flemish Baroque ornamentation.

THE OLD QUAYS. The names QUAI AUX BRIQUES and QUAI AU BOIS-À-BRÛLER mark the location of the old docks filled in during work on the metro line in 1976. The esplanade is lined with restaurants specializing in seafood. At one end stands part of the ANSPACH FOUNTAIN, an allegory of "Power and Communal Action", which originally stood on Place de Brouckère.

ST-JEAN-BAPTISTE
Following the local tradition, the façade does not have a grand portico in the Roman style. Instead, it has the triple gable typical of northern European houses.

QUARTIER DU BÉGUINAGE ★

THE CHURCH OF ST-JEAN-BAPTISTE. The church and the Rue du Béguinage are the last remnants of a Beguine convent founded outside the city walls in the 13th century. The street, its central axis, was incorporated in the star-shaped square created in 1855. The church illustrates the persistence of Gothic elements in the Baroque style of the Netherlands. The floor plan in the shape of a Latin cross, the cylindrical pillars and the ribbed vaults all reflect Gothic traditions. By contrast the façade, with its arches, broken pediments, niches, cartouches and candelabras, is typically Baroque; the interior, with cherubs and protruding cornices, uses the same architectural idiom.

BEGUINE CONVENTS
Lambert le Bègue, a Liège priest of the 12th century, is credited with founding the Beguine order. Beguine convents were established throughout northern Europe (the Netherlands, Belgium and Germany); in them women lived in a religious community without taking vows.

THE PACHÉCO HOSPICE. After the public authorities decided to take over the administration of charities, in 1819 the city council commissioned H.L.F. Partoes to build a hospice in the former gardens of the Beguine convent. The architect, imbued with rationalist theories, designed his building as part of a strictly rectangular urban complex. The austerely neoclassical building uses simple geometric shapes, avoiding all applied ornamentation. The hospice consists of two square courtyards (one for men and one for women), with pavilions at the center and corners, and internal galleries. The building, which was renovated and listed in 1980, still houses three hundred elderly people.

HARMONY
Place du Grand-Hospice and Rue de l'Infirmerie match the style of the hospice. The houses, with their smooth white façades, are incorporated in a harmonious overall composition.

THE THÉÂTRE FLAMAND. This was originally built for a popular theater troupe founded in 1852 by one of the first militant Belgian workers, named Kats. It was moved from the Alhambra in Place de Brouckère to the old arsenal at the far end of the Bassin au Foin (Hay Dock) in 1882. The foyer and the staircase are masterpieces of Flemish neo-Renaissance style.

The covering of the Senne
When the river was covered over ▲ *148*, the poor and run-down areas of the city center were demolished.
A boulevard in the Parisian style was created along this artery, running from the north to the south of the city. The aim was to give Brussels

the air of a great capital city, and to tempt back its wealthier citizens, who were already starting to move to residential districts on the outskirts.

Hôtel Métropole
Built according to plans by G. Bordiau in 1870 and renovated by A. Chambon in 1893, this palatial hotel (entrance hall below) has numbered sovereigns and other famous people, including Marie and Pierre Curie and Sacha Guitry, among its guests.

Around Place de Brouckère

This area features some highly diverse architectural elements, ranging from the 17th to the 19th century, though in recent times the growth of the city has to a large degree separated them from one another. They include Rue Neuve (built up in the 17th century), Place des Martyrs (18th century), Place de la Monnaie (early 19th century) and Place de Brouckère, which completes the grand perspective of the central boulevards.

The boulevards. Burgomaster Jules Anspach, who held office between 1864 and 1879, initiated the great public building program in the city. It was he who decreed the covering of the Senne, transforming the whole of the city center. Squares and grand monuments were built along the new axis thus created, stretching from the Gare du Nord to the Gare du Midi – among them the Palais du Midi (1875), Place Anneessens, Place Fontainas, the Bourse (1871) ▲ *163*, the covered market (1871) where the Philips Tower is now, and finally Place de Brouckère.

Place de Brouckère. The square was already very lively in the 19th century, with cafés, luxury hotels, theaters (the Alhambra and the Théâtre de la Bourse) and even the first movie theaters. The Eldorado complex and the famous Hôtel Métropole from this era can still be seen today. The magnificent façades on the square exhibit a broad range of styles, including French classicism, variants of neoclassicism, neo-Renaissance and eclectic styles. The Maison des Chats (3 boulevard Adolphe-Max) is especially interesting: Beyaert, the architect, sought to counter the French architectural influence by establishing a national style, taking his inspiration from the buildings of the Grand-Place. A genie, two cats and the inscription "*In den kater en de kat*" can be seen on the fourth story. The Philips Tower and the Administrative Center were built close to the square in 1967, in stark contrast to the style and scale of the surrounding buildings.

"[THE SENNE] WAS A FEATURE OF THE OLD BRUSSELS; YOU COULD STROLL OVER ITS BRIDGES, CATCHING SUDDEN VIEWS OF ROOFTOPS . . . , IT WAS ALMOST LIKE THE CANALS IN BRUGES."

CAMILLE LEMONNIER

THE PASSAGE DU NORD. This passage, connecting Boulevard Adolphe-Max with Rue Neuve, was built by Rieck in 1881. The gallery, which used to house a waxworks museum, theater and concert hall, is decorated with sculptures symbolizing the Arts and Science.

THÉÂTRE DE LA MONNAIE

A theater was first built here in 1695, after the bombardment of Brussels ● *34*, on the site of the former Brabant mint (1420–1531). J.-B. Vifquain designed the Place de la Monnaie in 1817, and two years later the Grand-Théâtre was built in the neoclassical style by French architect Damesne. The interior was destroyed by fire and completely redesigned by Poelaert in 1855, in the opulent style favored by the rising middle classes. Noteworthy features include, on the façade, the pediment by Simonis depicting *The Harmony of Human Passions* (1854); and, inside the building, a bust of the actor Albers by Jef Lambeaux and murals by the Symbolist painter E. Fabry (1909–30). The Opéra, as it is often called, was enlarged in 1985: contemporary artists contributed to the renovation of the foyer (floor by Sol Lewitt, ceiling by Sam Francis) and the Salon Royal.

THREE CENTURIES OF THEATER. Since the very first performance.

REVOLUTIONARY SPARKS IN 1830
"Sacred love of the homeland/ Give us boldness and pride/ To my country I owe my life/ To me it will owe its liberty."
These few lines at the first performance of the opera *La Muette de Portici* roused the audience to a frenzy ● *40*, even though it had been hand-

picked by the Dutch authorities. The opera by Auber, with libretto by Scribe and Delavigne, recounted the uprising of Naples against its Spanish oppressors in 1674. The analogy was all too clear.

THE SALON ROYAL
The new décor was designed by Charles Vandenhove, the floors and walls are by D. Buren and the sculpture by G. Paolini.

A MEMORIAL SQUARE
The Place des Martyrs was once planted with trees: first a string of miniature trees and then lime trees planted in staggered rows. Later it was completely cleared to make way for a monument dedicated to the patriots of 1830 ● *40*. The lithograph of 1830 on the right shows the burial of the revolutionaries who died in the fighting.

In 1830 the Place St-Michel (named after the patron saint of Brussels) was renamed Place des Martyrs, when the monument to the heroes of the Belgian revolution was erected here. The monument (above) was created by Willem Geefs between 1830 and 1848; its patriotic symbolism shows the Belgian lion and four angels watching over the dead.

(Lully's opera *Atys* in 1700) there have scarcely been any interruptions to the theater's program, and the theater became famous for its operas and ballets. Maurice Béjart and the Ballet du XXe Siècle staged all their productions here between 1960 and 1980; Béjart's ballet school, Mudra, was also based here. Director G. Mortier breathed new life into the theater, inviting guest orchestras or soloists for every production (including the baritone José Vandam and soprano Gwyneth Jones) and maintaining a program of consistently high quality. The theater has built up an international reputation, with innovative reworkings of the classical repertory and regular productions of new contemporary works. The present director is continuing the good work, seeking to attract a younger and wider public to the opera.

TOWARD THE PLACE DES MARTYRS

RUE NEUVE. This street was started in the 17th century and extended in 1839 to connect the Gare du Nord with the Gare du Midi – making it the first north–south axis in a city that had hitherto been arranged mainly in an east–west direction. Houses were soon built along it, followed by the first department stores, such as Grand Bazar, Bon Marché and Innovation (sadly the last of these, built by Victor Horta in 1900, was destroyed by fire in 1967). The Rue Neuve has been one of the city's main shopping streets ever since.

NOTRE-DAME-DE-FINISTÈRE (1713–30). Like the Church of the Minimes at Sablon, this church has a strikingly austere neoclassical façade. The octagonal lantern and the upper section of the façade were added in 1828. The interior is richly decorated with stuccos and Baroque furniture.

PLACE DES MARTYRS ★. In 1775 the city council commissioned Claude Fisco to create a square modeled on the neoclassical design of the new Place Royale ▲ *169*. The square forms an elongated rectangle, with six openings: four at the corners and two halfway along the sides. The council specified that the façades should be uniform and were to be painted in mid gray, with pearl gray for the woodwork. The Place des Martyrs was neglected for most of the second half of the 20th century: renovation work was delayed through conflicts of interest between various bodies wanting to make it either a grand showcase for the city or a multifunctional urban center. Work finally started in 1991.

The area around the Place Royale and the park was the result of a redevelopment project undertaken by the government of the Austrian Netherlands; work started in 1774 and was completed some ten years later. Previously the site was occupied by the old court, the palace and its park.

THE BURGUNDIAN PALACE. The palace had its origin in the castle built by Henri I, Duke of Brabant, in the 11th century. When the Duke of Brabant decided to live in Brussels rather than Louvain at the beginning of the 13th century, the Coudenberg was chosen as the home of his court. When the Netherlands were transferred to the House of Burgundy in the 15th century, the Brussels court acquired an international importance which it retained up to the abdication of Emperor Charles V in 1555. At that time the palace consisted of a disparate collection of buildings grouped around a courtyard. Most prominent among them was the *Magna Aula*, the great hall built by Philip the Good around 1455. The park covered an irregular area of around 86 acres, crossed by a small valley and divided roughly into a number of separate enclosures.

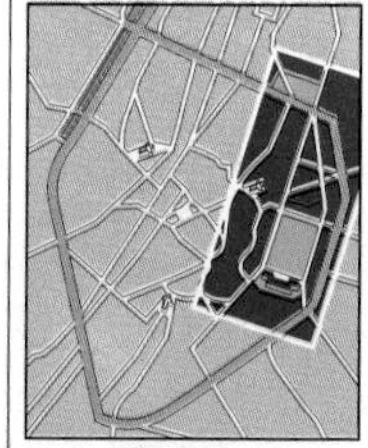

◷ One day

The Old Royal Palace in Brussels, painting by Jan Van der Heyden (17th century).

IMPROVEMENTS. In 1731 the palace was completely destroyed by fire. Charles de Lorraine, brother-in-law of Maria Theresa of Austria and governor of the Netherlands, decided to improve the palace he had just built nearby (on today's Place du Musée) by adding a park and a square in the French style, over the valley of the old estate (which was filled in). The project was designed by French architect Barnabé Guimard in the neoclassical style. The roads laid down at the time followed the lines of the old city wall; in the 19th century they provided the framework for the city's expansion toward Laeken ▲ *173*, Tervueren ▲ *189* and the Bois de la Cambre ▲ *181*.

THE PLACE ROYALE The Church of St-Jacques-sur-Coudenberg was built on the long side of the square, facing in the same direction as the Hôtel de Ville.

AROUND PLACE ROYALE

THE PLACE ROYALE ★. Originally this square was a rectangle surrounded by eight palatial residences joined by porticos. At the center of the square stood a statue of Charles de Lorraine, which was destroyed during the French Revolution; a copy now

THE "OLD ENGLAND" DEPARTMENT STORE
This magnificent Art Nouveau creation by Paul Saintenoy dates from 1899. The terrace café was famous for its view over the town. The building is currently being restored and will eventually house the collections of the Musée Instrumental ▲ *175*.

MODERN ART
The Musée d'Art Moderne was founded in 1984. It stands out from its European counterparts in placing emphasis on national productions rather than the great international artists of modern times. However, works by major 20th-century artists such as Rik Wouters (above, *The Flautist*) give it an important place among the great European galleries.

stands on the Place du Musée. The pavilions, built in Louis XVI style, are all identical. Later, the equestrian statue of Godefroi de Bouillon (a leader of the First Crusade and King of Jerusalem) and the bell tower gave this austere space a more dramatic air. The square was subsequently opened onto the Rue de la Régence, Rue Royale and Rue Montagne-de-la-Cour, transforming it into a major crossroads. On the main side of the square stands the CHURCH OF ST-JACQUES-SUR-COUDENBERG, with its model neoclassical interior: austerely monochrome, with a design strictly based on classical traditions. Most of the pavilions on the square are now public buildings, among them the Musée d'Art Ancien, Musée d'Art Moderne and Musée Bellevue (Musée de la Dynastie).

MUSÉES ROYAUX DES BEAUX-ARTS ★. With separate galleries devoted to historical and modern collections, the Royal Museums present a complete overview of the fine arts in Belgium from the end of the Middle Ages to the present day, including works by major artists.

THE PALACE OF CHARLES DE LORRAINE. This palace (1766) stands at the end of the Place du Musée; it supplanted the imposing 15th-century Nassau Palace, which stood on the site of today's Bibliothèque Royale. It forms an elegant semicircle, ending to the left in Louis XVI style apartments (now restored); and to the right in the former court chapel, known as the Protestant Chapel, because Napoleon gave it to the Protestant community in 1804. This beautiful neoclassical building is often used for concerts.

THE MONT DES ARTS. This replaced a square that was hastily created for the exhibition held in 1910. It was planned in 1939 and opened twenty years later, designed in a neoclassical variant of Art Deco style. At one end stands the equestrian figure of Albert I, opposite a standing figure of his wife, Queen Elisabeth. At the far end of the quadrangle is the PALAIS DES CONGRES; on one side there is a monumental arcade decorated with a clock, on the other the Bibliothèque Royale, which includes the old Nassau Chapel (15th century) – all that remains of the original Nassau Palace.

BIBLIOTHÈQUE ROYALE ALBERT IER (THE ALBERTINE). This library combined the collections of manuscripts belonging to the Dukes of Burgundy (Philip II, 1559) with a school created under the Republic (1795), encompassing a library, scientific collections, paintings and a botanical garden. The manuscript collection includes 34,000 items from the Burgundian library and monastic libraries (which proved a valuable source).

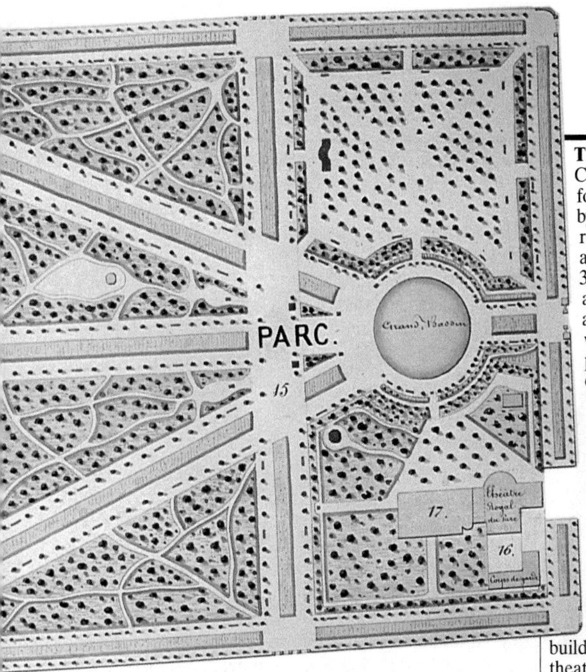

THE PARC ROYAL
Created after 1775 following designs by Guimard, the royal park covers approximately 30 acres. Its avenues border areas of mature woodland. The park has two ornamental lakes and some sixty sculptures, mainly from the 18th century (although most have been replaced by copies). There are a number of buildings, too, including the Vauxhall buildings, a charming theater, a café/restaurant and several kiosks.

The Albertine also has collections of prints, medals and maps, as well as a MUSEUM OF THE BOOK and a MUSEUM OF PRINTING.

THE PARK AND ITS SURROUNDING AREAS ★

The area around Place Royale and the park witnessed the triumph of the Belgian Revolution ● *40*. The symbolic importance of this district was reinforced when the new country's major institutions were established here, including Parliament, the royal palace and government ministries. Although attempts were made to establish a national architectural style, it is clear from these buildings that the Belgian public continued to favor the French style imposed in earlier years. The RUE ROYALE, flanking the northwest side of the park, is bordered by sober façades; toward the lower end is the PALAIS DES BEAUX-ARTS, one of Brussels' main cultural and artistic centers, which houses the MUSÉE DU CINÉMA. On the RUE DUCALE (southeast side of the park) are the former palace of the Prince of Orange and the present-day PALAIS DES ACADÉMIES, built in strict neoclassical style. On the *Rue de la Loi* (northeast side of the park), with its richly decorated façades, stands the *Palais de la Nation*, the seat of Parliament.

The entrance to the park on the Palais Royal side.

THE COLONNE DU CONGRÈS
The Column of Congress was erected by the side of the Rue Royale in 1850, to celebrate the fiftieth anniversary of Belgium and the drafting of the Constitution. The monument is a prominent feature of the area, a focal point for its views and avenues.

THE BOTANIQUE
Despite having undergone major alterations, the gardens are still very pleasant, with some remarkable trees.

THE PALAIS ROYAL. The fourth side of the PLACE DES PALAIS has undergone considerable modification. The first royal palacè was created by combining two older buildings behind an austere neoclassical façade. Leopold II commissioned architect Alphonse Balat to create magnificent new interiors, and in 1905 he got Jean Maquet to redesign the outside of the building. Maquet raised the level of the roof, added two curved galleries leading to new pavilions, and set the palace back from the present outline of the square.

FROM THE COLONNE DU CONGRÈS TO THE BOTANIQUE

The area in the northeast part of the city between Parliament, the Rue Royale, Boulevard Bischoffsheim and the Jardin Botanique was built up in Haussmann fashion in the second half of the 19th century. It was a residential area, intended for the wealthy middle classes, with large private houses built in the eclectic style typical of the late 19th century. Today this is no longer a residential area: the houses have mostly been converted into offices and shops. The names of the streets and squares conjure up characters and events connected with the beginnings of Belgian independence, like PLACE DE LA LIBERTÉ, which has a statue of Charles Rogier ● *40,* and the charming PLACE DES BARRICADES.

THE BOTANIQUE ★. The Jardin Botanique is located at the far end of the Rue Royale, beyond the inner ring road, and was severely disfigured when the Nord-Midi railway junction was built. It was designed in 1829, at the end of the Dutch régime: at that time it was one of the most remarkable botanical gardens in Europe. The gardens stretched over an irregular, sloping terrain arranged in terraces. At the top stood an imposing neoclassical building, designed by architects Meeus and Ginestre, incorporating the glasshouses and botanical museum. The building (below) is still standing, and in 1979 it was converted into a CULTURAL CENTER FOR BELGIUM'S FRENCH COMMUNITY. Sculptures by Constantin Meunier and Charles Van der Stappen were installed in the garden at the end of the 19th century: combining realism and symbolism, they depict themes such as time, the seasons, and plants associated with different emotions.

LAEKEN ▲ AND HEYSEL

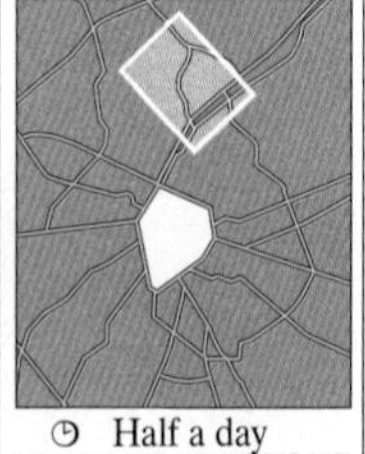

◷ Half a day

LAEKEN

Today the royal estate of Laeken is a landscape garden dotted here and there with buildings: the palace and the Belvedere (a Louis XIV style pavilion built in 1788 and modified in the 19th century), royal residences, glasshouses, a monument to Leopold I, a Chinese pavilion and a Japanese tower.

THE ROYAL ESTATE. The first palace, formerly the residence of the Austrian Governors General, was built by French architect Wailly, with the assistance of the Belgian Louis Montoyer (1782). It was given to King Leopold I. Major modifications were commissioned by Leopold II: from Girault, who built two pavilions and a chapel, and from Balat, who built the superb GLASSHOUSES ★ (above). The rotunda of the Winter Garden is the focal point of this construction; an elegant, brightly lit masterpiece. Opposite the palace is a neo-Gothic monument to Leopold I by Willem Geefs. Inspired by the Paris Exhibition of 1900, Leopold II set out to create a sort of architectural world tour, accompanied by copies of the major works of European sculpture; THE FOUNTAIN OF NEPTUNE by Jean de Bologne (1563–7) is one of the survivors from this project.

NOTRE-DAME-DE-LAEKEN. Fulfilling the wish of his wife, Louise-Marie d'Orléans, Leopold I decided to build a church with a royal crypt. A competition was held, and Joseph Poelaert ▲ *174* was chosen as the architect. Although this intriguing building (1852–1907) was never completed, its geometrical reworking of Gothic architecture is striking. The cemetery, which contains the graves of many famous people, has some interesting funerary sculpture, including a copy of Rodin's *The Thinker*. On the other side of the Avenue du Parc-Royal is a colonnade with a statue of Queen Astrid (the wife of Leopold III), who died in tragic circumstances.

HEYSEL. The Heysel Plateau remained undeveloped until the 1920's, when plans for an exhibition center were launched. The center was built in two phases, for the exhibitions of 1935 and 1958. Nevertheless, the mood of its architecture remained constant: the triumphalist Art Deco façade of the Grand Palais celebrates the technical achievement of its concrete supports, while the Atomium represents a similar celebration of science and technology. OSSEGHEM PARK has a number of attractions for the general public: the PLANETARIUM, various exhibition centers and BRUPARK, a leisure complex that includes an Oceadium (tropical swimming pool), a Kinepolis (movie theater complex) and theme parks called "MINI-EUROPE" and "THE VILLAGE".

Standing on either side of Avenue Van-Praet, the Japanese Tower and Chinese Pavilion bear witness to Leopold II's love of all things oriental. On the Heysel Plateau, the Atomium represents an enlarged molecule of iron – and the nine Belgian provinces.

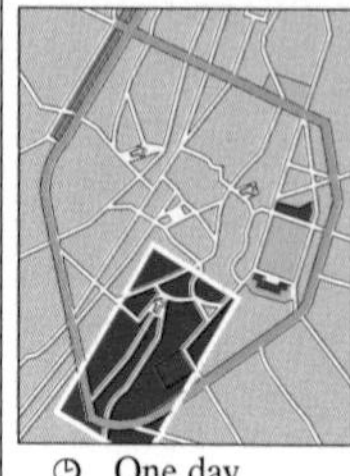

◷ One day

The southern part of the Pentagon ▲ *148* offers a striking contrast between two different districts. One area, higher up, stretches from the Palais de Justice to the Sablon: here the symbols of power and shops selling luxury goods stand side by side. Lower down is the Marolles quarter, centered around Rue Haute and the flea market, which has been a colorful, popular district since the Middle Ages.

PALAIS DE JUSTICE

"I went to the Palais de Justice where they have piled up imitations of monuments on top of monumental imitations, with no order or reason. . . . There is Assyrian on top of Gothic, Gothic on top of Tibetan, Tibetan on top of Louis XVI, Louis XVI on top of Papuan."
Octave Mirbeau

The Palais de Justice was built between 1866 and 1883, decisively altering the structure of the city: it closed off the royal vista, while opening up Avenue Louise toward the Bois de la Cambre.

THE ARCHITECTURE OF MEGALOMANIA. The Palais de Justice bears eloquent witness to the scale of middle-class aspirations in the last century: covering nearly 300,000 square feet and standing 670 feet high, it was the largest building erected in Europe in the 19th century. Embankments had to be built to support its massive weight: this accentuated the steep slope of the Galgenberg ("gallows hill"), which runs between the Palais de Justice and Rue des Tanneurs. Monumental entrances added to the imposing effect. The architect, Joseph Poelaert, drew on the full classical repertory of motifs to express the omnipotence of justice: pediments, columns, pilasters, statues and winged lions impart an air of grandeur and severity to the construction. The full impact of its megalomaniac architecture can best be appreciated by going through the peristyle to the hall (4,300 square yards). The extravagance did not meet with universal approval, however, and the compulsory purchase orders served on local residents left their mark. Even today the worst insult in Brussels slang is that of "architek"!

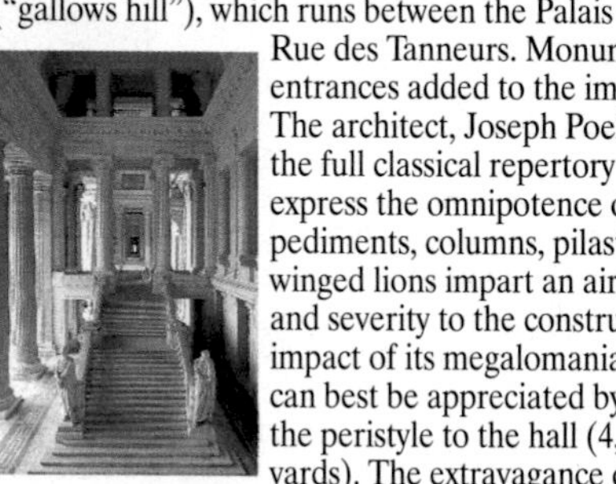

RUE DE LA RÉGENCE
A number of official buildings stand along the Rue de la Régence, which leads from the Palais de Justice toward Place Royale. In the section leading to the Sablon is the Romano-Byzantine Synagogue (De Keyser, 1875) and the Conservatoire de Musique (Cluysenaer, 1872), a mixture of French and Flemish neo-Renaissance styles.

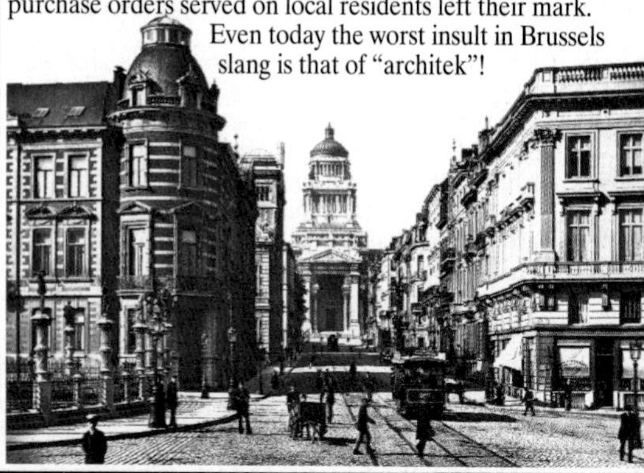

THE SABLON ★

SQUARE DU PETIT-SABLON. This square was created in 1890 on the orders of burgomaster Charles Buls ▲ *159* as a celebration of 16th-century Belgium. The wrought-iron balustrade, for example, is reminiscent of the railings in front of the old Burgundian palace ▲ *169*. The SCULPTURE GROUP FEATURING COUNTS EGMONT AND HORNES (Fraikin, 1864) was moved here from the Grand-Place. These two heroes, symbols of the resistance to Spanish occupation ▲ *32*, are surrounded by a semicircular group of ten 16th-century humanists.

THE PALAIS D'EGMONT. Not far from here is the Palais d'Egmont and its park. Only the central wing of the 16th-century palace remains, and this has been repeatedly altered. In 1753 the Dukes of Arenberg had it rebuilt in Italian classical style by Servandoni, who added the monumental portico crowned with cherubs. The palace was rebuilt in 1835 and again in 1905.

RUE AUX LAINES. The odd-numbered side of this street is lined with pre-19th-century residences; on the even-numbered side there is a beautiful group of twenty-six houses built by the Duke of Arenberg (1905) for occupation by the wealthy middle classes. On the corner of Rue de la Régence is the *Musée Instrumental*, at present housed in the former palace of the Princes of Thurn and Taxis, who founded the first international postal service in the 16th century. The quality and diversity of its collections make this one of the world's leading museums in its field. It is soon to be moved to the "Old England" building ▲ *170*.

PLACE DU GRAND-SABLON. This square, on the other side of Rue de la Régence, was where the aristocracy and the upper middle classes lived in sumptuous residences in the 17th century. For a long time it was a horse market, and then a fruit and vegetable

THE OLD TRADES
The railings in the Square du Petit-Sablon have forty-eight pillars in the Gothic style, all different. Each pillar bears a bronze statuette depicting one of the old trades, along with its traditional attributes.

MAISON DU PEUPLE
▲ *176*
This building was unusual in the way it was adapted to its sloping site, and in the ambitious and modern style of its design. The architecture symbolized the radical changes advocated by the Belgian Workers' Party, who built it. The opening of the building was marked by two days of celebrations.

NOTRE-DAME-DU-SABLON
In 1304 a small chapel was built on ancient marshland by the guild of crossbowmen, whose festivities are shown in this 17th-century painting. Worshippers crowded to see a miraculous statuette, brought from Antwerp and soon a settlement grew up around the chapel.

market. Today antiques and luxury goods are sold here, and there is an antique market near the church every weekend. Nearby, on Place Émile-Vandervelde, Victor Horta built the famous Maison du Peuple (1899) ▲ *175*. Despite angry protests, this building was demolished in 1965–6; in its place stands a functional 28-story tower block.

NOTRE-DAME-DU-SABLON. This oratory is a gem of Flamboyant architecture. It was extended in the 15th century, and completed with two bays and façades in the 16th century. The central nave has cylindrical columns with the foliated capitals typical of Brabant Gothic style. Elegant colonnettes made in a single casting can be seen in the choir (1435). Two Baroque chapels donated by the Princes of Thurn and Taxis stand on either side of the choir. Pinnacles, statues and turrets decorate the portals and the façades; these were restored (or completed) in the 19th century by J.-J. Van Ysendijck, a follower of Viollet-le-Duc.

RUE DES MINIMES. This street only became a respectable area during the last century. The famous anatomist Andreas Vesalius (1514–64) lived and supposedly carried out secret dissections here; a convent later stood on the site of his house. The CHURCH OF ST-JEAN-ET-ST-ÉTIENNE-AUX-MINIMES, built between 1700 and 1715, marks the transition between

MARCHÉ AUX PUCES (THE FLEA MARKET)
In 1873 the district council transferred the flea market from Place Anneessens to Place du Jeu-de-

Balle. The "old market" has been the true heart of the Marolles for more than a hundred years; it is well worth a visit. It is held every morning, until around one o'clock. Sunday is, of course, the busiest day.

two styles: although the monumental façade is still Baroque, its ornamentation (colossal order, arched pediment) prefigures neoclassicism.

THE TOUR ANNEESSENS. The Rue de Rollebeek follows the winding course of an old stream. It leads to the Boulevard de l'Empereur, where the Tour Anneessens stands. This 13th-century circular tower with loopholes is one of the few remnants of the first city wall.

THE MAROLLES ★

The Marolles district is named after the old convent of Apostolline nuns of the Mariam Colentes (or Marolles) community; it stretches from Notre-Dame-de-la-Chapelle to the Porte de Hal. This district, still very colorful, is arranged around two main axes: RUE HAUTE and RUE BLAES. Rue Haute was the first to be built up: from the Middle Ages onward it was a center for fullers and weavers, especially around Notre-Dame-de-la-Chapelle. Rue Blaes was built in 1851 to improve living conditions in the quarter. Some people still see this district as the true heart of Brussels: it is here that "brusseleir" is still spoken ● *48*.

NOTRE-DAME-DE-LA-CHAPELLE. Built in 1134 by Godefroi the Bearded, Duke of Brabant, this is one of Brussels' oldest and most beautiful churches. Some parts (the choir, transept and tower) date from the 13th century; others (such as the 15th-century nave and side aisles) from the Late Gothic period. The bell tower was added at the end of the 17th century. Neo-Gothic ornaments (gables, crockets, gargoyles and pinnacles) were added to the side walls during 19th-century restoration work. The painter Pieter Bruegel the Elder was buried here in 1569 (marble epitaph in the third chapel of the right-hand aisle). Bruegel lived in Brussels at the end of his life: his house can be seen, much restored, at 132, rue Haute.

THE BRIGITTINE CHAPEL. The district once bordered by the Senne and Rue Haute has altered greatly. Of the numerous religious institutions (convents of Ursulines, Visitandines and Brigittines) established here in the 17th century, only the Chapelle des Brigittines (1663) now remains, cut off from its surroundings by the railway. The design of the chapel's gabled façade is reminiscent of traditional local houses, while the ornamentation belongs to the Baroque repertory (volutes, broken pediments, niches). The chapel is now used as a theater and for exhibitions.

NURSERY SCHOOL. The nursery school at 40 rue St-Ghislain is one of the area's interesting buildings; built by Victor Horta in 1845, it is still in use today. The building is both functional and innovative. Its façade is almost reminiscent of typical railway-station design; behind it is a single space, brightly lit through a glass roof.

PLACE DU JEU-DE-BALLE. The RUE DES RENARDS runs at right angles to Rue Haute, connecting the antique dealers of the Sablon with the flea-market traders on Place du Jeu-de-Balle. The square was created in 1851, at the same time as RUE BLAES, as part of a renovation project for the area; it was designed for the very popular game of pelota ● *71*. The old

A VICTORY FOR LOCAL RESIDENTS
In 1969 the residents of the Marolles organized a campaign against huge property-development schemes in the quarter. A plaque at no. 10, rue Montferrat commemorates their victory. This proved to be the start of an exemplary urban-renovation program.

CITÉ FONTAINAS
This is a semicircular group of sixteen houses, overlooking the boulevard. It was built by Trappeniers in 1867, to house retired local teachers. The classical façade matched the style of the large private houses that were being built along the boulevard at the time.

Porte de Hal in the 19th century (lithograph).

ART NOUVEAU AT ST-GILLES
A detour via Rue Vanderschrick is a must for all Art Nouveau fans. The architect-developer Ernest Biérot built nos. 1–25 here between 1900 and 1902.

THE HOUSE OF ERASMUS
This house, on the Rue du Chapitre at Anderlecht, was the great humanist's home for five months, in 1521, when visiting his friend Canon Wijckmann. Today

the building (late 15th century) houses a museum that has important works by Metsys, Dürer, Holbein, Bosch and Poussin. Also worthy of note are the leather furniture and paneling from Malines (15th and 16th centuries) and valuable books from that period.

Caserne des Pompiers (Fire Station), built in the French classical style by Joseph Poelaert in 1861, is now used for shops and municipal housing.

CITÉ REINE-ASTRID. This municipal housing estate, between Rue de la Rasière and Rue Pieremans, was inspired by the "phalansteries" of French social theorist Charles Fourier (1772–1837). Built in 1914, the apartment blocks are arranged in six parallel rows joined by internal courtyards: the emphasis is on collective organization. The design, by architects Hellemans and Brunfaut, was determined by principles of functionality and hygiene that were very modern at the time. The chromatic brickwork shows the influence of Art Nouveau style.

HÔPITAL ST-PIERRE. Built on the site of a 13th-century leper-house with the same name, St-Pierre is still one of the city's main hospitals. Today's hospital was built by Jean-Baptiste Dewin in 1929, and is undergoing major renovation work.

BEYOND THE PORTE DE HAL

THE PORTE DE HAL. South of the Marolles, the Porte de Hal marks the end of the Pentagon. The boulevards of the Petite Ceinture (inner ring road), built on Napoleon's orders, starting in 1810, followed the outline of the second city wall (1357–83). The Porte de Hal is all that remains of this wall. Restored in the neo-Gothic style during the 19th century, it now houses the Musée du Folklore.

ST-GILLES. On the other side of Porte de Hal is the district of St-Gilles, which developed during the 19th century around the main traffic routes passing through the vicinity. It has a number of public buildings and amenities (prison, town hall, park etc.). Recent renovations reflect a concern to integrate the old bourgeois institutions into the fabric of the modern city. On Sundays the Marché du Midi takes place in front of the railway station, selling diverse mixture of goods.

ANDERLECHT ★. Further to the west is the district of Anderlecht, a busy and unpretentious shopping area which still has a number of charming medieval remains. Situated on the Chemin de St-Jacques, the COLLEGIATE CHURCH OF STS-PIERRE-PAUL-ET-GUIDON had a large chapter of canons, one of whom – Adrien Florisz Boyens (1459–1523) – became Pope Adrian VI. The church was built between 1350 (south porch) and 1470 (St-Sacrement Chapel, transept and chevet); it has mural paintings from the 15th and 16th centuries, and sculptures from the 14th and 15th centuries. The Chapel of Saint Guidon dates from the 16th century. The pillars of a Roman villa were used in the crypt (11th century). The PETIT BÉGUINAGE ▲ *165* was built to house eight nuns in the 13th century and extended in the 14th century; it is open to visitors.

AVENUE LOUISE

Avenue Louise was built in 1864 to connect the city center to the Bois de la Cambre. The avenue, a mile long and 180 feet wide, was rapidly built up with large private houses and became the fashionable place for a stroll, ousting the Allée Verte along the canal. Opulent residential areas grew up on either side of the avenue; today this is still a wealthy area with many luxury shops – especially toward the city center, around the Goulet Louise. The avenue soon became part of the network of boulevards designed as a framework for the residential suburbs to the southeast of Brussels, under Leopold II.

HÔTEL SOLVAY. Victor Horta excelled himself in designing this palatial residence (no. 224), in 1894–8, for industrialist Armand Solvay ▲ *184*. He also designed all the furniture and silverware for it. The focal point of the building is the monumental staircase, crowned by a glass roof which lights a magnificent neo-Impressionist painting by Theo van Rysselberghe.
HÔTEL MAX-HALLET (above), at no. 346, was also designed by Horta.

QUARTIER LOUISE-DEFACQZ

This residential suburb was developed between 1890 and 1905, and it was here that the architects of the Art Nouveau period created some of their most important œuvres. In 1893, just a few streets from each other, and almost simultaneously, Victor Horta built the MAISON TASSEL (6 rue Paul-Émile-Janson) and Paul Hankar built his MAISON PERSONNELLE (71 rue Defacqz). These two buildings, despite their very different idioms, are regarded as the earliest examples of Art Nouveau architecture.

AN ART NOUVEAU TOUR ● *98***.** Paul Hankar created one of the most impressive showpiece façades of Brussels Art Nouveau at 48, rue Defacqz for the house of painter Albert Ciamberlani, its two stories covered with sgraffiti. The back garden of this house connects with that of the Hôtel José-Ciamberlani

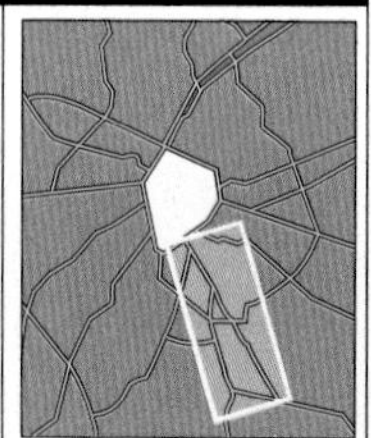

◷ One day

Paul Hankar's House, watercolor by P. Guimard.

EQUESTRIAN AVENUE
The Avenue Louise is a wide thoroughfare lined with rows of trees, with separate paths for pedestrians and horse riders. The entrance to the Bois de la Cambre is marked by two neoclassical pavilions, formerly tollhouses. Since 1950 traffic has spoilt this famous avenue

A GREEN AREA
When the area around the two lakes of Ixelles was developed, it was decided that all the houses should have gardens in order to create a smooth transition between the buildings and their natural surroundings. Victor Besme was responsible for the present appearance of the lakes, with a paved border.

Above: Victor Horta's dining room. Below: *The Abbaye de la Cambre*, a painting by Van Asloot.

(23 rue Paul-Émile-Janson), built by the same architect in 1900. In 1898 another painter, René Janssens, commissioned Hankar to build his house-studio at no. 50 rue Defacqz. At the same time, architect Octave Van Rysselberghe built a private house for Paul Otlet (48 rue de Livourne); the interior was designed by Henry Van de Velde. A few years later, Octave Van Rysselberghe built his own home (83 rue de Livourne) here. Alongside these major works, houses by Albert Rosenboom (83 rue Paul-Émile-Janson) and Armand Van Waesberghe (85 rue Faider) provide further examples of the popularity of Art Nouveau at the turn of the century.

THE HORTA MUSEUM. At 25 rue Américaine, in St-Gilles, is the house which was once the private residence and studio of Victor Horta (1861–1947) from 1899 to 1919. The house demonstrates clearly Horta's break with 19th-century house design, with its interconnecting rooms, which tended to be dark. Here the building is lit by a central light well with a spectacular staircase crowned by a double glass roof. Colored-glass windows, mirrors, white

A very popular place of recreation for the public, the Bois de la Cambre has been modified to meet the needs of large numbers of visitors.

earthenware and wrought ironwork add to the impression of brightness. Not far from here are two more Art Nouveau buildings worth a detour: the Hôtel Hannon (1 avenue de la Jonction), now a photograph gallery, and Maison Les Hiboux (53, avenue Brugmann).

Around the Étangs d'Ixelles

Beyond Avenue Louise, on the other side of the Jardins du Roi, are the two lakes of Ixelles. Before 1850 there were seven lakes in the Maelbeek valley, which runs from the Abbaye de la Cambre (where the river still has its source) up to the village of Schaerbeek; these two are the sole survivors. Victor Besme designed a new quarter on the land that had been reclaimed, from 1871 onward. Around the turn of the century this became a favorite area for Art Nouveau architects. Most of the houses on its steeply sloping streets (Rue de la Vallée, Rue du Lac, Rue Vilain-XIII) were designed by talented architects, though less well known than those who worked around the Avenue Louise. The quarter is still very stylish, and much in demand today. Among the architects who worked here were the Delune brothers and Ernest Blérot, who created at least fifteen houses here, most of them decorated with sgraffiti.

Abbaye de la Cambre

In 1201 the Duke of Lower Lotharingia and his wife, Mathilda, gave money to a young woman named Gisèle so that she could found an abbey, which was built near to the source of the Maelbeek. The building suffered serious damage during the Wars of Religion, and was rebuilt in the 17th and 18th centuries. At this stage it was one of the wealthiest religious foundations in the area. The church, (14th century), cloisters (16th century), main courtyard and terraced gardens (18th century) make this an exceptional architectural complex.

School of art. In 1926 Henry Van de Velde founded the Institut Supérieur des Arts Décoratifs de la Cambre. The revolutionary program of studies here was very similar to that of Gropius' Bauhaus in Germany, based on the principle of collaboration between art and industry. In the 1930's the institute was a center of modernist theory and production. The original buildings still house the departments dedicated to the visual arts.

Bois de la Cambre
This is one of the most beautiful public parks of the 19th century: a forest-like, landscaped park covering an area of 300 acres. It was created by the city authorities, from 1862 onward, under the direction of Eduard Keilig, a German landscape architect based in Brussels. The park was created on a mile of land taken from the Forest of Soignes ▲ *188*.

A resurrected façade
The Church of St-Augustin (1620) was demolished when the Place de Brouckère was built ▲ *166*; its Baroque façade was dismantled and re-erected, in 1893, on the Parvis de la Trinité in Ixelles. Not far from this is the leafy Place du Châtelain, with its restaurants and fashionable cafés: a very pleasant place to take a break.

The chariot group on top of the triumphal arch represents Brabant; allegories of the eight other Belgian provinces stand at the base of the arches.

The museums of the Cinquantenaire
The splendid displays of ancient Mesopotamian, Egyptian, Far-Eastern and Pre-Colombian treasures in the Musées Royaux d'Art et d'Histoire deserve a special mention; there are also extensive displays of decorative arts from the Middle Ages to Art Deco. A motor museum (Autoworld) and a military-history museum are located here, too.

The Parc du Cinquantenaire was the starting point of the first phase of urban expansion in the 19th century and the focus of the network of boulevards which shapes the elegant suburbs. This made the arch a sort of gateway to the city; later it was also to be linked with the colonial institutions that Leopold II planned to establish at Tervueren. In this way the king sought to demonstrate within the capital both the greatness of the young nation and its colonial future.

Parc du Cinquantenaire

The esplanade of the Cinquantenaire was built over a former military parade ground. Squares, roundabouts and parks were created, arranged around a few main roads and crossroads. The project started with the celebrations of 1880, commemorating fifty years of Belgian Independence. Gédéon Bordiau was commissioned to design the Cinquantenaire and the development of the northeastern quarter; the project was carried out in several stages, up to the end of the century.

An exhibition center. A complex designed for exhibiting the products of Belgian industry was created in the Parc du Cinquantenaire. Leopold II commissioned Bordiau to design two huge metal halls (1880); their span of 230 feet, made by the Cockerill factories, was a considerable engineering feat. Modifications were made for the international exhibitions of 1888 and 1897. There were further alterations in 1905, for the seventy-fifth anniversary of the kingdom, with the construction of an archway designed by Charles Girault, architect of the Petit Palais in Paris.

Finally came the construction of a semicircular double colonnade (1918), decorated with mosaics depicting the glorification of Belgium.

MUSÉES ROYAUX D'ART ET D'HISTOIRE. In 1888 the decision was taken to establish a museum of art and history here, to house collections going back to Charles V ● *33* and Albert and Isabella ● *34*. Some thirty rooms were recently reopened following renovation, with new displays.

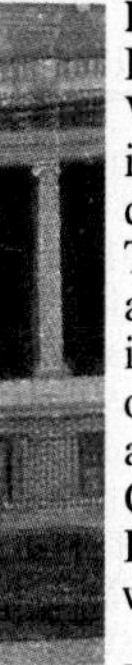

IN THE PARK. THE PAVILION OF HUMAN PASSIONS, the first building created by Victor Horta (1889), was built to house an impressive carved relief by Jef Lambeaux depicting the perversity of human passions. The subject scandalized the establishment, and the building was closed three days after its opening. It can now be visited by groups on request. The former Panorama of Cairo, a circular building decorated with views of Cairo and the Nile, created by the painter Émile Wauters for the exhibition of 1897, was converted into a MOSQUE in 1977.

PALAIS STOCLET

The Palais Stoclet stands half a mile away, on Avenue de Tervueren. It was commissioned in 1905 by Belgian banker Adolphe Stoclet, who was based in Vienna at the time; the architect was Josef Hoffmann. The building's unique decorations were produced by the Werkstätte, the Austrian workshops founded by Hoffmann himself. Two mosaics, 23 feet long, by Gustav Klimt should be mentioned: *Expectation* and *Fulfillment*, sumptuous compositions in mother-of-pearl, ceramics and glass, in the spirit of his famous work *The Kiss*.

QUARTIER DES SQUARES

The northeastern quarter, known as the "quarter of the squares", was planned in 1875. The parks with their many statues are very popular today; houses in the eclectic and Art Nouveau styles combine to create an unusually homogenous and extremely attractive area. Victor Horta designed three private houses here, including one for BARON VAN EETVELDE, general secretary of the Colonial Ministry. This house, at no. 4 avenue Palmerston, has a strikingly original façade with metal framework. The interior is arranged around a central spiral staircase, which winds around an octagonal winter garden; it is lit by a huge glass roof. The interior uses precious materials, covering a harmonious range of olive- and orange-greens, in its mosaic floors, onyx paneling and mahogany ceilings. This may seem very refined today, but Mme Van Eetvelde deplored the use of metal, which she considered "vulgar". Next to this building, at no. 6, Horta designed an apartment block in a strikingly different style; also, opposite, at no. 3, he created the HÔTEL DEPREZ-VAN DE

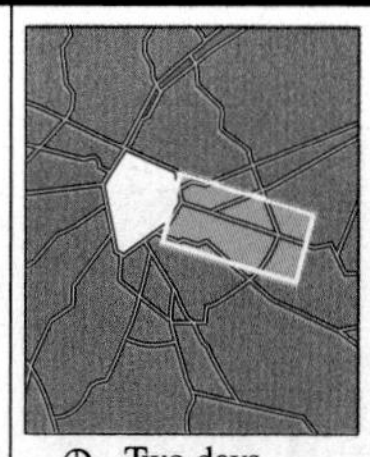

◷ Two days

ART NOUVEAU MASTERPIECE

The Palais Stoclet is perfectly preserved but closed to the public: this has if anything enhanced its reputation. On the exterior, smooth walls and asymetrical shapes prefigure modernist rationalism. However, the precious materials favored by Art Nouveau are still employed here (Norwegian white marble, bronze), as are historical motifs (the tower crowned by a flower-dome). The building's ornamentation is impressive and original, even though by this stage Art Nouveau was in decline in the city where it had flourished.

MAISON ST-CYR
At no. 11 square Ambiorix.

VELDE (1896). The neighboring streets offer examples of the work of other talented architects, including Hobé, Govaerts and Van Waesberghe. Gustave Strauven designed a splendidly extravagant façade for the Maison St-Cyr: the profusion of wrought ironwork, the striking shapes of the bay windows and the general exuberance of the design disguise the narrow dimensions of the house (a mere 13 feet) and its conventional structure.

PARC LÉOPOLD AND THE CITÉ SCIENTIFIQUE

Parc Léopold was created during the expansion of the city in the 19th century, as part of the development of the Quartier Léopold. A preliminary design by Fuchs in 1851 converted this former aristocratic estate into a zoological garden. The architect Alphonse Balat added the Victoria Regia Glasshouse, a precursor of the great glasshouse with palm trees at Laeken ▲ *173*. When the zoo went bankrupt in 1876, the city authorities took over the park; in 1880 it was renamed after the first two kings of Belgium and dedicated to scientific purposes. The natural history collections were housed in a former convent, and the glasshouses of botanist-explorer J.J. Linden were installed in the park. The idea of a "cité scientifique" was born at the start of the 20th century. The University of Brussels ▲ *186* decided to build its scientific institutes and School of Commerce here, with the financial backing of three industrialists, Ernest and Armand Solvay and Raoul Warocqué ▲ *293*, and bankers. Later the Pasteur Institute was added. The Solvay Library (recently restored) was created to promote the scientific study of social phenomena. Appropriately enough, the building was designed by sociologist E. Waxweiller.

THE WIERTZ MUSEUM
Antoine Wiertz (1806–65) was an artist of excess, in both the scale and sensationalism of his works. A Romantic painter deeply influenced by Rubens, he persuaded the Belgian government to build a huge studio for him near the Quartier Léopold. This has now been converted into a museum that houses the majority of his works, ranging from vast canvases such as *The Fall of the Giants* to more intimate portraits such as *The Beautiful Rosine*.

MUSÉE ROYAL D'HISTOIRE NATURELLE. Founded in 1876, the natural history museum was extended at the end of the 19th century, then again in the 1930's. It houses the awesome group of iguanodons discovered at Bernissart in 1878; the dinosaur galleries were designed with educational purposes in mind, and their pleasing layout has been preserved. More recent displays cover the fields of paleontology, mineralogy, paleobotanics, anthropology and prehistory. The museum regularly presents temporary exhibitions.

QUARTIER DE L'EUROPE

This quadrangular area, covering approximately 30 acres, grew up around two main centers. One of these is the ROND-POINT SCHUMMAN, where the European Commission and Council of Ministers are based; the other is the Quartier Léopold, with the huge European Parliament complex. The star-shaped PALAIS BERLAYMONT was the European Commission's first building, built by architects De Vestel, Gilson and

The Résidence Palace included a restaurant, a theater, reception rooms, a gym and a magnificent swimming pool in the Pompeian style, which can still be visited.

THE RÉSIDENCE PALACE
The Art Deco Résidence Palace was built by Michel Polak between 1923 and 1926, at no. 155, rue de la Lois; it was the largest complex of luxury apartments in Europe at the time. It was later converted into offices and incorporated into the European complex.

ERNEST SOLVAY
Born in 1838, the son of a salt refiner, Ernest Solvay was a

passionate scientist. His research led to the economic production of liquid ammonia and sodium bicarbonate (his invention of artificial sodium was to become the basis of the family's industrial empire). Solvay also took a keen interest in social questions: he established welfare organizations for employees in his factories and, as a senator, advocated workers' reforms.

Polak between 1962 and 1966; the shape of the building was modeled on the UNESCO headquarters in Paris. The European Parliament complex, designed by a group of Belgian architects, is scheduled for completion in 1996. THE LÉOPOLD BUILDING (nicknamed the "Caprice des Dieux" by locals) houses the conference center. Two semicircular units surround a central building crowned by a glass roof; office blocks line a pedestrian zone (the Mall) with the railway and new station beneath it.

RESIDENTS' PROTESTS. The proliferation of office blocks around these complexes have brought protests from groups of local residents since 1965. The protestors were seeking to save residential areas, and to retain a mixture of architectural functions in all districts. Although they were not able to prevent the demolition of the 19th-century artists' studios in Rue Wiertz and Rue Godecharle, it is likely that the almost rustic Rue Vautier, opposite the park, may now be spared.

QUARTIER LÉOPOLD. Entrusted to architect T.-F. Suys in 1838, the Quartier Léopold was the first large-scale extension of the capital; it was based on a neoclassical geometric design, starting from the avenues of the Parc Royal. Today its opulent private residences have made way for office blocks. Almost all that remains is the peaceful Square Frère-Orban with the CHURCH OF ST-JOSEPH (Suys, 1849), inspired by Trinità dei Monti in Rome, and the neo-Renaissance Conseil d'Etat (formerly a royal residence, the Palais d'Assche). The PLACE DU LUXEMBOURG, with its cafés and restaurants, has also survived. The monument dedicated to industrialist John Cockerill (Cattier, 1870) and the station (Saintenoy, 1889) have both been dwarfed by the colossal scale of the European institutions.

The Palais de la Folle Chanson was created by A. Courtens in 1925.

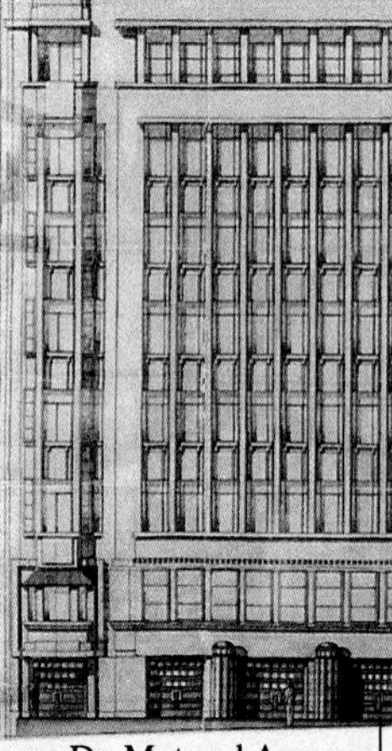

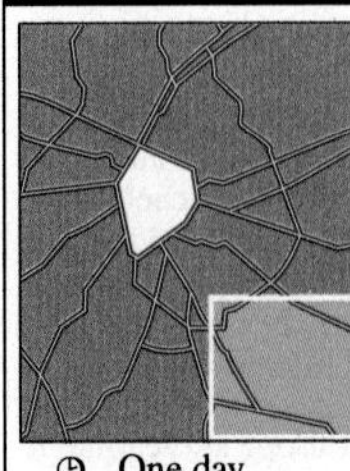

One day

For the tour below, unlike most of the others in Brussels, it is best to drive.

ART DECO AND MODERNISM

All the buildings that can be seen along the route from Avenue Émile-Duray to Avenue Franklin-Roosevelt date from the 1920's and 1930's, the period when Art Deco and modernism held sway. The development of new quarters in the city was spurred on both by the need for reconstruction after World War One and by the enthusiasm of the new generation of architects. Avenue De-Mot and Avenue Émile-Duray were created in 1910 to mark the entrance to the international exhibition. The Avenue des Nations (now Avenue Franklin-Roosevelt) continued on the same course. Affluent citizens moved into the new quarter, commissioning avant-garde architects to build houses, apartments and luxury villas. Stop at nos. 62–8, avenue Émile-Duray, built by Camille Damman in 1924 and inspired by the geometrical forms and hieratic figures of the Palais Stoclet ▲ *183*. Three remarkable Art Deco buildings stand at Rond-Point de l'Étoile, the junction between Avenue Louise and the outer ring road: the PALAIS DE LA FOLLE CHANSON at no. 2 (above); RÉSIDENCE ERNESTINE at no. 3; and the Palais du Congo at no. 2, avenue du Congo. The last two were built by Jean-Florian Collin, in a similar style, in 1939 and 1930 respectively. On Avenue Franklin-Roosevelt the most interesting buildings are nos. 27 and 29 (built by Henry Van de Velde in 1932) and, in particular, the HOUSE built by Michel Polak for BARON LOUIS EMPAIN in 1931 (no. 67). The latter, with its massive presence, the horizontal structure emphasized by string-courses, its granite facing, geometrical ornamentation and sumptuous interior decoration, is an outstanding example of Belgian architecture of the interwar years (it is not open to visitors). No. 52 is also striking: it was built by Adrien Blomsme in 1928, with bas-reliefs by sculptor Ossip Zadkine.

UNIVERSITÉ LIBRE DE BRUXELLES (ULB). The university was founded by Théodore Verhaegen in 1834. Initially it expanded into Parc Léopold ▲ *184*, before spreading along the avenue on the Plaine du Solbosch in 1922.

THE GLAVERBELL BUILDING
This remarkable product of 1960's architecture stands at no. 166, chaussée de la Hulpe. The impressive ring-shaped construction (380 feet in diameter, on four stories) surrounds an internal garden.

THE UNIVERSITY
The main building was designed by Alexis Dumont, in the Baroque style of the Netherlands.

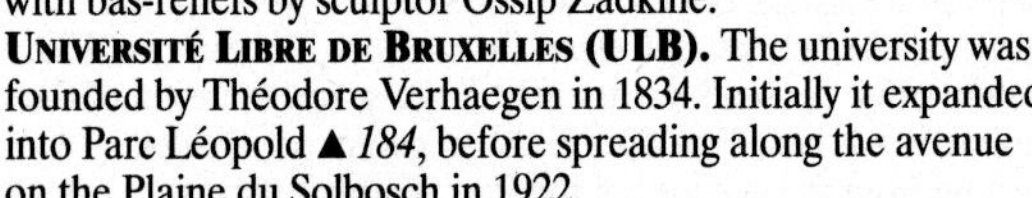

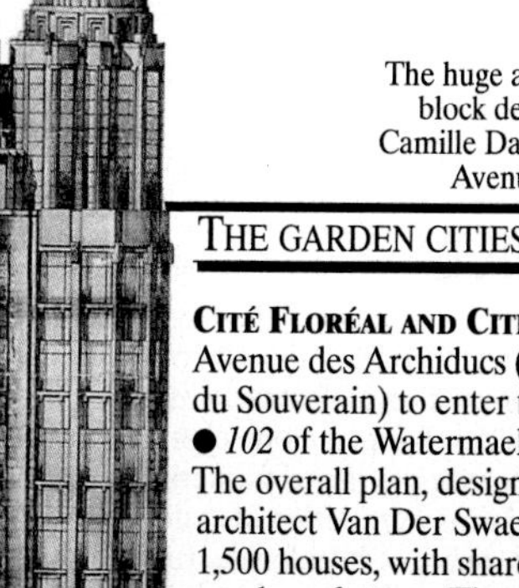

The huge apartment block designed by Camille Damman on Avenue Duray.

THE GARDEN CITIES

CITÉ FLORÉAL AND CITÉ DU LOGIS. Take Avenue des Archiducs (left off the Boulevard du Souverain) to enter the two garden cities ● *102* of the Watermael-Boitsfort district. The overall plan, designed by landscape architect Van Der Swaelmen, provided for 1,500 houses, with shared amenities and a number of stores. The greenery, public spaces and residential buildings were all planned with equal care. CITÉ FLORÉAL can be identified by its yellow window frames; it is dominated by the Fer à Cheval (The Horseshoe), a ten-story tower block designed by Eggericx in 1926–8. CITÉ DU LOGIS, arranged around the Place des Trois-Tilleuls, is larger, with green window frames and doors.

KAPPELLEVELD GARDEN CITY. Louis Van Der Swaelmen designed the overall plan for this garden city. The four districts within it were designed by the architects Hoste, Pompe, Hoeben and Rubbers. The city has 440 houses altogether; their nineteen different designs illustrate the diversity of modernism.

MUSÉE VAN BUUREN

The house of David and Alice Van Buuren at 21 avenue Léo-Ererra, in Uccle, is a monument to Art Deco: the original interiors are still intact. The house was designed by architects Govaerts and Van Vaerenbergh in 1927; its intimate interior displays a collection of paintings by old masters (including a *Fall of Icarus* by Pieter Bruegel the Elder) and modern artists. Adjoining the building are attractive gardens, with a maze, rose garden and exotic plants.

LOUVAIN-EN-WOLUWÉ

The architect Lucien Kroll created a group of buildings on this site: the Mémé (Maison Médicale) clinic, the ÉCOLE MATERNELLE (nursery school) and CRÈCHE, and the METRO STATION. He also designed the adjoining public space. These buildings are a unique illustration of ideological trends in Brussels after May 1968. For example, the overall design of the Mémé, the product of an extensive dialogue with students, expresses a vision of community life. The university authorities were horrified by Kroll's designs and withdrew the rest of the project from him.

The park at Woluwé is just one of the large open spaces for recreation and leisure in the city.

THE FOREST OF SOIGNES ★

Today's national park is a mere fragment of the huge forest which in the Middle Ages stretched from the Thiérache to the Louvain region. The forest, a royal domain, was not used only for hunting: it was plundered for iron ore, charcoal, and wood for burning and for beams; privileged farmers grazed their flocks here, and stud farms were set up in it; and it also served as a very useful source of land for the rulers of one of the most built-up regions of Europe. At a later date religious institutions were founded here, which now make pleasant excursions for the residents of Brussels. The forest currently stretches over an area of approximately 10,000 acres, jointly administered by Flanders, Brussels and Wallonia. At the beginning of the 19th century the forest covered 27,000 acres; the King of the Netherlands gave it to the "General Society for Promoting National Industry", which he created in 1822. After Belgian independence this company sold off a large part of the forest before returning it to the new national government in 1843. The new proprietors cleared large sections of the forest, making way for country estates, an agricultural complex and country houses. These large pieces of land have themselves been divided up more recently into smaller lots for new houses. The Bois de la Cambre ▲ *181*, a huge urban park, was created when the city of Brussels acquired a section of the forest in 1861. The Parc Solvay de la Hulpe, formerly owned by the Belgian chemist Ernest Solvay ▲ *185*, was also cut out of the Forest of Soignes, covering an area of more than 500 acres; the estate is now open to visitors. The Argentine river runs past the house and through the grounds, creating a setting of great beauty that will delight nature lovers: as well as beautiful cultivated plants (especially

◷ One and a half days

FOREST LANDSCAPE
The forest's appearance today is the result of intensive management, begun by Charles V in the mid 16th century and improved in the late 18th century. All trees cut down were systematically replaced to supplement the forest's natural regeneration, and gradually beech ■ *26* came to predominate. Today the vast stretches of evenly spaced trees of the same age and height give Soignes a distinctive, cathedral-like appearance.

The interior of the Musée de l'Afrique Centrale (drawing by the architect, Charles Girault, made in 1909).

“Now I had entered a dense forest, long and wide, and could not see any way in or out.”

G. Chastellain (15th century)

The series of tapestries showing Maximilian I hunting are set in the Forest of Soignes.

rhododendrons and azaleas), you can see rare species of wild flowers such as inulas and bee orchids, while in the ponds and woods you may spot crested grebes, kingfishers and black woodpeckers ■ *28*.

Tervueren ★

The Avenue de Tervueren was built at the end of the 19th century to connect the capital with a major scientific and residential complex that was being planned by Leopold II. Tervueren was initially a Carolingian settlement; it expanded after a ducal residence was built here in the 12th century.

Royal projects. The Tervueren estate still bears the mark of the projects planned by Leopold II, starting in 1895. Alongside the Museum of the Congo (now the magnificent Musée de l'Afrique Centrale), a college and research center were to be set up to train European officers for the African and Asian colonies. This grand scheme never came into being: only the museum was completed, commissioned from the Parisian architect Charles Girault and opening at the back onto French formal gardens. The Bois des Capucins, a former hunting estate to the south of the village of Tervueren, was partly converted into a “geographical arboretum” and opened to the public in 1905, with the same educational aims.

Chateau de Rixensart ★
This château, in Brabant, is less than 12 miles from Brussels. Despite its Renaissance-style façade, it was built in the 17th century; it is surrounded by beautiful formal gardens attributed to Le Nôtre.

Musée de l'Afrique Centrale
The museum was founded to make Belgians aware of the history and riches of their African colony. Since 1960 its collections have been extended to embrace art, ethnography, zoology and botany, and to cover a wider geographical area.

“Waterloo, Waterloo, Waterloo, mournful plain/ Like water boiling in a brimming pot/ In your arena of woods, hills, valleys,/ Pale death mixed the dark batallions.”
Victor Hugo

WATERLOO

THE BATTLEFIELD. The wide stretches of farmland along the main road leading to Charleroi, 12 miles south of Brussels, are the site of the famous battlefield where, on June 18, 1815, the 74,000 soldiers of Napoleon's army met the 77,000 men led by the Duke of Wellington ● *38*. The defeat of the imperial armies brought about Napoleon's downfall.

THE VILLAGE. Waterloo is also a village, whose residents included E.-P. Jacobs, the cartoonist who created Blake and Mortimer ● *59*. At the center of the village stands the CHURCH OF ST-JOSEPH, which has many commemorative plaques. Opposite is the WELLINGTON MUSEUM, a former inn where the English general set up his headquarters; it now displays his memoirs and sketches of the different stages of the battle. Several local farms were caught up in the action: the manor of Hougoumont; La Haie-Sainte, at the heart of the English batallions; La Belle-Alliance, meeting place of the victors Blücher and Wellington. The farm of La Caillou at Vieux-Genappe was Napoleon's headquarters; it was converted into a NAPOLEONIC MUSEUM in 1951.

THE BUTTE DU LION
This artficial hill was created by the Dutch around 1820 on the spot where Prince William of Orange was wounded. The whole battlefield can be seen from the top. A small group of museums and cafés has grown up at the foot of the hill. Visit the “Panorama of the Battle”: on the walls of this building the painter L. Dumoulin painted a continuous sequence of battle scenes.

LOUVAIN-LA-NEUVE

The first new town to be created in Belgium since 1666, Louvain-la-Neuve, situated to the south of Brussels, was founded in 1971 to house the French-speaking section of the Catholic University of Louvain. The town has expanded rapidly. The university buildings are integrated into the fabric of the town, which is designed specifically for pedestrian use – the railway station, parking lots and vehicular traffic all being banished below concrete paving in the town center. The town has a science park (which specializes in high technology), modern sports facilities and cultural institutions whose reputation has spread far and wide; these include the Théâtre Jean-Vilar and the Museum of Louvain-la-Neuve (with works by Delvaux, Magritte and others). There are guided tours, starting at the museum.

IN AND AROUND NAMUR

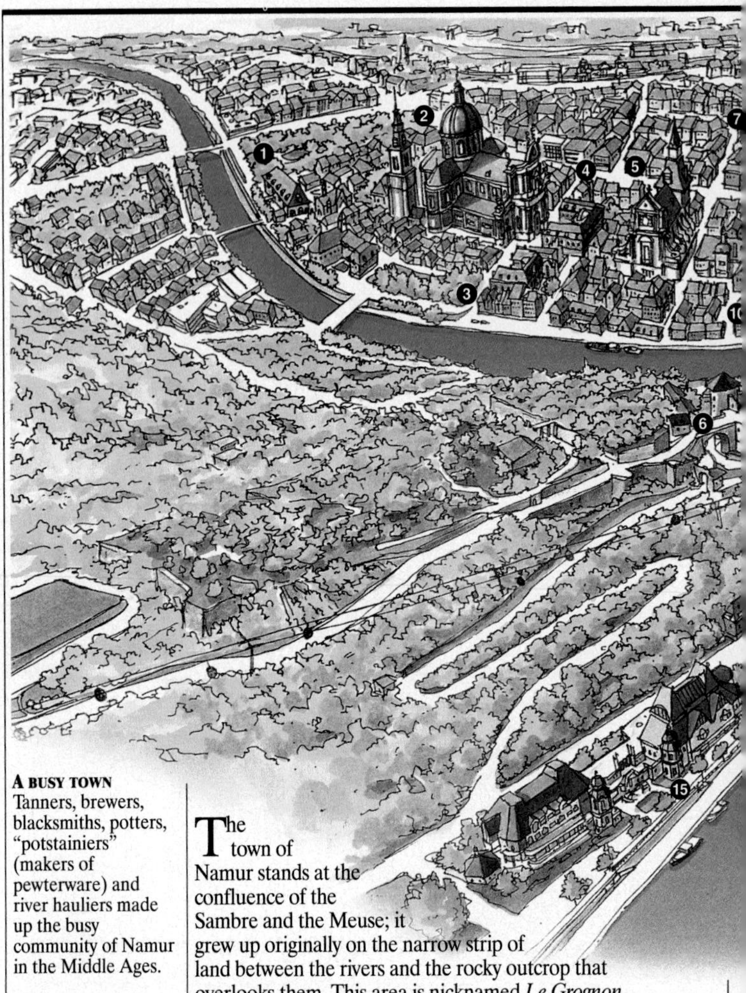

1. ARSENAL
2. ST-AUBAIN CATHEDRAL
3. HÔTEL DE GROESBEECK-DE-CROIX
4. PALAIS PROVINCIAL

A BUSY TOWN
Tanners, brewers, blacksmiths, potters, "potstainiers" (makers of pewterware) and river hauliers made up the busy community of Namur in the Middle Ages.

STRATEGIC SITE
Namur occupies a strategic site for controlling the lower Meuse valley. In the 17th century 10,000 soldiers lived here, alongside 9,000 civilians. Nine religious communities, established by Philip II of Spain, between them covered one third of the district known as the Quartier de la Corbeille.

The town of Namur stands at the confluence of the Sambre and the Meuse; it grew up originally on the narrow strip of land between the rivers and the rocky outcrop that overlooks them. This area is nicknamed *Le Grognon* ("the snorter"), because it is shaped like a pig's snout.

BEGINNINGS. In Roman times a settlement grew up around a river port on the left bank of the Sambre. The grid-like layout of this first town still persists in the street pattern of Namur today. Potters and jewelers were active in the town, which stretched for little more than 300 yards at this time. Christian shrines, including the Collegiate Church of Notre-Dame, were built between the rocky spur and the Meuse.

The Entry of Imperial Troops into Namur, on November 25, 1790 (engraving).

◷ One day

“Namur, before your walls Greece would have laid siege for twenty years in vain.”
Nicholas Boileau

Feudal fortifications. In the 10th century Count Bérenger built a stronghold on the spur, and Namur became a feudal holding. With the end of the Norman raids and the return of peace (11th and 12th centuries) the town grew rapidly in terms of both population and prosperity, and the Neuville quarter came into being. New city walls were built as the town expanded, reaching their furthest limit in the 15th century; at this time the district known as the Quartier de la Corbeille was built up, between the Sambre, the Meuse and the hills.
European power struggles. After a period of Burgundian rule Namur and its territory fell to the Spanish (from 1506), at which time Calvinism was gaining ground in Europe. In 1559 Namur became the seat of one of the new bishoprics, the spearheads of the Counter-Reformation led by Philip II of Spain. Philip set up camp here, from which

he set out to fight the Calvinists, and encouraged the establishment of religious orders. The city was captured by Louis XIV in 1692, reconquered by the combined forces of the English, Spanish and Dutch in 1695, taken by France again in 1701, and by Holland in 1715.

The Siege of Namur in 1692 (J.-B. Martin).

ART OF WARFARE
Namur's defenses reflect the evolution of military techniques – medieval (the fortified town was the last refuge of surrounding populations), classical (a bastioned wall allowed the town to resist while awaiting reinforcements) and modern (the wall is replaced by scattered forts, forming a barricade intended to hold back invaders).

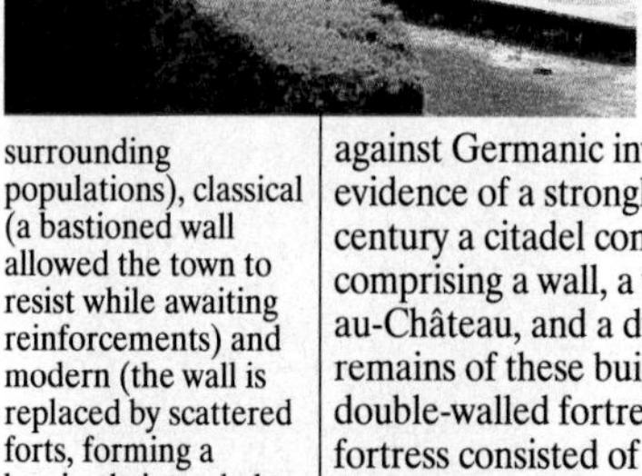

MODERN TIMES. The industrial revolution passed Namur by: the town retained a purely military function. In 1880 nine individual forts were built, with concrete walls and steel domes; these played a vital role during both world wars.

LOCAL TRADITIONS. The members of the whimsical Académie des Quarante Molons ("Academy of Forty Liars") are called *molons* (derived from *mintes*, an old word for lies). They pride themselves on elevating lying to a fine art form, only admitting to membership "the most worthy liars of Namur". Nowadays they devote their energies to charitable causes. Another local tradition is that of the *échasseurs*: combatants on stilts ● *70*, who confront each other in spectacular jousts.

THE CITADEL ★

HISTORY. In the 3rd and 4th centuries the Romans established a fortification at the end of the spur, to defend the settlement against Germanic invasions. From the 10th century there is evidence of a stronghold with a wooden keep. In the 12th century a citadel complex grew up around this center, comprising a wall, a well, a collegiate church called St-Pierre-au-Château, and a dungeon; though all built of stone, nothing remains of these buildings today. Between 1235 and 1245 a double-walled fortress replaced the old fortifications. The new fortress consisted of a wall with four towers (only the Tour aux Chartes and the Tour au Four survive), a keep (two of its towers are still standing) and the church. On the other side of

Between 1692 and 1703 the citadel of Namur became one of the largest fortifications in Europe.

the ditch stood an advance fortification, of which the last remnant is the Desseur Bordial Tower, incorporated in the Porte de Médiane. The César and Joyeuse towers were modified in the 15th century, with the advent of the cannon. Charles V had a citadel, the Médiane, built in front of the castle (1542–55): a self-contained miniature city for the use of soldiers protecting (and watching over) the town. The Terra Nova Fort (1633–83) was built to the west of the town during the Thirty Years' War. The Fort d'Orange, separate from the town's main defensive unit, was built on the Montagne du Diable in 1691, to defend a ravine, a weak point on the plateau. This fort doubled the area covered by the town's defenses, which were further extended by Louis XIV. The Dutch were the last to add to the defenses, in the 18th century, before the first fortress was destroyed (1782–1803).

Tour of the citadel. Today's citadel ● *88* follows the outline of its predecessor; it was built between 1816 and 1825. It consists of a keep (the Donjon), the Médiane and the Terra Nova. The arrangement of three lunettes and the artillery tower, all separate, was imitated from Napoleonic models; the cannons were kept in blockhouses. The neoclassical style of the whole can be seen most clearly in the infantry barracks, arsenal, forge and foundry. By 1860 the citadel had been overtaken by advances in weaponry, and it became a barracks. In 1939–40 a final series of alterations provided the underground fortifications with air conditioning, defenses against gas, and bomb-proof doors. A delightful open-air theater was added after the war.

Vault of the cathedral.

Quartier de la Corbeille

Parc Louise-Marie. This park, named after Queen Louise-Marie, wife of Leopold I, was created in 1878 among the remains of fortifications and a bridge. The ruins were used to create grottos.

The Arsenal ★. This was built by Vauban in 1693–5. Cannons and chariots were stored in the first story (which was divided into three sections),

Overexpansion
It soon became clear that the 200-acre area covered by the citadel made it difficult to defend. Gradually the outlying fortifications were abandoned.

Dismantling
The destruction of the old fortress was completed in 1803, on Napoleon's orders. He had pushed the borders of his Empire so far to the east that it no longer served any purpose for him.

The ceiling of the Church of St-Loup.

Louis XV style at Namur

The refuge of the former Abbey of Villers (1605) was used as the central body of the Hôtel de Groesbeeck, which replaced the abbey. This H-shaped mansion in Louis XV style was designed for Count Alexandre-François de Groesbeeck by Jean-Baptiste Chermann (1704–70), who was also in charge of rebuilding the cathedral.

rifles and tools in the second story and light equipment at the top.

The cathedral quarter. Head toward Place St-Aubain, leaving the Sambre. The old houses here still have windows with accolade lintels from the 16th century. The Collegiate Church of St-Aubain ★ with its Romanesque tower stood at the political heart of the medieval town. The present cathedral, by Italian architect Gaetano Pisoni, dates from 1751–67 and incorporates the Romanesque church, a medieval chapel and an early Christian cemetery. The church contains the heart of Don John of Austria, who died in Namur in 1578. The Diocesan Museum ★ (next to the cathedral) displays the cathedral treasures, among them a portable altarpiece (11th–12th century) and a reliquary containing two thorns from the Crown of Thorns (13th century). The Palais de Justice replaced the count's palace; its porchway (17th century) was built around the Tower of Jean de Namur, part of the city wall (12th–13th century). Opposite the cathedral, the Bishop's Palace (1730) has a vestibule decorated with stuccos by Moretti.

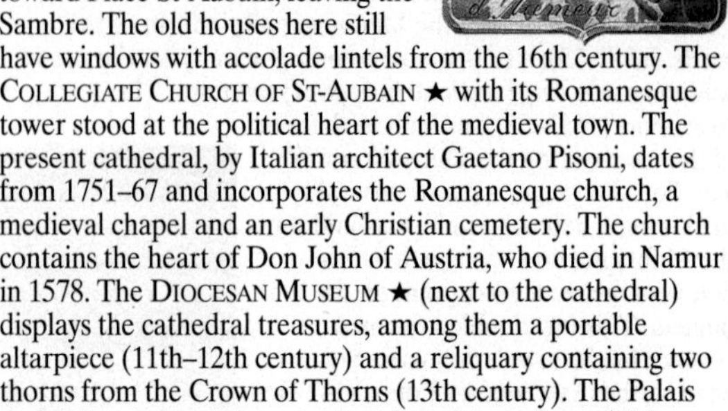

Hôtel de Groesbeeck de Croix ★. A dome decorated with rocaille stuccos crowns the staircase, which serves the various parts of the building (left). Everything has been preserved intact: stuccos, paneling, paintings, wallpaper, staircase. Exhibits include magnificent pieces of furniture in the Namur style and a collection of Vonêche crystal ★ ● *56* (below).

Church of St-Loup ★. The Jesuits moved into Namur in 1610. They founded a college and built the Church of St-Ignace (1621–45), later renamed St-Loup. The church is a splendid Baroque manifestation of the religious zeal that inspired its founder, Philip II of Spain, in his battles against the Calvinists.

Musée Félicien-Rops ★. The museum is at 12 rue Fumal, housed in an 18th-century building, which was converted in the 19th century. It is close to the Rue du Président, where Félicien Rops was born. Count Ferdinand Visart de Bocarmé donated his collection of works by Rops to the province of Namur some thirty years ago; later acquisitions have brought the total to about a thousand works, a quarter of which are on display.

In the town. From the Rops Museum, take Rue des Brasseurs (parallel to the Sambre). In 1704 it was decreed that wooden façades should be replaced by brick and stone: newer façades often mask earlier houses. The old markets for wool, wheat, hay and cloth stood in the area around Place Chanoine-Descamps and Place St-Jean. The Archeological Museum now occupies the former *Halle al' Chair* (meat market), built with brick and blue stone on a

A walk through old Namur

Take a leisurely stroll through the alleys of old Namur, stopping at one of the town's many cafés, where beer called *keute* used to be served.

Opposite page: the Café St-Loup.

limestone base in 1588–90. At 17 rue Julie-Billiard is the MAISON DES SŒURS DE NOTRE-DAME, the convent that houses the TREASURY OF HUGO D'OIGNIES ★ ▲ *198*. Hugo, a silversmith from Walcourt, came to Oignies at the end of the 12th century with his brothers Gilles, Robert and Jean, all priests. They founded a religious community; Hugo, who had become a monk, had his workshop there. In 1207 Marie d'Oignies, daughter of a wealthy family, came to live nearby and devoted herself to caring for lepers: this made the community famous and attracted the attention of Jacques de Vitry, a Parisian priest (later a cardinal). Vitry spent some years in the Holy Land: from here he sent back relics which, in the settings created by Hugo, attracted crowds of pilgrims. The treasury passed to the Diocesan Museum, and was finally housed in the convent. From here go to QUARTIER NEUVILLE. Tanners and metalworkers lived around Rue St-Nicolas, making use of the waters of the Hoyoux river, which flowed through the district.

THE BARRACKS AND QUARTIER LÉOPOLD. At the end of the 19th century the town was partly demilitarized and the large convent buildings were abandoned; after this, the north part of Namur grew rapidly. Town planners produced a design with roads radiating out from Square Leopold, next to the station (the railway follows the track of the old ramparts). Barracks and defensive buildings were replaced by large private houses. The town hall was built in RUE DE FER. This road, which follows the old road leading into the Roman town, was formerly known as the *Cuvierue*, because of the barrelmakers who lived here in the Middle Ages. The last stop is the *Musée des Arts Anciens du Namurois*, located in the Hôtel de Gaiffier d'Hestroy: the main building of this patrician residence dates from the 18th century.

FÉLICIEN ROPS
(1833–98)
A caricaturist and illustrator, Rops moved to Paris in 1874, after meeting Baudelaire when the latter was exiled in the Belgian capital.

Although his drawings are mainly of women, he also painted numerous landscapes. Above: *Le Gandin ivre* (*The Drunken Dandy*).

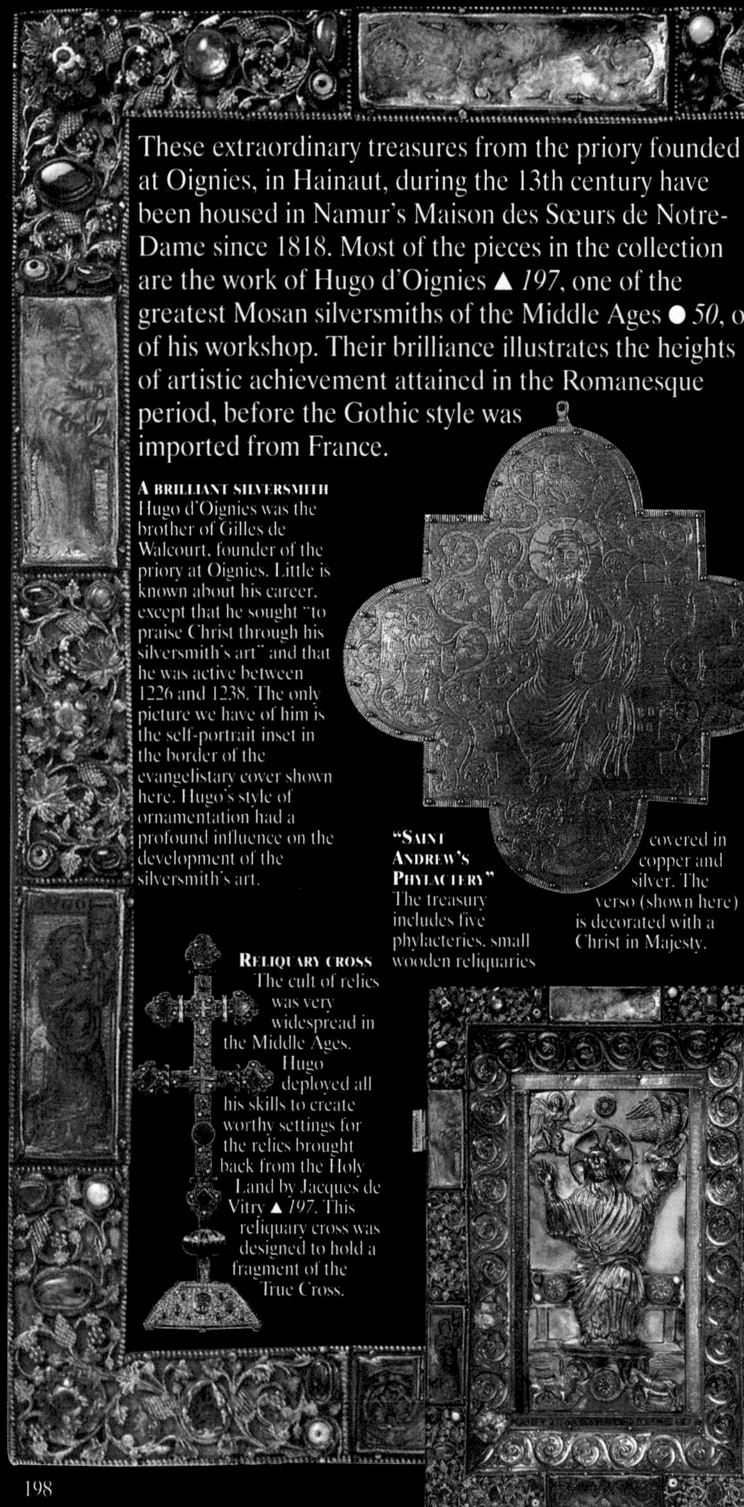

These extraordinary treasures from the priory founded at Oignies, in Hainaut, during the 13th century have been housed in Namur's Maison des Sœurs de Notre-Dame since 1818. Most of the pieces in the collection are the work of Hugo d'Oignies ▲ *197*, one of the greatest Mosan silversmiths of the Middle Ages ● *50*, o of his workshop. Their brilliance illustrates the heights of artistic achievement attained in the Romanesque period, before the Gothic style was imported from France.

A BRILLIANT SILVERSMITH Hugo d'Oignies was the brother of Gilles de Walcourt, founder of the priory at Oignies. Little is known about his career, except that he sought "to praise Christ through his silversmith's art" and that he was active between 1226 and 1238. The only picture we have of him is the self-portrait inset in the border of the evangelistary cover shown here. Hugo's style of ornamentation had a profound influence on the development of the silversmith's art.

"SAINT ANDREW'S PHYLACTERY" The treasury includes five phylacteries, small wooden reliquaries covered in copper and silver. The verso (shown here) is decorated with a Christ in Majesty.

RELIQUARY CROSS The cult of relics was very widespread in the Middle Ages. Hugo deployed all his skills to create worthy settings for the relics brought back from the Holy Land by Jacques de Vitry ▲ *197*. This reliquary cross was designed to hold a fragment of the True Cross.

Reliquary of the Virgin's milk
This reliquary was probably produced by one of Hugo's pupils, who followed his master's style closely. It holds a piece of galactite from the Cave of the Nativity near Bethlehem. The dove symbolizes purity.

Reliquary containing Saint Peter's rib (1238)
Although most of the pieces of the treasury can be attributed to Hugo or his workshop, only the three principal masterpieces are signed by him: the evangelistary cover, the chalice of Gilles de Walcourt ● *50* and this reliquary, which can be dated precisely thanks to a fragment of parchment accompanying it.

angelistary cover (1228–30). On each of the two leaves are subjects common to Romanesque conography: Christ in Majesty (surrounded by the mbols of the four Evangelists) and the Crucifixion. borders feature intertwining foliage and cabochons.

The master's technique
Hugo prefered the black-and-white niello technique (black enamel on metal) to the enamel decoration of the previous century. He was also a master of the techniques of filigree (gold and silver threads welded to a background) and *estampage* (motifs printed in relief).

1. NAMUR
2. GEMBLOUX
3. CORROY-LE-CHÂTEAU
4. VILLERS-LA-VILLE
5. NIVELLES
6. MARCHE-LES-DAMES
7. ANDENNE
8. WAREMME
9. HUY
10. CHÂTEAU DE JEHAY
11. AMAY
12. MODAVE

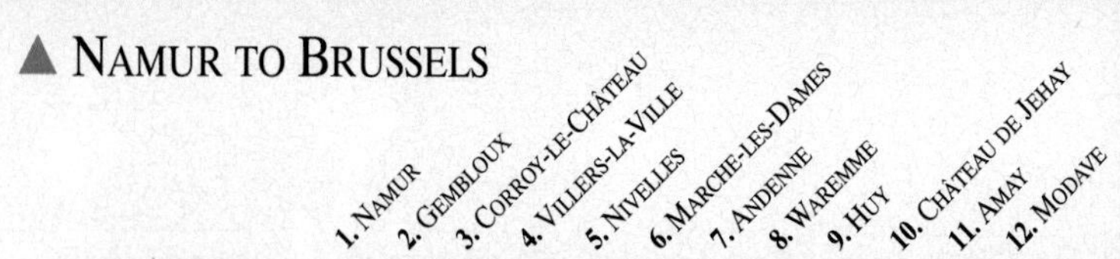

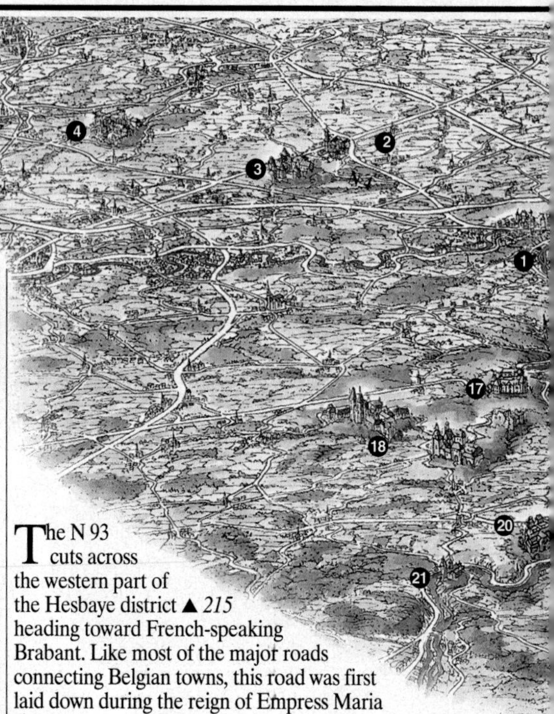

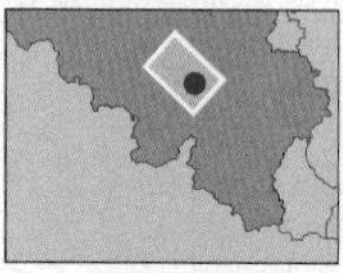

Half a day
30 miles

CORROY-LE-CHÂTEAU Although the castle's main buildings were greatly altered in the 17th and 18th centuries, much of the original structure (13th century) still remains.

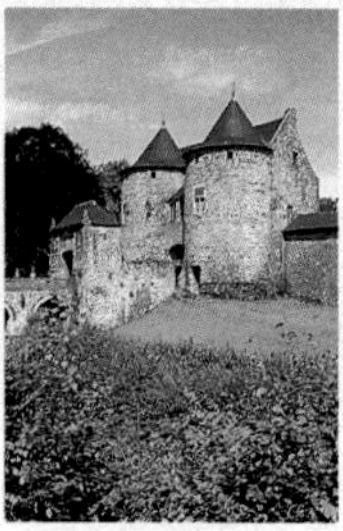

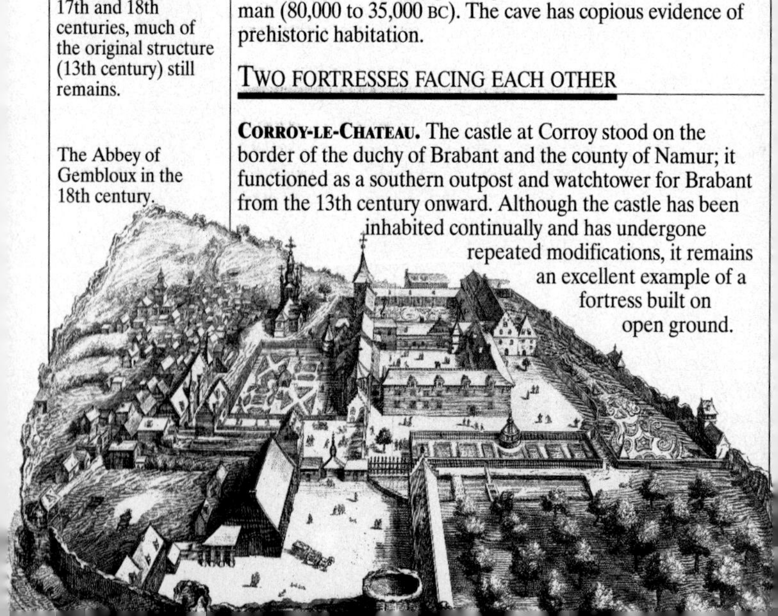

The N 93 cuts across the western part of the Hesbaye district ▲ *215* heading toward French-speaking Brabant. Like most of the major roads connecting Belgian towns, this road was first laid down during the reign of Empress Maria Theresa.

THE CAVE OF SPY

This is one of Belgium's most important Paleolithic sites: it became famous in 1866 when skeletal remains were discovered, definitively proving the existence of Neanderthal man (80,000 to 35,000 BC). The cave has copious evidence of prehistoric habitation.

TWO FORTRESSES FACING EACH OTHER

CORROY-LE-CHATEAU. The castle at Corroy stood on the border of the duchy of Brabant and the county of Namur; it functioned as a southern outpost and watchtower for Brabant from the 13th century onward. Although the castle has been inhabited continually and has undergone repeated modifications, it remains an excellent example of a fortress built on open ground.

The Abbey of Gembloux in the 18th century.

13. Bois-et-Borsu
14. Saint Séverin
15. Crupet
16. Spontin
17. Annevoie-Rouillon
18. Abbey of Maredsous
19. Dinant
20. Château de Freyr
21. Hastière-par-Delà
22. Vêves
23. Celles
24. Lavaux-Ste-Anne
25. Chevetogne
26. The Caves of Han
27. Rochefort

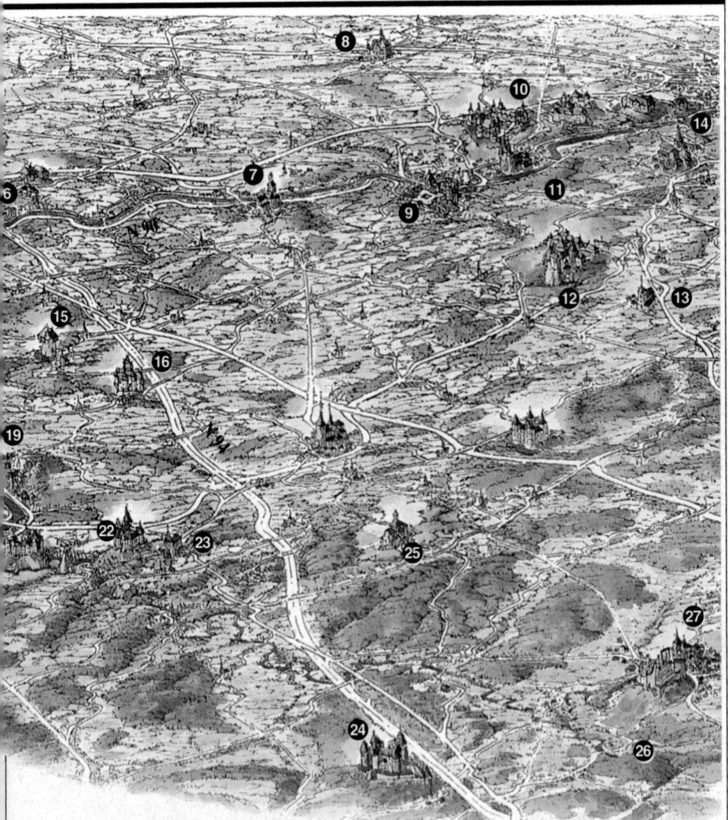

Among its most famous owners were the families of Brabant-Perwez in the 13th century and of Nassau in the 15th and 16th centuries.

Villeret ● *89.* Built in the mid 13th century, the stronghold of Villeret stands opposite that of Corroy; its function was to guard the border of Namur's territories. Its four walls, dotted with windows and arrow slits, stand at one end of a plain that was easily defended. The rectangular main tower was incorporated into a farm during the 18th century. The roof, which was destroyed in 1914, is currently being restored.

Gembloux

This was once the capital of the French-speaking part of Brabant; it now belongs to the present-day province of Namur. Gembloux still has a section of its 13th-century rampart. The town is known for its cutlery industry, which has flourished here since the 18th century, and for its ABBEY, founded by Saint Guibert around 940. Today the neoclassical abbey buildings house a college of agronomy. The former abbey church, which is now the parish church, has a

Sombreffe
This fortress belonged to the Sombreffe family, who owed allegiance to both Namur and Brabant in the 12th and 13th centuries. The castle still retains its 13th-century buildings, except for the main building (rebuilt in the 18th century). Its two dungeons are haunted by a knight who once came to lay siege to the fortress.

neo-Gothic shrine to Saint Guibert alongside a statue of the "Vieux Bon Dieu" – a painted-wood Ecce Homo regarded as a sacred object after blood was seen pouring from it in 1653. The Maison du Bailli (1589), where the bailiff of Gembloux lived in the 18th century, is also worth a visit.

BEAUTIFUL RUINS
In the 19th century the ruins of Villers became a mecca for the Romantics, and then for archeologists. Restoration work started in 1894 with the aim of preserving the buildings in their ruined state.

THE ABBEY OF VILLERS-LA-VILLE ★

This impressive collection of ruins is hidden away at the bottom of a valley, set in a rocky landscape near the winding course of the Thyle river.

PAST SPLENDOR. The magnificent site was chosen by Saint Bernard in 1147, and occupied by Cistercian monks for 650 years. The abbey reached its peak, in both worldly and spiritual terms, in the 13th century. The main surviving buildings date from this period and were constructed in local stone. The way they are arranged around the cloister is typical of Cistercian monasteries ● *86*. Three buildings are especially interesting: the church, the refectory and the hostelry. The first of these (1210–67) introduced Gothic architecture to the region; the other two are conventional Cistercian buildings.

REVIVAL. After four hundred years of decline, Villers had a second golden age in the 18th century. A magnificent abbey palace, complete with terraced gardens, was built to the southeast around 1720, and the old buildings were modified to suit 18th-century taste. In 1796 the monks were expelled; after this the abbey was plundered for building materials.

Abbey of Villers-la-Ville.

Nivelles

The town grew up, from the 11th century onward, around an abbey founded by Saint Gertrude four hundred years earlier. Initially Nivelles was a simple Merovingian villa; it expanded rapidly in the 12th century under the rule of the abbess. The town specialized in weaving, especially fine cloth. The Musée Communal, housed in the former refuge of the Abbey of Orval (18th century), displays objects found on the site of the Roman settlement of Liberchies, as well as a collection of Ancien Régime decorative art. But Nivelles is most famous for the Collegiate Church (Collégiale) of Ste-Gertrude, the former abbey church.

The Collégiale ★. The first abbess, Saint Gertrude, belonged to the Pipinnides, a powerful Merovingian family; in founding this abbey she contributed to the great Christian evangelical movement of the 7th century. Each year a procession makes a "tour" of the town, following the route the abbess is supposed to have taken when making her rounds. The Collégiale was rebuilt in the 11th century, for the sixth time since its foundation; it is a perfect example of Ottonian religious architecture, with two choirs facing each other. The *westbau* (front section of the church) is typical of Mosan architecture ● *82*; it was rebuilt, with very regular brickwork, in the 12th century. The church was altered in the 17th and 18th centuries, and then suffered serious bomb damage in 1940. After the war it was fully restored to its 11th-century state. The first tomb of Saint Gertrude and the remains of the earlier churches can be seen in the archeological crypt. The striking carved pulpit by Laurent Delvaux (1696–1778) is also worth seeing.

Bois-Seigneur-Isaac. This small village, located a few miles to the north of Nivelles, has two interesting buildings. The 15th-century Augustinian convent has a remarkable church, with a magnificent stucco ceiling in the Louis XVI style (1703) and a marble altarpiece by Delvaux. There is also a splendid classical palace (1720–40) built of stone, slate and whitewashed brick.

Restoration
Should the Collégiale have been restored to its original state, or as it had evolved during the course of the centuries? The local people were consulted and chose the former option.

Jean de Nivelles
This is the nickname given to the golden figure of an armed knight donated by Charles the Bold in 1469. ("Jean" is the nickname often given to an eccentric character.)

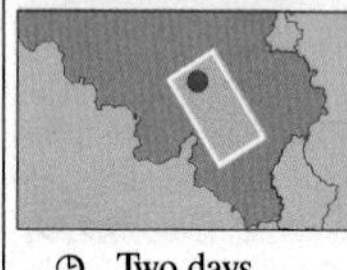

◷ Two days
🚗 45 miles

"[The Meuse] is a mediator. This long river . . . is the link which brings together the Saône and the Escaut, Burgundy and Flanders, the Rhine and the Seine. Even though its sloping course across the Ardennes takes it through other countries..., it remains resolutely French in character. Only after Liège does the Germanic world take over: it is here that the 'little France of the Meuse' comes to an end."

Vidal de La Blache

The Meuse is the backbone of southern Belgium: most of the rivers in the region flow into it, except for a few belonging to the basins of the Escaut or the Moselle. The source of the Meuse is in France, on the Langres plateau; by the time it reaches the Belgian border it has already flowed 300 miles. Its main tributaries in southern Belgium are the Semois, Lesse, Sambre and Ourthe. Between Hastière and Namur the river cuts across the Condroz plateau, with its alternating limestone and sandstone rocks. Steep slopes and spectacular rock formations, like those at Dinant or Freyr, are typical of the region.

LATE DEVELOPER. Until 1840–50 the Meuse was only navigable for eight to ten months of the year, through a narrow winding channel at the center of the river. Tolls were paid by the flat-bottomed boats propelled by small sails or pulled by draught horses on the banks. Flooding was common, causing considerable damage: a plaque in Namur (Rue St-Nicolas) lists all the great floods that have taken place since the 18th century. Major improvements were made: dams and locks were built to aid navigation and prevent floods, and the banks were rebuilt. Although the valley has retained much of its wild landscape, only a few oxbow lakes remain to indicate the river's original course. The photo reproduced here (center) shows fishermen on the banks of the Meuse in 1872.

The castle at Spontin, beyond Crupet, can accommodate visitors in its guest rooms.

CLIMATE, FLORA AND FAUNA. The climate of the Meuse valley is distinctly warmer than that of neighboring plateaus; vines used to be grown on the sunny slopes of Dinant, where remains of the old terracing can still be spotted here and there. Plants and insects from the south

Manuscript from the early 16th century, defining the borders between the county of Namur and the principality of Liège.

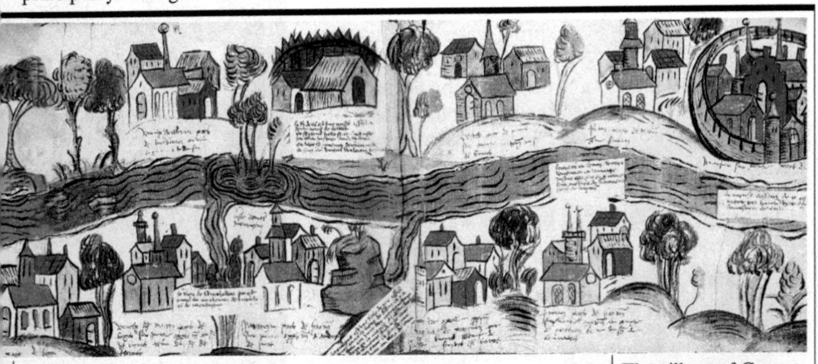

inhabit the sunniest slopes, giving them an almost Mediterranean air. The rocks (which, up to 1972, harbored the last nesting pairs of peregrine falcons) and dry grasslands ■ 22 offer a remarkable wealth of plant and animal life for this latitude, including rock roses, round-headed garlic, orchids, wall lizards and the swallowtail butterfly. This former pastureland has evolved into scrubland, where cornelian cherry, hawthorn and plum trees grow. Box trees, which seem to have taken refuge in the valley during the last ice age, form wild thickets on some sunny slopes. Forests of ash, maple and elm trees cover the lower slopes and some escarpments, with hart's-tongue fern growing in their shade.

Nature reserves. Several nature reserves have been created between Namur and Dinant, for example at Champalle ★, near Yvoir: here there are around 250 species of plants and ferns, including the drave-faux-aizon, originally from the Alps. The nature reserves at Fonds-de-Leffe and Devant-Bouvignes, the Colebi valley and Freyr (a popular spot for rock climbing) are well worth visiting.

From Namur to Dinant

Two routes are possible: along the right bank (on a road cut into the rock face ★) or along the left bank, on the main road, which has been widened to four lanes in places. If you choose the former, after Dave you pass alongside the Rochers du Neviau, a favorite haunt of rock climbers attracted by the rugged Meuse landscape.

Detour via Spontin. The Canon Gérard (1840–1932) decided to dedicate the caves in his parish at Crupet to Saint Francis. Since then, miracle cures have been witnessed in the cave, where life-size statues depict the miracles worked by the saint.

Spontin. The village makes the most of its natural resources: stone (Meuse limestone) and

The village of Crupet on the Condroz plateau ▲ 217 had a castle in the 13th century: only the keep stands today.

The holy caves of Crupet
When Canon Gérard decided to dedicate the local caves to a saint, he faced a difficult choice: which saint should he choose? The Franciscans, an order dedicated to making conversions, would have suggested Saint Antony, a great miracle worker and a favorite of their order – after Saint Francis, of course. Left: one of the statues in the cave.

The gardens of Annevoie (left and center).

spring water, famous since classical times. Spontin water is to be found on all the best tables. The Château de Spontin ▲ *204* was built around a 13th-century keep; its main building was redesigned in a lighter style in 1622.

THE BATHS AT CHAMPION. The Gallo-Romans, rich and poor, used to visit public or private baths. The baths at Champion, covering an area of around 400 square yards, are one of the largest private bath complexes discovered in Belgium. Only part of the site can be visited, in the summer: this includes the *hypocausts* (heating system, using pipes in the floor and walls), the *caldarium* (hot-water baths), the *tepidarium* (warm-water baths) and finally the *frigidarium* (cold-water baths). The remains, which date from the 3rd century, were built over earlier constructions from the 1st and 2nd centuries.

THE CHURCH OF FOY-NOTRE-DAME (heading back toward the valley). The church has a Baroque ceiling with caissons (1622–6). On the Monday of Pentecost and on September 8 the church hosts a pilgrimage to the miraculous Virgin of Foy: this dates back to 1609, when woodcutters discovered a statue in an oak tree. The statue had been placed in a hollow in the trunk, then forgotten, and gradually covered up by the tree as it grew.

CHATEAU D'ANNEVOIE ★. This château was built in the 18th century around an earlier tower and wing. Its owner was ironmaster Charles-Alexis de Montpellier (named after the town where his father had studied medicine). His forges are located away from the house, by the side of the road. The building is made entirely of limestone, which is abundant in the locality. Pass through the entrance porch and enter the main court. The 35 acres of gardens (27 acres of park) start beyond a passageway framed by two monumental terracotta vases. Charles-Alexis de Montpellier made magnificent use of the natural terrain, which slopes down from a hill to the bottom of the valley where the castle stands. He created ponds, fountains and canals, channeling water everywhere underneath the grass, directing it toward the melancholy lakes, which reflect the changing moods of the sky. He gave all these water features names: the Mirror, the Lake of the Water Lilies, the Oval Lake, and so on. Charles-Alexis derived much of his inspiration from memories of his grand tour of Europe. René Pechère, another garden lover, wrote: "At Tivoli there are terraces and a huge landscape. At Versailles there is a spectacle laid on for ambassadors to magnify the glory

“I WANT CHILDHOOD EVERYWHERE.”
LOUIS XIV’S INSTRUCTION FOR HIS GARDENS, ADOPTED AT ANNEVOIE

of the king . . . . Here, there is a man of refinement who loves his country and its forges, and nearby the River Meuse between its steep banks, the small stream of the Rouillon, and four springs. Eleven hectares and the gentle sound of water, which has not stopped for two hundred years. Landscape gardens: nonsense! This landscape has been wisely left to the care of nature, for the landscape to reveal itself.”

FORTRESS OF POILVACHE (near Yvoir). Only the west front survives of this castle, which was destroyed in 1154; it overlooks the whole valley. On the left bank of the river is a plain perfectly suited to military exercises. It was later to witness the uprising of Belgian patriots in 1789 and the maneuvers of German tanks during the *Blitzkrieg* of 1940.

THE MOLIGNÉE VALLEY ★. The CHÂTEAU DE MONTAIGLE (late 13th century), was the seat of one of the bailiffs of Namur. It guarded the winding course of the Molignée river in the Middle Ages: only its ruined walls stand today. A MUSEUM recreates the daily life of the castle during the periods when it was inhabited. Further on, the village of Sosoye is overlooked by beautiful dry grasslands ■ *22*. The impressive ABBEY OF MAREDSOUS houses a monastic community and an inn, which was once a school. The abbey was built by the architect Béthune in 1876, imitating the Gothic architecture of the late 13th century. “Maredsous beer” is in fact not brewed here at all: the local beer known as *crochon* comes from nearby FALAËN. At the end of this tour is the Gothic church at FURNAUX, built in the 16th century and heavily altered in the 18th and 19th centuries; it has Romaneqsue BAPTISMAL FONTS ★ from the 12th century. Baptismal fonts are the product of a long evolution. The baptisteries of early Christianity had hollowed-out pools in the floor, where baptism was performed by immersion. By the Middle Ages, when the majority of the population had been converted to Christianity,

INSIDE THE CHÂTEAU D’ANNEVOIE
Charles-Alexis commissioned the Moretti brothers to decorate the interior: do not miss their Rococo style stuccos, in the chapel and the Grand Salon Blanc.

THE LEGEND OF MIDIONE DE BIOUL
During a siege Midione, mistress of the Château de Montaigle (below), obtained permission to leave the castle with her most prized possession. She left with a heavy bundle of firewood on her shoulders, to the amusement of the besieging soldiers. In fact her husband was escaping from his enemies – hidden by the timber.

FORTIFICATIONS ALONG THE MEUSE
The Château de Poilvache (below) was one of the fortresses that guarded the Meuse in the Middle Ages.

RELIGIOUS SCULPTURE
The workshops where the Furnaux fonts were carved also made capitals for churches. Because so many of the latter have vanished, the fonts are an important source for the typical imagery of Romanesque architecture.

baptism was mainly for children (although not yet for infants, despite Charlemagne's move in that direction). Baptisteries gave way to basin-shaped baptismal fonts. The fonts at Furnaux (center) consist of a basin standing on a plinth supported by four lions, which hold a man or a book between their paws; a frieze depicts the baptism of Christ and the story of Abraham and Lot.

BOUVIGNES. The traditional rival of Dinant, Bouvignes has never recovered from being sacked by Henri II in 1554, during the wars against Charles V. In those days it was the second largest town in Namur. The town center is dominated by the 15th-century keep and tower. The CHURCH OF ST-LAMBERT, heavily restored between the wars, still has Romanesque features from the 12th century. The crypt used to house the treasures now displayed in the MUSEUM in the Maison Espagnole, in the Place Centrale. This building (16th century) also houses a MUSEUM OF LIGHTING, with collections ranging from the oil lamp to the light bulb. Bouvignes' 17th-century CHÂTEAU, formerly a Sepulchrine convent, faces the river, at the far end of a park; the main building, in a striking Baroque style, contrasts with the more traditional style of the wings.

Although named after the town of Dinant, originally "dinanderie" was a specialty of Bouvignes.

DINANT

Dinant (below, seen from Quai de la Meuse) was one of the leading towns of the principality of Liège. The town stretches along the banks of the Meuse below the steep cliffs; it also claimed jurisdiction over the water between the river bank and the end of a two-pronged stick held by an alderman. The local specialty was "dinanderie" – the manufacture of copper and brass articles (left), an industry in which it supplanted Bouvignes. Dinant's workshops produced cauldrons and dishes under the Ancien Régime. The town was sacked by the Duke of Burgundy in 1466, by Henri II in 1554 and by the Kaiser in 1914.

THE AYMON BROTHERS AT DINANT (▲ *268*). The horse Bayard, which carried the four Aymon brothers in their desperate flight from Charlemagne's wrath, is said to have crossed the Meuse at Dinant. According to legend,

its hoof cracked the great rock that can be seen at the entrance to the town – which has since been known as Bayard's Rock. **TOUR OF THE TOWN.** The bulbous bell tower of the COLLEGIATE CHURCH is a distinctive feature of the townscape, which can be viewed as a whole from the Viaduc Charlemagne. The church, in the Gothic style with a lovely side portal, dates from the 13th century – except for the stained-glass windows and the roof, which date from after 1914. At the end of the 17th century France decided to make Dinant, then under French rule, into a powerful fortress. Today all that survives of the ramparts is the TOUR TARAVISÉE; and only the base of the castle remains, occupied by a fort from the Dutch period. In August 1914 this fort was the scene of violent battles between the Germans and the French, during which Charles de Gaulle was wounded. In 17th-century buildings to the north of the town, the MONASTÈRE DE LEFFE houses a community of Benedictine monks, alongside the modern buildings of its brewery. The monks receive visitors for retreats and make a living from selling their beer (light or dark, with an alcohol content of 6° or 8°) ● 75.

ADOLPHE SAX (1814–94). The inventor of the saxophone was born in Dinant. He registered forty patents, and his workshops produced 20,000 instruments. Unusually, his genius earned him a host of enemies, who brought him to bankruptcy three times. Above: Sax's son with one of his father's inventions.

CHÂTEAU DE FREYR ★

The Château de Freyr was built in the Mosan style between 1571 and 1637. The southern wing was removed by its owners in the 17th century in order to open up the view over the gardens. These always took precedence for Freyr's owners: here, for once, the plants counted for more than brick and stone.

The gardens were in the classical style – and so those features of the building that were felt to be "too Renaissance" were modified, particularly the combination of brickwork and masonry. The interior decoration was adapted to suit 18th-century tastes.

THE GARDENS. Created by Guillaume and Philippe de Beaufort-Spontin (1760), the gardens were designed around a single main axis running parallel to the Meuse, leading to avenues, water features and groups of lime trees. After this they created a second garden, on the theme of card games. Statues of kings, queens and knaves on the wall separating the gardens illustrate this theme. The arbors are shaped like the different suits in a card game: hearts, diamonds, spades and clubs. Each arbor is divided into nine sections; two orangeries complete the design.

THE CLASSICAL IDEAL. The French-style formal garden, like that at Freyr, came into being with the Age of Enlightenment. It sought to demonstrate the pre-eminence of Reason by imposing order on nature, which was regarded as anarchic. As François Hiraux explains, "Classicism is the expression of a thoroughly different moral order from that which had characterized the western world for six or eight hundred years, through all sorts of crises. The classical age substituted the values and hallmarks of individualism for all the extravagance and excesses of collective life. . . . The classical garden is a spare, denuded space, properly outlined so you know quite clearly what is ordered and what is not. . . . The ordered garden represents a particular type of view and theory of society."

EVOLUTION OF FORMAL GARDENS
The French-style classical garden supplanted the

geometrically designed Renaissance garden, which itself continued the medieval tradition of an enclosed space protected from the dangers of the outside world.

HASTIÈRE-PAR-DELÀ

The abbey church of Hastière-par-delà, built in the Romanesque style, stands below the Rochers de Tahaux; the earliest records of the church date from the 10th century. The building as it stands today was first altered between 1033 and 1035. A Gothic chevet was added in the 13th century. The

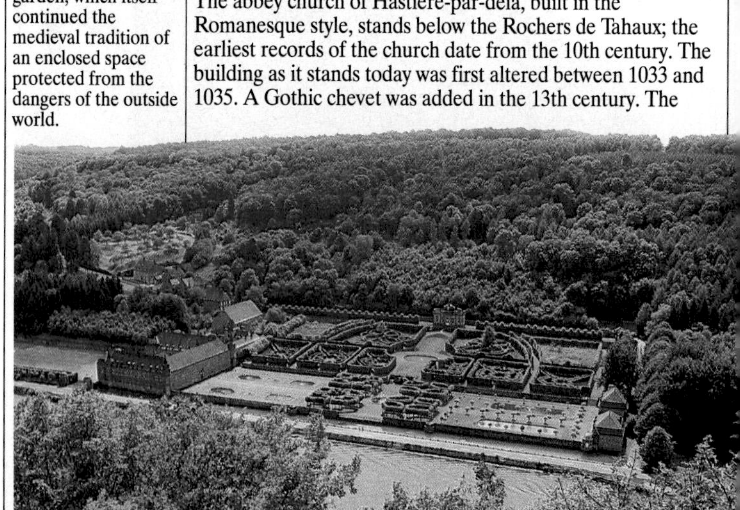

church consists principally of three naves with five bays, supported by rectangular pillars. The main nave, on two stories, originally had a ceiling. Before the 13th century the transept was joined to a semicircular apse, flanked by two apsidioles. The first story of the front section is decorated with blind arcade with a groined vaults. The square tower on the west side has a turret.

The church at Hastière-par-delà
The interior is very austere in appearance; in the past it was decorated with huge frescos, parts of which can still be seen (above).

From Dinant to St-Hubert

Leaving Dinant, and before reaching the exposed plateaus of the Ardennes around St-Hubert, the traveler crosses the Condroz and gradually descends into a huge trough, the Famenne ▲ *255*, which follows the narrow limestone strip of the Calestienne, a warm, sunny and attractive region with a hilly landscape that becomes less rugged around Han-sur-Lesse and Rochefort. The region is named after the Lesse and Lomme rivers, which flow together here. The natural landscape of the area is quite unusual, as in the valley of the Viroin ▲ *284* on the other side of the Meuse. It is made of limestone and schist rocks that were formed more than 370 million years ago, through the sedimentation and fusion of mineral particles deposited on the sea bed in the Primary era. The sea at this time was calm and quite shallow, encouraging the development of coral reefs – the origin of today's limestone terrain ■ *22*. The sediments were later raised and folded during the uprisings of the Ardennes massif at the end of the Primary era and the Alps at the end of the Tertiary era; they were then eroded by glaciers in the Quaternary era. The glaciers eroded the schists, but left the limestone intact.

Crossing the Condroz. The national park of Furfooz, created jointly by Gaume and the Ardennes, is an important archeological site. The numerous caves dotted throughout this limestone massif were inhabited during the Paleolithic period, and then used as a burial place in the Neolithic period (the objects that have been found here are kept in the Archeological Museum at Namur ▲ *196*). At Furfooz itself, a rocky outcrop was converted into a fortified settlement by the Letes, a Germanic tribe installed here by the Romans in exchange for serving in the imperial armies. A former bath building was used by the Letes for burying their dead. A keep was built in the 9th and 10th centuries, and human habitation of the site continued up to the 13th century. The blue waters of the Lesse, flowing below this hill, attract canoeists in the summer. After the Château de Vêves ▲ *212*, head for Celles-en-Condroz to see its beautiful Collegiate Church of St-Hadelin ★. Saint Hadelin was a disciple of Saint Remaclus ▲ *246*, and her cult developed in the region from the 8th

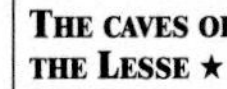

The caves of the Lesse ★
The Lesse and the Lomme have hollowed out the most extensive networks of caves in the country, including those at Han and Rochefort ▲ *213*. In both cases the water tunneled a direct channel through a bend in the river bank. The waters of the Lesse descend beneath a hill at the Gouffre de Belvau and resurface at the Trou de Han; the underground course in between was fully explored for the first time in 1988.

CHÂTEAU DE VÊVES
This fortress was built in the 15th century and converted into a manor house in the 16th and 17th centuries. The interior was divided into apartments, and windows were built into the forbidding walls. The castle stands out like a Wagnerian vision against its backdrop of wooded hills.

ROMANESQUE INFLUENCES
"Romanesque architecture [in Belgium] gained from the country's exposure to outside influences. The proximity . . . to the world of the Rhine on the one hand, and to what is now the northern part of France on the other, inevitably left its mark on the architecture along the banks of the Meuse. . . . Furthermore, trading links with Italy bore fruit in the evolution of the region's own architectural style."
Xavier Barral y Altet

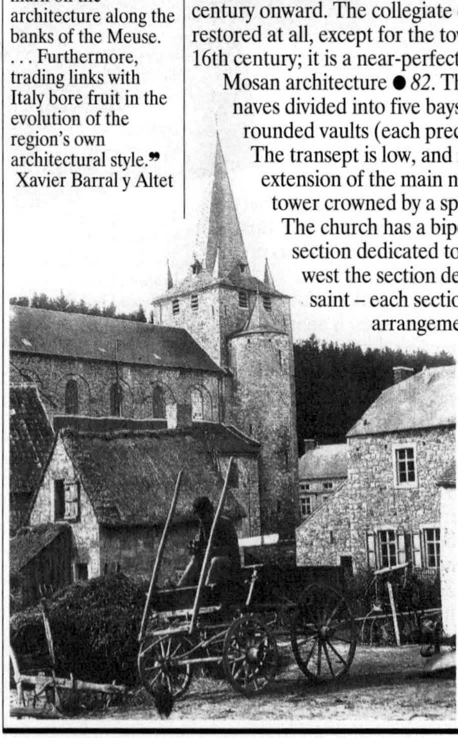

century onward. The collegiate church has hardly been restored at all, except for the tower, which was rebuilt in the 16th century; it is a near-perfect example of 11th-century Mosan architecture ● *82*. The interior consists of three naves divided into five bays, which end in three apses with rounded vaults (each preceded by a rectangular bay). The transept is low, and its crosspieces are joined to the extension of the main nave. To the west stands a huge tower crowned by a spire and flanked by two turrets. The church has a bipolar layout: to the east is the section dedicated to the worship of Christ; to the west the section dedicated to the worship of the saint – each section has an altar. This arrangement is also reflected in the presence of two crypts: the first is under the choir, which is slightly raised as a result, while the second, under the tower, houses the relics of the saint. The external ornamentation consists of arcades surrounding the small windows. A few miles away is CHEVETOGNE, which has a stunning Byzantine church built on the square floor plan of the Novgorod type (9th century). It was built in 1939, in response to a plea from Pope Pius XI for

the churches of East and West to come together. Move on to the village of LAVAUX-STE-ANNE, which has a plain-fortress dating from the 15th century. Its ground plan is an irregular trapezium, flanked by round towers and, at one corner, by a huge keep almost completely surrounded by moats. The site was not very favorable for defensive purposes, so the builders isolated the fortress by building it in the middle of a marsh, while the village stood on a nearby hillside.

THE LESSE AND LOMME NATIONAL PARK. The last remains of the dry grasslands ■ *22* of the Lesse and Lomme region have been made into a nature reserve. Here you can find many orchids, three types of gentian and the pasque flower (with purple flowers that appear in April), which is becoming increasingly rare. Some southern species of butterfly, such as the swallowtail (below), can be seen here, too. The most accessible grasslands are on the Belvedere near Han, looking down over the great oxbow lake on the Lesse (La Chavée); on the outskirts of Belvau (the Tienne des Pairées, with its junipers); or near to the village of Ave-et-Auffe. Nearby are the CAVES OF HAN, where people took refuge in times of trouble up to the 17th century. The MUSÉE DU MONDE SOUTERRAIN displays objects relating to habitation of the caves, from the Neolithic age up to Roman times. The objects were found in geological strata (some of them 10 feet thick) corresponding to the periods of occupation. Among the highlights of the collection are the Bronze Age jewelry and a bronze award presented to a veteran of Trajan's armies in AD 108.

ROCHEFORT. Once the capital of a small medieval county, this town was famous for its marble, which was exported throughout Europe. Today it is best known for its CAVE. Nearly all the buildings date from the 17th century or later – the village having been destroyed in 1650–3, first by mercenaries from Lorraine in the service of the Emperor and then by the Prince de Condé's troops. The Abbey of St-Rémy was founded by the Comte de Rochefort for the Cistercians in 1230; today it houses a community of Trappist monks. The CASTLE above the town has stood in ruins since 1807. Terraces were added to it in the 18th century, and the façades were given a Louis XIV style facing (having already been altered in the previous century). Nearby is the CHÂTEAU DE CIERGNON (19th century), the summer residence of the Belgian royal family.

JEMELLE. A large Roman villa has been discovered here. The main building, around 330 feet long, included baths with hypocausts. Furnaces have been found, too – evidence of the metalwork industry that developed here as iron ore was plentiful. The villa was occupied up to the 4th century, when the fortress of Vieux Château was built on an outcrop on the other side of the Lomme. Other discoveries include Roman fortifications from the 3rd and 4th centuries, as well as Roman and Merovingian cemeteries containing numerous funerary objects.

ROCHEFORT BEER
Rochefort (above) is famous for the brown ale ● *75* brewed by the Trappist monks of the Abbey of St-Rémy. In 1887 the monks moved back into the abbey, which they had abandoned during the French Revolution.

FROM FORTRESS TO COUNTRY SEAT
The impressive defensive apparatus of the Château de Lavaux-Ste-Anne was retained in 1630 when the buildings were updated to suit the tastes of the day. Brickwork was introduced at this stage, along with windows opening onto the courtyard above first-story arcades, all in the typical Baroque style. A museum of hunting and conservation has been established here.

Lundi 19 février 1934
5 HEURES DU MATIN DERN
La mort tragique

◷ One day
40 miles

THE BRUMAGNE LOTTO SET
The Musée Groesbeeck de Croix ▲ *196* owns this water-color lotto set (1779), which portrays the villages of Lives, Beez and Marche-les-Dames and various trades.

Le Village de Beez

MOUNTAINEERING AND QUARRIES
The Meuse landscape is dominated by limestone, a dolomitic rock which was used for the quarriers' houses at Lives, where stone was less expensive than brick or wood. The rugged terrain of this quarrying district has attracted climbers since the 19th century. King Albert I (below) ● *42*, a keen mountaineer, died at MARCHE-LES-DAMES in 1934 after a fall. He is commemorated there by a chapel, a monument and a museum.

The course of the Meuse gradually becomes calmer as it passes from the county of Namur into the episcopal principality of Liège ● *33*. The border used to be located just outside Huy, at Ben-Ahin. There is a town every 20 miles or so, the distance traveled daily by medieval boatmen: Dinant, Namur, Huy, and finally Liège. This area was one of the birthplaces of the industrial revolution, which has left its mark on the landscape around the river. Nevertheless, the old villages of the Condroz ▲ *217*, the farms of the Hesbaye (on the left bank of the Meuse), the woodland châteaux and the historic towns of the Meuse can still take you on a journey into the past.

STONE AND WATER

After LIVES (right bank), dependent on its stone quarries, you come to BEEZ (left bank), also an old quarrying center, although it acquired flour mills in the 19th century and a shipyard in 1937.

MARCHE-LES-DAMES. The village of Marche-sur-Meuse was renamed Marche-les-Dames when a Cistercian convent was established here in the 12th century. The convent building, extensively altered in the 18th century, now houses Carthusian nuns.

THE SAMSON VALLEY. On the right bank of the Meuse is a river of the Condroz, the Samson, after which this valley is named. From here you can walk through the undergrowth to the village of THON. The fortress at Thon, which was destroyed in 1691, was an outpost of Namur territory on the borders of Liège. The village of GOYET has beautiful stone houses from the 18th century, and caves that were inhabited by bear-worshipping tribes in Paleolithic times (a reconstruction of this prehistoric past can be seen).

ANDENNE

This was the only town on the Meuse in the Namur region without city walls, probably because it was founded by a community of nuns. Its status as church property theoretically exempted it from warfare and violence.

THE COLLEGIATE CHURCH OF STE-BEGGE. The church in its current state dates from the 18th century. It was rebuilt by Dewez ▲ *296*, replacing the Romano-Gothic Church of Ste-Marie-Majeure, the most important of the seven churches founded here by Saint Begge in the 7th century. This Merovingian saint came

EXCELSIOR 3

ÈRE HEURE 5 HEURES DU MATIN

S. M. Albert Ier, roi des Belges

La Hesbaye
To the north of the Meuse stretches the fertile plain of La Hesbaye, the agricultural heart of the country. Villages are grouped around château-farms ● *106* like the De la Tour farm at Wartet. From the 17th century onward, citizens who had made a fortune in the coal and metal industries purchased estates in this district, some of them covering an area of more than 2,500 acres. To tour round the district, first take the N 80. Built in 1750–5, the Château de Franc-Wartet ★ is a perfect example of an elegant Namur residence of the 18th century; it was designed in the classical style by Jean-Baptiste Chermann for the Groesbeeck de Croix family ▲ *196*. After the N 80, the N 69 follows, more or less, the Roman road from Bavai to Cologne. Here and there *tumuli* (burial mounds) stand out from the plain. These are the tombs of wealthy landowners, which were built on either side of the Roman road so as to be visible to all. The tombs were richly furnished, sometimes including the funeral pyre on which the dead person was cremated. Such tombs were common in Hesbaye and Condroz in the 1st and 2nd centuries. The best *tumuli* are the Tomb of the Emperor (Hannut), the Tomb of Avennes (Braives) and a group of five tombs near Omal.

from the same family as Saint Gertrude ▲ *203*. She is commemorated in an annual procession, during which her shrine (right) is carried through the streets of Andenne.

HUY

HISTORY. Huy developed, from the 6th and 7th centuries onward, around a nexus of rivers (the Meuse and the Hoyoux) and roads (from the Hesbaye to the Condroz, and from Namur to Liège). The oldest part of the town was on the left bank of the Meuse, at Batta, where a prosperous industrial area grew up (metalwork, pottery and coins). Between the 8th and 11th centuries the residential area spread to the right bank, at the foot of a rocky outcrop (later the site of a castle, then a citadel). In 1066 Huy was granted a charter by the Germanic Empire guaranteeing the political stability vital to its economic growth. The pewterware industry reached its peak here in the 16th and 19th centuries; faïence, similar to that produced in Andenne, developed around 1820, as did vine growing. The citadel at Huy was the main fortress of the principality under the Ancien Régime. A large number of 16th-century buildings can still be seen in the town, in the Late Gothic or Renaissance styles: the tourist information center itself is housed in the former Hospice d'Oultremont, built in a Gothico-Renaissance style. Festivals and a religious procession are held at Huy every seven years.

THE "FOUR WONDERS OF HUY". These are (in Walloon): *li chestia*, the château, replaced by a fort in 1818; *li rondia* (15th century), the Gothic rose window of the Church of Notre-Dame; *li pontia*, the bridge over the Meuse (13th century); and *li bassinia*, the fountain on the square in front of the town hall, with a basin dating from 1406. The treasury ★ of the collegiate church could equally well count as a fifth wonder: it consists mainly of shrines (12th and 13th centuries) that display the genius of Huy's casters, who used a local clay perfectly suited to their furnaces. Their works – for example, the plaque in *champlevé* enamel depicting the Tree of Life – are among the most distinctive creations of Mosan art ● *50*. In what was once a Minorite monastery (Renaissance), there is a museum showing the "Beau Dieu de Huy" (13th century), alongside displays devoted to the history of the town.

CRAFTS OF ANDENNE
From the 11th century onward the potters of Andenne made pottery from a local white clay, which they exported throughout Europe. In the late Middle Ages production declined, and the pottery was only sold locally. In the 18th century the production of faïence was started, prompting an industrial renaissance that continued into the 19th century with the production of porçelain. Since the 17th century Andenne has also been famous for its pipes, displayed in the town's Pipe Museum.

COLLEGIATE CHURCH OF HUY ● *82*
It took 225 years (1311–1536) for this church to be completed. Except for the French-style proportions of the interior, the building is a typical example of Liège architecture, a variant of the Mosan architectural style. Its transept is halfway along the nave, on a level with the side chapels; it has a polygonal chevet without radiating chapels or ambulatory. The entrances are at the side because of the tower, which has a rose window. Right: the Bethlehem Portal (13th century), showing the Nativity.

Colin Maillard
A mason named Colin Maillard, said to have been born in Huy in the 11th century, was blinded in a fight and subsequently achieved fame through a game named after him.

The church at St-Séverin
The church (below) is built mainly in Clunisian style: the tiered arrangement of the various elements contrasts with the local Mosan style ● *82*. The transept, choir and nave are at the same level; the lower, semicircular apse is flanked by apsidioles joined to the branches of the transept.

The fringes of the Condroz

The Condroz plateau is on the right bank of the Meuse, bordering on the Ardennes massif.

Château de Modave ★. The castle of the Counts of Marchin was built on a limestone cliff, 9 miles from Huy, above an estate with numerous springs. It was here that a machine for raising water was built in 1665: this served as the model for the Marly machine installed at Versailles. The present building is the product of modifications to the medieval fortress, which was rebuilt after its destruction by Lorraine forces in 1651 to create a residence in the classical style with pink brickwork. The counts retained the original layout, with the buildings arranged around a main court. Substantial outbuildings were added at the end of the 16th century.

From Modave to Liège. Toward St-Séverin, the church at Bois-et-Borsu has 14th-century frescos; the choir and nave date from the 11th century. St-Séverin is a small village of the Condroz, whose parish church (St-Pierre-et-St-Paul ★) dates from the 12th century. Just before arriving in Liège you can see the crystal factory ● *56* of Val St-Lambert, founded in 1826 in a 13th-century abbey that had been heavily restored during the 18th century.

Modave
The castle was acquired by wealthy industrialists from Liège in 1817. It is now owned by a water company.

CHÂTEAU DE JEHAY
Surrounded by water, the château (above) consists of a residential building, a farm and the Church of St-Lambert: each stands on an island, joined to the others by dykes and bridges. This group of buildings, with typically Gothic ornamentation, was restored by architect Alphonse Balat between 1859 and 1862.

SAINT ODA
Oda, or Chrodoara, a Merovingian noblewoman, founded the church dedicated to Saint George at Amay, and perhaps also a monastery. The sarcophagus (7th–8th century) in which she was buried can be seen in the crypt: its cover is decorated with a full-length portrait.

CHÂTEAUX OF THE REGION

The COLLEGIATE CHURCH OF ST-GEORGES-ET-STE-ODE AT AMAY was founded by Saint Oda in the 6th century. The present building dates from 1089, retaining from this period its *westbau* ("west building"), two square towers, and mural paintings from the 8th and 10th centuries. The nave and the choir date from the 18th century.

JEHAY-BODEGNÉE ★. The Château de Jehay stands in the middle of a marsh: its checkerboard-pattern walls (above) and complex arrangement are very striking. The L-shaped main building (16th century) was built with blocks of white stone and sandstone rubble, a common technique at the time. The interior has been refurnished by the Comte de Jehay.

CHÂTEAU D'AIGREMONT. The castle stands at the edge of a rocky escarpment, overlooking the Meuse. The present building (1717) took the place of a medieval castle. While the interior decoration and the portal (which has a grille decorated with arabesques) are in the Baroque style, the austere U-shaped main building is built in the traditional Mosan style in brick on a stone base.

CHÂTEAU DE CHOKIER. This 18th-century castle (below) is similar to Château d'Aigremont. It belonged to the regent Surlet de Chokier, who governed Belgium after the 1830 Revolution ● *40*.

In and around Liège

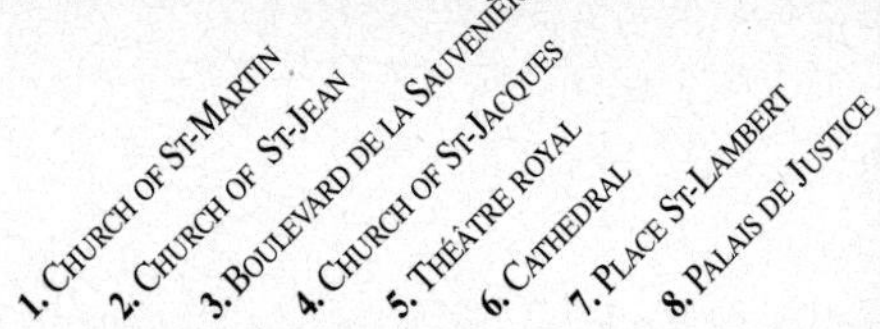

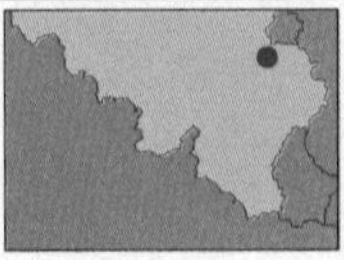

Four days

Liège was founded on the banks of the Meuse. However, it was another river that played the crucial role in its development: the Legia, a fast-flowing stream with its source on the edge of the Hesbaye plateau. At the confluence of the Legia and the Meuse is a rich alluvial plain: this is where the town was founded.

THE ASSASSINATION OF SAINT LAMBERT In the 7th century Lambert, Bishop of Tongres-Maastricht, decided to make Liège his second home: this was a turning point in the town's history. For it was here, around 700, that the bishop was assassinated, victim of a dispute between rival Merovingian clans. Miracles witnessed on the site of his "martyrdom" attracted businesses to the town, which grew rapidly from this time onward, soon becoming the capital of the principality.

HISTORY

The site is sheltered to the northeast by a double hill, the Publémont; it was inhabited as early as the Paleolithic era. In the early Middle Ages a small settlement took the place of a Gallo-Roman villa (farm-estate) on the fertile land where Place St-Lambert is today.

BISHOPRIC AND PRINCIPALITY. Three major events determined the history of the town: the assassination of Saint Lambert (left); the decision taken by his successor Saint Hubert ▲ *260* to make Liège the seat of his bishopric in the 8th century (Charlemagne built one of his palaces at Herstal around the same time); and Emperor Otto II's decision to invest Bishop

Notger with secular authority alongside his ecclesiastical powers. Notger is regarded as the founder of the state of Liège and the second founder of the city itself. His successors were the prince-bishops who ruled over both the principality and the diocese.

The Middle Ages. As the guilds became more powerful (the Peace of Fexhe in 1316 submitted the bishop to the will of the cathedral chapter, the nobility and the civic authorities) a sense of local identity grew up, setting Liège apart from the neighboring French and German territories. Although the bishopric belonged to the archdiocese of Cologne, and the principality came under the jurisdiction of the Holy Roman Empire, the Liégois have defended their neutrality through the centuries, while maintaining their linguistic allegiance to the French-speaking world. Inhabitants of Liège have

Palais de Justice
After a fire (1734) the south façade was rebuilt by Jean Anneessens in a strict neoclassical style. The right wing was built in 1879, in the neo-Gothic style (above).

"The Little France of the Meuse"
Liège received the Légion d'Honneur after World War One, and has always had very close ties with France: indeed July 14 is celebrated here with just as much enthusiasm as in Paris. Liège is the third-largest city of Belgium, with over 600,000 inhabitants.

also had to resist the ambitions of neighboring rulers, notably the Duke of Brabant and, in the 15th century, the Duke of Burgundy. Charles the Bold ordered the sacking of the town in 1468 – and even today the memory of this dreadful massacre lives on in Liège.

A modern city. Liège became prosperous again under Erard de La Marck, who made his "Joyous Entry" into the town on May 30, 1506. Liège and its surrounding region flourished under the patronage of the new bishop, who also actively encouraged commercial enterprise. New industries, such as the gunpowder industry, combined with the iron industry to produce the highly lucrative business of arms manufacturing ▲ *226*. This prosperity also provided the basis for a thriving artistic scene, and in the 17th century the flourishing Liège school of painters followed in the steps of Poussin, with artists such as Gérard Douffet, Bertholet Flémal and Englebert Fisen, while sculpture was dominated by Jean Del Cour ▲ *228*. As a result, Liège was naturally receptive to the ideas of the Enlightenment in the 18th century.

The 19th century. Oppressive tax legislation and the conspicuous privileges of the clergy had sowed the seeds of revolution. When the French Revolution erupted, Liège followed suit: on October 1, 1795 the Convention issued a decree annexing the former Netherlands and the principality of Liège to France. The Liégois also took an active part in the revolution of 1830 ● *40*. They greeted the new Belgian kingdom with enthusiasm, bringing to it the considerable benefit of their commercial expertise. Coal mines and iron and steel works had after all made Liège the leading town in Belgium's industrial revolution.

Today. In both world wars Liège displayed heroic resistance and suffered heavy damage. Today the town is reaffirming its historic role at the heart of southern Belgium: it is the third-largest river port in Europe, an active member of Euregio (Liège, Herleen, Maastricht, Aix-la-Chapelle and Hasselt) and the headquarters of the Economic Commission of the Wallonian Region.

Around Place St-Lambert

The best way to see Liège is to start at the heart of the town – with Place St-Lambert, which has been inhabited for thousands of years. It is here that the Cathedral of St-Lambert stood before it was destroyed by the revolutionaries.

Palais des Princes-Évêques. The Palace of the Prince-Bishops still stands on the square, on the site of Notger's first residence ▲ *221*: today it is the Palais de Justice (law courts). Commissioned by Erard de La Marck in 1526, the building exhibits a skillful combination of styles: Italian Renaissance in the ground plan and use of galleries, Gothic in its ornamentation. The building is arranged around two courts: the first of these is surrounded by porticos (left); the second, smaller court was the Prince-Bishop's garden. The palace was substantially altered in the 18th and 19th centuries.

The Perron. The former pillory on Place du Marché has become an emblem of Liège and a symbol of freedom. It stands on top of a perron, incorporating a fountain, and is crowned by *The Three Graces* by Jean Del Cour ▲ *228*. The significance of the pine cone at the very top remains a mystery.

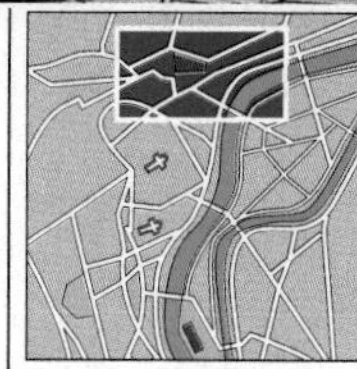

◷ Two days

The palace courtyard
The Gothic vaults of the first court are supported by sixty columns (today these are copies). All the columns are different, with decorations on the theme of Folly, a reference to the *Praise of Folly* by Erasmus, who was a friend of Erard de La Marck.

Place du Marché
Opposite the famous "A Pilori" café ★ is the Hôtel de Ville (1714–18). The town hall is still known as "La Violette" (The Violet), after the sign outside the building, where the city council have met since the 13th century.

A STUNNING COLLECTION OF INSTRUMENTS
The Museum of Walloon Life includes a highly renowned collection of chronometrical and astronomical instruments, assembled by the Antwerp poet Max Elskamp (1862–1931). Below: an astrolabe attributed to Liège instrument maker Lambert Damery (around 1600).

MASTERPIECES IN THE MUSEUM OF RELIGIOUS ART
The collection on the third story of the museum illustrates the development of Mosan art ● *50* from its beginnings up to the Gothic period, including a number of major works, among them the *Virgin of Evegnée* (11th century) and the Christ of Rausa (13th century). The Virgin with the Butterfly (right), from 1459, is one of the few paintings to have survived the sack of Liège in 1468. On the second story religious paintings by Blès and Patenier ● *120* can be seen alongside works from the 17th and 18th centuries (Del Cour, Bertholet Flémal, Fisen).

RUE HORS-CHÂTEAU ★

This delightful street, lined with 17th- and 18th-century buildings, follows the outline of the old rampart, with interesting little alleyways to explore on either side.

MUSÉE DE LA VIE WALLONNE ★. Founded in 1913, largely on the initiative of Joseph-Marie Remouchamp, the museum was moved to its present home, a former Minorite monastery (17th century), in the 1970's. The museum is intended primarily as an illustration of daily life in southern Belgium in the past, with reconstructions of traditional rooms and craft workshops (glassmakers, gunsmiths, brassware makers, coopers). Its collections include old shop signs, games and puppets, and terracottas by Léopold Harzé (1831–93). The museum also has a theater which presents traditional puppet shows ● *62*.

MUSÉE D'ART RELIGIEUX ET D'ART MOSAN. This museum traces the history of the diocese (a model of the Cathedral of St-Lambert, shows how the square looked before the revolution); it also displays a variety of liturgical and religious objects. To one side of the museum is the CHURCH OF ST-ANTOINE, former church of the Minorite monastery: once restoration is complete, this will become a venue for cultural events.

MONTAGNE DE BUEREN

Legend has it that this was the road used in 1468 by the famous six hundred men from Franchimont when they came to attack Charles the Bold's camp by night. Bueren, a citizen of Liège, surrounded the town with his men (the "Franchimontois") on September 9, 1468, seeking to inspire his fellow citizens with the will to fight on, after the defeat inflicted on them by the Burgundians. The enterprise failed: all Bueren's men died in the raid, and the town was sacked for seven weeks after. In fact the Franchimontois did not approach the town from here: the 402 steps of Montagne de Bueren were built in 1880 to allow troops in the citadel ▲ *235* to reach the town center without having to go through dangerous alleyways.

SENTIER DES COTEAUX ★. This pathway is reached through Impasse des Ursulines, to the left of Montagne de Bueren. The buildings on the right-hand side housed the Beguine convent of St-Esprit, founded in 1614. A former coaching inn houses the Art Nouveau studio of the violinist Eugène Ysaye (1859–1931), who was born in Liège and gave his name to one of the world's most famous musical competitions. The pathway ends in a terraced garden ★

"LIÈGE IS A TOWN WHICH UNMAKES AND REMAKES ITSELF TIRELESSLY."

JULES MICHELET

with a splendid view over the town. The Tour des Vieux Joncs, below this, was built for the Teutonic knights in the 13th century.

THE PIERREUSE ★. At the end of the Sentier des Coteaux is a colorful, popular district, traditionally the home of minority groups, where a large number of buildings still have

their attractive 18th-century timbering (above). The name of this quarter refers to the stone quarries that were mined here in the 13th century.

CHURCH OF ST-BARTHÉLEMY

Return to the Rue Hors-Château; this leads to PLACE ST-BARTHÉLEMY. The square, which features a metal sculpture, *The Principalitarians* (1992) by Mady Andrien, is dominated by the imposing façade of the Church of St-Barthélemy. This former collegiate church was founded by Notger's successor. The current building, in sandstone, goes back to the 11th century (east choir with flat chevet) and the 12th century (transept and triple nave). The forebuilding or *westbau* (the enormous block on the west side), which is typical of Mosan architecture ● *82*, dates from the late 12th century. By contrast the roofs of the twin towers are closer to the Rhenish Romanesque style.

EXCEPTIONAL INTERIOR ★. The interior was decorated with stuccos and paintings in the 18th century; it also houses splendid 12th-century baptismal fonts ★ (right), the *Exaltation of the Holy Cross* by Flémal and the *Crucifixion* by Fisen, a masterpiece of 17th-century Liège painting.

EN FÉRONSTRÉE. This street, the old road to Maastricht, was originally the home of the *ferons* or metalworkers. The former Hôtel d'Ansembourg (1738), at no. 114, houses the MUSÉE D'ARTS DÉCORATIFS ★, which displays some masterpieces of 18th-century Liège cabinetmaking.

THE FONTS ATTRIBUTED TO RENIER DE HUY

These fonts ● *50* were originally kept at Notre-Dame-aux-Fonts (next to the cathedral), before being transferred to St-Barthélemy in the 19th century.

LIÈGE GUNSMITHS
Liège hunting guns are among the most highly prized in the world. In the past this industry was a mainstay of the town's economy.

THE QUAI DE LA BATTE

Two squat, heavy mortars mark the entrance to the MUSÉE D'ARMES (18th century) at no.8. Here visitors can admire arms from all ages and all countries, although the emphasis is on firearms and especially rifles from Liège (around 13,000 exhibits). A portrait of *Napoleon* by Ingres commemorates the French general's visit to this building.

MAISON CURTIUS ★ (no. 13)**.** It was the firearms industry that made Jean Curtius' fortune, at the end of the 16th century. This supplier of arms to the King of Spain became the richest citizen of the town and built the palace that still bears his name today, a splendid emblem of his power. This imposing Mosan-style building from the early 17th century (brickwork alternating with stone, high mullioned windows ● *93*) houses remarkable collections of archeological treasures (rare Belgo-Roman and Frankish pieces), decorative arts, paintings, sculptures and Mosan art. The collections include such famous masterpieces as the Virgin by Dom Rupert ● *51* and Notger's evangelistary ● *50*. The MUSÉE DU VERRE at the far end of the court presents the art of glassmaking through the ages (including the glass of the classical age, Venice and Bohemia, Art Nouveau and Art Deco).

The banks of the Meuse today (above), and at the start of the century (below).

ÎLOT ST-GEORGES

The pedestrian Rue St-Georges leads to the heart of the old town, where all the façades were meticulously renovated during the 1970's. The tourist office, on the corner of En Féronstrée, is housed in a 17th-century building in the Mosan Renaissance style (with alternating bands of brickwork and windows).

MUSÉE DE L'ART WALLON. The museum was founded in 1952 and rehoused in 1978; it displays the work of Walloon artists from the 16th century to the present. It is arranged so that visitors work their way downward toward the first story,

"THE LIÉGOIS HAVE BEEN VANQUISHED MORE OFTEN THAN ANY OTHERS, BUT THEY HAVE ALWAYS LIFTED THEIR HEADS AGAIN"

MICHEL DE L'HOSPITAL

WALLOON ARTISTS
Below: *Woman with a Red Corset* (1880), a major work by Liège artist Adrien de Witte (1850–1935), which could be compared to a Degas. Left: *The Blindmen* by Anto Carte (1886–1954), who imbued these two figures with an expressive sense of gravity.

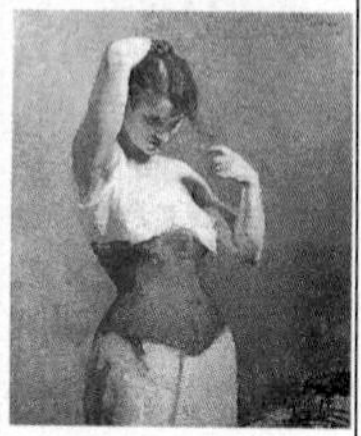

following a chronological display of artists (Henri Blès, Lambert Lombard, Léonard Defrance, Gérard de Lairesse, Rassenfosse, Heintz, Mambour and so on). The SALLE ST-GEORGES was recently refurbished: it is here that high-profile exhibitions are held (Monet, Gauguin etc.), as well as retrospectives of Walloon artists. Continue along the river bank. MAISON HAVART is a mecca of Liège cuisine; this 17th-century building is particularly charming, with its slate-covered corbeled stories. Opposite is the MAISON DES MANGONS ("House of the Butchers"), or meat market, built in limestone during the first half of the 16th century: it is one of the oldest buildings in Liège. On the right at the far end is the NEUVICE ("New Road"), which dates from the 13th century: some 17th-century buildings and the CHURCH OF STE-CATHERINE (18th century) can be seen here. Some old shops here still have their original shop signs, like the leather-goods shop with a Moor's head on the façade.

A LIVELY QUAYSIDE
The Quai de la Batte has the largest market in Liège, held on Sunday mornings ★. This jolly and colorful event should not be missed.

◷ One day

JEAN DEL COUR
On Place St-Paul stands a monument (1911) dedicated to Jean Del Cour (right), the greatest sculptor of Liège (1627–1707). This Baroque master, who was influenced by Bernini, achieved fame during his own lifetime. A number of his sculptures can be seen around Liège.

"CHRIST IN THE TOMB" (below)
As well as this masterpiece by Del Cour (1696), the cathedral's treasures include a stained-glass window depicting the *Coronation of the Virgin* (1530), a *Sedes sapientiae* (13th century), the Shrine of Saint Lambert (1896) and a neo-Gothic pulpit.

Liège was the capital of a state headed by a bishop who was a prince as well: inevitably it was a priests' paradise. From the Romanesque period onward it had many churches, attached to parishes and religious foundations: more than a hundred have been counted. One of the oldest shrines in Liège is the CHURCH OF ST-DENIS on Rue St-Étienne, which was founded by Notger in the 10th century. The church was altered from one century to another, and now presents a curious mixture of styles: Romanesque (the roof of the nave and the tower), Gothic (the choir) and Rococo (the interior decorations). RUE CATHÉDRALE leads to the square of the same name, with the fountain of the Vinâve d'Île (the Island Quarter), surmounted by Jean Del Cour's *Virgin and Child* ★ (1695).

CATHÉDRALE ST-PAUL

This church was also founded in the 10th century, then rebuilt in the 13th and 15th centuries, and finally altered in the 19th century after it had been elevated to the rank of cathedral in 1801, taking the place of the lost Cathedral of St-Lambert ▲ *223*. St-Paul follows the typical floor plan of Gothic churches in the Meuse region: three naves with seven bays bordered with chapels, and a northern entrance.

INTERIOR. The interior is striking, with its harmonious proportions and elegant frescos in the vaults (1557, renovated in 1860): Renaissance arabesques, human figures, birds and animals are fantastically intertwined. The treasury ★, reached through the 15th and 16th century cloister, includes beautiful 11th-century Mosan ivories, the splendid silver reliquary bust of Saint Lambert (16th century) donated by Erard de La Marck, and a small reliquary (left) donated by Charles the Bold in 1471, doubtless to make amends for sacking the town.

SURROUNDINGS. The pedestrian area is one of the delights of Liège (stores on the Rue St-Paul include Nagelmackers, Lemonnier and Magnette). Everywhere, given the slightest hint of sunshine, café terraces spill over onto the walkways.

THE CARRÉ ★

The Carré ("Square") is a bustling shopping center by day (right), and buzzes with lights and music by night. Formerly an island, this area is now bordered by Boulevard de la Sauvenière (once a branch of the Meuse) and Rue Pont-d'Avroy. The town's main theaters are located here.

CHURCH OF ST-JEAN. It was built in 981 or 982 by Notger, on the same octagonal floor plan as the Church of Notre-Dame at Aix-la-Chapelle. Only the forebuilding of this first church still stands, following reconstructions in the 16th century (west wing of the cloister) and the 18th century. Notger liked to meditate in the cloister of St-Jean, where he is now buried. Note the splendid Mosan oak statue ★ (1230) of the Holy Virgin enthroned as *Sedes sapientiae* ("the Seat of Wisdom") ● *50*. In the chapel is a painted woodcarving of *The Virgin and Saint John at Calvary* ★ (around 1250).

CHURCH OF ST-MARTIN

This former collegiate church was founded in the 10th century. Notger dedicated it to Saint Martin, patron saint of soldiers, highlighting the military origin of the building, which was built over fortifications. The church was burned down in 1291 and rebuilt in the 15th century (only the tower of this building survives); it was then sacked by the troops of Charles the Bold and rebuilt again in the 16th century. Despite its chequered history, St-Martin is still a lovely example of Mosan Gothic style. The interior was decorated with stuccos in the 18th century; a beautiful starred vault (1525) highlights the architectural qualities of the choir.

CORPUS CHRISTI. It was here, in the 13th century, that the feast of Corpus Christi, commemorating the holy sacrament, was celebrated for the first time. The feast-day was recognized by Pope Urban IV and extended to the whole Catholic world in 1264. The Rue MONT-ST-MARTIN is lined with 16th- and 17th-century buildings, many of them rebuilt in the 18th century. Rue St-Hubert follows the same course, descending steeply toward the city center as far as the COLLEGIATE CHURCH OF STE-CROIX (12th–15th century). With its three naves of the same height, this is one of the rare examples of a hall church in the region.

MONT ST-MARTIN (17TH CENTURY)
In the foreground, the branch of the Meuse that became Boulevard de la Sauvenière in the last century. In the background, standing out against the horizon, is the Church of St-Martin.

STAINED-GLASS WINDOWS IN ST-MARTIN
The interior of the basilica is lit by remarkable stained-glass windows, some of them donated by Erard de La Marck in 1526 and 1527.

The main post office and the Passerelle (footbridge), one of the bridges leading to Outremeuse.

SIMENON'S OUTREMEUSE

"At the age of seventy I act, think and behave like a child of Outremeuse": Georges Simenon grew up in Liège ▲ *232*. Although he set few of his novels here (only *Au Pont des Arches*, *Le Pendu de St-Pholien* and *Pedigree*), he often recreated its atmosphere under the guise of other towns. Simenon was born in the city center (at no. 24, Rue Léopold) but lived mainly in Outremeuse. Streets such as Rue Puits-en-Sock, where his uncle had a hat shop, and Rue de la Houpe (behind the Church of St-Pholien), where he met his bohemian friends as a young man, provided the setting of his early memories.

"THE HANGED MAN OF ST-PHOLIEN" Simenon's novel draws on the author's memories of his youth and the suicide of one of his friends at La Caque, a ruined house where young people gathered to discuss art and literature.

TOWN WITHIN A TOWN. Outremeuse is a colorful, eccentric town within a town. The quarter as a whole encompasses two parishes: St-Nicolas to the south (the old weavers' quarter, set up as the Free Republic of Outremeuse in 1927) and St-Pholien to the north (the old tanners' quarter, which has been the Free Commune of St-Pholien-des-Prés since 1959). No great monuments are to be found here, but the district has an atmosphere and traditions of which it is fiercely proud. The black madonna (16th century) in the Church of St-Nicolas (1710) is known as Notre-Dame d'Outremeuse, and the highlight of the year is the procession held in her honor on August 15, which is accompanied by various celebrations. On this day the quarter's many *potales* (little niches in the walls with statuettes of the Virgin) are covered with flowers, and the air is heavy with the aromas of *pékèt* – the local gin (left) – and *bouquettes*, the little pancakes that are eaten as snacks all through the day. The Trianon, the Walloon theater on Rue Surlet, presents plays in the local dialect; at no. 56 on the same street is the MUSÉE TCHANTCHÈS, home of the Liège puppet hero and also the headquarters of the Free Republic of Outremeuse, whose government ensures that traditions are upheld.

MUSEUMS. A walk through Outremeuse would not be complete without a visit to the birthplace of the famous composer André-Modeste Grétry (1741–1813), now a small museum. On Quai Van-Beneden, the MAISON DE LA SCIENCE houses the zoological museum with its famous aquarium, where exotic and indigenous, freshwater and seawater fish can be seen.

FROM THE UNIVERSITY TO THE CONSERVATOIRE

THE UNIVERSITY. Liège has a long intellectual tradition: it was known as the "New Athens" in the Middle Ages. The bishops who followed Notger on the episcopal throne fostered an educational system whose fame spread throughout the Western world. The schools of Liège were very influential and made a major contribution to the dissemination of the Mosan style (below, a miniature from the Evangelistary of Averbode). It was therefore quite natural that a university should be established here: this was ratified by royal decree on September 25, 1816. The university was founded on December 25, 1817 in a disused church, formerly of the Walloon Jesuits. In 1835 the Liège architect Rémont restored, enlarged and refurbished the buildings in the town center, on Place Cockerill and Place du 20-Août. Since the early 1960's the university, too cramped within Liège, has progressively moved out toward the hills of Sart-Tilman ▲ *252*.

LES CHIROUX. This is the name of Liège's new cultural center, referring to the rivalry in the 17th century between the *chiroux* or conservative party (from *tchirou*, meaning "wagtail", because of the type of coat worn by their supporters) and the more radical democratic party known as the *grignoux* or "grumpies".

THE CONSERVATOIRE. Walk alongside the Bishop's Palace before heading down BOULEVARD PIERCOT, one of the most fashionable boulevards in town. On this boulevard is the Liège Conservatoire de Musique, established after the Revolution on the model of the Conservatoire in Paris. Two famous Liège composers, César Franck and André-Modeste Grétry, studied here; names like Rouma, Vieuxtemps and Ysaye established the well-founded reputation of the Liège violin school. Continue along the boulevard. Steamships used to set down passengers at the foot of the present-day statue of Charlemagne (1868), surrounded by earlier figures of Liège history: Saint Begge, Pépin de Landen, Bertrade, Pépin le Bref, Charles Martel and Pépin de Herstal.

CHURCH OF ST-JACQUES ★

Take Rue Eugène-Ysaye. The Church of St-Jacques is probably the most beautiful church in Liège, and certainly the most striking. This former abbey church, founded in the 11th century, was a stopping point on the pilgrim route to

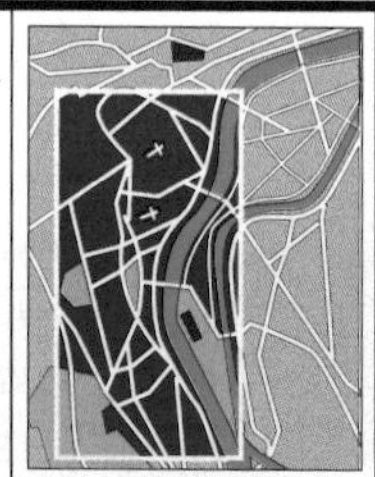

◷ Half a day

TCHANTCHÈS ● *63*
Tchantchès is the hero of Liège puppet plays, a little character who first appeared in the 19th century. As legend has it, he sprang from the ground between two paving stones around the year 760 – in Outremeuse, of course. As a baby Tchantchès could hardly be called a beauty, but he already smiles and prefers a good glass of *pékèt* to the milk he is offered. This irrepressible rebel (center), dressed in cap and smock, shamelessly dispensing deadly head butts, stubborn and good-hearted, represents the archetypal Liégois.

Creator of the famous police superintendent Maigret – a character who made him famous and with whom he came to be identified – Georges Simenon (1903–89) was one of the most prolific writers of our times. Born into an ordinary Liègeois family, he became one of the most popular novelists of the 20th century. His colossal output sold millions of copies; it was translated throughout the world, made into movies and repeatedly serialized on television.

EARLY YEARS
Simenon (right, with his parents and younger brother) was born in Liège to a modest family, and the nineteen years he lived among the ordinary folk of Liège left an indelible mark on his imagination. He began his writing career at the age of sixteen, as a junior reporter on the *Gazette de Liège*. But the town was too small for him, and he moved to Paris in 1922. He made a living by publishing light fiction and popular novels under a variety of pseudonyms.

SIMENON AND MAIGRET
Simenon launched the Maigret series in 1931, writing under his real name for the first time. The public immediately took the surly police inspector to heart: from this time onward Simenon and Maigret were inseparable. They had the same motto: "Do not judge, understand."

A writer's rituals
Simenon always observed the same rituals in his writing. After noting down his plan on a yellow envelope (this was the method which had first brought him success), he wrote the novel in a very plain style, with no embellishment, mostly within a week. On a calendar Simenon marked the days devoted to writing with a blue cross and those spent on revision with a red cross.

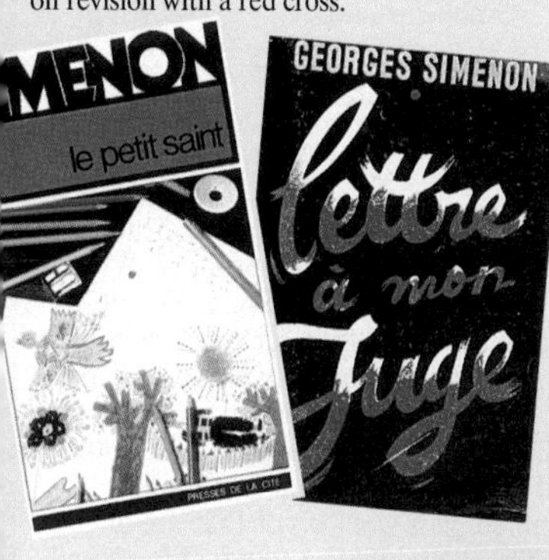

Novels of destiny
Without abandoning Maigret, Simenon also wrote novels (117 of them) where the main plot is not a detective story. These novels follow the tragic destiny of characters, mostly very ordinary figures, who are pushed to the limit by circumstance.

Simenon's own world, and in consequence that of his novels, gradually broadened from Liège to Paris, then to the French provinces and to the rest of the world, as he saw it on his travels.

A prolific writer
Simenon's unflagging productivity astonished commentators, who dubbed him the "steamship novelist" or the "Citroën of literature". He published 190 novels and more than 1,000 stories and novellas under pseudonyms; and 192 novels, 155 novellas and 25 autobiographical works under his own name.

Retirement
In 1972 Simenon abandoned fiction for autobiographical works. He wrote his last book, *Mémoires intimes*, in 1980 after the tragic suicide of his daughter.

Parc d'Avroy.

THE CEILING OF ST-JACQUES ★
The Gothic vaulting, covered with medallions and Renaissance arabesques (16th century), is considered to be among Europe's finest. There is a keystone at each rib crossing, making a total of more than 150 in the main nave ● *85.*

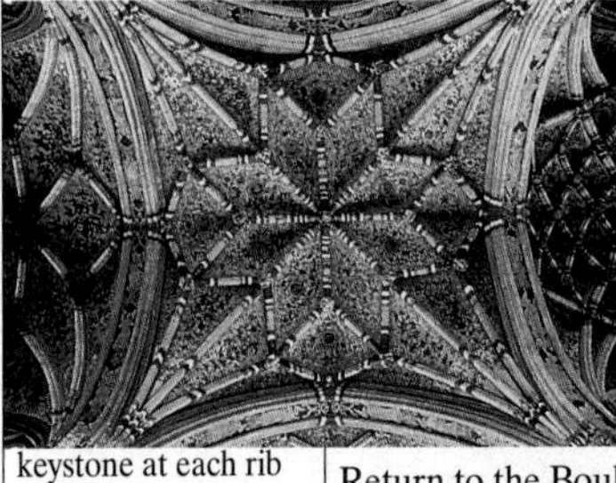

Santiago de Compostela; however, it was in fact dedicated to Saint James the Minor. It is an impressive repository of architectural styles: a 12th-century forebuilding is all that remains of the Ottonian church; the main section is built in the 16th-century Flamboyant style; and the Renaissance porch is decorated with carvings of *Jacob's Dream* based on drawings by Lambert Lombard. The interior decorations (17th–18th century) were restored in the 19th and 20th centuries.

THE INTERIOR. The stained-glass windows of 1525 are as stunning as ever, depicting their donators (the La Marck and Hornes families), Saint Lambert and Saint James. The balustrades are decorated with painted limewood statues by Del Cour. In the side chapel stands a gilded wooden statue of Notre-Dame-de-St-Jacques (1523). Also of interest are the 14th-century stalls and, above the entrance door, a 14th-century carved group depicting the Coronation of the Virgin.

PARC D'AVROY

Return to the Boulevard Piercot. On the left is the park, laid out over a former branch of the Meuse in 1835. A well as reproductions of classical statues, it contains the national monument to the Resistance (Louis Dupont, 1955). Liège, like all southern Belgium, with Hainault at the fore, was at the heart of the resistance to the German occupation. Overlooking the river are two squares, LES TERRASSES, flanked by four groups of animals in bronze.

"LI TORÊ"
The most famous statue of Les Terrasses and the most popular statue in Liège is the *Bullfighter* by Léon Mignon (1900), known as *Li Torê.* It is a traditional venue for student gatherings and ceremonies, on which occasions the animal's physical attributes inevitably attract lewd comments.

PARC DE LA BOVERIE

Cross Pont Albert-1er. Parc de la Boverie, behind the Palais des Congrès, was the setting for the World Fair of 1905. The unusual metal structure was erected by Nicolas Schöffer in 1961: the artist devised this "cybernetic" tower to create an effect of music

MUSÉE D'ART MODERNE
This museum came into being in 1952 when the Musée des Beaux Arts was split into a museum of Walloon art ▲ *226* and a museum of contemporary art; it is housed in a building dating from 1905. Works exhibited cover the period from 1850 to the present; French painting is especially well represented. Artists include Monet and Gauguin (*The Sorcerer of Hiva-Oa*, left), Picasso (*The Soler Family*, top), Chagall (*The Blue House*, above), Léger and Tapiès.

and movement from the light, sounds and atmosphere of its setting. At the far side of the park is the MUSÉE D'ART MODERNE, with a formal rose garden in front of it featuring busts of famous Liège artists (Rassenfosse, Heintz, Donnay, De Witte). At the end of the park there is a view over the Pont de Fragnée and the Union Nautique de Liège.

MAISON DE LA MÉTALLURGIE (on the opposite bank). This museum is devoted to metalworking in Liège. Pride of place goes to a display of steam-hammers (or *makas*, as they are called locally) and a forge that dates from the 17th century.

THE OUTSKIRTS

COINTE. The hills of Cointe, to the south of the town, offer a magnificent view over Liège and the confluence of the Ourthe and Meuse. Cointe was built up a century ago; its lovely avenues and villas have an air of faded elegance.

THE CITADEL. The citadel overlooks the town to the north, at the top of the Bueren Steps ▲ *224*; it also offers an impressive view over the Liège valley. The citadel was built in 1650, rebuilt by Vauban, and dismantled in the 18th century. It was rebuilt once again in 1816 under Dutch rule, along with the fort of La Chartreuse on the southern hills of the town, in order to protect Liège from the danger of French invasion. Today the citadel houses the university hospital, and its moats have been turned into public pathways. The ramparts of La Chartreuse have been classified as a sanctuary for bats.

THE ALBERT CANAL. Follow the river banks to the east as far as Coronmeuse. The canal joining the Meuse to the Escaut was completed in 1939, opening up a direct route to Antwerp and the North Sea for the industries of Liège.

ART NOUVEAU AT COINTE
Art Nouveau buildings can be seen throughout Cointe but especially on Avenue de la Laiterie: the Villa L'Aube (1903), at no. 2, was designed by Liège architect Gustave Serrurier (1858–1910) and decorated with a mosaic by Auguste Donnay. Serrurier was primarily a theorist and designed few buildings himself, but his architectural creations were praised by Victor Horta, who wrote to him: "You are the only Belgian architect to have achieved a truly modernist architecture."

▲ Liège to the Herve region

1. Liège 2. Visé 3. Blégny-Trembleur mine 4. Abbey of Val-Dieu 5. Henri-Chapelle 6. Tancrémont 7. Franchimont 8. Verviers 9. Eupen 10. Gileppe dam 11. Signal de Botrange 12. Robertville

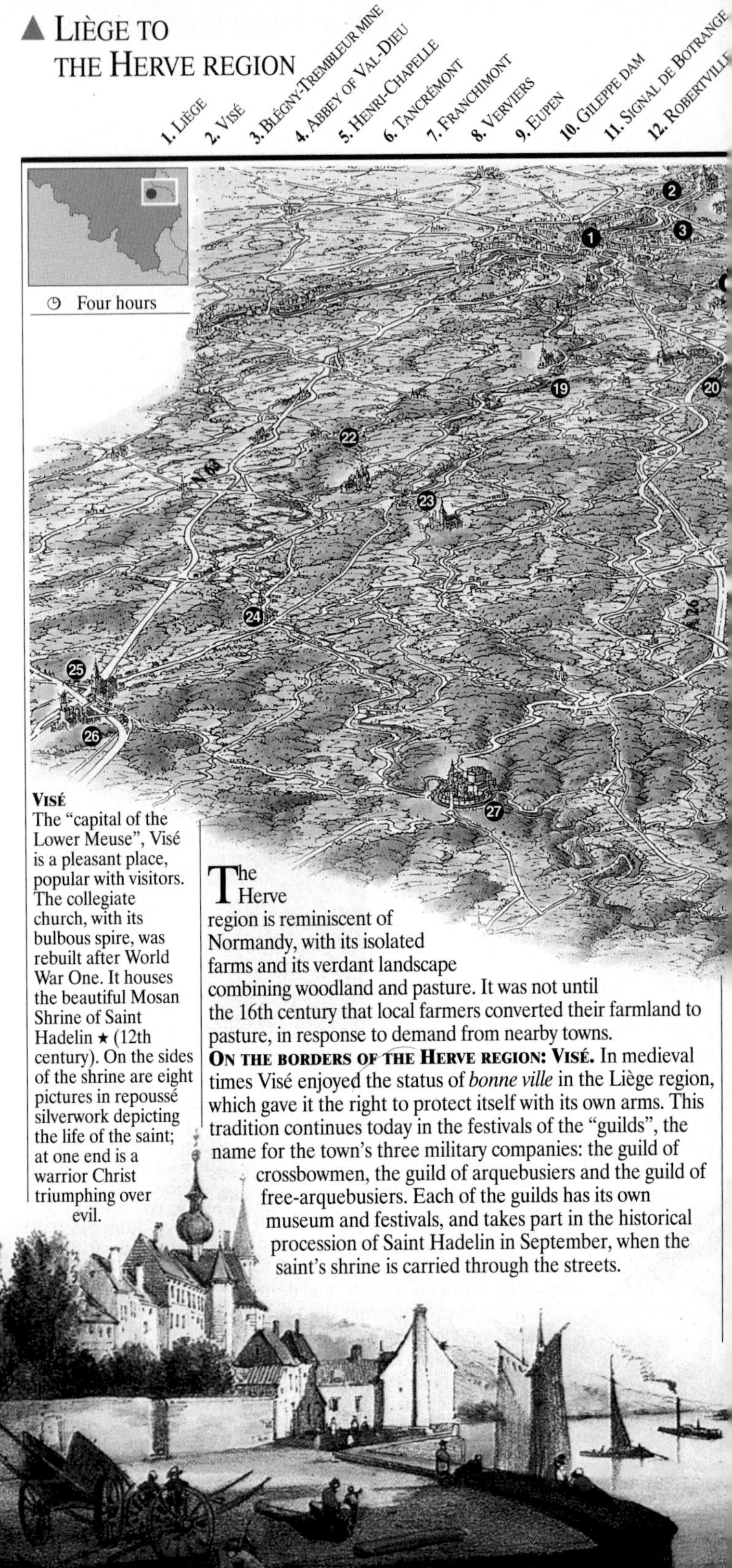

Visé
The "capital of the Lower Meuse", Visé is a pleasant place, popular with visitors. The collegiate church, with its bulbous spire, was rebuilt after World War One. It houses the beautiful Mosan Shrine of Saint Hadelin ★ (12th century). On the sides of the shrine are eight pictures in repoussé silverwork depicting the life of the saint; at one end is a warrior Christ triumphing over evil.

The Herve region is reminiscent of Normandy, with its isolated farms and its verdant landscape combining woodland and pasture. It was not until the 16th century that local farmers converted their farmland to pasture, in response to demand from nearby towns.

On the borders of the Herve region: Visé. In medieval times Visé enjoyed the status of *bonne ville* in the Liège region, which gave it the right to protect itself with its own arms. This tradition continues today in the festivals of the "guilds", the name for the town's three military companies: the guild of crossbowmen, the guild of arquebusiers and the guild of free-arquebusiers. Each of the guilds has its own museum and festivals, and takes part in the historical procession of Saint Hadelin in September, when the saint's shrine is carried through the streets.

13. BÜLLINGEN
14. ST-VITH
15. BURG-REULAND
16. MALMÉDY
17. STAVELOT
18. SPA
19. COMBLAIN-AU-PONT
20. SOUGNÉ-REMOUCHAMPS
21. CASCADES DE COO
22. DURBUY
23. WÉRIS
24. HOTTON
25. MARCHE-EN-FAMENNE
26. WAHA
27. LA ROCHE-EN-ARDENNE

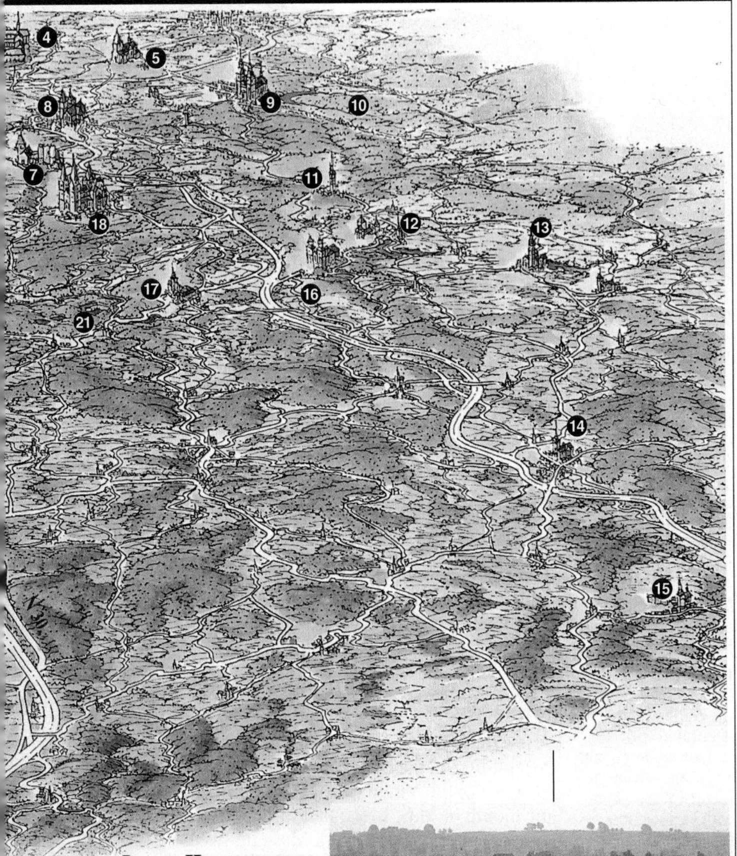

IN THE HERVE REGION. Leave the Fourons (Voeren) district to the north. Although this is a French-speaking area, having come under the jurisdiction of Liège in Napoleonic times, it was annexed to Limbourg in 1962. The Herve region begins at Mortroux. The CISTERCIAN ABBEY OF VAL-DIEU is approached down a hill leading into a valley; the church spire (19th century) can be seen among the treetops. The church in the VILLAGE OF HENRI-CHAPELLE is a composite building combining a Romanesque tower, a Gothic choir and an 18th-century nave; inside there is a decorated beam ★ (15th century) depicting the Last Supper. After this is Herve, the capital of the region, occupied by French soldiers during the 1830 Revolution and by German troops in World War One. Next comes the CHÂTEAU DE BOLLAND ★, seat of an independent manor that formed a separate enclave within the region. The buildings date from the 17th century, except for the towers (14th and 16th centuries). The last stop is the BLÉGNY COAL MINE ★, with one of the oldest mining buildings in Belgium, the Puits Marie (1816). Go down the shaft in a miners' cage to see the old mining gallery ● *96* ▲ *300*.

HERVE LANDSCAPE
The area is famous for its cheese ● *80*. It also has one of Belgium's most beautiful villages, Clermont-sur-Berwinne, which boasts a large number of 17th-century houses combining slate (roofs), brickwork (walls) and white stone (corner piers, frames of doors and windows).

THE CHAPEL OF CHEVREMONT
A group of British Jesuits fleeing religious persecution took refuge in Liège in 1613 and built a chapel on the hill of Chèvremont. The castle of Saint Begge ▲ *214* once stood here, a focal point for the cult of the Virgin from the 10th century onward. The Barefoot Carmelites built a convent and a basilica here in 1899.

CHURCH AT THEUX
In the 17th century the ceiling was decorated with caissons painted with 127 scenes from the life of Christ, along with various other figures.

On the heights of the Ardennes region are the Hautes Fagnes: "the spongy carpet of sphagnum moss which produced the peat marshes. . . . These marshes act as huge sponges, effectively creating huge reservoirs of water. Many rivers have their source here, flowing down into valleys which are quite shallow at first, but become deeper at around 1,600 feet above sea level." (Émile Merenne, *Pays de Liège, pays d'Europe*.) The Vesdre is one of the rivers that start on the Hautes Fagnes ▲ *244*: following its course upriver takes you through CHAUDFONTAINE (a spa town), Tancrémont and finally Verviers. The summit of the Hautes Fagnes is in the German-speaking cantons and on the plateau, with its peat bogs and lakes. Rivers that have their source here include the Warche, which flows through Malmédy, the Our, which flows as far as Luxembourg, and the Hoegne, which runs through Spa.

PILGRIMAGES

A few miles from CHÈVREMONT is BANNEUX-NOTRE-DAME, the end point of a pilgrimage in honor of the Virgin which takes place during the month of May. In the first three months of 1933 an eleven-year-old girl, Mariette Beco, witnessed eight apparitions of the Virgin here, some in the presence of witnesses. Since then millions of pilgrims have made the journey here, and the village has become famous for the miraculous cures brought about by water from the spring where the Virgin led Mariette.

THEUX ★

Under the Ancien Régime this little town was famous for its metalworking (kitchen utensils were produced here), its black marble quarries and its textile industry. It became a free town in 1457 and commemorated its independence by building a perron ▲ *223*, with four steps, in front of the town hall. However, this was destroyed – along with the whole town – by the Burgundians, after the Franchimontois ▲ *224* had attempted to free Louis XI in 1468. The present-day perron dates from 1768. The town has a wealth of architectural treasures, including houses in the Mosan Renaissance style (Rue Chaussée and Place du Perron), Baroque buildings (90 rue Hovémont), Rococo buildings (opposite the church) and neoclassical ones (the town hall and 80 rue Hovémont).

The Mosan figure of Christ at Tancrémont.

⏱ Three days
🚗 80 miles

CHURCH OF STS-HERMÈS-ET-ALEXANDRE ★ (11th century). Three naves of equal height and a flat roof make this a hall church, one of the few of its type to be found between the Loire and the Rhine. In the 13th century the building was fortified by the addition of a huge tower to the north, which was rebuilt a century later. The Gothic choir dates from 1500.

CHÂTEAU DE FRANCHIMONT ★. This fortress, which belonged to the episcopal principality of Liège, consists of two sections. The first comprises an 11th-century keep (reinforced with a thick mantle wall after 1387), a high courtyard bordered with buildings, and a barbican built to protect the eastern entrance in the 14th century. The second section, from the 16th century, consists of a pentagonal rampart, its corners reinforced with enormous circular towers, and an artillery tower adjoining the eastern entrance. The whole complex is a mine of information for those interested in the history of fortification.

THE CHRIST OF TANCRÉMONT ★. Before heading for Verviers, visit the nearby Chapel of TANCRÉMONT (19th century), which houses a large painted wooden sculpture of Christ on the cross (10th or 11th century). Works by Mosan artists ● *50* display a number of common stylistic features, such as soft shapes and figures characterized by serenity and humanity (dressed, as here, in a *colobium* or tunic). Generally these artists produced small pieces in ivory; here the sculptor was able to work on a much larger scale, without departing from the traditional style.

THE RUINS OF FRANCHIMONT
The fortress, built on an isolated outcrop overlooking the Hoegne, was damaged during the French Revolution. Restoration work is currently in progress.

VERVIERS

"Verviers, international wool center" says the sign at the entrance to the town. Today, however, only the SIMONIS FACTORY, founded in 1680, continues the traditions of an age when the Verviers wool industry could compete with that of Ghent or Bruges.

A CENTER FOR TEXTILES. The town's textile industry first began to emerge during the 14th century; it expanded rapidly in the 16th century, fueled by the rise of capitalism. A working class began to emerge, as spinners and weavers came to work in the factories. At the end of the 17th century

View of Franchimont in the 19th century.

RISE OF THE TEXTILE INDUSTRY
Several factors contributed to the rise of this industry in the 14th century: the presence of a river as a source of power; a lack of regulation, encouraging individual enterprise; and the support of local authorities, who gave Verviers manufacturers a special place at the Liège market in 1323 and built public tenters (frames for drying cloth) a century later. The merchants imported wool from all over Europe, and had it spun and woven by country workers before finishing the cloth in their factories in town and selling it at the great European fairs. Right: *The Home Weaver* (Léon Frédéric, 1896).

and during the 18th century Verviers became the main cloth-producing town in Liège and the second-largest town of the region, after Liège itself.

THE INDUSTRIAL REVOLUTION. William Cockerill (inventor of the spinning frame) arrived in Verviers in 1800, and the protectionist measures put in place by Napoleon held force until 1815. These factors, along with the entrepreneurial spirit of the manufacturers themselves, ensured that the Verviers textile industry stayed abreast of both technical developments and competitors during the 19th century. New manufacturing processes were quickly adopted: the flying shuttle in 1802, the spinning jenny in 1818, and the Leviathan in 1863. Mechanization itself spawned new industries: the construction of textile machinery, strap factories, shoe factories and so on. The advent of the railway in 1843 opened up new markets. The GILEPPE DAM ★, a mile or two to the east of the town, was built in 1878 to enable the textile factories to increase their output. However, the wool industry declined after 1914, undermined by international competition and the development of synthetic fabrics.

THE GILEPPE DAM
This carved lion (above) stands on the Gileppe Dam, built in 1848 to meet the water requirements of the Verviers textile industry. The wall of the dam is 200 feet high and 1,200 feet wide; it was built to create a reservoir of nearly 1 billion cubic feet and is still one of the largest dams in Europe.

Medieval weavers at work.

THE TOWN OF VERVIERS. The wool merchants built a number of magnificent houses in Verviers. The Mosan Renaissance style, much simpler here than in Liège, lasted until the end of the 17th century. After this came the Louis XIII style: notable features include lower first stories and window bases, the disappearance of mullioned windows and the appearance of projections on façades. In the 18th century wool merchants built residences in the neoclassical style: a typical example is the town hall (1775–80), designed by Jacques-Barthélemy Renoz (1729–86).

MUSEUMS IN VERVIERS. Preindustrial wool production is presented in the PRÉMUSÉE DE LA LAINE at no. 8, rue de Séroule (a museum encompassing the full history of the industry is due to open shortly). The MUSÉE D'ARCHÉOLOGIE ET DE FOLKLORE displays furniture, paintings and archeological items in a Louis XV style aristocratic residence, with interior decorations in the First Empire style (42, rue Renier); the Verviers crib ★, a unique animated nativity scene, is displayed here at Christmas. The MUSÉE DES BEAUX-ARTS ET DE LA CÉRAMIQUE (17, rue Renier) has a wide-ranging collection of paintings, including an early Italian work, pre-Impressionists, modern works and the work of local artists.

MECHANIZATION
Industrialization in the 19th century led to the disappearance of small-scale producers. From this time onward, spinners and weavers worked in the twenty or so remaining factories, forming a new "proletarian" class in the service of entrepreneurs, who themselves developed a paternalistic attitude to their workers. Below: a Verviers factory in the early 20th century.

LIMBOURG ★

This small town is perched on a promontory overlooking a bend in the Vesdre river; in the past it was the capital of a county and then a duchy of the same name ● *40*. Limbourg is made up of the lower town, which has most of the modern facilities and buildings, and the upper town, where the tightly packed houses along the main street date mainly from the 17th and 18th centuries. The upper town is built on the site of an old *burg* (castle) from around AD 1000. Some sections of the old castle wall survive.

SPECIALIZATION
The only factories to survive today are those which opted for specialization, like the Simonis factory: its cloths for billiard tables are famous throughout the world.

THE POPULATION OF VERVIERS
The residential areas of Verviers grew up around the riverside fulleries (left). The town expanded rapidly: at the start of the 19th century there were 10,000 inhabitants, which had risen to 50,000 by 1914. This demographic explosion brought about the fragmentation of the town, as districts such as Ensival, Heusy and Andrimont grew up around the town center.

Snow in the Haute-Ardenne
The region has plenty of pistes for cross-country skiing between November and March.

The Church of St-Nicolas at Eupen
Around the Church of St-Nicolas (1726) – façade (above) and interior (below) – are the Baroque-style patrician residences of the upper town, arranged in blocks and rows.

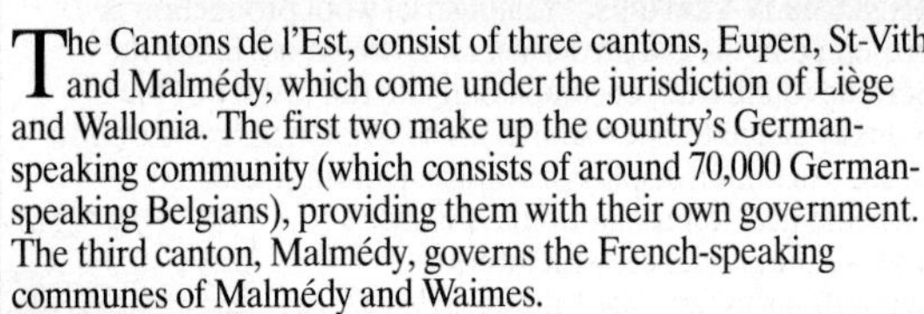

The Cantons de l'Est, consist of three cantons, Eupen, St-Vith and Malmédy, which come under the jurisdiction of Liège and Wallonia. The first two make up the country's German-speaking community (which consists of around 70,000 German-speaking Belgians), providing them with their own government. The third canton, Malmédy, governs the French-speaking communes of Malmédy and Waimes.

History. The cantons were combined to form the French département of Ourthe under Napoleon. They were annexed to Prussia in 1815, and then given to Belgium in 1919 under the Treaty of Versailles. In 1940 they were annexed by Hitler. They became part of Belgium again after World War Two.

Geography. The highest part of the Ardennes massif ▲ *256* is in the cantons; the three ridges here include the highest peaks in the country, among them the Signal de Botrange (2,275 feet). The region is divided geographically into a number of distinct areas, each with a different type of landscape: a marshy plateau, the Hautes Fagnes ▲ *244*; a relatively flat area of woodland and fields beginning to the south of the high plateau; and finally an area dominated by river valleys. Since 1971 this district has been part of the joint German-Belgian nature reserve of Hautes Fagnes-Eifel.

Itineraries

Eupen ★. Eupen has an upper and a lower town; it has been the home of the council of the German-speaking community since 1973. The Collège Patronné in the lower town was founded by Napoleon to impose the French language on this German-speaking area: it is a reminder of the Imperial age, when the town was renamed Néau. Each winter this old cloth-making town has a lively carnival.

The Vesdre Dam. The 30-acre reservoir created by the dam (3 miles from Eupen) stretches between deciduous forests and massifs covered with coniferous trees. Pathways for walkers have been laid down in the steep foothills.

Robertville. Cross the Hautes Fagnes ▲ *244* as far as Robertville, where the medieval fortress of Reinhardstein stands. Nearby, the artificial lakes of Robertville and Bütgenback are used for a variety of water sports.

THE SCHWALM VALLEY ★. A number of rivers have their source on the plateaus of Elsenborn, Rocherath and Losheimergraben, including the Olef, the Holzwarche and the Schwalm. The valley of the Schwalm is one of the best preserved in the Haute-Ardenne, where diversion channels used to be cut into the hillsides to irrigate the fields. One of these channels has been restored in the Schwalm nature reserve, where many semi-alpine flowers grow (spignel, bistort, knapweed and the very rare mountain arnica); birds that can be spotted here include gray shrikes and the stonechat ■ *23* and whinchat ■ *20*. The valley can be reached on foot from the road, heading toward the border to the north of ROCHERATH, or from the German village of KALTERHERBERG.

THE OUR VALLEY ★. ST-VITH, which was rebuilt after the Battle of the Ardennes ▲ *270*, is the starting point for the Our valley itinerary. Head for BURG-REULAND ★, a village huddled around the ruins of its 10th-century *burg*. The CHURCH OF ST-STÉPHANE has a schist portal by Recht (dated 1772); it also has a beautiful bulbous bell tower and, inside, a tomb of black Theux marble (17th century) made for a lord of Reuland and his wife. The valley runs along the German border up to the village of OUREN, which is close to the Luxembourg border. The Our winds between steep slopes covered with oak groves. Birds living around the river include the kingfisher, the dipper and the wagtail; otters can still be seen here, too. The rocky hillside habitat is well suited to the harsh winters.

EUPEN, CLOTH-MAKING TOWN
Eupen's prosperity, like that of Verviers, was founded on the textile industry. Rows of opulent-looking

houses can be seen in the residential area, in the upper town. A small museum recreates an 18th-century Eupen residence.

THE EUPEN CARNIVAL
As the carnival starts, the local authorities hand over their power to "Prinz Karneval", whose image is burned at the end of the festivities. The number eleven, almost a magic number in Eupen, plays a central role: on November 11, at eleven minutes past eleven, eleven laws are pronounced by the Council of Eleven, which holds sway throughout the carnival. The festival reaches its height on the Monday, in the *rosenmontag*, a grand costumed procession.

CHÂTEAU DE REINHARDSTEIN
This castle with its fairytale appearance was built in 1354. It was dismantled in 1799, and then sold as a source of building materials in the 19th century, before being rebuilt in 1965. Collections of armor and paintings can be seen inside.

▲ The Hautes Fagnes

A protected site
In 1957 the stretches of moorland and peat bog that had not been reforested were made into nature reserves.

They form part of the nature reserve of Hautes Fagnes-Eifel, a "green lung" at the heart of Europe that is a joint venture between German and Belgian parks, dating from 1985.

Use of peat
Peat was used as a fuel when wood started to become scarce, from the 16th to the 19th centuries. It was taken from the peat hills of the Hautes Fagnes by *troufleûrs*, who cut out the *troufes* (turfs of peat).

The Hautes Fagnes consist of 10,000 acres of peat bogs and moors, located in several separate areas around the high points of the Ardennes region: Signal de Botrange (2,275 feet) and Baraque Michel (2,200 feet). The climate at this altitude is cold and wet; rainfall is higher here than anywhere in the country, and fogs are frequent and persistent. These conditions create a habitat suitable for the plants and animals common to mountainous northern regions, such as andromeda, cranberry, chickweed wintergreen (*Trientalis europaea*) and various insects that took refuge here after the last ice age. The subsoil (mainly phyllite and quartzites) is among the oldest on the continent; some of the rocks date from as far back as the Primary era.

Birth of a landscape. The gentle relief, impermeable substrata and heavy rainfall (60 inches per year) favored the development of raised peat bogs or peat hills ■ *18*, some of them 7,000 years old. Analysis of the pollen contained in them shows that after the last ice age, 10,000 years ago, the landscape was dominated by deciduous forests, with clearings here and there in the marshy areas. The plant life changed radically from the early Middle Ages onward, as trees were cut down, the land was used for pasturing, rye was grown in the dry areas, and the peat hills were drained (after the 16th century). By the 19th century the landscape was very open, dominated by moorland with heather (*Calluna vulgaris*), cranberry and cross-leaved heath (*Erica tetralix*). At the end of the century, after farming was abandoned here, spruce was planted over large areas of moors and bogs. The draining of the bogs favored purple moor grass (*Molinia caerulea*) ■ *19* at the expense of flowering plants. However, increasing numbers of visitors have presented the most serious threat of recent decades – trampling the soil and disturbing wildlife, especially the black-grouse population (now below two hundred on the high plateau). Conservation measures had to be taken: signposted paths were laid, and access restricted to certain areas.

The palsas. At altitudes higher than 2,000 feet, "palsas" – or rather the remains of palsas – are numerous. Plant life has colonized the lakes in these basins: a variety of plants grow on the floating carpets of sphagnum moss (floating peat bogs). It can be dangerous to venture onto these areas: this unstable mattress of vegetation is loose in places, and liable to give way under the weight of imprudent walkers. Luckily most of the palsas can be easily spotted by the embankment of earth

which surrounds them, generally covered with moorland plants (heather, bilberry), or trees and bushes that contrast with the surrounding vegetation. The floating peat bogs and the lakes of the palsas have highly distinctive flora and fauna ■ *19.*

Across the Hautes Fagnes

These can only be explored on foot. Footpaths on the plateau offer walks at all levels of difficulty.

The Helle valley. This walk goes from Eupen to Baraque Michel along the Helle valley. Allow for 15 miles and a day's walking (make a very early start in winter). The path follows the fast-flowing course of the river and crosses the Hertogenwald Forest before ending on the fagne.

The summit of the plateau. There are many paths leading round or across the fagnes from Signal de Botrange and Baraque Michel. The paths heading toward the Helle river offer the widest views: over the southern Belgium fagne (with the largest peat hill of the region), if you start from Botrange; over the fagnes of the Potales and the Deux Séries, if you start from Baraque Michel. The mile-long nature trail marked out from the Fagne de la Polleûr gives a good idea of the plant life of the peat bogs. Half a mile to the south of Signal de Botrange, the Nature Center of Botrange presents the ecosystems of the high plateau.

Between Eupen and Montzen (Germany). Here the fagnes are less open than around Botrange: the woods have grown back again in places and the landscape is more varied. There are many remains of palsas and a good example of a peat hill. A path has been provided for visiting the Brackvenn, a fagne to the south of the road from Eupen to Montzen. The path crosses the peat hill of Misten (210 acres), where in places the peat is 23 feet thick. To the north of the road is a path crossing the Fagne de Puzen. Further north is the Fagne de Steinley, where the Vesdre river has its source; the Fagne de Kutenhart is a manmade moorland, resulting from the deterioration of the deciduous forest due to agricultural activities. These two fagnes can be visited by bicycle, on small forest roads.

Bilberry

The "palsas", remnants of the ice age

These depressions, from 80 to 160 feet in diameter, about 16 feet deep and surrounded by an embankment of earth, are filled with water and covered with a thick carpet of floating vegetation (**2**). The palsas appeared at the end of the last ice age. Huge spherical humps of ice formed in the surface of the ground (**1**), which must have looked like hillocks in the landscape. When the ice melted, hollows were left in the ground.

1

2

Spaghnum orchids

Around 650 Siegbert, King of Austrasia and Aquitaine and successor to the famous Dagobert, ordered the future Saint Remaclus to convert the people of the dark forest of the Ardennes. Remaclus' first abbey in the Semois valley was a total failure. After this he moved to the highlands where he founded two abbeys, one after the other, the first at Malmédy and the second at Stavelot. These twin monasteries, attached to the Benedictine order, played a key role in unifying the Ardennes region. The estate was enriched by a number of donations during the Middle Ages, and formed an independent principality within the Holy Roman Empire. A bitter rivalry divided the towns under the Ancien Régime: Malmédy, the larger of the two, resented the fact that the abbot lived at Stavelot, which was also the administrative capital of the principality. Their separation, which began under French rule, became final in 1815, when Malmédy was annexed to Prussia along with the other Cantons de l'Est, while Stavelot remained Belgian.

CARNIVAL COUNTRY
Famous carnivals include the Cwarmè at Malmédy and the Laetare Carnival (right) at Stavelot ● *68*.

APOLLINAIRE
(1880–1918)
During the night of October 3–4, 1899 two penniless young brothers left the inn at Stavelot without paying their bill: their mother had become bankrupt in Spa. One of the brothers was the poet Guillaume Apollinaire. He fell in love with a young Stavelot woman, Marie Dubois, who inspired the poems of *Le Guetteur mélancolique* and the *Caligrammes*. The town hall in Stavelot has a museum dedicated to him.

MALMÉDY

"The culture transmitted by the Abbey of Malmédy, essentially Latin and French, left the mark of its influence on the territories defined in 670. Today's linguistic border is a product of this, corresponding almost exactly to the old borders." (Jean-Marc Gay and Jean-Marc Huygen, *Les Cantons de l'Est*.) Malmédy, with its rows of slate-roofed houses set into the Warche valley, is in fact deeply Walloon: street signs are still given in Walloon as well as French. In 1944 ▲ *270* the town was completely destroyed by American bombs as the result of a command error; it was then occupied by Allied troops.

TOUR OF MALMÉDY. Formerly a Benedictine abbey church, the MALMÉDY CATHEDRAL was rebuilt in the 18th century after Louis XIV had almost completely destroyed the town (1689). The entrance façade of this grand, simple building is built in the Renaissance style. Only a few 18th-century buildings remain from the monastery that stood alongside it. Place du Châtelet, the heart of the old town, was formerly situated within the monastery grounds, which were enclosed by walls following the course of today's Rue Cavens and Rue de la Chemin-Rue. The old quarters of Haute-Vaulx, Vaulx and Outrelepont still have timbered houses built in 1690 and 1724. At no. 11, rue Cavens is the orphanage which was founded by Jean-Henri Cavens in the 19th century; it now houses the MUSÉE NATIONAL DU PAPIER and the MUSÉE DU CWARME (the local Shrove Tuesday carnival).

TANNERIES
Tanners were attracted to both Malmédy and Stavelot by the purity of the water. The first tanneries were established in the 16th century, and by 1885 there were no less than sixty-five in Malmédy.

STAVELOT ★

With its maze of little streets lined with timbered houses, its Grand-Place and its fountains, Stavelot is a lovely place to stay. It also has a very rich history and heritage.

THE ABBEY. The monastery was rebuilt in the 18th century, around two courtyards; it now houses the town hall and (in the outbuildings) the MUSÉE D'ART RELIGIEUX RÉGIONAL. The refectory (1778) in the second court houses the tourist office; the Duckers brothers created its stucco decorations. The ABBEY CHURCH was destroyed during the Revolution and plundered for building materials. As a result the only part still standing is the imposing tower porchway, a Romanesque building modified in 1534; the later additions (16th, 17th and 18th century) have all disappeared. Excavations are now under way to discover further remains – including the Merovingian chapel, the first Carolingian church and the 11th-century Ottonian building. The abbey church was very large (more than 330 feet long) because it had to accommodate large numbers of pilgrims, attracted by the relics of Saint Remaclus now on display in the TREASURY of the parish church of St-Sébastien (18th century).

SAINT REMACLUS
Remaclus (above) was the disciple and friend of Saint Eloi. His skull is preserved in a 19th-century shrine; the rest of his remains are kept in a Mosan-style tomb ★ (around 1265).

MOTOR RACING
The first motor races were held in 1896, on the road to Spa. They are commemorated in Stavelot's Musée du Circuit de Spa-Francorchamps.

PORTABLE ALTARPIECE FROM STAVELOT (1145)
The town was an important center of Mosan art ● *50*, as can be seen from this altarpiece detail, now in Brussels.

Pouhon Pierre le Grand
Named after Peter the Great, who took a cure at Spa in 1717, this is one of the resort's largest springs. The building (above), which dates from 1880, houses a monumental painting depicting famous visitors to the town.

The Fagnes de la Crête de Malchamps ★

The fagnes of the Malchamps Ridge are an extension of the Hautes Fagnes to the west: they act as a natural filter for the waters of Spa. The Spa Monopole company, which owns these fagnes, set up its buildings and installations below the ridge. The moorland and peat bogs offer a wide panorama over the lower hills of the Herve region ▲ *237*. Small pathways wind through the heather and bilberries. There are numerous remains of palsas ▲ *244*, especially in the area around the meteorological observatory: some still have lakes in them (providing a habitat for dragonflies), while andromeda and two species of sundew (a carnivorous plant) grow in abundance on the floating sphagnum-moss carpets. The black grouse has one of its last refuges in southern Belgium here: the very small population is stable, no doubt thanks to the regular influx of individual birds from the Hautes Fagnes ▲ *244*. The thick-billed nutcracker, the stonechat ■ *23* and the redpoll ■ *19* can also be seen here.

Walks around Spa
A dense network of paths was built up around Spa to meet visitors' needs. These include the "Tour of the Fountains" (which leads from the Lac de Warfaaz to the Tonnelet, Sauvenière and Reine springs) and the "Meyerbeer Tour" (which leads to the Géronstère and Barisart springs).

Spa

The Romans already knew Spa for its waters; the town's name comes from *espa* (fountain) and *sparsa* (from the Latin *spangere*, "to spring"). In the Middle Ages Spa was one of five towns belonging to the manor of Franchimont, ruled by the Prince-Bishop of Liège. At this time it was a small town, making the most of its abundant natural resources (deposits of iron and charcoal in its forests). However, when coal replaced charcoal, the metal industries gradually moved toward the Meuse valley. Then in the 16th century visitors started to flock to the town, and in later centuries Spa became known as "the Café of Europe" ▲ *250*.

Turbulent history. Despite its neutrality, Belgium was invaded by the German army on August 4, 1914.

From 1914 to 1918 Spa was a convalescent center for the German army, and in March 1918 it was the residence of Kaiser Wilhelm II. German leaders set out from Spa on the road to Rethondes.

TOUR OF SPA. The PRINCE DE CONDÉ SPRING is on Rue Gérardy, which leads to the *pouhon* (spring) of Peter the Great and then to the HÔTEL DE VILLE (18th century) with its perron (1596), an emblem of the town's freedom ▲ *223*. Follow the Rue Royale, with the CASINO standing on the south side (today's building dates from 1920). The Établissement des Bains, designed in the 19th-century eclectic style, offers peat baths and carbonated baths, along with a whole range of services such as fitness classes and beauty treatments, massage and other health treatments. The PARC DE SEPT-HEURES, on the PLACE ROYALE, acquired its name because visitors have been coming here for their evening stroll for over three hundred years. The Galerie Léopold II ★ is a prefabricated-metal gallery like those to be seen be seen in most spa towns; it was built between two small pavilions in 1878. The metal roof and wooden ceiling are supported by 160 cast-iron columns; originally the the colonnade would have been decorated with hanging baskets and gas lighting. The VILLA DE LA REINE MARIE-HENRIETTE on Avenue Reine-Astrid now houses the police station, the magistrate's court and two museums: the equestrian museum reflects the importance of horse racing in Spa, while the Musée de la Ville d'Eaux ★ presents local crafts, notably some lovely *jolités*, small objects in painted wood (left). The HÔTEL BRITANNIQUE on Rue de la Sauvenière was once the Kaiser's headquarters; it is now a boarding school.

SPORTS AND WALKS. Sports were popular from an early stage with visitors to Spa who had come to improve their health. Horse racing, tennis, swimming, shooting and golf suited the lifestyle of Spa's European elite, and were introduced as they became fashionable. Nevertheless, walking has remained the most popular activity, and there is plenty of choice provided by the dozens of footpaths in the woods and hills round about.

GALERIE LÉOPOLD II
Originally the gallery could be closed with panels on the town side or the hill side, according to the weather.

SOUVENIRS OF SPA
Spa virtually invented the tourist souvenir. Craft workshops initially produced walking sticks for visitors to use when walking from one spring to another. They then branched out into all kinds of wooden objects, inlaid with mother-of-pearl or metal, covered with lacquer, or decorated with paintings in gouache or oils (left). This art reached its peak in the 18th century.

The Source de la Reine.

THE SPRINGS
In Spa the springs are called *pouhons*. The most famous ones are the Sauvenière (below), the Tonnelet (right), the Géronstère and the Barisart.

Spa was for a long time the leading resort of its type. Indeed in the English language its name came to be synonymous with a spring town or water-cure center. The qualities of its water, containing iron and carbonates, were recognized from the 16th century onward and attracted Europe's elite right from the start. However, the 19th century was Spa's heyday: for many visitors its balls, beauty competitions, casinos and sporting events were just as important as taking baths and visiting the various springs.

FROM ONE CURE TO THE NEXT
At first the water was prescribed as a drink; it was probably not until around 1750 that baths were first taken. The water was heated (it is only 10° or 12°C when it rises from the ground). In 1868 the town council opened the present-day bath house, where heart patients came to take carbonated baths, and rheumatics were treated with peat from the fagnes.

THE MEETING PLACE FOR EUROPE
Europe's royalty often came to take the waters at Spa. After the Duchess of Orléans recovered her health here in 1787, her children erected a monument at the Sauvenière Spring (left).

GAMING AND CASINOS
A cure was accompanied by various distractions, among which gambling held a prominent place. In 1762 Spa became the first cure town where gambling was regulated by the ruling power (the Prince-Bishop, who of course imposed a tax payable to the treasury). However, putting the new law into effect proved problematic. Two other gaming houses were opened to compete with La Redoute (the official casino), before the three houses were finally merged.

A PASSION FOR SPORT

Sport also had a very important place among the visitors' amusements. Tennis was played from the first half of the 17th century onward, and the first European horse races were organized at Spa in 1773. The town was also a mecca for motorists in the early days of motoring: an automobile exhibition, with road tests, was organized in 1896.

SPA-MONOPOLE

Exports of water started in the 16th century: in 1583 mineral water from Spa was sent to Mézières, where Henri III, King of France, was staying.

The company Spa-Monopole started up in a small way just before World War One, and has grown steadily ever since. Today it manages all the town's springs.

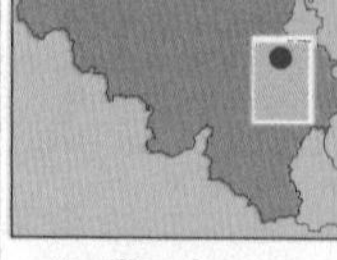

Two days
55 miles

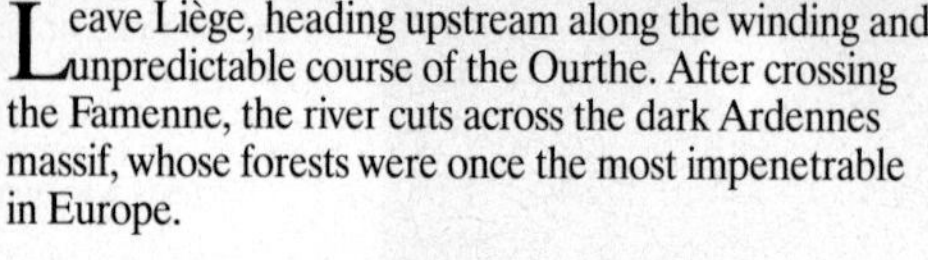

Leave Liège, heading upstream along the winding and unpredictable course of the Ourthe. After crossing the Famenne, the river cuts across the dark Ardennes massif, whose forests were once the most impenetrable in Europe.

From Liège to Comblain-au-Pont

The hills of Sart-Tilman have long been popular with walkers and painters. Since the 1960's part of Liège University has been located here ▲ *231*.

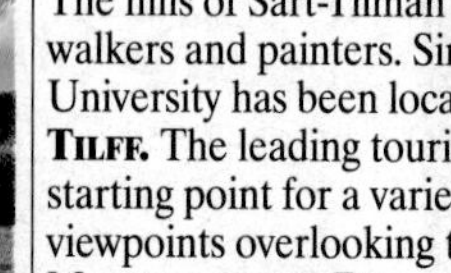

Tilff. The leading tourist resort after Liège, Tilff is the starting point for a variety of signposted walks leading to viewpoints overlooking the valley. The village has a small Museum of the Bee, and the church prides itself on owning a piece of the True Cross, donated by Godefroi de Bouillon ▲ *266* in 1100.

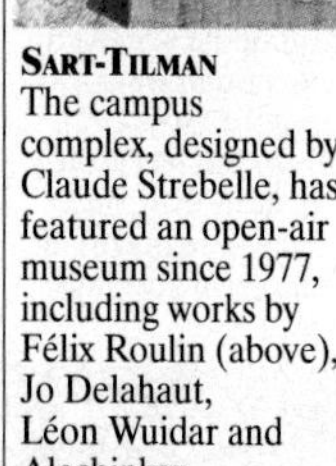

Sart-Tilman
The campus complex, designed by Claude Strebelle, has featured an open-air museum since 1977, including works by Félix Roulin (above), Jo Delahaut, Léon Wuidar and Alechinksy.

Comblain-au-Pont ★

Comblain's name derives from the Latin *confluentes*, and it is in fact located at the confluence of two of Belgium's most beautiful rivers, the Ourthe and the Amblève. Here the Ourthe valley is covered for a distance by the outlying ledges of the Condroz plateau ▲ *217* and flows past some spectacular dolomitic rock formations: the Roches-Noires (on a huge amphitheater created by a former bend in the river), the Chession and the Tartines. All the typical features of limestone hills ■ 22 can be seen here.

The Château de Colonster, in the park of Sart-Tilman, houses the Simenon archives, with manuscripts and other material donated by the writer in 1976 ▲ *230*.

TOUR OF COMBLAIN. A SMALL MUSEUM housed in the former 17th-century presbytery gives an overview of the region's archeology. Next door to it, the 19th-century church has baptismal fonts from the 16th century. The 12th-century TOUR ST-MARTIN, which overlooks the town, is all that survives of the 17th-century Comblenz Manor. A church was built alongside it in the 17th century, which explains the presence of a cemetery. Trails illustrating the geology of the area have been set up around the town; one of them leads to the GROTTES DE L'ABÎME. These caves were opened to the public in 1929.

THE AMBLÈVE VALLEY

The Amblève has its source at the heart of the Cantons de l'Est ▲ *242*. The first part of its course is gentle; after this it cuts out a deep valley (left), winding between steep slopes thickly covered with vegetation ★. In this dramatic setting, near to Aywaille, stand the ruins of the Château d'Amblève, where the Aymon brothers are said to have taken refuge ▲ *268*. It was also near here, in AD 716, that Charles Martel's soldiers, camouflaged with branches, crushed the Neustrian armies, giving rise to the legend of the walking forest used by Shakespeare in *Macbeth*.

AYWAILLE. This small town is huddled in a hollow between green hills. Overlooking the town is the HEID DES GATTES, one of the last Famenne sandstone outcrops that has not been quarried. A few miles to the south is the Château de Harzé (17th and 18th centuries), with its beautiful Renaissance gallery.

SPRIMONT (FRAITURE). To the north of Aywaille is the GROTTE DE LA BELLE-ROCHE, a fossil cave. Recent excavations uncovered exceptionally rich deposits from the middle of the Quaternary era (around half a million years ago). Traces of a stone industry have also been discovered (the earliest evidence of human occupation in Benelux), dating from the early Paleolithic era.

SOUGNÉ-REMOUCHAMPS ★. This charming little town stands on the border of the Condroz and the Ardennes. Its main tourist attraction is its cave, hollowed out by a tributary of the Amblève.

COO ★. Here the river forms a circular meander around a narrow rocky outcrop and explodes in a spectacular cascade. The passage between the two river beds is said to have been cut out by the monks of Stavelot in the 18th century. This is a popular spot, with a chairlift which gives a view over the whole valley. TROIS-PONTS ★, a few miles away, is a pleasant village at the confluence of the Amblève and the Salm.

ALONG THE AMBLÈVE
Paths have been laid down alongside the most beautiful stretches of the river. One, on the right bank, shortly after Sougné-Remouchamps, runs alongside what is known as the Fonds-de-Quareux: large quartzite blocks litter the river bed, which is very wild at this point. Legend has it that these are the remains of a mill built with the devil's assistance. Other paths lead up the valley of the Ninglinspo, a small tributary of the Amblève. The river, winding through a very narrow valley, has cut basins into the rock, which have been given poetic names such as Diana's Bath. This has been a protected conservation area since 1949.

THE CAVE OF SOUGNÉ-REMOUCHAMPS
This was excavated around 1820 and modified in 1912. Its chambers have very beautiful formations, which are cleverly lit. The cave's entrance served as a shelter for the last hunters of the ice age (around 9000 BC).

THE CHURCH OF ST-PIERRE DE XHIGNESSE
Notable especially for its apse decorated with blind arcades .

THE FAMENNE

The Famenne is a narrow strip of land stretching from Beauraing to Louveigné, bordered to the north by the Condroz ▲ *217* and to the south by the Ardennes. The soil is made of heavy clay over a base of sandstone and schists: it is not good farmland. However, the southern section, the Calestienne, is made of limestone and is therefore more fertile: it has been inhabited since the Neolithic era (the most famous remains are the dolmens and menhirs of Wéris). This section of the Ourthe valley is very narrow with steep slopes in places. The river has escaped alterations and mostly retains its natural appearance, with a winding course, wild river banks, and banks of gravel in midstream. Flooding is frequent and often dramatic. Dippers, kingfishers and swallows can be spotted here, nesting in the steep earth banks of the river bends; so can dragonflies, such as calopteryx, that live beside running water ■ *24*.

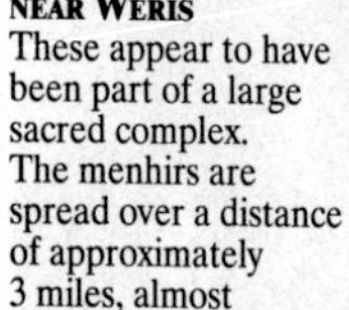

THE MEGALITHS NEAR WÉRIS
These appear to have been part of a large sacred complex. The menhirs are spread over a distance of approximately 3 miles, almost perfectly aligned on a north–northeast axis.

FROM COMBLAIN TO DURBUY. Long inhabited, this area has some beautiful buildings, such as the Romanesque CHURCH OF ST-PIERRE DE XHIGNESSE (around 1100). On the left bank of the river is the CHURCH OF ST-MARTIN DE TOHOGNE, with its typically Romanesque silhouette ● *82*, dating from the 12th and 17th centuries. However, the most impressive feature is the group of MEGALITHIC TOMBS AT WÉRIS ★. The smallest of these (32 feet long) was discovered in 1888; it is a covered underground passage consisting of a funeral chamber and an entrance passage, separated by two pierced slabs. The tomb was built around 2800 BC and may have held 150 bodies. The second tomb is also a covered passageway (35 feet long), but was built at ground level. The village of Wéris has a museum dedicated to the megalithic era.

DURBUY ★. This small town, with its network of charming little streets, nestles between the Ourthe and a spectacular rocky

The Château de Durbuy.

Waha under snow
Despite a few later additions, the overall shape of Waha's Romanesque church still reflects the Mosan style of the period, which followed Carolingian traditions ● *82*. The interior has some beautiful pieces, such as the 16th-century baptismal basin, the statues of Saint Roch and Saint Barbara and altarpiece of Saint Nicholas (17th century), and the 18th-century sculpture of the martyrdom of Saint Erasmus.

cliff, the Falize. Durbuy belonged to the county of Luxembourg in the Middle Ages: along with Marche and La Roche-en-Ardenne it formed a defensive line against the ambitions of Liège. Durbuy was therefore built around its castle, probably from the 11th century onward. The town was given its freedom in the 14th century and accorded a number of privileges, such as the right to build fortifications and form a company of crossbowmen; it also acquired the official status of *ville*, making it the smallest town in the world. It was merged with a number of other towns in 1977. Durbuy is dominated by the imposing castle of the Counts of Ursel, rebuilt in the 17th century and restored in the 19th century. As well as some very beautiful old houses, it has a splendid timbered corn market from the 14th century, the home of a SMALL ARCHEOLOGICAL MUSEUM. Its natural setting on the banks of the Ourthe makes Durbuy a place that is popular with tourists. Artists and craftworkers have moved to the town, and a variety of events are held here in the summer.

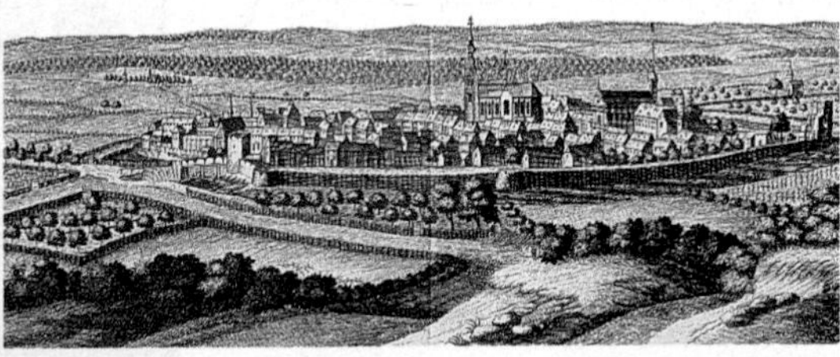

Exploring Marche
Strolling through the town center you will discover picturesque alleys (Ruelle Rosette) and beautiful brick and blue-stone houses from the 17th and 18th centuries, such as the Pot d'Étain ("Pewter Pot") which houses the tourist information center. The Gothic Church of St-Remacle dates from the 14th century, but was rebuilt in the 16th and 19th centuries.
Left: Marche in the 17th century.

Hotton. Hotton's slate-roofed houses are grouped along the banks of the Ourthe, on the border of the Famenne and the Ardennes. The town is notable for its GROTTE DES MILLE ET UNE NUITS, whose varied formations, some of them containing iron, display a stunning range of colors.

Marche-en-Famenne. Marche is the main town of the Famenne, situated on the main road that has connected the Netherlands to the southern provinces since the Middle Ages. The site has been occupied since prehistoric times. In 1311 the town acquired fortifications and privileges from the Counts of Luxembourg and rapidly became a thriving manufacturing and trading center. It was here, in 1577, that Don John of Austria signed the Pacification of Ghent ● *34*. In the 17th century a thriving lacemaking industry grew up. A SMALL LACE MUSEUM was opened in 1989, housed in the last surviving tower of the old ramparts. The MUSÉE DE LA FAMENNE, in the Maison Jadot (17th century), exhibits collections relating to the Famenne region (popular traditions, religious art, decorative arts, archeology and history). Do not leave Marche without trying the local *baisers* ("kisses"), small macaroons.

The church at Waha ★. This church, dedicated to Saint Étienne, is the oldest Romanesque church in Belgium. It was consecrated in 1050 and the dedicatory stone can still be seen in front of the south wall of the choir – a very rare feature.

Baptismal font in the church at Waha.

ARDENNES LANDSCAPE
The word Ardennes is said to come from the Celtic root *ardu* (meaning "high", and by extension "wooded height", then "wood"). The great forest, dark and mysterious, has given way to a landscape where farmland alternates with extensive areas of woodland.

THE ARDENNES

Moving further upstream along the course of the Ourthe, on the N 833, we leave the Famenne and reach the heart of the Ardennes massif.

AN ANCIENT LANDSCAPE. The Ardennes massif is a rocky platform from the Primary era, with poor soils (sandstone, schist, quartzite and phyllite) and hills reaching heights between 1,300 and 2,300 feet ▲ *244*. "The Ardennes" is used as a more general term, covering a huge wooded area – roughly the region bordered by the Meuse and the Rhine, the Vesdre, the Moselle and the Semois.

THE GREAT FOREST. For centuries the Ardennes Forest has been thought of as impenetrable and unchanging – but this immense area did not long remain untouched. Julius Caesar mentions paths cut through the forest, and in the Merovingian period further sections of the forest were cleared. Gradually humans encroached upon the austere but fertile land of the Ardennes, cultivating it defiantly and productively, right up to our own times. Villages and small towns grew up between

THE "REMUAGES"
Procession of Saint Monon, patron saint of cattle, in Nassogne (at Ascension).

THE ARDENNES, "THE GREATEST FOREST IN ALL OF GAUL."

JULIUS CAESAR

the forest and the fields, in the valleys and the clearings of the high plateaus, around the abbey estates and the fortresses of the local nobility. Despite all this the Ardennes remained on the margins of European civilization, and it was not until the 8th century that the region was christianized by Saint Remaclus ▲ *247* and Saint Hubert ▲ *260*. The Ardennes was a hunting ground for royalty in the Carolingian era, and the domain of metalworkers ▲ *263* under the Ancien Régime. Century by century the forest became smaller; then after 1866, in the wake of an agricultural crisis, it was replanted with coniferous trees, reclaiming a large part of the huge expanses of uncultivated moorland. At the start of this century it was composed of 70 percent deciduous trees (beech, oak, ash, maple and aspen) and 30 percent coniferous trees (spruce and pines); today it consists of 53 percent deciduous trees and 47 percent coniferous trees ■ *26*. Dark plantations of spruce now dominate the woodland of the massifs.

A WORLD OF THE IMAGINATION. The Ardennes was a separate world, a world of fantasy. For centuries this was a land beyond the jurisdiction of humans, who peopled it with imaginary pagan beings, both benificent and malign. In Roman times the goddess Dea Arduinna was said to ride through the copses astride a wild boar. There were legendary heroes ▲ *268*, fairies and werewolves. Little genies of the wood, clever and unpredictable dwarfs and a host of other supernatural creatures were said to hide in crannies in the rocks. Many place names reflect these traditional beliefs. There were stories of ghosts roaming the desolate expanses of forest in search of eternal peace. Inveterate hunters, punished for neglecting their duties, were supposedly condemned to wander in the forest forever, on an infernal hunt whose dreadful din can sometimes be heard at night.

THE SAINTS OF THE ARDENNES
Confronted by this harsh, austere world, the inhabitants of the Ardennes saw their saints as patrons or healers specializing in a particular field. Top to bottom: Saint Gôssé, a local saint worshipped at Compogne; Saint Druon, patron saint of shepherds; Saint Quirin, invoked to relieve leg ulcers. Above: an Ardennes village (Tavigny) in the early 1900's.

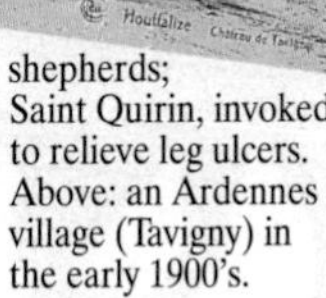

La Roche-en-Ardenne, early 20th century.

THE OURTHE
The river is rich in fish and invertebrates; gray wagtails, kingfishers and dippers can be spotted on its banks. The Ourthe is a popular place for fishing. Mâboge, Bérimesnil and Nadrin are excellent starting points for exploring the valley on foot.

WILDLIFE IN THE FOREST OF ST-MICHEL
In fall you can hear stags belling from the great clearing of Mochamps.
Below: a wild boar.

THE FOREST OF ST-MICHEL. Just before arriving at St-Hubert ▲ *260*, the road (the N 4, then the N 89) cuts across one of the largest wooded massifs of the Ardennes. The forest is dominated by deciduous trees (beech, oak, birches in the marshy areas, alders along the rivers). A number of peat bogs ■ *18* still survive at the heart of the forest (in the nature reserves of ROUGE PONCEAU and FAYI DE LUCI). The larger wild animals are common ■ *28*; the most common birds are the black woodpecker, the middle-spotted woodpecker and the honey buzzard.

DETOUR TOWARD HOUFFALIZE ★. Instead of heading directly for St-Hubert, you can follow the road beside the Ourthe. LA ROCHE-EN-ARDENNE, on a bend in the river, is an ideal stopping place for walkers (there are signposted footpaths). The town was badly damaged in 1944 ▲ *270* and has been almost completely rebuilt. The ruins of the 11th-century castle cast their shadow over the town: once a powerful feudal stronghold, it was demolished in the 18th century. Down below, the TOUR DES SARRASINS is all that remains of a small fort established by the Romans. Local specialties include blue sandstone pottery (right) and *baisers* ▲ *255*. Upstream from Roche the river winds ever more tightly through a narrow forest-covered ravine where deciduous species predominate. The woods here consist mainly of old copses of oaks, which used to be cut down for the tannin in their bark; there are also a few beautiful ravine forests of maple, which have been preserved in their wild state because of their inaccessibility. The rare hazel grouse and the goshawk nest here. The BOUCLE DU CHESLÉ, located to the southwest of Bérimesnil, makes a very interesting excursion on foot. At its summit are the remains of an ancient Celtic fortress, built largely between 700 and 470 BC, which has a complex system of fortification with a double line of defense. One of the most remarkable sights in this part of the valley is the BOUCLE DU HÉROU ★ (situated to the west of Nadrin), where the Ourthe describes a slow bend around steep slabs of rock. The rocks harbor an isolated population of wall lizards, and are a popular location for climbing enthusiasts.

In and around St-Hubert

1. Church of St-Gilles-au-Pré
2. Rue St-Gilles
3. Place de l'Abbaye
4. The abbey buildings
5. Basilica

◷ Four hours

A powerful abbey
The Abbey of St-Hubert was a revered shrine and an artistic and intellectual center (its library was said to be the best in the country), governing a dozen or so priories. It was also a powerful feudal manor, the focal point of an estate whose territories stretched from the Champagne region to the Moselle.

Nestling amid a ring of forests, the little town of St-Hubert is dominated by its imposing basilica, with houses grouped around it. The town grew up around a Benedictine abbey famous for its relics of Saint Hubert, which were deposited here in the 9th century.

History and legend

The conversion of Saint Hubert. A young Frankish nobleman and a keen hunter, according to legend Hubert was hunting at the heart of the Ardennes Forest on Good Friday in the year 685 when his attention was caught by a stag, which seemed to be inviting him to follow it. The count set off in pursuit of the stag, caught it, and was about to kill it. At this point he was dazzled by an unearthly light and had to stop: between the animal's horns was a vision of Christ on the Cross, reproaching him for this deadly passion and exhorting him to lead a more religious life. Hubert abandoned his title of count and decided to live as a hermit.

THE ROLE OF ST-HUBERT'S RELICS WAS TO "STRENGTHEN THE CHURCH OF LIEGE ON THE SOUTHERN BORDERS OF THE DIOCESE."

JEAN-LOUIS KUPPER

SUCCESSOR TO SAINT LAMBERT. A few years later Hubert went on a pilgrimage to Rome. Here he met the pope, who had been told in a dream that Lambert had just been assassinated in Liège ▲ *220* and that Hubert had been designated to replace him. Hubert refused this high honor, but God's will was shown by a miracle: an angel appeared to Hubert and placed a white stole, the bishop's insignia, around his shoulders. Hubert became Bishop of Tongres-Maastricht and dedicated the rest of his life to eradicating paganism in his diocese. He transferred the seat of the diocese to Liège, where he was buried when he died in 727. A number of miracles were witnessed around his tomb, and the bishop was made a saint on November 3, 743.

Buglers at St-Hubert.

ANDAGE BECOMES ST-HUBERT. In 825, perhaps to ensure that his cult did not eclipse that of Saint Lambert, Saint Hubert's body was transferred to the Ardennes, to a place called Andage. A monastery had been founded here around 700, and had just been restored by the Bishop of Liège. Pilgrims came to visit Andage, a church was built, and the village soon took the name of its patron saint.

THE SAINT'S MIRACLES. From the 9th century onward the shrine was renowned throughout the Western world for its miraculous cures for rabies, produced by making a small cut in the forehead of the afflicted person and inserting under the skin a thread from Saint Hubert's stole. Hunters were especially vulnerable to this terrible disease, and consequently chose Saint Hubert as their patron saint. Soon their example was followed by butchers and other trades connected with hunting, including buglers.

PILGRIMAGES AND EVENTS TODAY. Every year on November 3 hunters come to honor their patron saint. At 11am a solemn mass is held in the presence of the assembled hunters, buglers and others, culminating in a blessing of the animals on the old abbey square. An international festival of

SAINT HUBERT
It was not until the 15th century that the legend of Saint Hubert became firmly established. At this stage the conversion scene – Hubert kneeling at the feet of a stag bearing a cross between its antlers (above) – was the most popular iconographic motif, followed by that of the saint as bishop (next page, center).

THE INTERIOR OF THE BASILICA
The most striking features are the Baroque high altar, crowned with marble statues (1721) attributed to the Liège school of Jean Del Cour ▲ *228*, and the stalls, a masterpiece from 1733, with eighteen oak panels depicting episodes from the lives of saints Benedict (on the left) and Hubert (on the right). The treasury displays a number of objects (a liturgical comb, the head of a crook and a hunting horn) which are supposed to have belonged to the saint, along with a bronze key and, in pride of place, the holy stole – which is in fact later than the original but was brought into contact with the relics of the saint before they were lost, in the 16th century.

hunting and nature is held during the first weekend of September, when mass is also celebrated to the sound of horns, followed by the blessing and sharing of bread and by a historical procession. Finally the Lendersdorf pilgrimage, which goes back to 1720, brings together groups from Germany, Belgium and Luxembourg, who undertake a 200-mile walk to come and worship the saint at Ascension. On a more secular note, "Juillet musical" (part of the Festival of Wallonia) is one of the country's leading musical events.

THE OLD ABBEY

The Abbey of St-Hubert was a focal point of the Ardennes region for more than a thousand years, and one of the most famous religious communities of western Europe. The monks always kept abreast of the latest technical innovations of their time, becoming accomplished ironmasters, tanners and chemists. In 1796 the Benedictines were finally expelled from the town by the Revolutionaries: the abbey and its outbuildings were sold into private ownership. The abbey church became the parish church, and was given the title of basilica in 1927.

THE ABBEY BUILDINGS. The monastery buildings were rebuilt around 1725–30; they stand next to the north side of the church. Today they house various administrative offices and can only be visited when cultural events are held here. On these occasions visitors can admire the beautiful ironwork balustrade of the staircase (1731).

Crypt of the basilica.

THE BASILICA ★. This architectural treasure combines Gothic and Baroque styles to great effect. The church was rebuilt for the first time during the Middle Ages, but was later destroyed by fire in 1525. The abbot decided to have it completely rebuilt. Construction work started in 1526 and was finished in 1564. The result is a magnificent building in the Flamboyant style, in the shape of a Latin cross. The façade was rebuilt in a Classico-Baroque style between 1700 and 1702, with three distinct stories. At the top, the tympanum of the pediment is decorated with a relief showing the *Conversion of Saint Hubert*, and flanked by two bell towers with rounded roofs. Behind it the last remains of the 13th-century towers can be seen. The interior is flooded with light, highlighting subtle variations of color in the stone (limestone and sandstone). The central nave is divided into five bays; the choir, which is very deep, was built to accommodate a large number of monks.

IN THE TOWN. St-Hubert is a very small town, a charming place to take a stroll. The Church of ST-GILLES-AU-PRÉ at the end of Rue St-Gilles is well worth a visit, if only for its large square tower, the last remnant of the original building (1064). The church was substantially altered in the 16th century (choir and ceiling) and the 18th century (the porch); it has a delightfully simple high altar from the 17th century.

THE FOURNEAU ST-MICHEL

A few miles to the north of the town, in the middle of the forest, is a group of highly informative museums: a museum of metallurgy, the Redouté Museum and a museum of rural life. Nature trails have also been laid out to encourage visitors to discover the natural riches of the Masblette valley.

MUSÉE DE LA MÉTALLURGIE ★. The St-Michel "furnace" is actually a collection of forges from the 18th century, which were set up under the instigation of Abbé Spirlet, the last abbot of St-Hubert. In 1959 a museum of iron gave a new lease of life to the old buildings. Old tools and equipment are now on exhibition here, illustrating all the main metal-related activites: coal mining, cooperage, the manufacture of nails and pans. Tan mills and flour mills are shown alongside the *maka*, or power hammer, driven by the water of the river. This museum gives a more or less complete picture of industrial life on the Famenne under the Ancien Régime.

MUSÉE REDOUTÉ. In the same building is a small museum presenting the life and work of the artist Pierre-Joseph Redouté, who was born at St-Hubert in 1759 and died in Paris in 1840. You can also visit Redouté's birthplace in St-Hubert, where a number of items relating to the artist are on display.

MUSÉE DE LA VIE RURALE ★. Five hundred yards away in a picturesque setting is a remarkable museum that gives a vivid impression of traditional country life in the region to the south of the Sambre-et-Meuse valley. Some twenty buildings have been transplanted here, including farmhouses from the Ardennes and the Gaume, a chapel, a school and tobacco stores; furniture and tools complete this reconstruction of the local past.

METAL INDUSTRIES IN THE ARDENNES
The iron industry flourished for a long time in the Ardennes, which had a plentiful supply of all the necessary raw materials (iron ore, wood for burning, water). However, this industry died out with the rise of mechanization and the growth of the coalfields in the Sambre-et-Meuse valley.

"THE RAPHAEL OF ROSES"
Redouté had a brilliant career at the courts of Louis XVI and Napoleon. Professor of Plant Iconography in the royal gardens, he produced and illustrated a number of botanical works.

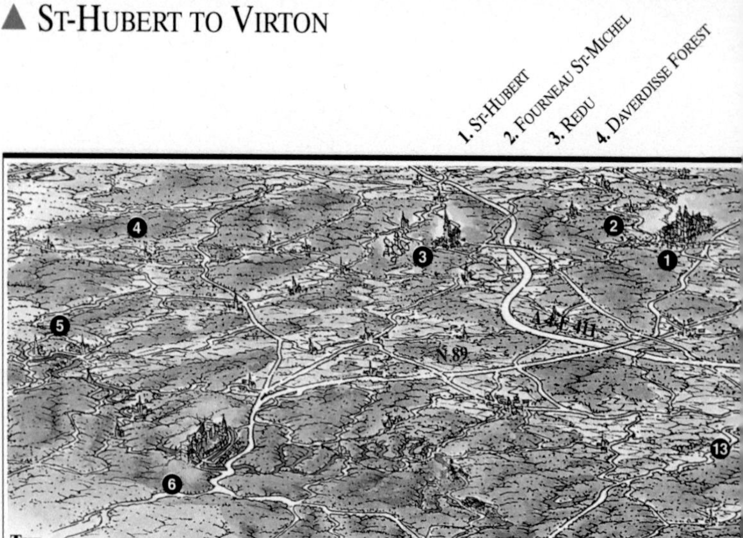

1. St-Hubert
2. Fourneau St-Michel
3. Redu
4. Daverdisse Forest

The Semois
This lovely river is some 125 miles long, with its source near Arlon, in the pleasant landscape of the Belgian Lorraine ▲ *271*. It enters the Ardennes region just outside Herbeumont: here the landscape is much wilder, dominated by forests and steep slopes. The valley becomes narrower and the river follows a tightly winding course until it meets the Meuse, in France. The river bends are known as *hans* in the local dialect: this word features in many village names.

This itinerary follows the Semois upstream, crossing the southern part of the Ardennes as far as the Gaume, known as the "Provence of Belgium".

From St-Hubert to Vresse

Redu-Transinne. A European space station for telemetry was built in the village in 1964; then the Eurospace Center, retracing the story of space exploration, was opened in 1991. Redu is also a mecca for secondhand book lovers ★: it has many bookstores (for new and secondhand books) and has been twinned with the British town of Hay-on-Wye since 1984.
Daverdisse. The village is surrounded by extensive forests, mainly tall copses of deciduous trees (beech, oak, maple) ■ *26*. Birds that nest here include species that are relatively uncommon in southern Belgium (middle-spotted woodpecker, hazel grouse, pied flycatcher). For the best views walk along the river banks (Lesse, Our and Almache).

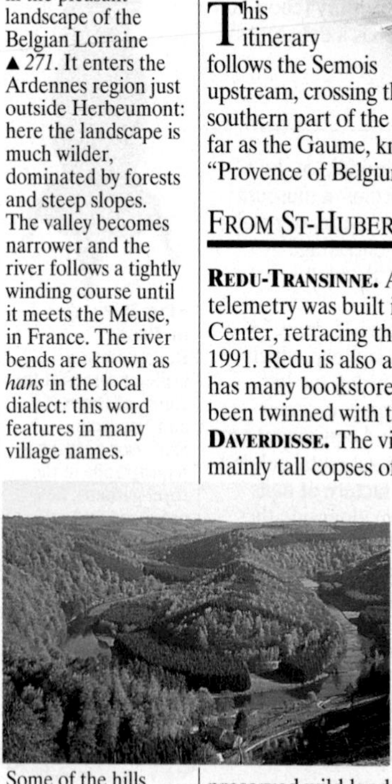

Some of the hills caught between the river bends have highly evocative names, like the Giant's Tomb downriver from Bouillon (above).

The Semois valley ★

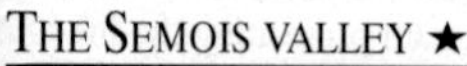

The course of the Semois through the Ardennes offers some of the best preserved wild landscapes on the massif ▲ *256*. Here the forest has suffered relatively little human intervention: the tree plantations are close to their original state, particularly on the steep slopes of the river valley, and consist mainly of deciduous species. Because of the acid subsoil, flowering plants are quite sparse among the undergrowth; lichens, on the other hand, thrive in the humid air of this ancient woodland. The forest wildlife includes some notable species, such as the *mouflon* (wild sheep), introduced in the 1950's, the wildcat and

5. Vresse-sur-Semois
6. Bouillon
7. Florenville
8. Abbey of Orval
9. Montquintin
10. Virton
11. Buzenol-Montauban
12. Bastogne
13. Neufchâteau
14. Habay-la-Neuve
15. Anlier Forest
16. Arlon

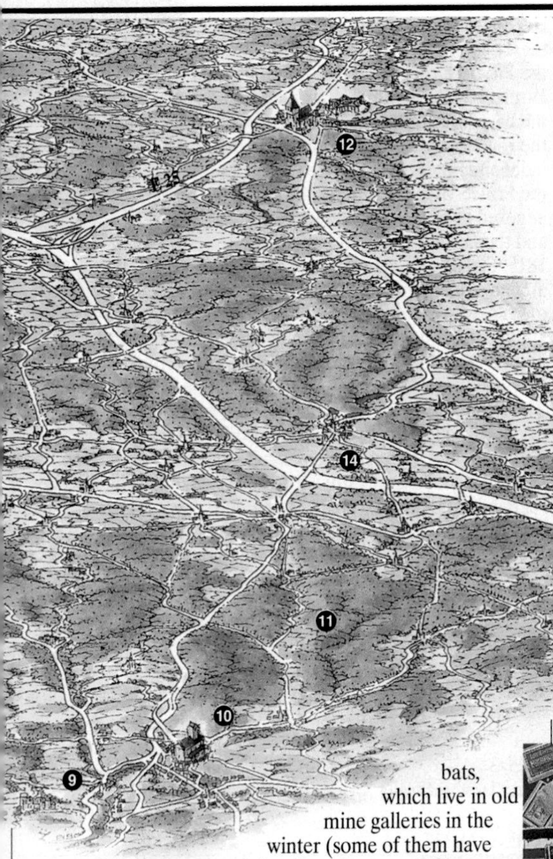

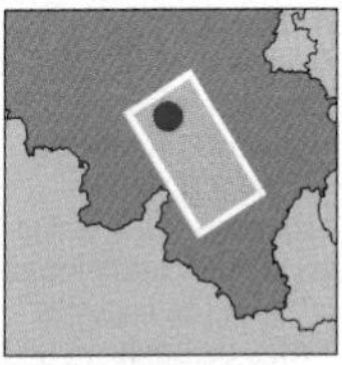

One day
55 miles

bats, which live in old mine galleries in the winter (some of them have been classified as protected sites for this reason). The rare hazel grouse takes refuge in the dense copses of hazel and birch.

Vresse to Herbeumont ★. A long footpath (the GR AE-E3) follows the valley from the French border to Florenville. To cover its full course takes from four to six days on foot, or three days on a mountain bike. It is one of the most beautiful routes of its type in southern Belgium. Downriver from Bouillon the chief points of interest along the footpath are Bohan-Membre with its nature reserve on a wooded hillside,

Semois tobacco
Tobacco plantations once flourished along the banks of the Semois: the soil here, dry on the surface and humid below, provided the perfect growing conditions. Tobacco cultivation reached its peak in the early 20th century (by 1905 there were over a million plants here). A small museum at Vresse-en-Semois is dedicated to the local tobacco industry. Opposite: *Visit to the Tobacco Factory*, by Léonard Defrance (1735–1805), the most gifted Liégois painter of his generation.

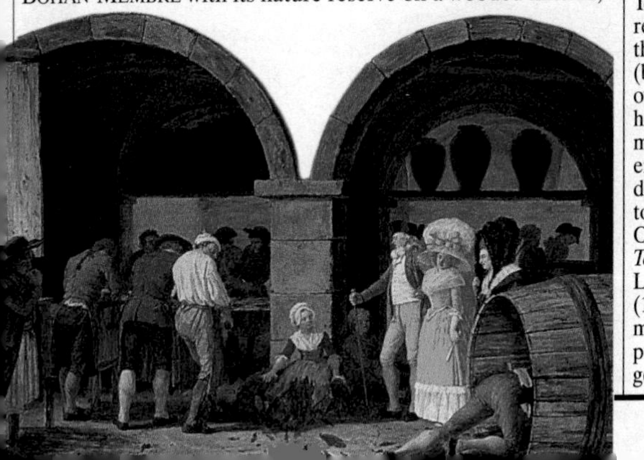

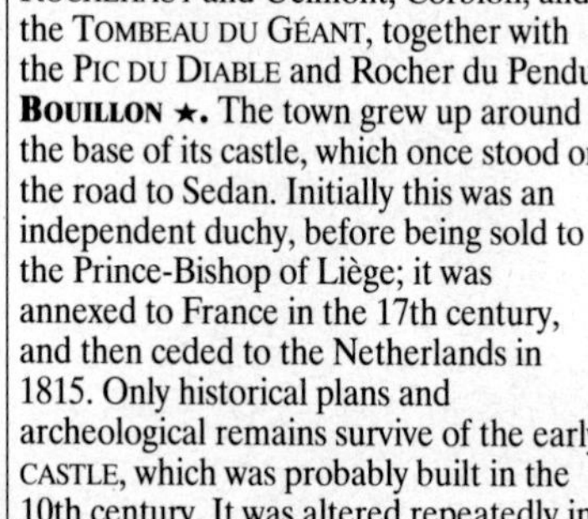

WATERS OF THE SEMOIS
The river's fish population is among the highest in the Ardennes. This is due to the high nutritional value of the water as it runs through Gaume. Common species include carp, barbel and chub.

The Petit-Fays Gorge; rooftops in Gaume.

ROCHEHAUT and Ucimont, Corbion, and the TOMBEAU DU GÉANT, together with the PIC DU DIABLE and Rocher du Pendu.

BOUILLON ★. The town grew up around the base of its castle, which once stood on the road to Sedan. Initially this was an independent duchy, before being sold to the Prince-Bishop of Liège; it was annexed to France in the 17th century, and then ceded to the Netherlands in 1815. Only historical plans and archeological remains survive of the early CASTLE, which was probably built in the 10th century. It was altered repeatedly in later centuries, notably in the 16th century when it was converted to a bastioned fortress with an artillery tower and canon casemates. The castle was modernized by Vauban, who also built a rampart around the town (1679); it still has its triple-slitted loopholes and underground passageways for munitions and supplies. Bouillon was still a fortified town under the Dutch regime (1815–30); the great 12th-century keep was demolished during this time. Next to the castle is the MUSÉE DUCAL, devoted to the town's history and traditions. The main points of interest upriver from Bouillon are BOHAN and the ROCHER DE DAMPIERRÉE; the Ruisseau des Gorges and the ROCHE PERCÉE; the remains of a Celtic fortress at CUGNON on the Fayet; HERBEUMONT (with the ruins of its 12th-century castle); the Tombeau du Chevalier; and the FOREST OF CONQUES AND STE-CÉCILE, which overlooks magnificent oxbow lakes on a former bend of the Semois river.

GODEFROI DE BOUILLON
King of Jerusalem and conqueror of the Holy City (in 1099), he sold his duchy to the bishopric of Liège before departing for the crusades.

THE GAUME

Around Ste-Cécile and Chasse-Pierre the road leaves the Ardennes Forest, opening out onto the pasturelands of the Gaume. The traveler is likely to feel something like relief: the landscape here is gentler and the plant life reflects the richer subsoils (of the marls, in the Semois valley). The Gaume, like the Arlon region, is part of the Belgian Lorraine ▲ *271*. It is protected to the north by the Ardennes and exposed to the southern

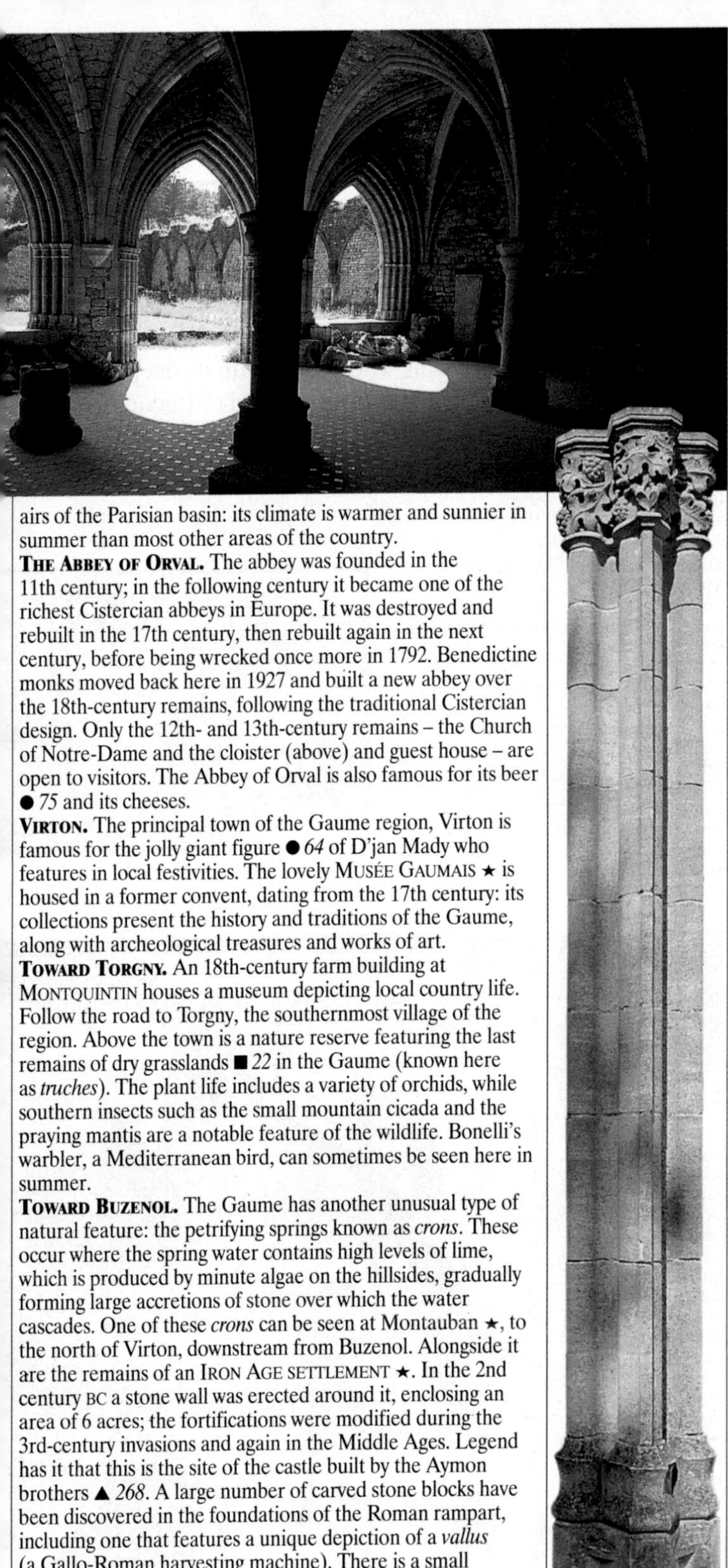

airs of the Parisian basin: its climate is warmer and sunnier in summer than most other areas of the country.

THE ABBEY OF ORVAL. The abbey was founded in the 11th century; in the following century it became one of the richest Cistercian abbeys in Europe. It was destroyed and rebuilt in the 17th century, then rebuilt again in the next century, before being wrecked once more in 1792. Benedictine monks moved back here in 1927 and built a new abbey over the 18th-century remains, following the traditional Cistercian design. Only the 12th- and 13th-century remains – the Church of Notre-Dame and the cloister (above) and guest house – are open to visitors. The Abbey of Orval is also famous for its beer ● *75* and its cheeses.

VIRTON. The principal town of the Gaume region, Virton is famous for the jolly giant figure ● *64* of D'jan Mady who features in local festivities. The lovely MUSÉE GAUMAIS ★ is housed in a former convent, dating from the 17th century: its collections present the history and traditions of the Gaume, along with archeological treasures and works of art.

TOWARD TORGNY. An 18th-century farm building at MONTQUINTIN houses a museum depicting local country life. Follow the road to Torgny, the southernmost village of the region. Above the town is a nature reserve featuring the last remains of dry grasslands ■ *22* in the Gaume (known here as *truches*). The plant life includes a variety of orchids, while southern insects such as the small mountain cicada and the praying mantis are a notable feature of the wildlife. Bonelli's warbler, a Mediterranean bird, can sometimes be seen here in summer.

TOWARD BUZENOL. The Gaume has another unusual type of natural feature: the petrifying springs known as *crons*. These occur where the spring water contains high levels of lime, which is produced by minute algae on the hillsides, gradually forming large accretions of stone over which the water cascades. One of these *crons* can be seen at Montauban ★, to the north of Virton, downstream from Buzenol. Alongside it are the remains of an IRON AGE SETTLEMENT ★. In the 2nd century BC a stone wall was erected around it, enclosing an area of 6 acres; the fortifications were modified during the 3rd-century invasions and again in the Middle Ages. Legend has it that this is the site of the castle built by the Aymon brothers ▲ *268*. A large number of carved stone blocks have been discovered in the foundations of the Roman rampart, including one that features a unique depiction of a *vallus* (a Gallo-Roman harvesting machine). There is a small EXHIBITION OF ROMAN SCULPTURE on the site.

The Ardennes has been identified with the Broceliande of the *chansons de geste*. Its landscape still echoes to the gallop of the magic horse Bayard, who helped the four Aymon brothers escape after they had been banished by Charlemagne. This dark forest, peopled with terrifying wild beasts, with its deep valleys and its high desolate plateaus, was also a land of freedom, a refuge for exiles and rebels. The rough, harsh landscape with its thick mists and hidden clearings became a fairytale land of the imagination.

THE LEGEND OF THE AYMON BROTHERS
The brothers were the sons of Aymon de Montaubon, a vassal of Charlemagne. Their adventures fall into three main episodes. Having been unjustly banished by Charlemagne, they took refuge in the Ardennes, where they built their castle, Montessor (bottom); then, pursued by the emperor, they spent

many years wandering in the forest, all four astride their faithful horse Bayard (above); after being welcomed in Gascony by King Yon, the fugitives took shelter in the Castle of Montauban. In the end the brothers were reconciled with the emperor, but the eldest, Renaut, had to undertake a penitential pilgrimage to the Holy Land. He ended his life piously in Cologne.

AT THE HEART OF THE ARDENNES
The epic of the four Aymon brothers is firmly rooted in the Ardennes. The names of landmarks and castles all along the Meuse commemorate the four fugitives' adventures. Excavations at Montauban ▲ *267* in the 1950's cast new light on the story's historical location.

MAUGIS THE ENCHANTER
He was the heroes' cousin; his magic (above) helped them escape Charlemagne's fury.

"BAYARD FELL INTO THE MEUSE, WHICH IS COLD AND FAST-FLOWING, AND IN A MOMENT SANK TO THE BOTTOM."

MANUSCRIPT OF 1250

THE PONT DES ARCHES. Bayard, the faithful horse with supernatural powers who helped the brothers to escape, symbolizes their rebellious spirit. After Renaut's surrender, Bayard was handed over to Charlemagne and thrown headlong from the Pont des Arches in Liège (depicted above by Jan Van Eyck in the background of *The Virgin of Autun*). The horse escaped, fleeing into the Forest of the Ardennes, where he is said still to roam.

THE WAR AGAINST CHARLEMAGNE. The war forms the backdrop to the story (above), making the tale of the Aymon brothers into an epic of rebellion and freedom.

HISTORY OF AN EPIC
The *Chanson des Fils Aymon* was one of the most famous epics of the Middle Ages. It was probably written in the 12th century (perhaps at Stavelot), and was reworked several times from the 13th century onward. The story was popularized after the advent of printing, and adopted as one of the main themes of puppet theaters throughout Liège.

CHARLEMAGNE
The emperor (below) was very popular in the Meuse valley and the Ardennes. His family, who owned many estates here, grew more and more powerful, culminating

in Charlemagne's reign in the 8th century. His history is central to local legends and epics.

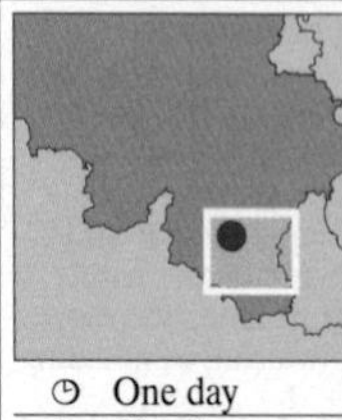

◷ One day
🚗 50 miles

Painted vaults (15th century) of the Church of St-Pierre at Bastogne.

The Porte de Trève
This gateway, a few yards from the church, is all that survives of Bastogne's medieval city walls.

Saint Isidore
The Musée en Piconrue chose Saint Isidore, the patron saint of farmers, as its emblem. The museum is a center for the study, protection and presentation of religious art and popular beliefs in the Ardennes and Luxembourg. Each year it presents an exhibition relating to one of its chosen themes: popular worship, patron saints and the religious and artistic history of the region. It also has an audiovisual display.

Bastogne

Bastogne grew up at the junction of two Roman roads (Reims to Cologne and Arlon to Tongres). Today it is still a major crossroads at the heart of the Ardennes. In medieval times it was a fortified town; now it is better known as the scene of a decisive battle in 1944–5.

Battle of the Ardennes. In June 1944, as the Allies were landing in Normandy, the German armies retreated into Belgium in disarray. Hitler would not admit defeat, however: he ordered his forces to advance across the Belgian Ardennes and Luxembourg to recapture Antwerp and isolate the Dutch front. The attack was launched on Saturday, December 16, 1944. The entire eastern part of the region from Echternach to Monschau was invaded by a formidable military machine. By Christmas, when one unit had almost reached Dinant, the tide had started to turn. While the British artillery shelled German positions, General Patton performed a perfect reverse maneuver, broke through the enemy lines and liberated Bastogne.

Tour of the town. The Church of St-Pierre ★ was founded in the 8th century and rebuilt in the 12th century (today's Romanesque tower is all that remains of this building); it was rebuilt again in the Flamboyant style in the 13th and 15th centuries. Inside the church are beautiful 12th-century baptismal fonts. Opposite is the Musée en Piconrue ★ (named after a district of the town), housed in a former convent from the late 17th century. The museum opened in 1986.

The Anlier Forest ★

This is without any doubt the most beautiful forest in southern Belgium today. Its southern edge follows close to the border between the Ardennes ▲ *256* and the Belgian Lorraine, the Secondary-era land formations that

Refuge
When the black stork moved back into southern Belgium in the 1980's, it settled in the Anlier Forest.

enclose the Gaume ▲ *266* and the Arlon region. Deciduous trees (mainly oak and beech) predominate in the forest, and wildlife is abundant ■ *28*. The forest has largely preserved its natural appearance: foresters have concentrated on maintaining trees of varying height throughout, rather than creating monotonous plantations of uniform trees. Clearings and marshes are dotted around the forest, especially near its many rivers.

Walks. Habay-la-Neuve is the ideal starting point for a walk. One popular route leads up the valley of the Rulles, a tributary of the Semois, which runs through the forest for over 6 miles above the town. The lakes here are a reminder of the forges that once prospered here ▲ *263*. Another very pleasant route runs upriver alongside the Arlune, a tributary of the Rulles, toward the nature reserve of Louftémont.

Arlon

Arlon is the main town of the Belgian province of Luxembourg; today it has around 24,000 inhabitants. Although Arlon and the Gaume together form what is known as the Belgian Lorraine, a German dialect is still spoken in Arlon.

History. Arlon (Orolanum) is one of the oldest towns in Belgium. At first it was just a trading post, but its location at the junction of two major roads (Reims to Trier and Tongres to Metz) meant that it rapidly developed into an important trading center. In the second half of the 3rd century it came under threat from repeated attacks by Germanic tribes, and was converted into a *castrum*: funerary and public monuments were dismantled to build the ramparts. After Trier was captured by the Germans in 451, Arlon was occupied by the Franks, which explains the persistence of a German dialect up to the present day. The town was annexed to the county of Luxembourg in the Middle Ages, and suffered repeated destruction under the Ancien Régime. Between 1794 and 1815 it was included in the French département of Les Fôrets ● *35*. In the 19th century the town underwent substantial alterations to establish an infrastructure worthy of a provincial capital.

Battle of Bastogne
"Nuts!" was General MacAuliffe's response to the Germans on December 22, 1944, when they demanded the surrender of Bastogne. The town held out.

On December 26 it was liberated by Patton (above), who attacked the German forces from the rear. A few miles from here, at Mardasson, is the Bastogne Historical Center, which provides records of these events (movies, uniforms and tanks). Although the Battle of Bastogne had a decisive impact on the outcome of the war, fighting continued for a month longer. St-Vith, Malmédy and Houffalize were completely destroyed (left).

Neufchâteau
This town nestling at the heart of the Ardennes between Bastogne and Habay-la-Neuve offers a wide range of open-air activities.

HILL OF ST-DONAT This hill (below), bathed by the source of the Semois ▲ *264*, is where the town began. It was here that the Romans built their *castrum*, and the medieval lords their fortress. A Capuchin monastery was founded in 1621, and the hill was fortified following plans by Vauban during a brief occupation by the French. The former monastery church has been a parish church since 1825.

TOUR OF ARLON. The tourist information center (2 rue des Faubourgs) is housed in a late-18th-century coaching inn: it was from here that the Luxembourg revolutionaries set out for Brussels in 1830 ● *40*. PLACE LÉOPOLD was redesigned for pedestrian use in 1845; on it stand the headquarters of the provincial government (neoclassical style, 19th century) and the former Palais de Justice (Gothic style, 19th century). The MUSÉE LUXEMBOURGEOIS, founded in 1846, stands on Rue des Martyrs. This historical and archeological museum has extensive collections of prehistoric, Frankish and Carolingian items. Its collection of religious art includes some remarkable works, among them a very beautiful altarpiece (1510) by the Antwerp school. However, the museum is best known for its impressive Gallo-Roman collection ★, which encompasses more than 450 carved stone blocks from funerary monuments, incorporated in the 3rd century rampart or discovered during excavations of the Roman baths. Daily life in Gallo-Roman times is depicted in more than 600 carved scenes (below, *The Travelers*). Head for the Grand-Place, lined with cafés where you can sample *maitrank*, a local alcholic drink. A tower from the Roman wall can be seen in the basement of one of the houses. Rue des Thermes-Romains leads to the Jardin Archéologique, which has remains of the Roman baths (pools for steam baths and urinals). The baths were built in the 1st century AD, destroyed during 3rd-century invasions, and rebuilt in the following century. Nearby are the foundations of the first Christian basilica in Belgium (5th century), where rich Frankish families buried their dead.

EXCURSIONS. Three miles to the south of the town is the Victory Memorial Museum devoted to World War Two. To the west the N 83 runs alongside the most striking area of marshland in southern Belgium, between Heinsch and Chantemelle. Grass of Parnassus, cotton grass and orchids all flourish here; acid peat bogs, similar to those of the Ardennes, have formed in places ▲ *244*.

In and around Charleroi

BATTLEGROUND
Many battles have been fought here over the centuries, including the battles of Fleurus (1690), Charleroi and Fleurus (1794, below), Ligny (Napoleon's last victory, 1815) and Charleroi (1914).

In 1666 the Spanish built a fortress at Charnoy, a small village inhabited by a handful of metalworkers. The star-shaped fortress ● *88*, with six bastions and a concentric ground plan, was named Charles-Roy in honor of Charles II; its purpose was to resist the territorial ambitions of Louis XIV. The French occupied Charleroi between 1667 and 1678, extending it to create the present arrangement of upper and lower towns.

INDUSTRIAL CENTER. Coal power was the driving force behind the Industrial Revolution, and the Sambre valley had this commodity in abundance. However, the revolution spared Charleroi's town center, which retained its distinctive street pattern – a striking contrast to other towns of the region, where the urban fabric and the industrial buildings are intermeshed. New quarters were created after the city wall was destroyed in 1867, and Charleroi became established as the central town of Belgium's Black Country (Pays Noir) ▲ *278*.

1. Lower town 2. Palais des Beaux-Arts et des Expositions 3. Tour Baudoux 4. Hôtel de Ville 5. Beffry 6. Place Albert-1er 7. Place Charles-II 8. Basilica of St-Christophe 9. Boulevard Joseph-Tirou 10. Upper town 11. Musée du Verre 12. Caserne Trésignies

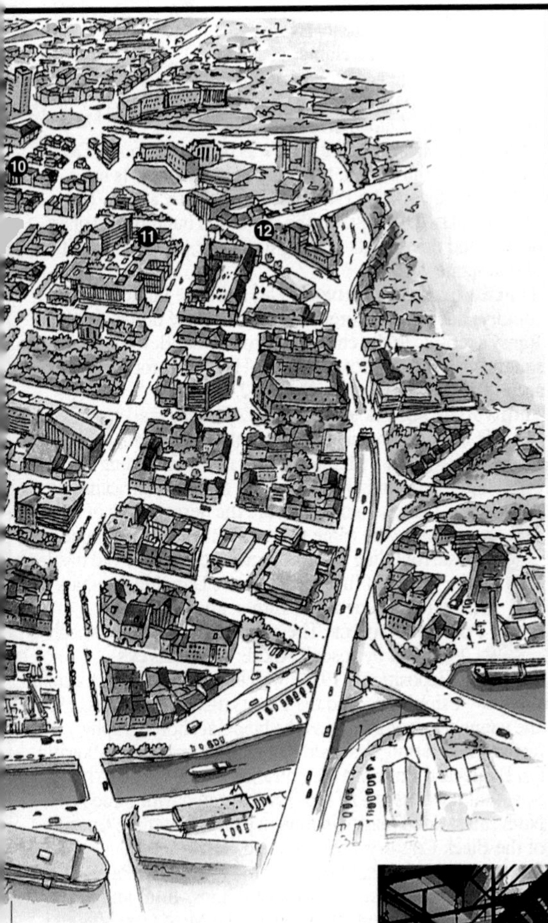

◷ One day

Jules Destrée (1863–1936) ▲ *276* Brilliant orator, a passionate advocate of socialism and Walloon interests, a statesman, man of letters and journalist. Destrée was Charleroi's parliamentary representative from 1894 to his death, playing a major role in the great debates of the time; he was the first to raise the Flanders-Wallonia issue in 1912 ● *36*.

Redeployment. In the 1970's the coal mines were closed, and the steel and glass industries suffered a major crisis. Efforts have since been made to regenerate the town's industry, with the creation of hi-tech business centers and the conversion of unused industrial sites. Since the town merged with its neighboring communes, its population has increased to more than 200,000, or twice that number if outlying districts are included.

Musée des Beaux Arts. The museum displays works by Hainaut artists, or works connected with Charleroi (Delvaux, Magritte ● *122*, Meunier ● *115*).

The upper town

Administrative buildings, museums and educational establishments are located here. There are many cafés and restaurants around the two main squares, especially Place Charles-II, the historical heart of the town with its checkerboard fountain.

Hôtel de Ville. The town hall was built by Joseph André (1936), with a neoclassical façade made of alternating

MUSÉE DU VERRE
Charleroi glassblowers developed their craft to a peak of perfection, carrying the town's reputation as far afield as the United States ● *56*. Charleroi's glass museum is one of the finest in Europe, not only displaying the history of local glassmaking but also explaining the properties and applications of glass as a material.

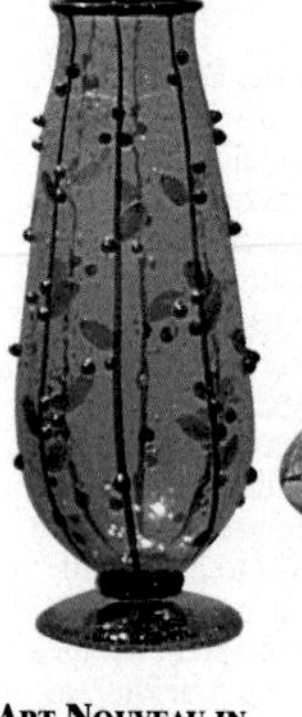

ART NOUVEAU IN CHARLEROI
Several districts of the town were built up less than a century ago. Explore the town and you can discover unexpected treasures here, like this house on Boulevard Defontaine.

bluestone and white stone. Every quarter of an hour the chimes of the belfry ring out the notes of a traditional tune: *Pays de Charleroi* (on the hour), *Skeujè l'feu* and *Lolotte* are some of the ones you can hear. The interior ★ is decorated in Art Deco style. On the third story, the Musée des Beaux Arts has a collection of works by 19th- and 20th-century artists. The MUSÉE JULES-DESTRÉE (at the top of the building) displays objects and documents relating to the great Walloon politician of that name ▲ *275*.

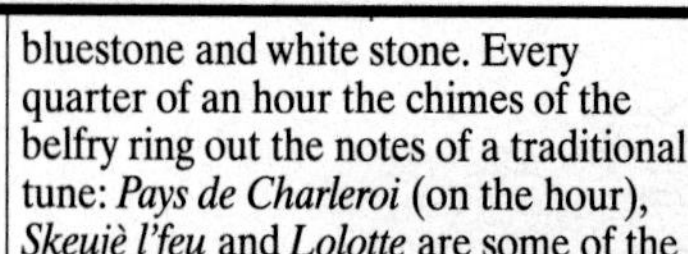

BASILICA OF ST-CHRISTOPHE. This Baroque building (18th century) has been restored several times: the dome and Jean Ransy's mosaic in the choir date from 1956. Before leaving the square, visit the MAISON DES HUIT-HEURES, a focal point of social struggles in the Pays Noir ▲ *278*.

AROUND THE SQUARE ★. Charleroi's Sunday market goes back to 1709; it has a very friendly atmosphere, attracting a colorful crowd with a Mediterranean flavor, including Italians, Spaniards and Greeks, as well as North Africans and Turks. These communities are the descendants of immigrants who came to work in the local coal mines. The surrounding streets are named after the old bastions of the fortress (Turenne, Orléans, Dauphin, Vauban, etc.); they are lined with 18th-century buildings.

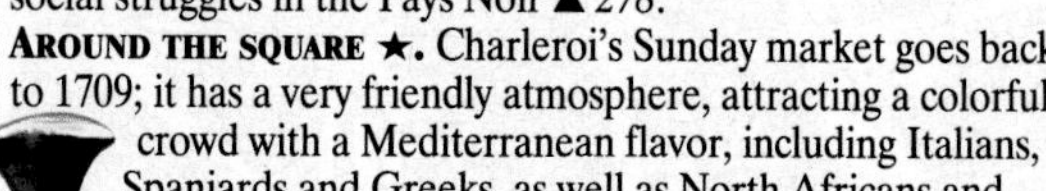

PLACE DU MANÈGE. The square has two neoclassical buildings by Joseph André: the Palais des Expositions (1954), which holds prestigious annual exhibitions, and the PALAIS DES BEAUX ARTS (1957), the venue for events such as the biennial choreography festival, in a setting designed by Paulus, Marini and Magritte. On Boulevard Bertrand the entrance hall of the INSTITUT SUPÉRIEUR INDUSTRIEL (1907) is decorated with three Art Nouveau stained-glass windows depicting the three treasures of the Black Country: coal, iron and glass.

ON THE BOULEVARDS. Head downhill toward the Palais de Justice. In the park stand two carved lions, Tutur and Totor, which are a popular meeting place. The MUSÉE DU VERRE is also located here. The new boulevards were built between the wars, over the town's old fortifications. This gave the modernist and Art Deco architects of the 1930's, such as Leborgne and Depelsenaire, a whole new area to build on.

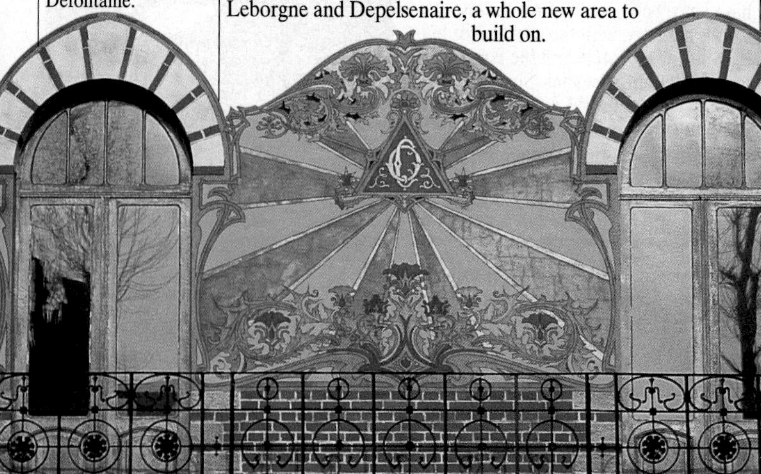

Relief on the Palais des Expositions.

Rue de la Montagne, at the beginning of the 20th century.

THE LOWER TOWN

The town's commercial and financial institutions are concentrated here, including banks and company headquarters.
TOWARD THE FORTIFICATIONS. Below the pedestrian zone, to the right, is the town's oldest street, Rue de Dampreny. Its steps once led toward the ramparts; nowadays the street is lined with restaurants and bistros, some occupying casemates from the old fortifications. At the end stands the CHAPEL OF ST-FIACRE (17th century). The Sambre used to flow close by here: its old course was diverted to make way for Boulevard Tirou, the main road in the lower town.
AROUND THE PLACE ALBERT-1ER. This is where the town's carnival is held. Rue de Marcinelle, to the left of the square, has the town's most beautiful classical building, the INSTITUT NOTRE-DAME. To the right, in Rue de Marchiennes, is the CHURCH OF ST-ANTOINE (1829): its columns, crowned by a triangular pediment, give it the appearance of a classical temple. In the left nave is a painting by François-Joseph Navez, a follower of David, in a strict neoclassical style: *Our Lady of the Afflicted and Saint Antony of Padua*. On the left of the square is the PASSAGE DE LA BOURSE (1890), a smaller version of the Galeries St-Hubert in Brussels ● *160*. Its stucco elevation conforms to classical models. At the end of the passageway, on Rue Léopold, is a wall decorated with a monumental plan of the fortress of Charleroi, engraved by Alphonse Darville in 1966 for the town's tricentenary.
TOWARD THE RIVER. The footbridge that leads to the station of Charleroi-Sud is decorated with two sculptures by Constantin Meunier: *The Miner* and *The Blacksmith*. The buildings along the quaysides offer a panorama of all the architectural styles to be seen in the town: neoclassical, eclectic, neo-Gothic, Art Nouveau, modernist and Art Deco. A huge flea market is held here during the last weekend of June.

BALLS AND CARNIVALS
Charleroi is a lively town, with a highly developed predilection for festivities. On Mardi Gras (Shrove Tuesday) the carnival procession takes over the streets of the town (left). The Charleroi carnival is a family occasion, centered around the children. The most spectacular event is the grand ball of the Climbias, held in the Ruche Verrière ▲ *278* at Lodelinsart on the Saturday following Shrove Tuesday. The Climbias are members of a charitable organization who dress in the costumes of 18th-century gentlemen-glassmakers (the *climbia* was a kind of tong used by the glassmakers). The Marche de la Madeleine at Jumet is one of the most impressive parades of its kind ● *165*. It takes place at the end of July, bringing together some 50 organizations, 2,000 marching soldiers and 250 horses.

THE "TERRILS"
There are nearly one hundred terrils (heaps of waste material from the old coal mines) in the Charleroi region. Trees have been planted on most of them today. More surprisingly, vines are now grown on the slagheap at Herlaimont in the Chapelle district. In fact this loose, friable earth provides excellent conditions for growing grapes.

ARTIST OF THE PAYS NOIR
A room in the Musée des Beaux Arts ▲ *275* is dedicated to Pierre Paulus (1881–1959), an outstanding painter of industrial scenes of the Sambre and the Black Country (right), depicting its coal mines, mining villages and slagheaps.

THE GREAT STRIKES OF 1886
The history of Charleroi's glassblowers is tragically intertwined with the bloody riots of March 1886, provoked by the poverty and famine of that dreadful year. During the riots the glassworks and Château de Baudoux were set on fire, and more than twenty strikers died. These dramatic events prompted the first serious consideration of social issues in Belgium, leading to the beginnings of proper legislation in this area.

In this region heavy industry has created a landscape of chimneys, blast furnaces, cooling towers, pithead frames and slagheaps. Upriver from Charleroi factories still occupy most of the Sambre valley. A disorderly mass of workers' houses grew up around the factories. There was no overall plan: some are grouped in mini-villages, others are arranged in alleys, courtyards or passages; the contrast with the small number of pit managers' residences is striking. The area is full of surprises: a row of houses may end in a wooded slag heap or even a large field. The old village-style groups of houses grew up independently of each other, leaving green spaces between them: today these offer great potential for town-planning and economic-development projects.

LODELINSART, THE GLASS TOWN. The Chaussée de Bruxelles and Chaussée de Châtelet lead to Place Edmond-Gilles. This square is named after the founder of the Nouvelle Union Verrière, the association of glassblowers ● *56* established in 1894, which held its meetings in the RUCHE VERRIÈRE (1909). Chaussée de Ransart at Gilly leads to CHÂTEAU MONDRON (1881), the most splendid of the private residences built by the great Charleroi industrialists of the 19th century. The building was equipped with an armored room after the troubles of 1886; it was converted into a church in 1929.

JUMET AND ITS HISTORICAL PROCESSION. The Marche de la Madeleine procession is held in Jumet each year on the Sunday closest to July 22. Crossing the district from east to west, you will see the CHAPELLE D'HEIGNE, a 13th-century Romanesque building that has undergone several alterations.

MARCINELLE AND COUILLET. Marcinelle's Grand-Place has a beautiful Romanesque church; the Avenue de Philippeville joins this town to Couillet. The MUSÉE DES SCIENCES at Parentville acts as an observatory, offering a view over the whole industrial basin. The road through Blanche-Borne leads to the BOIS DU CAZIER coal mine (1907), the scene of the worst mining disaster in Belgium, in 1956, in which 262 miners died. The mining buildings, lamp store and changing rooms give an insight into the surface life of a coal mine.

Musée de la Photographie ★
These negatives (left) come from the extensive collection in the photographic museum of Mont-sur-Marchienne, housed in a neo-Gothic building from the late 19th century (formerly a convent). The museum also acts as a contemporary-art center and presents temporary exhibitions.

Musée de l'Industrie ★
The stunning museum of industry at Marchienne-au-Pont is housed in the old Forges de la Providence. It features permanent displays and events relating to the area's industrial heritage. Industrial techniques are presented, including metalwork and printing, as are real factory workshops and a forge that was once used for repairs to the rolling mill. The manor house in this town was owned by the Cartier de Marchienne family, into which the novelist Marguerite de Yourcenar was born.

1. Charleroi
2. Abbey of Aulne
3. Thuin
4. Lobbes
5. Beaumont
6. Barbançon
7. Rance

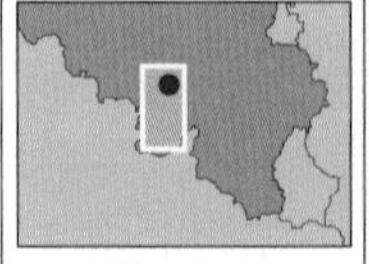

One day
25 miles

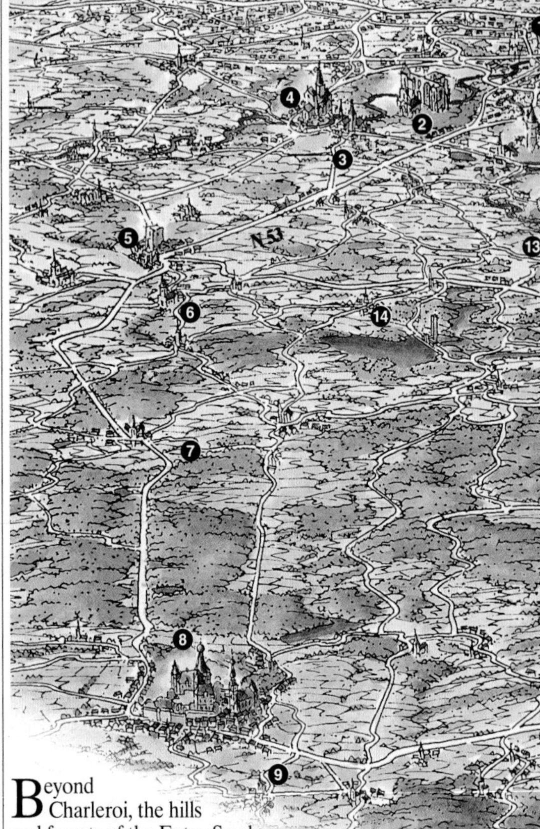

Church of St-Ursmer at Lobbes
Monks could not be buried in the abbey church at Lobbes because of the holy relics preserved there. For this reason another church was built on the hill (below). It was dedicated in 697 and took the name of St-Ursmer in 823. Some precious remains from the 9th-century reconstruction still survive (the nave and western section), which are rare examples of Carolingian architecture in Belgium. The crypt, entrance porch, tower and choir are in the Mosan style ● *82*, while the central spire is the product of misguided restoration in the 19th century. The crypt houses the tomb of Saint Ursmer (8th century).

Beyond Charleroi, the hills and forests of the Entre-Sambre-et-Meuse region offer a foretaste of the Ardennes, on a gentler note. The metalworking industry flourished here under the Ancien Régime: this has left its mark in the names of towns and lakes (old reservoirs).

Land of processions. French influence is more apparent here than anywhere else in southern Belgium (in the village squares bordered by trees, for example). The area has a lively tradition of local customs and festivities, most notably in its traditional processions or marches ● *65*: there are more than sixty of these, held in different villages across the region from the month of May onward.

Charleroi to Chimay

The Abbey of Aulne. The abbey was founded in 657 by Saint Landelin, a reformed robber; it became a Cistercian abbey in the 12th century and was soon one of the most powerful abbeys in the region. It flourished in the 13th century, but was plundered and ransacked in the 15th and 16th centuries, before recovering its former splendor for the next two hundred years. The monastic buildings were completely rebuilt in the 18th century, but the abbey was burned down in 1794. Today all that remains is an attractive group of ruins (remains of arcades and sections of walls) set deep in the Sambre valley.

Thuin. This town, once an advance fortress of the principality of Liège, is divided into an upper town (on a rocky outcrop that was fortified in the past) and a lower town on the banks of the Sambre, which still has its old harbor district.

Lobbes. The town was built on the left bank of the Sambre. The abbey founded here in the 7th century became one of the most important cultural and religious centers of the region in

The "marche" at Walcourt
Walcourt's marches are processions of saints accompanied by a ceremonial military escort. They were suppressed during the Revolution, and reintroduced under the First Empire, which explains the style of the uniforms worn by the soldiers. The memory of Napoleon is still very much alive in this region next to the French border.

the 10th century. Originally the town had three churches: the first was destroyed in the 10th century; the second was demolished along with the abbey in 1794; only the Church of St-Ursmer survives.

FROM BEAUMONT TO RANCE. BEAUMONT still has its Tour Salamandre, all that survives of the ramparts built by Richilde, Countess of Hainault, in the 10th century (later modified by the Princes of Croy). BARBANÇON had the first glassworks in Hainaut, founded in the 16th century ● *56*. Houses from the 16th and 17th centuries can still be seen here today, with mullioned windows and stone staircases on the façades. RANCE once had thriving marble quarries and sawmills: a MUSEUM commemorates these activities.

CHIMAY. This picturesque town with its narrow alleys and stone stairways nestles at the heart of a beautiful forest. On its Grand-Place stand the Hôtel de Ville (18th century) and the Collegiate Church of St-Pierre-et-Paul (Jean Froissart, chronicler of the Hundred Years' War, was a canon here). The CHÂTEAU DES PRINCES DE CARAMAN-CHIMAY stands on a rocky outcrop washed by the waters of the Eau-Blanche; it was rebuilt, following Charles de Croy's plans (1607), after a fire in 1935.

ÉTANG DE VIRELLES. The metalworking industry flourished in the western part of the Entre-Sambre-et-Meuse region in the 15th and 16th centuries. River water was held back by dykes and chaneled toward mills which powered the forges. After the forges closed at the end of the 19th century, the lakes were used for hunting and fishing. The rushes are used for basketwork, and the reeds for making thatched roofs. The Étang de Virelles is the largest of these old reservoirs; since 1985 it has been managed by three conservation groups. It has numerous dragonflies, prey to the hobbies (falcons) that come here to hunt. The reeds give refuge to a variety of aquatic birds in the summer, and to migratory birds in the winter.

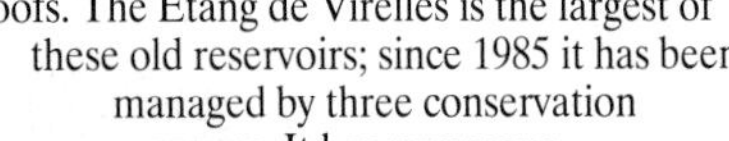

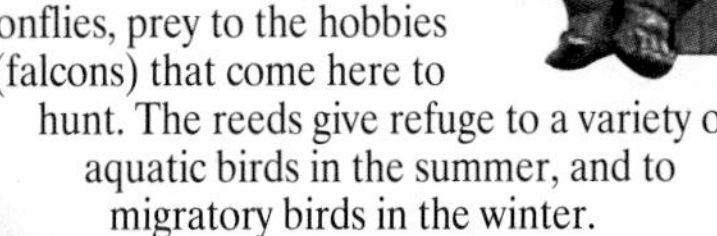

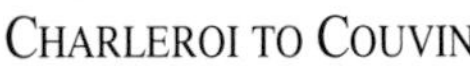

CHARLEROI TO COUVIN

FLOREFFE. Make a detour to see this town, which has the first abbey founded by Saint Norbert (founder of the Premonstratensian order) in Southern Belgium. The land was donated by Godefroid, Count of Namur, and his wife in 1121. Most of the present abbey buildings date from the 18th century.

FOSSES-LA-VILLE. The town is famous for its carnival, with Doudous and Chinels ● *69*, and for the Collegiate Church of St-Feuillen, founded in the 7th century. The church was rebuilt in

THE THEATER OF MME TALLIEN
Formerly the mistress of Barras, the French revolutionary, Mme Tallien married a member of the Caraman-Chimay family in 1805 and moved to his château, where she died in 1835. She was interested in music and had a charming theater built, a replica of the one at Fontainebleau. This was replaced by the present theater in 1863; it was restored in 1991 and now hosts a music festival.

ABBEY OF FLOREFFE
The abbey was altered in the 17th and 18th centuries (below). The stalls were carved by Pierre Enderlin in the 17th century (detail, right).

the 18th century, retaining its forebuilding and an external crypt from the 11th century. The interior has 13th-century baptismal fonts, and a reliquary by Hugo d'Oignies ▲ *198* in the treasury.

Gerpinnes. The Church of St-Michel is notable for its crypt, its tower and its Romanesque baptismal fonts. It also has a Merovingian tomb (8th century) which may be that of Saint Rolende, daughter of King Didier of Lombardy, and a shrine (1599) that is carried in a 22-mile procession on the Monday of Pentecost (the longest procession in Entre-Sambre-et-Meuse).

The lakes of the Eau-d'Heure. In 1978 1,500 acres of land on the borders of the Condroz and the Fagne were submerged in order to reduce the pollution of the Sambre and supply

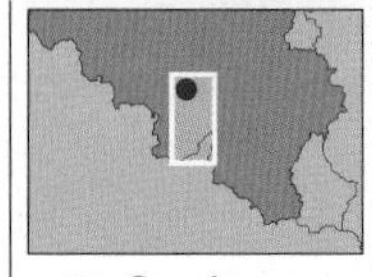

◷ One day

🚗 25 miles

Couvin

Flowing through this walled town (above) is the Eau-Noire, the main river of the Ardennes in Entre-Sambre-et-Meuse; its name (meaning "black water") probably comes from the color of the stones on the river bed. Couvin is a pleasant place to stay, with a large number of footpaths across the woods and hills. Nearby are the Grottes de Neptune, hollowed out by the Eau-Noire, which are open to visitors.

Walcourt

The medieval town of Walcourt is built on the slopes of a promontory between Gerpinnes and Philippeville. Remains of fortifications still mark the outline of the old fortress. The Basilica of St-Materne was rebuilt in the 15th century; its bulbous spire was made this century, following a 17th-century model. The interior is no less interesting, with Gothic stalls and rood screen, a miraculous Virgin with a silver mask, and a splendid treasury ★.

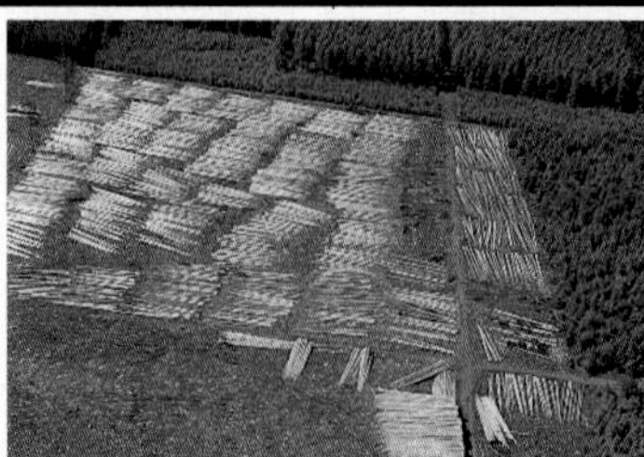

THE VIROIN VALLEY
Nowhere else is the contrast between the limestone hills of the Calestienne to the north and the great wooded slopes of the Ardennes to the south more clearly apparent: the river runs almost exactly along the dividing line between these two natural regions.

drinking water and hydroelectric power. Together the lakes, which have been adapted for water sports and birdwatching, constitute the largest reservoir in southern Belgium.

FORTIFIED TOWNS. The towns of Philippeville and Mariembourg remained under French rule from 1659 to 1815. MARIEMBOURG was founded on the orders of Charles V in 1546 and named after Mary of Hungary, regent of the Netherlands. PHILIPPEVILLE, named after King Philip II of Spain, was founded by Charles V in 1555, a year after Mariembourg was captured by Henri II of France. The town as it looks now was designed by Vauban under Louis XIV.

"RIEZES" AND "SARTS". In the region stretching to the south of Couvin ▲ *283* there are hundreds of *rièzes*: isolated marshes created by the presence of impermeable rocks in the subsoil. Rainwater stays on the surface, forming lakes covered with dull-colored vegetation. *Sarts* or *brûlys* (both terms appear frequently in place names) are large sections of forest that were cleared in the past to make way for crops of rye. In the process of essartage, or grubbing (top left), the tree stumps were burned in the ground: the ashes, rich in potassium, acted as a natural fertilizer. Near Brûly-de-Pesche is HITLER'S BUNKER, which served as his headquarters in June 1940.

The valley has many villages; the warm, well-drained soils provide perfect conditions for growing cereal crops (top, right).

NISMES. The Eau-Noire and the Eau-Blanche flow together in this old clog-making village, forming the Viroin river. The most accessible examples of the dry grasslands ■ *22* that covered the hills of the Calestienne ▲ *211* in the last century can be seen near here: TIENNE-BREUMONT, MONTAGNE-AU-BUIS, the ROCHE-À-LOMME and the ABANNETS nature reserve. Orchids (left, *Ophrys insectifera*) and gentians flower here. Some of these sites have deep cavities, initially formed when the limestone melted in the tropical climate of the Tertiary era. Iron ore accumulated in the holes, which were exposed once again when the ore was mined. These cavities are known locally as *fondrys*; the best example can be seen in the town of FONDRYS DES CHIENS.

TREIGNES, THE "MUSEUM VILLAGE". This village is packed with museums. These include the "ECOMUSEUM" OF RURAL LIFE AND TECHNOLOGY, a MUSEUM OF AGRICULTURAL MACHINERY, the MUSÉE DU MALGRÉ-TOUT (dedicated to the archeology of the region) and the impressive MUSÉE PAUL-DELVAUX (devoted to industrial and railway history). The remains of a Roman villa were discovered nearby in 1979, which had been destroyed around 260, during the first invasions.

TREIGNES
Being a border town, Treignes has a remarkably large and busy station, despite its rural setting.

In and around Mons

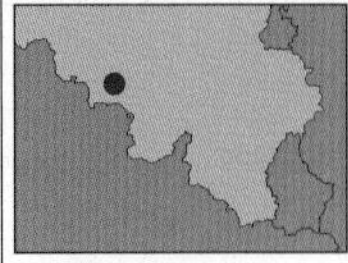

◷ One day

HISTORY

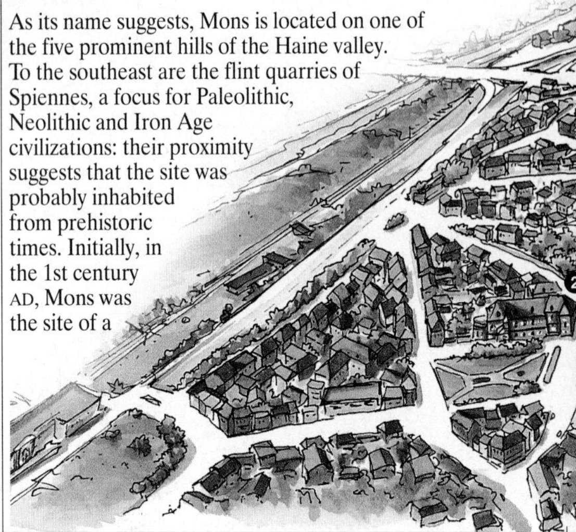

As its name suggests, Mons is located on one of the five prominent hills of the Haine valley. To the southeast are the flint quarries of Spiennes, a focus for Paleolithic, Neolithic and Iron Age civilizations: their proximity suggests that the site was probably inhabited from prehistoric times. Initially, in the 1st century AD, Mons was the site of a Roman encampment (*castrilocus*), set up on the road connecting Bavay to Utrecht. Waudru, a noblewoman, founded a monastery here in the 7th century. During the 9th and 10th centuries the Count of Mons and then the Count of Hainaut built a castle on top of the hill, reinforced in the 12th century by a rampart with a circumference of half a mile. The town grew up around this castle.

THIRTEENTH-CENTURY RAMPARTS. A century later another wall was built around the town, at the foot of the hill. The wall had stone gateways opening onto the main routes (four roads and a river) connecting the town with the outside world. It also acted as a barrier to the town's growth, and within the walls the town became ever more densely populated. Beyond the fortifications lay huge marshy and wooded areas, which prevented the incorporation of neighboring villages. Up to the 19th century various fortifications were built outside the wall, sometimes at a considerable distance from the main citadel, under different regimes (Burgundian, Spanish, French and Austrian). When the town fell to Louis XIV after the siege of 1691, new fortifications were built by Vauban: these made Mons one of the strongest border forts of the time.

THE 19TH-CENTURY FORTIFICATIONS. The Dutch demolished the 13th-century ramparts between 1815 and 1820 to make way for new fortifications. These encroached on the surrounding countryside and were themselves dismantled between 1861 and 1865. From this time onward the town began to grow rapidly, especially in the mid 20th century when the walls were replaced by boulevards, paving the way for expansion onto the foothills and the surrounding area. In 1976 eighteen neighboring villages were merged with the town, including Jemappes to the west of Mons, famous for the battle that took place there in November 1792. The French Revolutionaries were victorious; after this Hainaut was annexed to France, as the "département" of Jemappes.

THE ARCHITECTURE OF MONS
From the 16th century onward secular buildings were generally constructed in the materials that came to be typical of

Mons architecture: brick and stone for the facing, and tiles and slate for the roof. In the 17th century gables with finials or steps took the place of pointed gables on the tall, narrow buildings. After the town was bombarded by Louis XIV, entire quarters were rebuilt in French classical style. The grand styles (Louis XIV, Regency, Louis XV, Louis XVI) that held sway in France in the 18th century were also eventually adopted here.

1. Collegiate Church of Ste-Waudru
2. Musées Chanoine Puissant
3. Belfry
4. Grand-Place
5. Hôtel de Ville
6. Musées du Centenaire
7. Musée de la Vie Montoise
8. Church of Ste-Elisabeth
9. Church of St-Nicolas-en-Havré

An administrative and military town. Mons was the capital town of the county of Hainaut and the seat of important judicial, legislative, administrative and military bodies from the Middle Ages onward. These included the regional government, the supreme court, the Grand Bailliage (Great Bailiwick), the Provost's Office and the Échevinage, which acted as a court of appeal for a number of outlying villages. From the 13th century onward Mons was governed by a mayor appointed by the count and the aldermen. Today it is the home of Hainaut's government and still has a court of appeal. However, the town no longer has a military function and has not had a garrison since the last war.

Rue des Clercs with the belfry in the background. Bottom: the siege of Mons by Louis XIV's armies in 1691.

Concentric plan
Generally history and topography together determine a town's layout. This is particularly true of Mons: the town within the ramparts was adapted to the shape of the hill, and today's street plan is still the same as in the Middle Ages.

THE "CAR D'OR"
In the 14th century the town's religious authorities called upon Saint Waudru to help end a plague epidemic, and the traditional observances were intensified. Every Trinity Sunday the golden carriage carries the saint's shrine through the town.

COLLEGIATE CHURCH OF STE-WAUDRU ★

Place Léopold (in front of the station) is part of the western quarter that was developed from 1870 onward, after the Dutch fortifications were dismantled. From here, Rue de la Houssière leads to the old town.

A HILLSIDE CHURCH. This street leads toward the Gothic Collegiate Church of Ste-Waudru – a prominent feature of the townscape, anchored halfway up the hill. The present church, built in Brabant Gothic style, took the place of earlier churches built on the same site in Merovingian, Carolingian and Romanesque times. Building work started in 1450 and was not completed until 1690. Several generations of builders were involved but all adhered to the initial plans, resulting in an impressive overall unity of style. The chapter of canonesses, which took the place of the religious community founded by Saint Waudru in the 7th century, were closely involved in the construction of their church. Building work came to an end in the late 17th century due to lack of funds: the 620-foot tower that the canonesses had planned to build on the western façade was never completed.

SOARING VERTICALITY. On the outside the building appears as a huge solid mass: the tower on the façade has a solid base (like the tower porchway of the Church of St-Rombaut at Malines) and the chevet forms a solid triangular shape (its chapels are contained between short buttresses and joined to the vault of the choir by flying buttresses). The effect of the interior is quite different: visitors are immediately struck by the strong upward thrust of the architecture; the soaring verticality of the pillars and the stone ribs is unimpeded by any horizontal elements over the building's three stories, from the beveled bases of the pillars to the keystones of the vault.

HIGHLIGHTS OF STE-WAUDRU. A marble ROOD SCREEN separated the nave and the choir in the 16th century (1535–48). The screen, a triumphal arch with three rounded arches and caissons, was made in black Dinant marble by Jacques Dubroeucq, assisted by Jean de Thuin and Hubert Nonnon. The screen was destroyed at the time of the French Revolution: only the bas-reliefs and the alabaster statues of the Virtues (all by Dubroeucq) survived. These were moved to the choir and the transept around 1930. On the other

side of the choir, underneath the organ, stands the 18th-century CAR D'OR (Golden Carriage), made in painted and gilded wood by Ghienne and Midavaine. On Trinity Sunday it carries the shrine of Saint Waudru through the town, accompanied by musicians, choirs, banners and horses. Legend has it that disaster will befall the town if the six horses pulling the carriage stumble on the slope leading up to Ste-Waudru. Painted WINDOWS from the 16th century can be seen in the choir; the five stained-glass windows of the chevet were produced by Claix Eve, a master glassmaker from Mons, in 1510–11; the stained-glass windows in the transept also date from the 16th century. The treasury, in the former chapter house, includes items connected with Saint Waudru and the chapter of canonesses, as well as silversmiths' works from the 13th to the 19th centuries.

NEARBY MUSEUMS. The MUSÉE FRANÇOIS-DUESBERG (12, square Franklin-Roosevelt) was opened in 1994. It is named after the donator of this collection of 18th-century gilded-bronze clocks. Next door is a former Ursuline convent, built in 1710. A few yards from the church are the Musées Chanoine Puissant (entrance in Rue Notre-Dame-Débonnaire), whose artistic and historical collections are in two buildings: the 16th-century Vieux Logis (formerly part of the Abbey of Ghislenghien) and the Chapel of Ste-Marguerite (in Rue Sars).

"A SECOND MICHELANGELO"
Jacques Dubroeucq was born in Mons. In Italy he discovered the Renaissance style, which he expressed in the rood screen for the collegiate church of his home town. He became official architect to Mary of Hungary, for whom he designed a number of buildings (at Binche ▲ *292* and Mariemont ▲ *293*) and was later granted the title of "master artist" by Charles V.

THE BELFRY

The belfry (nearly 300 feet high) is the most prominent feature of the townscape, visible from a great distance. To reach it, take the Rue des Clercs, lined with 16th- and 18th-century houses, and the Rampe du Château. This tower was built by the architect Louis Ledoux between 1661 and 1669, within the walls of the medieval castle, to replace a late-15th-century clock tower that had collapsed. It is the only Baroque belfry in Belgium. The walls are made of Bray sandstone, while

THE BELFRY
The slate roof covers a complex construction, which Victor Hugo described in the following terms in a letter to his wife, written in 1837: "Imagine an enormous coffee pot, surrounded at the base by four slightly smaller teapots. It would be ugly if it were not so big. . . ."

The monkey
This wrought-iron monkey, from the Middle Ages, can be seen to the left of the portal of the town hall. Since 1930 it has been viewed as a bringer of good luck – but before 1914 it was seen as a "bogeyman" who would punish naughty children.

The lock of the Hôtel de Ville
The left-hand door of the portal opening onto the porch is decorated with this lovely ornamental lock. The 15th-century original, made of wrought iron, is kept in the Musée de la Vie Montoise.

the pilasters, columns, bossed window frames, balustrades, pediments and coats of arms are made of limestone blocks.

The Grand-Place ★

This is the commercial center of the town, at the junction of the town's main roads. The square was first laid out, on an old marketplace, in 1348. Today it offers examples of most of the architectural styles to be seen in the town, providing a kind of panoramic view of secular architecture in Mons over six centuries.

Hôtel de Ville. The principal building on the Grand-Place is the town's administrative center, situated on the curved side of the square. It dates from 1458, when it replaced the 14th-century Maison de Paix. Mathieu De Layens supervised its construction (he was also responsible for the town hall in Louvain). It is a unique example of secular Gothic architecture from the 15th century, with a broad façade that has eight windows and a portal at ground level and ten windows on the upper story. A third story was planned, but the aldermen were not able to complete it due to lack of funds. In 1718, Tirou and Caffiaux added a bell tower and replaced the original roof tiles with slate. The internal courtyard shows how administrative functions expanded over the course of the centuries: several buildings were added here, including a room for weddings (16th century), the aldermen's Chapel of St-Georges (17th century), and the antechamber of the burgomaster's office (18th century). In the porch, on the left, is the original spiral STAIRCASE, a typically medieval construction: its steps are made of single stone blocks, and it is set in an external polygonal tower. At the far end of the main courtyard is an underground passageway leading to the JARDIN DU MAÏEUR (Mayor's Garden). At the end of the garden is an old pawnshop (1625): this houses the MUSÉES DU CENTENAIRE, consisting of a museum covering the two world wars (on the first and fourth stories), a museum of ceramics (on the second story) and a museum of prehistoric and Gallo-Roman archeology, along with a numismatics museum (on the third story).

Houses on the Grand-Place. The oldest buildings date from the 16th century (on the the square's southern crossroads, by Rue de la

Chaussée). Typical of this Gothico-Renaissance period is the house known as "Au Blanc-Lévrié" (The White Greyhound) ● *92* because of the greyhounds on its sign. The town hall is flanked by two 17th-century Baroque buildings: the Hôtel de la Toison d'Or on the right (1650), and the Chapel of St-Georges on the left (1601). The siege of 1691 caused considerable damage, and so a large proportion of the buildings date from the 18th century. These are built in the French classical style, like the houses on the corner of the Grand-Place and Rue des Clercs (1702–9). These façades are wider than they are tall, featuring side gables with finials, high stone bases, straight piers and wide windows with movable frames. Local examples of Louis XIV style can be seen at nos. 6, 7, 28, 29 and 30; Regency and Louis XV style in the Hôtel de la Couronne (1765) at no. 23; and Louis XVI style in L'Âne-Rayé (1780) at no. 4. The most striking 19th-century building is the neoclassical theater (1842). Twentieth-century additions include a pastiche of Flemish Renaissance style on the corner of Rue La Coupe, dating from the 1930's.

Saint George and his escort of ten *chinchins* ("protectors") confront the dragon, who is accompanied by eight devils, seven savages or "leaf-men" and twelve civilized men, all to the sound of a tune called *The Doudou*. The people of Mons pluck hairs from the dragon's tail, which are traditionally supposed to bring good luck.

Mons traditions

The Lumeçon ● *65.* This processional game re-enacting the combat between Saint George and the dragon is held on the Grand-Place every year on Trinity Sunday. The Lumeçon is said to date from the 14th century.

The Ducasse des Messines. Every year on the Sunday nearest to Ascension the Messines quarter honors a 16th-century painting – depicting the Virgin appearing to a nun – that is renowned for its miraculous healing powers. The religious pilgrimage is accompanied by secular festivities.

Local customs. Next to the Musée des Beaux Arts is the Musée du Folklore et de la Vie Montoise, housed in the Maison Jean-Lescarts, formerly a convent infirmary. The displays illustrate aspects of everyday life and local customs.

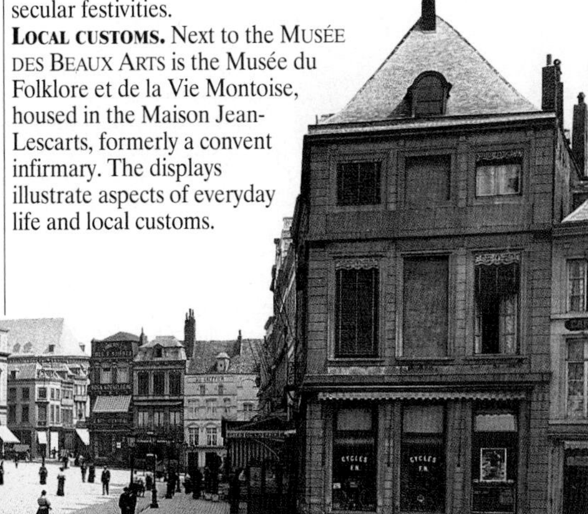

Art Nouveau in Mons
Numerous examples of Art Nouveau and Art Deco architecture can be found along the 3 miles of boulevards built from 1865 onward. However, the most striking example is the Maison Léon-Losseau, designed by Paul Saintenoy, in the city center (at no. 37, rue Nimy, next to the Palais de Justice).

1. Mons 2. Binche 3. Mariemont 4. Seneffe 5. La Louvière 6. Bois-du-Luc 7. Le Rœulx 8. Boussu 9. Le Grand-Hornu 10. Elouges

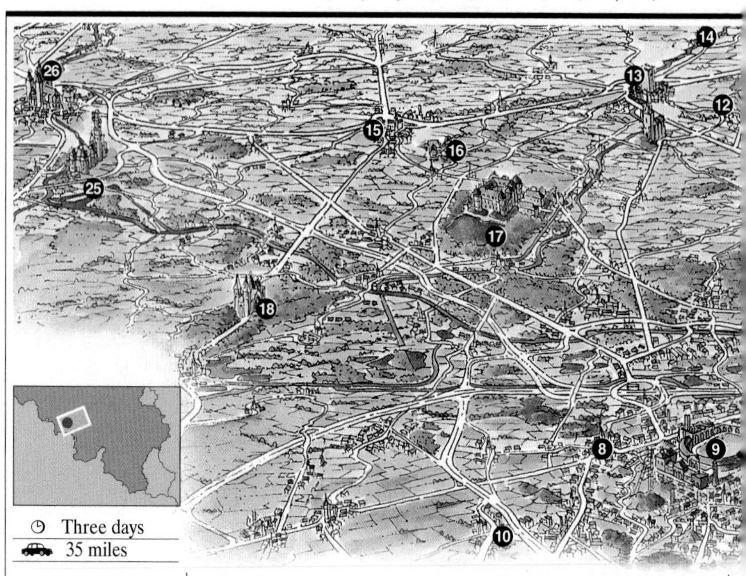

Three days
35 miles

A fortified town
Binche still has part of its old rampart, with twenty-five towers and over a mile of Bray-sandstone wall; a thick covering of ivy softens its austere appearance. These are the remains of a 12th-century fortress where Margaret of York, widow of Charles the Bold, lived in the 15th century. Subsequently, in 1545, Mary of Hungary, sister of Charles V and regent of the Netherlands, built a Renaissance palace in place of the medieval fortress. This was destroyed when the town was sacked by Henri II in 1554.

The Centre region is a product of the Industrial Revolution, a coalfield set between those of Mons-Borinage and Charleroi. It owes its prosaic name to the unimaginative mine owners who called it simply the Bassin du Centre (central coalfield). This started as an agricultural area, acquiring its industrial status initially through coal mining and then through the metal and glass industries that developed here. Since the 1960's the Centre has been hard hit by the decline of coal as an industrial fuel, and by the emergence of competition from developing countries.

Binche

Binche, on the southern edge of the Centre region, is famous for its carnival: this is the home of the Gilles ▲ *294*, and an international museum of the carnival is located here. The town was an important lacemaking center in the 17th and 18th centuries, giving its name to a type of lace that can be identified by its very fine thread, together with its *fond de neige* patterns, incorporating little balls or stars, combined with motifs such as flowers or palm leaves. Today the town has around twenty lacemakers and a hundred or so pupils, thanks to a school of lacemaking founded in 1954. To find out more, visit the Centre de la Dentelle et des Métiers d'Art (Lace and Craft Center) on the Grand-Place.
The Grand-Place. The Hôtel de Ville has a Gothic façade (14th century) and a 16th-century belfry with a peal of twenty-six bells, of which twelve were cast between 1597 and 1630. The Collegiate Church of St-Ursmer (12th–15th century), built in the Romanesque style, has an organ from the Grand

11. Parc de Paradisio
12. Château d'Attre
13. Ath
14. Lessines
15. Leuze
16. Aubechies archeological site
17. Château de Belœil
18. Bon-Secours Forest
19. Soignies
20. Écaussinnes-Lalaing
21. Écaussinnes d'Enghien
22. Sloping lock of Ronquières
23. Enghien
24. Nivelles
25. Antoing
26. Tournai

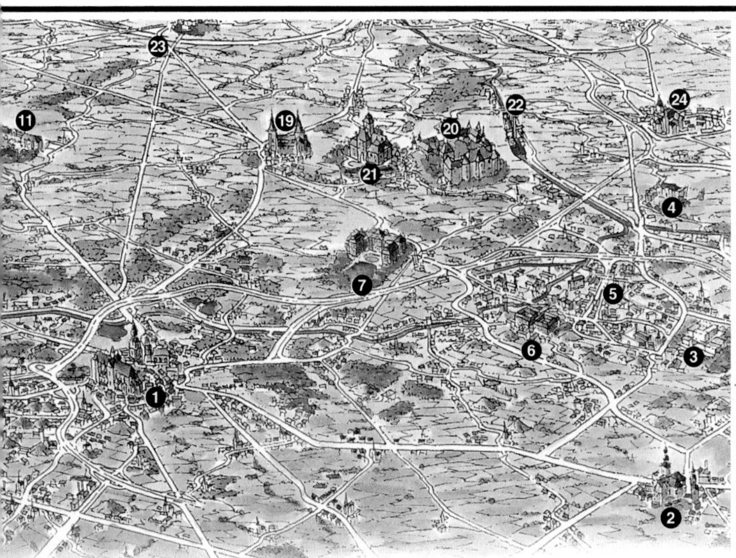

Synagogue in Berlin (acquired in 1907) and a treasury that includes an enameled gold crucifix, decorated with pearls and jewels, donated by Margaret of York in 1479.

Mariemont ★

Mary of Hungary built a hunting pavilion here in 1546. It was extended by Archduke Albert and Archduchess Isabella, and then completely rebuilt in the classical style by Charles de Lorraine in the 18th century, to accommodate his court of "drinkers, diners and hunters".

New owners: the Warocqué family. Mariemont was state-owned when it was destroyed, on the eve of the French victory at Fleurus, in 1794. Later it was acquired by entrepreneurs, attracted by the estate's large coal deposits. When the Société Minière du Parc de Mariemont was founded in 1802, one of the shareholders was Nicolas Warocqué (1773–1838), a Mons businessman who amassed a fortune through nationalization and founded an industrial dynasty that owned Mariemont from 1813 to 1917. Warocqués of successive generations managed the coal mines of Mariemont and held the office of Mayor of Morlanwelz. Nicolas Warocqué commissioned a neoclassical palace from Tilman-Frans Suys, the king's architect, along with landscaped gardens, designed by C.-H. Petersen in 1832. It was Raoul Warocqué, the last representative

The golden age of Mariemont
Mariemont acquired the status of royal residence under the Archduke Albert and Archduchess Isabella. They rebuilt the castle in two phases (1606–10 and 1618)

and redesigned the gardens. This was a brilliant period in Mariemont's history, a time when its visitors included Rubens and Jan ("Velvet") Bruegel.
Above: Raoul Warocqué.

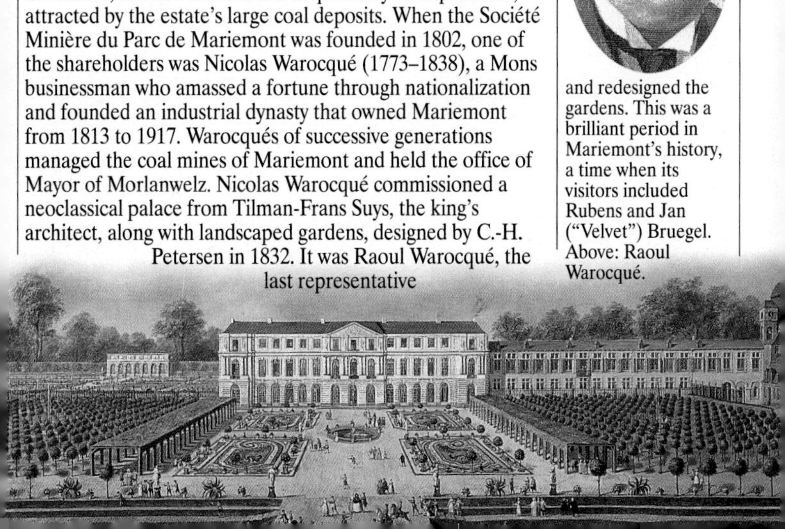

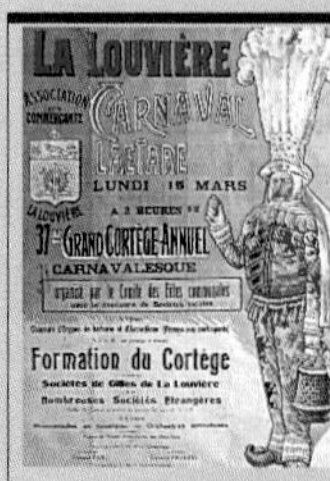

A Gille at La Louvière, a few miles from Binche.

Binche's annual carnival is one of the most famous carnivals in Europe. It is a thoroughly traditional affair, not one devised for tourists – an authentic expression of local traditions, governed by a strict set of rules. The carnival spans several weeks, during which preparations and events steadily build up to a climax. Only on the last day, Mardi Gras (Shrove Tuesday), do the Gilles finally make their appearance. Binche's Gilles are masked figures with a complex and ancient history. The Gilles of the neighboring towns are pale comic variations on these archetypcal ritual figures, without the same magical significance or authenticity.

THE GILLE
This male figure acquired his name in the 18th century, but in fact goes back much further and is rooted in a long European tradition of masked ritual dancers. Legend has it (wrongly, in fact) that he is a distant descendant of the Incas displayed at Binche in 1549, during festivities in honor of Mary of Hungary. The Gille of Binche is close to the heart of all the townsfolk, a symbol of their collective identity. His costume holds clues to his rural past (clogs, bells, and the ear of corn embroidered on the hat).

DIMANCHE GRAS
On the Sunday before Lent the Gilles do not yet wear their traditional costume, but the whole town wears fancy dress. A huge procession of costumed dancers passes through the streets toward the town center.

MARDI GRAS
On Shrove Tuesday the Gilles appear and perform their dances. In the morning they wear masks; in the afternoon they wear heavy hats (nearly 7 pounds, and 3 feet high) decorated with three hundred ostrich feathers.

Preparations
Carnival preparations begin weeks ahead. The first rehearsal, held six weeks before the carnival, is for the drums. Then, after four Sundays of *soumonces*, the Gilles practice their steps. The festivities are officially opened on Candlemas (Feb. 2), with costumed balls

and the "Trouilles de Nouille" night, when everyone wears rags. The last three days are the climax of the carnival: after the fancy-dress parade on the Sunday, the Monday is the traditional day for family gatherings; finally the Gilles make their appearance on the Tuesday.

Dance of the Gilles
The Gilles wear masks and perform jerky movements, forming an imposing, anonymous mass of figures. Around midday they remove their masks, after performing their dance outside the town hall. In the afternoon they come together again, wearing the high hats bristling with ostrich feathers. They parade through the town, throwing oranges at the crowd (above). After this, the nine hundred or so Gilles join with all the other carnival figures (sailors, peasants, harlequins and pierrots) to dance late into the night.

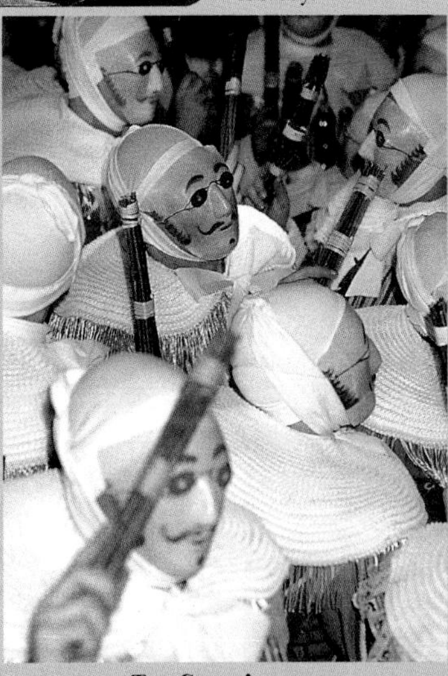

The Gilles' masks
These are made of waxed cloth, with green glasses, sideburns and a moustache.

of the family, who bought the ruins of the archducal castle and replanted the estate to restore its original appearance.

Musée Royal. Raoul Warocqué died in 1917. His legacy to the state formed the basis of this museum. Warocqué's château was destroyed by fire in 1960; today's building, which houses the museum, was built by Roger Bastin in 1975, incorporating the remains of the 19th-century building. The grounds have some 120 acres, planted with rare trees and adorned with oriental bronzes, works by Belgian sculptors of the 19th and 20th centuries, and the romantic ruins of Charles de Lorraine's castle. The museum's collections consist mainly of works assembled by Raoul Warocqué, including treasures from the Mediterranean and Far East, archeological finds and Tournai porcelain. Later acquisitions have added to the original collection.

Château de Seneffe ★

The Château de Seneffe (above) was built by the architect Laurent-Benoît Dewez in 1763–8. It stands in its own grounds, to the east of the village. On either side of the main building (built in bluestone from Feluy) are two long galleries with Ionic columns, ending in pavilions. The grounds (covering 54 acres) include a formal garden called the Trois Terrasses, a small neoclassical theater, an ice house and an orangery. General von Falkenhausen, the German military governor of Belgium under the Occupation, used the château as his residence. A museum of silverwork is soon to be opened here.

Industrial sites

La Louvière. This hamlet expanded during the Industrial Revolution, becoming a commune in 1869. The museum of

Bois-du-Luc
A fine assembly of buildings was erected in this coal-mining town in the mid 19th century. Alongside the industrial buildings are tightly packed rows of workers' houses, framed to the north by schools, the hospital, the hospice and the church, and to the south by the director's house. Wooded slagheaps overlook the scene.

Laurent-Benoît Dewez, architect
The Château de Seneffe was this architect's first creation. He was the official architect of the Netherlands from 1767 onward, under the rule of Charles de Lorraine.

Canal du Centre
The canal has six locks and four lifts, which are unique pieces of machinery; they make up a difference in ground level of nearly 300 feet. The lifts, driven by the power of the water, carry the boats over a distance of 55 feet.

Left: cross section of a mine drawn by a miner for his grandson.
Below: a poster on display at the Musée du Gravure.

prints and engravings displays a wide-ranging collection covering the graphic arts and all types of print. THE CENTRE DE LA FAÏENCE is housed in the buildings of the Boch factory, official supplier to the court of Belgium since 1841; it displays antique pieces and offers a practical introduction to the techniques of painting and decorating porcelain and earthenware.

THE CANAL DU CENTRE. This canal, 13 miles long, was built to connect the Nimy–Blaton Canal with the Charleroi–Brussels Canal. Work started in 1888 and the canal was operational by 1917. It was withdrawn from commercial use in 1957 and now features the Living MUSEUM OF THE CANAL DU CENTRE, which encompasses a wide array of buildings and exhibits, including a lock keeper's cottage, an Italian *cantina* (dedicated to the Italian immigrant community), hydraulic lifts, some remarkable pieces of machinery and traditional boats: *sabots* and *baquets* from Charleroi, *wallons* from the Borinage, and the *Grisette*, the last wooden barge still afloat in Belgium.

BOIS-DU-LUC ★ (Commune of Houdeng-Aimeries). The ÉCOMUSÉE RÉGIONAL DU CENTRE, housed in the former offices of the coal mine, celebrates the Centre region's industrial past. However, this is more than just a museum: it is also the venue for a variety of events, including workshops, debates and theatrical performances. The MUSÉE DE LA MINE on the same site is dedicated to the life of mineworkers in the 19th century.

LE RŒULX

THE CASTLE ★. The castle's exact origins are uncertain, but it goes back beyond the 12th century. The building commissioned by the Princes of Croy (1713) has an emblazoned pediment and seventy-two symmetrically-arranged windows, giving it a palatial air. The castle still retains the walls and base of the 15th-century Tour du Bailli (Bailiff's Tower). The interior has huge rooms displaying many objets d'art, furniture of the period, and paintings by Van Dyck, Van der Meulen and Fragonard.

MINERS' MEMORIES
The Musée de la Mine at Bois-du-Luc includes some very moving exhibits, such as the painting (left) by a former miner and self-taught artist named Castelain and cross section of a mine (top).

THE GARDENS AT RŒULX
The Château de Rœulx stands in grounds covering 100 acres, with magnificent formal gardens (below). The rose garden (near the Orangery) has over 100,000 rose plants.

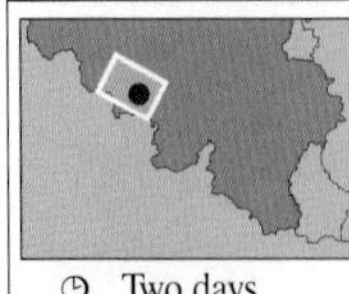

◷ Two days
55 miles

Coal mining was already a long-established activity in the Borinage region by 1248, when an act was passed to regulate the industry: it limited the number of pits in operation and stipulated that mines should not be worked from Pentecost to mid September, so that farmers would not neglect their fields at harvest time. Borinage depended exclusively on this single industry for its prosperity, which reached a peak in the 19th and 20th centuries and fell into decline after World War Two.

FROM FRAMERIES TO ST-GHISLAIN

At the COAL MINE OF CRACHET-PICQUERY (in the Commune of Frameries), the viewing platform and communication tunnel (over a mile long) are open to visitors. Next comes WASMES, at the heart of Borinage: this town had the largest number of mine shafts in the region. Its last coal mine closed in 1960. The WAGNAUX MINE was one of the largest: a practical training school for miners was established here by the mine owners in 1932. After the war the school trained immigrant workers, who formed an ever larger section of the workforce. The school included a remarkable model mine, which can now be seen in the basement, with over 200 yards of purpose-built galleries. There is also a museum here, with exhibits (some of them very moving) illustrating the life of coal miners. Leave Wasmes and head for St-Ghislain; this town's MUSÉE DE LA FÊTE FORAINE ET DU THÉATRE ITINÉRANT is an unusual museum devoted to fairgrounds of the past.

THE FUNERARY CHAPEL AT BOUSSU
The chapel has a group of Renaissance tombs of local lords (detail below); one of the figures, in the Mannerist style, is attributed to Jacques Dubroeucq ▲ *289*; another, *L'Homme à Moulons*, represents a corpse being eaten by worms.

BOUSSU

LE GRAND-HORNU ★. The industrialist Henri de Gorge acquired the Hornu concession in the early 19th century and set about renovating the mine, which had been operational since 1778. His insistence on quality and his philosophy of social innovation resulted in the creation of a mining complex that has immense historical value. De Gorge was confronted by a shortage of workers – so he built the Grand-Hornu estate ● *94* of four hundred houses to attract them. The houses, built in 1822, stand on wide, straight, paved streets and display a level of comfort that was unheard of at the time (with hot water, a bread oven, a well and a garden). The miners of the Grand-Hornu had the best living conditions in Borinage. De Gorge built workshops and offices, forming an arc around a large courtyard (460 feet by 260 feet): this was the nerve center of his mining company, which operated a total of twelve mine shafts. The pits themselves were equipped to ensure maximum profitability, producing bituminous coal, which was in great demand at the time. During its most prosperous period (1870–1920) the company had nearly 2,300 workers and produced an annual output of 245,000 tons. The site was abandoned after the last mine shaft was closed in 1953; then in 1971 it was acquired by Henri Gauchez, a Hornu architect, who gave it to the

“THE COAL INDUSTRY WAS A WORLD AT THE FOREFRONT OF TECHNOLOGY; IT WAS ALSO A WORLD OF TERRIBLE SUFFERING, AND OF WONDERFUL BROTHERHOOD.”

BROCHURE OF THE MUSÉE DE LA MINE (LES WAGNAUX)

Le Borinage by Gromaire (1952).

province of Hainaut. The buildings have now been renovated; they house a museum dedicated to the history of the estate, exhibition galleries, and the headquarters for several different companies. A museum of modern art is planned.

CHAPELLE FUNERAIRE DES SEIGNEURS. This chapel, built in the 12th century and modified in the 16th century, houses tombs and a crypt containing the remains of the lords who ruled over Boussu from the 12th to the 19th century. In the upper galleries is a religious museum, displaying works in silver (15th–19th century) and painted wood statues (12th–18th century).

THE CASTLE. The ruins of the castle that belonged to the lords of Boussu stand in 30 acres of wooded grounds. This was the first Renaissance-style castle built in the Netherlands; it was designed by Jacques Dubroeucq ▲ *289*, and took the place of a medieval fortress. The buildings formed a square around a central courtyard (with sides measuring 330 feet) which incorporated stables for 300 horses. A covered gallery and a small castle completed the complex, later destroyed during the wars of the 16th and 17th centuries. A new residence was built at the end of the 19th century; this was destroyed by the German army in 1944. Excavations are currently under way.

FROM FARMERS TO MINERS

The act of 1248, which sought to restrict the activities of farmer-miners, indicates that farming was considered the priority at the time. When coal became the region's main source of income, this order of importance was reversed.

A PATERNALIST VISIONARY

Originally from Lilles, Henri de Gorge (1774–1832) was the archetypal paternalist mine owner. Workers' houses were grouped around his own residence and workshops, and he dreamed of creating his own town: “Degorgeville”. For his workers he provided a clinic, school, library, village hall and public baths: in this he was a pioneer, far in advance of the social initiatives of his time. Left: the Grand-Hornu.

Coal mining is a very old industry in southern Belgium; for a long time it was a seasonal activity. In the 19th century the coal mines became the heart of industrial life in the Haine-Sambre-et-Meuse valley. Growth in the industry was encouraged by technical innovations and by the involvement of financial investors in the mining companies; this growth was founded on the exploitation of a large and overworked body of laborers. Belgium's ratification of the European Community's coal-and-steel treaty in 1951, coupled with the growth of non-European competition, sounded the industry's death knell. The last mine shaft closed in 1984.

MINEWORKERS
The *bouveleur* cut out the *bouveaux*, the tunnels used as the main route through the mine. The *boutefeu* positioned the dynamite used to open up the seams of coal.

Moulineurs collected the coal on the surface and sent it for sorting and washing. *Hiercheurs* (women and children) carried the coal away: originally on their backs, and later in trucks when the pits were mechanized.

The *abatteurs*, the "kings of the mine", extracted the coal. Their work was carried out under extremely difficult conditions: the seams were very narrow, sometimes so narrow that the miners had to work doubled up (using a pick that weighed 26 pounds on average); the mines were hot and airless. The picks were equipped with sprinklers to ensure that miners did not breathe in too much dust: this meant the men were working in mud. The *abatteurs* had to shore up the tunnel with timber as they worked, to stop it caving in ● *96*.

Hiercheur (coal carrier).

FIREDAMP
This colorless, odorless and highly explosive methane gas was the biggest danger in the mines, since spontaneous explosions could ignite coal dust and start fires. Naked flames could also trigger explosions: Davy lamps were therefore made obligatory, in 1823, in mines with high firedamp levels. Named after its English inventor, the Davy lamp had a protective metal grille; when oxygen became scarce the lamp's flame died out, indicating a high level of firedamp in the air. Left: explosion in the Anderlues mine in April 1892.

MECHANIZATION
The seams of coal in southern Belgium were thin (between 16 inches and 5 feet high), awkwardly shaped and irregular. It was partly for this reason that mechanization was late in the coalfields of the region: horse-drawn trucks did not appear until 1825, and the horses were not replaced by motorized tractors until 1945. Although mechanization made the miners' work easier, the use of pneumatic drills created larger quantities of the dust that caused silicosis: this was not recognized as an occupational illness of miners until 1964.

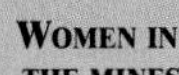

WOMEN IN THE MINES
Women were allocated the menial tasks: they carried coal (on their backs, before the advent of trucks) and performed a number of jobs on the surface, such as washing and sorting coal and cleaning lamps.

THE ROAD TO ATH

PARC DE PARADISO. A neoclassical palace built in the 19th century and the remains of a Cistercian abbey stand in the Domaine de Cambron. The estate has been converted into an ornithological paradise: more than 2,500 birds live in its aviaries, including toucans, pelicans, penguins and swans. The larger aviaries and the gardens are open to the public.

CHÂTEAU D'ATTRE ★. This small castle was built, in composite style, in 1752. "Its architectural style has been described as French, with some Austrian touches. Is this surprising, in the Belgium of this period?" wrote René Pechère, referring to the proximity of France and to the fact that Spain had ceded the Catholic Netherlands to the Austrian Hapsburgs in 1713.

LESSINES. The town is famous for its procession of "black penitents" on Good Friday, who parade by torchlight to the sound of drums. Another attraction is the HÔPITAL NOTRE-DAME-À-LA-ROSE ★. As the historian Gertrude Raulier explains, "From the 12th century onward many towns had a hospital . . . to take in sick pilgrims, and later poor invalids of the locality. Alix de Rosoit decided to found one of these hospitals in Lessines, near the Dendre river, in the locality of Monciel." Work began in 1242 and the building was completed in 1246; the hospital was later modified, in the 16th century, when the great quadrangle was built. Initially both monks and nuns lived here, caring for invalids of their own sex; later only the nuns remained, and the hospital was closed in 1970. The buildings were maintained by a farm on the other side of the Dendre. Today the Hôpital houses a local museum, with collections of paintings, china, medical

FRANCO-AUSTRIAN ARCHITECTURE
Attre was the product of a very fruitful partnership between the architect-decorator François de Cuvillès and architect-builder Jacques-François Blondel. The former produced collections of motifs that were used in many European castles; the latter founded a school of architecture and helped to disseminate Louis XIV style throughout the continent. In the gardens is the "Rocher", an artificial hill planted with spruces and crowned with a tower: it is said to have cost more than the castle itself.

René Magritte ● *122* was born at Lessines.

BELŒIL: WAR AND PEACE. The aristocrats who built Belœil were constantly involved in wars; in their palace at Belœil it seems they were seeking to demonstrate that there could also be a paradise on earth. Right: the Château de Belœil (19th-century engraving).

instruments, and exhibits relating to the life of the nuns. Beyond the parlor are the 17th-century cloisters, built in the Gothic style, the pharmacy and the internal apartments, including a nun's cell and "Monseigneur's quarters" (the bishop stayed here when he visited the hospital).

ARCHEOLOGICAL SITE AT AUBECHIES. Traces of human habitation were discovered near Blicquy-Aubechies, the earliest dating from the 5th milennium BC. Neolithic, Bronze Age and Iron Age dwellings have been recreated here, along with a Gaulish house. The dwellings, built of wattle and daub, housed a sedentary farming population. The Neolithic house is a long, communal dwelling; after this came the more complex communal houses of the Bronze Age. The Gauls lived in smaller houses, in smaller family units. Although the overall principles of construction stayed the same over the ages, building methods (assembly and finishing) developed as tools improved.

CHÂTEAU DE BELŒIL ★

The Ligne family played an important part in European history from the 12th century onward. The Belœil estate must be seen in the context of the family's history: the Princes of Ligne were warriors and diplomats, living on the border between the

"THE GARDENS OF BELŒIL
The gardens were designed at a time when, as René Pechère has pointed out, "Le Nôtre's theories had been disseminated in book form, in Dezalliers d'Argenville's *Théorie et pratique du jardinage* (the fourth edition of 1747 was the best known)." Prince Charles-Joseph introduced landscape elements into the garden, creating an eclectic impression. His garden designers made highly effective use of perspective effects, which are the key to landscaping: for example, the large lake was designed to give the illusion of being less rectangular than it really is.

"Because Belœil is one of the most beautiful gardens in the world, it has long been assumed that it was designed by Le Nôtre, which is not the case. It has been called the Belgian Versailles. It must be recognized that Belœil is, quite simply, Belœil: complete in itself."
René Pechère

THE TREASURES OF BELŒIL
The entrance hall has a collection of clocks. The Chambre d'Épinoy has three Brussels tapestries from the workshop of De Vos. Four large Chinese lacquer wardrobes (18th century) can be seen in the Chambre d'Amblise. Beyond the gallery on the second story is the library, with beautifully bound books including Charles Perrault's

Contes du temps passé (below). After the Salon des Ambassadeurs, there are the tapestries of the Salon des Feld-Maréchaux. The chapel has an 18th-century coral writing-desk from Sicily and two 16th-century triptychs. Above (medallion): Sidonie de Ligne. Right: *Portrait of Anne Murat* by Winterhalter (19th century).

Hapsburg territories and France. The de Lignes owed allegiance to the Hapsburgs, but were thoroughly European in their love of French civilization. That war was a way of life for them is clear from Prince Charles-Joseph de Ligne's letter to his son regarding the latter's first battle: "It would be very agreeable my dear Charles . . . if we were to acquire a little wound together." The princes acquired the Belœil estate in the 14th century. From this time onward the castle and the grounds were repeatedly modified: the main building and the wings were built by Claire-Marie de Ligne between 1682 and 1699; the garden was redesigned by Claude-Lamoral II, Claire-Marie's second husband, who enlarged the main lake, widened the canals and created the kitchen garden with its Pomome pavilion. At the end of the 18th century Charles-Joseph (the son, 1735–1814) landscaped the gardens, creating the Parc aux Daims (deer park) and Île de Flore in the fashionable English style. Today the grounds cover 300 acres, half of this laid out as a single garden. The hornbeam arbors cover an area of 5 acres: in other words, 6 miles of bushes needing regular trimming.

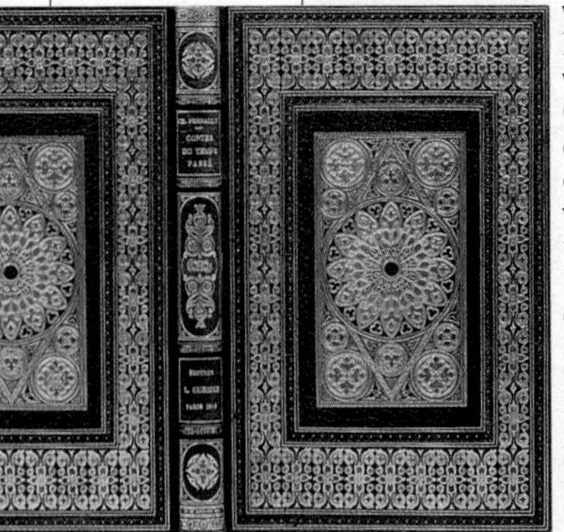

Château. The castle and its outbuildings stand on two islands, surrounded by moats and connected by a bridge. The oldest parts date from the late 18th century. The residential section was destroyed by fire in 1901 and rebuilt in 1901–6, preserving the U-shaped design, the façades matching the entrance pavilions, the wings of the outbuildings and the gardens. All the buildings were designed in "classical" French style.
The interior. The main staircase in the entrance hall is set to one side in order to open up the widest possible view of the gardens. After this come the bedrooms, including the Chambre d'Épinoy and the Chambre d'Amblise, named after family estates. The gallery on the second story leads to the library, the Salon des Ambassadeurs (with 17th- and 18th-century paintings) and then the Salon des Feld-Maréchaux, named by Charles-Joseph in honor of military glory – "the dearest idol of my heart". The chapel (at the end of the tour) is in the stable block, which is the oldest surviving part of the château.

Forests and marshes ★

The marshes of Harchies-Hensies-Pommerœul. This nature reserve is located on the far western edge of the Haine's alluvial plain. The marshes and lakes attract many different species of nesting and migratory birds. In the winter you can see ducks, grebes, divers, cormorants and buzzards; spring brings shore birds, birds of prey, terns and sparrows, in addition to the birds that nest here, such as the lovely whitethroat, the sedge warbler, the bittern and the shelduck. Migratory birds can be seen here from the end of the summer: the osprey, the great white egret and the bearded tit. A footpath provides a tour of the reserve, which takes half a day.
Forêt de Stambruges and Le Mer de sable ● *20*.
The N 50, which connects Mons with Tournai, passes through Hautruge before crossing the Stambruges Forest. The forest ■ *29*, home of the black woodpecker, consists mainly of deciduous trees (beech, sessile oaks, ash, poplars, wild cherry and maple). It also includes the Mer de Sable nature reserve, which protects the last surviving area of moorland in the Haine valley; the name refers to an old reservoir that was drained and filled with sandy soil. Typical moorland plants can be seen here: cross-leaved heath ■ *19*, heather, cotton grass and sundews (these small carnivorous plants grow in some ditches). To reach the nature reserve, leave the N 50 near the village of Stambruges and take a small road at the entrance to the forest. The reserve has five signposted footpaths.
Forêt de Bon-secours. A wide variety of plant life grows under its oaks and beeches, including wood hyacinths and wood anemones, which flourish in rich soil, while the bracken and lily of the valley grow in sandy, acid soil. The forest also has a museum, which makes a good introduction to a visit.

Naturalists' paradise
To the west of Mons, the Haine valley presents a patchwork of urban and industrial areas (including the Borinage). However, in between these areas are a number of natural features. The north of the valley is bordered by a huge belt of forestland, the largest in southwest Belgium. The soil here is mainly sandy and not well suited to agricultural use: because of this, the forests have been left largely untouched. To the east are a number of marshy areas with lakes; these isolated marshlands (Douvrain, St-Ghislain, Hautrage, Harchies, Hensies, Pommerœul) have formed in the depressions created by collapsed coal mines. Above: hen harrier in flight.

Wood hyacinths carpet the floors of the forests in the west of the region.

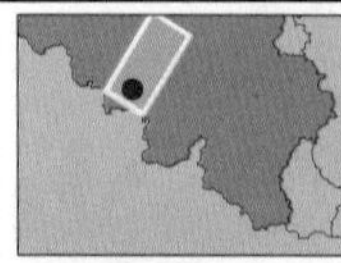

One and a half days

SOIGNIES

This town in the Senne valley grew up around a monastery, founded in the 7th century by Saint Vincent (husband of Saint Waudru ▲ *286*), and the Collegiate Church of St-Vincent built in the 11th and 12th centuries. The town's economy expanded rapidly in the 14th century thanks to its cloth industry. The 16th-century Halle aux Draps (former cloth market) bears witness to this prosperity. Today Soignies is a major stone-quarrying town: "little granite" (bluestone) has been mined here since the 19th century.

COLLEGIATE CHURCH OF ST-VINCENT ★. The church stands on a promontory overlooking the Senne. It has two towers: a lantern tower above the transept crossing and another tower at the western end. The naves offer a remarkable example of Romanesque architecture, while the choir is covered with what is probably the largest and oldest Romanesque vault in Belgium. The church escaped destruction during the French Revolution, and its splendid interior has remained intact: including the retable with six English alabaster statues in the Chapel of St-Vincent (15th century), the stalls in the main church (1650), a Baroque rood screen (1632), two statues of the Virgin (15th century) and some magnificent funerary monuments in the 13th-century cloister.

COLLEGIATE CHURCH OF ST-VINCENT
The collegiate church in Soignies is built on an impressive scale: it is 233 feet long and 72 feet high. It houses the relics of Saint Vincent: the "Grand Tour de St-Vincent" and a historical procession are held in their honor on Pentecost Monday.

ÉCAUSSINNES-LELAING AND ÉCAUSSINNES-D'ENGHIEN

Marie de Lalaing, daughter of the lord of Écaussinnes, married Englebert d'Enghien, owner of the Château de la Follie, in 1384. This marriage was the origin of the names of these two villages.

CHÂTEAU D'ÉCAUSSINES-LALAING ★. The fortress was built on a rocky outcrop overlooking the right bank of the Sennette river, to guard a ford on the borders of Hainaut. It was reinforced by Count Baudoin V of Hainaut in the 12th century, and still has three round towers that were added in the 14th century. The castle lost its military significance in the 15th century, after which the Croy family converted it into a more comfortable residence; work was continued by the Van der Burch family, who owned the castle from 1624 to 1854. In 1928 Count Adrien van der

CHÂTEAU D'ÉCAUSSINNES-LALAING
Jean de Croy and his son converted the fortress (right) in the 15th century. They built the east wing to let in more light, widened the loopholes to form large windows, and added another story to the buildings. The nave of the Gothic chapel juts out to the north; this was built on the site of the old drawbridge. The present entrance tower was built in the 18th century.

Château d'Enghien and its grounds were acquired by the town council in 1986 and opened to the public. Restoration work is currently under way.

Burch reacquired his ancestors' castle and established a museum here. Both the Salle d'Armes and the Grand Salon (which has Charles X style furniture) contain magnificent fireplaces, with mantelpieces of single blocks of stone bearing the Croy arms and bas-relief allegories symbolizing the struggle between good and evil. The Gothic chapel houses a 14th-century Romanesque Virgin attributed to Beauneveu.

Écaussinnes-d'Enghien. The Chateau de la Follie dates from the early 16th century. Its chapel has beautiful stained-glass windows produced after designs by Bernard van Orley, whose splendid tombstone, made by Jean Mone (1508), can be seen in the Church of St-Rémy.

Enghien ★

Enghien was named after the first lords of the manor, who probably became established here in the 11th century. It stands on the borders of the duchy of Brabant and the county of Hainaut, a strategic location that led to the development of a fortress and a town. Later the manor of Enghien had various owners, before being sold by Henri IV of France to Charles d'Arenberg and his wife, Anne de Croy, in 1607.

Château d'Arenberg. The medieval castle, built from 1250 onward, consists of a group of residential buildings flanked by projecting towers; it is reached from Rue du Château through a Renaissance portal (1541). The castle moat also encircled the town. Once the defenses had become redundant, the medieval castle was converted into a residential palace: the ditches were filled in and towers knocked down, the main building was renovated and a main courtyard bordered by four pavilions laid out at the front (1720). The castle was ruined during the French Revolution and demolished in 1806, except for the chapel tower, which still stands today, richly decorated with carved stone and wood altarpieces, paintings and stained-glass windows. In 1904 Baron Empain acquired the estate and built a castle surrounded by a landscaped garden.

Goûter Matrimonial
An amazing "matrimonial tea" for single people is held at Écaussinnes-Lalaing on Pentecost Monday. Prospective brides and bridegrooms come from miles around.

Ronquières
The sloping lock enables barges of 1,330 tons to cope with the 220-foot difference in ground level. The boats are placed in a water tank, 300 feet long and 40 feet wide, which is pulled by eight cables. Visitors can climb to the top of the great tower, which offers a panoramic view of the lock; an audiovisual display explains how the lock works.

The Pavilion of Seven Stars
If you stand at the center of this little temple at Enghien, you are at the focal point of fourteen avenues.

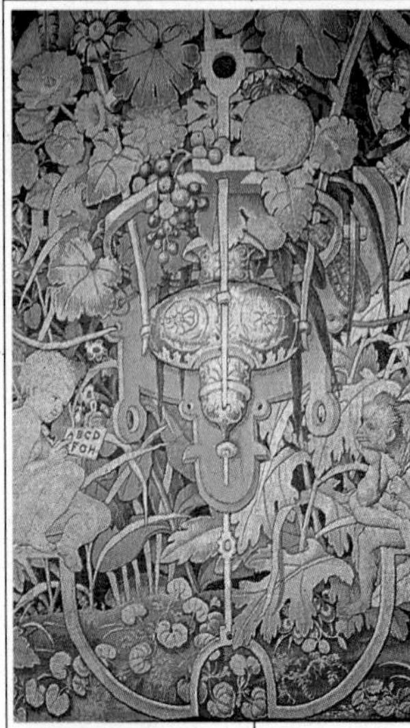

Tapestry making at Enghien
Following the example of Brussels, Enghien exported its tapestries throughout Europe. The Musée de la Tapisserie is housed in the Maison Jonathas, a 12th-century keep which was converted in the 16th century.

The grounds. The Arenberg family, who acquired the estate of Enghien in 1607, carried out a series of major improvements to it. A farm, gardens and fishponds near the gates of the castle ensured that it was more or less self-sufficient. Practical features were designed with care: the kitchen garden was converted into Renaissance-style walled gardens from 1650 onward. A network of roads and pathways was laid out, punctuated by ornamental lakes and fountains at the crossroads. Four pavilions were erected at the corners of the largest garden. Two of these can still be seen: the Chinese Pavilion and the Pavilion of Paintings, named after their interior decoration. Beyond the steps the grounds are arranged in a Baroque design around the Pavilion of Seven Stars, which stands at the center of an ornamental lake: this is the crowning glory of the masterpiece of landscaping created by Charles d'Arenberg.

Church of St-Nicolas. This simple church, built in the shape of a Latin cross with a tower over the transept crossing, is typical of the architecture of the Escaut basin. A side portal in Brabant Gothic style was grafted onto the north side of the church in 1457. The church was destroyed by fire in 1497 and partially rebuilt. The Chapel of Notre-Dame-de-Messines contains a 16th-century altarpiece from Antwerp depicting the life of the Virgin. The building was restored in 1964, revealing the full impact of its austere, traditional Hainaut Gothic style – a style that in this region lasted until well into the 17th century.

Capuchin monastery. Eight religious foundations and four hospitals were founded in Enghien over the centuries. Several of these can still be seen today: the Augustine monastery, founded in 1254 and converted into a college in the 19th century; the Couvent des Clarisses (formerly Hôpital St-Antoine), founded in 1266; and above all the Capuchin monastery, worth visiting for the treasures it contains. The monastery's church was built by Charles d'Arenberg and Anne de Croy in 1614 to house their tomb. The crypt holds over sixty tombs belonging to this illustrious family, while the Chapel of St-Joseph contains the tomb of Guillaume de Croy, Archbishop of Toledo (a masterpiece by Jean Mone, 1525) as well as an altarpiece above the high altar showing the Adoration of the Magi, carved by Servaes de Coulx (1616). The monastery's museum has an impressive art collection, as well as splendid models of the park and castle (the latter can be taken apart to reveal the rooms inside).

The park at Enghien
The grounds have two long vistas – one looking toward the canal, the other toward the Mall.

In and around Tournai

1. GRAND-PLACE
2. CATHEDRAL
3. BELFRY
4. CHURCH OF ST-QUENTIN
5. CHURCH OF ST-JACQUES
6. CHURCH OF STE-MARGUERITE
7. CHURCH OF ST-PIAT

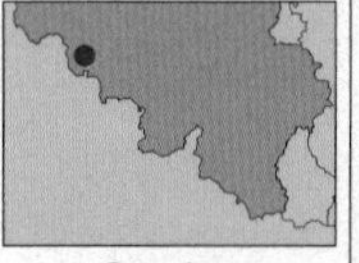

◷ One day

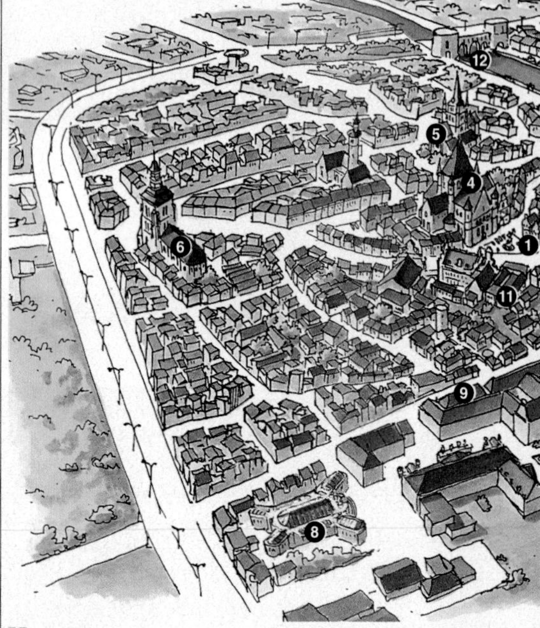

Seal of the town, 14th century.

CLOVIS
Clovis (right) left Tournai for Soissons, then Paris. This undoubtedly diminished the importance of France's first capital.

SIEGE BY LOUIS XIV
Louis XIV captured Tournai in 1667 and made it a French bastion, building a new citadel, canalizing the Escaut, and establishing the Parliament of Flanders (the main government for his new territories).

HISTORY

ROMAN TOWN. A country settlement was established on the left bank of the Escaut around 50 BC. A century later the great road from Cologne to Boulogne was built, making this settlement, *Civitas Turnacensium*, into an important town that became the capital of its province. Later, in imperial times, it was surrounded by a rampart.

A ROYAL CITY. Like all northern European towns, Tournai was repeatedly pillaged by the "barbarians" who were battering the Roman Empire. Around AD 431 the Salian Franks captured the town and made it their capital. Under the Merovingian kings Chlodio, Meroveus, Childeric and Clovis, Tournai became a royal city; in Childeric's time the town was made the seat of a bishopric that has lasted to the present day.

MEDIEVAL GREATNESS. From the 11th century onward Tournai flourished, along with the whole of northern Europe. As the religious center of Flanders and a key trading center, the town attracted pilgrims and merchants. Although the Hundred Years' War diminished the town's political standing, it became a great artistic center in the 15th century, with notable achievements in the fields of

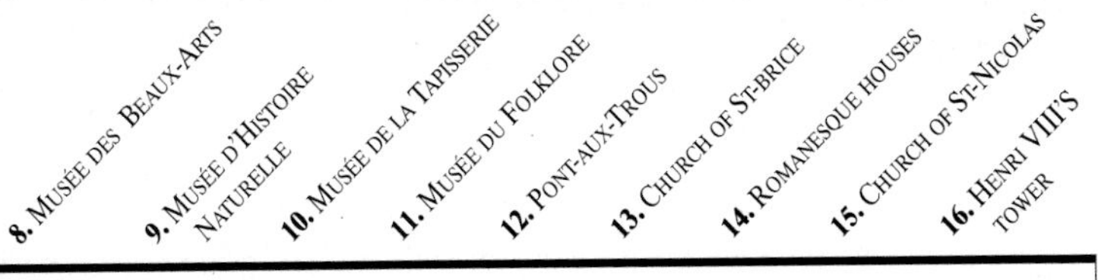

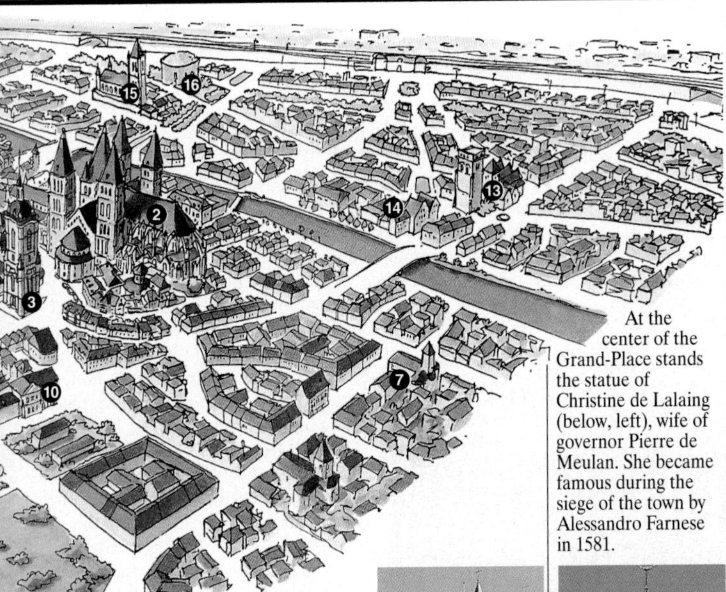

At the center of the Grand-Place stands the statue of Christine de Lalaing (below, left), wife of governor Pierre de Meulan. She became famous during the siege of the town by Alessandro Farnese in 1581.

painting (Jacques Daret, Robert Campin and Roger van der Weyden ● *120*), tapestry (Pasquier Grenier), sculpture (stone funerary steles), brassware and bronze casting.

Under foreign rule. In 1553 the town was taken by Henry VIII (which makes it the only town in Belgium to have come under British rule). Soon after, Tournai became part of the Spanish Netherlands. Like other towns, it saw troubled times in the 16th century (the Iconoclastic Fury of 1566). Louis XIV, determined to extend his kingdom to the north, embarked on the conquest of the Netherlands and seized the city. In 1713, under the treaty of Utrecht, Tournai, along with the rest of the Spanish Netherlands, passed into the hands of the Austrian Hapsburgs. This cut the town off from its commercial outlets in France. As a result, efforts were made to revive the town's economy, including the establishment of the royal porcelain factory and the manufacture of tapestries ● *52*.

From the Revolution to Independence. During the French Revolution Tournai lost a significant part of its artistic heritage. In 1830 it became part of the new kingdom of Belgium. It fell victim to German air raids in May 1940, which destroyed the center of the town.

The Belfry
At the end of the 12th century Tournai, then under French jurisdiction, was granted the power to govern itself as a *république commune*. The belfry was built as an emblem of this independence.

THE HALLE AUX DRAPS
This beautiful Renaissance building was strongly influenced by the town hall of Ghent (1602). To the rear is a huge courtyard with galleries, with apartments above them, on the Italian model.

Today Tournai is again a thriving commercial and artistic center, with its quarries, cement works and the publishing house Éditions Casterman, which produces the famous *Tintin* books.

AROUND THE GRAND-PLACE ★

THE GRAND-PLACE. The square is lined with beautiful façades, reconstructed after the bombardment of 1940. LA HALLE AUX DRAPS (cloth market) is a reminder of Tournai's main industry: textiles were weighed and sold here. The high-gabled building is the former GRANGE DES DIMES (tithe barn) of the Abbey of St-Martin: grain produced on the abbey's estate was stored here for selling. Beyond this is the ROMANESQUE CHURCH OF ST-QUENTIN (12th century): its robust façade hides a 14th-century choir, decorated with a 17th-century altarpiece and a marble screen.

THE OLD QUARTERS OF ST-JACQUES AND ST-NICAISE. Rue Piquet leads toward a group of streets that have retained their original façades. The interior of the beautiful GOTHIC CHURCH OF ST-JACQUES has magnificent neo-Gothic furniture. Tournai's ARCHEOLOGICAL MUSEUM is housed in a former pawnshop, a 17th-century building. At the center of PLACE DE LILLE is a monument in honor of the French soldiers who came to the assistance of Belgium in 1831, when the country was invaded by the Dutch. The square is dominated by the impressive tower of the CHURCH OF STE-MARGUERITE (14th century). Rue Dorée and the small Place Roger-de-la-Pasture lead to Rue Roc-St-Nicaise, named after a stone quarry that was worked here in the Middle Ages. The square displays early 19th-century private residences and a row of houses in brick and stone from the late 17th century. A stone tower from the town's second rampart can be seen on Rue St-Georges. Near to the charming Place de Nédonchel, on Réduit des Sions, is the curious MUSÉE DU FOLKLORE, housed in 17th-century buildings, with displays presenting the urban and rural life of the past.

❝Ah! that enormous vessel that stood out among the rooftops of the town. . . . Nothing was comparable to the cluster of towers with their uniform spires: from far off across the countryside they looked like knights armed for a grand cause.❞
M. Des Ombriaux

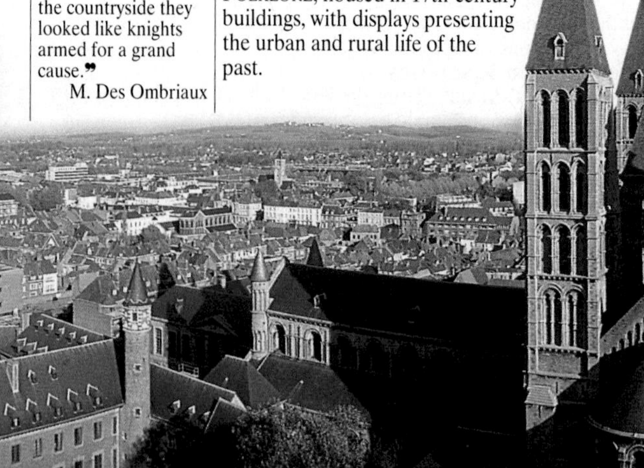

“TOURNAI, ONE HUNDRED SPIRES, FOUR HUNDRED BELLS.”
(OLD SAYING)

PLACE DE L'ÉVÊCHÉ
This hand-colored engraving from the 19th century shows the cathedral and (on the right) the Bishop's Palace, which is joined to the cathedral by the Fausse Porte, itself overlooked by the Episcopal Chapel of St-Vincent (1198). It was here that the town's magistrates pledged to respect the privileges of the church in Tournai in a ceremony held every year up to the end of the 18th century.

THE CATHEDRAL ★

Tournai's Cathedral of Notre-Dame is an important example of Western architecture of the Middle Ages, with its subtle mix of Romanesque and Gothic styles.

THE NAVE. The Romanesque nave, with ten bays, was built between 1140 and 1171. Horizontal lines clearly mark the four stories of the building: the first story, the huge galleries, the ornamental gallery and finally a story of windows. Among the most striking features of the nave is a stunning collection of stone capitals: there are hundreds of them (be sure to see the capital of “The Falling Man”). On the right side of the nave, near to the 18th-century pulpit, is a Gothic chapel with small 14th-century stained-glass windows and magnificent oak panels (1729) depicting the life of Saint Benedict.

THE TRANSEPT. This is a huge Romanesque construction, built between 1171 and 1200. The northern section (on the left) has a collection of mural paintings from the late 12th century, depicting the legend of Saint Margaret. On the opposite wall is a monumental wooden statue of Saint Michael, a typical work of the Enlightenment by Nicolas Lecreux (1763). The stained-glass windows of the northern transept (around 1500) depict the story of the separation of the dioceses of Tournai and Noyon in 1146. At the center of the transept is a large rood screen, a Renaissance work dating from 1572. The southern part of the transept (on the right) is lit by stained-glass windows called the “Privileges”, which recount the origins of the authority of the bishop and canons over the town.

THE ROOD SCREEN
The rood screen gives access to the choir, while also screening it off. Its design was influenced by the triumphal arches of antiquity, but its ornamentation holds true to the medieval tradition, showing scenes from the Old and New Testament side by side.

The Plague of Tournai in 1090, painting (1883) by L. Gallait in the town's Musée des Beaux Arts.

THE CHOIR OF THE CATHEDRAL. This large Gothic construction was begun by Bishop Gautier de Marvis in 1243. The quality of light is created by 19th-century stained-glass windows. The decorations are striking: the high altar and its marble altarpiece (1727, from the local Abbey of St-Martin), an array of brass lecterns and chandeliers (some cast in the 13th century), and the episcopal throne in gilded bronze (19th century).

THE CRYPT OF THE ABBEY OF ST-MARTIN
The remains of the abbey can only be entered through the town hall. They consist of the 12th-century crypt, probably once the monastery cellar, and one section of the Gothic cloister (15th century).

THE CHAPELS. The chapels around the choir display 15th-century stone steles – masterpieces from the workshops of Tournai. At the entrance to the ambulatory (on the left) is a painting by Peter Paul Rubens depicting *The Deliverance of Souls from Purgatory* (1635). This painting was one of a pair: its companion piece, *The Triumph of Judas Maccabaeus*, was stolen by the French revolutionaries and is now displayed in the Musée Municipal in Nantes.

THE TREASURY. The chapter houses are exceptionally interesting. Among the major works on display here are an early-15th-century Arras tapestry and two large reliquary shrines (*châsses*) from the 13th century. The *Châsse de Notre-Dame* by Nicolas de Verdun dates from 1205, while the *Châsse de St-Éleuthère*, a gem of medieval silverwork, was completed in 1247. Also worthy of note are the Byzantine cross (11th century) and ivories from the Merovingian period.

THE EPISCOPAL QUARTER. The façade of the cathedral, which stands on Place de l'Évêché, has been repeatedly altered; the second level was recently restored. On the right is the Bishop's Palace, a 17th-century building, joined to the cathedral by a stone arch called the FAUSSE PORTE. On the left is the HÔTEL DES ANCIENS PRÊTRES (18th century), a rest home for retired priests.

Designs for tapestries Tournai produced tapestries of a very high quality in the 19th century ● *52*.

Enclos Saint-Martin and the museums

Enclos St-Martin. The Benedictine Abbey of St-Martin was founded on this site in the late 11th century. The elegant abbey palace is now used as the town hall: it was built in 1763, following a design by Laurent-Benoît Dewez ▲ *296*. A nearby passageway leads to the Musée des Beaux Arts.
Musée des Beaux-Arts ★. The building was specially designed by the architect Victor Horta ● *98* to house the private collection of Brussels businessman Henri Van Cutsem. Painting of the 19th and early 20th century is especially well represented, with two works by Édouard Manet (*Argenteuil* and *Chez le père Lathuille*). A collection of full-size color photographs reproduces all the works attributed to the painter Roger van der Weyden (Roger de la Pasture, in French) ● *120*, who was born in Tournai around 1400.
More museums. Near to the town hall are three specialist museums: the Musée d'Histoire Naturelle, the Musée des Arts Décoratifs and the Musée de la Tapisserie et des Arts du Tissu. The tapestry museum, which is housed in a former aristocratic residence, also has a research center. At the museum of decorative arts visitors can see porcelain produced locally between 1750 and the early 20th century, as well as some silversmiths' works. Blue motifs on a white background are typical of the local china, although there are also pink and white pieces with imitation-wood decorations or with motifs taken from Buffon's *Natural History of Birds* (1764). The factory's most famous order was for 1,603 pieces; it was placed by the Duke of Orléans (later Philippe Égalité) in 1787.

A museum designed by Victor Horta The architecture of the Musée des Beaux Arts is striking, especially for the natural light provided by its unusual windows. The main façade is decorated with a bronze sculpture, *La Vérité inspiratrice des Arts*, some 45 feet long, donated to the town by the sculptor, Guillaume Charlier.

The quarters of St-Pierre and St-Piat

Rue des Chapeliers and Rue du Puits-Wagnon lead to the quarter of St-Pierre, an old medieval port now converted into a pedestrian zone. At the heart of the quarter markets are held on Place du Vieux-Marchée-au-Beurre (including a flea market on Sundays). The little streets that lead onto the square are named after traditional trades. Rue de la Ture, which has several old façades, leads to the Église du Séminaire Épiscopal, a former Jesuit college (17th century); the Rue de Jésuites also has some lovely Gothic façades (13th century).

The treasures of Childeric Excavation of the royal tomb▲ *316* yielded discoveries that are important for our knowledge of the Middle Ages. The tomb was unequivocally identified as Childeric's by a seal ring bearing a portrait of the king and the inscription *Childirici Regis*.

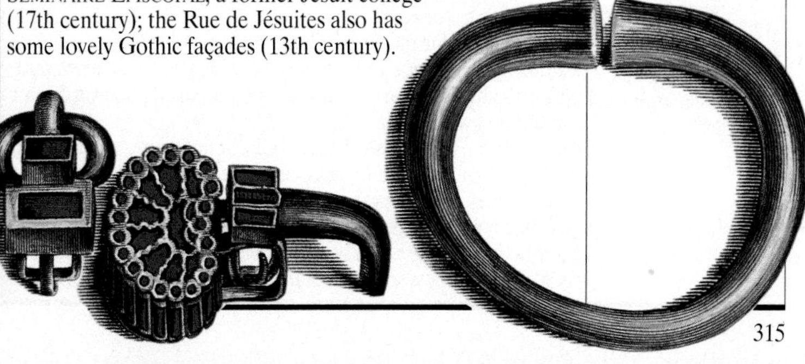

The CHURCH OF ST-PIAT, named after the first Christian missionary in Tournai, has a Romanesque nave, a Gothic choir and elegant interior ornamentation from the 17th century. Excavations carried out in 1970 uncovered remains of earlier churches, dating from the 6th century onward.

THE ROMANESQUE HOUSES
These are among the earliest examples of bourgeois residences in western Europe. Originally these opulent houses were

covered with lead, like the churches. This type of house was adopted by merchants throughout the Escaut valley (the Stapelhuis at Ghent is another example).

THE RIGHT BANK OF THE ESCAUT

CHURCH OF ST-BRICE. The right bank of the Escaut is dominated by the impressive tower of a church dedicated to Saint Brice, a bishop of Tours and one of the patron saints of Merovingian Gaul. The Romanesque church was extended in the 13th century through the construction of a huge choir with three naves of uniform height – creating a *hallekerk*, or hall church, the first example of an architectural type that was to become widespread in maritime Flanders. The tomb of the Merovingian king Childeric (father of Clovis), who died in Tournai in 482, was discovered near to this church in 1653; the treasures ▲ *315* found in the tomb were given to Louis XIV (since Meroveus was considered to be the founder of the French monarchy) and are now kept in Paris, in the Cabinet des Médailles. Not far from here, opposite the church in Rue Barre-St-Brice, are two famous ROMANESQUE HOUSES (left).

THE RIVER BANKS. Quai Notre-Dame has a group of 17th-century houses built by Vauban, Louis XIV's minister. The Parliament of Flanders, built by Louis XIV, no longer exists. However, the quarter where it once stood still has some magistrates' residences and has retained its peaceful atmosphere.

HENRY VIII'S TOWER. The great tower built by Henry VIII in the 16th century stands at the end of Place Verte. It formed part of the city wall, and in 1911 the ditches alongside it were filled in. Rue du Curé-du-Château leads to the medieval CHURCH OF ST-NICOLAS.

PONT-DES-TROUS
This bridge formed part of the great rampart that guarded the city and its river from the 13th century onward. The river was defended by huge grilles that could be lowered from the bridge, blocking the way into the town.

EXCURSIONS AROUND TOURNAI

MONT-SAINT-AUBERT. This hill reaches an altitude of 486 feet; its summit offers a magnificent view over Tournai and the surrounding area, including northern France, the Escaut valley and the village of Kain.

KAIN. The old farms in this village include interesting examples of the rural architecture of Tournai. These brick and bluestone buildings are arranged around paved courtyards and surrounded with moats.

ESQUELMES. The parish church, built in limestone rubblework by the side of the Escaut, offers a remarkable example of 12th-century Romanesque architecture. The arrangement of its different elements is very effective: the single nave is extended to the east by a second, lower choir with a shallower roof, and then by a semi-circular apse with a semi-conical roof.

THE ECONOMY OF SOUTHERN BELGIUM

THE ECONOMY OF SOUTHERN BELGIUM

A TRULY EUROPEAN AREA

THE GEOGRAPHICAL HEART OF EUROPE
Southern Belgium has always been a great European crossroads. Today Brussels enjoys the added privilege of being the seat of the headquarters of the European Community. Situated only a few hours' journey from Liège, Mons, Namur and Charleroi, both the European Union – which is the largest world market – and the many businesses that have opted to establish offices here are now on the very doorstep of Belgian industry. Southern Belgium is therefore at the heart of an area of intense commercial, industrial and financial activity bounded by lines connecting Paris, Luxembourg, Bonn, Amsterdam and London. This major industrial and trading region, which has Brussels at its center, covers approximately 7 percent of the total area of the European Union, yet it houses some 20 percent of the population of the European Community and receives as much as 25 per cent of its gross national product. Southern Belgium also boasts a rich and varied culture, and has learned how to derive the maximum benefit from its unique geographical location.

LINES OF COMMUNICATION

FREEWAYS
Brussels, which is only about an hour's drive from the coast, is served by what is probably the most concentrated systems of freeways in the world, and undoubtedly one of the best. In a continual state of expansion, it links Brussels to Paris, Cologne, Amsterdam, and Frankfurt, each less than 200 miles away. Thanks to the opening of the Channel Tunnel in 1994, Belgium is even accessible by car from the UK.

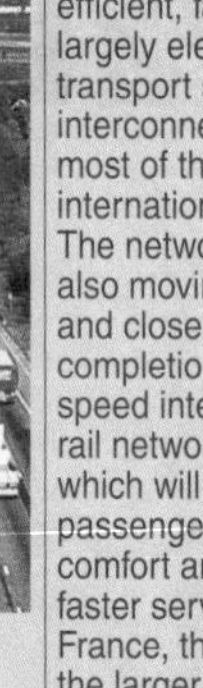

RAILWAYS
In the arena of rail transport, yet again southern Belgium has the good fortune to be extremely well placed. The country's efficient, fast and largely electrified rail transport system interconnects with most of the major international cities. The network is also moving closer and closer to the completion of a high-speed international rail network (TGV), which will offer future passengers additional comfort and a much faster service to France, the Ruhr, the larger ports on the north coast, and the UK via the Channel Tunnel.

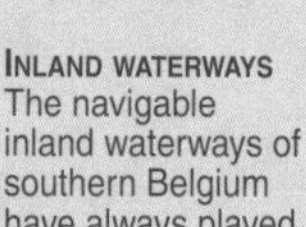

INLAND WATERWAYS
The navigable inland waterways of southern Belgium have always played an important role in the national economy. The Meuse, Escaut (Scheldt) and Rhine, together with their many tributaries and the canals between the rivers, provide an excellent shipping network. Indeed the Albert Canal, which is an incredible feat of civil engineering, is able to accommodate vessels of up to 9,000 tons, allowing them to sail as far inland as Liège. In addition the complex lock system at Ronquières has provided a link between Antwerp and Charleroi; and the construction of a hydraulic lift at Strépy-Thieu will soon allow large vessels to make a quick and easy transition between the Rhine, the Meuse and the Escaut.

A WINDOW ON THE WORLD

For Brussels and southern Belgium, having an extensive involvement in affairs worldwide is not an unusual or new situation, but rather an ongoing tradition. A variety of statistics dramatically illustrate this. While scarcely one European in a hundred comes from southern Belgian, the region commands 1 percent of world trade, and the region's industries derive as much as two-thirds of their gross national income from export.

In the light of these statistics, it is not surprising to learn that southern Belgium has one of the highest levels of export in the world – which is one reason why it has proved such an attractive proposition for foreign investors. In this respect the region created an excellent organization, the Office for Foreign Investors (OFI).
The OFI has various functions: one of these is to approach foreign markets with a view to setting up collaborative ventures and overseas consultancy assignments. Another is to provide a central point of contact for potential investors wishing to explore the possibility of projects in southern Belgium.
A variety of other organizations have been set up to promote the abilities and special interests of the region and to provide support for activities that have a foreign input, whether from companies or academic institutions and research centers.

The most notable of these initiatives was the formation of the Agence Wallonne à l'Exportation (AWEX), which is very much concerned with the worldwide image of southern Belgium. This organization deploys a network of more than fifty representatives who promote the commercial interests of southern Belgium abroad.

The geographical situation of southern Belgium is something of a paradox in that it is continental, in view of its central location in Europe, but also possesses many of the characteristics of a coastal economy, thanks to its proximity to the major ports of Antwerp, Rotterdam, Dunkirk, Zeebrugge and Ghent.

Airports

Most of the towns and industrial centers of southern Belgium are at least an hour's journey from Brussels' international airport at Zaventem.
To compensate, there are two major regional airports, namely Liège Airport and Brussels-South-Charleroi Airport.
The first of these regional airports is located at the center of Euregio, the international association that groups together the adjacent regions of Belgium (the provinces of Liège and Limbourg), Holland (Maastricht) and Germany (the Cologne region).
The second, which is located at Gosselies, is at the heart of a new 500-acre airport complex. This has the potential capacity to handle a thousand travelers at a time and was constructed in response to the increasingly urgent problem of overcrowding at the larger neighboring airports, especially Brussels' international airport at Zaventem.

THE ECONOMY OF SOUTHERN BELGIUM

A SOUND INDUSTRY

A land of iron and coal, southern Belgium has known intensive industrial activity since the Middles Ages. Indeed, this area was the cradle of the continental Industrial Revolution. At one time the economy of the country relied almost entirely on its heavy industry. Inspired by the 19th-century pioneers of industry such as John Cockerill (steel), Solvay (production of chemicals), Gramme, Jadot, Empain and Nagemackers, in the 20th-century Belgium has spread its technical expertise worldwide. In terms of employment, and with the closure of many of the mines, southern Belgium has undergone a move away from heavy industry toward light and service industries and is also rapidly developing in the field of new technology. A proliferation of small companies (around 2,500) has emerged to meet this challenge, and their efforts are continually being reinforced by the public sector.

Two of the most important economic centers in the region are the Liège and Charleroi basins, both of which clearly demonstrate this evolution. The iron and steel industries, the construction industry, electrical engineering, coal, chemicals and glassmaking were originally the major sources of prosperity in these areas. Having undergone a period of profound restructuring, these industrial sectors are now equipped with sophisticated equipment, both in terms of computers and robotics, and have diversified and become extremely successful. This has paved the way for the development of new activities based on advanced-technology products. Thus recent industrial prosperity in Liège, for example, has been associated with the space program, software engineering, telecommunications and new materials, while Charleroi has become a well-known center for the aeronautical industry, petrochemicals and computer graphics; and in Mons the University of Hainaut now specializes in neoceramics.

It would be invidious to single out instances of joint ventures between university departments and individual firms. Nevertheless, there are two outstanding examples of dynamic interaction between the academic world and industry that deserve to be mentioned. First that of Louvain-la-Neuve, which has had the effect of

transforming the part of Brabant situated outside the Sambre-et-Meuse industrial area into a huge industrial park specializing primarily in biomedicine and pharmaceuticals. Moreover, a number of major international companies have now chosen this as a location for setting up research centers.
Namur's suburbs have witnessed a similar phenomenon, in that they have acted as a magnet for the development of biotechnology and food processing – thanks to the setting up of a science park attached to the University of Namur and the science and agronomy faculties at Gembloux.

Investment incentives

Investing in economic recovery
The chief objectives of the authorities in southern Belgium have been to foster diversification of the region's existing industries, boost employment, make the most of local skills and encourage the development of new technology.
For these reasons, although the extra-ordinary success with which southern Belgium has taken up the challenge of economic recovery in the world market is in large measure due to the energy and enthusiasm of businesses in the region, it has also been greatly aided by the unfailing support of the region's policy makers.

Regional and local infrastructures
Southern Belgium is made up of nine local councils that between them are responsible for the running of some three hundred industrial estates, all of which are fully equipped and situated close to the country's major road and rail networks.
In order to promote the implantation and development of new businesses and to encourage economic activity in general, southern Belgium has at its disposal an attractive system of incentives. This system has on the one hand to take into account the specific needs and characteristics of the economic development of southern Belgium, and on the other the guidelines and regulations laid down by the the European Commission. With this in mind, the regional government of southern Belgium is particularly keen to promote the development of an infrastructure of small and medium-sized companies that will form the basis of increased economic activity in the area.

One form of incentive is that any company with less than 250 employees is entitled to apply for an investment bonus of up to a maximum of 21 percent. This incentive is open to any company in the area, whether of Belgian or foreign origin. The obvious benefits of such financial assistance have attracted a great deal of interest in the scheme. This should in turn lead to an increase in employment and also give a boost to the general economy and trade of the area. The regional government is particularly keen to foster investment in such economically strategic sectors as the development of new materials, telecommunications, microelectronics, aeronautics, biotechnology and food processing. Larger companies, provided that they are situated in the redevelopment zones (which comprise more than two-thirds of the total area of the region), are also able to benefit from investment bonuses (of up to a maximum of between 21 and 24 percent). Moreover, this system of incentives is not the only action taken by the authorities of southern Belgium in order to encourage investment in the region. In tandem with local investment companies and the organization Société Régionale d'Investissement de Wallonie (SRIW), the regional government has at its disposal a variety of other valuable economic benefits. The primary function of the SRIW, which is a public service company, is to make a contribution, through its financial interventions, to the restructuring, modernization and further development of the region's industrial fabric. In contributing to the capitalization of more than two hundred businesses, the organization has to date paid out some twenty two thousand million belgian francs. In this way, as well as fulfilling the role of a public development and holding bank, the SRIW is in effect the financial arm of the regional government's industrial policy.

Economic recovery: a matter of minds

Another factor that makes southern Belgium attractive to modern businesses is its highly qualified labor force. Because the level of training is so high, it is able to handle the manufacture of sophisticated high-technology products, which is a measure of its industrial competitiveness – and to compete in terms of skill and creativity, the region has to rely on its academic record. Thanks to a history of several centuries of excellent education, today southern Belgium is able to maintain extremely high standards of education and training, supplied by some 130 schools and 9 university centers. In addition, various interface units support the efforts undertaken to promote the industrial development of academic research.

PRACTICAL INFORMATION

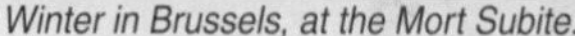

Winter in Brussels, at the Mort Subite.

Summer in the Gaume.

What could be better than a holiday or short break in Brussels or southern Belgium? The location of Brussels makes it an excellent base from which to visit neighboring countries, and there is a wide variety of accommodation to choose from. Wherever you go in Belgium, you will invariably find the people helpful and friendly.

ADDRESSES

UK

◆ BELGIAN TOURIST OFFICE
29 Princes Street,
London W1R 7RG
Tel. (0171) 629 0230

US

◆ BELGIAN TOURIST OFFICE
780 Third Avenue
Suite 1501,
New York 10017
Tel. (212) 758 8130

BRUSSELS

◆ TOURIST OFFICE (O.P.T.)
61 rue du Marché-aux-Herbes,
1000 Brussels
Tel. (2) 504 02 00
◆ BRITISH EMBASSY
85 rue Arlon
1040 Brussels
Tel. (2) 287 62 11
◆ US EMBASSY
27 bd du Régent,
1000 Brussels
Tel. (2) 513 38 30

DOCUMENTATION

Visitors to Belgium from the UK require a passport or British Visitor's Passport as identification and are also recommended to take an E111 form (available from main post offices in the UK), which entitles you to treatment in the event of an accident or medical emergency. Visitors from the US require a passport. There are no visa requirements for visitors from the UK, US, Canada or Australia.

POINTS OF INTEREST

WINTER

There is an art to making the most of winter in Belgium. Visit Brussels and the many other towns, where the cozy bars and cafés and the colorful carnivals will help you forget the cold weather. Or take a trip to the Hautes Fagnes, and enjoy the snow-capped mountain landscape.

SUMMER

Water is plentiful in southern Belgium: waterfalls, fountains, ponds and lakes are to be found everywhere. Visit the numerous parks and châteaux, or take to the water in a barge, sailing boat or kayak.

FALL

Fall is the season for the smell of dead leaves, the ritual of the hunt, and warm, inviting firesides. Visit the Ardennes and enjoy its wild beauty and rich colors at this time of year, when the forests are a mass of glorious reds, browns and purples.

SPRING

Visit the Viroin valley and the reservoir at Virelles; spring is also a good time for a visit to the Hautes Fagnes. It offers an ideal opportunity to go birdwatching, too, and to enjoy the sight of the mountain slopes covered with wild flowers.

TOURIST INFORMATION

Tourist offices in Belgium, local and regional alike, are generally extremely helpful and efficient. They will provide you with brochures and leaflets (usually free of charge, or for a small fee) giving information on a variety of subjects. If you are interested in architecture, you will want to ask for the specialist booklet describing the history of Art Nouveau in Brussels; or you may want to obtain one of the excellent local maps showing the region's lakes (from the tourist information center in Botte du Hainaut), so you can plan your own trips. Some towns, such as Namur, sell a mini-directory. Most tourist offices will supply you with a comprehensive list of local hotels and restaurants.

TELEPHONING FROM ABROAD

Dial 00 (international) and then 32 (the code for Belgium), followed by the local code (without the initial zero, which is only used for calls within Belgium) and the number of the person you are calling. Telephone numbers have seven digits in Brussels, and six digits in other parts of southern Belgium.

Stay in a palace (like the Astoria) or a cottage (like this one in Vielsalm).

HOTELS

Brussels offers accommodation of every type, ranging from youth hostels to top-quality luxury hotels. The middle-range hotels tend to be either family-run operations or branches of one of the larger hotel groups; these can be useful sources of information for the visitor, since some belong to European chains such as Relais et Châteaux, Relais du Silence or Étapes du Bon Goût.

RESERVATIONS

It is best to make hotel reservations in advance. This can be organized, without extra charge, through
◆ B.T.R. (Belgian Tourist Reservations)
111 bd Anspach
1000 Brussels
Tel. (2) 513 74 84
Fax (2) 513 92 77

ACTIVITY HOLIDAYS

Sports enthusiasts, nature lovers and those on walking or cycling holidays have some additional possibilities available to them:

◆ GÎTES D'ÉTAPE DU C.B.T.J.
(Centre Belge du Tourisme des Jeunes) "Type 2" houses are reserved solely for groups, whereas "Type 1" houses are open to individuals.

◆ GÎWAL
(Gîtes and Itinéraires de Wallonie)
This organization offers a dozen or so lodging houses along the walks of the Grande Randonnée ◆ *336*.

◆ LES MAISONS DES AMIS DE LA NATURE
These eight houses are open to non-members at a slightly higher rate than that charged to members of the association.

BUDGET ACCOMMODATION

For a cheaper holiday, there are a number of options that you may want to consider:

◆ CAMPING
There are plenty of campsites. They are classified from one to four stars.

◆ YOUTH HOSTELS
There are six youth hostels in southern Belgium (which are open to all ages).
There are also the following possibilities:

◆ LEISURE VILLAGES
These variations on holiday villages are mostly situated close to towns, and offer accommodation for as little as half a day.

◆ BED AND BREAKFASTS
Since 1981 bed and breakfast accommodation with a family has become increasingly common throughout southern Belgium.

◆ The "GÎTE"
Another popular type of accommodation (also introduced in 1981) is the "gîte". This kind of rented self-catering accommodation is exclusive to southern Belgium.

INFORMATION

For information on rural holidays:
◆ U.T.R.A.-U.P.A.
94–96 rue Dansaert
1000 Brussels
Tel. (2) 511 07 37
◆ FETOURAG
30 rue de la Science
1000 Brussels
Tel. (2) 230 72 95
◆ AGROTOURISME (Lux.)
Tel. (62) 21 25 88
◆ AGRI-ACCUEIL (Liège)
Tel. (87) 33 17 83
◆ AGRI-VACANCES (Hainaut)
Tel. (71) 66 62 89
◆ AGRI-TOUR MOSAN (Namur)
Tel. (81) 21 15 52

ACTIVITY AND BUDGET HOLIDAYS

ACCOMMODATION	INFORMATION	HOLIDAY LOCATION
YOUTH HOSTEL	52 rue Van-Oost 1050 Brussels Tel. (2) 215 31 00	Bouillon, Champlon, Malmédy, Namur ◆ *358*, Tilff ◆ *364*, Tournai ◆ *374*
GÎTES D'ÉTAPE DU C.B.T.J. (Type 1)	31 rue Montoye 1040 Brussels Tel. (2) 512 54 47	Eupen, Wanne Han-sur-Lesse, Ovifat, Rochefort
GIWAL	32 av. Montefiore 4130 Esneux Tel. (41) 80 15 82	Rièzes, Jalhay, Jambes-Namur, Trooz-Nessonvaux, Sourbrodt, Gemmenick, La Gleize, Glons, Poulseur, Houffalize, Limerlé, Rensiwez
MAISONS DES AMIS DE LA NATURE	Maison Verte 18 rue des Frères-Descamps 7800 Ath Tel. (68) 28 09 09	Fraipont, Stavelot, La Reid, Trois-Ponts, Melreux-Hotton, Chiny-sur-Semois, Godinne, Grandglise

HOW TO BOOK

To book rural rented accommodation, holiday villages and holiday apartments, contact Belsud, a department of Office de Promotion du Tourisme (O.P.T.)
◆ Belsud Réservation
61 rue du Marché-aux-Herbes
1000 Bruxelles
Tel. (2) 504 02 80.
For accommodation in the Luxembourg region, contact:
◆ Relobel-Locations
c/o F.T.L.B. - BP 18
6980 La Roche-en-Ardenne.

Hôtel Métropole.

IN BRUSSELS

BUDGET ACCOMMODATION
The most reasonably priced accommodation can be found in the Jacques Brel, Bruegel and Jean Nihon youth hostels, at the C.H.A.B. (Brussels Accommodation Center) and at the Sleep Well-Auberge du Marais. Young people can also apply to the Maison Internationale des Étudiants and to the ACOTRA organization (the latter have a help desk in the entrance hall at Zaventem Airport). There aren't any campsites in Brussels itself; the nearest ones are to be found at Beerzel (about 14 miles to the south of the city), at Ohain (12½ miles to the southeast), Wezemberg-Opem (6 miles to the east) and Hudenberg (about 12½ miles to the east).

SPECIAL RATES AND PACKAGE DEALS
Many of the hotels in Brussels offer special cut-price deals during the week throughout January, February, July, August and December, and some luxury hotels offer special weekend deals throughout the year.

THE "VISIT BRUSSELS" PASSPORT
S.N.C.B. offer a reduction of 60% on journeys to Brussels, plus a whole day of free travel around Brussels by metro, tram and bus. "Visit Brussels" also entitles the holder to reductions on tickets to museums and exhibitions, as well as discounts in some restaurants, hotels and stores. These "passports" can be purchased at a cost of 220BF from tourist offices and are also available in Brussels at 700 different outlets (such as tour operators, bookstores and hotels) or by calling the S.N.C.B. Tel. (2) 513 89 40.

DISCOVERING BELGIUM

PLACES TO VISIT
Be warned: apart from some of the major museums and monuments, many of the places of cultural interest have varying opening times, depending on the day of the week or time of year, and some places are only open during the summer months. Many of the country's art treasures are in religious institutions or in châteaux or other buildings that are privately owned or run by charities, and are therefore not generally accessible to the public.

TOURS OF BRUSSELS
A number of tour operators, including De Boeck, offer comprehensive coach tours of the city. There are also organizations that offer specialized cultural or thematic tours. Among these are Arcadia (the association of art historians) and A.R.A.U (the Atelier de Recherche et d'Action Urbaine, or action committee for the preservation of Brussels), which has devised five thematic itineraries around Brussels – including its "Brussels 1900" tour, which is a must for anyone interested in Art Nouveau. The official tourist organization, the O.T.B. (Office du Tourisme Bruxellois), runs a different tour on different days of the week, each on a particular subject or theme (the press, food etc.).

◆ DE BOECK INCOMING
48 place De Brouckère
Tel. (2) 218 68 98
◆ ARCADIA
58 rue Wafelaerts
Tel. (2) 534 38 19
◆ A.R.A.U. TOURVILLE
2 rue du Midi
1000 Brussels
Tel. (2) 513 47 61
◆ O.T.B.
34 rue aux Laines
1000 Brussels
Tel. (2) 512 12 80

TOURS AROUND SOUTHERN BELGIUM
The Tourist Federation of Brabant ◆ *350* offers a one-day tour of local abbeys, including Nivelles and Villers-la-Ville. From the Tourist Federation of Hainaut ◆ *371* you can obtain day passes to the cliffs at Ronquières or the Abbey of Aulne. The federation of the province of Liège ◆ *362* offers an all-inclusive tour that takes in the Cantons de l'Est and the scenic delights of the Ourthe-Néblon, as well as a visit to the industrial-archeology site at Blégny-Trembleur. The tourist office in Liège caters for music lovers and fans of Simenon's novels alike in its range of excursions and tours.

FLIGHTS TO BRUSSELS

FROM	AIRLINE	FREQUENCY
LONDON	British Airways	7 flights daily
	Sabena	7 flights daily
MANCHESTER	British Airways	4 flights daily
	Sabena	4 flights daily
GLASGOW	Sabena	2 flights daily
NEW YORK	American Airways	1 flight per day
	Sabena	1 flight per day
CHICAGO	Sabena	1 flight per day

FLIGHTS TO ANTWERP

FROM	AIRLINE	FREQUENCY
LONDON	Sabena	2 flights daily

BY AIR

Sabena, Belgium's national carrier, has flights from Brussels to many major cities; and most of the larger airlines offer direct flights to Brussels.

◆ **FROM THE UK**

There are direct flights to Brussels from London, Birmingham, Bristol, Edinburgh, Leeds, Manchester, Newcastle and Glasgow. Economy fares start as low as £69 for a special-rate return ticket, and can be as high as £190. Expect to pay between £250 and £320 for a business-class return ticket.

◆ BRITISH AIRWAYS
Tel. (0345) 222 111

◆ SABENA
Tel. (0181) 780 1444

◆ **FROM THE US**

There are direct flights to Brussels from most of the major airports throughout the US, including Atlanta, Boston, Chicago, Los Angeles and New York. The cost of a ticket may vary greatly depending upon where you are flying from. The price of a round-trip ticket from New York, for example, ranges from around $550 to $800.

◆ AMERICAN AIRWAYS
Tel. (800) 624 6262

◆ SABENA
Tel. (212) 247 8390

TRAVELING INTO THE CITY CENTER

Brussels is said to be the 11th busiest European airport (5th for freight transport, and 16th for passengers). Brussels' international airport, Zaventem, is situated 9 miles from the city center. In June 1994 Zaventem 2000, the new airport station, was opened. This runs a train service into Brussels' Gare Centrale and Bruxelles-Nord every 20 minutes throughout the day. The journey time is 15 minutes, and tickets cost 75BF. The first and last trains are at 6.09am and 11.46pm respectively from Zaventem, 5.39am and 11.14pm from Gare Centrale, 5.43am and 11.18pm from Bruxelles-Nord.

BY RAIL

There are regular international train services into Belgium from France, Holland, Germany and the UK (with the addition of a sea crossing).

BY FERRY

The main ports serving Belgium are Dunkirk, Ostend and Zeebrugge; and the common routes from the UK are Ramsgate to Dunkirk (which takes 2½ hours), Ramsgate to Ostend (taking 5 hours by ferry or 1¾ hours by jetfoil), Felixstowe to Zeebrugge (which takes 5¾ hours), and Hull to Zeebrugge (taking 14 hours). There are also ferry services from Dover and Harwich to the Belgian ports.

VIA THE CHANNEL TUNNEL

EUROSTAR

Eurostar heralds the start of a new era in international travel. Every day a fleet of trains whisks passengers direct from Waterloo International in London or Ashford International in Kent to the Gare du Midi/Zuid, in the center of Brussels, at speeds of up to 186mph. The journey takes just 3¼ hours from London to Brussels (an hour less from Ashford). At both Waterloo and Ashford International the automatic check-in saves time and hassle. Passport control is normally carried out on the train. All Eurostar's carriages are air-conditioned; there are two bar-buffets offering a selection of refreshments, and two areas devoted to disabled passengers. Telephones, taking credit cards and Eurostar phonecards, are available; and mobile phones work on board, except in the tunnel itself. Passengers traveling First Class enjoy a meal served at their seat. A competitive range of fares is available.

TAXI

A taxi ride from the airport into the center of town costs around 1,400BF.

◆ EUROSTAR
IN THE UK
Tel. (0345) 881881
IN BRUSSELS:
Tel. (2) 224 8856

LE SHUTTLE

Le Shuttle transports car passengers from Folkestone to Calais and the journey takes only 35 minutes.
Tel. (0990) 353535

T.E.C. (Transports en Commun) coach.

BY TRAIN

A DENSE NETWORK
The fact that Belgium is such a small country and the efficiency of the Société des Chemins de Fer Belge (S.N.C.B.) make the railway the principal means of transport, along with the car. "Intercity" (I.C.) trains only stop at the larger stations, whereas "Interregional" (I.R.) trains also stop at intermediate stations, and the "L" trains stop at all stations along the way.

TRAIN TIMES
In principal all trains run at the same time each hour and there is usually a minimum of one train per hour between the major cities: if the first train on a given route leaves the station at 6.41am, there should be a train at the same time each hour throughout the day.

TICKET PRICES
These are according to distance traveled: 210BF for 15 miles, 690BF for 60 miles, 1,340BF for 120 miles.

TICKETS
◆ Tickets can be purchased five days in advance of the date of travel.
With the exception of weekend tickets, return tickets are only valid for one day.
Reservations are obligatory on trains for which a supplement must be paid.
◆ Tickets are not on sale on the trains themselves. Warn the ticket inspector before getting onto a train if you have been unable to buy your ticket beforehand.
An additional payment of only 50BF will be charged (the fine for being caught without a ticket is 1,000BF).

COMBINED TICKETS
◆TRAIN + CYCLE
On arriving at the station, you can rent a bicycle (150–300BF a day), or a tandem (340BF) ◆ *331*.
◆TRAIN + CAR
You can either rent a car on arrival or reserve one in advance.

S.N.C.B. SPECIAL RATES

B. TOURAIL TICKET	5 days of unlimited travel
WEEKEND TICKET	40% reduction for lone travelers, or 40% reduction for the first passenger and 60% for a second passenger
DAY TICKET TO THE ARDENNES	Available during high season only
MULTI-PASS	One return ticket or two single tickets, for two, three, or four people
B-EXCURSION	Visit various sites for an all-in price (which includes reduced-price train fare, plus complimentary bus or tram journey and entrance tickets)

BY COACH

The S.N.C.B. network is complemented by the important T.E.C. system – the public-transport coaches that serve the whole of southern Belgium. Stations where connections can be made between coach and trains are listed in the S.N.C.B. timetables, which also give times of all the Intercity trains and Interregional trains.

INFORMATION
◆ BELGIAN NATIONAL RAILWAYS, Presnick House, 10 Greyroad Pl., London SW1
Tel. and Fax (0171) 233 0360
◆ S.N.C.B. (Brussels)
National information office
Tel. (2) 219 26 40
◆ T.E.C. BRUSSELS Tel. (2) 515 20 00
PROVINCE OF BRABANT Tel. (10) 48 04 04
PROVINCE OF HAINAUT Tel. (65) 38 88 15
PROVINCE OF LIÈGE Tel. (41) 61 84 44
PROVINCE OF LUXEMBOURG Tel. (61) 23 21 78
PROVINCE OF NAMUR Tel. (81) 72 08 40

BY CAR

There is no toll on freeways throughout Belgium, and they are all well lit at night.

SPEED LIMITS
The speed limit is 75mph on four-lane freeways, 55mph on all other main roads, and 35mph in built-up areas.
◆ BREAKDOWN SERVICE
S.O.S. Tel. 736 59 59

CAR RENTAL
The main car rental companies all have branches in the larger towns. It is advisable to organize car rental before you travel, as renting on site can be more expensive.

CAR RENTAL COMPANIES

IN THE UK
◆ AVIS
Tel. (0181) 848 8733
◆ EUROPCAR
Tel. (0171) 387 2276
◆ HERTZ
Tel. (0171) 730 8323
◆ EURODOLLAR
Tel. (0171) 272 2273
◆ BUDGET RENT A CAR
Tel. (0171) 495 5533

IN BELGIUM
◆ AVIS
Tel. (2) 735 23 88
◆ EUROPCAR
Tel. (2) 348 92 12
◆ HERTZ
Tel. (2) 735 40 50
◆ EURODOLLAR (Ada)
Tel. (1) 49 58 44 44
◆ RENT A CAR
Tel. (1) 46 82 60 60

STREET SIGNS

Street signposting can be irregular. Some crossroads seem to have been missed out entirely, and this can make it difficult, on occasion, to find your way around Brussels' back streets. Equip yourself with a good street map.

ROAD AND FREEWAY SIGNS
Signs on roads and freeways conform to standard European conventions. Main roads are given in white on a blue background, and freeways in white on green.

TOURIST SIGNS
There are all sorts of tourist signs to look out for. Prominent signs indicate the location of virtually all the places of interest, as well as most sports centers and the various tourist routes.

COMMUNES AND DISTRICTS
In the 1970's a bout of administrative reorganization took place throughout Belgium, which grouped districts together to form larger units called *communes* ◆ 345. These are sometimes referred to under the name of the place itself, and sometimes under the name of the district. In some cases the name of the former principal town has been adopted as the name of the new unit: such is the case with Ath, which now also includes Rebaix. In other cases an entirely new name has been coined: this is the case with the commune of Sivry-Rance, which owes its name to the grouping together of the towns of Sivry and Rance. For this reason signposts at the approach to towns frequently carry two names: at the top the present name of the district itself, and underneath it the name of the places to which it has been linked.

GLOSSARY

CITIES AND TOWNS
Brussels: *Bruxelles/Brussel*
Courtrai: *Kortrij*
Ixelles : *Elsene*
Liège: *Luik*
Mons: *Bergen*
Muscron: *Mouscron/Moeskroen*
Namur: *Namen*
Soignies: *Zinnik*
Tournai: *Doornik*

USEFUL PHRASES
Exit: *Sortie/Uitrit*
Slow: *Ralentir/ Vertragen*
Diversion: *Déviation/ Wegamlegging*
Roadworks: *Travaux/Werken*
Bad road: *Route en mauvais état/ Weginschechtestaat*
Difficult drive: *Passage difficile/Moeilikke doorgang*

TRAVELING THROUGH FLEMISH AREAS

Traveling between Mons and Brussels presents a challenge, since it involves passing through both Flemish-speaking and French-speaking areas; consequently the signposting alternates between the two languages. For the same reason getting around the suburbs of Brussels may prove equally confusing, as the same place can have two different names.

RING ROADS AROUND BRUSSELS

The city of Brussels is surrounded by a ring road in the shape of a pentagon, which is called the *Petite Ceinture*. You can take this road, with its numerous tunnels, to get to the outskirts of Brussels. This inner ring road is surrounded by a much larger outer one, known simply as the *Ring*, which encircles the neighboring districts and takes traffic out to the provinces.

The outer ring road is subdivided into the *Ring Ouest* (west ring) and the *Ring Est* (east ring).

THE CANTONS DE L'EST

The Cantons de l'Est is a German-speaking area – so you may find it useful to take a German phrasebook with you and to arrive there equipped with a few useful phrases.

FRENCH/GERMAN NAMES

Liège	*Lüttich*
La Calamine	*Kelmis*
Bullange	*Büllingen*
Trois-Vierges	*Ulflingen*
Waimes	*Weismes*
Wécercé	*Weywertz*
Rénastène	*Reinhardstein*
Vesdre	*Wese*
Amblève	*Amel*
Meuse	*Maas*

In Brussels art and transport sometimes converge.

INDIVIDUAL TRANSPORT

BY CAR

Certain areas are best avoided during the rush hours (8am to 10am and 5pm to 7pm). These are the Petite Ceinture, the Ring and freeway entrances and exits. The inhabitants of Brussels enjoy access to excellent public-transport systems and are encouraged to leave their cars at home in order to reduce traffic jams and to improve the quality of the air in the city. Visitors to Brussels can leave their vehicles in parking lots.

PARKING

In some areas, such as around Avenue Louise and the Bourse, it is almost impossible to park: parking on the street is penalized by the immediate removal of the vehicle. Use the underground parking lots (from 60BF to 80BF an hour), but don't forget that some close at midnight. Parking discs for the *zone bleue* areas can be obtained from service stations.

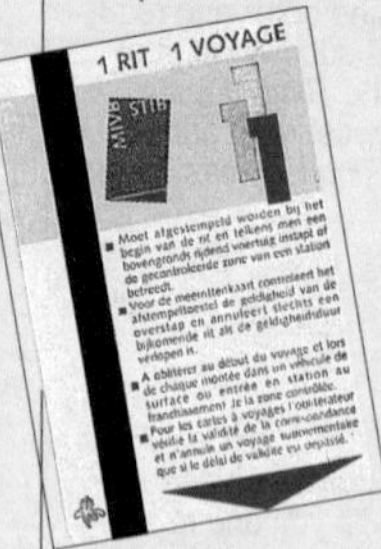

BY TAXI

A 1992 survey estimated that there were around 1,500 taxis in operation in Brussels.

◆ TIPS

A service charge is included in the price, but most people round the amount up.

◆ FARES

There is a charge of 75BF, plus 31BF per kilometer if the journey is within the nineteen districts that make up the city of Brussels or 63BF per kilometer for journeys beyond the city limits.

TAXI COMPANIES

◆ A.T.R.
Tel. (2) 242 22 22
◆ AUTO LUXE
Tel. (2) 512 31 23
◆ TAXI ORANGE
Tel. (2) 513 62 00
◆ TAXI VERT
Tel. (2) 511 22 44

PUBLIC TRANSPORT

S.T.I.B. NETWORK

The metro, trams and buses are run by S.T.I.B. (Société des Transports Intercommunaux de Bruxelles). Free public-transport maps are available from information offices in most metro stations, or from the S.T.I.B. head office:

◆ S.T.I.B.
20 galerie
de la Toison-d'Or
Tel. (2) 515 20 63

THE METRO

◆ LINE 1A links the Heysel metro station, in the northwest, to Hermann-Debroux in the southeast.

◆ LINE 1B connects Veeweyde station, in the southwest, to Stockel station in the northeast. The overlapping section (which runs east–west) means that all trains on lines 1A and 1B stop at stations between Beekant and Mérode.

◆ LINE 2 is a short line which curves from Clemenceau station to the Place Simonis.

◆ There are also two PRÉ-MÉTRO (old metro) lines. The first runs north–south, linking the Gare du Nord to the Gare du Midi. The second (very short) passes through Montgomery station. Metro station signs are a white "M" on a blue background. Trains run from 6am to midnight.

TRAVEL CARDS

◆ Tickets valid for one, five, or ten journeys allow you to make transfers between metro, bus and train for up to one hour from the start of each journey. They can be used throughout the whole S.T.I.B. network.
◆ The "24-hour" card offers unlimited travel over the entire S.T.I.B. network system.
◆ The monthly M.T.B. season ticket (Junior and Senior, at concessionary or normal rates) provides unlimited transport on the S.T.I.B. network. A monthly season ticket is a very worthwhile purchase for visitors making an extended stay in Brussels.

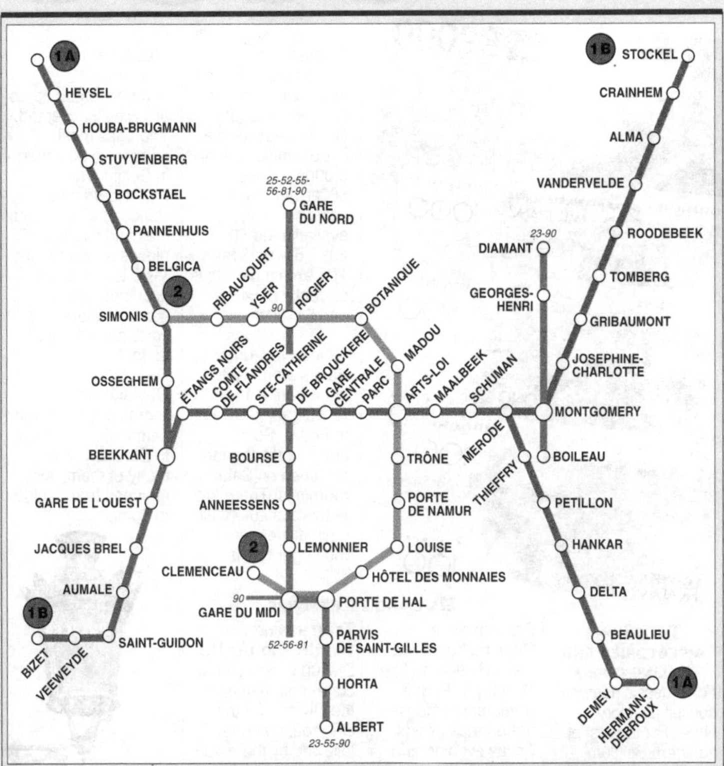

ART IN THE METRO

For over twenty years fifty-five works of art have been exhibited in Brussels metro stations. Among the various designers and artists whose works are on display, some of the best-known are:

◆ Pol Bury with *Moving Ceiling* and Paul Delvaux with *Nos vieux trams bruxellois* at Bourse station.

◆ Jean-Michel Folon with *Magic City* at Montgomery station.

◆ Pierre Alechinsky and Christian Dotremont with *Sept écritures* at Anneessens station.

Art forms such as the comic strip are well represented on the metro, too:

◆ In 1980 a fresco produced by Studios Hergé, packed with characters from the books by Georges Rémi (better known as Hergé), was completed along the walls of the Stockel metro station.

◆ Twelve years later Schuiten, making use of a theme frequently dealt with in his books, the history and transport of the city, decorated the new levels at the Porte de Hal station with bas reliefs made out of parts from old trains.

The S.T.I.B. arranges free guided tours of the metro stations where art (mainly frescos and comic strips) is on display. For information and reservations, contact the head offices ◆ *330*. Tours need to be booked 21 days in advance.

BRUSSELS BY BICYCLE

If a tram, a car and a bike were to set out simultaneously on a 6-mile journey across the city of Brussels, which would arrive first? The bicycle, of course. Turning away from the designers of urban freeways (who naturally have a vested interest in building more roads) and intent on transforming Brussels into a more pleasant and comfortable place in which to live, the Bruxelles-Capitale region took the decision to create eighteen cycle routes (five of which converge at the Rue de la Loi). These now constitute an efficient alternative method of traveling around the city.

BICYCLE RENTAL

◆ BIKE IN
18 rue Kelle
1200 Brussels
Tel. (2) 763 13 78

◆ CYCLES C.Y.D.
14 avenue E.-Pirmez
1040 Brussels
Tel. (2) 640 17 60

◆ J.O. BIKES
4 rue Général-Fives
1040 Brussels
Tel. (2) 647 46 71

◆ VLERICK
20 boulevard d'Anvers
1000 Brussels
Tel. (2) 219 92 28

MONEY

CURRENCY

The official currency in Belgium is the Belgian franc (BF). Notes are available in denominations of 5,000BF, 1,000BF, 500BF and 100BF; coins currently available are 50BF, 20BF, 5BF and 1BF. The exchange rate is currently £1=45BF and $1=30BF.

CHANGING MONEY

Banks are usually open from 9.15am to 3.30pm, Monday to Friday. Some bureaux de change are open on Saturday mornings. There are numerous automatic cash dispensers in all the larger towns.

METHODS OF PAYMENT

In theory credit cards are widely accepted. The ones most commonly accepted in Belgium are Mastercard and Bancontact; and you may find that some places refuse to take Visa. Eurocheques, accompanied by a check-guarantee card, are accepted up to 7,000BF.

OPENING HOURS

Stores are open from 9am to 6pm, Monday to Saturday; however, many of them close for lunch from midday to 2pm.

MAIL AND TELEPHONES

TELEPHONE DIRECTORIES AND DIALING CODES

For Brussels numbers, consult directory No. 1. For the rest of southern Belgium, use directories No. 6 (east), No. 7 (central) and No. 8 (west). The code for each area is given under the name of the principal town.

Brussels 02

Liège 041
Waremme 019
Huy 085
Durbuy 086
Stavelot 080
Verviers 087

Wavre 010
Charleroi 071
Chimay 060
Namur 081

Dinant 082
Ciney 083
Marche-en-Fam. 084
Libramont 061
Arlon 063

La Louvière 064
Mons 065
Nivelles 067
Ath 068
Tournai 069

POST OFFICES

Opening hours are normally 9am to 5pm, Monday to Friday. Some post offices are open later on Friday evening and are also open on Saturday morning.

MAIL

Letters (up to 20g) or postcards to any part of Europe cost 16BF. An express letter (up to 20g) costs 180BF.

TELEPHONING THE UK AND THE US

Dial 00 (international code) and then 44 for the UK or 1 for the US (country code), followed by the area code (dropping the first zero for the UK) and the number you are calling.

PUBLIC TELEPHONES

Both coin-operated and card-operated public telephones exist in Brussels and southern Belgium. Telephone cards (200BF, 400BF, 600BF or 1,000BF) are available from Belgacom offices.

EMERGENCY SERVICES

Fire brigade: 100
Police: 101
Red Cross (ambulance): 105
Directory enquiries (Belgium): 1307
International directory enquiries: 1304 (telephone numbers)
1324 (country and area codes)

COST OF A TELEPHONE CALL (PER MINUTE)

Telephoning within Belgium

	before 8am	8am–8pm	after 8pm
Mon–Sat	18.08BF	20.95BF	18.08BF
Sunday	18.08BF		

Telephoning Europe

	before 8am	8am–8pm	after 8pm
Mon–Sat	5.47BF	7.23BF	5.47BF
Sunday	5.47BF		

The above rates for dialed calls to Europe from Belgium are valid for area codes 056, 057, 058, 060, 061, 063, 064, 065, 069, 071 and 082 (see left).

Window shopping . . .

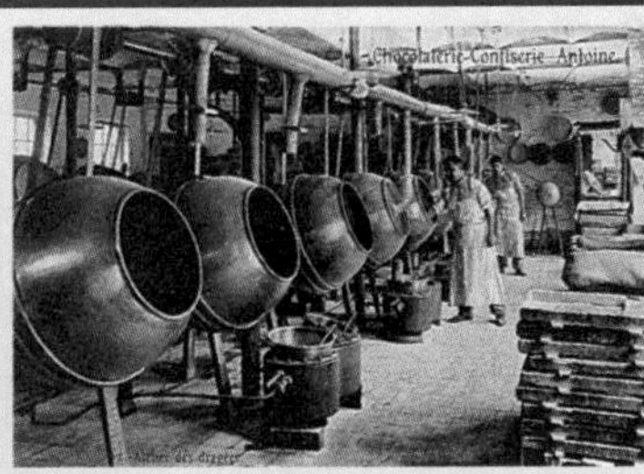
Roasting cocoa beans.

There are chocolate lovers with differing inclinations: some crave the delicate sweetness of creamy white chocolate, while others prefer the slightly bitter quality and rich taste of dark chocolate. The most famous Belgian chocolate houses are renowned for their handmade pralines, but the commercially produced variety are also delicious and are characteristically presented in attractive ribboned boxes containing a tempting selection of flavors.

THE HISTORY OF CHOCOLATE

Around 1520, while in Mexico, Cortez encountered a beverage made from cocoa mixed with pepper and honey, which the Aztecs served at the grand banquets given in his honor. This drink was quickly introduced into Spain, and by the next century its use had spread across Europe: indeed this exquisite but inexpensive beverage was even recommended for its supposed medicinal properties. Until the 18th century the manufacturing technique was known only to the Aztecs, who ground the cocoa beans by hand on a stone held between the knees.

The chocolate industry in Belgium, which developed in the middle of the 19th century, had a slow beginning. In 1870 Belgium had no more than a dozen chocolate makers. By 1900 the number had increased to around sixty, who were exporting some 2,000 tons of cocoa powder, cocoa butter and chocolates.

The Belgian Conseil Supérieur d'Hygiène Publique exercised such a rigid control over manufacturers that there was no question of supplying inferior quality products. The future was set: Belgian chocolate became famed for its superior taste and quality.

THE MANUFACTURE OF CHOCOLATE

Once they have been cleaned and sorted, the cocoa beans are roasted in a large rotating drum. After being left to cool, they are broken up in a crushing machine. The hulls are then separated out from the broken pieces of bean, which are tipped into a mill: the cocoa emerges from the mill in the form of a syrupy paste. The cocoa paste thus obtained can either be used directly in the manufacture of chocolate or be put into a hydraulic press in order to extract the fat (known as cocoa butter). The next stage is for sugar and flavorings to be added; the cocoa is then coarsely ground in a mixer until the various ingredients are blended together. But the product is still of a very coarse nature, and in order for it to reach a soft, smooth consistency it must be ground several times between granite cylinders.

The mixture is then transferred to huge "shells", or round steel tanks, where it is stirred continuously for twenty-four hours, until all the sugar granules have completely dissolved and the mixture has acquired a velvety-smooth consistency. It is then at last ready to be molded. Once it has been molded, the finished product is chilled in enormous refrigerators.

CHOCOLATE SPECIALISTS

LÉONIDAS
46, bd Anspach
Much cheaper in Brussels than abroad (360BF per kilo). However, although Léonidas chocolates are very well-known internationally, Belgian connoisseurs often favor two of the other great chocolate houses, namely:

NEUHAUS
1 rue de l'Étuve, close to the Grand Place
(980BF per kilo)

GODIVA
22 Grand-Place,
Open until 10pm
(1,080BF per kilo)

CHOCOLATE TERMS

◆ The *chocolat de couverture* used in the fabrication of pralines, pâtisseries and confectionery, has a special taste. It is a very fine chocolate and generally contains less sugar but more fat than other types.

◆ The famous filled Belgian candies known as *pralines* have a coating of *chocolat de couverture.*

Comic-strip production in Brussels and southern Belgium is an impressive industry, and there are specialist libraries and a museum devoted to the subject. The country inspires the setting for many of the stories, and the heroes themselves can be found in every town and city in the form of murals or statues.

A BRIEF HISTORY

PREWAR

Comic strips made their first appearance in children's weeklies and the children's supplements in daily newspapers: *Le Petit Vingtième*, the Thursday supplement published between 1929 and 1940, was produced by Hergé, who quadrupled its circulation.

POSTWAR TO 1960

This was the era of the specialist weeklies (twenty-one of them were published in France after 1945). The most famous are *Bravo* (1936–51), which launched E.-P. Jacobs' *Héroïc-Albums* (1945–56) and then, for a long time, *Spirou* (1938) and *Tintin* (1946). This was the melting pot from which three waves of comic-strip creators emerged.

FROM 1960 TO THE PRESENT DAY

Between 1960 and 1970, the golden age of the comic strip, the number of books multiplied. They were the pride and joy of two Walloon publishing houses: Dupuis (*Spirou*), in Marcinelle, and Casterman (*Tintin*) in Tournai.

"TINTIN"

◆ 1929. Start of the adventures of Tintin.
◆ 1946. Birth of the weekly. Here Hergé trained and formed among others E.-P. Jacobs (Blake and Mortimer), P. Cuvelier, J. Martin (Alix) and R. Macherot.
◆ 1967. Greg became chief editor and attracted a new wave of brilliant creators (Craenhals, Herrman).

"SPIROU"

◆ 1938. Jean Dupuis launched the weekly *Spirou*. Rob Vel created the character of the same name. The graphics were later taken over by Jijé, then by Franquin, future creator (1957) of Gaston Lagaffe.
◆ 1944. This was the renaissance: Sirius (Timour), Will (Tif and Tondu) and the Liégeois Charlier and Hubinon were soon joined by Morris (Lucky Luke) and then in 1952 by Peyo.
◆ 1956. With Yvan Delporte a new group blossomed: Roba, Tillieux, Lambil, then Seron and Walthéry.
◆ 1969. Birth of the amazing but short-lived supplement *Le Trombone illustré*.

CENTRE BELGE DE LA BANDE DESSINÉE

20 rue des Sables, 1040 Bruxelles
A museum, but unlike others this one is housed in a former department store, Waucquez, built by Victor Horta in 1906. As well as such treasures as Tintin's rocket and thousands of original plates, there are a "Museum of the Imagination", a cinema, video and reference libraries, a bookstore, and a relaxing reading room.

BRUSSELS, COMIC-STRIP CITY

◆ LE DEUXIÈME SOUFFLE
2 rue Braemt
The best known store (10,000 titles, collectors' items and original plates)
◆ BANDE DES SIX NEZ
179 chaussée de Wavre
◆ FIL À TERRE
198, chaussée de Wavre
Buy-and-exchange stores line the entire street.
◆ CHIC BULL
46 bd M. Lemonnier
◆ LE DÉPÔT
108 rue du Midi
◆ DURANGO
9 rue de l'Athénée
◆ ESPACE BD
2 place C. Cocq
◆ ESPACE TINTIN
13 rue de la Colline
◆ FANTÔME ESPAGNOL
71 bd M. Lemonnier
◆ JONAS
142 chaussée d'Ixelles
◆ MULTI BD
126 bd Anspach
◆ PEPPERLAND
7 rue du Baudet
◆ SANS TITRE
7 rue Léopold
◆ SCHILRF BOOK
752, chaussée de Waterloo

MURALS

Out of the desire to brighten up buildings was born the idea of a "mural trail" that would encourage people to rediscover forgotten areas of the city center. Several murals are dedicated to cartoonists or comic-strip heroes.

◆ RUE DE NAMUR: Schuiten
◆ RUE DU CHEVREUIL: Roba's Boule & Bill
◆ RUE DU MARCHÉ AU CHARBON: Carin
◆ RUE DE LA BUANDERIE: Morris' Lucky Luke
◆ BOULEVARD DU MIDI: Geluck

As you travel across southern Belgium, there are many nature reserves and areas of scenic beauty to explore. To the east, beginning with the Ardennes Forest, which has many streams and rivers running through it, is a vast expanse of natural countryside, a "green lung" in the heart of urban and industrial northwest Europe.

DISCOVER THE NATURE RESERVES

RESTRICTIONS

Nature reserves in Belgium are divided into four zones, according to the degree of protection that is needed.
ZONE A:
unrestricted access.
ZONE B:
access restricted to paths and signposted areas.
ZONE C:
guided visits only.
ZONE D:
no access permitted.

FOREST FIRES

Since 1991 72 percent of the Hautes Fagnes has been categorized under Zone C. During periods when there is a high risk of forest fires, access may be forbidden; red flags are then raised.

VISITING RESERVES

Half-day visits to the nature reserves of southern Belgium are organized on a regular basis. For details, contact:

◆ RÉSERVES NATURELLES ET ORNITHOLOGIQUES DE BELGIQUE (R.N.O.B.)
103 rue Royale
Ste-Marie
1030 Brussels
Tel. (2) 245 43 00
◆ ASSOCIATION NATURE ET TERROIR
Tel. (71) 33 12 63

Some nature reserves have their own discovery centers.
◆ CENTRE BOTRANGE (HAUTES FAGNES)
4950 Robertville. Tel. (80) 44 57 81.
In case of forest fire, call (80) 44 72 72.
Guided walks and cycle rides; one-day or week-long group tours.
◆ VIRELLES NATURE (ÉTANG DE VIRELLES)
20 rue E.-Hermant 6200 Bouffioux
Tel. (71) 38 17 61
or 21 13 63 (in peak season)
Guided tours, introduction to nature treks, and off-track rambles on demand.

UNDERSTANDING NATURE

On a more general note, the association named ÉDUCATION-ENVIRONNEMENT (which is active throughout the whole of the Brussels and southern Belgium area) is of help to visitors who want to undertake walks with a view to increasing their understanding of nature and the environment:
◆ without a guide, with the help of their booklets for walkers;
◆ or with a guide (on demand), which can be for either half a day or a whole day. Guided walks on a specific theme can be arranged.
For more detailed information, contact:
UNIVERSITÉ DE LIÈGE
DÉPARTEMENT DE BOTANIQUE
Bâtiment B 22
Domaine du Sart-Tilman
4000 Liège
Tel. (41) 56 38 57
Fax (41) 56 38 40

BEWARE

During the game-hunting seasons (from July 15 to August 15 and from September 15 to October 15) access to forest areas is restricted to the hours between 9am and 5pm. Between October 1 and December 31 the local forestry authorities put up posters indicating specific areas out of bounds to walkers.

Forest lovers will want to obtain the leaflets with detailed fold-out maps of the most beautiful state-owned forests (Bon-Secours, Rance and Stambruges), available from:
DIRECTION GÉNÉRALE DES RESSOURCES NATURELLES ET DE L'ENVIRONNEMENT
15 av. Prince-de-Liège
5100 Namur
Tel. (81) 32 12 11

Hautes Fagnes.

The Viroin valley.

The Giant's Tomb (Semois valley).

Treks

◆ The Belgian walking association (Association Belge Sentiers de Grande Randonnée) has marked out more than 2,800 miles of cross-country paths, making some twenty walks, all described in their guides which are available from bookstores or from: S.G.R. A.S.B.L. 27 rue Chéra 4141 Louveigné-Sprimont Tel. (41) 60 81 77. Some of the paths follow the course of a river, such as grande randonnée (GR) 57 (112 miles) along the Ourthe valley or GR 571–572 (94 miles) along the Amblève and the Salm. Other routes cover areas of natural beauty, such as GR 575 (71 miles) in the Namur section of the Condroz plateau. For a grand tour of the Ardennes-Eifel area, follow the G.R.A.E. long-distance path: this intersects with GR 12 and circles the whole of the Semois valley, then traverses the Bastogne and Tailles plateaus and crosses the Hautes Fagnes before eventually joining up with the German Eifel-Verein. The visitor is also sure to enjoy GR 56 (91 miles) across the Cantons de l'Est.

◆ In addition, the Namur tourist federation (F.T.P.N.) – responsible for marking out the Belgian section of the Route St-Jacques – has organized seven different itineraries (from 28 miles to 90 miles long). Most of them include half-board and baggage transport. For information and reservations, contact: C.A.P. Nam, F.T.P.N. 3 rue Notre-Dame 5000 Namur Tel. (81) 22 29 98

Walking across the Ardennes

The depths of the forest
The G.R.A.E. path allows you to explore the east Ardennes and its plateaus, whereas the Transardennaise route runs further to the west through Daverdisse, Redu, St-Hubert and La Roche-en-Ardenne, culminating at the heart of the massif. The G.T.A.-Belgique association (which is a non-profit-making organization) offers a choice of three different packages, allowing you to go at your own pace:

◆ the entire walk (100 miles) in five or six days

◆ a route with at least one overnight stop

◆ walks departing from a fixed base.

The prices (from 4,500BF to 16,500BF for a break of two to eight nights) include half board (you can choose between a hotel, self-catering accommodation or camping), as well as transportation of baggage or people between overnight stops. The association will also organize a guide for a specific period, if desired. Reservations can not be made during the hunting season.

Information center
(Maison de la Randonnée)
Grande Traversée des Ardennes
G.T.A.-Belgique
41 Sprimont
6680 Ste Ode
Tel. (61) 68 86 11
Fax (61) 68 86 95

Equipment
Compass and maps nos. 59, 60, 64 and 67 from the I.N.G. (◆ *337*), a whistle for scaring away wild boar, and sturdy walking shoes (since you will be crossing a rocky massif area).

Warning
Do not touch bait (brown-colored cubes or cylinders) left to vaccinate foxes against rabies.

Simple walks

Each part of southern Belgium has its own walks. The area where marked paths are most numerous is in the Cantons de l'Est, with a total of several hundred miles. Recommended walks can be found in the various publications available from the provincial federations that have offices in Brussels (for the Brabant area), Mons (for walks in Hainaut), St-Vith (for the Cantons de l'Est), and in Liège and Namur for the provinces of the same name. For walks in the province of Luxembourg, you will need to contact the local or regional information centers.

HORSE RIDING AND PONY TREKKING
ASSOCIATION NATIONALE DU TOURISME ÉQUESTRE
12 rue du Moulin
1331 Rosières
DOMAINE PROVINCIAL DE MONT-LE-SOIE
6698 Grand-Halleux
Tel. (80) 21 64 43
Courses of lessons are offered, and one- to nine-day treks for all levels.

MAPS
You can obtain I.N.G. (Institut National Géographique) maps from Touring Club agencies or from the I.N.G. sales office:
13 Abbaye de la Cambre
1050 Brussels
Tel. (2) 648 52 82
Fax (2) 646 25 18

RAMBLING ORGANIZATIONS
◆ AUSTRAL BORÉAL
Two- and three-day walks and rambles throughout the year.
◆ CARAVANES DE LA JEUNESSE BELGE
Weekend rambles, open to all ages.
◆ MAISON DE LA RANDONNÉE
For information and a variety of walks.
◆ PASSEPORT AVENTURE A.S.B.L.
Weekend walks, and introduction to trekking.

Although mountain bikes are enormously popular in the provinces of Liège and Luxembourg, they are almost never seen in Brabant and Hainaut and are still a rare sight in the province of Namur.

TRAILS IN THE CANTONS DE L'EST
Obtain a guide map from the Cantons de l'Est tourist office: this shows all the mountain-bike trails throughout the region (375 miles of trails, mostly along country lanes and through forests, graded according to degree of difficulty).

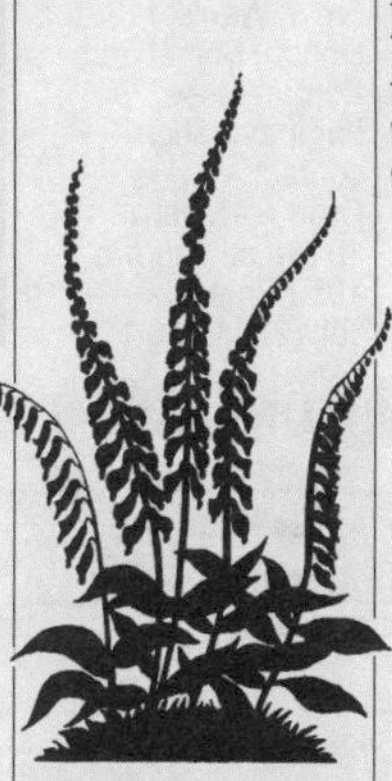

TOURING
There is always the option of taking guided bike tours to various places, such as Spa (one-day or two-day rides, guided or not), Bouillon (staying in a youth hostel) and Vielsalm. Mountain-bike rides (minimum of two days, with a choice of half-board or room-only accommodation) are also available at Baraque de Fraiture (on the high plateau of the Ardennes) now that a bike trail, inspired by the Trans-ardennaise footpath, has been established on tarmac paths.

MOUNTAIN BIKES

SHORT BIKE RIDES
In the province of Liège there is a picturesque ride around Sart-Tilman and a much more testing route from Tour des Fontaines to Spa (22 miles), which is reserved for experienced cyclists.

JUNE MEETING
SART-TILMAN (V.T.T. Live):
Two-day event – cycle ride, rally and open cycle races, for the truly dedicated.
HOUFFALIZE
Belgian branch of the Grundig Mountain Bike World Cup.

In the province of Luxembourg there are tours around Arlon (19 miles on sandy terrain, cyclable all year round), Houffalize, Bouillon (where there is a choice of hilly rides, or flat rides alongside the Semois river) and Vielsalm. In the province of Namur go for a ride along the Lesse valley, departing from Namur (three routes) or from Houyet, and discover the cultural heart of the region, without ever having to leave the high ground, thanks to the Bioul trail.

INFORMATION
FÉDÉRATION BELGE FRANCOPHONE DE VÉLO TOUT TERRAIN
44 rue de la Hoëgne
4910 Theux
Tel. (87) 54 24 28
For information on mountain-bike trails, including the length of each and the degree of difficulty.

TOUR COMPANIES
◆ VÉLODREAM (Spa)
1 Hoctaisart
Tel. (87) 77 11 77
◆ ARDENNES MOUNTAIN BIKES (Vielsalm and Baraque de Fraiture)
16 Chaufheid, Theux
Tel. (87) 54 22 28

MOUNTAIN BIKE RENTAL
Bicycles and cycling accessories can be hired in the following places:
◆ In the province of Luxembourg, in the towns of Arlon, Barvaux, Bomal, Borzée, Bouillon, Herbeumont, Hotton, Houffalize, La Roche-en-Ardenne, Ste-Ode and Virton
◆ In the province of Liège, at Spa, Stavelot, Comblain-Remouchamps, also at Burg-Reuland, Butgenbach, Eupen, Malmédy and St-Vith (Cantons de l'Est)
◆ In the province of Namur, at Han-sur-Lesse and Houyet and in Namur itself.

◆ WATERSPORTS, ROCK CLIMBING AND CAVING

The Haute Meuse seen from the water.

LAKES AND RIVERS

Hire a boat or jump on a barge ◆ *356* and watch the beautiful, imposing countryside of the Meuse valley gradually unfold before you.

Artificial lakes – Eau d'Heure or Lake Robertville, for example – offer a range of watersports, including windsurfing and jetskis, while the meandering rivers typical of the Ardennes are perfect for canoeing and kayaks, and some of them for rafting. In the fast-flowing waters you may be lucky enough to catch a trout as it glides between the rocks. Use a flexible fishing rod fitted with a reel, a weighted line and a large hook.

FISHING PERMITS

Fishing is forbidden in the forest areas and outside the licensed zones of Chiny, Azy-Épioux, Ste-Cécile and Herbeumont on the Semois, and Pesche-Couvin on the Eau Noire. Fishing permits, which are valid for a year, are available from post offices.

ROCK CLIMBING

Along the edge of many of the rivers in the Ardennes the water has cut into the ancient rocks of the massif, creating cliff faces that are ideal for rock climbing. This sport is practiced mostly at Freyr, Waulsort, Hotton, Bomal and Pont-à-Lesse. For information, contact:
CLUB ALPIN BELGE
19 rue de l'Aurore
1050 Brussels
Tel. (2) 648 86 11.

CAVING

Thousands of caves and underground shelters, oriented northeast–southwest, have been carved out of the band of calcareous rock by the water as it flows from the fissure of the Sambre-et-Meuse to Couvin and Han-sur-Lesse, in the south. Enthusiasts, wishing to visit caves other than the eleven that are open to the general public should contact:
L'UNION BELGE DE SPÉLÉOLOGIE
Château de Géronsart
1 rue du Pont de briques
5100 Jambes

WATERSPORTS ON THE ARDENNES RIVERS

WATERWAY	FROM/TO	SPORTS CENTERS	ACTIVITIES
BASSE-LESSE	from Houyet to Anseremme	Lesse Kayak Anseremme ◆*360*	kayak
		Meuse et Lesse Dinant ◆*360*	
		Kayaks Ansiaux Anseremme ◆*360*	
HAUTE-LESSE	from Lessive to Houyet	Kayaks Ansiaux Anseremme ◆*360*	sports kayak
	from Han to Wanlin (2 runs)	Kayaks Lesse et Lomme Han-sur-Lesse ◆*362*	kayak–bicycle
OURTHE	from Barvaux or from Bomal (7 runs)	Bonjean Sports Aywaille ◆*363*	kayak and canoe
	from Nisramont to La Roche (2 runs)	Ardennes Aventure La Roche-en-Ardenne ◆*364*	kayak and raft (November–March)
AMBLÈVE	from Coo to Lorcé (2 runs)	Cookayak Stavelot ◆*366*	kayak
SEMOIS	from Bouillon to Cugnon (4 runs)	Moulin de la Falize Bouillon ◆*366*	canoe, mountain bike, kayak (2- or 3-day descents)
	from Bouillon to Alle from Poupehan to Bohan (4 runs)	Récréalle Alle-sur-Semois ◆*369*	kayak (longer trips available on demand)

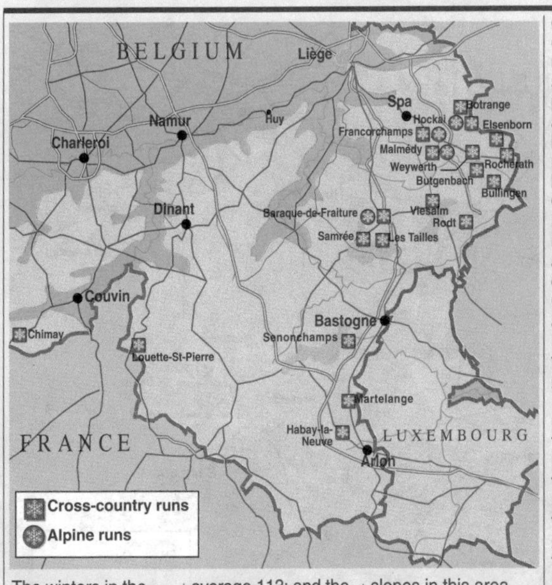

The winters in the Ardennes can be extremely harsh. The average temperature in January is 32°F; the number of days each year when the temperature falls below freezing is on average 113; and the ground is usually covered with snow for two months of the year. This provides a perfect opportunity to enjoy the delights of skiing (cross-country, that is, since all the slopes in this area are very gentle). Some resorts (Spa, Baraque-de-Fraiture) have nursery slopes, and several resorts offer the opportunity to rediscover the childhood pleasures of tobogganing or to experience the more modern delights of snow scooters. The provinces of Liège and Luxembourg each have around thirty resorts. Concentrated here, in the West Cantons and the Fagnes, they make up two axes at right angles to each other: one bordering the Grand Duchy (easy access via freeway E 25), the other along the French border.

SNOW BULLETINS

Recorded information:

LIÈGE
Tel. (41) 22 43 87

LA ROCHE-EN-ARDENNE
Tel. (84) 41 10 11

NAMUR
Tel. (81) 22 29 98

ST-VITH
Tel. (80) 22 76 64

From 10am you can obtain live information regarding La-Roche-en-Ardenne, Namur and St-Vith on the same numbers or dial:
(84) 41 19 81
or (41) 22 42 10
or (41) 52 44 19

PRINCIPLE CROSS-COUNTRY SKI SLOPES

LOCATION	ALTITUDE	RESORT CAPACITY	NUMBER OF RUNS	LENGTH
BOTRANGE	2,264 ft	250 and 800	2	31 and 12 miles
ELSENBORN	2,067 ft	700	1	8¾ miles
ROCHERATH	2,133–2,274 ft	350	1	9¼ miles
BULLINGEN	2,067 ft	300	1	9¼ miles
BUTGENBACH	1,804–1,968 ft	300 and 300	2	7½ miles
WEYWERTZ	1,870–1,968 ft	250 and 1,000	2	8¾ and 11¼ miles
HOCKAI	1,837–1,968 ft	400 and 50	2	6¼ and 10¼ miles
FRANCORCHAMPS	1,640–1,903 ft	150 and 500	3	4¼, 6¼ and 10 miles
MALMÉDY	1,640–1,870 ft	250 and 300	5	2½ and 10 miles
VIELSALM	1,804–1,968 ft	50, 70, 100 and 150	4	4 and 7½ miles
RODT-ST-VITH	1,919 ft	1,000	1	9¼ miles
BARAQUE-DE-FRAITURE	2,132 ft	300 and 800	2	13 miles
LES TAILLES	2,018 ft	400	1	8¾ miles
SAMRÉE	1,739–1,968 ft	200	1	13¾ miles
SENONCHAMPS	1,739–1,968 ft	200	1	12 miles
MARTELANGE	1,634 ft	100	1	12 miles
HABAY-LA-NEUVE	1,378–1,427 ft	100 and 40	2	12 miles
LOUETTE-ST-PIERRE	1,654 ft	150	1	12 miles
CHIMAY	1,132–1,214 ft	100 and 250	2	10 and 9¼ miles

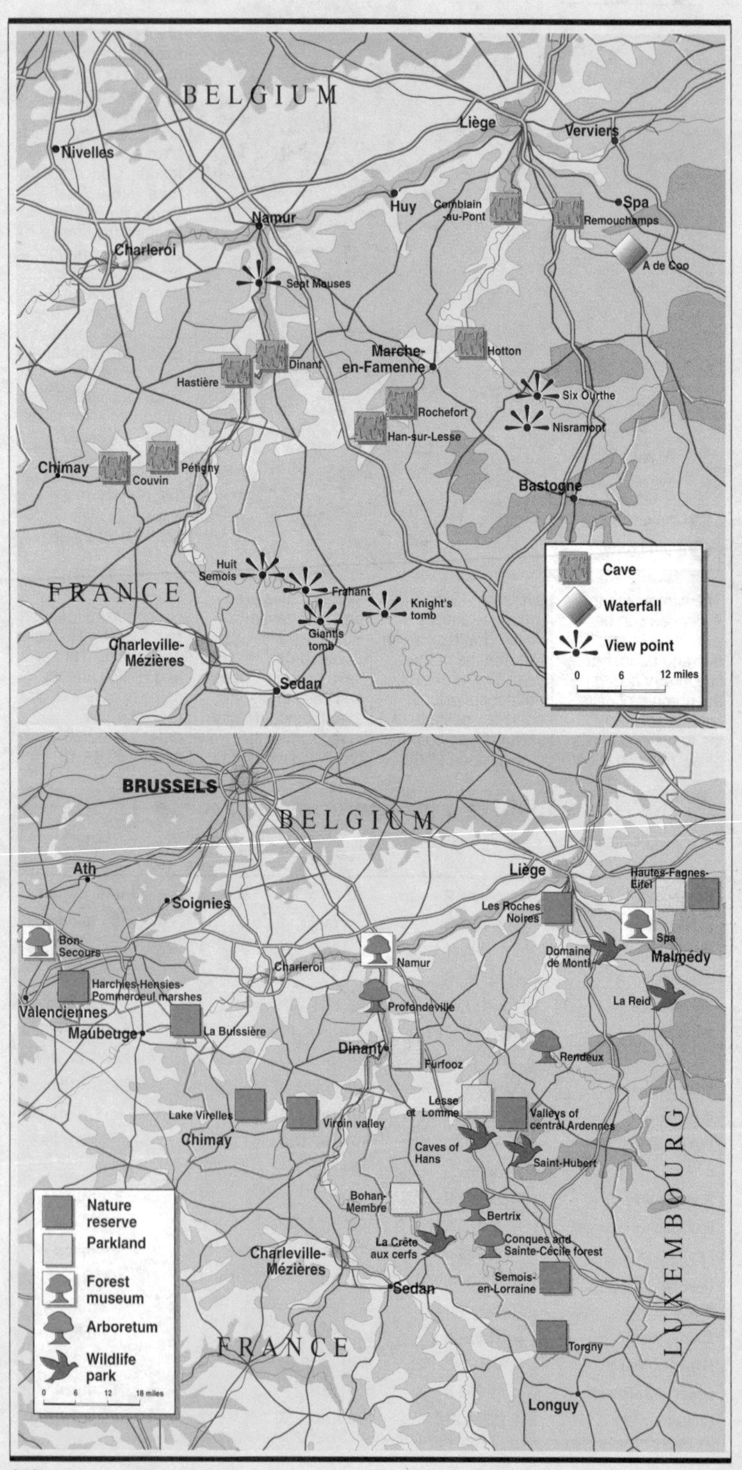
BELGIUM
Liège
Verviers
Nivelles
Huy
Comblain-au-Pont
Spa
Namur
Remouchamps
Charleroi
A de Coo
Sept Meuses
Hotton
Marche-en-Famenne
Dinant
Hastière
Six Ourthe
Rochefort
Nisramont
Han-sur-Lesse
Chimay
Pétigny
Couvin
Bastogne
Huit Semois
FRANCE
Frahant
Knight's tomb
Giant's tomb
Charleville-Mézières
Sedan
Cave
Waterfall
View point
0
6
12 miles
BRUSSELS
BELGIUM
Ath
Liège
Hautes-Fagnes-Eifel
Soignies
Les Roches Noires
Bon-Secours
Spa
Domaine de Monti
Namur
Malmédy
Charleroi
Harchies-Hensies-Pommeroeul marshes
La Reid
Valenciennes
Profondeville
Maubeuge
La Buissière
Dinant
Furfooz
Rendeux
Lesse et Lomme
Lake Virelles
Viroin valley
Valleys of central Ardennes
Chimay
Caves of Hans
Saint-Hubert
LUXEMBOURG
Bohan-Membre
Nature reserve
Bertrix
Parkland
La Crête aux cerfs
Conques and Sainte-Cécile forest
Charleville-Mézières
Forest museum
Semois-en-Lorraine
Sedan
Arboretum
FRANCE
Torgny
Wildlife park
Longuy

PRACTICAL DETAILS

CHÂTEAUX AND PARKS

AROUND BRUSSELS		
CHÂTEAU SOLVAY	1310 La Hulpe	*Park only; 8am–dusk*
NAMUR TO BRUSSELS		
CORROY-LE-CHÂTEAU *TEL. (81) 63 32 32*	5032 Corroy-le-Château, Gembloux	*Open May–Sep., Sat. –Sun. and pub. hols. 10am–noon and 2–6pm*
BOIS-SEIGNEUR-ISAAC *TEL. (67) 21 38 80*	1421 Entité de Braine l'Alleud	*Open only the last two Sundays in June and the first Sunday in July, 2–6pm*
NAMUR TO ST-HUBERT		
ANNEVOIE *TEL. (82) 6115 55*	5181 Annevoie-Rouillon, Anhée	*Garden: Apr.–Oct., daily, 9am–7pm; May–Aug. Château: Jul.–Aug., daily, 9.30am–1pm and 2–6.30pm; Easter–Jun. and Sep., Sat. and Sun. and pub. hols., same times*
CRUPAND *TEL. (83) 69 90 93*	5332 Crupand, Assesse	*Groups by appointment. Contact Mme Limbosch–Blomme,18 rue Basse, Crupand*
SPONTIN *TEL. (83) 69 90 55*	5530 Spontin, Yvoir	*Open daily, 10am–1pm and 2–5pm*
RUINS OF POILVACHE *TEL. (82) 61 35 14*	5530 Houx, Yvoir	*Open Jul.–Aug., daily 10.30am–6.30pm; Apr.–Jun. and Sep., Sat. and Sun., same times*
RUINS OF MONTAIGLE *TEL. (82) 69 95 85*	5522 Falaën, Onhaye	*Open Jul.–Aug., daily, 11am–7pm; Apr.–Jun. and Sep.–Nov., Sat. and Sun. and pub. hols.*
WALZIN	Dinant	*Park only Jul.–Aug. from 10am.*
FREYR *TEL. (82) 22 22 00*	5540 Waulsort, Hastière	*Open Jul.–Aug., Sat. and Sun. and pub. hols. 2pm–6pm.*
VÊVES *TEL. (82) 66 63 93*	5561 Celles-sur-Lesse, Houyand	*Open Jul.–Aug., Tue.–Sun., 10am–6pm; Easter–Jun. and Sep.–Oct., Tue.–Sun., 10am–12.30pm and 1.30–6pm*
LAVAUX-STE-ANNE *TEL. (84) 38 83 62*	5580 Lavaux-Ste-Anne	*Open Jul.–Aug., daily 9am–7pm; Mar.–Jun. and Sep.–Oct., 9am–6pm.; Nov.–Feb., 9am–5pm*
CHÂTEAU DES COMTES *TEL. (84) 21 44 09*	Rochefort 5580 Rochefort	*Open Jun. 15–Sep. 15, daily, 10am–noon and 1–6pm, Easter–Jun. 15 and Sep. 15–30 , Sat. and Sun. and pub. hols, same times*
NAMUR TO LIÈGE		
FRANC-WARAND *TEL. (85) 83 34 04*	5380 Franc-Warand, Fernelmont	*Open Jun.–Sep., Sat. and Sun. and pub. hols., 2–5.30pm.*
JEHAY *TEL. (85) 31 17 16*	4540 Jehay-Bodegnée, Amay	*Open Jul.–Aug., Sat.–Sun., pub. hols., 2–6pm*
AIGREMONT *TEL. (41) 36 16 87*	4400 Awirs, Flémalle	*Open Jul.–Aug., Easter, Tue.–Sun., 10am–noon and 2–6pm; Apr.–Oct., Sat.–Sun., pub. hols.*
MODAVE *TEL. (85) 41 13 69*	4577 Modave	*Open Apr.–mid-Nov., daily 9am–6pm; mid-Nov.–Mar., groups by appointment*
LIÈGE TO SPA		
REINHARDSTEIN *TEL. (80) 44 64 40*	4950 Robertville, Weismes	*Tours Jul.–Aug., Tue., Thur., Sat., 3.30pm; Jun. 15–30 and Sep. 1–15; Sun. and pub. hols., 2pm–5pm; 16 Sep.-Jun. 14, by appointment*
RUINS OF FRANCHIMONT *TEL. (87) 54 10 27*	4910 Theux	*Open Apr.–Sep., Tue.–Sun.,10am–7pm; Oct. –Mar. Sat. and Sun. and pub. hols., same times*
LIÈGE TO LA ROCHE-EN-ARDENNE		
RUINS OF ROCHE-EN-ARDENNES *TEL. (84) 41 13 42*	6980 La Roche-en-Ardenne	*Open Jul.–Aug., daily,10am–7pm; Apr.–Jun. and Sep.–Oct., daily 10am–noon and 2–5pm; Nov.–Apr., daily, 2–4pm and Sat. and Sun., 10am–noon*
ST-HUBERT TO VITRON		
BOUILLON *TEL. (61) 46 62 57*	6830 Bouillon	*Open Jul.–Aug., daily, 9.30am–7pm; Apr.– Jun. and Sep., 10am–6pm; Mar., Oct.–Nov., 10am–5pm Feb. and Dec., 1–5pm; Jan., Sat. and Sun.*
RUINS OF HERBEUMONT	6887 Herbeumont	*Free access*
CHARLEROI-CHIMAY		
CHIMAY *TEL. (60) 21 14 68*	6460 Chimay	*Open Apr.–Oct., daily, 10am–noon and 2pm–6pm; Nov.–Mar., by appointment*

MONS TO CHARLEROI		
ROEULX	7070 Le Roeulx	*Closed for restoration work*
MARIEMONT	7140 Morlanwelz-Mariemont	*Park: Nov.–Jan., 9am–4pm; Feb.–Mar. and Oct., 9am–5pm; Apr.–Sep. 9am–7pm*
SENEFFE	7180 Seneffe	*Closed for restoration work*
MONS TO TOURNAI		
ATTRE *TEL. (68) 45 44 60*	7940 Brugelandte	*Open Jul.–Aug., Thur.–Tue., 10am–noon; 2–6pm, Apr.–Jun., Sep.-Oct., Sat.– Sun. and pub. hols.*
ATH *TEL. (68) 28 01 41*	7800 Ath	*Visits by appointment all year round*
BELOEIL *TEL. (69) 68 94 26*	7970 Beloeil	*Open Apr.–Oct., daily 10am–6pm,*
ANTOING	7140 Antoing	*15 May–Sep., Sun. and pub. hols., 3–5.30pm (guided tours)*
MONS TO BRUSSELS		
ECAUSSINNES-LALAING *TEL. (67) 44 24 90*	7191 Ecaussinnes-Lalaing	*Open Jul.–Aug., Tue.–Fri., 10am–noon; 2–6pm; Apr.–Jun. and Sep.–Oct., .Sat. and Sun., pub. hols.*
ENGHIEN *TEL. (23) 95 83 60*	7850 Enghien	*Park only: Easter–Sep., daily, 10am–8pm; Feb.–Easter and Oct., Sat. and Sun. and pub. hols. 1–6pm; Nov.–Jan., same days, 1–5pm*

ABBEYS

CHARLEROI-CHIMAY		
AULNE *TEL. (71) 51 52 98*	6534 Gozée, Thuin	*Open Apr.–Sep., Tue.–Sat., 10.30am–noon and 1.30–6pm, Sun. and pub. hols., until 7pm*
CHARLEROI-COUVIN		
FLOREFFE *TEL. (81) 44 53 03*	5150 Floreffe	*Guided tours: Jul.–Aug., from 10.30am; May–Oct., 1.30–5pm*
NAMUR TO ST-HUBERT		
LEFFE *TEL. (82) 22 23 77*	5500 Dinant	*Visits by request*
NAMUR TO BRUSSELS		
VILLERS-LA-VILLE *TEL. (71) 87 98 98*	1495 Villers-la-Ville	*Open Jul.–Sep., Wed.–Sun., 10am–6pm, Mon.–Tue., 10am–5pm; Easter–Jun., Wed.– Sun., 10am–6pm; Oct.–Mar., Wed.–Sun., 1–5pm*
GEMBLOUX (ANCIENNE ABBAYE) *TEL. (81) 62 21 11*	5030 Gembloux	*Open Mon.–Fri., 9am–noon and 2–4pm*
LIÈGE TO PAYS DE HERVE		
VAL-DIEU *TEL. (87) 68 73 81*	4880 Aubel	*Visits to the church and courtyard only*
LIÈGE TO SPA		
STAVELOT (ANCIENT ABBEY) *TEL. (80) 86 23 39*	4970 Stavelot	*Open Apr.–All Saints Day, 10am–12.30pm and 2.30–5.30pm*
ST-HUBERT TO VIRTON		
ST-HUBERT	6870 St-Hubert	*Open for viewing outside of cultural events*
ORVAL *TEL. (61) 31 10 60*	6823 Villers-devant-Orval	*Open Easter-Sep., 9.30am–12.30pm and 1.30–6.30pm; Oct.–Easter, 10am–12.30pm and 1.30–6pm*

If you are looking for cultural entertainment in Belgium, there is plenty to choose from. In the capital there are endless theaters, café-theaters, movie theaters and concert halls and all over the rest of the country there are shows and festivals from summer through to the fall.

IN THE CAPITAL

For information consult *M.A.D.* (*Magazine des Arts et du Divertissement*), the Thursday supplement to the daily publication *Le Soir.*
Do not miss classics such as the Théâtre de la Monnaie ◆ *352* and the Théâtre de Toone; two unusual locations are Les Halles de Schaerbeek ◆ *351* and the Raffinerie du plan K ◆ *352.*
Theater lovers can take the opportunity to visit Varia ◆ *352*, at the "National" ◆ *352*, at the "Parc" ◆ *352* and at the Atelier Ste-Anne ◆ *351*.
Movie lovers will enjoy a trip to the Kinépolis ◆ *341* (24 screens), the Musée du Cinéma ◆ *351* and two major festivals ◆ *351*.

FROM THEATER TO MUSIC

FESTIVAL OF SPA
Over fifteen days, several shows are put on each evening in various venues all over the city. There are new plays, revivals and also café-théâtre pieces.
For information and reservations contact Spa's tourist office, located on the Place Rotonde du Casino ◆ *365.*

MOSAN SUMMER FESTIVAL
This festival celebrates music, nature and architecture, since concerts are held in the most beautiful sites around the Meuse, occasionally crossing boundaries to take place in France as well as Luxembourg. Information and accommodation in Dinant.

FESTIVAL OF WALLONIA
This is a collection of five regional festivals. There are more than seventy concerts held from the summer through to the fall, often in splendid settings such as the Collégiale de Nivelles, Abbatiale de Floreffe, St-Hubert basilica, Château de Seneffe, Stavelot Abbey. Concerts are also held in Brussels from June to October. Each festival has a specific address for information and reservations:
◆ JULY MUSIC FESTIVAL OF ST-HUBERT
St-Hubert ◆ *367* (reservations from mid-June).
◆ FESTIVAL DE NAMUR
(July and Sep.–Oct.)
Namur ◆ *358*
◆ FESTIVAL OF STAVELOT
(Aug.–Sep.)
Stavelot ◆ *366*
◆ MUSIC FESTIVAL OF BRABANT
(Sep.–Oct.)
Court-St-Etienne
FESTIVAL OF HAINAUT
(Sep.–Oct.)
Mons ◆ *371*
◆ NUITS TRANSFIGURÉES DE LIÈGE
(Sep.–Oct.)
Liège ◆ *362* (reservations from Aug. 16).
For this last festival, tickets can also be purchased at:
INFO. SPECTACLES
Tel. (41) 22 11 11
FNAC
Tel.(41) 22 12 12

CALENDAR OF FESTIVALS		
APR.–MAY	BRUSSELS	Brussels-Europe festival
MAY 1–31	BRUSSELS	International arts festival (theater, music, contemporary dance, movies)
MAY 27–9	BRUSSELS	Jazz Rallye (each Saturday or Sunday in sixty cafés and on the Grand-Place)
JANUARY	BRUSSELS	Brussels International Film Festival (new movies and retrospectives)
JUNE–NOV.	ALL OVER SOUTHERN BELGIUM	Festival of Wallonia
JUL. 8–10	CHINY	Storytelling festival (storytellers, musicians, comic books and ephemera market)
JUL.–AUG.	DURBUY	Festival of Music (chamber music and classical music recitals)
JUL.–SEP.	VALLÉE DE LA MEUSE	Mosan Summer Festival (classic music concerts in beautiful monuments in the province of Namur)
AUG. 5–20	SPA	Theater festival
AUG. 20–1	SEMOIS (CHASSEPIERRE)	Festival of street theater
OCT. 21–NOV. 13	ALL OVER BELGIUM	Belga Jazz Festival (major European and American jazz and world music artists)

FOLKLORE

Feb. ("Brandons" Sun.) **Namur-Bouge**
Great Fire
Seven huge bonfires to burn away winter

March 26–7 **Mons**
Ducasse de Messines
Traditional procession of the giants, concerts and exhibitions.

Easter Monday **Herve**
Cavalcade
Procession and rondel

June 11 and 12 **Tournai**
Four processions
Historical processions and pageants concerts.

June 25 **Ellezelles**
Witches sabbath
March across the countryside, then on the sabbath, trial and execution of the witches on the square.

July 20 **Viesam**
Macralles sabbath
Taking of the keys to the city, sabbath comic revue in the local dialect.

August 9 **Brussels**
Plantation du Meiboom
May tree planted at the corner of Rue du Marais and Rue des Sables before the clock strikes five.
Celebrations all through the night .

August 19 **Jambes (Namur)**
Festival of Folklore
International festival: several hundred dancers from various countries.

August 27 **Bouillon**
Medieval fair
Tournament, archery, bear baiting.

FROM FOLKLORE TO RELIGION

May 29 **Mons**
Procession of the Golden Carriage and "Lumeçon"
Procession starting from the Collégiale, and a fight between St George and the dragon on the Grand-Place.

June 26 **Wavre**
Procession du Grand Tour
Cavalcade of fire and fireworks on Saturday evening.
Procession ends on Sunday with the breaking of the "wastia", an enormous decorated loaf.

July 31 **Furnes**
Procession of the Penitents
Re-enactment of scenes from the old and new testaments.
Procession of the cross .

August 15 **Liège**
Festivals in Outre-Meuse
Three days and three nights of celebrations
Processions, Mass.
Burial of the Mati l'Ohé.

Fourth weekend in August **Ath**
Vêpres Gouyasse, (Parade of the Giants)
Famous parade with giant models and a staging of David slaying Goliath, in front of the church on the Sunday.

September 11 **Tournai**
Grand historical procession
In honor of the Virgin who saved the city from the plague.
Brotherhoods and choral groups form part of the procession.

October 2 **Nivelles**
Tour of St-Gertrude
Journey of nine miles around the city walls as in the time of the abbesses.

Date varies **Cantons de l'Est**
Festival of Saint Martin
Procession by lantern light.
Dividing the mantle.

HISTORICAL COMMEMORATIONS

July 5 and 7 **Brussels**
Ommegang
Re-enactment of the festival held in 1549 in honor of Charles V and his son, Philip.

September 3 and 4 **Lessines**
Historical feast day
Commemoration of the victory of the bourgeois militia of Sébastien de Tramasure in 1583.

FESTIVAL OF THE HUNT

September 3 and 4. **St-Hubert**
International festival of hunting and nature
Grand mass in front of hunting troupes and a blessing of animals. Historical procession.
Hunting horns.

November 3 **St-Hubert**
Pilgrimage of Saint-Hubert
Grand mass with hunting horns and a blessing of animals.

CARNIVALS

February 12–15 **Malmédy**
Tel. (80) 22 76 64

February 13–15 **Binche**
Tel. (64) 33 37 21

February 14 **Eupen**
Tel. (80) 22 76 64

March 13 **Stavelot**
Tel. (80) 88 25 95

March 13–15 **La Louvière**
Tel. (64) 22 85 71

March 15 **Fosses-la-Ville**
Tel. (85) 84 10 77

March 21 **Andenne**
Tel. (67) 21 54 13

PAGEANTS

3rd Sunday in May **Thuin**
Pageant of Saint Roch

Pentecost Monday **Gerpinnes**
Procession of Sainte Rolende

Sun. after Pentecost **Walcourt**
Pageant of Sainte Trinité

Closest Sun. to July 22 **Jumet**
Pageant of the Madeleine

Every seven years **Fosses-la-Ville**
Procession of Saint Feuillen

The annual calendar of the 71 processions is published by: the Association des Marches Folkloriques de l'Entre-Sambre-et-Meuse, 25, rue de Liège 6280 Villers-Poterie/ Gerpinnes.

◆ Glossary of terms: French / Flemish

Alternative place names

French	Flemish (English)	French	Flemish (English)
Aix-le-Chapelle	Aken	Le Coq	De Haan
Alost	Aalst	Lessines	Lessen
Anvers	Antwerpen (Antwerp)	Lille	Rijsel
Audenarde	Oudenaarde	Lierre	Lier
Ath	Aat	Looz	Borgloon
Baarle-Duc	Baarle-Hertog	Louvain	Leuven
Braine-le-Château	Kasteelbrakel	Lys	Leie
Braine-le-Comte	's Gravenbrakel	Malines	Mechelen
Bruges	Brugge	Menin	Meen
Bruxelles	Brussel (Brussels)	Messines	Mensen
Bullange	Büllengen	Meuse	Maas
Campine	Kepen	Mons	Bergen
Clabecq	Klabbeek	Mouscron	Moeskroen
Comines	Komen	Namur	Namen
Courtrai	Kortrijk	Nivelles	Nijvel
Dixsmude	Diksmuide	Oreye	Oerle
Dunkerque	Duinkerke (Dunkirk)	Othée	Elch
Enghien	Edingen	Ostende	Oostende (Ostend)
Escaut	Schelde (Scheldt)	Renaix	Ronse
Furn	Veurne	Saintes	Sint Renelde
Gand	Gent (Ghent)	Soignies	Zinnik
Grammont	Geraardsbergen	Termonde	Tendermonde
Hainaut	Henegouwen	Tongres	Tongeren
Hal	Halle	Tournai	Doornik
Hesbaye	Haspengouw	Tubize	Tubeke
Hulpe, La	Ter Hulpen	Waremme	Borgworm
Huy	Hoei	Wavre	Waver
Jodoigne	Geldenaken	Ypres	Ieper
La Flandre	Vlaanderen (Flanders)	Yser	Ijzer
La Panne	De Panne	Zeebrugge	Zeebruges

English	French	Flemish
Monday	lundi	maandag
Tuesday	mardi	dinsdag
Wednesday	mercredi	woensday
Thursday	jeudi	donderdag
Friday	vendredi	vrijdag
Saturday	samedi	zaterday
Sunday	dimanche	zondag
today	aujourd'hui	vandaag
yesterday	hier	gisteren
Tomorrow	demain	morgen
morning	matin	morgen/ochtend
afternoon	après-midi	namiddag
evening	soir	avond
yes	oui	ja
no	non	nee
please	s'il vous plaît	astublieft
thank you	merci	dank u
Hello	bonjour	goedemorgen
good evening	bon soir	goedenavond
goodbye	au revoir	tot ziens
How are you?	Comment allez vous?	Hoe maakt u het?
Very well thank you	Très bien merci	Goed, dank u
How much?	Combien?	hoeveel?
Do you speak English?	Parlez-vous anglais?	Spreekt u engels?
My name is . . .	Je m'appelle . . .	Mijn naam is . . .
I do not understand	Je ne comprends pas	Ik Begrijp het niet
I don't know	Je ne sais pas	Ik weet het niet
I would like	Je voudrais	Ik wil graag
Could I have the bill please	L'addition s'il vous plaît	De rekening, alstublieft
Where is . . .?	Où est . . .?	Waar is . . .?
I'm looking for . . .	Je cherche . . .	Ik zoek . . .
open	ouvert	open
closed	fermé	gesloten
What is the time?	Quelle heure est-il?	Hoe laat is het?

USEFUL ADDRESSES

◆ "Communes" and "Entités"

The *communes* (districts) of southern Belgium were restructured, following administrative changes in the 1960's, into larger units or *entités*. Some of these are made up of only one former *commune* while others, made up of more than one district, carry the name of the former principal *commune*, and yet others have been given a new name which is a combination of two of the original names.
The places referred to in the useful addresses section have been grouped by *entité* (the largest units). For each of these the full address, giving the exact district *commune* has been supplied. Thus, in the section concerning the *entité* of Dinant, under the heading "places to visit", you will find the "Spanish House", and also the name of the exact place where this is located: Bouvignes-sur-Meuse.
The following list gives a reference list for all the *communes* and their corresponding *entités*. In the first column is the name of the *commune* (in bold where it is also the name of the *entité*), then, next to it, that of the *entité* to which it belongs. For example, Alle-sur-Semois is part of the *entité* of Vresse-sur-Semois.

Alle-sur-Semois ◆ *369*	**Vresse-sur-Semois**
Andenne ◆ *359*	**Andenne**
Anhée ◆ *359*	**Anhée**
Annevoie-Rouillon ◆ *359*	**Anhee**
Anseremme ◆ *359*	**Dinant**
Antoing ◆ *372*	**Antoing**
Arbre ◆ *362*	**Profondeville**
Arlon ◆ *367*	**Arlon**
Ath ◆ *372*	**Ath**
Aubel ◆ *363*	**Aubel**
Awenne ◆ *367*	**St-Hubert**
Awirs ◆ *360*	**Flemalle**
Aywaille ◆ *363*	**Aywaille**
Baisy-Thy ◆ *362*	**Villiers-la-Ville**
Basse-Bodeux ◆ *366*	**Trois-Ponts**
Bastogne ◆ *367*	**Bastogne**
Baulers ◆ *371*	**Nivelles**
Beaumont ◆ *370*	**Beaumont**
Beloeil ◆ *372*	**Belœil-Quevaucamps**
Binche ◆ *372*	**Binche**
Blégny-Trembleur ◆ *356, 372*	**Blégny**
Bouffioulx ◆ *370*	**Chatelet**
Bouillon ◆ *367*	**Bouillon**
Boussu-lez-Walcourt ◆ *370*	**Froid Chapelle**
Bouvignes-sur-Meuse ◆ *359*	**Dinant**
Braine l'Alleud ◆ *355*	**Braine l'Alleud**
Braine-le-Comte ◆ *373*	**Braine-le-Comte**
Brugelette ◆ *373*	**Brugelette**
Brussels ◆ *351*	**Brussels**
Burg-Reuland ◆ *363*	**Burg-Reuland**
Cambrom-Casteau ◆ *373*	**Brugelette**
Celles ◆ *360*	**Houyet**
Charleroi ◆ *369*	**Charleroi**
Chaud Fontaine ◆ *364*	**Chaud Fontaine**
Chimay ◆ *370*	**Chimay**
Comblain-la-Tour ◆ *364*	**Comblain-au-Pont**
Corbion ◆ *367*	**Bouillon**
Corroy-le-Chateau ◆ *360*	**Gembloux**
Couvin ◆ *370*	**Couvin**
Crupet ◆ *359*	**Assesse**
Dalhem ◆ *364*	**Dalhem**
Daverdisse ◆ *368*	**Daverdisse**
Dinant ◆ *359*	**Dinant**
Dorinne ◆ *362*	**Yvoir**
Durbuy ◆ *364*	**Durbuy**
Écaussinnes-Lalaing ◆ *373*	**Écaussines**
Ellezelles ◆ *373*	**Lessines**
Enghien ◆ *373*	**Enghien**
Eupen ◆ *364*	**Eupen**
Falaen ◆ *361*	**Onhaye**
Frameries ◆ *373*	**Frameries**
Franc-Waret ◆ *360*	**Fernelmont**
Francorchamps ◆ *366*	**Stavelot**
Furfooz ◆ *359*	**Dinant**
Gembloux ◆ *360*	**Gembloux**
Genval ◆ *355*	**Rixensart**
Gerpinnes ◆ *370*	**Gerpinnes**
Gesves ◆ *360*	**Gesves**
Godarville ◆ *357*	**Chapelle-lez-Herlaimont**
Goesnes ◆ *361*	**Ohey**
Gozée ◆ *371*	**Thuin**
Grand Halleux ◆ *366*	**Vielsalm**
Habay-la-Neuve ◆ *368*	**Habay**
Ham-sur-Heure ◆ *370*	**Ham-sur-Heure**
Han-sur-Lesse ◆ *362*	**Rochefort**
Hanzinne ◆ *370*	**Florennes**
Harzé ◆ *363*	**Aywaille**
Hastière ◆ *360*	**Hastière**

- VIEW
- CITY CENTER
- ISOLATED
- PARKING
- SUPERVISED GARAGE
- TELEVISION
- QUIET
- SWIMMING POOL
- CREDIT CARDS
- REDUCTIONS FOR CHILDREN
- NO PETS
- MUSIC
- LIVE BANDS
- PARK, GARDEN
- OUTDOOR TABLES
- AIR CONDITIONING
- CONFERENCE ROOMS

UK/US

UK

BELGIAN TOURIST OFFICE
29 Princes Street,
London W1
Tel. (0171) 629 0230

US

BELGIAN TOURIST OFFICE
780 Third Avenue,
Suite 1501,
New York 10017
Tel. (212) 758 8130

TRANSPORT

UK

AIRLINES
BRITISH AIRWAYS
Tel. (0345) 222 111
SABENA
Tel. (0181) 780 1444

BELGIAN NATIONAL RAILWAYS
Presnick House
10 Greyroad Place
London SW1
Tel. and Fax
(0171) 233 0360

BRITISH RAIL INTERNATIONAL
Tel. (0171) 834 2345

NATIONAL EXPRESS/ EUROLINES
Tel. (0171) 730 0202
or (0171) 730 3499
(credit card bookings)

CHANNEL TUNNEL
LE SHUTTLE
Tel. (0990) 353535
EUROSTAR
Tel. (0345) 881881

FERRIES
SALLY LINE
Tel. (01843) 595522
P&O
Tel. (0181) 575 8555

US

AIRLINES
AMERICAN AIRWAYS
Tel. (800) 624 6262
SABENA
Tel. (212) 247 8390

TOUR OPERATORS

UK

HOLTS BATTLEFIELD TOURS
Golden Key Building
15 Market Street
Sandwich, Kent CT13
Tel. (01304) 612248

SWAN HELLENIC ART TREASURES TOURS
77 New Oxford Street
London WC1
Tel. (0171) 831 1676

CAR RENTAL

UK

AVIS CAR RENTAL
Tel. (0181) 848 8733

BUDGET RENT A CAR
Tel. (0171) 495 5533

EURODOLLAR
Tel. (0171) 272 2273

EUROPCAR
Tel. (0171) 387 2276

HERTZ
Tel. (0171) 730 8323

GENERAL

USEFUL INFORMATION

AMERICAN EMBASSY
27 boulevard du Régent
1000 Brussels
Tel. (2) 518 38 30

BRITISH EMBASSY
85 rue Arlon
1040 Brussels
Tel. (2) 287 62 11

TOURIST PROMOTION OFFICE AND THE TOURIST FEDERATION OF THE PROVINCE OF BRABANT
61 rue du Marché-aux-Herbes
1000 Brussels
Tel. (2) 504 02 00

EMERGENCIES

ACCIDENT EMERGENCY/ FIRE BRIGADE
Dial 100
POLICE
Dial 101

RED CROSS (AMBULANCE)
Dial 105

TRANSPORT

SNCB
(Belgian national railways)
Information office
Tel. (2) 219 26 40
Tel. (2) 219 28 80
Open 6am–10.30pm

TEC
(Bus company serving the whole of southern Belgium)
Bruxelles-Capitale
Tel. (2) 515 20 00
Province of Brabant
Tel. (10) 48 04 04
Province of Hainaut
Tel. (65) 38 88 15
Province of Liège
Tel. (41) 61 84 44
Province of Luxembourg
Tel. (161) 23 21 78
Province of Namur
Tel. (81) 72 08 40

CAR RENTAL

CENTRAL RESERVATIONS
AVIS
Tel. (2) 735 23 88

EUROP CAR
Tel. (2) 348 92 12

HERTZ
Tel. (2) 735 40 50

EURODOLLAR (ADA)
Tel. (1) 49 58 44 44

RENT A CAR
Tel. (1) 46 82 60 60

ROAD INFORMATION

TOURING CLUB OF BELGIUM
441 rue de la Loi
1000 Brussels
Tel. (2) 233 22 11
Eleven other branches throughout Brussels.

ROYAL AUTOMOBILE CLUB OF BELGIUM
53 rue d'Arlon
1040 Brussels
Tel. (2) 230 08 10

ACCOMMODATION

AGRITOURISME
31 rue du Sablon
6600 Bastogne
Tel. (61) 21 31 06
◆ *325*

BELSUD RÉSERVATION
61 rue du Marché-aux-Herbes
1000 Brussels
Tel. (2) 504 02 80
◆ *325*

BTR
(Belgian Tourist Reservations)
111 bd Anspach
Box 4
1000 Brussels
Tel. (2) 513 74 84
◆ *325*

FÉDÉRATION WALLONNE DES AMIS DE LA NATURE
MAISON VERTE
18 rue Frères Descamps
7800 Ath
Tel. (68) 28 09
◆ *325*

GÎTES D'ÉTAPE DU CBTJ
31 rue Montoyer,
Box B
1040 Brussels
Tel. (2) 512 54 47
◆ *325*

GIWAL
32 av. Montéfiore
4130 Esneux
Tel. (41) 80 15 82
◆ *325*

UTRA – UPA
94–96 rue Dansaert
1000 Brussels
Tel. (2) 511 07 37
◆ *325*

YOUTH HOSTEL
52 rue Van Oost
1050 Brussels
Tel. (2) 215 31 00
◆ *325*

NATURE AND LEISURE

ASSOCIATION NATIONALE DU TOURISME ÉQUESTRE
12 rue du Moulin
1331 Rosières
Information on horseriding and pony treks throughout southern Belgium.
◆ *337*

AUSTRAL BORÉAL
41 rue Auguste Danse
1180 Brussels
Tel. (2) 345 52 10
Two- and three-day walks throughout the year.
◆ *337*

CARAVANES DE LA JEUNESSE BELGE
216 chaussée d'Ixelles
1050 Brussels
Tel. (2) 640 97 85
Fax (2) 646 35 95
Weekend rambles open to all ages.
◆ 337

CLUB ALPIN BELGE
19 rue de l'Aurore
1050 Brussels
Tel. (2) 648 86 11
◆ 338

DIRECTION GÉNÉRALE DES RESOURCES NATURELLES ET DE L'ENVIRONNEMENT
15 av. Prince de Liège
5100 Namur
Tel. (81) 32 12 11
◆ 338

ÉDUCATION-ENVIRONNEMENT
Université de Liège
Department of Botany
Building B 22
Domine du Sart-Tilman
4000 Liège
Tel. (41) 56 38 57
Fax (41) 56 38 40
Nature walks.
◆ 337

MAISON DE LA RANDONNÉE
30 rue Ravenstein
1000 Brussels
Tel. (2) 514 32 72
Passes for the international network of major walks and the Transardennaise. There is also an office at 83 rue St-Gilles 4000 Liège Tel. (41) 23 71 64.
◆ 337

MAISON LIÉGEOISE DE L'ENVIRONNEMENT
36 rue de la Régence
4000 Liège
Tel. (41) 22 19 61
Sells booklets and guides to the walks offered by the Éducation-Environnement.
◆ 335

NATIONAL GEOGRAPHICAL INSTITUTE
Abbaye de la Cambre,
1050 Brussels
Tel. (2) 648 52 82
Publishes and sells extremely detailed maps for the major walks.
◆ 337

PASSEPORT AVENTURE ASBL
18 av. des Bouleaux
1959 Kraainem
Tel. (2) 731 16 63
Weekend walks and introductions to trekking in the Fagnes, in Gaume, and in the valleys of the Semois and Warche.
◆ 337

RÉSERVES NATURELLES ET ORNITHOLOGIQUES DE BELGIQUE
103, rue Royale Ste-Marie
1030 Brussels
Tel. (2) 245 43 00
Regularly organizes half-day guided walking tours of the nature reserves and bird sanctuaries in southern Belgium.
◆ 335

"SENTIERS DE GRANDES RANDONNÉES" ASSOCIATION (SGR ASBL)
27 rue Chéra
4141 Louveigné
Tel. (41) 60 81 77
Head office of the walking association. Maps and guides for all the major walks in southern Belgium.
◆ 336

UNION BELGE DE SPÉLÉOLOGIE
CHÂTEAU DE GÉRONSART
1 rue du Pont-de-Briques
5100 Jambes
Potholers association of Belgium.
◆ 338

BRUSSELS

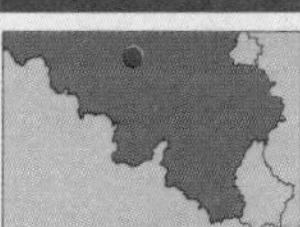

POSTAL CODE 1000

PRACTICAL INFORMATION

ACOTRA
38 rue de la Montagne
1000 Brussels
Tel. (2) 513 44 80
Information for the young.
◆ 326

ARAU TOURVILLE
2 rue du Midi
1000 Brussels
Tel. (2) 513 47 61
Brussels coach tours.
◆ 326

BICYCLE RENTAL
BIKE IN
18 rue Kelle
1200 Brussels
Tel. (2) 763 13 78
CYCLES CYD
14 av. E.Pirmez 1040 Brussels
Tel. (2) 640 17 60
JO BIKES
4 rue Général Fives
1040 Brussels
Tel. (2) 647 46 71
VLERICK
20 bd d'Anvers1000 Brussels
Tel. (2) 219 92 28

DE BOECK
8 rue de la Colline
1000 Brussels
Tel. (2) 513 77 44
Coach tours of Brussels.
◆ 326

DE BOECK INCOMING
48 pl. de Brouckère
Tel. (2) 218 68 98
Coach tours of Brussels.
◆ 326

EUROLINES
Boarding reservations
50 pl. de Brouckère
1000 Brussels
Tel. (2) 21 70 00 25
◆ 327

OTB (BRUSSELS' TOURIST OFFICE)
34 rue aux Laines
1000 Brussels
Tel. (2) 512 12 80

STIB
20 galerie de la Toison d'Or
1000 Brussels
Tel. (2) 515 20 00
Information on Brussels transport.
◆ 330

TAXI COMPANIES
ATR
Tel. (2) 242 22 22
AUTOLUXE
Tel. (2) 512 31 23
TAXI ORANGE
Tel. (2) 513 62 00
TAXI VERT
Tel. (2) 511 22 44

ENTERTAINMENT

ATELIER STE-ANNE
75–77 rue des Tanneurs
1000 Brussels
Tel. (2) 513 19 28

BRUSSELS INTERNATIONAL FILM FESTIVAL
30 chaussée de Louvain
1030 Brussels
Tel. (2) 218 10 55
The festival takes place every January and shows a selection of international movies, new Belgian productions, and a retrospective of a famous personality.

BRUSSELS INTERNATIONAL FESTIVAL OF FANTASY, SCIENCE FICTION AND THRILLERS
144 av. de la Reine
1210 Brussels
Tel. (2) 242 17 13

CONCOURS INTERNATIONAL REINE ÉLISABETH
20 rue aux Laines
1000 Brussels
Tel. (2) 513 00 99
An important musical event: the finals of the competition from which the twelve best entries go on to be staged at the Palais des Beaux-Arts.

HALLES DE SCHAERBEEK
22A rue Royale-Ste-Marie
1030 Brussels
Tel. (2) 218 00 31
Equally interesting for its architecture as for the performances which are given here, since this former covered market is a superb example of the glass architecture of the 19th century.

KINÉPOLIS
Bruparck
1 bd du Centenaire
1020 Brussels
Tel. (2) 478 04 50

MUSÉE DU CINÉMA
9 rue Baron Horta
1000 Brussels
Tel. 507 83 70
Permanent exhibition.

Old movies shown. Silent movies (two screenings per day with piano accompaniment).

THÉÂTRE NATIONAL DE BELGIQUE
Centre Rogier
Place Rogier
1210 Brussels
Tel. (2) 217 03 03

THÉÂTRE DE LA MONNAIE
Place de la Monnaie
1000 Brussels
Tel. (2) 218 12 11
Box office open from 11am to 6pm (Rue de la Reine).

THÉÂTRE ROYAL DU PARC
Rue de la Loi
1000 Brussels
Tel. (2) 511 41 49
Box office open from 11am to 6pm. This theater is renowned for its varied program of the classics, new plays and grand and spectacular productions.

THÉÂTRE VARIA
78 rue du Sceptre
1040 Brussels
Tel. (2) 640 82 58
Box office open Mon.–Fri., 11.30am–2pm and 4.30–7pm
Close to the European Community headquarters, the program includes classics and major new plays.

RAFFINERIE DU PLAN K
21 rue de Manchester
1070 Brussels
Tel. (2) 511 83 01
Performance space famous for its experimental theater.

CULTURE

AUTOWORLD
PALAIS MONDIAL DE L'AUTOMOBILE
11 parc du Cinquantenaire
1040 Brussels
Tel. (2) 736 41 65
Open Apr.–Sep. 10am–6pm, Oct.–Mar. 10am–5pm
Closed Christmas Day and Jan. 1.
History of the automobile.

LE BÉGUINAGE
8 rue du Chapelain
1070 Brussels
Tel. (2) 521 13 83
Open 10am–noon and 2–5pm

BIBLIOTHÈQUE ROYALE ALBERT IER (OR ALBERTINE)
Mont des Arts
1000 Brussels
CABINETS DE DONATIONS AND MUSÉE DU LIVRE
Tel. (2) 519 53 54
Open Mon., Wed. and Sat. 2–4.45pm
Museum of books and collections of donated works.
MUSÉE DE L'IMPRIMERIE
Tel. (2) 519 53 56
Open Mon.–Sat. 10am–5pm
Museum of printing.

CATHEDRAL OF ST-MICHEL
Parvis Ste-Gudule
Tel. (2) 219 68 34
Open summer 7am–7pm, winter 7am–6pm.
Visits to the crypt by appointment only.

CENTRE BELGE DE LA BANDE DESSINÉE
20, rue des Sables
Open 10am–6pm
Closed Mon., Jan. 1, Nov. 1 and Dec. 25
Comic strip museum.

DOMAINE ROYAL DE LAEKEN
1020 Brussels
SERRES ROYALES
av. du parc Royal
These glasshouses are open for a few days each year from April to May. For information contact TIB.
PAVILLON CHINOIS
44 av. Van Praet,
Tel. (2) 268 16 08
Open Tue.–Sun. 9.30am–12.30pm and 1.30–4.50pm
TOUR JAPONAIS
44 av. Van Praet,
Tel. (2) 2868 16 08
Open Tue.–Sun. 10am–4.45pm
Closed Jan. 1., May 1, Nov. 1, Nov. 11, Christmas Day

HÔTEL DE VILLE
Grand-Place
1000 Brussels
Tel. (2) 512 75 54
Open Apr.–Sep., Tue.–Fri. 9.30am–12.30pm and 1.45pm–5pm, Sun. and public holidays 10am–noon and 2–4pm; Oct.–Mar., Tue.–Fri. until 4pm Sun. and public holidays same opening times. Closed some public holidays

HÔTEL E.-HANNON
GALERIE CONTRETYPE
1 av. de la Jonction
Open Tue.–Sun. 2–5.30pm
This beautiful Art Nouveau house is now a gallery of photography.

HÔTEL SOLVAY
224 av. Louise
1050 Brussels
Tel. (2) 647 37 33
Visits by appointment; apply in writing giving telephone number.

HÔTEL VAN EETELDE
4 av. Palmerston
1040 Brussels
Visits by request only. Contact the ARAU *◆ 351 ◆ 326*

MAISON D'ÉRASME
31 rue du Chapitre
1070 Brussels
Tel. (2) 521 13 83
Open 10am–noon and 2–5pm.

MAISON DU ROI
MUSÉE DE LA VILLE DE BRUSSELS
29–33 Grand-Place
Tel. (2) 511 27 42
Open Apr.–Sep., Mon.–Fri. 10am–12.30pm and 1.30–5pm, Thur. 10am–5pm, Sat., Sun. and public holidays 10am–1pm; Oct.–Mar., Mon.–Fri. until 4pm
Closed Jan. 1., May 1, Nov. 1, Nov. 11 and Christmas Day

MAISON TASSEL
6 rue P.-E.-Janson
1040 Brussels
Tel. (2) 380 17 81
Group visits only, by appointment.

MUSÉE DU FOLKLORE
Bd du Midi
1000 Brussels
Tel. (2) 534 25 52
Open Tue.–Sun. 10am–5pm

MUSÉE HORTA
23–25 rue Américaine
Tel. (2) 338 42 20
Open 2–5.30pm
Closed Mon.
Art nouveau gems.

MUSÉE INSTRUMENTAL
Currently closed to the public. The museum is housed in a beautiful Art Nouveau building in an Old English style. Located on on the corner of Rue Villa-Hermosa.

MUSÉE ROYAL DE L'ARMÉE ET D'HISTOIRE MILITAIRE
3 parc du Cinquantenaire
1040 Brussels
Tel. (2) 733 44 93
Open 9am–noon and 1–4.45pm
Closed Mon. and public holidays

MUSÉE ROYAL D'HISTOIRE NATURELLE
260 chaussée de Wavre
1040 Brussels
Tel. (2) 6327 42 38
Open Tue.–Sat. 9.30am–4.45pm
Sun. 9.30am–6pm
Closed Mon.
Natural history museum. *◆357*

MUSÉE VAN BUREEN
41 av. Léo Errera
Tel. (2) 343 48 51
Guided tour Monday at 2pm, other days by appointment. 1930's building which houses a collection of pictures from the 16th to 20th centuries.

MUSÉE WIERTZ
62, rue Vautier
1040 Brussels
Tel. (2) 648 17 18

Open Apr.–Sep.
10am–noon and
1–5pm, Oct.–Mar.
until 4pm

MUSÉES ROYAUX D'ART AND D'HISTOIRE
Parc du Cinquantenaire
Av. des Nerviens
Tel. (2) 773 96 10
Open Tue.–Fri. 9.30am–5pm, Sat.–Sun. 10am–5pm
Closed Mon. and public holidays

MUSÉES ROYAUX DES BEAUX-ARTS DE BELGIQUE
1000 Brussels
ANCIENT ART
3 rue de la Régence
Tel. (2) 508 32 11
Open Tue.–Sun. 10am–noon and 1–5pm Closed Mon.
MODERN ART
1–2 place Royale
Tel. (2) 508 32 11
Open Tue.–Sun. 10am–1pm and 2–5pm Closed Mon.

HOTELS, ACCOMMODATION

LE XVIIe ***
25 rue de la Madeleine
1000 Brussels
Tel. (2) 502 57 44
Fax (2) 502 64 24
This elegant hotel was once a private residence. Located close to the central station and the gilded gables of the Grand-Place.
Double rooms: 5500–6100BF

ATLAS**
30 rue du Vieux-Marché-aux-Grains
1000 Brussels
Tel. (2) 502 60 06
Fax (2) 502 69 35
In the heart of the old part of Brussels.
Double rooms: 3,800–4,300BF

BREUGHEL YOUTH HOSTEL
2 rue de St-Esprit
1000 Brussels
Tel. (2) 511 04 36
Fax (2) 512 07 11

LE CHAMBORD***
82 rue de Namur
1000 Brussels
Tel. (2) 513 41 19
Fax (2) 514 08 47
69 rooms, some with south-facing terraces and a view over the city.
Double rooms: 4295–4795BF

JACQUES BREL YOUTH HOSTEL
30, rue de la Sablonnière
1000 Brussels
Tel. (2) 218 01 87
Fax (2) 217 20 06

JEAN NIHON YOUTH HOSTEL
4 rue de l'Éléphant
1080 Brussels
Tel. (2) 410 38 58
Fax (2) 410 39 05

HOTEL-RESTAURANTS

ASTORIA*****
103 rue Royale
1000 Brussels
Tel. (2) 217 62 90
Fax (2) 217 11 50
HOTEL
Built in 1908, this delightful Belle Époque hotel is now part of the Pullman-Sofitel chain.
Double rooms: 6,500–12,500BF
RESTAURANT AND BAR
The Palais Royal in a Louis XVI style setting. The Pullman bar is an exact copy of its original on the European express train La Flèche d'Or.

AMIGO*****
1–3 rue de l'Amigo
1000 Brussels
Tel. (2) 547 47 47
Fax (2) 513 52 77
Spanish renassance-style hotel built on the site of a 16th-century gaol. The motto of the establishmentment is "Comme un ami chez soi" ("Like a friend in his own home").
Restaurant and bar.
Double rooms: 6,750–8,550BF

CONRAD HILTON*****
71 av. Louise
1050 Brussels
Tel. (2) 542 42 42
Fax (2) 542 42 00
HOTEL
Double rooms: 8,500–16,000BF
RESTAURANT
LA MAISON DE MAÎTRE
Superb cuisine. Rated Michelin 1-star.
Café Wiltcher's, bar.

HILTON INTERNATIONAL
38 bld de Waterloo
1000 Brussels
Tel. (2) 504 11 11
Fax (2) 504 21 11
HOTEL
441 rooms.
Rooms: 8,800–13,700BF
RESTAURANT
Maison du Bœuf
Hotel restaurant with Michelin 1-star rating. Specialties: roast quail with fresh thyme. Roast ribs of beef with salt, Maison du Bœuf steak tartare.
Menus: lunch 1,590–2,690BF
À la carte: 2,500–2,750BF
CAFÉ
Café d'Egment
Menus: lunch 1,040BF
À la carte: 1,100–1,400BF

MÉTROPOLE*****
31 pl. de Brouckère
1000 Brussels
Tel. (2) 217 23 00
Fax (2) 218 02 20
Founded in 1894. The only remaining 19th-century hotel in Brussels. The interior décor of the palace was designed by the architect Alban Chambon in Renaissance and Empire styles.
Double rooms: 8,400–11,400BF
RESTAURANT
The Alban Chambon restaurant is among the ten best in the region of Bruxelles-Capitale.
BAR
Le XIXe.

MONTGOMERY*****
134 av. de Tervuren
1150 Brussels
Tel. (2) 741 85 11
Fax (2) 741 85 00
HOTEL
Sauna, gym.
Double rooms: 11,500–18,000BF
RESTAURANT
La Duchesse.

NEW SIRU***
1 pl. Rogier
1210 Brussels
Tel. (2) 217 75 80
Fax (2) 218 33 03
HOTEL
Double rooms: 3,500–5,900BF
RESTAURANT
New Brasserie Siru. Numerous pictures on the walls.

RADISSON SAS ROYAL*****
47 rue Fossé-aux-Loups
1000 Brussels
Tel. (2) 219 28 28
Fax (2) 219 62 62
HOTEL
281 rooms.
Double rooms: 11,900BF
RESTAURANT
Sea Grill Jacques Le Divellec
Closed Sat. lunchtime and Sun.
Seafood restaurant. Specialties: Marinated St-Jacques pan-fried foie gras.
À la carte: 3,000–4,000BF
HOTEL RESTAURANT:
L'Atrium
À la carte: 1,500–2,000BF

RENAISSANCE*****
19 rue du Parnasse
1040 Brussels
Tel. (2) 505 29 29
Fax (2) 505 25 55
HOTEL
Double rooms: 8,500–9,500BF
RESTAURANTS
La Brasserie and le Marché Parnasse
À la carte: 900–1,200BF
Specialties: European and asiatic cuisine.

ROYAL WINDSOR****
5–7 rue Duquesnoy
1000 Brussels
Tel. (2) 511 42 15
Fax (2) 511 60 04
HOTEL
Double rooms: 10,150BF
RESTAURANT
Les 4 Saisons
Closed Sat. lunchtime
Specialties: cappucino de moules.

À la carte: 1,600–2,100BF

STANHOPE***
9 rue du Commerce
1040 Brussels
Tel. (2) 506 91 11
Fax (2) 512 17 08
HOTEL
English-style rooms. Sauna, fitness center. Double rooms: 12,500–14,500BF
RESTAURANT
Le Brighton

RESTAURANTS

AUX ARMES DE BRUSSELS
13 rue des Bouchers
1000 Brussels
Tel. (2) 511 55 50
Closed Mon.
Belgian cuisine: carbonnade of beef with beer, mussels in white wine. À la carte: 1,000–1,500BF Menus: 990BF and 1,695BF

LES BAGUETTES IMPÉRIALES
70 av. J. Sobieski
1020 Brussels
Tel. (2) 479 67 32
Fax (2) 479 67 32
Closed Tue., Sun. eve, 2 weeks at Easter and Aug.
Michelin 1-star establishment serving Vietnamese cuisine. Specialties: lobster, crispy pancakes with Vietnamese-style lobster, baby pigeon stuffed with swallow's nest. À la carte: 2,050–2,400BF

BLEU DE TOI
73 rue des Alexiens
1000 Brussels
Tel. (2) 502 43 71
Closed Sat. and Sun. lunchtime
Brasserie-style cooking in a theater-inspired setting. À la carte: 1,000–1,500BF

BRUNEAU
73–75 av. Broustin
1080 Brussels
Tel. (2) 427 69 78
Closed Sat. lunchtime and Tue. eve and Wed., May 15–Jun. 5 and Dec. 24–Jan. 3
Michelin 3-star establishment serving French cuisine. Lunchtime menu: 1,850BF À la carte: 3,000–5,000BF

CLAUDE DUPONT
46 av. Vital Riethuisen
1080 Brussels
Tel. (2) 426 00 00
Michelin 2-star restaurant. Specialties: coquille St-Jacques in a beurre blanc and parsley sauce, lobster and sole fricassée, roast saddle of goat with thyme and pepper. Menus: lunch 1,750–3,200BF À la carte: 2,150–2,700BF

COMME CHEZ SOI
23 pl. Rouppe
1000 Brussels
Tel. (2) 512 29 21
Closed Sun. and Mon.
French cuisine. Founded in 1926. One of the best restaurants in Belgium. Art Nouveau décor. Awarded Michelin 3-stars. À la carte: 3,000–5,000BF. Menus: 1,875, 3,250 and 4,250BF

ÉCAILLER DU PALAIS ROYAL
18 rue Bodenbroek
1000 Brussels
Tel. (2) 511 99 50
Fax (2) 511 99 51
Closed Sun., Apr. 5–13, Aug. and public holidays
Seafood restaurant with a 1-star Michelin rating. Specialties: Coquilles St-Jacques with cep mushrooms, turbot with sesame and parsley sauce, Lobster pot-au-feu with celery. À la carte: 2,700–3,000BF

LA GRIGNOTIÈRE
2041 chaussée de Wavre
1160 Brussels
Tel. and fax (2) 672 81 85
Closed Sun., Mon., public holidays and Aug.
Michelin 1-star establishment. Specialties: Steamed cod with tomato and basil, crispy baby pigeon with foie gras and almonds, langoustines with asparagus. Menu: 1,300–1,900BF

IN'T SPINNEKOPKE
1 pl. du Jardin-aux-Fleurs
1000 Brussels
Tel. (2) 511 86 95
Closed Sat. lunchtime and Sun.
Belgian-beer cuisine in a bar dating from 1762. One hundred varieties of local beers. À la carte: 1,000–1,500BF

T'KELDERKE
15 Grand-Place
1000 Brussels
Tel. (2) 513 73 44

MAISON DU CYGNE
9 Grand-Place
1000 Brussels
Tel. (2) 511 82 44
Closed Sat. lunchtime and Sun.
French cuisine in a 17th century house. À la carte: 3,000–5,000BF. Menus: lunch 1,300BF and 1,600BF, dinner 2,200BF and 2,500BF

RESTAURANT DES TROIS COULEURS
453 av. de Tervuren
1150 Woluwe-St-Pierre
Tel. (2) 770 33 21
Closed Mon. and Tue.
French cuisine. À la carte: 2,500–3,000BF. Menu: 1 900BF

LES PETITS OIGNONS
13 rue Notre-Seigneur
Tel. (2) 512 47 38
Closed Sun.
French cuisine in a 17th-century residence. À la carte: 1,500–2,000BF Menus: lunch 650BF, dinner 950–1,500BF

LA QUINCAILLERIE
45 rue du Page
1050 Brussels
Tel. (2) 538 25 53
Closed Sat. lunchtime
Brasserie-style cuisine. Original décor. À la carte: 1,500–2,000BF

LA ROUE D'OR
26 rue des Chapeliers
1000 Brussels
Tel. (2) 514 25 54
Brasserie cuisine in an old café which has been redecorated in an Art Nouveau style. Murals in homage to Magritte. À la carte: 1,000–1,500BF

SEA GRILL
47 Fossé aux Loups
1000 Brussels
Tel. (2) 217 92 25
Fax (2) 219 62 62
Closed Apr. 7–14, Jul. 21–Aug. 18, Sat. lunchtime, Sun. and public holidays
Seafood restaurant with a 1-star Michelin rating. Specialties: steamed scallops, cress soup (in season), lobster, warm crab with parsley butter. Menu: 1,650–2,400BF À la carte: 2,050–2,600BF

LA TAVERNE DU PASSAGE
30 galerie de la Reine
1000 Brussels
Tel. (2) 512 37 32
The oldest brasserie in Brussels. Art Deco dating back to 1928. Belgian cuisine.

LA TORTUE DU ZOUTE
31 rue de Rollebeek
1000 Brussels
Tel. (2) 513 10 62
Closed Tue. and Sun. eve.
Seafood restaurant with an exotic décor. Specialties: crab soup, medallion of monkfish with puréed tomato and basil. À la carte: 1,500–2,000BF Menus: lunch 650BF, dinner 850BF and 1,350BF

LA TRUFFE NOIRE
12 bd de la Cambre
1050 Brussels
Tel. (2) 640 44 22
Fax (2) 647 97 04

Brussels – European Capital and Business City

Office for foreign affairs
2 rue Royale
1000 Brussels
Tel. (2) 518 17 11
Fax (2) 518 17 39

Conferences and fairs

Brussels Congress
61 rue Marché-aux-Herbes
1000 Brussels
Tel. (2) 504 02 75
Fax (2) 513 07 50

Palais des Congrès
3, Coudenberg
1000 Brussels
Tel. (2) 513 41 30
Fax (2) 514 21 12

Brussels International Fair
Pl. de Belgique
1020 Brussels
Tel. (2) 477 02 77
Fax (2) 477 03 90

Commerce and industry

Brussels chamber of commerce and industry
500 av. Louise
1050 Brussels
Tel. (2) 648 50 02
Fax (2) 640 93 28
Brings together more than two thousand firms. Seminars, meetings, language courses for foreign businesses.

Office for foreign investment
25 rue du Champ-de-Mars
1050 Brussels
Tel. (2) 513 97 00
Fax (2) 511 52 55
Services and information for new investors

Office for foreign trade
162 bd É.-JacqMayn
Box 36 WTC -Tour 1
1210 Brussels
Tel. (2) 209 35 11
Fax (2) 217 61 23

Société de Développement Régional de Brussels (SDRB)
6 rue Gabrielle-Petit
1210 Brussels
Tel. (2) 422 51 11
Fax (2) 422 51 12
Administrative office for the region's nineteen industrial and scientific parks. Also keeps a list of all available industrial buildings.

Société Régionale d'Investissement de Brussels (SRIB)
13 av. Mamix
1050 Brussels
Tel. (2) 511 64 83
Fax (2) 511 90 74
Regional office for investment in Brussels.

Union des Entreprises de Brussels
75 rue Botanique
1030 Brussels
Tel. (2) 219 32 23
Fax (2) 218 56 06
Offer its Promexport service – the first club for the country's exporters – and publishes the Brussels Export Directory containing more than a thousand addresses.

Services

EEBIC (Erasmus European Business and Innovation Centre)
40 av. Joseph-Wijbran
1070 Brussels
Tel. (2) 529 58 11
Fax (2) 529 59 11
Logistical support, management and technological assistance for small businesses.

Technopol
64 rue de la Fusée
1130 Brussels
Tel. (2) 215 92 00
Fax (2) 215 83 08
Program of health and safety, communication, food industry, precision engineering.

Téléport
Buro and Design Centre
Esplanade du Heysel
Box 4, 1020 Brussels
Tel. (2) 475 20 00
Fax (2) 475 20 10
Advanced technology: telematics and telecommunication.

Closed Sat. lunchtime, Sun., one week at Easter, Aug. 1–15 and Christmas
Elegant décor. Specialties: Carpaccio with truffles, white truffles (Oct.–end Dec.), St-Pierre with leek and truffles. Menu: lunch 1,450–3,475BF À la carte: 2,800–3,200BF

Villa Lorraine
75 av. du Vivier-d'Oie
1180 Brussels
Tel. (2) 374 31 63
Restaurant with 1-star Michelin rating. French cuisine. Specialties: Fricasséed lobster and oysters with Riesling, saddle of goat with raisins and spices. À la carte: 3,000–5,000BF Menus: lunch 1,750BF, dinner 3,000BF

Braine l'Alleud

Postal code 1420

Culture

Château de Bois-Seigneur-Isaac
1421 Ophain-Bois-Seigneur-Isaac
Tel. (67) 21 38 80
Only open the last two Sundays in June and the first Sunday in July, 2–6pm.

Musée de Cire
319 rte du Lion
1420 Braine l'Alleud
Tel. (2) 384 67 40
Open Apr.–Oct.
9am–6.30pm
Waxworks museum.

Restaurants

Le Cheval Fou
2 rue de l'Église
1421 Ophain
Tel. (2) 385 07 76

La Hulpe

Postal code
1310

Tourist information center
73 rue Delpierre
Tel. (2) 354 73 02

Culture

Château Solvay
Park open 9am–5pm

Rixensart

Postal code
1330

Hotel-restaurants

Château du Lac****
87 av. du Lac
1332 Genval
Tel. (2) 654 11 22
Fax (2) 653 62 00
Restaurant
Le Trèfle à 4
Closed Mon. and Tue.
Lakeside palace with an atmosphere of northern Italy. French cuisine. Double rooms: 4,500–8,600BF Menus: lunchtime 1,600BF, dinner 2,400 and 2,950BF

Tervuren

Postal code
3080

Culture

Musée Royal de l'Afrique Centrale
13 Leuvensesteenweg
Tel. (2) 769 52 11
Open Mar. 16–Oct.15
9am–5.30pm,
Oct. 16–Mar. 15
10am–4.30pm
Closed Mon.
The richest central African collection in the world. More than 250,000 pieces. Temporary exhibitions.

Woluwé St-Pierre

Restaurant

De Bijgaarden
20 I. Van Beverenstraat
(close to the castle)
Tel. (2) 466 44 85
Closed Sat. lunchtime and Sun., Apr. 7–15, Aug. 13–Sep. 4
Two-star Michelin establishment. Specialities: pheasant with white truffle, roast turbot with lobster bearnaise sauce. Menus: lunch 1,950–4,500BF À la carte: 3,350

BOAT TRIPS

FERRY TO TOURNAI
Tel. (69) 22 20 45
or (65) 36 04 64
Runs from May to October except on Mondays and public holidays.
Boat trips along the Escaut. An alternative way of discovering Tournai, the oldest city in Belgim.

BOAT TRIPS ALONG THE MEUSE

Sail across the Basse-Meuse departing from Huy (for information contact the tourist office ◆ 361) or from Blégny. The most beautiful crossings are across the Haute-Meuse: they give a totally different view of this delightful holiday spot dotted with its elegant, romantic villas stretching between Namur and Dinant. Other boat trips, going up-river toward the French border, enter into a world which consists of meandering waters, bare rocks, and gentle forests.

COMPAGNIE DES BATEAUX
64 rue Daoust
5500 Dinant
Tel. (82) 22 23 15
or (82) 22 43 97
Fax (82) 22 53 22

BATEAUX BAYARD
13 rue Caussin
5500 Dinant
Tel. (82) 22 30 42
Fax (82) 22 60 16

BATEAUX ANSIAUX "LE COPÈRE"
15 rue du Vélodrome
5500 Dinant
Tel. (82) 22 23 25
Fax (22) 33 44

TRAIN RIDES

RAILWAY MUSEUMS

CHEMIN DE FER DES TROIS VALLÉES
Information and reservations at
49–51 chaussée de Givet
5660 Mariembourg
Tel. (60) 31 24 40
Runs Jul.–Aug., Tue.–Thur. and Sat.–Sun. (from Mariembourg), Tue.–Wed. and Fri.–Mon. (from Dinant); Apr.–Jun. and Sep., Sat.–Sun. and public holidays
Discover the beautiful valleys of the Eau-Blanche, the Eau-Noire, of the Viroin (across Mariembourg, Treignes, Chimay) and of the Haute-Meuse (across Dinant-Givet) in an ancient steam train.

CHEMIN DE FER DES HAUTES FAGNES
Information and reservations
VENNBAHN V.O.E.
BAHNHOF RAEREN
70 Bahnhofstrasse
4730 Raeren
Tel. (87) 85 24 87
Fax (87) 85 16 18
Open Mon.–Sun., 9am–noon 9.30am–11.30am
Runs April to Oct. on Sun., the first Sat. of the month and public holidays.
This railway line links Eupen to Weywert, then branches toward Bullingen, and Trois-Ponts. There are connections with the national and local railway networks (SNCB and TEC), which also offer reduced rates and travel passes. Information on SNCB service is available in all stations; for information on TEC telephone (87) 74 25 92.

TOURIST TRAIN RIDES

BOUILLON
12 rue de Laitte
Tel. (61) 46 70 04
Runs from Feb. to Nov., at weekends., from Jul. to Aug.,daily Five-mile circuit.

LA LOUVIÈRE
Tel. (64) 66 25 61
Runs from May to Oct., Sat. and Sun., 10am–4pm, from Jul. to Aug., daily 10am–6pm.
Discover diverse modes of haulage. Reservations essential. Departure from the Italian cantina or the machine room at Bracquegnies.

NAMUR
Information and reservations
COMITÉ D'ANIMATION DE LA CITADELLE
8 rte la Merveilleuse
Tel. (81) 22 68 29
Runs from Apr. to Sep. 11am–7pm
Journey to one of the most important strongholds in Europe across its lush, green 20-acre setting.

NISMES
Tel. (60) 31 11 28
Runs from Apr. to Sep. 9am–7pm.
Discover in one hour the region's principle places of natural interest. One departure every hour.

REBECQ
Tel. (67) 67 01 20
Runs from May to Sep., Sun. and public holidays, from 2.45pm.
Take the 4-mile return journey which follows the Vallée des Oiseaux and the Senne between Rebecq and Rognon.

ROCHEFORT
SI (information and reservations)
5 rue de Behogne
Tel. (84) 21 25 37
Forty-five minute tour of the area: Apr.–Oct., weekends. and public holidays; Jun.–Sep. 15, daily. Three-hour circuit across this wooded region as far as Lavaux-Ste-Anne: May 15–Sep. 15, Wed. and Fri.

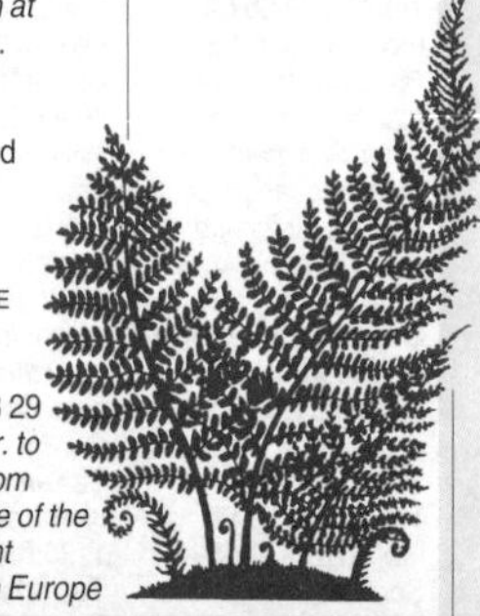

BOAT TRIPS ON THE HAUTE-MEUSE, SINGLE TICKETS AND ROUND TRIP (RT)

From Namur	Boat company	Namur – Wépion	1¾ hrs. RT	Jul.–Aug.
		Namur – Dinant	9am RT	Jul.–Aug.
		Panoramic Sambre-et-Meuse		Apr.–Aug.
From Dinant	Compagnie des Bateaux	Dinant – Anseremme	45 mins. RT	Apr.–Aug.
		Dinant – Freyr	1¾ hrs RT	Jul.–Aug.
		Dinant – Hastiere	4 hrs. RT	Jul.–Aug.
		Dinant – Namur	3½ hrs.	Jul.–Aug.
	Compagnie Bayard	Dinant – Anseremme	45 mins. RT	Apr.–Oct.
		Dinant – Freyr	1½ hrs. RT	May–Oct.
		Dinant – Agimont		May–Oct.
		Dinant – Namur	Single ticket	May–Sep.
	Société Ansiaux	Dinant – Givet	9am	Jul.–Aug.
		Dinant – Anseremme	45 mins.	Apr.–Oct.
		Dinant – Freyr	1¾ hrs.	Apr.–Oct.
		All journeys by request		Apr.–Oct.

AMUSEMENTS

FUN PARKS

MONDE SAUVAGE SAFARI
3 Fange de Deigné
4 920 Deigné-Aywaille
Tel. (41) 60 90 70
or (41) 60 81 40
Fax (41) 60 91 08
Open Mar. 15 – Nov. 15 10am–7pm
215-acre park made up of four different sections. One section of the safari park is full of African animals roaming freely. Take the tiny train or drive through this section. Another section is laid out as a kind of zoo; this can be visited on foot. There is also a children's farm with domestic animals, next to a children's park. An aviary full of exotic birds is situated right next to the restaurant.

TELECOO
4970 Stavelot
Tel. (80) 68 42 65
or (80) 68 42 45
Fax (80) 68 44 43
Open Apr.–Oct., 10am–7pm
Open throughout winter, weekends and school holidays
Situated at the foot of the Cascade de Coo. Largely suitable for adolescents. The chair lift ride gives you a view over the Amblève valley and the lake. Amusement park with bobsleigh rides, go-carts, rollercoaster, dodgems. Two-hundred acre game with a 40-minute train ride around it.

WALIBI
1300 Wavre
Tel. (10) 41 44 66
Fax (10) 41 10 66
Open May–Sep. 15, 10am–6pm
The many rides at this amusement park include a loop-the-loop train ride, a big wheel, rafting and canoeing and water ski-ing. There are also various thematic water rides, including the world of "A Thousand and One Nights" and a magic castle where you can take part in the adventures of Tintin. There is also Kangarooland for smaller children.

RECREATION CENTERS

MONT MOSAN RECREATION PARK
Plaine de Sarts
4500 Huy
Tel. (85) 23 29 96
Open Apr.–Oct.
10am–8pm

CENTRE DE DÉLASSEMENT DE CLAIRE-FONTAINE
7160 Godarville
Rue Clémenceau
Tel. (64) 44 86 75

CENTRE DE LOISIRS DE L'ORIENT
8 chemin de Mons
7500 Tournai
Tel. (69) 22 26 35

DOMAINE DES GROTTES DE HAN
Han-sur-Lesse
◆ *362*

RÉCRÉALLE
Alle-sur-Semois
◆ *369*

EDUCATIONAL

HISTORY

MINI-EUROPE-BRUPARCK
1020 Brussels
20 bd du Centenaire
Tel. (2) 478 05 50
or (2) 477 03 77
Open Apr.–Jun. 9.30am–6pm,
Jul.–Aug. 9.30am–8pm,
Sep.–Oct. 9.30am–6pm;
May–Sep., Sun.and public holidays closes one hour later
This 6-acre park contains some three hundred models of major European buildings and the great technological structures of the European Community at one twenty-fifth of the actual size. The catalog, included in the entrance price, gives information on European sociology, economy, technology, history and culture.

NATURAL SCIENCES

AQUARIUM DUBUISSON AND MUSÉE ZOOLOGIQUE
22 quai Van-Beneden
4020 Liège
Tel. (41) 66 50 00
Fax (41) 66 50 10
Open Mon.–Fri. 10.30am–12.30pm and 1.30–5.30pm,
weekends and public holidays, 10.30am–12.30pm and 2–6pm
Closed Dec. 24–26, 31 and Jan. 1.
Forty carefully constructed biotopes house more than 1,500 creatures. Three species of fish, coral and invertebrates. The museum contains skeletons and stuffed or preserved animals representing 18,000 species and showing the evolution of animal life.

ATOMIUM
1020 Brussels
Bd du Centenaire
Tel. (2) 477 09 77
Fax (2) 477 03 98
Open 10am–6pm
Two-hour guided visits. The atomium is built in the shape of an iron atom 165 million times its actual size. Four of the spheres contain a permanent biological research exhibition and one is dedicated to an exhibition of the cells of the human body and recently discovered viruses. The Biogénium offers a journey to the heart of our biological universe. Superb view from the highest point of the building, at 335 feet, open until 9.30pm from spring to summer. Combined tickets to the Atomium and Mini-Europe, with the Musée des Sciences Naturelles and the Meise botanical gardens.

MUSÉE DES SCIENCES NATURELLES
260 chaussée de Wavre
1040 Brussels
Tel. (2) 627 42 38
or (2) 627 42 34
Fax (2) 4646 44 66
Open 9.30am–4.45pm, Sun., 9.30am–6pm
Closed Mon., Jan. 1. and Christmas Day
Minerals from around the world and Belgium fauna. Termitiarium and a collection of live spiders. Fossils and some models of dinosaurs. Exhibitions on human evolution and different cultures and genetics.

SPACE TECHNOLOGY

BELGACOM
5 580 Lessive
63 rue de l'Antenne
Tel. (78) 11 88 22
Fax (84) 37 79 07
or (2) 217 50 05
Open Apr.–Nov., 5pm, Jul.–Aug. 9.30am–5.30pm
Land-based satellite telecommunication station. Discover state-of-the-art technology, learn how to set up a space communication program, or watch a movie of the launch of a satellite.

EUROSPACE CENTER
6890 Transinne
Tel. (61) 65 64 65
Fax (61) 65 64 61
Open 10am–5pm
Education and leisure center containing permanent exhibitions and a display of the astronauts' various procedures.

BIRDS AND BUTTERFLIES

EUROBUTTERFLY CENTER
5530 Yvoir
Domaine de Champalle
Tel. (82) 61 10 84
Open Jun. 15–Sep. 15
Butterfly farm and glasshouses with exotic butterflies and flowers. No dogs.

PARC DE PARADISO
Cambron Casteau
Open, Apr.–Oct. 9am–7pm
Tropical greenhouses and giant aviaries in enormous grounds.

WATERLOO

POSTAL CODE
1410

TOURIST INFORMATION CENTER
149 chaussée de Brussels
1040 Waterloo
Tel.(2) 354 99 10

CULTURE

MUSÉE WELLINGTON
147 chaussée de Brussels
1040 Waterloo
Open Apr.–mid-Nov. 9.30am–6.30pm, mid-Nov.–Mar. 10.30am–5pm

HOTEL-RESTAURANTS

HÔTEL LE 1815***
367–369 rte du Lion
Tel. (2) 387 00 60
Fax (2) 387 12 92
At the foot of the famous commemorative mound to the memory of Napoleon.
Double rooms: 4,500BF

RESTAURANTS

MAISON DU SEIGNEUR
389 chaussée de Tervuren
Tel. (2) 354 07 50
Closed Mon. and Tue.
French cuisine.
À la carte: 2 500–3 000BF
Menus: lunchtime 1,350BF, dinner 1,650 and 2,000BF

NAMUR

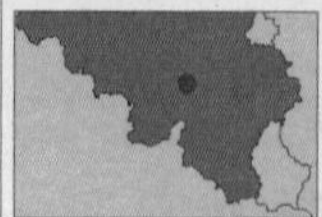

POSTAL CODE 5000

TOURIST FEDERATION OF THE PROVINCE DE NAMUR
3 rue Notre-Dame
5000 Namur
Tel. (81) 22 29 98

ENTERTAINMENT

FESTIVAL OF NAMUR
(Jul. and Sep.–Oct.)
Théâtre Royal de Namur
Pl. du Théâtre
5000 Namur
Tel. (81) 22 27 74

CULTURE

CITADEL
8 rte Merveilleuse
Tel. (81) 22 68 29
5000 Namur
Open Apr.–Sep.,daily 11am–7pm
Closed Aug. 1
One of the largest citadels in Europe.

HÔTEL DE GROESBEECK DE CROIX
3 rue J. Saintraint
Tel. (81) 22 21 39
5000 Namur
Visits by guided tour only Wed.–Mon. at 10am, 11am, 2pm, 3pm and 4pm.
Delightful museum with an interesting decorative arts collection.

MUSÉE ARCHÉOLOGIQUE
Halle à l'Chair
Rue du Pont
5000 Namur
Tel. (81) 23 16 21
Open 10am–5pm, Sat.–Sun. 10.30am–5pm
Collection of Roman and French archeological pieces.

MUSÉE FÉLICIEN ROPS
12 rue Furnal
Tel. (81) 22 01 10
5000 Namur
Open Easter–Nov. 1 10am–6pm, off season 10am–5pm.
Closed Tue. except during Jul. and Aug.
Late 19th-century works by the artist Félicien Rops.

MUSÉE DES ARTS ANCIENS DU NAMUROIS
HOTEL DE GAIFFIER D'HESTROY
24 rue de Fer
5000 Namur
Tel. (81) 22 00 65
Open Easter–Oct. 10am–12.30pm and 1.30pm–6pm.
Closed Tue.

TRANSPORT

In 1835, Léopold I founded the first railway line on the European continent. The line ended up in Brussels where soon, the rattle of a thousand tramlines would be heard. This modernity showed the enterprising spirit and economic power of Belgium, which, along with England, France and Bohemia, was one of the pioneers of the industry.
Several museums have now been dedicated to transport in general and the railway in particular.

MUSÉE DES CHEMINS DE FER BELGES
Gare du Nord
70 rue du Progrès
1210 Brussels
Tel. (2) 224 62 79

MUSÉE DU TRANSPORT URBAIN BRUXELLOIS
346B av. de Tervuren
1050 Brussels
Tel. (2) 515 31 08
Open Apr.–Sep., Sat., Sun. and public holidays 1–7pm
More than sixty locomotives from 1868 to the present day. Trams, which started running at the beginning of the 20th century, run across the Forest of Soignes and on the Musées de Woluwé line to Cinquantenaire.

MUSÉE ARCHÉOLOGIQUE AND FERROVIAIRE
22 rue de la Gare
Treignes
Open Apr.–Sep. 10am–12.30pm and 2–5.30pm, Oct.–Mar., Tue.–Sat., same opening times
A collection of 19th-century railway carriages and locomotives freshly painted in bright colors.

NATURE AND LEISURE

CAP NAM
Tourist Federation of the Province of Namur
3 rue Notre-Dame
5000 Namur
Tel. (81) 22 29 98
Offers package deals which include half-board accommodation and baggage transport for walks in the province of Namur.

MUSÉE PROVINCIAL DE LA FORÊT
7 rte Merveilleuse
5000 Namur
Tel. (81) 22 48 94
Open Jun. 15–Sep. 15 daily, Apr.–Jun. 15 and Sep. 1–15, Sat.–Thur., Nov.–Mar. by appointment only

ACCOMMODATION

BED & BREAKFAST
– M. AND MME DE RIBAUCOURT
38 chemin du Beau-Vallon
5100 Wépion
Tel. (81) 41 15 91
– MONSIEUR JACQUET
19 rue des Perce-Neige
5024 Marche-les-Dames
Tel. (81) 58 94 10

HÔTEL LE BEAU REGARD
1 av. Baron de Moreau
5000 Namur
Tel. (81) 23 00 28
Fax. (81) 24 12 09

HÔTEL LE ST-LOUP
4 rue St-Loup
5000 Namur
Tel. (81) 23 04 05
Fax (81) 23 09 43

YOUTH HOSTEL
8 av. Félicien Rop
5000 Namur
Tel. (81) 22 36 88
Fax (81) 22 44 12

HOTEL-RESTAURANTS

L'ESPIÈGLERIE***
13c, rue des Tanneries
5000 Namur
Tel. (81) 22 30 24

Not to be missed

Jazz
Brussels Jazz Club
13, Grand-Place
1000 Brussels
Tel. (2) 512 40 93
Travers
11, rue Traversière
1030 Brussels
Tel. (2) 218 40 86

Beer and bars
Musée de la Brasserie
10 Grand-Place
1000 Brussels
Open all year round, Mon.–Fri. 10am–noon and 2–5pm; Apr.–Oct., aussi Sat. 10am–noon
Musée Bruxellois de la Gueuze
56 rue Gheude
1070 Brussels
Open all year round, Mon.–Fri. 8.30am–4.30pm; Jun.–Oct., Sat. 9.30am–1pm; Nov.–Mar., Sat. 10am–6pm
Brussels beer museum.
Bièrodrome
21 pl. Fernand-Cocq
1050 Brussels
Tel. (2) 512 04 56
Falstaff
17–23 rue Mauss
1000 Brussels
Tel. (2) 511 87 89

Restaurant closed Sat. lunchtime and Sun.
Specialties: pheasant with chicory, baked perch with fennel.

Restaurants

La Bergerie****
100 rue de Mosanville
5101 Lives-sur-Meuse
Tel. (81) 58 06 13
Closed Sun. eve., Mon. and Tue.
Excellent restaurant. Specialties: pan-fried duck's liver with caramelized apples, poached trout.

Le Bietrume Picar**
15 rue Haute-Marcelle
5000 Namur
Tel. (81) 23 07 39
Closed Sun. eve. and Mon.

Brasserie Henry
3 pl. St-Aubain
5000 Namur
Tel. (81) 22 02 04
Menus: 490 and 780BF

Amay

Postal code 4540

Culture

Château de Jehay
Rue du Parc
4540 Jehay-Bodegnée
Tel. (85) 31 17 16
Open Jul.–Aug., Sat. Sun. 2–6pm

Andenne

Postal code 5300

Andenne tourist office
48 pl. des Tilleuls
5300 Andenne
Tel. (85) 84 62 72

Culture

Musée Communal de la Céramique
29 rue Charles Lapierre
Tel. (85) 84 41 81
5300 Andenne
Open Jul.–Aug., daily 2.30pm–5pm; May–Jun. and Sep., Tue., Fri.–Sun. and public holidays same opening times

Hotel-restaurants

La Ferme Beckaert**
330 pl. Moinnil
5300 Landenne-sur-Meuse
Tel. (85) 82 68 61
Fax (85) 82 50 81
Closed Sun.eve. and Mon.
Restaurant specializing in local dishes. 7 rooms. Menus: 975BF, 1,650BF and 1,850BF

Anhée

Postal code 5537

Tourist information center Meuse-Molignée
Pl. communale
5537 Anhée
Tel. (82) 61 12 61

Culture

Château d'Annevoie
5537 Annevoie-Rouillon
Tel. (82) 61 15 55
Gardens
Open Apr.–Nov. 1 9am–7pm, May–Aug., by guided tour only
Château
Open Jul.–Aug., 9.30am–1pm and 2pm–6.30pm, Easter–Jun. and Sep., Sat. Sun. and public holidays same opening times

Hotel-restaurants

Ferme de Grange
2 Ferme de Grange
5537 Anhée
Tel. (82) 61 21 08

Hostellerie Wachter
140 chaussée de Namur
5537 Yvoir
Tel. (82) 61 13 14
Fax (82) 61 28 58

Restaurants

Les Jardins d'en-Bas
1 rue d'En-bas
5537 Annevoie-Rouillon
Tel.(82) 61 37 06
Closed Tue., Wed. and Thur.
Local cuisine: pot-au-feu with snails, crayfish soup. Menu: 750BF

Assesse

Postal code 5330

Culture

Château de Crupet
5332 Crupet
Tel. (83) 69 90 93
Visits for groups only by appointment, write to Madame Limbosch-Blomme: 18 rue Basse, Crupet.

Restaurants

Les Ramiers***
32 rue Basse
5332 Crupet
Tel. (83) 69 90 70
Closed Mon. eve. and Wed.
Specialties: couscous with crayfish, warmed calves-head jelly. Menus: 950BF, 1,450 and 1,950BF

Dinant

Postal code
5500

Tourist information center
37 rue Grande,
Tel. (82) 22 28 70

Festival

Mosan summer festival
For information and accommodation contact:
30 rue des Fossés
5500 Dinant
Tel. (82) 22 59 24

Culture

Château de Walzin
5500 Dinant
Grounds open Jul.–Aug., Thur. from 10am. Castle itself closed to the public.

Citadel
25 Le Prieuré
5500 Dinant
Tel. (82) 22 36 70
Open Easter–mid-Nov., daily 9.30am–6pm; mid-Nov.–Easter 10am–4pm; Closed Jan. 1–15 and Fri. from Nov. to Mar.

Monastère de Leffe
1 pl. de l'Abbaye
5500 Dinant
Tel. (82) 22 23 77
Visits on request.

Musée du Cuivre et de la Dinanderie
27 rte de Givet
5500 Dinant
Tel. (82) 22 30 17
Open Easter–Sep., Tue.–Sun. 1.30pm–6pm
Closed Mon.
Copper- and brassmaking museum.

Spanish House
(Museum of Lighting)
Pl. du bailliage
5500 Bouvignes-sur-Meuse
Tel. (82) 22 49 10 or 22 45 53
Open May–Oct. 9, 1–6pm
Closed Mon.

NATURE AND LEISURE

FURFOOZ NATIONAL PARK
Rue du Camp-Romain
5500 Furfooz
Tel. (81) 22 47 65
Open Jul.–Aug. 10am–6pm, Apr.–May 10am–5pm, Sep.–Oct. 10am–4.30pm; Nov.–mid-Dec., Sat.–Sun. by appointment. Closed Jan. 5–Feb. 15

KAYAKS ANSIAUX
15 rue du Vélodrome
5500 Anseremme
Tel. (82) 22 23 25
Open 15 Mar.–Oct.
Reservations essential. Offers courses in kayak sailing, nature trails and mountain bike treks. Accommodation available in the Aquatel complex which is open all year round.
◆ 338

LESSE KAYAK
2 pl. de l'église
Tel. (82) 22 43 97
5500 Anseremme
Open Apr.–Oct. 8.30am–7pm
Embarcation at Houyet between 9am and 11.30am.
◆ 338

MEUSE ET LESSE
13 rue Caussin
5500 Dinant
Tel. (82) 22 61 86
Open 15 Mar.–Oct.
Kayak rental. Departure from Houyet between 9am and 11am or from Gendron between 9am and 3pm.
◆ 338

HOTEL-RESTAURANTS

AUBERGE DE BOUVIGNES
112 rue Fétis
5500 Bouvignes
Tel. (82) 61 16 00
Fax (82) 61 30 93
Restaurant closed Sun. eve. and Mon.
Specialties: lobster ragoût with fresh pasta, spicy perch. 6 rooms. Menus: 1,490BF, 2,200BF and 2,400BF

MOULIN DE LISOGNE
Rte de la petite-vallée-de-la-Leffe
5501 Lisogne
Tel. (82) 22 63 80
Fax (82) 22 21 47
Fresh local produce: beef carpaccio flavored with truffle, poached river trout. 10 rooms. Menus: 1,450BF, 1,650BF and 1,950BF

RESTAURANTS

LE JARDIN DE FIORINE
3 rue Cousot
5500 Dinant
Tel. (82) 22 74 74
Closed Sun. eve. and Wed.
Specialty: ris de veau braised in Sauternes. Menus: 1,000BF, 1,495BF, 1,995BF and 2,500BF

FERNELMONT

POSTAL CODE 5380

CULTURE

CHÂTEAU DE FRANC-WARET
5380 Franc-Waret
Tel. (81) 83 34 04
Open Jun.–Sep., Sat. Sun. and public holidays 2–5.30pm

FLEMALLE

POSTAL CODE 4400

CULTURE

CHÂTEAU D'AIGREMONT
4400 Awirs
Tel. (41) 36 16 87
Open Jul.–Aug. and Easter, Tue.–Sun. 10am–noon and 2–6pm; Apr.–Oct., Sat.–Sun. and public holidays same opening times

HOTELS-RESTAURANTS

CHÂTEAU DES COMTES DE HORION
27 rue de Horion
4460 Horion-Hozemont
Tel. (41) 50 53 93
Fax (41) 50 47 60
Unusual 13th-century site surrounded by a moat. Specialties: suprême de Basse-Meuse, goose liver with apple. Menus: lunch 1,250BF, dinner 1,850BF and 2,500BF

GEMBLOUX

POSTAL CODE 5030

GEMBLOUT TOURIST OFFICE
Parc d'Epinal-Caves de la Maison du Bailli
Tel. (81) 61 51 71

CULTURE

ANCIENT ABBEY
FACULTY OFAGRONOMY
2 passage des Déportés
5030 Gembloux
Tel. (81) 62 21 11
Open Mon.–Fri., 9am–noon and 2–4pm

CHÂTEAU DE CORROY-LE-CHÂTEAU
5032 Corroy-le-Château
Tel. (81) 63 32 32
Open May–Sep., Sat.–Sun. and public holidays, 10am–noon and 2–6pm

RESTAURANTS

LE PRINCE DE LIÈGE
96B chaussée de Namur
5030 Gembloux
Tel. (81) 61 12 44
Closed Sun. eve. and Mon.
Specialties: langoustine and asparagus lasagne, Vendée baby pigeon. Menus: 1,000BF, 1,900BF and 2,675BF

GESVES

POSTAL CODE 5340

ACCOMMODATION

L'AUBERGESVES
4 Pourrain
5340 Gesves
Tel. (83) 67 74 17
Fax (83) 67 81 57
Specialties: coquilles St-Jacques with truffle sauce, local quail. 6 rooms. Menus: 950BF, 1,350BF, 1,800BF and 1,950BF

HASTIÈRE

POSTAL CODE 5540

TOURIST INFORMATION CENTER
55 rue Marcel-Lespagne
5540 Hastière
Tel. (82) 64 44 34

CULTURE

ABBEY CHURCH
Tel. (82) 64 42 66
5540 Hastière
Open Jul.–Aug. 9am–noon and 2pm–7pm, Apr.–Jun. and Sep.–Oct. 2–5pm

CHÂTEAU DE FREŸR
5540 Waulsort
Tel. (82) 22 22 00
Open Jul.–Aug., Sat. Sun. and public holidays 2–6pm

NATURE AND LEISURE

GROTTE DU PONT D'ARCOLE
2 rue d'Inzemont
5540 Hastière
Tel. (82) 64 44 01
Open Jul.–Aug. 9am–6pm, Apr.–Sep. 10am–5pm; Oct.–Nov., Sat.–Sun. and public holidays 1–4pm

RESTAURANTS

LA MEUNERIE
17 rue Larifosse
5540 Hastière
Tel. (82) 64 51 33

HOUYET

POSTAL CODE 5560

TOURIST INFORMATION BUREAU
Allée de Rasteau
5560 Houyet
Tel. (82) 66 72 13
Open mornings only.

CULTURE

CHÂTEAU DE VÊVES
5561 Celles
Tel. (82) 66 63 93
Open Jul.–Aug., Tue.–Sun. 10am–6pm; Easter–Jun. and Sep.–Oct., Tue.–Sun. 10am–12.30pm and 1.30–6pm

HOTEL-RESTAURANTS

HOSTELLERIE DU VAL-JOLI
2 rue St-Hadelin
5561 Celles
Tel. (82) 66 63 63
Fax (82) 66 67 68
Specialties: lobster with beurre blanc, game. 7 rooms
Menus: 1,900BF, 2,200BF and 2,700BF

HUY

POSTAL CODE
4500

TOURIST OFFICE
1 quai de Namur
4500 Huy
Tel. (85) 21 29 15

HOTEL-RESTAURANTS

L'AIGLE NOIR
8 quai Dautrebande
4500 Huy
Tel. (85) 21 23 41

HÔTEL DU FORT
6 chaussée Napoléon
4500 Huy
Tel. (85) 21 24 03
Fax (85) 23 18 42

MODAVE

POSTAL CODE 4577

TOURIST INFORMATION CENTER
9 rue Pont-de-Bonne
4577 Modave
Tel. (85) 41 29 69

CULTURE

CHÂTEAU DE MODAVE
4577 Modave
Tel. (85) 41 13 69
Open Apr.–mid-Nov.
9am–6pm

HOTEL-RESTAURANTS

CASTEL DU VAL-D'OR
64 Grand-rue
4560 Ocquier
Tel. (86) 34 41 03
Fax. (86) 34 49 56
17 rooms.
Restaurant closed Mon. eve., Tue. and Wed.
Menus: 835BF, 1,200BF and 1,265BF

FERME BAYA
Ferme de Baya
5353 Goesnes
Tel. (85) 61 12 20

LA ROSERAIE**
80 rte de LImet
4577 Modave
Tel. (85) 41 13 60
4 rooms.
Restaurant closed Mon. eve., Tue. and Wed.
Menus: 1,100BF, 1,495BF and 1,980BF

NIVELLES

POSTAL CODE 1400

TOURIST OFFICE
'Waux-Hall"
Pl. Albert Ier
Tel. (67) 88 22 75

CULTURE

COLLÉGIALE
Grand-Place
Tel. (67) 21 93 58
Open summer 9am–6pm, out of season 9am–5pm

RESTAURANTS

FREDDY COLLETTE
7 square Gabrielle-Petit
1400 Nivelles
Tel. (67) 21 05 30
Closed Sun. eve. and Mon.
Specialties: slab of perch stuffed with tomato, smoked fillets of eel with leeks.
An extremely good gastronomic restaurant.
Menus: lunch 900BF, dinner 1,200BF, 1,850BF and 2,350BF

LE VIEUX MARRONNIER
7 pl. de Baulers
1401 Baulers
Tel. (67) 21 86 66

ONHAYE

POSTAL CODE 5520

CULTURE

RUINS OF THE CHÂTEAU DE MONTAIGLE
Rue du Marteau
5522 Falaën
Tel. (82) 69 95 85
Open Jul.–Aug.
11am–7pm;

FLEA MARKETS

Brussels is full of different markets. Many visitors may already be familiar with the two major antiques markets – the Place du Jeu de Balle and the Place du Grand-Sablon – but there are also many other smaller markets worth exploring, both in Brussels and throughout southern Belgium.

MAJOR MARKETS

PLACE DU JEU DE BALLE
FLEA MARKET
Daily 8am–1pm
Located in an area which is undergoing an enormous transformation, the Marolles. A maze of stalls where prices tend to be lower throughout the week than at the weekend. In the surrounding area antique dealers and stall holders (books, old manuscripts, furniture, secondhand clothes, Art Deco pieces and memorabilia from the Universal Exposition of 1958.

LE SABLON
ANTIQUES AND BOOK FAIR
Sat. 9am–6pm,
Sun. 9am–2pm
Numerous attractive covered stalls go to make up this chic antiques market. In the square and adjacent streets (particularly the Rue des Minimes) are a string of shops specializing in glassware and African art.

OTHER BRUSSELS MARKETS

ABATTOIRS OF ANDERLECHT
24 rue Ropsy-Chaudronstraat
(covered market)
Sat.–Sun. until 1pm

AUDERGHEM
Under the Debroux viaduct
1st Sun. of the month
Tired of bargain hunting? Those with a special interest in embroidery and lace should pay a visit to the Costume and Lace Museum.

MUSÉE DE L'ARMÉE
1st Sat. of the month,
Books and old manuscripts.

MUSÉE DU COSTUME AND DE LA DENTELLE
6 rue de la Violette
1000 Brussels
Tel. (2) 512 77 09
Open Apr.–Sep., Mon.–Thur. 10am–noon and 1.30–5pm; Sat.–Sun. and public holidays, 2–4.30pm
Closed some public holidays

ELSEWHERE IN BELGIUM

NAMUR
BRIC-A-BRAC MARKET
Quai de Meuse
Jambes
Sunday morning

LIÈGE
MARCHÉ DE LA BATTE
Sun. 8am–2pm
Unusual objects in the middle of a fruit and vegetable market.

SPA
FLEA MARKET
Parc de Sept-Heures
Galerie Léopold II
(behind the OT).
Sun. 8am–2pm

ANTIQUE FAIRS

NAMUR	bric-a-brac	Jan. 13–16
BRUSSELS	Eurantica (antiques)	Mar. 18–27
LIÈGE	antiques	May 5–9
BRUSSELS	bric-a-brac	Jun. 16–19
TOURNAI	antiques/ bric-a-brac	Aug. 12–15
LIÈGE	bric-a-brac	Sep. 30–Oct. 2
NAMUR	antiques	Nov. 4–13

Apr.–Jun. and Sep.–Nov., weekends and public holidays, 11am–6pm; Nov.–Mar., Sun. weather permitting

PROFONDE VILLE

POSTAL CODE 5170

RESTAURANTS

L'EAU VIVE
37 rte de Floreffe
5170 Arbre
Tel. (81) 41 11 51
Closed Mon. eve. and Tue.
Specialties: crispy baby pigeon with an orange dressing.
Menus: lunch1,000BF, dinner 1,450BF and 1,950BF

MARTEAU LONGE
51 rte de Floreffe
5170 Arbre
Tel. (81) 41 10 95

ROCHEFORT

POSTAL CODE 5580

TOURIST INFORMATION CENTER
5 rue de Behogne
5580 Rochefort
Tel. (84) 21 25 37

TOURIST OFFICE
1 rue des Sarrasins
5580 Han-sur-Lesse
Tel. (84) 37 75 96

CULTURE

CHÂTEAU DE LAVAUX-STE-ANNE
5580 Lavaux-Ste-Anne
Tel. (84) 38 83 62
CHÂTEAU
Open Jul.–Aug. 9am–7pm; Mar.–Jun. and Sep.–Oct., 9am–6pm; Nov.–Feb., 9am–5pm
MUSÉE DE LA CHASSE ET DE LA NATURE
Open 9am–noon and 1–6pm

RUINS OF THE CHÂTEAU DES COMTES
Rue Jacquet
5580 Rochefort
Tel. (84) 21 44 09
Open Jun. 15–Sep. 15,daily 10am–noon and 1–6pm; Easter–Jun. 15 and 15–30 Sep., Sat.–Sun. and public holidays same opening times

NATURE AND LEISURE

DOMAINE DES GROTTES DE HAN
5580 Han-sur-Lesse
Tel. (84) 37 72 13
CAVES
Open Jul.–Aug. 9.30am–11.30am and 1–6pm, Apr.–Jun. until 5.30pm, Sep.–Oct. until 5pm, Nov.–Mar. 9.30am–3.30pm
Tours every half hour. Constant temperature of 54°F.
MUSÉE DU MONDE SOUTERRAIN
3 pl. Théo-Lannoy
Open Jul.–Aug. 11am–7pm, Apr.–Jun. 11am–5pm
SPÉLÉOTHÈME
Ferme de Dry Hamptay
46 rue des Grottes
Open Jul.–Aug. noon–8pm, Apr.–Jun. and Sep.–Nov. 15, noon–6pm

KAYAKS LESSE ET LOMME
5580 Han-sur-Lesse
Tel. (82) 22 43 97
Open Jun. 15–Sep. 15 9.30am–18 h
Offers combined kayak and mountain bike tours.

HOTEL-RESTAURANTS

AUBERGE LES FALIZES
90 rue de France
5580 Rochefort
Tel. (84) 21 12 82
Fax (84) 22 10 86
Restaurant closed Mon. eve. and Tue.
Specialties: ballotine of sole with leeks.
6 rooms.
Menus: 1,395–2,000BF

HÔTEL DES ARDENNES
2 rue des Grottes
5580 Han-sur-Lesse
Tel. (84) 37 72 20
Fax (84) 37 80 62

RESTAURANT DU CHÂTEAU
10 rue du Château
5580 Lavaux-St-Anne
Tel. (84) 38 88 83
Restaurant closed Mon. and Tue.
Specialties: creamed potatoes with foie gras and wild mushrooms, ris de veau in balsamic vineger.
8 rooms.

SERAING

POSTAL CODE 4100

CULTURE

VAL ST-LAMBERT CRYSTAL FACTORY
245 rue du Val
4100 Seraing
Tel. (41) 37 09 60
Open Tue.–Sun. 9.30am–5pm
Closed Jan. 1 and Christmas Day

VILLIERS-LA-VILLE

POSTAL CODE 1495

TOURIST INFORMATION CENTER
53 rue de l'Abbaye
1495 Villiers-la-Ville
Tel. (71) 87 98 98

CULTURE

ABBEY
53 rue de l'Abbaye
Tel. (71) 87 98 98
1495 Villiers-la-Ville
Open Easter–Jun., Wed.–Sun. 10am–6pm, Jul.–Sep., Wed.–Sun. 10am–6pm, Mon.–Tue. 10am–5pm; Oct.–Mar., Wed.–Fri. 1–5pm, Sat.–Sun. and public holidays 11am–5pm

HOTEL-RESTAURANTS

HOSTELLERIE LA FALISE
7 rue La Falise
1470 Baisy-Thy
Tel. (67) 77 35 11
Fax (67) 79 04 94

YVOIR

POSTAL CODE 5530

TOURIST INFORMATION BUREAU
Rue du Maka
5530 Yvoir
Tel. (82) 71 11 40

CULTURE

CHÂTEAU DE SPONTIN
5530 Spontin
Tel. (83) 69 90 55
Open 10am–1pm and 2–5pm

RUINS OF THE CHÂTEAU DE POILVACHE
5530 Houx
Tel. (82) 61 35 14
Open Jul.–Aug., daily 10.30am–6.30pm; Apr.–Sep., Sat. Sun.same opening times

HOTELS, ACCOMMODATION

BED & BREAKFAST
Château de Spontin
8 chaussée de Dinant
5530 Spontin
Tel. (83) 69 90 55
Fax (83) 69 92 14

RESTAURANTS

LE VIVIER D'OIES
7 rue de l'État
5530 Dorinne
Tel. (83) 69 95 71

LIÈGE

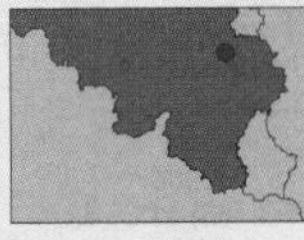

POSTAL CODE 4000

TOURIST FEDERATION FOR THE PROVINCE OF LIÈGE
77 bd de la Sauvenière
Tel. (41) 22 42 10
Fax (421) 22 10 92

ENTERTAINMENT

THÉÂTRE ROYAL ANCIEN IMPÉRIAL
56 rue Surlet
4000 Liège
Puppet shows

THÉÂTRE AL BOTROULE
4 rue Hocheporte
4000 Liège
Puppet shows.

CULTURE

MAISON GRÉTRY
34 rue des Récollets
4000 Liège
Tel. (41) 43 16 10
Open Wed.–Fri.
2–4pm

MUSÉE D'ANSEMBOURG
114 Féronstrée
4000 Liège
Tel. (41) 23 20 68
Open Tue.–Sun.,
1–6pm
Closed Mon.
Eighteenth-century decorative arts from Liège.

MUSÉE D'ARMES
8 quai de Maastricht
4000 Liège
Tel. (41) 23 15 62
Open Mon., Thur. and Sat. 10am–1pm, Wed. and Fri. 2–5pm, 1st and 3rd Sun. of the month 10am–1pm

MUSÉE D'ART MODERNE
3 parc de la Boverie
4020 Liège
Tel. (41) 43 04 03
Open 1–6pm,
Sun. 11am–4.30pm
Closed Mon.

MUSÉE DE L'ART WALLON
Îlot St-Georges
86, Féronstrée
Tel. (41) 22 08 00
Open Tue.–Sat.
1–6pm, Sun.
11am–4.30pm

MUSÉE CURTIUS
13 quai de Maastricht
4000 Liège
Tel. (41) 23 20 68
Open Mon., Thur. and Sat. 2–5pm; Wed. and Fri. 10am–1pm
Open 2nd and 4th Sun. of the month
10am–1pm
Contains within its collection some important Mosan masterpieces, made of Notger ivory.

MUSÉE TCHANTCHÈS
56 rue Surlet
Tel. (41) 42 75 75
Open Tue. and Thur.
2–4pm
Collection of puppets from the Théâtre Royal and traditional Liège costumes.

MUSÉE DU VERRE
13 quai de Maastricht
Tel. (41) 23 20 68
Open Mon., Thur. and Sat. 2–5pm; Wed., Fri. 10am–1pm; 2nd and 4th Sun. of the month
10am–1pm
Closed Tue.
Museum holds more than ten thousand pieces, of which two thousand are regularly on display.

MUSÉE DE LA VIE WALLONNE
Cour des Mineurs
Tel. (41) 23 60 94
Open 10am–5pm,
Sun. 10am–4pm
Closed Mon.
Superb collection of puppets; shows are put on in the museum.

HOTEL-RESTAURANTS

LE CYGNE D'ARGENT
49 rue Beeckman
4000 Liège
Tel. (41) 23 70 01
Fax (41) 22 49 66

HÔTEL BEDFORD
36 quai St-Léonard
4000 Liège
Tel. (41) 28 81 11
Fax (41) 27 45 75

LE SIMENON
16 bd de l'Est
4020 Liège
Tel. (41) 42 86 90
Fax (41) 44 26 69

RESTAURANTS

AL'PILORI
Pl. du Marché
4000 Liège

AS OUHES
21 pl. du Marché
4000 Liège
Tel. (41) 23 32 25

AU VIEUX LIÈGE
41 quai de la Goffe
4000 Liège
Tel. (41) 23 77 48

CAFÉ LEQUET
17 quai sur Meuse
4000 Liège
Tel. (41) 22 21 34

LE FIACRE
2 pl. St-Denis
4000 Liège
Tel. (41) 23 15 45

ROBERT LESENNE
9 rue de la Boucherie
4000 Liège
Tel. (41) 22 07 93

AUBEL

POSTAL CODE 4880

CULTURE

ABBAYE DU VAL-DIEU
4880 Aubel
Tel. (87) 68 73 81
Visits to the abbey church and the courtyard only.

RESTAURANTS

LE CLOS ST-JEAN
94 Cosenberg
4880 Aubel
Tel. (87) 68 77 18
Closed Sat. lunchtime and Mon.
Local cuisine using fresh produce from the local market.
Menus: 1,050BF, 1,350BF and 1,650BF

AYWAILLE

POSTAL CODE 4920

NATURE AND LEISURE

BONJEAN SPORTS
30 rte des Trois-Ponts
4920 Aywaille
Tel. (41) 84 63 12
Open Apr.–Oct.
Bicycle rental. Departures from Barvaux start at Rue Bassecour, after the dam. Departures from Bomal start from Le Sassin sports center.

CAVE OF REMOUCHAMPS
4920 Sougné-Remouchamps
Tel. (41) 84 46 82
Open Feb.–Nov. 15
9.30am–5pm

RESTAURANTS

LE BORGHÈSE
8 rue de Louveigné
4920 Sougné-Remouchamps
Tel. (41) 84 76 72
Closed Fri.
Specialty: steak cooked in Aubel beer.
Menus 350–800BF

LES JARDINS 1900
20 rue Henri-Orban
4920 Aywaille
Tel. (41) 84 44 65
Fax (41) 84 44 54
Closed Wed. and Thur.
Specialty: goose liver pâté and confit de canard.
Menus: 550BF, 895BF, 1,150BF and 1,450BF

HOTELS, ACCOMMODATION

RURAL "GÎTE"
Monsieur Wolters
25 Pouhon
4920 Harzé
Tel. (86) 43 41 16

BURG-REULAND

POSTAL CODE 4790

HOTEL-RESTAURANTS

LE VAL DE L'OUR
150 rue du Village
4790 Burg-Reuland
Tel. (80) 32 90 09
Fax (80) 32 97 00
Menu starts from 850BF. 16 rooms.

LA CALAMINE

POSTAL CODE
4720

TOURIST INFORMATION
27–29, Thimstrasse
4720 La Calamine
Tel. (87) 65 37 44

HOTEL-RESTAURANTS

HÔTEL PARK CAFÉ
2 rue des Carabiniers
4720 La Calamine
Tel. (87) 65 99 94
Fax (87) 65 34 28

CHAUD FONTAINE

POSTAL CODE 4050

CULTURE

MAISON SAUVEUR
Parc des Sources
Tel. (41) 65 18 34
Open 9am–noon and 1.15–5pm

COMBLAIN-AU-PONT

POSTAL CODE 4170

HOTEL-RESTAURANTS

HOSTELLERIE ST-ROCH
1 rue du Parc
4180 Comblain-la-Tour
Tel. (41) 69 13 33
Fax (41) 69 31 31
HOTEL
Double rooms with 18th-century Liègeois furniture. Private tennis court. One of the Relais et Château group.
Rooms: 3,800–6,800BF
RESTAURANT
Ancient hostelry situated in the Ourthe valley. Excellent view across the Ourthe from the terrace.
Menus: 1,200–2,300BF

DALHEM

POSTAL CODE 4607

RESTAURANTS

LE JARDINET
14 pl. de la Reine-Astrid
4607 Dalhem
Tel. (41) 79 24 15
Closed Mon.
Specialties: goose à l'instar de Visé, quail salad.
Menus: 1,250BF, 1,950BF and 2,600BF

DURBUY

POSTAL CODE 6940

ROYAL TOURIST INFORMATION CENTER
HALLE AUX BLÉS
6940 Durbuy
Tel. (86) 21 24 28

HOTEL-RESTAURANTS

LE LIGNELY
6941 Heyd
Tel. (86) 49 96 50
Fax (86) 49 96 55
Specialties: braised turbot with shallots, poêlée de St-Jacques.
Menu: 1,895BF

LE SANGLIER DES ARDENNES
99 rue d'Ursel
6940 Durbuy
Tel. (86) 21 32 62
Fax (86) 21 24 65
Excellent restaurant. Specialties: chicken baked in salt, game.
Rooms: 3,800–6,000BF
À la carte: 1,950–2,250BF

ACCOMMODATION

RURAL "GÎTE"
MADAME PIRET
22 rue de Blhay
6991 Heyd
Tel. (86) 49 91 84

ESNEUX

POSTAL CODE
4130

HOTELS, ACCOMMODATION

YOUTH HOSTEL
4 rue Blandot
4130 Tilff
Tel. (41) 88 21 00

RESTAURANTS

LA MAIRIE
15 rue Blanchot
4130 Tilff
Tel. (41) 88 24 24
Closed Sun. eve. and Mon.
Specialty: foie gras.
Menus: lunch 1,000BF, dinner 980BF and 1,350BF

EUPEN

POSTAL CODE
4700

TOURIST INFORMATION CENTER
7 Marktplatz
4700 Eupen
Tel. (87) 55 34 50

HOTEL-RESTAURANTS

HÔTEL RATHAUS
13 Rathausplatz
4700 Eupen
Tel. (87) 74 28 12
Fax (87) 74 46 64

HERVE

POSTAL CODE
4650

HOTEL-RESTAURANTS

LE DÉJEUNER SUR L'HERBE
80 rue Maigre-Cense
4650 Julémont
Tel. (41) 87 66 24
Restaurant closed Tue., Wed. and Thur.
Menus: 1,150BF, 1,300BF, 1,550BF and 1,800BF

HOTTON

POSTAL CODE
6990

NATURE AND LEISURE

GROTTE DE HOTTON
6990 Hotton
Tel. (84) 46 60 46
Open Apr.–Oct. 10am–5pm, Jul.–Aug. 10am–6pm
Unusually beautiful underground cave of "A Thousand and One Nights".

HOUFFALIZE

POSTAL CODE
6660

TOURIST INFORMATION CENTER
1 rue de Schaerbeek
6660 Houffalize
Tel. (61) 28 81 16

HOTELS, ACCOMMODATION

PIERRET RURAL "GÎTE"
M. AND MME PIERRET
14 Chabrehez
6661 Tailles
Tel. (80) 41 88 06

HOTEL-RESTAURANTS

LA VALLÉE DES FÉES
8 rue Achouffe
6660 Houffalize
Tel. (61) 28 81 48
Fax (61) 28 93 55
Specialty: lapin à la chouffe.
Menus: 790–1,650BF

JALHAY

POSTAL CODE
4845

NATURE AND LEISURE

GILEPPE DAM
4845 Jalhay
Tel. (87) 64 81 25

HOTEL-RESTAURANTS

LE VIEUX HÊTRE
18 rte de la Fagne
4845 Jalhay
Tel. (87) 64 70 92

LA-ROCHE-EN-ARDENNE

POSTAL CODE
6980

TOURIST INFORMATION CENTER
Pl. du Marché
6980 La-Roche-en-Ardenne
Tel. (84) 41 13 42

CULTURE

ARDENNE AVENTURE
27 rue de l'Église
6980 La-Roche-en-Ardenne
Tel. (84) 41 21 45

Open all year round. Offers kayak trips (Apr.–Oct.), rafting (Nov.–Mar.) and mountain biking all year round.

RUINS OF THE FEUDAL CHÂTEAU
6980 La-Roche-en-Ardenne
Tel. (84) 41 13 42
Open Jul.–Aug. 10am–7pm, Apr.–Jun. and Sep.–Oct. 10am–noon and 2–5pm; Nov.–Apr., Sat. Sun. 10am–noon and 2–4pm, Mon.–Fri. 2–4pm.

HOTEL-RESTAURANTS

HOSTELLERIE DE LA CLAIRE FONTAINE
64 rte de Hotton
6980 La-Roche–en-Ardenne
Tel. (84) 41 24 70
Fax (84) 41 21 11
Specialty: ris de veau with crayfish.
Double rooms: 3,000–3,800BF
À la carte: 900–12,500BF

MALMÉDY

POSTAL CODE
4960

TOURIST INFORMATION CENTER
10 pl. du Châtelet
4960 Malmédy
Tel. (80) 33 02 50

CULTURE

MUSÉE DU CARNAVAL AND MUSÉE DU PAPIER
MAISON CAVENS
11 pl. de Rome
4960 Malmédy
Tel. (80) 33 70 58

HOTEL-RESTAURANTS

HOSTELLERIE TRÔS-MARETS
2 rte des Trôs-Marets
4960 Malmédy
Tel. (80) 33 79 17
Fax (80) 33 79 10
Delightful setting in grounds lined with 100-year-old trees.
Rooms: 4,850–7,500BF
Menus: 1,750BF and 2,750BF

HÔTEL DU MOULIN
28 Grand-Rue
4960 Ligneuville
Tel. (80) 57 00 81
Fax (80) 57 07 88
Restaurant closed out of season, Tue. eve. and Wed.
Ardennois cuisine in a 19th-century inn.
Menus: lunch 1,500BF, dinner 1,950BF

YOUTH HOSTEL
Hohes Venn-Hautes Fagnes
4960 Malmédy
Tel. (80) 33 83 86

RESTAURANTS

A VI MAM'DI
41 pl. Albert Ier
4960 Malmédy
Tel. (80) 33 96 36

MARCHE-EN-FAMENNE

POSTAL CODE 6900

TOURIST INFORMATION CENTER
"Le Pot d'Étain"
7 rue des Brasseurs
6900 Marche-en-Famenne
Tel. (84) 31 21 35

CULTURE

MUSÉE DE LA FAMENNE
17 rue du Commerce
6900 Marche-en-Famenne
Tel. (84) 31 46 54
Open Tue.–Sat. 10am–1pm and 2–5pm
Information at Maison Jadot.

HOTEL-RESTAURANTS

LE CHÂTEAU D'HASSONVILLE
6900 Marche-en-Famenne
Tel. (84) 31 10 25
Fax (84) 31 60 27
Restaurant closed Mon. eve. and Tue.
Twelfth-century castle in 125 acres of grounds.
Excellent quality hotel and restaurant.
Rooms: 4,400–6,400BF
À la carte: 2,100–2,600BF

LE QUARTIER LATIN
2 rue des Brasseurs
6900 Marche-en-Famenne
Tel. (84) 32 17 13
Fax (84) 32 17 12
Double rooms: 2,700–3,800BF
À la carte: 800 à 1,300BF

OUPEYE

POSTAL CODE
4680

HOTEL-RESTAURANTS

HOSTELLERIE AU COMTÉ DE MERCY
5–6 rue du Tilleul
4681 Hermalle-sous-Argenteau
Tel. (41) 79 35 35

PEPINSTER

POSTAL CODE
4860

HOTEL-RESTAURANTS

HOSTELLERIE LAFARQUE
20 chemin des Douys
4860 Pepinster
Tel. (87) 46 06 51
Fax (87) 46 97 28
Restaurant closed Mon. eve. and Tue.
Specialties: coucou de Malines à l'instar de Visé, langoustine en olivade. 6 rooms.
A member of the Relais et Château group.
Menus: 2,150BF, 2,250BF and 2,550BF

SPA

POSTAL CODE
4900

TOURIST OFFICE
41 pl. Royale
Tel. (87) 77 25 10
or (87) 77 25 19

ENTERTAINMENT

FESTIVAL DE THÉÂTRE DE SPA
Tickets available at the at the venue
ROTONDE DU CASINO
Open 10am–6pm

CULTURE

MUSÉE DE LA VILLE D'EAU AND MUSÉE DU CHEVAL
VILLA ROYALE MARIE-HENRIETTE
77 av. de la Reine-Astrid
Tel. (87) 77 13 06
Open Jun. 15–Sep. 15 and school holidays 2.30pm–5.30pm; other times, Sat.–Sun. and public holidays 2.30pm–5.30pm
Closed Jan. 1.–15 Mar.

NATURE AND LEISURE

MUSÉE DES EAUX ET FORÊTS
Rte de la Gleize
Berinsenne
4900 Spa
Open Jul.–Aug. and Easter holidays, Tue.–Sun. 2–5pm; Sep.–Nov. 15 and Mar.–Jun., Wed., Sat. and Sun. 2–5pm
For all information write to: Eaux et Forêts, 28 Vieille route de Stavelot, 4880 Spa Tel. (87) 77 11 06

VÉLODREAM
1 Hoctaisart
4900 Spa
Tel. (87) 77 11 77
Organizes mountain bike tours.

HOTEL-RESTAURANTS

HÔTEL LA HEID DES PAIRS
143 av. Professeur-Henri-Jean
4900 Spa
Tel. (87) 77 43 46
Fax (87) 77 06 44
Bar, swimming pool.
Double rooms: 2 700–5 200BF

RESTAURANTS

LA BELLE ÉPOQUE
15 pl. du Monument
4900 Spa
Tel. (87) 77 54 03

ST-VITH

POSTAL CODE
4780

CANTONS DE L'EST TOURIST OFFICE
2 Mühlenbachstrasse
4780 St-Vith
Tel. (80) 22 76 64

HOTEL-RESTAURANTS

HOTEL ZUR POST***
39 Hauptstrasse
4780 St-Vith
Tel. (80) 22 80 27
Fax (80) 22 93 10
Restaurant closed Sun. eve. and Mon.
Specialties: baby pigeon de Bresse, foie gras and game. Good restaurant. 8 rooms.
Menus: 1,800BF, 2,500BF and 3,000BF

STAVELOT

POSTAL CODE
4970

TOURIST OFFICE
Ancient abbey
Tel. (80) 88 23 39

ENTERTAINMENT

FESTIVAL DE STAVELOT
(Aug.–Sep.)
Ancient abbey
Tel. (80) 86 27 34
From Jul. 15, Mon.–Sat. 10am–12.30pm
Closed Sun. and public holidays

CULTURE

MUSÉE DU CIRCUIT DE SPA-FRANCORCHAMPS
Courtyard of the Hôtel-de-Ville
Tel. (80) 86 27 06
Open Easter–Nov. 10am–12.30pm and 2.30pm–5.30pm, Nov. 4–Easter 10am–12.30pm and 2–4.30pm

MUSÉE GUILLAUME APOLLINAIRE
Rue du Châtelet
Tel. (80) 86 21 24 or (80) 86 23 25
Open Jul.–Aug., 10am–12.30pm and 2.30pm–5.30pm
Out of season, by appointment only.

NATURE AND LEISURE

COOKAYAK
4970 Stavelot
Tel. (80) 68 42 45
Open Mar.–Nov.
Reservation recommended for groups of more than ten people. Circular tour.

HOTEL-RESTAURANTS

HÔTEL D'ORANGE
In front of Les Capucins
4970 Stavelot
Tel. (80) 86 20 05
Fax (80) 86 42 92
Restaurant closed Tue. and Wed. except Jul. and Aug.
Former 17th-century inn.
Double rooms: 1,900–2,200BF
Menus: 510–1,520BF

HOSTELLERIE LE ROANNAY
155 rte de Spa
4970 Francorchamps
Tel. (87) 27 53 11
Fax (87) 27 55 47
Restaurant closed Tue.
Bar, private swimming pool, sauna.
Specialties: foie gras à la golden cooked in muslin, roast baby pigeon en cocotte.
Double rooms: 3,200–4,450BF
Menus: 850–1,500BF

THEUX

POSTAL CODE
4910

CULTURE

RUINS OF THE CHÂTEAU DE FRANCHIMONT
24 rte de Sassor
4910 Theux
Tel. (87) 54 10 27
Open Apr.–Sep., Tue.–Sun. 10am–7pm; Oct.–Mar., Sat.–Sun. and public holidays10am–7pm
Closed Jan.
To arrange visits contact: Tel. (87) 54 16 23

NATURE AND LEISURE

ARDENNES MOUNTAIN BIKES
16 Chaufheid
4910 Theux
Tel. (87) 54 22 28
Organizes tours to Vielsam and from Baraque to Fraiture.

PARC DE LA REID
583A, rue Fond-Marie
4910 Theux
Tel. (87) 54 10 75
Open 9am–5pm

RESTAURANTS

LE RELAIS DU MARQUISAT
13 rue Hocheporte
4910 Theux
Tel. (87) 54 21 38
Closed Sun. eve. and Mon.
Specialties: tourin à l'ail doux, magrets de canard.
Menus: 725BF, 995BF and 1 200BF

TROIS-PONTS

POSTAL CODE
4980

HOTEL-RESTAURANTS

AUBERGE DU PÈRE BOIGELOT
1 rue du Pèlerin
4983 Basse-Bodeux
Tel. (80) 68 43 22
Double rooms: 1,750–1,950BF
Menu from 690BF

VERVIERS

POSTAL CODE
4800

HOTEL-RESTAURANTS

AMIGO
1 rue Herla
4800 Verviers
Tel. (87) 22 11 21
Fax (87) 23 03 69
Menus: 980–1,500BF

VIELSALM

POSTAL CODE
6690

VAL DE SALM TOURIST INFORMATION CENTER
Tel. (80) 21 50 52

CULTURE

MUSÉE DU COTICULE
Salm-Château
Tel. (80) 21 57 68

NATURE AND LEISURE

DOMAINE DU MONTI
6698 Grand Halleux
Tel. (80) 21 45 45
Open 9am–5pm
Wildlife park.

DOMAINE PROVINCIAL DE MONT-LE-SOIE
6698 Grand-Halleux
Tel. (80) 21 64 43
Nine-day pony treks and courses of lessons at the riding stables.

HOTEL-RESTAURANTS

LE VAL D'HÉBRON
10 Hébronval
6690 Vielsalm
Tel. (80) 41 88 73
Fax (80) 41 80 73
Double rooms: 1, 000–1,550BF
Menus: 610–1,500BF

WAIMES

POSTAL CODE
4950

CULTURE

CHÂTEAU DE REINHARDSTEIN
4950 Robertville
Tel. (80) 44 64 40
Guided tours Jul.–Aug., Tue., Thur. and Sat. to 3.30pm; Jun. 15–Jul. and Sep. 1–15, Sun. 2–5.15pm, every hour

NATURE AND LEISURE

CENTRE NATURE BOTRANGE
4950 Sourbrodt
Tel. (80) 44 57 81
Open 10am–6pm
Closed 21 Nov.–9 Dec.
Situated in the heart of the Hautes-Fagnes, at the highest point in Belgium. Its service for groups offers guided nature walks and bicycle rides.
Its educational service offers day- and week-long nature trips. Cross-country skis

and mountain bikes available for rent .

HOTEL-RESTAURANTS

LE CYRANO
23–25, rue de la Gare
4950 Robertville
Tel. (80) 67 99 89
Fax (80) 67 83 85
Restaurant closed Wed. and Sat. lunchtime.
Local cuisine based on fresh products in season.
Specialties: pot-au-feu de langoustines, ris de veau with port.
12 rooms.

HÔTEL DES BAINS
2 Lac de Robertville
4950 Robertville
Tel. (80) 67 95 71
Fax (80) 67 81 43
Restaurant closed Wed.
Specialty: ravioles de veau.
Heated swimming pool.
14 rooms.
Menus: 1,250BF, 1,950BF and 2,600BF

RESTAURANTS

LE MONT-RIGI
Rte de Botrange
4950 Robertville
Tel. (80) 44 48 44

HOTELS, ACCOMMODATION

FARMHOUSE "GÎTE"
Monsieur Marichal
4950 Waimes
Tel. (80) 67 94 62

ST-HUBERT

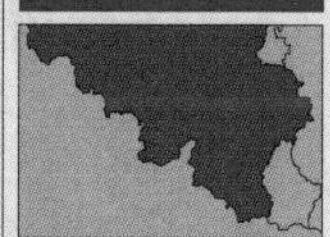

POSTAL CODE
6870

TOURIST INFORMATION CENTER
ABBEY PALACE
6870 St-Hubert
Tel. (61) 61 30 10

ENTERTAINMENT

ST-HUBERT JULY MUSIC FESTIVAL
ABBEY PALACE
6870 St-Hubert
Tel. (61) 61 33 50
Reservations from Jun. 15 10am–noon and 1.30pm–5pm.

CULTURE

FOURNEAU ST-MICHEL
6870 St-Hubert
Tel. (84) 21 08 90
Fax (84) 22 19 36
Open 9am–5pm
RURAL LIFE MUSEUM
Open Apr.–Sep. 15

NATURE AND LEISURE

PARC ST-HUBERT
6870 St-Hubert
rue St-Michel
Tel. (61) 61 17 15
Open 9am–6pm
Wildlife park.

HOTEL-RESTAURANTS

L'AUBERGE DU SABOTIER
21 Grande-Rue
6870 Awenne
Tel. (84) 36 65 23
Fax (84) 36 63 68
Restaurant closed Tue. and Wed. out of season
Specialty: pigs' trotters crépinettes with mushrooms.
Rooms: 1,500–1,800BF

LE CLOS ST-MICHEL
46 rue St-Michel
6870 St-Hubert
Tel. (61) 61 25 69
Fax (61) 61 28 25
Restaurant closed Mon. eve. and Tue.
The newly converted hotel has only recently opened.
Specialties: braised ris de veau, cottage pie with carrot and coriander. Good restaurant.
Menus: 1,750–2,200BF

ARLON

POSTAL CODE
6700

PRACTICAL INFORMATION

TOURIST PAVILION
Parc Léopold
6700 Arlon
Tel. (63) 21 63 60

CULTURE

MUSÉE LUXEMBOURGEOIS
13 rue des Martyrs
6700 Arlon
Open Mon.–Sat. 9am–noon and 2–5pm, Sun., 10am–noon and 2–5pm

ROMAN TOWER
6700 Arlon
Open Tue.–Sat., and Sun. afternoon
Contact the Café d'Alby: 1 Grand-Place Tel. (63) 21 64 47

HOTEL-RESTAURANTS

HOSTELLERIE DU PEIFFESCHOF
111 chemin du Peiffeschof
6700 Arlon
Tel. (63) 22 44 15
Restaurant closed Tue. eve. and Wed.
Specialty: Calves kidneys with bacon.

Double rooms: 2,200–2,600BF
Menus: 1,850BF

BASTOGNE

POSTAL CODE
6600

TOURIST INFORMATION CENTER
24 pl. Mac-Auliffe
6600 Bastogne
Tel. (61) 21 27 11

CULTURE

MUSÉE EN PICONRUE
24 pl. St-Pierre
6600 Bastogne
Open mid-Jun.–mid-Oct., Tue.–Fri. 1.30pm–6pm, Sat.–Sun. 10am–6pm

BASTOGNE HISTORICAL CENTER
Colline du Mardasson
Tel. (61) 21 14 13
Open Jul.–Aug. 9am–6pm, May–Jun. and Sep. 10am–4pm, Mar.–Apr. and Oct.–Nov. 15 10am–4pm

RESTAURANTS

WAGON RESTAURANT LÉO
6 rue du Vivier
6600 Bastogne
Tel. (63) 21 93 93
Closed Mon.
Specialties: mussels, sauerkraut paysan.
Menus: 385–725BF
À la carte: 1,000BF

BOUILLON

POSTAL CODE
6830

TOURIST INFORMATION CENTER
FORTIFIED CASTLE
6830 Bouillon
Tel. (61) 46 62 57

CULTURE

BOUILLON FORTIFIED CASTLE
6830 Bouillon
Tel. (61) 46 62 57
Open Jul.–Aug. 9.30am–7pm, Apr.–Jun. and Sep. 10am–6pm, Mar. and Oct.–Nov. 10am–5pm; Feb. and Dec., Sat.–Sun. 10am–5pm, Mon.–Fri. 1–5pm

NATURE AND LEISURE

LA CRÊTE DES CERFS
19 rue du Christ
6830 Bouillon
Tel. (61) 46 69 81
Wildlife park.

MOULIN DE LA FALIZE
6830 Bouillon
Tel. (61) 46 62 00
RECREATION CENTER
Open all year round
WATERSPORTS
Open Mar.–Oct.
Rental of kayaks and mountain bikes. Trip down the Semois in 1 to 5 days.

HOTELS, ACCOMMODATION

YOUTH HOSTEL
16 chemin du Christ
Tel. (61) 46 81 37

HOTEL-RESTAURANTS

AUBERGE DU MOULIN HIDEUX
1 rue de Dohan
6831 Noirefontaine
Tel. (61) 46 66 21
Fax (61) 46 77 30
Restaurant closed Wed.
Specialties: ham and woodcock mousse, slow-cooked calves feet with mushrooms. Superb situation next to a lake in wooded surroundings. Double rooms: 7,500BF
À la carte: 1,750–2,500BF

UN BALCON EN FORÊT
120 rte de Alle
6830 Rochehaut
Tel. (61) 46 65 30
Fax (61) 46 68 16
Specialties: turtle-dove pâté with duck-liver. Restaurant surrounded by trees. Tennis courts. Covered swimming pool. Double rooms: 2,300–2 800BF

HÔTEL DES ARDENNES
43 rue des Abattis
6838 Corbion
Tel. (61) 46 70 30
Fax (61) 46 77 30
Specialty: baby pigeon with ris de veau and goose-liver pâté. Gardens with a fountain and a view over the hills. Tennis. Double rooms: 2,900–3,500BF
Menus: 900–1,850BF

DAVERDISSE

POSTAL CODE 6929

HOTEL-RESTAURANTS

LE MOULIN DE DAVERDISSE
61 rue de la Lesse
6929 Daverdisse
Tel. (84) 38 81 83
Fax (84) 38 97 20
Specialty: lobster jamaïque. Situated in wooded surroundings. Double rooms: 1,700–2,500BF
Menus: 900–1 900BF

FLORENVILLE

POSTAL CODE 6820

TOURIST PAVILLION
Pl. Albert Ier
Tel. (61) 31 12 29

CULTURE

ABBEY OF NOTRE-DAME D'ORVAL
6823 Villers devant Orval
Tel.(61) 31 10 60
Open Sun. from Easter–Sep. 9.30am–12.30pm and 1.30pm–6.30pm, Oct.–Easter 10am–12.30pm and 1.30pm–6pm, Sun.

HOTEL-RESTAURANTS

LA ROSERAIE
2 rte de Chiny
6821 Lacuisine
Tel. (61) 31 10 39
Fax (61) 31 49 58
Restaurant closed Wed.
Specialty: gratin de lobster. Attractive chalet on the banks of the Semois. Double rooms: 1,935–2,940BF
Menus: 950–1,875BF

HABAY

POSTAL CODE 6720

TOURIST INFORMATION CENTER
Portail de Lorraine
6720 Habay-la-Neuve
Tel. (63) 42 22 37

HOTEL-RESTAURANTS

LE CHÂTEAU DU PONT-D'OYE
1 rue du Pont-d'Oye
6720 Habay-la-Neuve
Tel. (63) 42 21 48
Fax (63) 42 35 88
Restaurant closed Sun. eve. and Mon.
Specialties: ris de veau au Maitrauk, crispy quail with truffle sauce. Restaurant in a delightful natural setting. Exceptionally quiet and peaceful location. Double rooms: 2,400–5,000BF
Menus: 1,080–2,000BF

LES FORGES DU PONT-D'OYE
6 rue du Pont-d'Oye
6720 Habay-la-Neuve
Tel. (63) 42 22 43
Fax (63) 42 28 52
Delicious local cuisine using market-fresh produce. Tiered garden. Double rooms: 1,200–1,850BF
Menus: 1,350–2,550BF

RESTAURANTS

CHEZ TANTE LAURE
6 rue Émile-Baudrux
6720 Habay-la-Neuve
Tel. (63) 42 23 63
Closed Wed. eve. and Thur.
Specialty: rabbit à la Rochefort.
Menu: 760BF

HERBEUMONT

POSTAL CODE 6887

TOURIST PAVILION
Av. des Combattants
Tel. (61) 41 24 12 (during peak season)
Tel. (61) 41 20 84 (out of season)

CULTURE

RUINS OF THE FEUDAL CHÂTEAU
6887 Herbeumont
Free access.

PALISEUL

POSTAL CODE 6850

HOTEL-RESTAURANTS

LE GASTRONOME
2 rue de Bouillon
6850 Paliseul
Tel. (61) 53 30 64
Fax (61) 53 38 91
Restaurant closed Sun. eve. and Mon.
Specialties: calves head, tongue and brains in vinaigrette. Excellent cuisine. Swimming pool. Flower garden.
Menus: 1,950–2,600BF

ROUVROY

POSTAL CODE 6767

HOTEL-RESTAURANTS

AUBERGE DE LA GRAPPE D'OR
Rue de l'Ermitage
6767 Torgny
Tel. (63) 57 70 56
Fax (63) 57 03 44
Restaurant closed Sun. eve. and Mon.
Specialties: crayfish with zucchini flowers and frogs' leg mousse.

Double rooms: 1,800–2,100BF
Menus: 1,100 and 1,995BF

VIRTON

POSTAL CODE 6760

TOURIST PAVILLION
2 rue Croix-le-Maire
6760 Virton
Tel. (63) 57 89 04

CULTURE

MUSÉE GAUMAIS
38–40 rue d'Arlon
6760 Virton
Tel. (63) 57 03 15
Open 9.30am–noon and 2–6pm
Closed Tue. and Nov.–Mar.

HOTEL-RESTAURANTS

LE CHÂTEAU DE LATOUR
Rue du 24-Aug.
6761 Latour
Tel. (63) 57 83 52
Restaurant closed Wed.
Specialty: snails in puff pasty à la gournaise. Peaceful setting in the ruins of an ancient residence.
Menus: 850–1,750BF

VRESSE-SUR-SEMOIS

POSTAL CODE 5550

CULTURE

MUSÉE DU TABAC ET DU FOLKLORE
112 rue Albert-Raty
5550 Vresse-sur-Semois
Tel. (61) 50 08 27
Open Jul.–Aug. 11am–1pm and 3–7pm; Mar.–Jun. and Sep.–Dec., Mon.–Fri. 10am–noon and 1–5pm, weekends. 11am–1pm and 2–5pm

NATURE AND LEISURE

RÉCRÉALLE
16 rue Léon-Henrard
Tel. (61) 50 03 81
5550 Alle-sur-Semois
For all watersports, transport is provided to the departure point.

HOTEL-RESTAURANTS

AU RELAIS
72 rue Albert-Raty
5550 Vresse-sur-Semois
Tel. (61) 50 00 46
Fax (61) 50 02 26
Restaurant closed Wed. eve. and Thur.
Specialty: confit of spring chicken in garlic and onions.
Menus: 850 and 1,500BF

◆

CHARLEROI

POSTAL CODE 6000

DEPARTMENT FOR TOURISM
100 av. Mascaux
Marcinelle
Tel. (71) 44 87 11

CHARLEROI INFORMATION PAVILION
Square de la Gare du sud
Tel. (71) 44 87 11

CULTURE

MUSÉE DES BEAUX-ARTS AND MUSÉE JULES DESTRÉE
HÔTEL DE VILLE
Pl. Charles-II
6000 Charleroi
Tel. (71) 23 02 94
Beautifully presented collections, in a sumptuously decorated building.

MUSÉE DU VERRE
10 bd Defontaine
6000 Charleroi
Tel. (71) 31 08 38
Open 9am–5pm
Closed Sun., Mon. and public holidays
Tourist office by appointment. Glass museum and exhibtion of the history of the techniques of glassmaking.

CHURCH TREASURIES

ST-HUBERT

TREASURY OF THE BASILICA OF STS-PIERRE-AND-PAUL AND ST-HUBERT
On display in the basilica on Pentecost Monday and Nov. 3
Several beautiful ivory pieces.

STAVELOT

TREASURIES OF THE ÉGLISE PRIMAIRE
Rue de l'Église
Tel. (80) 86 44 37
Open Jul.–Aug. 10am–noon and 2–5pm
By appointment all year round except during services
The reliquary of Saint Remacle is the most impressive work in this collection.

LIÈGE

TREASURY OF ST-PAUL'S CATHEDRAL
Pl. Albert 1er
Visits outside of church service times. Contact the sexton. Good examples of Mosan gold- and ivory work.

HUY

TREASURY OF THE COLLEGIATE CHURCH OF NOTRE-DAME
Quai de Namur
Tel. (85) 21 20 05
Open Sat.–Thur. 9am–noon and 2–5pm, except during services
Guided tours on request, reserve 15 days in advance. Reliquaries from the 12th to 16th centuries. Superb enamel medallion from the Mosan school.

ANDENNE

TREASURY AND MUSEUM OF THE COLLEGIATE CHURCH OF STE-BEGGE
Pl. du Chapitre
Tel. (85) 84 13 44
Open Jul.–Aug., Sun. 2.30–6pm; May–Jun. and Sep., first Sun. of the month, same opening times
Closed Nov.–Apr.

NAMUR

DIOCESAN MUSEUM AND TREASURY OF THE CATHEDRAL
1 pl. du Chapitre
Tel. (81) 22 03 20
Open Easter–Oct., 10am–noon and 2.30–6pm, Sun. 2.30–6pm; Sun. and Nov.–Easter, 2.30–4.30pm
Closed Mon.
Contains several interesting pieces including a Merovingian reliquary.

TREASURY OF HUGO D'OIGNIES
INSTITUT DES SŒURS NOTRE-DAME
17 rue J-Billard
Tel. (81) 23 04 49
Open 10am–noon and 2–5pm, Sun. 2–5pm
Closed Tue., public holidays. and Dec. 11–26
Includes some very beautiful pieces by one of the major Mosan goldsmiths, Hugo d'Oignies (17th century).

MONS

TREASURY OF THE COLLEGIATE CHURCH OF STE-WAUDRU
Open Jun.–Oct., Tue.–Sun., 2–5pm and on request at the tourist office.
Chalices and reliquaries, also a rare illuminated manuscript.

TOURNAI

TREASURY OF NOTRE-DAME CATHEDRAL
Pl. de l'Évéché
Open summer 10.30–11.45am and 2–5.45pm, Sun. and public holidays, 2–4.45pm; winter 10.30–11.45am and 2–4pm; Sun. and public holidays 2–4pm
Contains two exquisite pieces of gold work: the reliquaries of Our Lady of Saint Eleuthère.

Musée de la Photographie
11 av. Paul-Pastur
6030 Marchienne-au-Pont
Tel.(71) 43 58 10
Open 10am–6pm
Closed Mon. and public holidays
Museum of photography.

Hotels, accommodation

Holiday Inn
1 rue du Poirier
6000 Charleroi
Tel. (71) 30 24 24
Fax (71) 30 49 49
Double rooms: 2,500–2,950BF

Restaurants

La Mirabelle
7 rue de Marcinelle
6000 Charleroi
Tel. (71) 33 39 88
Closed Sun.
Specialty: sea bass, Seafood cuisine.
Menus: 850–1 500BF

Beaumont

Postal code 6500

Tourist office
10 Grand-Place,
6500 Beaumont
Tel. (71) 58 81 91

Culture

Salamandre Tower
6500 Beaumont
Tel. (71) 58 81 91
Open May, Jun. and Sep., Sat. Sun. and public holidays 10am–6pm; Jul.–Aug., Mon.–Fri. 10am -6pm, Sat. Sun. and public holidays 10am–7pm

St-Géry's Priory
9 rue Lambot
6500 Solré-St-Géry
Tel. (71) 58 97 00
Fax (71) 58 96 98
Restaurant closed Sun. eve. and Mon.
Specialty: gaufrette of goose liver pâté with asparagus.
Menus: 1,250–1,950BF

Châtelet

Postal code 6200

Nature and leisure

Virelles Nature
Tel. (71) 21 13 63
20 rue E.-Hermant
6200 Bouffioulx
Tel. (71) 38 17 61
Open May–Sep. 10am–6pm
From Oct. to April, Sunday guided tours only. From May 15 to Sep. 15 boat trips and pedal-boat rides.

Chimay

Postal code 6460

Tourist information center
Hôtel de ville
Grand-Place
6460 Chimay
Tel. (60) 21 18 46

Culture

Château de Chimay
6460 Chimay
Tel. (60) 21 14 68
Open Apr.–Oct. 10am–noon and 2–6pm
Out of season, visits by appointment only.

Restaurants

Edgard and Madeleine
35 rue du Lac
6461 Virelles
Tel. (60) 21 10 71
Closed Tue.
Specialty: escavèche with trout. Local produce served in a lively atmosphere.
À la carte: 1,000–1,600BF

Couvin

Postal code 5660

Tourist information center
2 av. de la Libération
6400 Couvin
Tel. (60) 34 49 85

Nature and leisure

Neptune's cave
Rte de l'Adugeoir
5 660 Pétigny
Tel.(60) 31 19 54
Open Jul.–Aug.,daily 9.30am–6pm; Apr.–Jun. and Sep., 9.30am–noon and 1.30–6pm; Oct., Sat.–Sun. 9.30am–noon and 1.30–6pm

Caverne de l'Abîme
5660 Couvin
Open Jun.–Aug. 10am–noon and 2–6pm; Apr.–Jun. and Sep., Sat.–Sun. same opening times

Restaurants

Le Sacavin
2 rue de la Marcelle
5660 Couvin
Tel. (60) 34 40 87
Closed Sun. eve. and Mon.
Menus: 650–1,500BF

Florennes

Postal code 5620

Accommodation

Rural "gîte"
Mme Sprimont
1 rue Ste-Barbe
5621 Hanzinne
Tel. (71) 50 35 74

Froid Chapelle

Postal code 6440

Nature and leisure

Plate-Taille Informations
6440 Boussu-lez-Waulcourt
Tel. (71) 63 35 34
Open Easter–Sep.
Visits to the dam, series of galleries up to the top of the tower with its panoramic view. Forty-five minute boat trip across the lake with commentary.

Gerpinnes

Postal code 6280

Restaurants

Clos de la Rochette
16 rue Anys
6280 Gerpinnes
Tel. (71) 50 11 40
Fax (71) 50 30 33
Closed Sun. eve., Mon. and Wed. eve.
Specialty: rouget de roche served with cream and rosemary.
Menus: 1,200–2,050BF

Ham-sur-Heure

Postal code 6120

Restaurants

Le Pré Vert
24 chemin de la Folie
6120 Ham-sur-Heure
Tel. (71) 21 56 09
Closed Mon.
Menus: 795–1,595BF

Momignies

Postal code 6590

Hotel-restaurants

Hostellerie du Gahy
2 rue du Gahy
6590 Momignies
Tel. (60) 51 10 93
Fax (60) 51 28 79
Restaurant closed Sun. eve., Mon. and Wed. eve.
Specialty: lobster with vanilla. Formerly a private residence. Renowned for its peace and quiet. Tennis.
Double rooms: 3,000BF
Menus: 900–1,900BF

Philippeville

Postal code 5600

Hotel-restaurants

La Côte d'Or
1 rue de la Gendarmerie
5600 Philippeville
Tel. (71) 66 81 45
Fax (71) 66 67 97
Restaurant closed Sun. eve. and Mon.
Specialty: foie gras with caramelized apple.
Double rooms: 1,900–2,900BF
Menus: 1,290–2,000BF

Sivry-Rance

Postal code 6470

TOURIST OFFICE
31 Grand-Place
6470 Sivry
Tel. (60) 45 57 93

TOURISME SANS FRONTIÈRE EN SUD-HAINAUT
52 rte de Mons
6470 Sivry-Rance
Tel. (60) 45 62 07

CULTURE

MUSÉE DU MARBRE
Pl. Albert-Ier
6470 Sivry-Rance
Tel. (60) 41 20 48
Open Apr.–Oct., Tue.–Fri. 9.30am–6pm, Sun. and public holidays 2–6pm; Nov.–Mar., Tue.–Fri. 8.30am–5pm
Closed Sun., Mon., public holidays. and Dec. 15.–1Jan. 5

HOTEL-RESTAURANTS

LA BRAISIÈRE
13 rte de Chimay
6470 Sivry-Rance
Tel. (60) 41 10 83

THUIN

POSTAL CODE
6530

REGIONAL TOURIST INFORMATION OFFICE
Tel. (71) 59 41 41

CULTURE

AULNE ABBEY
6534 Gozée
Tel. (71) 51 52 98
Open Apr.–Sep., Tue.–Sat. 10.30am–noon and 1.30–6pm, Sun. and public holidays, 10.30am–noon and 1–7pm
Closed Mon. and out of season except by appointment.

RESTAURANTS

LES BUISSONNETS
2 rue de Leernes
6534 Gozée
Tel. (71) 51 51 85

LE PRÉ GOURMAND
159 rte d'Anderlues
6530 Thuin
Tel. (71) 59 41 21

VIROINVAL

POSTAL CODE
5670

CULTURE

MUSÉE DU MALGRÉ-TOUT
28 rue de la Gare
5670 Treignes
Tel. (60) 39 02 43
Open Feb. 15–Apr. 15 and May–Dec. 15., Tue.–Sat. 9am–5.30pm, Sun. and public holidays 10.30am–6.30pm
Closed Mon.

HOTEL-RESTAURANTS

LE SANGLIER DES ARDENNES
4 rue J.-B.-Périquet
5670 Oignies-en-Thiérache
Tel. (60) 39 90 89
Fax (60) 39 02 83
Restaurant closed Mon. and Tue.
Excellent restaurant.
Double rooms: 1,500BF
Menus: 1,150–2,400BF

RESTAURANTS

LE CHÈVREFEUILLE
85 rue de la Gare
5670 Treignes
Tel. (60) 39 03 60

WALCOURT

POSTAL CODE 5650

TOURIST OFFICE
25 Grand-Place
5650 Walcourt
Tel. (71) 61 25 26

HOTEL-RESTAURANTS

HOSTELLERIE DE L'ABBAYE
7 rue du Jardinet
5650 Walcourt
Tel. (71) 61 14 23
Fax (71) 61 11 04
Restaurant closed Wed.
Specialties: sautéed langoustine and carpaccio de foie gras. Winter garden.
Double rooms: 1,800–2,600BF
Menus: 1,290–1,850BF

◆

MONS

POSTAL CODE 7000

TOURIST FEDERATION FOR THE PROVINCE OF HAINAUT
31 rue des Clercs
Tel. (65) 36 04 64

ENTERTAINMENT

FESTIVAL OF HAINAUT
(Sep.–Oct.)
Centre RTBF
Esplanade Anne-Charlotte-de-Lorraine
7000 Mons
Tel. (65) 32 71 42

CULTURE

MUSÉE DU FOLKLORE AND DE LA VIE MONTOISE
MAISON JEAN LESCART
Rue Neuve
7000 Mons
Tel. (65) 31 43 57
Open 10am–12.30pm and 2–6pm; May–Sep., Fri. until 5pm; Oct.–Apr., Sun. until 5pm
Closed Mon.

MUSÉES DU CENTENAIRE
Jardin du Mayeur
7000 Mons
Tel. (65) 33 52 13
Open 10am–12.30pm and 2–6pm; May–Sep., Fri. until 5pm; Oct.– Apr., Sun. until 5pm. Closed Mon.
Include the Numismatic Museum, the War Museum, the Museum of Prehistoric and Gallo-Roman archeology and the Ceramic Museum.

MUSÉE DES BEAUX-ARTS
8 Rue Neuve
7000 Mons
Tel. (65) 34 77 63
Open 10am–12.30pm and 2–6pm; May–Sep., Fri. until 5pm; Oct.–Apr., Sun. until 5pm
Closed Mon.

MUSÉE CHANOINE PUISSANT
THE OLD LODGE
22 rue Notre-Dame-Débonnaire
7000 Mons
Tel. (65) 33 66 70
Open 10am–12.30pm and 2–6pm; May–Sep., Fri. until 5pm; Oct.–Apr., Sun. until 5pm
Closed Mon.

HOTEL-RESTAURANTS

LE CHÂTEAU DE LA CENSE-AU-BOIS
135 rte d'Ath
7020 Nimy
Tel. (65) 31 60 00
Fax (65) 36 11 55
Restaurant closed Sun. eve. and Mon.
Nineteenth-century manor house.
Double rooms: 4,500–5,500BF
Menus: 1,450–2,150BF

LA FORÊT
3 chaussée de Brunehault
7020 Masnuy-St-Jean
Tel. (65) 72 36 85
Fax (65) 72 41 44
Restaurant closed Sat. and Sun. eve.
Specialty: salmon lasagne with basil. Verdant setting.

Double rooms: 3,000BF
Menu: 1,250BF

RESTAURANTS

DEVOS
7 rue de la Coupe
7000 Mons
Tel. (65) 31 60 00
Fax (65) 36 11 55
Closed Sun. eve. and Wed.
Specialty: fillet of beef montois. Seventeenth-century building with a courtyard.
Menu: 1,850BF

ANTOING

POSTAL CODE 7640

CULTURE

CHÂTEAU D'ANTOING
7640 Antoing
Guided tours mid-May–Sep., Sun. and public holidays 3–5.30pm

ATH

POSTAL CODE 7800

CULTURE

CHÂTEAU D'ATH
7800 Ath
Tel.(68) 28 01 41
Open by appointment.

RESTAURANTS

CHALET NORMAND
384 chaussée de Brussels
7822 Meslin-L'Évêque
Tel. (68) 55 11 05
Closed Mon.
Specialty: duck liver par-cooked in Armagnac.
Menus: 950–1,495BF

BELŒIL-QUEVAUCAMPS

POSTAL CODE 7972

TOURIST INFORMATION CENTER
27 rue du Château
7970 Belœil
Tel. (69) 68 94 26

CULTURE

CHÂTEAU DE BELŒIL
7970 Belœil
Tel. (69) 68 94 26
Open Apr.–Oct.
10am–6pm

BINCHE

POSTAL CODE 7130

TOURIST OFFICE
Grand-Place
Tel. (64) 33 40 73

CULTURE

CENTRE DE LA DENTELLE AND DES MÉTIERS D'ART
Grand-Place
7130 Binche
Lace-making center.

COLLEGIATE CHURCH OF ST-URSMER
Rue Haute
7130 Binche
Tel. (64) 33 37 21
Open Mon.–Thur. 8am–noon and 12.30–4.30pm, Fri. 8am–noon
Visits during office hours only.

MUSÉE INTERNATIONAL DU CARNAVAL ET DU MASQUE
10 rue du St-Moustier
7130 Binche
Tel. (64) 33 57 41
Open Apr.–Oct., Mon.–Thur. 9am–noon and 2–6pm, Sat. 2–6pm, Sun. and public holidays 10am–noon and 2–6pm; Nov.–Mar., Mon.–Thur. 9am–noon and 1–5pm, Sat.–Sun., 2–6pm

RESTAURANTS

RESTAURANT BERNARD
37 rue de Brussels
7130 Binche
Tel. (64) 33 37 75
Closed Tue. eve., Wed., Sun.
Specialty: fillet of lamb à la binchoise.
Menus: 1,350–1,600BF

BOUSSU

POSTAL CODE 7300

RESTAURANTS

L'ORANGERIE
102 rte de Mons
7331 Hornu
Tel. (65) 78 50 29
Closed Tue. and Wed. eve.

INDUSTRIAL ARCHEOLOGY

INDUSTRIAL ARCHITECTURE

LE GRAND-HORNU
7301 Hornu
82 rue Ste-Louise
Tel. (65) 77 07 12 or (65) 38 23 95
Fax (65) 78 73 98
Open Mar.–Sep. 10am–noon and 2–6pm, Oct.–Feb. 10am–noon and 2–4pm
Closed Mon.
Guided tours of around 1½ hours.

STEEL INDUSTRY

FOURNEAU ST-MICHEL
6870 St-Hubert
Tel. (84) 21 08 90
Fax (84) 22 19 36
Open 9am –5pm
MUSEUM OF IRON
Open Mar.–Jan.

MUSÉE DE L'INDUSTRIE
134 rue de la Providence
6030 Marchienne-au-Pont
Tel. (71) 27 56 10
Open 9am–4pm, Sat. by appointment.
Guided tours.

MAISON DE LA MÉTALLURGIE
17 bd R.-Poincaré
4020 Liège 2
Tel. (41) 42 65 63
Open 9am–5pm
Closed Sat.–Sun.

MINING

DOMAINE DE BLÉGNY
4670 Blégny
Tel. (41) 87 43 33
Fax (41) 87 58 50
Open May–Sep. 10am–4.30pm, Apr.–Oct., weekends 10am–4.30pm
Visit the mine and the surface installations. Boat trips along the the Meuse from May to September.

MUSÉE DE LA MINE
7110 Bois-du-Luc
5 bis rue St-Patrice
Tel. (64) 28 54 48
Open 8.30am–5pm, Sat. and public holidays 2–5pm
Visit the museum or the museum and a miner's dwelling. Free tour.

MUSEUM OF MARBLE
Pl. Albert Ier
6470 Rance
Tel. (60) 41 20 48
Open Apr.–Oct., Tue.–Fri. 9.30am–6pm, Sun. and public holidays 2–6pm; Nov.–Mar., Tue.–Fri. 8.30am–5pm; Closed Mon. and Dec. 15.–Jan. 15

CHARLEROI

Three different tours around Charleroi's industrial area. For information contact:

GEVERU (ULB)
CAMPUS DE LA PLAINE
CP 246 bd Triomphe
1050 Brussels
Tel. (2) 650 21 11
This organization offers a 24-mile circuit called: "Itinéraire d'une grande cité industrielle" (Tour of a major industrial city).

MUSÉE DE L'INDUSTRIE
Tel. (71) 23 71 20
The "Circuit du patrimoine industriel" (Tour of the industrial fatherland) is offered by Charleroi's department of tourism in collaboration with Archéologie Industrielle de la Sambre. Thirty-six points have been retained. Complete your tour with a visit to a company.

ESPACE ENVIRONNEMENT
29 rue de Montigny
6000 Charleroi
Tel. (71) 30 03 00
This organization is responsible for the most recent of the three tours – "Parcourir Charleroi industriel" (Visit industrial Charleroi) – which allows you to discover seventy important industrial sites.

Menus: 1,650–1,950BF
▭ P ♣

BRAINE-LE-COMTE

POSTAL CODE 7090

CULTURE

SLOPING LOCK AT RONQUIÈRES
Open May–Aug.
Visits 10am–6pm, river boat, Mon.–Tue. and Thur.–Sun.
For all information contact:
Tourist federation for the province of Hainaut
7000 Mons
Tel. (65) 36 04 64
◆ 371

RESTAURANTS

AU GASTRONOME
1 rue de Mons
7090 Braine-le-Comte
Tel. (67) 55 26 47
Closed Sun. and Thur. eves., Mon.
Specialty: lobster gastronome.
Menus: 650–1,600BF
▭

BRUGELETTE

POSTAL CODE 7940

CULTURE

CHÂTEAU D'ATTRE
7940 Brugelette
Tel. (68) 45 44 60
Open Jul.–Aug., Thur.–Tue., 10am–noon and 2–6pm; Apr.–Oct., Sat.–Sun. and public holidays 10am–noon and 2–6pm

ÉCAUSSINNES

POSTAL CODE 7190

CULTURE

CHÂTEAU D'ÉCAUSSINNES
7191 Écaussinnes-Lalaing
Tel.(67) 44 24 90
Open Jul.–Aug., Fri.–Tue. 10am–noon and 2–6pm; Apr.–Jun. and Sep.–Oct., weekends. and public holidays same opening times

RESTAURANTS

LE PILORI
10 rue du Pilori
7191 Écaussinnes-Lalaing
Tel. (67) 44 23 18
Closed Mon., Tue. and Wed. eves., Sat. lunchtime
Specialty: crispy lobster with coriander.
Menus: 750–1,950BF
▭ ✝ ♣

ENGHIEN

POSTAL CODE 7850

OFFICE OF CULTURAL AND TOURIST INFORMATION
50 Grand-Place
7850 Enghien
Tel. (2) 395 83 60

CULTURE

CHÂTEAU D'ENGHIEN
7850 Enghien
Tel. (2) 395 83 60
GROUNDS
Open Easter–Sep. 1–8pm; Feb.–Easter and Oct., Sat. Sun. and public holidays 1–6pm; Nov.–Jan. Sat. Sun. and public holidays 1–5pm

HOTEL-RESTAURANTS

AUBERGE DU VIEUX CÈDRE
1 av. Élisabeth
7850 Enghien
Tel. (2) 395 68 38
Fax (2) 395 38 62
Restaurant closed Fri. and Sat. lunchtime, Sun. eve. and Mon.

Double rooms: 2,600–3,400BF
Menus: 1,100–1,675BF
▭ P ♣

FRAMERIES

POSTAL CODE 7080

RESTAURANTS

L'ASSIETTE AU BEURRE
278 rue de l'Industrie
7080 Frameries
Tel. (65) 67 76 73
Closed Sun. eve., Wed. eve. and Thur.
Specialty: fricasséed rabbit with saffron.
Menus: 1,300BF and 1,950BF
▭ P

HONNELLES

POSTAL CODE 7387

RESTAURANTS

LES TOURELLES
12 rue du Château
7387 Honnelles
Tel. (65) 75 90 95
Closed Mon.eve.–Thur. eve
Specialties: pot-au-feu de ris de veau, lamb's tongue. 17th-century setting.
Menus: 650–1,500BF
▭ P ♣

LESSINES

POSTAL CODE 7860

RESTAURANTS

LE NAPOLÉON
25, rue Lenoir-Scaillet
7860 Lessines
Tel. (68) 33 39 39
Closed Wed. and eves.
À la carte: 725–1,045BF
Menu: 750BF
▭ P

CHÂTEAU DU MYLORD
35 rue St-Mortier
7890 Ellezelles
Tel. (68) 54 26 02
Closed Sun. eve. and Mon.
Specialties: tartare de bar and langoustines served with caviar. Set in beautiful grounds.
Menus: 1,000–3,500BF
▭ P ✝ ♣

LA LOUVIÈRE

POSTAL CODE 7100

REGIONAL INFORMATION CENTER
18 rue de la Loi
7100 La Louvière
Tel. (64) 27 79 61

HOTEL-RESTAURANTS

DJORBI, LA PALIS DES LOUPS
2 rue Hamoir
7100 La Louvière
Tel. (64) 26 22 92
Fax (64) 21 49 73
Specialty: Groenland turbot with melon.
Double rooms: 2,150–2,450BF
Menus: 550–950BF
▭ P 🚗

RESTAURANTS

LE DAMIER
59 rue de l'Hospice
7110 Houdeng-Aimeries
Tel. (64) 22 80 70
Closed Sun. eve. and Mon.
Menus: 1,100–2,500BF
▭ P ✝ ♣

LE RŒULX

POSTAL CODE 7070

CULTURE

CHÂTEAU DU RŒULX
7070 Le Rœulx
Castle and grounds temporarily closed for restoration work.

HÔPITAL ST-JACQUES
7070 Le Rœulx

RESTAURANTS

AUBERGE ST-FEUILLIEN
1 chaussée de Mons
7070 Le Rœulx
Tel. (64) 66 22 85
Closed Sun. eve., Mon.
Specialty: fricasséed lobster à la Hocgaarden.

MORLANWELZ

POSTAL CODE 7140

CULTURE

DOMAINE DE MARIEMONT
100 chaussée de Mariemont
7140 Morlanwelz-Mariemont
Tel. (64) 21 21 93
MUSÉE ROYAL
Open Tue.–Fri., 9am–noon and 2–4pm; Sat., 2.30pm–7am; Sun., 10am–noon
Closed public holidays.

PÉRIWELZ

POSTAL CODE 7600

NATURE AND LEISURE

MAISON DE LA FORÊT
Plaine des Sapins
7600 Péruwelz
Tel. (69) 77 20 45
Open Mar.–Oct., Sat. Sun. and public holidays. 2–7pm

SENEFFE

POSTAL CODE 7180

CULTURE

CHÂTEAU DE SENEFFE
7180 Seneffe
Temporarily closed for restoration work.

HOTELS, ACCOMMODATION

LE REFUGE DU BOIS DE NAUWES
9 rue Infante-Isabelle
7180 Seneffe
Tel. (64) 55 79 26
Guest rooms.

SOIGNIES

POSTAL CODE
7060

HOTELS, ACCOMMODATION

BED & BREAKFAST
49 rue de la Procession
7061 Thieusies
Tel. (65) 72 83 94
Fax (65) 73 02 53

RESTAURANTS

LA FONTAINE ST-VINCENT
7 rue Léon-Hachez
7060 Soignies
Tel. (67) 33 95 95
Closed Sun., Mon. eve. and Tue.
Specialties: tuna carpaccio and marinated salmon.
À la carte: 1,200–1,600BF

◆

TOURNAI

POSTAL CODE 7500

TOURNAI TOURIST CENTER
14 Vieux-Marché-aux-Poteries
7500 Tournai
Tel. (69) 22 20 45

CULTURE

MUSÉE D'ARMES DE LA TOUR HENRY VIII
Rue du Rempart
7500 Tournai
Tel. (69) 22 38 78
Open Wed.–Mon. 10am–noon and 2pm–5.30pm
Arms museum.

MUSÉE DES BEAUX-ARTS
St-Martin's enclosure
7500 Tournai
Tel. (69) 22 20 43
Open Wed.–Mon. 10am–noon and 2–5.30pm

MUSÉE DU FOLKLORE
MAISON TOURNAISIENNE
34–36 réduit des Sions
7500 Tournai
Tel. (69) 22 40 69
Open Wed.–Mon. 10am–noon and 2–5.30pm

MUSÉE D'HISTOIRE, D'ARCHÉOLOGIE ET DES ARTS DÉCORATIFS
8 rue des Carmes
Tel. (69) 22 16 72
Open Wed.–Mon. 10am–noon and 2pm–5.30pm; Closed Mon. on market days

MUSÉE D'HISTOIRE NATURELLE
Main courtyard of the Hôtel de Ville
7500 Tournai
Tel. (69) 23 39 39
Open Wed.–Mon. 10am–noon and 2pm–5.30pm
Museum of natural history.

ACCOMMODATION

HÔTEL D'ALCANTARA
2 rue des Bouchers-St-Jacques
7500 Tournai
Tel. (69) 21 26 48
Fax (69) 21 28 24
Double rooms: 2,700–4,200BF

HÔTEL DE LA CATHÉDRALE
Pl. St-Pierre
7500 Tournai
Tel. (69) 21 50 77
Double rooms: 2,450–3,100BF

YOUTH HOSTEL
64 rue St-Martin
7500 Tournai
Tel. (69) 21 61 36

RESTAURANTS

LE CHARLES QUINT
3 Grand-Place
7500 Tournai
Tel. (69) 22 14 41
Closed Wed. eve., Thur.
Specialty: duck liver pâté with chicory.
Menus: 1,400–1,600BF

LE PRESEVE
2 Marché-aux-Poterles
7500 Tournai
Tel. (69) 22 35 13
Closed Mon.–Thur. eve., Sun.
In a 17th-century house overlooking the cathedral. Specialty: spiced lobster.
Menu: 995BF

L'EAU À LA BOUCHE
8 A–B quai du Marché-aux-Poissons
7500 Tournai
Tel. (69) 22 77 20
Closed Mon. and Thur. eve.
Specialty: kidneys in a mustard sauce.
Menus: 850–1,650BF

LE MANOIR DE ST-AUBERT
14 rue des Crupes
7542 Mont-St-Aubert
Tel. (69) 21 21 63
Closed Sun. eve. and Mon.
Specialties: Anjou baby pigeon with creamed maize. Grounds set around a stretch of water.
Menus: 1,700–2,250BF

APPENDICES

ESSENTIAL ◆ READING ◆

◆ *Belgian Art 1880–1914*, Brooklyn Museum, New York, 1980
◆ SIMENON (G.): *Maigret Mystified*, trans. Stewart (J.), Penguin, London, 1987
◆ THOMPSON (H.): *Tintin, Hergé and his creation*, Sceptre, London, 1992
◆ WIGHTMAN (E.M.): *Gallica Belgica*, B.T. Batsford Ltd, London, 1985

GENERAL ◆ INTEREST ◆

◆ BARNES (A.): *Introducing Belgium*, Harrap, London, 1981
◆ BLACK (C.):*Belgium*, Longman, London 1978
◆ BRISTOW (P.): *Through the Dutch and Belgian canals*, Nautical, London c. 1988
◆ BRYSSINCK (R.), BOUDART (M.) and BOUDART (M.) eds.: *Modern Belgium*, Modern Belgium Association, Brussels, 1990
◆ COWIE (D.): *Belgium: the land and the people*, A.S. Barnes, New York, 1977
◆ D'HAENENS (A.) ed.: *150 years of communities and culture in Belgium 1830–19080*, Ministry of Foreign Affairs, Brussels, 1980
◆ EDWARDS (T.): *Belgium & Luxembourg*, B.T. Batsford, London, 1955
◆ FROMMER (A.): *A masterpiece called Belgium*, Sabena, Brussels, 1984
◆ GERSON (N.B.): *Belgium*, Collier-Macmillan, London, 1964
◆ GORIS (J.-A.): *Belgium*, University of California Press, Berkeley and Los Angeles, 1945
◆ HENROT (T.): *Belgium*, trans. Wolf (R.E.) and Henrot (T.), Vista Books, London, 1961
◆ HUGGETT (F.E.): *Modern Belgium*, Pall Mall, London, 1969
◆ IRVING (R.E.M.): *The Flemings and Walloons and Belgium*, Minority Rights Group, London, 1980
◆ LAZAREFF (A.): *Brussels*, Lannoo, Belgium, 1990
◆ LYON (M.): *Belgium*, Thames & Hudson, London, 1971
◆ NEWMAN (B.): *The Lazy Meuse*, Herbert Jenkins, London, 1949
◆ PILKINGTON (R.): *Small Boat through Belgium*, Macmillan, London, 1957

◆ HISTORY ◆

◆ BOND (B.): *Britain, France and Belgium 1939–1940*, Davis-Poynter, London, 1975
◆ BROWNE (A.): *A nation in bondage, a chronicle of Belgian history from 1384 to 1950*, New Horizon, Bognor Regis, 1981
◆ DRINKWATER (J.F.): *Roman Gaul: the three provinces, 58 BC–AD 260*, Croom Helm, London, 1983
◆ EMERSON (B.): *Leopold II of the Belgians, king of colonialism*, Weidenfeld & Nicolson, London, 1979
◆ ESSEN (L. VAN DEN): *A Short History of Belgium*, University of Chicago Press, Chicago, 1928
◆ EYCK (F.G.): *The Benelux countries; and historical survey*, Van Nostrand, Princeton, New Jersey, 1959
◆ GEYL (P.): *History of the Low Countries. Episodes and Problems*, Macmillan, London, 1964
◆ GILLIAT-SMITH (G.): *The Story of Brussels*, J.M. Dent & Co., London, 1906
◆ VAN HOUTTE (J.A.): *An Economic History of the Low Countries 800–1800*, St Martin's Press, New York, 1977
◆ HUIZINGA (J.): *The Waning of the Middle Ages*, Penguin, Harmondsworth, 1968
◆ DE MEEÛS (A.): *History of the Belgians*, trans. Gordon (G.), Praeger, New York, 1962
◆ MOKYR (J.): *Industrialisation in the Low Countries 1795–1850*, Yale University Press, New Haven, 1976
◆ MONRO (J.H.): *Wool, Cloth, and Gold. The Struggle for Bullion in Anglo-Burgundian Trade, 1340–1378*, University of Toronto Press, Toronto, 1972
◆ NICHOLAS (D.): *Medieval Flanders*, Longman, London/ New York, 1992
◆ SIBORNE (W.): *History of the war in France and Belgium in 1815, History of the Waterloo campaign*, Greenhill, London, 1990
◆ STEEN (C.R.): *A chronicle of conflict*, Tournai 1559–1597. HES, Utrecht, 1985
◆ STEEN (C.R.) ed.: *The time of trouble in the Low Countries, the chronicles and memoires of Pasquier de la Barre of Tournai, 1559–1567, P. Lange, New York, c. 1989*

POPULAR ◆ CULTURE ◆

◆ GROSS (J.E.): *Transformations of a popular culture form in northern France and Belgium, Anthropological Quarterly*, Vol. 60, 1987
◆ DE LAET and MARTENS (T.): *Beyond the seventh art: the art and practice of cartoons in Belgium*, Ministry of Foreign Affairs, Brussels, 1979
◆ DE LAET (D.) and VARENDE (Y.): *Beyond the seventh art: history of the Belgian strip cartoon*, Ministry of Foreign Affairs, Brussels, 1979
◆ MAELSTAF (R.): *Animated cartoons in Belgium*, Ministry of Foreign Affairs, Brussels, 1976
◆ DE VRIELYNCK (R.) ET AL: *Beyond the seventh art: animated cartoons in Belgium*, Ministry of Foreign Affairs, Brussels, 1979

◆ ARCHITECTURE ◆

◆ BARRAL I ALTET (X.): *Belgique Romane*, Zodiaque, La Pierre-qui-Vive (Yonne), 1989
◆ BOCHGRAVE D'ALTENA (COUNT J.A.P.G. DE.): *Castles of Belgium*, trans. Bardwell (B.), Desoer, Belgium, 1967
◆ BORSI (F.), DELEVOY (R.-L.) and WIESER-BENEDETTI (H.): *Bruxelles 1900: capitale de l'art nouveau*, Officina Edizioni, Rome, 1972
◆ DIERKENS-AUBRY (F.): *Musée Horta: Bruxelles-Saint-Gilles*, Musea nostra, Credit communal, Brussels, 1988
◆ GOEDLEVEN (E.): *The Grand'Place in Brussels, centre of five hundred years of history*, Editions Racine, Tielt, 1993
◆ OOSTENS-WITTAMER (Y.): *Victor Horta: the Solvay House*, trans. Gray (J.A.), Institut Supérieur d'archéologie et d'historie de l'art, Collège Érasme, Louvain-la-Neuve, 1980

PAINTING AND ◆ SCULPTURE ◆

◆ *Art in Belgium*, Lannoo, Tielt, 1985
◆ AVERMAETE (R.): *Rik Wouters*, Arcade, Brussels, 1962
◆ BLOCK (J.): *Les XX and Belgium avant-gardism 1868–1894*, UMI Research, Ann Arbor, Michigan, 1984
◆ BUSSY (C.): *Anthologie du Surréalisme en Belgique*, Editions Gallimard, Paris, 1972
◆ CAMPBELL (L.): *Van der Weyden*, Oresko Books, London, 1979
◆ *Catalogue Inventaire de la Peinture Moderne*, Musés royaux des Beaux-Arts de Belgique, Brussels, 1984
◆ COLIN (P.): *La peinture belge depuis 1830*, Brussels, 1930
◆ GABLIK (S.): *Magritte*, Thames & Hudson, London, 1985
◆ GEIRLANDT (K.J.) and VAN TIEGHEM (J.P.): *Hyperréalisme*, Y. Brachot, Brussels, 1973
◆ GODDARD (S.H) ed. *Les XX and the Belgian avant-garde, prints, drawings and books ca 1890*, Spencer Museum of Art, University of Kansas, Lawrence, 1992
◆ FRY (R.): *Flemish Art, a critical survey*, Chatto and Windus, London, 1927
◆ GORIS (J.-A.): *Modern sculpture in Belgium*, Ministry of Foreign Affairs, Brussels, 1982
◆ HAMMACHER (A.M.): *Magritte*, Thames & Hudson, London, 1986
◆ LOZE (P.): *Belgium Art Nouveau, from*

Victor Horta to Antoine Pomp, Snoeck-Ducaju, Ghent, 1991

◆ MARIEN (M.) ed.: *René Magritte: Manifestes et autres écrits*, Les Lèvres Nues, Brussels, 1972

◆ PICON (G.): *Surrealism, 1919–1939*, Editions d'art Albert Skira, Geneva, 1977

◆ *Rik Wouters, Palais des Beaux-Arts*, Brussels, 1935

◆ REVENS (L.) and HUYSMANS (J.K.): *The graphic work of Félicien Rops*, Land's End, New York, 1968

◆ *Rogier van der Weyden, Rogier de la Pasture, Official painter to the city of Brussels, portrait painter of the Burgundian court*, Crédit Communal, Brussels, 1979

◆ SCHIMMEL (P.) et al: *Flemish Expressions: Representational Painting in the Twentieth Century*, Newport Harbor Art Museum, Newport, 1986

◆ SMEETS (A.): *Un Musée: Des chef-d'œuvres: Le Musée d'art moderne de Liège*, Le Botanique, Brussels, 1984

◆ SYLVESTER (D.): *Magritte*, Thames & Hudson, London, 1992

◆ TORCZYNER (H.): *Magritte: the True Art of Painting*, trans. Miller (R.), Thames & Hudson, London, 1969

◆ VOVELLE (J.): *Le Surréalisme en Belgique*, André de Rache, Brussels, 1972

◆ DE WILDE (E.): *Landscape in Flemish and Dutch drawings of the 17th century from the collections of the Musées Royaux des Beaux-Arts de Belgique, Brussels*, Belgian Government and Greater Manchester Council, Manchester, 1976

◆ WILENSKI (R.H.): *Flemish Painters*, 2 vols., Faber & Faber, London, 1960

Decorative ◆ Arts ◆

◆ DUNCAN (A.): *Art Nouveau*, Thames & Hudson, London, 1994

◆ EARNSHAW (P.): *A dictionary of lace*, Shire, London, 1982

◆ D'HULST (R.-A.): *Flemish tapestries from the fifteenth to the eighteenth century*, Editions Arcade, Brussels, 1967

◆ LEWIS (F.): *Belgian textiles*, F. Lewis, Leigh-on-Sea, England, 1975

◆ SELZ (P.) and CONSTANTINE (M.) eds.: *Art nouveau: art and design at the turn of the century*, Museum of Modern Art, New York, 1975

◆ WATELET (J.-G.): *Serrurier-Bovy: from art nouveau to art déco*, trans. Williams (A.) and Carlton (N.), Lund Humphries, London, 1987

Walloon ◆ Literature ◆

◆ DOMINIQUE (J.): *Poêmes choisis*, La Renaissance du Livre, Brussels, 1955

◆ ELSKAMP (M.): *Œuvres complètes*, Seghers, Paris, 1967

◆ GILLES (V.): *Œuvres choisies et poêmes inédits*, La Renaissance du Livre, Brussels, 1955

◆ MERTENS (P.): *Les chutes centrales: nouvelles*, Verdier, Lagrasse, c. 1990

◆ MERTENS (P.): *Les Éblouissements*, Seuil, Paris, 1987

◆ SEVERIN (F.): *Poêmes*, Bricage, Paris, 1951

◆ VERHAEREN (E.): *Les campagnes hallicucinées, les villes tentaculaires*, Gallimard, Paris, 1982

◆ WOUTERS (L.) and BOSQUET (A.) eds.: *La Poésie francophone de Belgique 1804–1884*, Editions Traces, Belgium, 1985

◆ Literature ◆

◆ BRONTË (C.): *The Professor*, J.M. Dent & Sons, London/E.P. Dutton & Co., New York, 1910

◆ BRONTË (C.): *Villette*, J.M. Dent, London, 1909

◆ CLAUS (H.): *The Sorrow of Belgium*, trans. Pomerans (A.J.), Viking, London 1990

◆ GASKELL (E.M.): *The Life of Charlotte Brontë*, J.M. Dent, London/E.P. Dutton, New York

◆ MALLET-JORIS (F.): *Cordelia*, trans. Green (P.), W.H. Allen, London, 1965

◆ MALLET-JORIS (F.): *Into the Labyrinth*, trans. Briffault (H.), Secker & Warburg, London, 1953

◆ MALLET-JORIS (F.): *A Letter to Myself*, trans. O'Brien (P.), W.H. Allen, London, 1964

◆ MALLET-JORIS (F.): *The Paper House*, trans. Coltman (D.), W.H. Allen, London/ New York, 1971

◆ MALLET-JORIS (F.): *Signs and Wonders*, trans. Briffault (H.), W.H. Allen, London, 1967

◆ MALLET-JORIS (F.): *The Underground Game*, trans. Briffault (H.), W.H. Allen, London/ New York, 1974

◆ MALLET-JORIS (F.): *The Witches – three tales of sorcery*, trans. Briffault (H.), W.H. Allen, London, 1970

◆ SIMENON (G.): *Intimate memoirs*, trans. Salemson (H.), Hamilton, London, 1984

◆ SIMENON (G.): *Letter to my mother*, trans. manheim (R.), Hamilton, London, 1976

◆ SIMENON (G.): *The stain on the snow*, trans. Petrie (J.), Penguin, Harmondsworth, 1976

◆ WILLINGER (D.) ed.: *An Anthology of Contemporary Belgian Plays, 1970–1982*, The Whitston Publishing Co., Troy, New York, 1984

Travelers' ◆ Tales ◆

◆ BRERETON (SIR W.): *Travels in Holland, the United Provinces, England . . . 1634–35*, ed. Hawkins (E.), Chetham Society, 1844

◆ COSTELLO (D.): *A Tour through the Valley of the Meuse*, 1845

◆ DURER (A.): *The Writings of Albrecht Dürer*

◆ EVELYN (J.): *Diary and Correspondence*, Henry Colburn, London, 1827

◆ GUICCHARDINI (L.): *The Description of the Low Countreys*, Theatrum Orbis Terrarum Ltd., Amsterdam, 1976

◆ IRVING (W.): *Journals and Notebooks, Vol. 1, 1803–1806*, University of Wisconsin Press, Madison/Milwaukee/ London, 1969

◆ KAHRL (G.M.): *Tobias Smollett; Traveler-Novelist*, University of Chicago Press, Chicago, 1945

◆ OVERBURY (SIR T.): *Observations in his Travailes upon the State of the XVII Provinces as they stood Anno Domini 1609*

◆ SMITHERS (H.): *Observations made during a residence in Brussels*, The British Press, Burssels, 1820

◆ SOUTHEY (R.): *Journal of a Tour in the Netherlands in the Autumn of 1815*, William Heinemann, London, 1903

◆ TEMPLE (SIR W.): *Observations upon the United Provinces of the Netherlands*, 1672

◆ TROLLOPE (F.): *Belgium and Western Germany in 1833*, John Murray, London, 1835

◆ Guides ◆

◆ BLYTH (D.): *Flemish cities explored, Bruges, Ghent, Antwerp, Mechelin and Brussels*, Bodley Head, London, 1990

◆ DUNFORD (D.), HOLLAND (J.) AND LEE (P.): *Holland, Belgium and Luxembourg, the Rough Guide*, Rough Guides, London, 1990

◆ List of illustrations

Front cover: (top) Poster © coll. CIDEP.
Spine: Statue of Saint-Druoun © Musée en Piconrue.
Back cover: (clockwise from top left) *The Adventures of Tintin*, Hergé © Castennan. Fan © Musée du Costume et de la Dentelle, Brussels. Detail from Spa poster © MVW Liège. Glassware © Hugo Maethens/Editions Ludian, Ghent. Bird illustrations, coll. P. Goffart.
1 *Man with a cock, Jumet*, Théodore Mansy, photo c. 1890 © Musée de la Photo, Charleroi.
2–3 Omnibus Wavre-Bruxelles, photo © Van Parys agency, Brussels.
4 *The old sidewalk*, Charleroi, 1933, photo, Léonard Misonne © ASBL Léonard Misonne/Musée de la Photo, Charleroi.
Quid, Brussels, 1930, photo Léonard Misonne © ASBL Léonard Misonne/Musée de la Photo, Charleroi.
4–5 *Woods in winter*, 1935, photo Léonard Misonne © ASBL Léonard Misonne/ Musée de la Photo, Charleroi.
6–7 *Haulers of Charleroi*, 1932, Émile Chavepeyer © Musée de la Photo, Charleroi.
9 Château de Spontin, collection J.J. Rousseau.
10 *Bèreke, Un ketje des Marolles (Young Albert)*, Chaland © Editions Lumpia, Anvers/Les Humanoïdes Associés, Genève.
Vierge de Dom Rupert, 1149–1158, stone statue, polychrome and gold plate, Musée Curtius, Liège © Hugo Maertens/Éditions Ludion.
11 Statue of Saint-Druon © Musée en Piconrue, Bastogne.
Gilles de Binche, collection Bastin-Evrard.
14 Interior of the Théâtre de la Monnaie, collection B. Roland.
Façade of the Théâtre de la Monnaie, collection Bastin-Evrard.
Courtyard of the Bishop's Palace, collection B. Roland.
15 Brussels parliament, collection B. Roland.
18–19 Moor grass peat bog, collection P. Goffart.
Libin peat bog, collection P. Goffart.
22–3 Spoye, dry grasslands recolonization, collection P. Goffart.
24–5 Schalm, river of the Ardennes, trout region, collection P. Goffart.
26–7 Redu beech tree, collection P. Goffart.
31 *Coq hardi*, Pierre Paulus, watercolor drawing © MVW, Liège/ADAGP.
32 Column of a horse god, 3rd century, Musée Luxembourgeois, Arlon © Éditions Ludion/H. Maertens.
Charlemagne, watercolor engraving © Léonard de Selva-Tapabor.
32–3 *Roman horseman*, 60–70 AD, Musée Luxembourgeois, Arlon © Éditions Ludion/ H. Maertens.
Raoul de Zähringen, Bishops' Palace at Liège, wax seal © Archives de l'État, Liège.
Charles V, medal, 1599, Théry © BN.
Portrait of Philippe le Bon, Van der Weyden, 15th century, Musée des Beaux-Arts, Anvers © Giraudon.
34 Silver Belgian coin for the Brabant revolution, 1790, coll. Thomas © Roger-Viollet.
La Fonderie, Léonard Defrance, oil on canvas, coll. part., collection J.J. Rousseau.
34–5 *Arrival of the Duke of Alba in Brussels in 1567*, Hogenberg, colored engraving, 16th century © Giraudon.
Map of the Low Countries, *Leo Belgicus*, engraving, 1559 © BN.
35 *Emperor Joseph II and his brother the Archduke Léopold*, Andreas Rosci, after P. Batoni, engraving © Roger-Viollet.
36–7 *One evening of the strike/The Red Flag*, Eugène Laermans, oil on canvas, 1893 © Musées Royaux des Beaux-Arts, Brussels.
37 Poster of the Belgium Workers' Party before 1914, priv. coll. © Jean-Loup Charmet.
Belgian manœuvres, September 1913 © Roger-Viollet.
38 *La garde meurt et ne se rend pas*, Cambronne, Musée Royal de l'Armée, Brussels © Giraudon.
The Battle of Waterloo, image d'Épinal © BN.
38–9 *Battle of Waterloo*, L. Dumoulin, panoramic painting of the battle, 1912, collection Bastin-Évrard.
39 *Map of the battle of Mont-St-Jean* © BN.
Bataille de Waterloo, le 18 juin 1830, engraving, coll. F. Masson, Paris © Dagli-Orti.
Cuirassiers français à la bataille de Waterloo, watercolor engraving, 19th century © de Selva-Tapabor.
40 *Madame Abts confectionne le premier drapeau belge*, Constantin Coene, oil on canvas, 1830, coll. Musée Royal de l'Armée, collection J.J. Rousseau.
Combattant de 1830, oil on wood, anon., coll. Musée de l'Armée, Brussels © Giraudon.
Porte de Louvain à Bruxelles, retrait des troupes hollandaises le 27 septembre1830, litho., De Dewasme, coll. Musée de la Dynastie, Brussels © Giraudon.
41 *Le Gouvernement provisoire de 1830*, oil on canvas, Charles Picqué, Maison du Roi, Brussels, collection J.J. Rousseau.
Barricades devant le Parc royal de Bruxelles, Constantin Coene, oil on canvas,1830, Musées Royaux des Beaux-Arts, Brussels © BPK, Berlin.
Charlier Jambe de Bois, poster, anon., all rights reserved.
Le Départ des volontaires liégeois pour Bruxelles, le 4 septembre 1830, Charles Soubre, oil on canvas, 1878, donated by Me Dumont-Lamarche on exhibition at the Hôtel de Ville de Liège, collection J.J. Rousseau.
42 *Léopold II*, 1865, photo Louis Ghémar, Brussels © Musée de la Photo, Charleroi.
Albert Ier, photo © Roger-Viollet.
42–3 *Mariage de Léopold Ier avec la princesse Louise d'Orléans*, Joseph Court, oil on canvas © Giraudon.
43 Albert II and Paola © Sygma/J. Orban.
Baudouin Ier à Bruxelles le 2 juin 1959, photo © Roger-Viollet.
Léopold III lors de l'inauguration du Canal Albert, chromo © J. L. Charmet.
La Reine Astrid avec ses enfants en 1932, chromo, Belgian photo, coll. part. © J.L. Charmet.
44 Anti-tank cannon and Belgian soldiers, Belgium, 1939–40 © Roger-Viollet.
44–5 Poster for the legislative elections of 1925 © Crédit communal, Brussels.
Poster for the fiftieth anniversary of the Liberation of Brussels, 1944–94 © OPT, Brussels.
"Capitulation du roi Léopold III sans prévenir le commandement allié", in *Paris-Soir*, May 29 1940 © Roger-Viollet.
45 Secours Ouvrier International, Belgian section, child victims of the flood of Namur c. 1930 © Roger-Viollet.
46 Street sign, Liège, collection Gallimard.
Calligramme d'Albert Maquet, 1945, coll. A. Maquet © BU, Liège.
Jean Haust, photo © MVW, Liège.
46–7 *Hommage des écoles primaires*, A. Roumer and L. Titz, watercolor,1896 © AVB.
47 First written proof of the word "wallon", Jean de Haynin, manuscript © BR, Brussels.
Book cover *Chansons wallonnes* © coll. CIDEP.
48 *Bèreke, Un ketje des Marolles/Young Albert*, Chaland © watercolor, Éditions Lumpia, Anvers/Les Humanoïdes Associés, Geneva.
Book cover for Marcel Rémy's *Les Ceux de chez nous*, 1941 edition © BU, Liège.
49 Tintin, in *Le Temple du Soleil*, Hergé © Casterman.
50 *Les Trois Vertus théologales et les Sept Dons du St-Esprit*, Floreffe bible, miniature, 1165 © British Library, London.
Notger ivory panel, c. 980, Musée Curtius, Liège, collection J.J. Rousseau.
Chalice of Gilles de Walcourt, c. 1228, Treasury of Hugo d'Oignies, Namur, collection Bastin-Évrard.
50–1 Baptismal fonts of Notre-Dame, 1107–1118, Church of St-Barthélemy, Liège, collection J.J. Rousseau.
51 Reliquary bust of Pope Alexander, silver head, copper stand with gold leaf, engravings and enamel, Musées Royaux d'Art et d'Histoire, Brussels, collection J.J. Rousseau.
Virgin of Dom Rupert, 1149–1158, stone statue, polychrome and gold leaf, Musée Curtius, Liège © Hugo Maertens/Éditions Ludion.
52 Mark "B-B" (Brabant-Bruxelles), corner of a tapestry in the series *L'Histoire de Jacob* © Musées Royaux d'Art et d'Histoire, Brussels.
La Bataille de Ronceveaux, Tournai, mid-15th century © idem.
Detail of *La Bataille de Ronceveaux* © idem.
53 Detail of *L'Histoire de Jacob, Le Partage des troupeaux entre Jacob et Laban*, composition by B. Van Orley, mid-16th century, made by Willem de Kempeneer, Brussels © idem.
L'Histoire de Jacob, Le Partage des troupeaux entre Jacob et Laban, composition by B. Van Orley, mid-16th century, made by Willem de Kempeneer, Brussels © idem.
La Déploration de Croix, detail, early 16th century, Brussels © idem.
54 Sign of the lacemaker, Grand-Place, Brussels © Bastin-Évrard.
La Dentellière, Caspar Netscher, oil on canvas, 1664 © The Wallace Collection, London.
Handkerchief in Brussels lace, 1863 © Léonard de Selva-Tapabor.
54–5 *Dentellières dans un atelier à Bruxelles*, photo © Van Parys agency, Brussels.
55 Benediction veil, Brussels lace, N.D. de Laeken, c. 1720 © Musée du Costume et de la Dentelle, Brussels.
English needlepoint of the 19th century © idem. Fan, gauze point of the 19th century © idem.*L'Impératrice Eugénie* X. Winterhalter, oil on canvas, Château de Belœil © Hugo Maertens/Éditions Ludion, Ghent.
56 *Porteuses de canons en verre*, Charleroi region, c. 1910, photo anon. © Archives de Wallonie/ Musée de la Photo, Charleroi.
Vonêche crystal clock, Musée Grœsbeeck de Croix, Namur, collection J.J. Rousseau.
56–7 *The Glassblowers*, Masson, oil on canvas © MVW, Liège/coll. M. Bockiau.

List of illustrators

Cover:
Catherine Lachaud, Jean Chevallier,
F. Guiol, J. C. Sénée.

Nature:
18–19: C. Felloni, A. Larousse, D. Mansion.
20–1: C. Felloni, A. Larousse, J. Guiol, J. Chevallier.
22–3: A. Larousse, C. Felloni, J. Chevalier, D. Mansion, B. Duhem.
24–5: F. Desbordes, J. Chevallier, P. Robin, J. Guiol, D. Mansion, C. Felloni, J. Wilkinson.
26–27: F. Desbordes, C. Lachaud, J. Wilkinson, F. Desbordes.
28–9: F. Desbordes, J. Chevallier, J. Guiol.
29–30: A. Larousse, F. Desbordes, J. Chevallier.

History:
46: coloring by J.B. Héron.

Architecture:
82–3: Jean-Marie Guillou.
84–5: J. C. Sénée.
86–7: Claude Quiec, Françoise Lenormand. Coloring by Catherine Totems.
88–9: Claude Quiec, Catherine Totems.
90–1: Jérôme Deborde.
92–3: M. Ballay.
94–5: Valérie Gevers, Michel Sinier.
96–7: Maurice Pommier.
98–9: Valérie Gevers.
99: Paul Hankar © AAM, Brussels.
100: Jean-Claude Senée.
101: Louis Hermann de Koninck, Lucien François © AAM, Brussels.
102–3: Françoise Lenormand ; colorists: Catherine Totems.
104–5: Bruno Lenormand.
106–7: Pierre de Hugo.
108: Pierre de Hugo.

Itineraries:
202–3: coloring by J.B. Héron.
244-245: A. Larousse, Claire Felloni, D. Mansion.

Practical information:
Maurice Pommier.

Maps:
Patrick Mérienne, Vincent Bruno, Stéphane Girel, Éric Gillion.
Colorists: Christine Adam, Carole Picard, Catherine Totems, Olivier Verdy.

Computer graphics:
Paul Coulbois, Florence Picquot, Patrick Alexandre, Xavier Garnerin (Latitude), Emmanuel Calamy, Patrick Mérienne.

We would like to thank the following for their invaluable help in creating this guide:

Mme Christine Bastin and M. Jacques Évrard (photographs, Brussels)
Mme Dubois (MVW, Liège)
M. Robert Gérard (Bibl. des Chiroux, Liège)
M. Goedleven
Mme Anne De Knop (Maison du Roi, Brussels)
Mme Léonard-Etienne (Cab. des Est., Liège)
Mme Anne Lernout and M. Willy Branders (Atelier et Perspective, Brussels)
Mme Liesen et M. Éric Hennault (AAM, Brussels)
Mme Mengeot (Musée des Beaux-Arts, Charleroi)
Mme Anne Molitor and M. Serge Creuz (Maison "La Bellone", Brussels)
Mme Geneviève Muzin (Cab. des Dessins, Musée des Arts Déco, Paris)
Mme Opsomer (BU, Liège)
Mme Renier (BU, Mons)
Mme Liliane Sabatini (Musée d'Art Wallon, Liège)
Mme Simons (Archives de la Ville de Bruxelles)
M. Christian Spapens (CIDEP, Brussels)
M. Vanrie (AGR, Brussels)
Mme Martine Van Romphey (OPT, Brussels)
M. Georges Vercheval, M. Marc Vausort,
Mme de Naeyer (Musée de la Photo, Charleroi)
Mme Walch (Cab. des Est., Brussels)

In some cases we have been unable to contact the heirs to certain documents, or their publishers; an account remains open for them at our offices.

Abbreviations:
AGR : Archives Générales du Royaume, Brussels.
AVB: Archives de la Ville de Bruxelles.
BM: Bibliothèque Municipale.
BN: Bibliothèque Nationale, Paris.
BR: Bibliothèque Royale, Brussels.
BU: Bibliothèque de l'Université.
Cab. des Est.: Cabinet des Estampes.
CIDEP: Centre d'Information, de Documentation et d'Étude du Patrimoine, Brussels.
MICM: Musée International du Carnaval et du Masque, Binche.
MVW: Musée de la Vie Wallonne, Liège.
OPT: Office pour la Promotion du Tourisme.
RMN: Réunion des Musées Nationaux, Paris.

Index

Page numbers in bold refer to the Practical information section

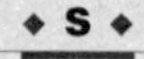

◆ T ◆

◆ U ◆

◆ W ◆